INTERNATIONAL BANKING IN THE NEW ERA: POST-CRISIS CHALLENGES AND OPPORTUNITIES

INTERNATIONAL FINANCE REVIEW

Series Editor: J. Jay Choi

International Finance Review is an annual book series in the international finance area (broadly defined). The IFR will publish theoretical, empirical, institutional, or policy-oriented articles on multinational financial management and strategies, global corporate governance and risk management, global capital markets and investments, emerging market finance, international financial economics, or related issues. Each volume generally will have a particular theme. Those interested in contributing an article or editing a volume should contact the series editor (J. Jay Choi, Temple University, jjchoi@temple.edu).

Volume 1: Asian Financial Crisis: Financial, Structural and International Dimensions, edited by J. Choi, Elsevier 2000

Volume 2: European Monetary Union and Capital Markets, edited by J. Choi and J. Wrase, Elsevier 2001

Volume 3: Global Risk Management: Financial, Operational, and Insurance Strategies, edited by J. Choi and M. Powers, Elsevier 2002

Volume 4: The Japanese Finance: Corporate Finance and Capital Markets in Changing Japan, edited by J. Choi and T. Hiraki, Elsevier 2003

Volume 5: Latin American Financial Markets: Developments in Financial Innovations, edited by Harvey Arbeláez and Reid W. Click, Elsevier 2004

Volume 6: Emerging European Financial Markets: Independence and Integration Post-Enlargement, edited by Jonathan A. Batten and Colm Kearney, Elsevier 2005

Volume 7: Value Creation in Multinational Enterprise, edited by J. Choi and Reid W. Click, Elsevier 2006

Volume 8: Asia-Pacific Financial Markets: Integration, Innovation and Challenges, edited by Suk-Joong Kim and Michael McKenzie, Elsevier 2007

Volume 9: Institutional Approach to Global Corporate Governance: Business Systems and Beyond, edited by J. Choi and Sandra Dow, Emerald 2008

Volume 10: Credit, Currency, or Derivatives: Instruments of Global Financial Stability or Crisis? edited by, J. Choi and Michael G. Papaioannou, Emerald 2009

INTERNATIONAL FINANCE REVIEW VOLUME 11

INTERNATIONAL BANKING IN THE NEW ERA: POST-CRISIS CHALLENGES AND OPPORTUNITIES

EDITED BY

SUK-JOONG KIM
The University of Sydney, Australia

MICHAEL D. MCKENZIE
The University of Sydney, Australia

Emerald

United Kingdom – North America – Japan
India – Malaysia – China

Emerald Group Publishing Limited
Howard House, Wagon Lane, Bingley BD16 1WA, UK

First edition 2010

British Library Cataloguing in Publication Data
A catalogue record for this book is available from the British Library

ISBN: 978-1-84950-912-1
ISSN: 1569-3767 (Series)

CONTENTS

LIST OF CONTRIBUTORS

Pierre-Richard Agénor	School of Social Sciences, University of Manchester, Manchester, UK
Wahida Ahmad	School of Economics and Finance, La Trobe University, Melbourne, Victoria, Australia
Folarin Akinbami	Durham Law School, Durham University, Durham, UK
Jonathan A. Batten	Department of Finance, Hong Kong University of Science & Technology, Sai Kung, Hong Kong
Leonardo Bortolotto	CASS Business School, City University of London, London, UK
Thi Ngoc Tuan Bui	Faculty of Business and Economics, Center of International Finance, Katholieke Universiteit Leuven, Leuven, Belgium
Maria Carapeto	CASS Business School, City University of London, London, UK
Luiz A. Pereira da Silva	Central Bank of Brazil, Brazil
Sinclair Davidson	School of Economics, Finance and Marketing, RMIT University, Melbourne, Australia
Anna Faelten	CASS Business School, City University of London, London, UK
Warren P. Hogan	School of Finance and Economics, University of Technology Sydney, Sydney, Australia

Aneta Hryckiewicz Goethe University Frankfurt, Frankfurt am Main, Germany; Kozminski University, Warsaw, Poland

Bang Nam Jeon Department of Economics and International Business, Drexel University, Philadelphia, PA, USA

Suk-Joong Kim Discipline of Finance, The University of Sydney, Sydney, NSW, Australia

Oskar Kowalewski Warsaw School of Economics (SGH), Warsaw, Poland

Siqiwen Li Accounting and Finance Discipline, School of Business, James Cook University, Townsville, Queensland, Australia

Alina C. Luca International Monetary Fund, Washington DC, USA

Robin H. Luo School of Economics and Finance, La Trobe University, Melbourne, Victoria, Australia

Michael D. McKenzie Discipline of Finance, The University of Sydney, Sydney, NSW, Australia

Scott Moeller CASS Business School, City University of London, London, UK

Thi Tuong Van Nguyen Faculty of Business and Economics, Center of International Finance, Katholieke Universiteit Leuven, Leuven, Belgium

John O'Keefe Federal Deposit Insurance Corporation, Washington DC, USA

William V. Rapp School of Management, New Jersey Institute of Technology, Newark, NJ, USA

Christian Rauch Finance Department, Goethe University Frankfurt, Frankfurt am Main, Germany

Piet Sercu — Faculty of Business and Economics, Center of International Finance, Katholieke Universiteit Leuven, Leuven, Belgium

Ola Sholarin — Department of Economics and Quantitative Methods, University of Westminster, London, UK

Peter G. Szilagyi — Judge Business School, University of Cambridge, Cambridge, UK

Valeriya Vitkova — CASS Business School, City University of London, London, UK

Ji Wu — School of Business Administration, Penn State University at Harrisburg, Middletown, PA, USA

PART I
AN OVERVIEW

INTRODUCTION TO INTERNATIONAL BANKING IN THE NEW ERA: POST-CRISIS CHALLENGES AND OPPORTUNITIES

Suk-Joong Kim and Michael D. McKenzie

1. OVERVIEW

International banking refers to the activities of providing financial services (banking) to clients (both institutional and individual) located in many different countries. This encompasses a wide range of activities, including transactions with foreigners and domestic residents relating to deposits and lending in domestic and foreign currencies, facilitating foreign currency transactions and foreign exchange risk hedging, participating in international loan syndications, and facilitating international trade finance for clients.

International banking activities were traditionally the domain of multinational banks, who enjoyed an overwhelming advantage in engaging in international banking activities as they operated across multiple banking jurisdictions. This meant that they were able to arbitrage bank regulations and systemic risks at the national level by internationalizing into offshore

International Banking in the New Era: Post-Crisis Challenges and Opportunities
International Finance Review, Volume 11, 3–11

ISSN: 1569-3767/doi:10.1108/S1569-3767(2010)0000011004

centers and those jurisdictions with lenient regulations of banking activities. For example, the Eurodollar market in London and the continental European countries with universal banking tendencies presented attractive opportunities for U.S. multinational banks in the 1960s.

In the early 1980s, many advanced economies began the process of deregulating their banking sectors, which reshaped the traditional boundaries of commercial and investment banking activities. This change has served to blur the distinction between domestic and international banking activities. Commercial banks diversified their asset and liability activities and actively participated in sophisticated financial engineering activities. This change meant that multinational as well as national banks were developing a capacity to service clients located in multiple jurisdictions and to engage in international banking activities.

By the early 1990s, the banking sectors of many emerging economies followed this trend and underwent their own wave of deregulation and liberalization. This change led to a significant penetration of foreign banks into these emerging market regions. For example, multinational banks from the United States and Western Europe are well represented in most emerging economies although each region has dominant players – European banks in emerging Europe, U.S. banks in East Asia, and Spanish and U.S. banks in Latin America (see Domanski, 2005). More recently, banks from the emerging economies themselves are venturing into international markets. The important difference here is that the emerging market bank internationalization is mostly limited to intraregion expansions. For example, 100% of foreign emerging market bank assets in East Asia and Latin America and 97% in Europe in 2004 were from other emerging economies in the same region (see Van Horen, 2007).

In the current environment of global deregulated banking systems, the role of banks is no longer limited to that of the traditional financial intermediation in national markets. Instead, banks in advanced economies are active in every aspect of the financial services industry. Furthermore, banks are not only active in their respective home markets, but globally, and both sides of their balance sheets will typically have international exposures. In addition, the banks from emerging markets also have both direct and indirect exposures to international banking markets.

Against this backdrop of a deregulated and truly integrated global banking system, we have watched a dramatic financial credit crisis unfold. The U.S. mortgage origination industry created a supply of assets for Wall Street investment banks, who in turn created and marketed asset-backed

Asset Backed Securities (ABS). It is these asset-backed securities that have been marketed globally have been identified as one of the most important causes of the current global financial crisis. Multinational banks have played a key role in creating linkages across the financial markets of both advanced and emerging economies, through which the adverse consequences of the U.S. subprime market collapse were able to spread to other financial systems. Western European banking systems were directly impacted, and banking systems around the world suffered both direct and indirect spillovers. The tightening in the international financial markets exposed the structural weakness of the economies of some the Euro zone countries, and this led to the current sovereign debt issues of Greece, Spain, Hungary, and potentially many others in Europe.

The scale of the financial crisis, in terms of its impact on the global economy and the size of the bailout/stimulus packages (e.g., US$787tr in the United States and US$586tr in China), has caused policy makers to question their past decisions to deregulate the banking sector. Ongoing discussions in numerous forums hark back to the era of regulation as a cure for the current problems and a means to prevent future crisis. For example, De Grauwe (2009) proposes a return to the "narrow banking" of the Glass–Steagall era as the Basle approach of regulation has not been effective. Thus, the roles of banks are once again being redefined with the possibility of a return to a more controlled environment.

This volume of the *International Finance Review* focuses on international banking in the postcrisis era. A total of 14 original chapters, not published elsewhere, have been selected from a competitive field. The chapters utilize various methods, including theoretical, empirical, and qualitative. Several papers offer combinations of these different categories, and among the empirical papers, there are a wide variety of datasets analyzed. These chapters serve to contribute to the knowledge on issues related to the field of international banking.

The chapters are divided into four parts. Part II formalizes much of what has been discussed in this introduction and discusses the role played by banks in the recent global financial crisis. The implications of the crisis on financial regulation are discussed in Part III. Part IV includes three chapters on operational aspects of banks during financial crises and one chapter on the relative performance of conventional versus Islamic banks in general and during financial crises. The last part of the book concentrates on the determinants of multinational banking presence in emerging markets.

2. THE ROLE OF BANKS AND LAWYERS IN THE GLOBAL FINANCIAL CRISIS

Part II considers the various roles played by banks and lawyers during the global financial crisis. The discussion begins with a chapter from Ola Sholarin entitled "The Subprime Mortgage Crises: How the Market Was Failed and Manipulated." This chapter investigates the roles played by the Wall Street investment banks and commercial banks in triggering the worst financial crisis of the modern era. In addition, this chapter also discusses the shortcoming of the rating agencies, as well as failures of financial regulators during and after the crisis. The main proposition is that the financial derivatives and other exotic financial instruments – including Credit Default Swaps (CDS), ABS, and Collateralized Debt Obligations (CDO) – are not, in themselves, the financial "weapons of mass destruction." Instead, the blame for the financial crises squarely and unreservedly rests with the unscrupulous and reckless institutional market practitioners, the unprofessional attitude and approach of the rating agencies as well as the regulatory failure on the part of the financial regulators and other gate keepers.

The second chapter in this section, "Bank Fragility and the Financial Crisis: Evidence from the U.S. Dual Banking System", is by Christian Rauch, and it compares the stability of the U.S. dual banking system's two bank groups, national and state banks, in light of the current financial crisis. The main finding of this chapter suggests that, ceteris paribus, national banks reduced their potential balance sheet fragility after the escalation of the crisis in August 2007 by reducing lending and liquidity creation stronger than state banks. Anecdotal evidence supports the empirical findings. Although both The Federal Deposit Insurance Corporation (FDIC) and The Office of the Comptroller of the Currency (OCC) did not anticipate the adverse effects of the crisis, the OCC publicly showed an earlier reaction to liquidity-related problems than the FDIC.

The third chapter is by Jonathan A. Batten, Warren P. Hogan and Peter G. Szilagyi and is entitled "Asia-Pacific Perspectives on the Global Financial Crisis 2007–2009." They consider recent events in financial markets and the subsequent responses by monetary and fiscal authorities, which are impressive for their scale, innovation, and flexibility in the face of sharply deteriorating circumstances. Internationally, the economic malaise brought perverse responses not least being the apparent quest for higher capital adequacy requirements than was thought necessary before the downturn. Where possible, the uniqueness of the responses by authorities in the Asia-Pacific region is highlighted. Other features impeding recovery cannot be dealt with immediately. Among these, the most important is the valuation procedures associated with accounting rules.

The fourth paper entitled "Bankers and Scapegoats" by Sinclair Davidson considers the issues surrounding the subprime crisis and explores arguments relating to regulation and the political economy of the recent crisis. He concludes that as long as the political cost-benefit of having inefficient banking regulation dominates an economic cost-benefit of having efficient regulation, we can expect that perverse incentives will remain, and financial crises will be a regular feature of the economic landscape.

The fifth and the last chapter in this section is by William V. Rapp and is entitled "The Lawyers and the Meltdown: The Role of Lawyers in the Current Financial Crisis." He argues that lawyers, not just bankers, for good and bad have been involved in all aspects of the current financial crisis and that if lawyers had been less involved or had raised warnings about legal risks as well as economic ones, the financial impact may not have been so disastrous and widespread. This chapter then highlights a public policy need not only for financial regulatory reform but also for a tightening in the professional standards and regulatory penalties imposed on lawyers involved in such transactions.

3. POST-CRISIS FINANCIAL REGULATION

Following from the discussion on the global financial crisis and the role banks and lawyers played, the implication of these discussions on the financial market regulation are presented in Part III. The first chapter in this part is entitled "The Global Financial Crisis – Causes, Effects and Issues to Consider in the Reform of Financial Regulation" by Folarin Akinbami. Following the global financial crisis, the need for the reform of financial regulations in several jurisdictions across the globe, including the United Kingdom and the United States, has been highlighted. This chapter critically examines some of the areas where reforms are most needed and concludes that market fundamentalism and over-reliance on the alleged self-correcting powers of the market have led to excessive deregulation and liberalization in world financial markets. Financial regulatory reforms will therefore have to be substantial and comprehensive to properly address the problems caused by excessive financial liberalization.

The second chapter is by Pierre-Richard Agénor and Luiz A. Pereira da Silva and is entitled "Reforming International Standards for Bank Capital

Requirements: A Perspective from the Developing World." In this chapter the authors discuss recent proposals for reforming international standards for bank capital requirements, from the perspective of developing countries. After evaluating the effectiveness of capital requirements reforms and progress in implementing existing regulatory accords, they discuss the pro-cyclical effects of Basle regimes and suggest a reform proposal. Their main finding is that the minimum bank capital requirements proposals in developing countries should be complemented by the adoption of an incremental, size-based leverage ratio.

The third chapter is entitled "Financial Fragility and Securitisation: The Discussions with Australian Regulators and Bank Risk Managers" by Siqiwen Li. Among divergent approaches to understanding the global financial crisis, Minsky's Financial Instability Hypothesis has gained increased attention. In part, the chapter draws upon Minsky's notion that the seeds of instability are sown when banks, households, and firms move from hedge, to speculative, and then into Ponzi financial positions. Financial innovations such as securitization contribute to this transformation. Furthermore, this chapter includes the findings arising from an analysis of interviews that focus on securitization-related issues after the subprime crisis with practitioners who were closely involved in regulation and risk management. The need for fundamental reform in the financial sector with a more consistent regulatory platform and enhanced supervision is highlighted, to facilitate rapid healing from the damage arising from the financial crisis in Australia.

4. FINANCIAL MARKETS AND BANKING

Part IV of this volume contains four chapters on operational aspects of banks. The first chapter in this group is "The Effects of Underwriting Practices on Loan Losses: Evidence from the FDIC Survey of Bank Lending Practices" by John P. O'Keefe. This chapter investigates the influence of U.S. bank loan underwriting practices on loan losses and identifies potential determinants of lending practices for five categories of loans: business, consumer, commercial real estate, home equity, and construction and land development loans. For business loans, the likelihood that bank management will adopt low-risk lending practices increases with bank financial performance, management quality hierarchical complexity and decreases with market competition. Results for the selection of lending practices for consumer loans and three categories of real estate loans are similar to those found for business loans but show weaker statistical relationships to all explanatory variables. In addition, lower (higher) risk underwriting practices are generally associated with lower (higher) gross loan charge-offs (as percentage of gross loans and leases) for the five categories of loans.

The second chapter is by Thi Ngoc Tuan Bui, Thi Thong Van Nguyen, and Piet Sercu and is entitled "Banks, ABSs and CDSs: Information Production, Risk Bearing, and Incentive Compatibility." The focus of investigation is on the discussion on the microeconomic pros and cons of bank loan-backed securities and credit default swaps. "Micro" implies comparative advantages for banks versus other holders of the loans or risks, not the macro pros and cons of higher credit volumes. The major conclusion is that securitization and CDS seem to destroy value because they move loans and risks away from the party best informed about the risk and best placed to deal with default toward worse-placed parties. Therefore, ABSs and CDSs should be confined to the highest-quality type of paper where no information asymmetries exist, like in Europe where the traditional Mortgage Backed Securities have not caused problems for centuries.

The third chapter in this part of the book is "Distress Resolution Strategies in the Banking Sector: Implications for Global Financial Crises" by Maria Carapeto, Scott Moeller, Anna Faelten, Valeriya Vitkova, and Leonardo Bortolotto. This chapter evaluates the effectiveness and the motivation behind the choice of different types of distress resolution strategies in the banking sector. This is a global study that analyzes key financial characteristics of distressed banks that were either acquired by other banks or were subject to government intervention, as well as the change in the financial profile of those distressed institutions from one year pre-deal to three years post-deal. The results show that governments intervene in the (relatively) best performers that only underperform in liquidity ratios, an indication of critical short-term flow problems. Distressed sellers enjoy much improved performance, in particular, in cross-border deals. There is some evidence of foreign acquirers "cherry picking" the least distressed banks, although no significant differences in target performance remain post-deal between cross-border and domestic deals.

The fourth and final chapter of this section is "Comparison of Banking Efficiency in Europe: Islamic Versus Conventional Banks" by Wahida Ahmad and Robin H. Luo. This research measures and compares Islamic banking efficiency to conventional banking efficiency using a sample of three European countries – Germany, Turkey, and the United Kingdom. The study covers the period from 2005 to 2008 in measuring the X-efficiency using the nonparametric method, known as Data Envelopment Analysis (DEA). It reveals that Islamic banks are technically more efficient than conventional banks but are beset by lower allocative efficiency. This results in lower cost efficiency for Islamic banks in comparison with the more conventional banks in the European countries considered.

5. LOCATION AND DETERMINANTS OF INTERNATIONAL BANKING

Part IV contains two chapters examining the determinants of foreign banks' presence in emerging market countries. The first chapter is "The Economic Determinants and Behavior of Foreign Banks in Emerging Countries during a Period of Global Economic Downturn" by Aneta Hryckiewicz and Oskar Kowalewski. This study uses panel data to examine the economic determinants of foreign banks' entry modes into emerging European countries during the period 1994–2008. The results suggest that a parent bank's choice of an organizational structure is a function of its strategic plans in the region and the countries' characteristics. After further consideration of the financial crisis of 2007–2010, it is revealed that as a result, parent banks tend to behave differently toward their foreign affiliates depending on its organizational structure. Their findings suggest that these differences are especially observable during periods of economic expansion and home financial distress.

The second chapter in this part is by Ji Wu, Bang Nam Jeon, and Alina C. Luca and is entitled "Does Distance Affect the Performance of Foreign Banks? Evidence from Multinational Banking in Developing Countries." This chapter investigates whether the geographic distance between subsidiaries of multinational banks and their headquarters is an important factor in determining the performance of the subsidiaries. Using various performance indicators of 340 subsidiaries in 54 emerging and developing economies from 69 global banks during the years 1994–2008, it is found that first, the distance constraint adversely affects loan growth, profitability, and performance of foreign bank subsidiaries, and second, the unfavorable information asymmetry faced by foreign banks, due to the distance constraint, in financing foreign clients cannot be fully overcome by establishing their presence abroad such as setting up their foreign subsidiaries.

REFERENCES

De Grauwe, P. (2009). *Lessons from the banking crisis: A return to narrow banking*. CESifo DICE Report 2/2009, 19–23. Available at http://www.cesifo-group.de/DocCIDL/dicereport209-forum4.pdf

Domanski, D. (2005). Foreign banks in emerging market economies: Changing players, changing issues. *BIS Quarterly Review* (December), 69–81. Available at http://www.bis.org/publ/qtrpdf/r_qt0512f.pdf

Van Horen, N. (2007). Foreign banking in developing countries; origin matters. *Emerging Markets Review*, *8*, 81–105.

PART II
THE ROLE OF BANKS AND LAWYERS IN THE GLOBAL FINANCIAL CRISIS

THE SUBPRIME MORTGAGE CRISES: HOW THE MARKET WAS FAILED AND MANIPULATED☆

Ola Sholarin

ABSTRACT

This chapter investigates the roles played by the Wall Street investment banks and commercial banks in triggering the worst financial crisis the markets have ever witnessed. The chapter also examines the shortcoming of the rating agencies, as well as failures of financial regulators during and after the crisis. The author proffers that the financial derivatives and other exotic financial instruments – including CDS, asset-backed securities (ABS), and collateralized debt obligation (CDO) – are not, in themselves, the financial "weapons of mass destruction" as it is being alleged. The author places the blame for the financial crises squarely and unreservedly at the doorstep of the unscrupulous and reckless institutional market practitioners, the unprofessional attitude and approach of the rating agencies as well as the regulatory failure on the part of the financial regulators and other gate keepers.

☆The author thanks the discussants at the 2009 Infinity Conference on International Finance, Dublin, where earlier draft of this chapter was discussed, for insightful comments and suggestions received.

International Banking in the New Era: Post-Crisis Challenges and Opportunities
International Finance Review, Volume 11, 15–32

ISSN: 1569-3767/doi:10.1108/S1569-3767(2010)0000011005

1. INTRODUCTION

The subprime mortgage crises sent unprecedented shockwaves to every corner of the globe and seriously unnerved major financial and economic indicators from every continent. The magnitude of its devastation and the boundary of its effect are unparalleled so much so that it has been dubbed the financial tsunami of modern times.

From Washington to London and from Tokyo to Reykjavik, the scale of economic and financial losses has terminated the existence of some of the most powerful financial institutions ever built. The crisis continues to threaten economic existence of sovereign states in the heart of Europe including Greece, Iceland, Spain, and Portugal. The impact on the East European countries is still unraveling, and their situations may be worse.

What started as a default of relatively small fraction of mortgage obligors in America has degenerated into massive liquidity crisis and credit crunch, the ripple effect of which has now returned to threaten the national currency of 27 member countries and global economic powerhouse in the heart of Europe. Following the recent turmoil in Greece, the European Central Bank embarked on the biggest gamble in its 11-year history by pledging US$1 trillion to ensure liquidity in the European debt markets and to stabilize the Euro. The monetary injection is also meant to stem the contagion in Athens and prevent it from altering financial equilibrium in Spain, Portugal, and Ireland, as well as in other potentially vulnerable states within the monetary union. When the financial crisis struck 23 years ago in 1987, it took only $11 billion to get the US economy up and run again and to calm global markets. The subprime mortgage crisis has swallowed well over $11.6 trillion in pledges by countries around the globe as bailout packages, and there appears to be no end in sight judging by the recent action of the European Central Bank.

It must be noted that although the crises were triggered by exposures to subprime mortgage write-downs in Europe and America, it was the consequential and rapid evaporation of liquidity that effectively transformed the relatively small ripple of mortgage write-downs into a financial tsunami of truly global proportion and magnitude according to Brunnermeier (2009).

The subprime mortgage crisis was not as a result of any natural disaster, and neither was its emergence played out as an abrupt or precipitous occurrence. According to Sholarin (2009), the subprime mortgage crisis was as a result of a catalog of systematic errors, sustained manipulation of market fundamentals, deliberate disregard for due diligence procedures, as well as disregard for risk management techniques and procedures on the part of market players and practitioners. It was also as a result of errors of judgment and professional ineptitude on the part of the rating agencies, as well as regulatory failures, blunders, and neglect on the part of the regulators – the custodians of market integrity and financial gatekeepers.

In this regard, the specific roles played by the investment banks and their commercial counterparts in this crisis deserve to be espoused and critically appraised, as is the manner and ways in which the rating agencies and market regulators have failed the markets.

According to the *Wall Street Journal* article of March 27, 2007, the trail of regulatory failures is not confined to one geographic location; it stretches from Canberra's Australian Securities and Investment Commission to London's Financial Services Authority, and from Washington's Securities and Exchange Commission to Berlin's Federal Financial Supervisory authority among others.

2. THE GENESIS OF THE CRISIS

2.1. Availability of Cheap Credit

Following almost two decades of sustained economic prosperity in Brazil, Russia, India, China, and most western countries, credit facilities became readily available and extremely cheap within the global financial system. As a result of this, bid-ask spread on major credit transactions around the globe, especially in Europe and America, became profoundly narrowed and severely tightened. This availability of cheap credit presented unusual opportunities for major financial institutions, especially Commercial banks, investment banks, and hedge funds. According to Greenlaw, Hatzius, Kashyap, and Shin (2008), these institutions used the cheap credit facilities in three major ways including: by creating a large army of obligors through which a stream of receivables could be pooled and securitized, by embarking on Merger and Acquisitions, and by using the cheap credits to fund Leveraged Buyouts. As a result of this, the market practitioners recorded a substantial level of profit margin for themselves and their clients. This high level of profitability however did not go without equally high level of systemic risk.

Sharp-minded market analysts were expressing concerns about the unusually low level of credit spread everywhere across the globe[1] and were openly discussing their potential danger. Those profiting from the situation were, however, more interested in enhancing further their profit from the credit bubble, hoping to exit before the bubbles burst.[2]

2.2. Unhealthy Mortgage-Lending Practices

The ease with which cheap credit became available, and the ferocious appetite for mortgage-backed security (MBS) among originators and investors combined to engender dangerous lending practices. By virtue of the depth and breadth of their mortgage markets, Europe and America were best placed, and they became the natural destinations for most of these credit facilities from the credit-surplus states from Europe, Asia, and Middle Eastern petro-dollar states.

Cheap mortgages were readily available to almost everyone including an army of high-risk borrowers through subprime mortgage lending according to The Goldman Sachs' Report (2007) on global assessment of loss and contango from subprime issue.

In their quest to reap the potential benefits of having large number of mortgage receivables assets, loan originators (mainly commercial banks) ignored standard procedures and were aggressively extending mortgage loans to a large number of borrowers with little or no regard for the borrowers' credit worthiness.

Some commercial banks and their surrogate mortgage providers were even offering cash-back incentives to new mortgagers, while others were offering teaser rates to incentivize people with unstable stream of earnings to take on mortgages. At some point in Europe and America, a loan-to-value ratio of 125% of property value was widely and easily available. Extra incentives to raise personal loan on the same property (for furniture, holidays, and cars) were being piled on the mortgagers thereby pushing the loan-to-value ratio in some cases beyond 150% loan-to-value threshold argues Sholarin (2009). With such low level of hair cut and credit risk exposures, one would expect effective repayment measures to be in place. To the contrary, most of these subprime mortgage owners had no income, no jobs, and no assets – the so-called NINJA group by market practitioners.

The risk level became heightened even further when buy-to-let mortgage facilities were intensified. This engendered self-certification of earnings to be introduced. It entitled anyone, regardless of credit history and earning potentials, to acquire a mortgage simply by self-certifying his or her ability to repay the loan.

In no time, a large number of people were able to secure credit to buy two, three, four, or more properties on buy-to-let terms with very questionable ability and/or incentive to repay the mortgage loan. Many low-income earners (particularly in Europe and America) saw this as an opportunity to get on to the property ladder and become multiproperty land lords.

Before the crises, an implied loan-to-value ratio was maintained by various mortgage lenders, and this used to be pegged to a specific coefficient of mortgager's salary. A loan-to-value ratio 4 (×) the gross annual and verifiable salary was not uncommon, and mortgagers were required to provide a reasonable proportion of the loan as up-front deposit. This was intended to serve as credit enhancement facilities and to provide adequate cushion in case of credit events. It was also intended to serve as a precautionary measure to deter moral hazards and information asymmetry among borrowers. In what was to be perceived later as one of the greatest regulatory failures ever committed, some commercial banks and other mortgage providers were openly offering up to 6 (×) the annual and unverifiable salary in loan mortgages, and some were even offering to fund the statutory mortgage tax for new customers as incentives in a desperate move by commercial banks and their surrogate mortgage lenders to increase their pool of mortgage obligors according to Sholarin (2008).

As home markets were getting saturated, major European and American banks moved aggressively to newly found markets among the new EU member states and started offering differentiated mortgages in Pound sterling and Euro for West European mortgagers to own properties in the new EU member states mainly in Bulgaria, Ukraine, Poland, and Czech Republic in the form of buy-to-let schemes.

Judging by their legal and macroeconomic infrastructures, it was clear that these new-found markets were clearly not ready and dangerously ill-equipped to absorb the vast amount of credit facilities that were being piled on them. It became evident later that commercial banks in Western Europe abated and helped finance the East-European frontiers to facilitate home-selling for their surrogate property development entities in which the commercial banks themselves were major stake holders.

2.3. Unchecked Spate of IPOs, M&A and LBOs

As credit facilities became visibly cheap, leveraged buy outs (LBOs), initial public offerings (IPOs), and Mergers and Acquisitions (M&As) reached levels that could hardly be sustained by the markets. Private equity firms and hedge funds were on a spending spree. There was rapid and unprecedented flow of cheap capital to equities, bonds, and real estate markets in Greece, Ukraine, Russia, Bulgaria, and Czech Republic. This was despite the political, operational, legal, and credit risks to which most of these countries were, and still are, exposed. As a result of this, most of these countries embarked on highly ambitious projects relying on continued and uninterrupted influx of foreign capital into their economies.

The abruptness with which these loans were being withdrawn and/or terminated as the crises mounts was a major reason behind credit crises that later engulfed Greece, Ukraine, Spain, Ireland, and Portugal immediately after the crises, and for which about $1 trillion had to be pledged by the European Central Bank in early May 2010 to, in part, enhance liquidity and calm investors.

3. THE ROLES OF INVESTMENT BANKS AND THEIR COMMERCIAL COUNTERPARTS

3.1. Securitization of "Toxic Assets"

Mainly within Europe and North America, the investment banks and their commercial counterparts who had assembled a huge army of mortgage obligors embarked on paradigm shift away from the fundamental ethics of banking. These institutions started to swap the "originate and keep" concept on their mortgage loan stock into "originate and sell." These investment banks and their commercial counterparts initiated massive securitization of their toxic mortgage loan receivable by passing them on as financial securities in the debt markets. When it was clear that the financial regulators were impliedly less concerned about the potential risk of such acts, the investment bankers and their commercial allies went further and started repackaging the securitized toxic loan stock yet again and passing them on as collateralized debt obligations (CDOs), CDO of CDOs and other exotic structured financial instruments (Sholarin, 2008).

Although the first layer of the securitized mortgage receivables were highly risky, owing to the subprime quality of their mortgage components, the CDOs, which were created as a result of second layer warehousing of the risky mortgage instruments, assumed risks of even higher magnitude. When the newly created CDOs were being warehoused in a third-layered securitization process to create CDO of CDOs, then the overall layer of assets so created quickly became "poisonous", highly unstable and extremely dangerous.

At a point, it was technically not feasible to attempt applying VaR to quantify the maximum amount of possible loss at a point in time on an investment portfolio owing to the multilayered and highly interconnected level debt obligation among institutional investors involved.

The bulk of the funding being channeled into the toxic securitized assets was coming from the same investment banks themselves albeit through a third-party intermediary. This significantly increased the level of counterparty risk exposure of the entire financial markets as correlation coefficient of the securitized assets moved from negative to positive in the portfolio universe of the commercial and investment banks concerned.

Three fundamental errors of judgment were made by the investment, and commercial bank participants in these multilayered CDOs and other mortgage-related structured financial products. First, the investment banks and their commercial bank counterparts wrongly assumed that market value of the original assets (the properties) upon which the value of the multilayered financial instruments was based will remain perpetually high; they were wrong.

Second, the investment and commercial banks wrongly assumed that the influx of cheap credits, which the market had been enjoying for over a decade and with which they could refinance and achieve maturity transformation on their short-dated capital injection and, thereby, maneuver their ways out of any credit events, will remain perpetually cheap and available; again, they were wrong.

The third error of judgment was their desire to ignore the prospect of interest rate rising to reflect the risk of subprime lending, which reflected highly imprudent and weak stress testing measures among participants; the market practitioners were wrong again.

The rating agencies were later accused by public investors of being complacent for eagerly awarding investment grade status to those CDOs, CDO of CDOs, and other structured financial instruments, which were priced on such incoherent and inconsistent assumptions and questionable macroeconomic fundamentals Keys, Mukherjee, Seru, and Vig (2008).

In compliance with the market expectation theory, the interest rate started to rise to reflect the risk premium on loan advancements to the high-risk "NINJA" mortgage borrowers, and it was not long before mortgage owners started to default under the burden of sharp and sudden rise in interest payment. As the market value of properties started to fall below the nominal value of loan credits, mortgage borrowers exercised their option to walk away from further loan and interest repayments as they would have been "out of the money," and this triggered massive write-downs in mortgage loans among mortgage providers.

Following the massive write-downs that followed the sudden increase in interest rates, investors were forced to recalibrate their balance sheets to account for the write-downs in the market value of their "poisonous" assets. This is in compliance with the fair value accounting rules. The diminished value of the "poisonous" assets was far outweighed by the liabilities of these asset owners (Allen & Carletti, 2008).

As a result of this, the rating agencies invoked the "credit event" clause and started reviewing downwards the ratings on the "toxic assets," which they had rated as "investment grade assets" only a few days earlier.

These inconsistencies seriously damaged investors' confidence in the financial markets and further heightened their bearish outlook on the financial markets. According to Adrian and Shin (2008), this led to acute liquidity shortage, which caused interbank lending activities to be suspended at a time when demand for liquid capital was at its peak.

3.2. Market Timing and Manipulation

A number of investment banks and their boutiques engaged in severe market manipulations, which went unchecked by the regulators. On March 11, 2008, the market perceived an email sent by Goldman Sachs' derivative group to mean that Goldman was no longer prepared to step in for clients on Bear Stearns's derivative deals. In technical language, this meant that Goldman would not facilitate netting of multilateral obligations that involved Bear Stearns' financial transactions. This development seriously and fundamentally agitated the financial market in ways that turned the already desperate situation into a stampede. Many of the Bear Stearns' hedge fund clients, most of whom had well over US$60 billion in margin accounts exposure in Bear Stearns' derivative-related transactions, decided to dump Bear Stearns unceremoniously and in mass.

As a result of this, it became almost impossible for Bear Stearns to secure its much-needed daily liquidity financing. Bear Stearns was faced with imminent collapse. With well over 150 million transactions outstanding with various counterparty hedge fund clients, Washington knew clearly well that Bear Stearns' was highly interconnected, and its demise was certain to trigger unimaginable systemic failure – the "too big to fail" paradox started gaining momentum at this stage. Within three days, March 14, 2008, to be precise, the U.S. Federal Reserve had concluded a massive financial bailout for Bear Stearns with JP Morgan fronting as the conduit for the Federal Reserve. By this time, its market rating and financial image had been seriously impaired. Bear Stearns, whose shares had been valued at US$150, a share less than a year earlier, was acquired by JP Morgan Chase for US$2 per share. Although JPMorgan Chase agreed to assume the first US$1 billion of related losses, the unspoken acrimony that followed in the financial circle was deafening and unimaginable. Similar giant institutions were left pondering who was next on the casualty list. Bear Stearns shareholders lost almost everything as did the Halifax Bank of Scotland's (HBOS) shareholders who were offered 58.4 cents per dollar on their HBOS shares on October 24, 2008, following a merger proposal with Lloyds TSB (Shin, 2009).

Goldman Sachs has been particularly singled out as one of the serious offenders in market manipulation with regard to the subprime mortgage crises. It was accused recently of deliberately selling financial assets to investors with full knowledge that other Hedge Funds, with which it had commercial interest, was already planning to sell-short the same assets.

3.3. Engendering Liquidity Shortage

Following the massive write-downs on mortgage-related toxic assets, the asset-liability mismatch among commercial and investment banks became very serious and significantly widened. The interbank lending came to a complete stand still as banks suspended lending to one another (Morris & Shin, 2004).

The spreads between LIBOR, EURIBOR, and Fed Funds Rate were stretched to unprecedented limits compared with return on the U.S Treasury bill (Table A1).

IKB in Germany was the first victim of the liquidity crisis outside the United States. In August 2007, it was forced to seek 3.5 billion euros liquidity fund from one of its major shareholders as it was unable to assist one of its conduits to roll over an ABCP-related credit line. This was followed by the BNP Paribas' declaration on August 9, 2007, that it would freeze redemptions for three major investment funds. This sent fear across the markets as banks started to be reluctant in lending to one another.

As a result of this, by August 2007, LIBOR was significantly higher than other major credit risk indicators as its spreads began to widen significantly in relation to the alternative lending indicators. This was particularly well pronounced in LIBOR-OIS Spread, T-Bill-OIS Spread, Agency Spread as well as MBS-GC Repo Spread. On the basis of data supplied by the U.S

Federal Reserve Board, the spread between LIBOR and OIS was well in excess of +100 basis points as at December 2007, and that between the T-Bill and OIS was close to −200 basis points as at September 2007, indicating that OIS was significantly higher than the T-Bill. These findings were strongly corroborated by other independent research outputs offered by Bloomberg, Lehman Live, and Global Insight. The magnitude of spread among these credit-risk indicators was also found to be robustly supported by, and consistent with, the findings of Brunnermeier (2009).

The European Central Banks responded almost immediately by injecting 95 billion euros in overnight credit facility into their interbank lending market on August 9, 2007. On their part, the U.S Federal Reserve responded by pumping US$24 billion into their money markets. The Fed also reduced the discount rate by 50 basis points, lengthened the lending period to 30 days, and broadened the range of collateral acceptable at its discount windows.

On September 6, 2008, the Bank of England decided to maintain its bank rate at 5.75%. Twelve days later, on September 18, 2007, the U.S Federal Reserve opted to lower its own discount rate by 50 basis points to 5.25%. This seriously exposed a substantial number of British financial institutions, which relied heavily on short-term financing. In particular, this affected Northern Rock, which was experiencing a wild run on its branches across the United Kingdom, and could not secure the short-term liquidity it desperately required to service its long-term loans. The bank was nationalized in September 19, 2007. This was the first bank run in the United Kingdom in more than a century (Shin, 2009) and Diamond and Rajan (2005). This was followed by the demise of the internet banking pioneer – Net Bank – which was taken over by the ING bank on September 28, 2007, following a liquidity-related crisis.

By October 2007, the level of sub-prime-related write-downs was beyond what could be considered as sustainable (see Tables A2–A4). Between mid-September and early October 2008, over US$ 19 trillion had been wiped off stock markets from across the globe as investors' confidence hit the rock bottom. Some were offering, rather than receiving, incentives to invest in American TB. As the liquidity crises evolved further, the U.S. Federal Reserve introduced US$200 billion Term Security Lending Facility (TSLF) on March 11, 2008.

This was designed to enable investments banks to tap into government funding assistance by swapping their mortgage-related bonds (and other toxic assets) for Treasury bonds for up to 28 days duration.[3] Although, this sent the OIS-T-Bill spread to widen further, it provided a temporary relief only for a small number of financial institutions.

4. THE ROLES OF THE RATING AGENCIES

The erratic and inconsistent rating activities of the rating agencies also contributed to the financial crises as well as the liquidity shortage that followed. The rating inconsistencies caused the cost of short-term interbank lending to be dramatically raised to unprecedented levels as was the cost on CDS for major borrowers. At some point, the CDS cost was well over 2,000 basis points for AAA-rated borrowers and over 3,000 basis points for BBB-rated borrowers according to the information provided in the ABX Spread series 7-1 by the Lehman Live. The ABX spreads series 7-1 is based on credit default swaps on 20 asset-backed securities (ABS) (of different ratings) that contain subprime mortgages.

A sizable proportion of institutional investors – notably pension funds, mutual funds and investment trusts – are prevented by regulations from holding or investing in sub-investment-grade assets according to Allen and Gale (2007). This prompted originators and arrangers to use various and often questionable credit enhancement means to acquire AAA rating for their toxic assets (especially MBS asset class) to meet the regulatory demands of these institutional investors. Rating agencies often played direct role in abetting this practice by directly offering assistance in selecting and engineering credit enhancement facilities preferred by the rating agencies themselves for awarding a predetermined rating level for their client's products; a practice highly uncommon and considered unprofessional in financial markets. The suspicion grew even bigger when it became known that originators (who were mainly commercial banks and investment banks) were offering substantial return to the rating agencies for engineering such credit enhancements, and rating alphabets on structured financial instruments. This unscrupulous activity on the part of the rating agencies made it possible for high-caliber originators and arrangers to secure the highly coveted AAA rating for their "toxic assets" through the back door and sell same to institutional investors as investment-grade products (Gorton, 2008).

Aided by the rating agencies, the originators were able to exploit a vital loophole in the securitization exercise. They (the originators) were able to mask the mismatch that exists in the rating profile of an originator of financial instruments, and tranches of investment products that such originator was offering to the market. The judgments of the rating agencies were openly queried also because it was perceived that the rating outcome offered for most of the SIV did not fully incorporate the exposure of their clients to include sponsored off-balance sheet credit risks.

In their quest to "originate and distribute" their junk loans for profit, the originators were, in essence, virtually "buying" their preferred rating points for various tranches of their "toxic" structured financial products on the shelves of the rating agencies, which they then sold on to unsuspecting investors, who erroneously relied on the AAA ratings of such product as being truly reflective of the inherent risk and, hence, market value of such financial products.

This perception is substantiated by the fact that the rating agencies earn far more income from rating structured products than from any other rating contracts within the last decade.[4] The rating agencies were, at some point, also found to be unprofessional and reckless in their rating activities.[5]

According to Duffie (2008), one of the most disturbing outcomes of the rating arbitrage highlighted above is the fact that a huge proportion of the credit risk, which the rating mismatch has created, actually remains within the banking industry as the bankers themselves were among the most active investors in the "toxic" structured financial products. As a result, many of them became overexposed as they inadvertently went over-weighted in structured financial products including CDOs and other exotic instruments. The story of Societe Generale trader (Jerome Kerviel), who lost US$7.1 billion in 2008, serves to corroborate this view.

5. CONCLUSION

This chapter posits that the subprime mortgage crises are not about derivatives and other modern financial instruments. The problem lies with the users and also the abusers of derivatives and other financial products. Derivative instruments are like guns. They do not kill, but their misuse could result in fatality. The subprime financial debacle was as a result of recklessness and professional ineptitude of the stakeholders – mainly the investment banks and their commercial counterparts. The list also includes the rating agencies that were sacrificing and, still continue to, sacrifice financial due diligence, and allowing themselves to be used by financial originators of ABS to literarily buy investment-grade rating level for money. Next on this list are the financial gate keepers – the FSA, SEC, and a host of other regulators – for failing to supervise, manage, and regulate the financial markets.

In the word of Nicolas Taleb, VaR only offers X% probability of incurring a specific amount of daily loss. Impliedly, this can also be interpreted to mean there is (1−X) probability of incurring unlimited amount of financial loss. It is the sacred duty of financial gate keepers to ensure that such events with very low probability, but high severity are closely monitored and regulated.

A new world order will be required to address the problem, which, judging by the recent developments in Greece, Portugal, and Spain, can be said to be perennial financial problem. However, it must be in the form of regulations that will not reverse, but rather strengthen, the achievements of the past decades. The politicians in Berlin and Paris appear to be experimenting on what needs to be done. At the moment, their efforts appear to lack coherence and sound economic and financial judgment.

Specifically, what is needed is a deterrence to prevent the ongoing misuse of the financial tools while engendering introduction of new ones, as well as strengthening the regulatory supervision without stifling smooth operation of the system.

For long, it has been perceived that the best minds and brains in the financial world are the financial operatives themselves. They, therefore, ought not to be controlled by regulators who are, at best, less qualified to be employed as financial operatives. It is high time the regulators, the rating agencies and other financial gate keepers matched the pay packages of financial market operatives and attract the best minds and brains to deliver effective supervision of financial markets. This will enable them to attract well-qualified personnel to narrow the knowledge gap that now exists in area of market supervision.

NOTES

1. The *Wall Street Journal* article by Berman of March 27, 2007, "Sketchy Loans Abound with Capital Plentiful, Debt Buyers Take Sub-prime-Type Risk" was amongst the first to hint at this potential "Credit Bubble."

2. In the words of the former CEO of Citigroup – Chuck Prince – "When the music stops, in terms of liquidity, things will be complicated. But as long as the music is playing, you've got to get up and dance. We are still dancing." *The Financial Times*, July 10, 2007.

3. As at this date, Bear Stearns had approximately US$16 billion in CMBS. In addition to this the investment bank also had almost US$15 billion in prime and Alt-A, and another US$2 billion in sub-prime mortgage assets that could be pledged for high-grade Treasury bonds.

4. Moody's income went from $159 million in 2000 to $705 million in 2006, primarily because of increases in fees from "structured finance" (*Fortune Magazine*, March 19, 2007).

5. An exchange between two analysts of a rating agency, printed in the Economist of November 13, 2008, quoted one of the analysts saying "we rate every deal ... it could be structured by cows and we would rate it."

REFERENCES

Adrian, T., & Shin, H. S. (2008). *Liquidity and financial cycles*. BIS Working Paper No. 256.

Allen, F., & Carletti, I. (2008). Should financial institutions mark to market? *Banque de France Financial Stability Review*, October Review.

Allen, F., & Gale, D. (2007). *Understanding financial crises*. Oxford, UK: Oxford University Press.

Berman, D. K. (2007). Sketchy loans abound with capital plentiful, debt buyers take sub-prime-type risk. *The Wall Street Journal*, March 27, Dow Jones and Company, Inc. Available at http://online.wsj.com/article/SB117495177692049687.htm

Brunnermeier, M. K. (2009). Deciphering the 2007–08 liquidity and credit crunch. *Journal of Economic Perspectives*, *23*(1), 77–100.

Diamond, D. W., & Rajan, R. G. (2005). Liquidity shortage and banking crises. *Journal of Finance*, *60*(2), 615–647.

Duffie, D. (2008). *Innovations in credit risk transfer: Implications for financial stability*. BIS Working Paper 255. Available at http://www.bis.org/publ/work255.pdf

Goldman, S. (2007). *The sub-prime issue: A global assessment of losses, contagion and strategic implications*. Goldman Sachs Market Report, November 20.

Gorton, G. (2008). The panic of 2007. Federal Reserve Bank of Kansas. Available at http://www.kc.frb.org/publicat/sympos/2008/Gorton.10.04.08.pdf

Greenlaw, D., Hatzius, J., Kashyap, A. K., & Shin, H. S. (2008). *Leveraged losses: Lessons from the mortgage market meltdown*. U.S. Monetary Policy Forum Report No. 2.

International Monetary Fund. (2008). *Global financial stability report*. Washington, DC: International Monetary Fund.

Keys, B. J., Mukherjee, T. K., Seru, A., & Vig, V. (2008). *Did securitization lead to lax screening? Evidence from loans*. European Finance Association, 2008 Athens Meetings Paper. Available at SSRN: http://ssrn.com/abstract=1093137.

Morris, S., & Shin, H. (2004). Liquidity black holes. *Review of Finance*, *8*(1), 1–18.

Shin, H. S. (2009). Reflections on modern bank runs: A case study of northern rock. *Journal of Economic Perspectives*, *23*(1), 101–119.

Sholarin, O. O. (2008). Growth financing in emerging markets: How does privatization compare with securitization? *Journal of Money, Investment and Banking*, (2).

Sholarin, O. O. (2009). *The 2007–2009 global financial-liquidity crisis: Causes, consequences and policy implications*. Working Paper Series, Faculty of Finance, Pablo De Olavide University, Seville, Spain.

APPENDIX

Table A1. AAA-Rated Bank Bond Index Spreads Relative to Government Bonds (in Basis Points).

Year	Financial Indicators					
	EUR 1-year	EUR 10-years	USD 1-year	USD 10-years	GBP 1-year	GBP 10-years
2003	31.83	42.86	35.4	84.82	37.24	66.17
2004	31.68	37.34	36.22	68.72	34.48	69.76
2005	18.71	27.06	41.08	64.16	35.2	62.16
2006	23.73	33.73	35.45	74.87	30.48	65.75
2007	49.55	56.17	82.34	86.52	84.97	103.67
2008	87.65	103.07	160.13	200.51	157.33	181.38

Source: IMF Global Financial Stability Report (2008).

Table A2. Comparison of Financial Loss Estimates, October 2008 (in Billion of U.S. Dollars).

	Outstanding	Estimated Loss (April 2008 GFSR)	Estimated Loss (October 2008)
Subprime residential	300	45	50
Alt-A residential	600	30	35
Prime residential	3,800	40	85
Commercial real estate	2,400	30	90
Consumer loans	1,400	20	45
Corporate loans	3,700	50	110
Leveraged loans	170	10	10
Total for loans	12,370	225	425
	Outstanding	Estimated Mark-to-Market Loss (April 2008 GFSR)	Estimated Mark-to-Market Loss (October 2008)
Base case estimates of mark-to-market losses on related securities			
ABS	1,100	210	210
ABS CDOs	400	240	290
Prime MBS	3,800	0	80
CMBS	940	210	160
Consumer ABS	650	0	0
High grade corporate debt	3,000	0	130
High yield corporate debt	600	30	80
CLOs	350	30	30
Total for securities	10,840	720	980
Total for loans and securities	23,210	945	1,405

Source: IMF Global Financial Stability Report (2008).

Table A3. Global Financial Sector Losses (in Billions of U.S. Dollars).

Bank Write-Downs by Region		Bank Write-Downs by Type		Financial Sector Write-Downs	
Americas	334	Mortgages	243	Banks	587
Europe	229	Loans/leveraged loans	202	Hedge funds/other	60
Asia	24	Other	54	Insurers	80
		SIVs	5	Government-sponsored enterprises	20
		Trading	33		
		Mono-lines	49		

Source: IMF Global Financial Stability Report (2008).

Table A4. Estimates of Financial Sector Potential Write-Downs (Billions of U.S. Dollars).

	Base Case Estimates of Write-downs on U.S. Loans			Write-downs on U.S. Loans			GSEs and Government	Other (Hedge Funds, Etc.)
	Outstanding	April estimates	October estimates	Banks	Insurance	Pensions/ savings		
Subprime	300	45	50	35–40	0–5	0–5	–	October 2015
Alt-A	600	30	35	20–25	0–5	0–5	–	October 2005
Prime	3,800	40	85	25–30	0–5	0–5	45–55	0–5
Commercial real estate	2,400	30	90	60–65	October 2005	0–5	–	October 2020
Consumer loans	1,400	20	45	30–35	0–5	0–5	–	October 2015
Corporate loans	3,700	50	110	80–85	0–5	0–5	–	25–30
Leveraged loans	170	10	10	October 2005	0–5	0–5	–	0–5
Total for loans	12,370	225	425	255–290	May 2040	0–35	45–55	60–100

Table A4. *(Continued)*

	Base case estimates of mark-to-market losses on related securities			Losses on securities			GSEs and Government	Other (Hedge Funds, Etc.)
	Outstanding	April estimates	October estimates	Banks	Insurance	Pensions/ savings		
ABS	1,100	210	210	100–110	40–45	35–55	October 2015	October 2025
ABS CDOs	400	240	290	145–160	55–75	30–45	15–20	15–30
Prime MBS	3,800	0	80	20–25	October 2015	October 2020	20–25	0–5
CMBS	940	210	160	80–90	20–25	15–35	October 2020	15–20
Consumer ABS	650	0	0	–	–	–	–	–
High-grade corporate debt	3,000	0	130	65–75	20–30	20–35	–	
High-yield corporate debt	600	30	80	45–50	October 2015	15–20	–	
CLOs	350	30	30	15–20	0–5	0–5	–	October 2008
Total for securities	10,840	720	980	470–530	155–210	125–215	55–80	55–125
Total for loans and securities	23,210	945	1,405	725–820	160–250	125–250	100–135	115–225

Sources: Goldman Sachs; JPMorgan Chase & Co.; Lehman Brothers; Markit.com; Merrill Lynch; and IMF staff estimates.
Notes: ABS = asset-backed securities; CDO = collateralized debt obligation; CLO = collateralized loan obligation; GSE = Government-sponsored enterprises; CMBS = commercial mortgage-backed security; MBS = mortgage-backed security; the prime residential loans category includes a portion of GSE-backed mortgage securities.

BANK FRAGILITY AND THE FINANCIAL CRISIS: EVIDENCE FROM THE U.S. DUAL BANKING SYSTEM

Christian Rauch

ABSTRACT

Purpose – *This chapter compares the stability of the U.S. Dual Banking system's two bank groups, national and state banks, in light of the current financial crisis. The goal of the chapter is to answer three distinct questions: first, is there a difference in the (balance sheet) fragility between the two groups and, second, to what extent has the balance sheet fragility of both groups changed after the escalation of the financial crisis beginning in August 2007? Building on that, the third question asks to whether or not the respective regulatory agencies of both bank groups are responsible for these changes in balance sheet fragility in light of the financial crisis.*

Methodology – *To answer these questions the chapter uses U.S. Call Report data containing full quarterly balance sheets and P&Ls of all U.S. commercial banks over the period 2005–2008. Anecdotal evidence as well as univariate and multivariate difference-in-difference methodology focusing on the immediate pre-crisis period Q1/2005–Q3/2007 and the crisis period Q3/2007–Q4/2008 are applied.*

International Banking in the New Era: Post-Crisis Challenges and Opportunities
International Finance Review, Volume 11, 33–86

ISSN: 1569-3767/doi:10.1108/S1569-3767(2010)0000011006

Results – *Highly significant and robust results show that, ceteris paribus, national banks reduced their potential balance sheet fragility after the escalation of the crisis in August 2007 by reducing lending and liquidity creation stronger than state banks. Anecdotal evidence supports the empirical findings. Although both FDIC and OCC did not anticipate the adverse effects of the crisis, the OCC publicly showed an earlier reaction to liquidity-related problems than the FDIC.*

Originality – *The chapter is the first of its kind to analyze bank fragility around the escalation of the financial crisis and the role of the regulatory agencies. The chapter holds especially interesting policy implications in the light of the current discussion about the future regulation of the banking markets.*

INTRODUCTION

Bank fragility has been at the heart of the discussions about causes and consequences of the financial crisis 2007/2008. Researchers and practitioners alike have always recognized the importance of a safe and sound banking system, yet the amount of failures and instabilities within the banking system over the past 3 years from the likes of Bear Stearns, Lehman Brothers, AIG, or Merrill Lynch remind everybody again what the systemic consequences of big and unexpected bank failures – especially in times of crisis – can be. A thorough understanding of bank fragility with its determinants and economic implications is thus of high importance, even more so in times of crisis in which sudden exogenous shocks can cause an unanticipated systemic instability. Although past research has brought forward many theoretical and empirical results which provide the basis for a fundamental understanding of banks and their proneness to instability, new times and changing economic environments also call for new analyses to gain an understanding of new crises. Consequently, academia has reacted quickly in analyzing the current crisis. First papers dealing with bank stability and the financial crisis are for example Puri, Rocholl and Steffen (2009), analyzing changes in banks' lending behavior during the course of the crisis, Freixas, Martin, and Skeie (2009), in which interbank lending markets are observed, or Berger and Bouwman (2009b) who analyze the liquidity creation of banks before financial crises. This chapter follows the body of literature on crisis-related subjects. It will thereby tackle a research question focusing on a central issue to the full understanding of the crisis, which has not been analyzed before: the stability of all banks in the U.S. banking system shortly before and after the escalation of the financial crisis in August 2007. The chapter thereby focuses on one aspect which has been largely ignored by research so far: the role of regulatory and supervisory agencies for bank and bank system stability, especially in the United States where the current financial crisis originated.

These agencies play a pivotal role in keeping the banking system healthy by not only constantly monitoring and preventing banks from conducting business which might endanger their stability but also by deciding on the survival of distressed banks and taking failed banks safely out of business. In the United States the major supervisory agencies are the Office of the Comptroller of the Currency (OCC), the Federal Deposit Insurance Corporation (FDIC), the Federal Reserve (Fed) as well as local state supervisory authorities. These agencies have the regulatory and supervisory power over almost 95% of all U.S. commercial banks. The OCC has authority over all national banks and bank holding companies. State banks can be both member and nonmember banks of the Federal Reserve System. Member banks are jointly supervised by the FDIC, the Fed and state supervisors, whereas nonmember banks are supervised by the FDIC (in case they obtain deposit insurance) and state authorities. All agencies monitor banks by regularly examining the banks' operating business in terms of risk with special regard to "safety and soundness and consumer protection."[1] The scope of their tasks allows the agencies to influence the operating business of the banks if the respective agency deems the bank too unstable or risky. System stability and individual banks' fragility are hence directly linked to the respective supervisory agency and its supervision policy. To analyze the subject, this chapter focuses on the two major banking groups in the United States, the OCC-supervised national banks and the FDIC-supervised state banks. The first major research question of this chapter is thus: to what extent does the (balance sheet) fragility of the two banking groups change after the escalation of the current crisis in August 2007?

The second aspect of bank fragility on which this chapter focuses is liquidity. The chapter thereby follows the works of Berger and Bouwman (2009a, 2009b), who introduced a new measure of bank liquidity creation (2009a) and subsequently applied this measure to U.S. commercial banks (2009a, 2009b). Liquidity is a crucial aspect when it comes to bank stability. Especially in the current crisis, the liquidity aspect of banks has been a major factor: what is now known to be a "liquidity crunch" has contributed significantly to not only the escalation of the crisis but also to the magnitude and number of bank failures. Why is liquidity creation so pivotal for banks and their stability? The reason is the liquidity mismatch between assets and liabilities as a result of maturity transformation processes by which the bank creates liquidity (as explained by Diamond & Dybvig, 1983). Banks offer depositors short-term availability of deposited money and grant borrowers long-term availability of loan money. By transforming maturities of short-term liabilities (i.e. deposits) into long-term assets (i.e. loans), banks hold illiquid items instead of the general public and are able to offer liquidity to both depositors and borrowers. Instability arises in times of heightened deposit demand or increased loan charge-offs. Whenever banks cannot meet the liquidity demand on the liabilities side of the balance sheet, for example in case of a bank run, they become illiquid and run the risk of being taken out of business by the respective supervisory agency. The fact that most bank failures during the current crisis as well as the instabilities of system relevant banks are a direct consequence of liquidity problems calls for a new and thorough analysis of bank liquidity creation and its influence on bank stability. Although the theoretical idea of banks as liquidity creators was already developed by Bryant (1980) and Diamond and Dybvig (1983) back in the 1980s and had already been used for empirical research by Deep and Schaefer (2004) and Berger and Bouwman (2009a, 2009b), there are to the best of my knowledge only two papers covering liquidity aspects in the current crisis: Freixas et al. (2009) and Berger and Bouwman (2009b). It is especially interesting to include the liquidity issue when analyzing the regulatory and supervisory authorities of U.S. banks. FDIC and OCC both mentioned liquidity-related issues as a potential source of trouble for banks, however only late in 2008 after the crisis had already escalated. It will thus be interesting to see whether the banks acted before the agencies addressed the issue or if the agencies raised the issue first. The second major research question of this chapter is thus: to what extent do the two banking groups differ in their liquidity creation and to what extent does that liquidity creation contribute to the banks' fragility?

The chapter measures bank fragility using four CAMEL indicators as well as four liquidity indicators. CAMEL scores are balance sheet-based ratios or figures indicating the stability of banks; they have long been used by regulators and supervisors around the world. The liquidity indicators are newly developed techniques by Deep and Schaefer (2004) and Berger and Bouwman (2009a) which allow detailed analysis of total and relative liquidity amounts per bank as well as the extent of liquidity mismatch on the balance sheet. The differences in fragility between the groups and the changes in fragility from before to after the beginning of the current crisis are measured with a univariate and multivariate difference-in-difference methodology. Additionally, this chapter uses anecdotal evidence to analyze the supervisory agencies' evaluation of the crisis as well as their (policy-) reactions to it. Anecdotal evidence is collected through public statements of FDIC, Fed, and OCC officials and publicly available internal communication between the agencies and the banks. Comparing the empirical results with the anecdotal evidence allows for a more detailed analysis of the influence the agencies have on the banks and whether or not the agencies reacted timely to the escalation of the crisis and the looming instability of banks caused thereby. The results show that national banks, as compared to state banks, reduced their potential balance sheet fragility after the escalation of the crisis in August 2007 by subsequently reducing lending and liquidity creation. Anecdotal evidence supports these findings: the OCC, regulator and supervisor of national banks, reacted more quickly to liquidity-related problems than the FDIC.

By tackling these research questions, the chapter addresses two topics. First, the chapter aims at providing evidence on the stability of the U.S. banking system before and during the beginnings of the current financial crisis. This insight allows for a thorough analysis of how stable U.S. banks are in times of regular economic conditions and how the current crisis changed this stability for better or for worse. Second, the chapter distinguishes between the safety and soundness of the two major banking groups in the United States, state and national banks. The results will thus allow for a comparative analysis of the way authorities conduct bank supervision. This comparison also has a political dimension. For years, there has been an ongoing debate about the benefits and concerns about the duality of the U.S. banking system (see e.g. Robertson, 1966; Kreps, 1966; Scott, 1977 or, recently, Blair & Kushmeider, 2006; Telser, 2007). Although there are many arguments in favor of the system, there are also many critics asking for changes in the system or abandoning the system altogether. The results of this study can serve as arguments in this debate by answering the question of whether or not one part of the system might be more stable than the other part. More importantly, the analyses of the chapter also address a most recent political debate on the restructuring of the banking system as a consequence of the current financial crisis. Government has proposed new and different roles for all regulatory and supervisory authorities: plans of Secretary of the Treasury Timothy Geithner and President Barack Obama see the Federal Reserve as a new "super-"authority supervizing all other regulatory and supervisory authorities. The chapter can contribute to the discussion on these plans by providing insight into the work of the supervisory authorities.

The chapter is structured as follows: section "The U.S. dual banking system: Chartering process and supervisory authorities" discusses the theoretical background on the concept of bank liquidity creation to cover the most important subject of this chapter. The third part explains the way bank fragility is measured for the analyses at hand and elaborate on the univariate and multivariate difference-in-difference analysis. The fourth part discusses the results of the different analyses. The fifth part elaborates on robustness tests which are performed to validate the results of the chapter's main analyses. The sixth part summarizes the results and interpret them.

THE U.S. DUAL BANKING SYSTEM: CHARTERING PROCESS AND SUPERVISORY AUTHORITIES

Upon chartering, a bank has two possibilities: it can either charter with state authorities and become a state bank or charter with federal authorities and become a national bank.[2] National banks charter with the OCC and become a member of the Federal Reserve System, state banks charter with local state authorities and remain within state regulatory and supervisory boundaries. State banks are not members of the Federal Reserve System, unless they choose to become a member: after chartering with state authorities, each state nonmember bank has the possibility to apply for a membership of the Federal Reserve System, which is usually granted contingent upon the fulfillment of certain requirements. The Fed-membership causes certain obligations and rights for the respective banks. For a start, member banks "buy into" their respective regional Fed-branch by acquiring a certain share of stock. This share of stock serves as additional safety equity capital which the bank can sell back to the Fed in case of distress. Nonmember banks do not keep mandatory capital with the Fed and do not have to "buy into" any state authority. In contrast to nonmember banks, member banks can also use the Fedwire interbank payment transfer system which allows for the quick transfer or large amounts of money. This can be of advantage in case of threatening illiquidity or distress when banks need large amounts of short-term money. Another difference is regarding the cost for supervision: Fed membership is usually associated with higher costs as compared to state and/or FDIC supervision. A similarity between the groups is that both member and nonmember banks can use the Federal Reserve Discount Window. The Discount Window serves as a complementary monetary policy tool next to open market operations to provide short-term lending, i.e. liquidity, to the market, either to allow banks to meet the overnight Fed reserve requirements on rather short notice or in times of distress. Financial services offers by the Fed, such as check clearing, electronic funds transfers. automated clearing house payments, and coin and currency services, can also be used by both member and nonmember banks.

The main difference between national and state banks, which is also the relevant difference for the purposes of this chapter, is the way supervision is exercised for the different bank groups. Table A1 in the appendix provides an overview of these differences. After obtaining the initial bank charter, each bank has a primary and a federal supervisor. The primary supervisor is the chartering authority, which is the state supervisor for state banks and the OCC for national banks. The respective federal supervisor for national banks is the OCC. For state banks a distinction has to be drawn between member and nonmember banks of the Federal Reserve System. For member banks, the federal supervisor is the Federal Reserve, more precisely the respective regional Fed-branch which is responsible for the region in which the bank is located. For nonmember banks, the federal supervisor is the FDIC in case the bank obtains deposit insurance through the FDIC (which about 95% of all state nonmember banks have). State nonmember banks without deposit insurance are solely supervized by state authorities. For national banks, the sole supervisor is the OCC. This means that the OCC is the only authority to monitor the banks in a variety of ways: they talk to the management, analyze daily operations and the risk associated with them and examine mandatory bank reports consisting of full balance sheets, profit and loss accounts, special risk and capital reports and all off-balance sheet items. They can also issue rules and regulations for the respective banks to follow. For state member and nonmember banks, there is no single authority exercizing these rights. Instead, supervision is conducted by a joint group of authorities. For FDIC insured nonmember banks, the supervisory authorities are the respective state supervisors (from the state in which the bank's headquarters are located) and the FDIC. For FDIC insured member banks, the supervisory authorities are the FDIC, the regional Fed-branch which is responsible for the geographical region in which the respective bank is located in, as well as the FDIC. In case a bank does not have FDIC deposit insurance, the FDIC is not a supervisor. The different authorities exercise the supervisory rights jointly for each bank. This means that each bank is monitored by supervisors of FDIC, Fed, and state supervisors, depending on which group they belong to. The stark difference here is that national banks are only supervised by the OCC, whereas state banks are not supervised by the OCC at all but instead by the FDIC, Fed, and state supervisors.

BANK SUPERVISION IN THE UNITED STATES

What types of risks the agencies look for or when risky operations become intolerable for the supervisor is a very opaque process. All supervisors are rather intransparent in the way they disclose safety and soundness standards for banks and the way they are enforced. A source of rules and standards are FDIC and OCC supervision handbooks. Both of these manuals contain detailed information about the stability-relevant areas of banks such as capital, liquidity, market risk exposure, or earnings. For all these areas, the manuals describe on which factors a supervisor will focus on and in which way she will evaluate these factors. The factors both agencies rely on are CAMEL scores, as represented by capitalization, management efficiency/quality, and liquidity. Using a number of balance sheet and P&L proxies, a final score is derived for each bank which indicates the bank's safety and soundness. In order to evaluate banks the same way as supervisors do, I also look at the banks' CAMEL factors for the paper's analyses. However in spite of a large amount of "soft" information, these manuals do not contain any "hard" information such as target ratios for certain risk relevant assets or liabilities. The only exception is made for capital: both manuals include the standard Basel numbers for capital calculation and required magnitude of capitalization. As much relevant "hard" information is not disclosed, it is thus very difficult to tell when a supervisor will deem a bank in danger of distress. Additionally, examination reports are not made public. Drawing on past bank examinations to derive possible distress thresholds is hence not possible. The official term used in supervision legislation is the "safety and soundness" of a bank: whenever a supervisor regards a bank as "unsafe and unsound" she is allowed to take action against the bank. Again, the term "unsafe and unsound" is not defined by any "hard" numbers, i.e. there is no list of ratios providing thresholds a bank must not fail. For determining the safety and soundness, a supervisor (or a court) will look at a bank's resilience and whether or not it is "robust in its operations." Speaking in very simple terms, this means to which degree a bank is likely to go into illiquidity or insolvency within a given amount of time without the help of third parties. The likelihood of distress and the loss given default, i.e. the size of bank, are also the crucial factors in determining the action taken to either keep the bank in business or take the bank safely out of business. For doing so, the supervisors have a variety of possibilities. They can informally or formally advise the bank's management of possible unsafe or unsound operations and leave the resolving of the issues to the bank. They also have the power to force mandatory precautionary or corrective measures upon the bank if they believe that management is either incapable or unwilling to take the necessary steps needed to restore the safety and soundness of the bank. Next to these informal or formal measures – which are mostly used – the authorities can also fine the bank for not implementing informal or formal advice of the supervisors. In tougher cases, supervisors are empowered to issue Cease and Desist orders against the bank and/or its managers to force the bank into complying with the authority. To take a bank out of business without the bank's management approval, both agencies can retrieve the bank charters and therefore end the operations of the bank. All these measures show that the agencies can take any action necessary to influence the operating business of the bank to keep the banks safe and sound. In most cases, the supervisors work together with the banks on a so called "control as influence" basis, meaning that the supervisors are in constant dialogue with the bank, its risk, legal and compliance departments and management and give recommendations which the bank follows. The harsher "control as command" basis as represented by cease and desist orders or charter retrieval comes into play whenever there is serious misconduct by the bank or the immediate threat of financial distress.

The way in which supervisors monitor banks clearly shows the large influence that supervisors have on the day-to-day operations of a bank and hence on its safety and soundness. They also show that supervisors can not only exert corrective but also precautionary measures to keep banks stable, for example in anticipation of times of economic turmoil. Yet, there is no possibility to determine any differences in the way supervision is conducted or how the different agencies deal with crisis situations or financial distress of banks.

MEASURING BANK FRAGILITY

The chapter applies two proxies to measure bank stability, both related to the fragility of individual banks' balance sheets. First, classic "CAMEL" score methodology is applied. The term "CAMEL" stands for capital adequacy, management efficiency and liquidity, as represented by the first capital letters of each term, and refers to a number of indicators which give evidence of a bank's operative strength and balance sheet stability. There are many possible ratios or figures which can indicate whether or not a bank is adequately capitalized, its management works efficiently and it is liquid enough. This analysis uses four of the most widely accepted and well-known factors for capitalization and efficiency: loan loss coverage, return on assets, loan growth, and cost efficiency. All factors are explained in Table A4 of the appendix. The chapter thereby closely follows the methodology as proposed by Bongini, Claessens and Ferri (1999) and Bongini, Laeven and Majnoni (2002). As liquidity indicators, the chapter uses two newly proposed indicators by Deep and Schaefer (2004) and Berger and Bouwman (2009a), as explained in more detail further below.

Loan loss coverage is measured by the ratio of excess loan loss reserves and capital (as in Tier-1 and Tier-2 capital) to total loans. It measures to which degree a bank covers its total loans to meet sudden loan defaults. The higher the ratio, the more loans are covered by capital and the more stable is the bank. Cost efficiency is measured by the ratio of operating expenses to total revenues. The higher the ratio, the more inefficient is the bank. This inefficiency is seen as an indicator for instability because it reduces a bank's profits and thus makes it more prone to sudden exogenous shocks which affect their operating business. The general economic health of a bank is measured by the annualized loan growth. Although an increasing loan growth ratio can be positive for the general economy, it is widely perceived in a negative way in terms of bank stability. By expanding the loan volume, banks are regarded to accept loan applications from less credit-worthy borrowers. This increases the overall default risk of the loan portfolio and thus makes banks more fragile. Finally, the return on assets is calculated as the ratio of net income to total assets. It measures the profitability of each dollar in assets. Banks which "operate" their assets in a more profitable way and hence show a higher margin, are regarded as more stable. The reasoning is the same as for the cost efficiency ratio.

These (or similar) figures are used by banks' supervisory authorities in the United States and can therefore serve as valid indicators of bank instability for the purposes of this chapter. However, since most of the bank failures as well as the bank system instability during the current crisis are caused by a sudden liquidity dry-up in the market, a special focus should be laid on liquidity as a stability indicator. To do so, the chapter applies four distinct and newly developed liquidity measures to exactly determine the absolute and relative extent of liquidity creation of each bank both with and without off-balance sheet items as well as the amount of maturity transformation a bank performs to create liquidity: the Berger and Bouwman (2009a, 2009b) "CAT"[3] method and the Deep and Schaefer Liquidity Transformation (LT) Gap, as shown in Tables A3a, A3b of the appendix. The CAT method measures the absolute monetary (U.S. Dollar denominated) amount of liquidity from the asset and liabilities side of each bank's balance sheet. It thus yields the volume of liquid monetary means which each single bank provides to the economy, as represented by each bank's lenders and borrowers, or retains for itself. In contrast, the LT Gap measures the relative amount of liquidity created in terms of the relationship between deposits and assets. The LT Gap value not only shows into what kind of assets a bank converts its deposits, but it is thereby also a measure of the fragility of a bank's balance sheet. The CAT and LT Gap values taken together therefore allow for three interpretations of a bank's liquidity creation: first, what is the total amount of created liquidity? Second, to what extent exhausts a bank its liquidity creation capabilities with given liquidity amounts? And third, taken all these answers together, how fragile is the bank in its liquidity creation? To gain further insight into bank liquidity creation, the chapter also reports the values including and excluding off-balance sheet items. Furthermore, a relative value of the Berger and Bouwman CAT measure is included: the ratio of total liquidity as represented by the CAT measure to a bank's total assets. This measure helps to compare liquidity creation of banks of different sizes.

The CAT methodology is based on a three-step procedure. The first step of the procedure determines which balance sheet item is liquid or illiquid. This is done by categorizing each items based on the ease, cost, and time at which the respective item can be liquidated, i.e. turned into cash. The perspective is thereby always from the owner of the balance sheet item. For loans, the ease, cost, and time reference is seen from the bank's perspective. The easier and less costly it is to sell off a loan or the quicker it is repaid, the more liquid the loan is. The same logic applies for all assets: consequently, the most liquid asset is cash. For the liabilities, the ease, cost, and time applies for the depositors. Following the asset labeling, the most liquid liability is a checking account which can be demanded on a daily basis. In contrast, a savings account with a maturity of 5 years would be labeled illiquid as it could only be withdrawn after 5 years. In the second step of the procedure each asset is weighted positive or negative according to its label. For liquid assets and illiquid liabilities, the label is negative, whereas for illiquid assets and liquid liabilities the label is positive. The weights are either +0.5 or −0.5, in order to calculate one U.S. dollar of liquidity for each liquid liability which is turned into and illiquid asset. The third label, semi-liquid, is weighted with 0. Berger and Bouwman do this for all balance sheet items which cannot clearly be determined as being either liquid or illiquid. As those would blur the final result, they are taken out of the calculation. The last step then consists of summing up the weighted values to get to the absolute amount of liquidity. For all category labels, we adapt the suggestions of Berger and Bouwman, a detailed list of balance sheet and off-balance sheet items with liquidity label can be found in the appendix.

The LT Gap calculations follow the guidelines as presented by Deep and Schaefer in 2004. As stated earlier, the LT Gap value shows the relationship of liquid assets to total deposits, standardized by the total assets. The value thus shows how many dollars of deposits were turned into liquid or illiquid assets. The underlying notions are the same as in the Berger and Bouwman methodology. To calculate the liquid assets value, I add up the positions cash and balances from depository institutions, government and nongovernment securities, federal funds sold and acceptances of other banks. Additionally, all loans with a maturity of less than 3 months are regarded to be liquid. To calculate the total value of deposits I add the total volume of all savings, time and transactions accounts up. To calculate the LT Gap, I subtract the liquid assets from the deposits and divide that number by the total assets.

It is to be noted that there are further distress or fragility indicators for banks, some also focusing on efficiency or capitalization factors, others focusing on different aspects such as asset price- or debt-related factors. Most prominent factors are the "Distance to Default" and the "Subordinated Debt Spread," as explained by e.g. Gropp, Vesala and Vulpes (2002 and 2004).[4] Both factors can give short-term indications of the level of distress of a bank and are widely used by regulatory and supervisory agencies. However, we forego an inclusion of these factors for two reasons. First, to observe all national and state banks and to avoid a sample selection bias, we observe both stock-listed and nonstock listed banks. The two mentioned factors can only deliver useful results for stock-listed banks due to their strong focus on market prices for assets and liabilities. Second, both factors do not take bank liquidity into account, which is at the focus of this chapter's analysis.

UNIVARIATE AND MULTIVARIATE FRAGILITY ANALYSES

To find answers to the chapter's research questions, the analysis follows a simple and clear-cut two step procedure. The first step contains a detailed analysis of the actual crisis-related comparison of both banking groups' fragility. I therefore apply a difference-in-difference methodology which allows for a comparison of both banking groups before the beginning of the crisis, after the beginning of the crisis and a comparison of the changes in the differences among the groups from before to after the beginning of the crisis. A difference-in-difference analysis can be applied whenever differences between two groups are to be measured, before one of the groups has undergone a certain kind of treatment or change and after this treatment or change has affected the group. The methodology was made popular by Card and Krueger (1994) and has since been a widely accepted and well-known methodology to measure differences between so-called treatment and control groups before and after a treatment.[5] The treatment group is the national banking group, the control group is the state banking group. The pre-treatment period is from the first quarter of 2005 to the second quarter of 2007, the post-treatment period starts on the escalation of the crisis in the third quarter of 2007 and ends in the fourth quarter of 2008. The choice for state banks as treatment group and the choice for the period of Q3/2007 to Q4/2008 might seem rather arbitrary: it is ex ante unclear whether or not any supervisory authority has exerted any "treatment" on banks and, if so, when this "treatment" has happened. However, these obstacles and the arbitrary choice for treatment group and period should not pose a problem for the analysis at hand: the goal of this chapter is to detect possible differences in the fragility of the observed banking groups before and after the beginning of the current financial crisis. I thus apply the difference-in-difference analysis not to detect a certain treatment but to detect these differences between the banking groups. As can be seen in this section of the chapter, a robustness test is applied to account for the choice of the treatment group and the observed time frame.

The difference-in-difference analysis is not only applied for descriptive comparisons of the two groups, but also in a multivariate regression setting. A specific goal of this chapter is to determine whether or not the regulatory and supervisory agencies are responsible for possible differences and changes in differences between the two groups. Yet, a large number of factors might be responsible for changes in fragility after the beginning of the crisis apart from the supervisory agencies. To only observe the absolute and relative changes between the groups might explain how the groups differ but not why. I apply a multivariate regression setting including a difference-in-difference estimator to determine to what extent the supervisory agency is responsible for the observed changes, thereby controlling for other possible influence factors. The estimated model is

$$Y_{i,t} = \beta_1 A_t + \beta_2 B_{i,t} + \beta_3 C_t + \beta_4 D_i + \beta_5 \text{Crisis}_{\text{dummy}} + \beta_6 \text{Treatment}_{\text{dummy}} + \beta_7 \text{Crisis}_{\text{dummy}} * \text{Treatment}_{\text{dummy}} + \varepsilon_{i,t} \quad (1)$$

The dependent variable $Y_{i,t}$ is the respective CAMEL factor or liquidity indicator, varying between the banks and over time. Used dependent variables are the four "classic" CAMEL indicators return on assets, loan growth, cost efficiency, and loan loss coverage as well as the four liquidity indicators total liquidity, total liquidity including off-balance sheet items, LT Gap and ratio of total liquidity to total assets. A_t represents time dummy variables to capture possible trend effects, $B_{i,t}$ are bank-specific control variables to account for heterogeneity among the banks. Included are the ratio of agricultural loans to total loans, total assets, total equity, the ratio of private to institutional loans, the ratio of trading assets to total assets, the ratio of short-term to long-term deposits, the loan charge offs and the net income. These variables control for the business model of the bank (private versus institutional clients, rural focus, and investment focus), the size of the bank (total assets) and the operative strength of the bank (net income). C_t contains macroeconomic control variables which might affect all banks to a similar degree. These factors have to be included in order to differentiate the effect of the supervisory agency from other influence factors, especially since some fragility indicators might be driven by exogenous factors. I include the federal funds rate, the interest rate spread between T-Bills with maturities of 1 month and 10 years, the U.S. GDP in bn. U.S. dollars and the average savings quota of U.S. households. D_i contains unobserved bank fixed effects to account for all other unobserved factors which might influence bank fragility and/or differences between the banking groups. $\text{Crisis}_{\text{dummy}}$ is a dummy variable indicating whether or not the respective time period is before (dummy = 0) or after the start of the financial crisis (dummy = 1) in the third quarter of 2007. $\text{Treatment}_{\text{dummy}}$ is a dummy variable indicating whether or not the respective bank is part of the control (state bank, dummy = 0) or treatment (national bank, dummy = 1) group. The last dummy variable $\text{Crisis}_{\text{dummy}}*\text{Treatment}_{\text{dummy}}$ is the most important variable: it is the interaction term of the crisis and the treatment dummy variable. The estimate β_7 thus shows by how much the treatment group (state banks) changed compared to the control group (national banks) and compared to the pre-crisis period. I finally include an error term $\varepsilon_{i,t}$.

One thing should be stressed at this point: although the inclusion of fixed effects accounts for bank-specific differences in the sample, I use the mentioned bank characteristic variables as well as macroeconomic control variables to distinguish between "supply and demand" effects of bank fragility. Liquidity creation is not only the result of active banking policy, it can also be driven by the availability of deposits or the demand for loans. Interest rate spreads also play a major role, not only due to profitability reasons but also because they influence loan demand, especially for long- versus short-term loans. The analysis wants to determine whether or not changes in fragility – mainly represented by liquidity factors – are driven by active policy management of banks' supervisory agencies. The control variables control for these influence factors. The yielded estimators for the difference-in-differences estimators are thus able to only reflect the influences of the supervisory agencies and the crisis.

To run the regression, I use a dynamic-panel difference GMM estimation model with heteroskedasticity robust standard errors and the inclusion of lags of the dependent variable as explanatory variable to account for auto-regressive effects.[6] This estimation technique is chosen due to the specifics of the dataset. First, the regressors might not be fully exogenous and correlate with current and past realizations of the error. I regress bank balance sheet variables on other bank balance sheet variables, possible endogeneity of the variables is thus to be expected. To account for that, the lags of the regressors serve as instrumental variables which are used for the estimation. I furthermore test on a dependent variable which is expected to depend on its past realizations, thus being dynamic. In case the supervisory agency might pursue boundaries for certain fragility indicators and hence adjusts these indicators accordingly, the analysis can account for that. Third, I include unobserved fixed effects for which this estimation technique accounts. As we apply a panel dataset we expect panel-typical heteroskedasticity and autocorrelation within the individuals. This estimation methodology thus allows for an unbiased estimation of the regression and yields reliable results.

DATA

The analyses in this chapter are performed with U.S. Call Report data. The dataset contains full balance sheets, profit and loss accounts, all off-balance sheet items as well as excerpts on risk-based capital for all U.S. commercial banks on a quarterly basis from the first quarter of 2005 to the last quarter of 2008. For reasons of simplicity, banks which merged during this period of time are treated as if they had already been merged at the beginning of the observation period by means of adding up their balance sheets and netting out the profit and loss accounts. Additional data containing all necessary information on the charter- and regulatory agent are taken from public official FDIC supervisory statistics. The final dataset contains a total of 5,460 banks, of which 1,238 are national banks, and 4,222 are state banks. A detailed description of the dataset can be found in Table A5 of the appendix.

ANECDOTAL EVIDENCE – OFFICIAL STATEMENTS OF REGULATORY AGENCIES ON CRISIS

In the first step of the empirical analysis, I analyze the anticipation of and reaction to the financial crisis by the observed regulatory and supervisory bank agencies. The reactions are taken from official statements as recorded in press clippings or public speeches/interviews by FDIC, OCC, or Fed officials from the first quarter 2007 to the last quarter of 2008, as presented in Table A2 of the appendix.[7] In the first quarter of 2007, no official statement is released or comment made by any of the agencies regarding the crisis. First comments by the FDIC and the OCC are made in the second quarter of 2007. The FDIC reported that bank asset indicators were less favorable at the time, but that the banking sector as a whole was in good condition. First slight signs of subprime-related problems were admitted by the FDIC in June 2007: in two separate statements, the FDIC called for stricter bank regulation in the light of the increase in subprime lending and was in favor of banning high-risk bank operations. In the second half of 2007, the FDIC continued to acknowledge the looming risks within the banking sector but stressed that these problems would not pose any kind of significant risk for the banking sector. Although the FDIC started to look closer at banks' CDO exposure and expected an increase in the number of defaults for smaller banks, they kept indicating that the industry was in good shape and banks would be able to cope with the problems. Towards the end of 2007, the FDIC suggested that the subprime-related problems were more severe than previously assumed. In several statements, FDIC officials said that banks may need to increase capital as the subprime market could cause bigger problems for banks than previously expected. It was in December 2007 that the FDIC first acknowledged the possibility of a large bank failure. However, at the time the FDIC believed that the struggling subprime mortgage market would have more adverse effects on bank clients than on the banks themselves.

The statements made in the beginning of 2008 show that the FDIC was both preparing their banks for adverse market effects but at the same time strongly underestimated the magnitude of the effects and the problems these effects already had on banks at the time. Just weeks before the almost-failure of Bear Stearns, the FDIC told investors not to worry about the health of the banking system and that bank failures would only become more likely with smaller banks. In spite of these rather soothing statements, the FDIC internally warned their banks about the perils of the subprime meltdown and urged them to increase loan loss provisions. Additionally, the FDIC increased both reserves and the examination staff to deal with anticipated problems. Yet, Selma Blair was mistaken to believe that the markets were past the worst of the turmoil in May 2008, as she stated at the time. The third quarter of 2008 saw the FDIC again publicly calming markets and bank customers by stating that larger institutions are not expected to fail (July 2008). However, the FDIC took an important step to deal with the increasing troubles of the banking markets by increasing the deposit insurance threshold from USD 100,000 to USD 250,000. In the last quarter of 2008, the FDIC publicly only addressed problems related to the subprime crisis, no more positive outlooks. Selma Bair talked about liquidity problems of banks, and the FDIC "Supervisory Insight" report featured a long article on the same issue. Additionally, the FDIC reacted to the crisis by implementing certain remedial steps aimed at supporting banks in distress and the FDIC itself. Among these steps was the increase of the insurance premium to cover larger deposit losses or the public urge for small banks to apply for federal financial aid.

In comparison to the FDIC, whose officials commented frequently on the crisis and related problems, the OCC kept public comments to a minimum, especially regarding warnings and/or estimations concerning the health of national banks. This can be seen from the number of official statements included in Table A2 of the appendix. A first sign of this minimum in communication was that there was no public statement on the crisis or related issues in the first half of 2007. In the third quarter of 2007, John Dugan addressed the House committee and stated that the banks were healthy and the system was safe, although the market turmoil surrounding mortgage lending had already begun to surface. In spite of this public statement, the OCC had just before Mr. Dugan's speech released a report on foreclosure prevention, in which it stated that the mortgage meltdown could be stressful on the banking system. To follow up on this report, the OCC released another study in the last quarter of 2007, showing that lending standards had eased considerably for the fourth consecutive year. The report concluded that this might have adverse effects on the banking system. In 2008, the OCC increased the number of official releases and comments regarding the crisis. In early 2008, Mr. Dugan publicly warned banks to "clean up" loan portfolios and to prepare for losses stemming from subprime loans. Additionally, Mr. Dugan announced his concern with the overall real estate lending development and suggested several steps to keep banks from failing. The OCC again repeated its anticipation of mortgage-related losses from banks for 2009 and drew attention to potential risks for banks posed by home equity loans, which were also closely tied to the developments in the real estate market. The first mention of liquidity risk by the OCC took place in the third quarter of 2008, hence one quarter before the FDIC first publicly acknowledged banks' liquidity situation. The OCC thereby urged banks to pay attention to potential illiquidity risks. A very interesting statement was finally made by Mr. Dugan in the last quarter of 2008, in which he addressed the roles of the different regulatory and supervisory agencies. He specifically stated that the U.S. banking system could benefit from a consolidation of the different supervisory authorities. Details as to how this consolidation should take place were not provided.

In conclusion it can be said that both agencies, FDIC and OCC, underestimated the magnitude of the subprime-related problems not only for their banks but also for the banking system as a whole, at least publicly. Whether or not internal and publicly unavailable communication addressed banks' problems more clearly or contained stronger warnings about the perils of the looming crisis is unclear. However, judging by the public statements of the agencies, both banking groups were provided with too little red flags too late. The same goes for liquidity risks. Although the crisis escalated in August 2007 because of liquidity drying up in interbank markets, both agencies first addressed potential liquidity problems towards the end of 2008. The OCC first mentioned that liquidity-related problems could pose a risk for banks, the FDIC addressed this issue only after the failure of Lehman Brothers. However, a distinction has to be drawn between public statements made by FDIC and OCC officials and publicly available internal communication between the agencies and their banks. At times when both agencies drastically warned banks of current and future problems, statements directed at the general public contained mostly positive outlooks or muted warnings. Whether or not this was meant to calm markets and customers or a mere underestimation of the bank-inherent problems and their effects on banks, remains unclear. However, a conclusion that can be drawn from the available communication is that both agencies did not anticipate the escalation of the crisis and reacted too late to the risks, especially posed by illiquidity. Whether or not the empirical results support this conclusion will be discussed in the sub-chapters 'Descriptive results and univariate Difference-in-Difference analysis' and 'Multivariate Difference-in-Difference analysis results'.

DESCRIPTIVE RESULTS AND UNIVARIATE DIFFERENCE-IN-DIFFERENCE ANALYSIS

In the first step of the analysis, the chapter provides a broad overview of the actual ratios and figures for the four classic CAMEL as well as the newly introduced four liquidity factors for both banking groups. Starting with the classic CAMEL factors of loan growth, loan loss coverage, cost efficiency and return on assets, the chapter does not detect any strong visible effects of the crisis on the banks, neither in terms of anticipation nor in terms of reaction after the escalation of the crisis in August 2007. As can be seen in Table A7, an exception to that is only the rate of loan growth. Overall, loan growth remains fairly stable over the observed period from Q1/2005 to Q4/2008 with values of between 1% and 2%. A notable drop in lending can be seen in the two quarters following Q3/2007, in which national bank lending growth decreased from 2.3% to 0.2% and state bank lending growth from 2.2% to −0.3%. This shows that both banking groups strongly decreased the amount of newly lent money. If this effect can be attributed to the escalation of the crisis, it is a very initial and short-lived reaction: lending increased thereafter to pre-crisis levels and average values for the full year 2008 are consequently at 0.9% for national and 1.6% for state banks in lending growth. A strong and persistent adjustment of lending following the events of Q3/2007 can thus not be detected from a purely descriptive point of view. The analyses of the three other CAMEL factors loan loss coverage, return on assets and cost efficiency yield fairly similar results, as Table A7 shows. Both banking groups show a strong homogeneity in cost efficiency with average values of 74% at the beginning of the observation period increasing to values of about 79% towards the end of the period for both banking groups. The increase seems to be stable and does not show any crisis-related jumps. The same goes for the return on asset values, which decrease on average from 0.8% in 2005 to 0.5% in 2008, again for both groups. The time series shows very little volatility and no overall trend which could be attributed to the beginning of the crisis. The last factor, loan loss coverage, exhibits very similar features. Both groups show a slight increase over the observation period, yet again no sharp in- or decreases after Q3/2007. The only real difference lies in the level of coverage: national banks have average values of about 22–23% whereas state banks are at 26–27%. In terms of loan loss protection, state banks therefore seem to be more secure than national banks.

Although the univariate difference-in-difference results support the descriptive findings of the four classic CAMEL factors they add a little more insight into possible crisis-related changes in the factors. To measure the differences between the groups as well as the changes within and between the groups over time, the chapter calculates mean values for each CAMEL factor for the period before and after Q3/2007. Looking at the average values of the pre-crisis period in Table A9, the analyses detect significant differences between the banking groups for loan loss coverage and return on assets. Loan growth and efficiency do not seem to differ significantly between the groups. These results are not surprising as they support the descriptive findings above. The second period from Q3/2007 to Q4/2008 exhibits the same results. Detected are significant differences between the groups for return on assets and loan loss coverage but not for efficiency. Loan growth, however, is now significant. The interpretation of the values is thus straight forward: in both periods, the groups do not show any significant differences in average values of efficiency but do show slightly significant differences in return on assets and loan loss coverage. Loan growth is an exception, since it is only strongly different in the second period, which could be an indicator that one of the bank groups adjusted lending following the escalation of the crisis. The second step of the analysis is the univariate difference-in-difference analysis which shows to what extent the relationship (i.e. the differences in the given CAMEL factors) between the groups changed over the two periods. Here, the chapter does not find any significant values, except for loan growth (as seen in Table A9). The interpretation is thus that the differences between the groups did not change over time, or – more precisely – that the escalation of the crisis in Q3/2007 did not trigger any changes within the four CAMEL factors in one of the groups which would have lead to a stronger difference between the groups with the exception of loan growth. The reason is a slight increase in lending of state banks at a contemporaneous decrease of national banks. From a purely descriptive and univariate point of view it can thus be said that the groups only differ in their lending behavior after the escalation of the crisis.

For the second part of the CAMEL factors, the liquidity indicators, the analyses find more heterogeneity between the groups as well as stronger changes over time as seen in Table A8. The first interesting finding is that national banks have a larger liquidity creation, both including and excluding off-balance sheet items. The finding makes intuitive sense since, as the description of the dataset in Table A6 shows, national banks are much larger in terms of deposits, loans, and consequently asset size. Looking at the changes in the numbers over time, a slight reaction to the escalation of the crisis can be detected. National banks decrease their overall liquidity after Q3/2007. Total balance sheet liquidity starts to decrease after Q4/2007 and, disregarding a slight jump from Q2/2008 to Q3/2008, continues to decline steadily and strongly, especially towards the end of the observation period. Liquidity including off-balance sheet items even turns negative in the last quarter of 2008. State banks show a slightly different development of total liquidity. Both liquidity numbers, in- and excluding off balance sheets, show a slight decline following Q4/2007, which is followed by two quarters of increase. Finally, the sharp drop comes in Q4/2008.

Interesting results are also found for the two relative liquidity ratios, the LT Gap and the total liquidity divided by total assets (Table A8). The first thing to note about the liquidity-to-asset ratio is that state banks have on average higher ratios than national banks. This means that state banks create more liquidity relative to their asset size. The finding is interesting, since national banks are much larger and also create more absolute liquidity for the markets. Furthermore, there seems to be only a marginal reaction to the events in Q3/2007 with slight drops in Q1 and Q4/2008. The drop in Q4/2008 could be attributed to the events surrounding the failure of Lehman Brothers in Q3/2008. What can be seen, however, is that the ratios for both groups increase strongly at the beginning of the observation period in 2005 and stagnate thereafter. The analysis of the LT Gap also yields some interesting results. The LT Gap values for national banks start at a higher level than state banks' LT Gap, but subsequently decline over the observation period until they almost reach the low level of state banks' LT Gap in Q4/2008. A sharp drop following Q3/2007 can however not be detected, neither for national nor for state banks.

The univariate difference-in-difference analysis for the liquidity values again supports the descriptive results, as can be seen in Table A9. In the period before the crisis escalation, the analysis finds highly significant differences between the two groups for all four liquidity values. I find that national banks create more absolute liquidity both with and without off-balance sheet items, have on average a higher LT Gap but create significantly less liquidity relative to their asset size as compared to state banks. The mean values over the period following Q3/2007 are slightly different: I only find the same results as in the pre-crisis period for the relative liquidity values LT Gap and the ratio of liquidity to assets. The liquidity values are only slightly significantly different (total liquidity) or not significant at all anymore (total liquidity plus off-balance sheet liquidity) between the groups. It can be seen that on average national banks decreased their absolute liquidity creation after the escalation of the crisis whereas state banks continued to raise their amounts of liquidity. The same goes for the relative ratio of total liquidity to assets. A similar pattern can be seen with the LT Gap development: although both banking groups decrease their LT Gaps, national banks do so much stronger than state banks. It can thus be stated that national banks, on average, reduced their fragility in terms of liquidity creation in comparison to state banks following the escalation of the crisis in Q3/2007.

Consequently, the univariate difference-in-difference analysis supports these results by showing the degree to which national banks reduced their fragility as compared to state banks. For the three values of LT Gap, the ratio of liquidity to assets and the total liquidity including off-balance sheet items, the differences between the groups have decreased significantly over time because national banks reduced their absolute and relative amounts of liquidity creation as compared to state banks. The conclusion drawn from the time series of values can thus be supported by the univariate difference-in-difference analysis: national banks reduced their fragility over the escalation of the crisis in Q3/2007 as compared to state banks.

MULTIVARIATE DIFFERENCE-IN-DIFFERENCE ANALYSIS RESULTS

The results of the descriptive and univariate part of the analysis can only show to what extent the two banking groups differ in the given stability factors. To determine the causes of the changes within and between the groups and to attribute the underlying reason for the change to a supervisory agency, a multivariate difference-in-difference analysis is performed. This analysis allows to disentangle market- or bank-inherent factors from supervisory influence on the banks. The three variables in questions are $Crisis_{dummy}$, $Treatment_{dummy}$, and, most importantly, the interaction term of crisis and treatment indicator $Crisis_{dummy}*Treatment_{dummy}$.[8] The general finding is that all three indicators support all the findings from the univariate analysis. The results show that overall and in the presence of a number of controlling factors, the differences between the groups can be attributed to the supervisory agents.

From the regressions with the four classic CAMEL score factors, only loan growth has a significant coefficient for the $Crisis_{dummy}*Treatment_{dummy}$ interaction term variable, as can be seen in Table A10. This means that national banks – given that other possible influence factors are controlled for – reduced lending activity after the escalation of the crisis in Q3/2007 stronger than state banks did. Since the variable in question is the loan growth, the result does not mean that they cut back on total lending. They merely reduced the amount of newly lent money to borrowers stronger than state banks did. The $Crisis_{dummy}$ and $Treatment_{dummy}$ variables support the finding: both are significantly negative, meaning that total loan growth of both bank groups was reduced following the escalation of the crisis and that, in total, national banks had a smaller loan growth than state banks over the whole observation period. Interaction term and treatment indicator are insignificant for all other factors, which shows that the supervisory agents had no influence on the way the factors developed. In contrast, the $Crisis_{dummy}$ indicator is significant for the efficiency and return on asset factors. For the whole sample average return on asset has therefore declined over the observation period, whereas cost efficiency increased. Both developments can be seen in the descriptive data.

Looking at the liquidity factors in Table A11, the analyses yield highly significant results for all of the $Crisis_{dummy}*Treatment_{dummy}$ interaction term variables, with the exception of total liquidity. For total liquidity including off-balance sheet items, the coefficient is highly significant and negative, just as for the ratio of total liquidity to assets and the LT Gap. The interpretation is therefore the same as in the univariate setting: national banks reduced their liquidity creation after the beginning of the crisis stronger than state banks. The two other dummy variables $Crisis_{dummy}$ and $Treatment_{dummy}$ support these findings and reflect the findings of the descriptive analysis. The coefficients for the treatment indicator are highly significant and positive for the total liquidity including off-balance sheet items as well as the LT Gap and highly significant and negative for the ratio of total liquidity to assets. The interpretation is here that national banks create on average more absolute liquidity over the whole observation period and also use more maturity transformation for doing so (as represented by the higher LT Gap). However, relative to their size they create less liquidity than state banks. The coefficients for the crisis indicator variable are highly significant and negative for LT Gap, total liquidity with off-balance sheet items and the ratio of liquidity to assets and insignificantly negative for the total liquidity without off-balance sheet items. What is shown here is that all banks reduced their total liquidity creation and the amount of maturity transformation.

In a second step of the multivariate analysis, I compare the OCC-supervised national banks only with state nonmember banks, excluding all state member banks. The results are presented in Tables A12 and A13 of the appendix. I do that to compare federally regulated banks with banks which are not regulated or supervised by the Fed but only by state authorities and the FDIC. As OCC banks are also part of the Federal Reserve System, just as state member banks, the groups might exhibit certain similarities which cannot be accounted for if the state member banks are not separated from state nonmember banks. Additionally, in state nonmember banks, state supervisors play a much more important role in examining the bank and in "keeping it stable." This analysis will therefore allow for a more detailed comparison of federal versus state supervisors. However, in spite of these differences, the results largely support the results of the first specification of the multivariate difference-in-difference analysis as presented in Tables A10 and A11. Looking at the four CAMEL factors excluding liquidity, the results show almost the exact same significances and signs of the coefficients. The interaction term $Crisis_{dummy}*Treatment_{dummy}$ for loan growth is significant at the 5% level and negative and loan loss coverage, cost efficiency and return on assets are insignificant. The same results can be found in Table A10 in the comparison of national and state banks including state member banks. I find slight differences in the $Crisis_{dummy}$ variable, indicating the change in variables during the escalation of the crisis. Although the sample of all state and national banks showed especially strong reactions to the crisis in loan growth, cost efficiency and return on assets, the sample without the state member banks only shows a strong and negative reaction in loan growth and a slightly negative reaction in loan loss coverage. This result implies that the crisis affected smaller banks less in earnings or efficiencies but only in loan growth. As the reduction in loan growth is stronger for the sample excluding state member banks, the conclusion can be drawn that smaller nonmember banks must have reduced their lending stronger as a reaction to the crisis than larger member banks.

Looking at the four liquidity factors, I also find the results of the initial model specification including state member banks supported. The main variable $Crisis_{dummy}*Treatment_{dummy}$ has for the liquidity indicators the same significant coefficients with the same signs as in the initial model. The major difference to the initial model can be seen in the magnitude of the coefficients. The coefficients are larger in the second specification of the model, meaning that national banks decreased their liquidity creation stronger than state banks excluding member banks as compared to state banks including member banks. An example, as shown in Table A11 and A13, is the coefficient of the variable "Total Liquidity OBS": comparing all national to all state banks (Table A11) results in a highly significant coefficient of −137,488 meaning that national banks decreased their liquidity creation on both the balance sheet and through off-balance sheet items as compared to state banks and as compared to the period before the crisis by 137,488 USD. The same coefficient in the second model, as reported in Table A13, is at −256,371, hence more negative. $Crisis_{dummy}$ and $Treatment_{dummy}$ support the results of the main model, both in terms of significances and signs of the coefficients.

ADDITIONAL ANALYSES AND ROBUSTNESS TESTS

To validate the results yielded by the major analyses, different robustness tests are performed. In a first step, a test accounts for the large heterogeneity in the dataset. By observing almost all U.S. commercial banks, the dataset is comprised of large multinational stock-listed banks as well as small and only regionally active savings banks. The fact that both bank groups also contain very large and very small banks makes a comparison of the two groups difficult and can bias the results. Although this heterogeneity is already accounted for by including bank-specific control variables in the regression, a further check is included in a separate analysis: by means of propensity score matching, all observed banks are clustered into subsamples to obtain three groups of mostly homogeneous state and national banks. The groups are displayed in Table A15. As can be seen in Table A14, a probit regression methodology is applied to calculate a propensity score for each observed bank. The propensity score indicates to what extent – given a certain number of influence factors – a bank is more or less likely to be a state or national bank. The model

$$Y_{\text{dummy}} = \beta_D A_i + \beta_1 B_i + \varepsilon_i \tag{2}$$

is estimated where Y_{dummy} is the dependent variable indicating whether or not each observed bank is either a state or an national bank. A_i is a set of bank-specific control variables. Included are the number of deposits as size indicator, the ratio of agricultural loans to total loans to indicate whether or not the bank is located in a rural or urban area, the ratio of private to institutional loans and the ratio of short- to long-term deposits to indicate whether the bank has a stronger focus on private versus commercial business and the ratio of trading assets to total assets to indicate whether a bank has a more investment or retail driven business. Furthermore, a dummy variable indicating whether or not each bank is part of a bank holding company structure is included. B_i is another set of bank-specific control variables, containing bank fragility indicators. ε_i is the error term. The estimation is performed using figures as of the fourth quarter of 2005, i.e. at a neutral pre-crisis period. In a second step, the banks are sorted according to their propensity scores and divided into thirds. After excluding the propensity scores outside the common support region, the subsamples lie within a propensity score range between 0.05765 and 0.87525. As can be seen in Table 15, this procedure delivers three homogenous groups of banks which are subsequently used for the same multivariate difference-in-difference analysis as given by Eq. (1). For reasons of brevity, the chapter will forego a detailed description of all results. The important finding of the subsample difference-in-difference analysis is that they support the results of the analysis for the whole sample. Comparing various subsamples comprised of homogeneous banks, it is found that they yield the same kinds of significances and coefficients as the analysis for the whole sample. This supports the results and their interpretations of the main analysis.[9]

The second robustness test is directed at validating the choice of pre-crisis and crisis period. A validation can be obtained by testing the difference-in-difference analysis for different time periods in which no "treatment" effect takes place. It has to be checked whether or not the difference-in-difference analysis yields significant results for periods in which no "treatment" effect hast taken place. Should the results be significant without a treatment effect, the analysis might capture a time trend which could also be responsible for the results during the actual treatment period. In this case, results are not robust. For this analysis, the multivariate difference-in-difference analysis for two time periods before the crisis period is tested. The first test period has the first quarter of 2003 to the second quarter of 2004 as "pre-treatment" period and the second half of 2004 and the full year 2005 as "post-treatment" period. The second test period is outside our actual observation period and has the second quarter of 1998 to the third quarter of 1999 as "pre-treatment" period and the fourth quarter of 1999 and the full year 2000 as "post-treatment" period. Both validation periods yield no significant differences between the groups in fragility from post- to pre-treatment period. The observed differences among the groups are the same as in our main observation, which is what was to be expected. It can thus be said that the difference-in-difference analysis does capture the full crisis effect in the third quarter of 2007.[10]

CONCLUSION

This chapter analyzes the aggregate bank fragility of the national and state banking groups in the United States with a special focus on the period immediately preceding the current financial crisis and the period after the escalation of the crisis beginning with the third quarter of 2007. The goal of the analysis is to determine if the banks' supervisory agencies can be deemed responsible for any kinds of changes in fragility during the course of the crisis. The chapter also tries to account for the natures of the crisis by measuring bank fragility through bank liquidity indicators as opposed to classic CAMEL fragility indicators. The two major research questions of the chapter are: to what extent has the balance sheet fragility of the two banking groups changed after the escalation of the current financial crisis in August 2007? Do the two banking groups differ in their liquidity creation and to what extent does that liquidity creation contribute to the banks' fragility? To answer these questions, the chapter uses univariate and multivariate difference-in-difference analysis to determine variations between the groups and crisis-related changes of fragility.

The chapter's analyses yield one central finding: as measured by the two CAMEL factors liquidity and loan growth, national banks have reduced their fragility after the escalation of the financial crisis in August 2007 as compared to state banks. National banks drastically reduced their liquidity creation and thereby their exposure to possible liquidity crunches. They also reduced the amount of loan growth as compared to state banks and thereby limited the risk of future losses in case of a further escalation of the crisis. These findings are supported by the anecdotal evidence this chapter detects. Public statements and publicly available information from agency officials or the agencies themselves show that both, FDIC and OCC, failed to anticipate the full scope of the crisis. However, it was the OCC which first reacted to liquidity-related issues by publicly warning their banks about it. The fact that national banks were quicker and stronger in reducing their liquidity creation in comparison to state banks might thus be a sign that the supervisors' statement on liquidity did indeed have an effect on these banks.

The results are especially interesting in the light of the regulatory and supervisory background of national versus state banks in the U.S. national banks are solely supervised by their chartering authority, the OCC, whereas state banks are supervised by a consortium of agencies comprised of state authorities, regional Fed branches and the FDIC. The ongoing discussion about whether or not supervisory agencies "did enough" after the escalation of the crisis to shelter their banks – or whether or not they should have anticipated the crisis or at least the dire consequences of it – is addressed by the results of the chapter. Although the data show that neither of the agencies foresaw the crisis and reduced fragility in anticipation of it, the OCC reacted at least in terms of liquidity creation and lending behavior. It could thus be concluded that a single authority might be able to react quicker and stronger to adverse changes in the economic environment than a multitude of agencies. Given this argument and the fact that the OCC anticipated liquidity-related problems earlier than the FDIC, might lead to the conclusion that the OCC could be given a more important role in the future of U.S. banking regulation.

Finally it can be said that once the crisis will be over and the whole magnitude of it can be seen, further and more detailed analyses will be able to shed more light on these chapter's research questions. This study sees itself as a stepping stone for further research and encourages other researchers to build on its results and help further understand bank fragility and the role of supervisory agencies.

NOTES

1. Quote taken from www.fdic.gov – Mission, Vision, and Values.
2. An overview of the U.S. banking system is given in Table A1 of the appendix.
3. The name "CAT" is derived from "Category," by which the balance sheet items are labeled according to Berger and Bouwman.
4. A detailed description of both factors, which I omit for reasons of brevity, can be found in the given source of Gropp et al. (2002, 2004).
5. A recent crisis-related paper applying the methodology is e.g. Puri et al. (2009). A more detailed analysis of difference-in-difference can be found in Wooldridge (2006).
6. GMM estimator as developed by Arellano and Bond (1991) and Arellano and Bover (1995). The Arellano and Bover (1995) version is applied in the chapter.
7. Fig. A1 of the appendix provides an additional overview over the development of the crisis by displaying six crucial factors. This table can be used to compare the timeline of the agencies' statements with actual crisis developments.
8. To focus on the analysis and interpretation of the three dummies, the chapter will forego a detailed description of the control variable coefficients and significances. For a list of all control variables, please refer to the section "Measuring bank fragility" of the chapter or Tables A8 and A9. All variables are described in Table A3a, A3b.
9. For reasons of brevity, only liquidity validation results are reported in the chapter.
10. For reasons of brevity, the full results from the validation difference-in-difference estimates will not be reported in the chapter.

ACKNOWLEDGMENTS

For valuable comments and suggestions I would like to thank Bolong Cao, Bjoern Imbierowicz, Sascha Steffen, Marcel Tyrell, Mark Wahrenburg, and Larry D. Wall. All remaining errors are my own.

REFERENCES

Arellano, M., & Bond, S. (1991). Some tests of specification for panel data: Monte Carlo evidence and an application to employment equations. *Review of Economic Studies*, *58*(2), 277–297.

Arellano, M., & Bover, O. (1995). Another look at instrumental variables estimation of error-components models. *Journal of Econometrics*, *68*(1), 29–51.

Berger, A., & Bouwman, C. (2009a). Bank liquidity creation. *Review of Financial Studies*, *22*(9), 3779–3837.

Berger, A., & Bouwman, C. (2009b). *Financial crises and bank liquidity creation*. Working Paper. Available at http://papers.ssrn.com/sol3/papers.cfm?abstract_id=1231562

Blair, C. E., & Kushmeider, R. (2006). Challenges to the dual banking system: The funding of bank supervision. *FDIC Banking Review*, *18*(1), 1–22.

Bongini, P., Claessens, S., & Ferri, G. (1999). *The political economy of financial distress in East Asian financial institutions*. Working Paper. Available at http://papers.ssrn.com/sol3/papers.cfm?abstract_id=202050

Bongini, P., Laeven, L., & Majnoni, G. (2002). How good is the market at assessing bank fragility? A horse race between different indicators. *Journal of Banking and Finance*, *26*(5), 1011–1028.

Bryant, J. (1980). A model of reserves, bank runs and deposit insurance. *Journal of Banking and Finance*, *4*(4), 335–344.

Card, D., & Krueger, B. (1994). Minimum wages and employment: A case study of the fast-food industry in New Jersey and Pennsylvania. *American Economic Review*, *84*(4), 772–793.

Deep, A., & Schaefer, G. (2004). *Are banks liquidity transformers?* KSG Working Paper No. RWP04-022, Cambridge, MA.

Diamond, D. W., & Dybvig, P. (1983). Bank runs, deposit insurance, and liquidity. *Journal of Political Economy*, *91*(3), 401–419.

Freixas, X., Martin, A., & Skeie, D. (2009). Bank liquidity, interbank markets, and monetary policy. *Federal Reserve Bank of New York Staff Report*, *371*, 1–37.

Gropp, R., Vesala, J., & Vulpes, G. (2002). Equity and bond market signals as leading indicators of bank fragility. *European Central Bank Working Paper Series*, *150*(02), 1–59.

Gropp, R., Vesala, J., & Vulpes, G. (2004). Market indicators, bank fragility, and indirect market discipline. *Federal Reserve Bank of New York Economic Policy Review*, *2004*(09), 53–62.

Kreps, C. H. (1966). Modernizing banking regulation. *Law and Contemporary Problems*, *31*(4), 648–672.

Puri, M., Rocholl, J., & Steffen, S. (2009). *The impact of the U.S. financial crisis on global retail lending*. Working Paper. Available at http://www.cepr.org/meets/wkcn/5/5567/papers/RochollFinal.pdf

Robertson, J. L. (1966). Federal regulation of banking: A plea for unification. *Law and Contemporary Problems*, *31*(4), 673–695.

Scott, K. E. (1977). The dual banking system: A model of competition in regulation. *Stanford Law Review*, *30*(1), 1–50.

Telser, L. (2007). Solvency vs. competition: Hobson's choice for the Fed. *Journal of International Money and Finance*, *26*(7), 1151–1173.

Wooldridge, J. (2006). *Introductory econometrics*. New York: Cengage Learning Services.

APPENDIX

Table A1 shows the different banking groups with their charter/charter agent as well as their primary and federal supervisory agency. Relevant for the purposes of the chapter are only national and state banks. To provide a thorough picture of the U.S. banking system, investment banks and thrifts are also reported. The last column of the table shows the number of banks which fall into that category as of the first quarter of 2005 (the numbers in italics show the number of banks as of the fourth quarter of 2008).

Figure A1 shows the evolution of the current financial crisis as represented by nine indicators. The upper part of the figure shows the number of banks on the FDIC "troubled banks" – watchlist as well as the development of total real estate loans in the U.S. banking system and the average loan loss allowance of all U.S. banks (both rebased to the levels of January 1, 2005). The middle part of the graphic shows the price of crude oil, the market capitalization of Citigroup (both rebased to the levels of January 1, 2005) and the Dow Jones Industrials Average Index. The lower part shows the Federal Funds Rate and the U.S. unemployment rate (both

Table A1. US Dual Banking and Bank Supervision.

	Charter/ Charter Agent	Primary Supervisor	Federal Supervisor	Fed Member	Number of Banks
National banks	National/OCC	OCC	OCC	Yes	1751 *(1539)*
State member banks	State/state	State	Fed	Yes	954 *(862)*
State nonmember banks	State/state	State	FDIC[a]	No	5245 *(5104)*
Other banks					
Investment banks	OCC	SEC	SEC/Fed[b]	No	Not included in dataset
Thrifts	OTS	OTS	OTS/FDIC[c]	No	Not included in dataset

[a]The FDIC is only federal supervisor for FDIC-insured banks, which account for about 95% of all state nonmember banks. All noninsured banks are only supervised by state authorities.
[b]Investment Banks are mainly supervised by the SEC, the Fed (especially the regional New York Fed-branch) serves as additional supervisor.
[c]If a thrift (or savings institution) possesses FDIC-insurance, the FDIC is additional supervisor.

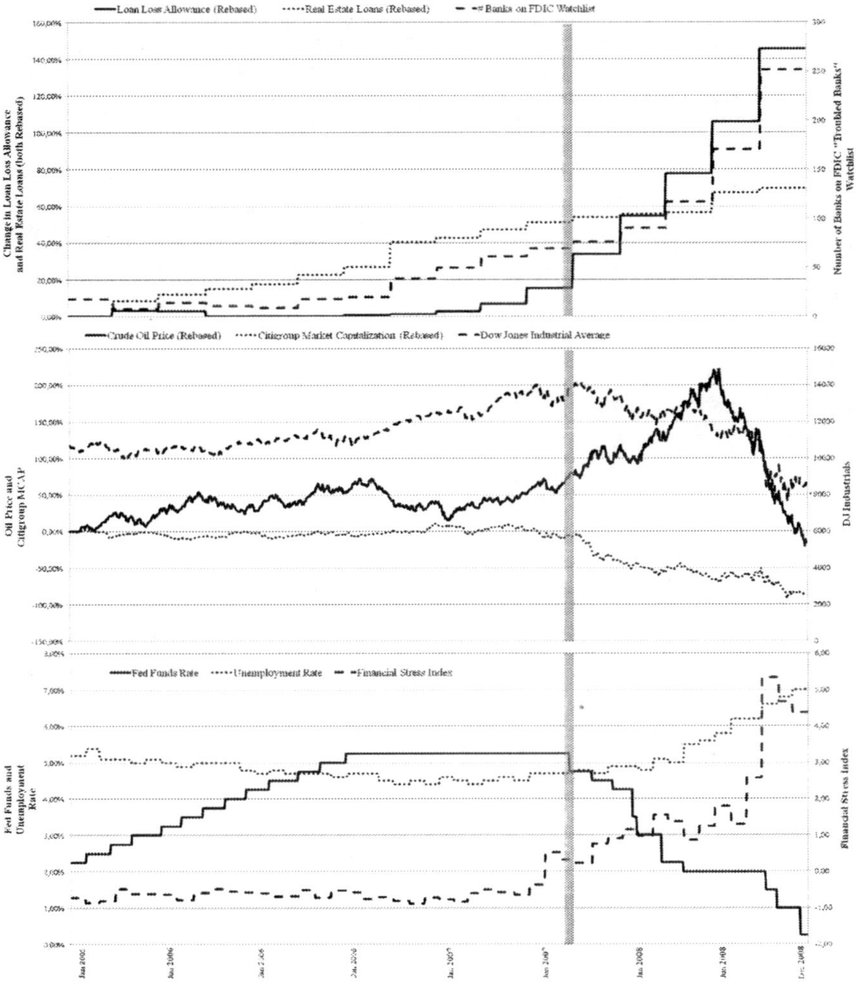

Fig. A1. Evolution of the Crisis.

in percent) and the Federal Reserve Bank of Kansas' Financial Stress Index. The highlighted period shows the third quarter of 2007 in which the crisis escalated.

Table A2 contains statements and/or press releases of the major regulatory and supervisory agencies in the quarters surrounding the escalation of the financial crisis in the third quarter of 2007. The table

Table A2. Statements of Regulatory Agencies on Crisis before and after its Escalation.

Quarter/Year	FDIC	OCC	Timeline of Events/Fed
Q1/2007	No official comment	No official comment	No significant event/no Fed comment
Q2/2007	– FDIC reports that "asset quality indicators are less favorable" than in previous year but "industry's overall condition is good." (*Hoosier Banker Volume 91; Issue 6, 06/01/2007*) – Ms. Bair calls for stricter bank regulation, especially in the light of subprime mortgage lending (*Wall Street Journal, 06/11/2007*) – FDIC is in favor of banning high risk bank operations (see Timeline of Events) (*Dow Jones Capital Market Report, 06/13/2007*) – FDIC opposes Basel II capitalization rules, says is not sufficient and calls for higher capitalization (*Dow Jones International News, 06/25/2007*)	– Publicly declares it is in favor of implementing Basel II, disagreeing with FDIC that capitalization is not enough (*Dow Jones Capital Market Report, 06/13/2007*) – Supreme Court rules that mortgage lending entities of national banks are also subject to supervision and regulation by the OCC, not state authorities. OCC is thus responsible for the safety and soundness of these entities (*Reuters News, 04/19/2007*)	– FDIC, OCC, and Fed release joint risk management program for clustering in real estate lending (*06/01/2007*) – Dispute between FDIC and Fed regulators whether or not to ban high risk bank operations (subprime lending), FDIC says ban, Fed says will cut off access to credit (*06/13/2007*) – Fed is against banning high risk bank operations (subprime lending – see Timeline of Events) (*06/13/2007*) – Dispute between FDIC, OCC and Fed about how to adopt Basel II (*06/25/2007*) – Fed publicly declares it is in favor of implementing Basel II, disagreeing with FDIC that capitalization is not enough (*06/25/2007*)
Q3/2007	– FDIC looking into banks' CDO exposure, expecting downgrades due to higher defaults (*Reuters News, 07/11/2007*) – FDIC says "Banking system is in good shape and well-capitalized"; Ms. Bair says on subprime-market problems "we'll be just fine on this" (*Reuters News, 08/10/2007*)	– OCC publishes report "Foreclosure Prevention: Improving Contact with Borrowers," also including estimations on volume of mortgage "meltdown," saying situation could be stressful (*Reuters News, 08/01/2007*) – Mr. Dugan addresses House committee, stating that banks are	– Senate discusses whether or not FDIC/OCC should also be allowed to supervise lending practices by banks (*07/26/2007*) – European commercial banks, in spite being flush with cash, increase the rates they charged each other for interbank lending sharply (*08/07/2007*) – Fed FOMC meets but leaves interest rates unchanged (*08/07/2007*)

– Ms. Bair says: "Industry is very strong" (*Reuters News, 08/22/2007*) – FDIC acknowledges problems with strong increase in defaulting real estate loans (up almost 30% to previous year) (*Reuters News, 08/27/2007*) – Ms. Bair says: "Golden age of banking is over in market environment turmoil" (*Reuters News, 08/27/2007*)	healthy and the system is safe, in spite of the market turmoils surrounding mortgage lending (*Federal Reserve News, 09/05/2007*)	– St. Louis Fed Director asks for permission to cut the discount rate (*08/09/2007*) – BNP Paribas announces that it would suspend withdrawals from three funds that invested in U.S. subprime mortgages. The reason: bank could not value fund assets because of "complete evaporation of liquidity in certain market segments in U.S. securitization market." European banks hence pushed overnight lending rate to 4.7% (with target being 4%!). Later that same day, ECB announces it would lend unlimited amounts at the 4% rate, additional to pumping 94.8 bn USD in the European banking system (*08/09/2007*) – Fed decides to open discount window (*08/10/2007*) – Countrywide announces that it would draw down credit lines for 11.5 bn USD as a consequence of the drying up of the tri-party repo market which it used heavily for financing (*08/16/2007*) – Fed decides to cut lending rate by 0.5 basis point and to lend for 30 days instead of overnight (*08/16/2007*) – Fed announces rate cut for discount window and discount window opening, urging banks to use it; Bernanke also hints at Fed funds rate cut (*08/17/2007*)

Table A2. (*Continued*)

Quarter/Year	FDIC	OCC	Timeline of Events/Fed
			– As no banks were using the discount window at reduced rate for 30 days and would not lend to each other, Fed decides to auction off funds anonymously instead of giving them through the discount window (*08/25/2007*)
Q4/2007	– Ms. Bair: "Banks may need to increase capital" in market turmoil. She also expects subprime to get worse before getting better (*Dow Jones News Service, 10/22/2007*) – FDIC says mortgage problems are troubling for consumers, not for banking system (*Dow Jones News Service, 11/01/2007*) – FDIC acknowledges earnings problems for banks, says that loan loss provisions are increased to a total of 16.6 bn (most since 1987) (*Dow Jones Capital Markets Report, 11/28/2007*) – FDIC investigates scenarios for the "unlikely event" that a big bank might fail (*American Banker, 12/09/2007*) – FDIC eliminates "MERIT" program to conduct thorough supervisions in all banks (*Wall Street Journal, 12/20/2007*)	– OCC announces final implementation of Basel II framework (*Federal Reserve News, 11/01/2007*) – OCC study shows that lending standards eased considerably for the fourth consecutive year, OCC highlights risks associated with it (*Bank News, 11/01/2007*)	– Chairman Geithner says that capitalization of banks is strong enough to withstand any possible subprime-related crisis (*October 2007*) – Chairman Bernanke says that banking infrastructure is "robust" and system is "healthy" (*October 2007*) – FOMC decides another quarter point rate cut (*10/31/2007*) – Fed says must look for sustainable solution to mortgage problems, FDIC urges quick action (*Reuters News, 11/27/2007*) – Fed cuts rate again by 0.25 basis point, markets react disappointed (*12/11/2007*) – Chairman Geithner hints for the first time that problems might be deeper than "just" liquidity related (*12/13/2007*) – Fed announces use of Term Auction Facility (TAF) to auction funds off to banks directly, giving out money to much laxer collateral requirements than banks would have had to fulfill for going to the

	– FDIC "Supervisory Insights" publication features article about liquidity risks, however more in general terms. Only marginally related to market turmoil at the time (*FDIC Supervisory Insights, Q4/2007*)		discount window or in dealing with primary dealers in usual open market operations (*December 2007*) – Spread between Fed Funds Rate and LIBOR had increased to full percentage point (*December 2007*) – Fed auctions off 40 bn USD through TAF (*December 2007*)
Q1/2008	– Ms. Bair says that big bank failure is highly unlikely; failures among smaller banks are more likely and expected with higher frequency (*Reuters News, 02/05/2008*) – FDIC announces an increase in staff to deal with increasing number of bank failures (*Wall Street Journal, 02/26/2008*) – Ms. Bair announces publicly that subprime situation will pose a problem for banking industry for "near future" (*American Banker, 02/27/2008*) – Ms. Bair says that investors should not be worried about the health of the U.S. banking system, as relatively few banks are troubled, and those that are tend to be small (*Dow Jones Financial Wire, 02/29/2007*) – FDIC sends out letter to banks urging them to increase loan loss provisions due to expected increase in loan defaults (*Dow Jones Financial Wire, 03/01/2008*)	– OCC publicly urges banks to estimate values/expected profits of loan portfolios realistically in the wake of the crisis, especially in market turmoil (*Dow Jones Capital Market Report, 01/31/2008*) – Mr. Dugan publicly announces concern with CRE lending development and names measures the OCC is taking against it, to prevent banks from failing (*PR Newswire, 01/31/2008*) – Mr. Dugan suggests steps to deal with losses stemming from CDOs (*American Banker, 02/28/2008*) – OCC demands large banks to disclose monthly mortgage data in anticipation of future losses from low-income clients (*States News Service, 02/29/2008*) – Mr. Dugan warns banks to "clean up" loan portfolios before supervisor examination and prepare for losses (*Mortgage Servicing News, 03/01/2008*)	– Chairman Bernanke acknowledges amount and severity of problems, delivers speech saying that further monetary policy easing is necessary (*01/09/2008*) – Fed decides to cut rate by 0.75 basis points in between FOMC meetings (first time they did that since 9/11) (*01/21/2008*) – Moody's announces downgrade of mortgage-backed debt issued by a Bear Stearns fund which started rumors that Bear had liquidity troubles (*03/10/2008*) – Fed starts talking to securities houses, offering them to buy troubled assets through Term Securities Lending Facility (TSLF) to buy 200 bn worth of "troubled" assets in exchange for T-bills (*10/03/2008*) – Bear informs Fed of instability – at the time, strange move of Bear because Fed is not the federal regulator of investment banks, the SEC is. However, SEC does not have cash or monetary means to "rescue" any securities house, which is why the Fed was informed (*03/12/2008*)

Table A2. (*Continued*)

Quarter/ Year	FDIC	OCC	Timeline of Events/Fed
	– FDIC expects "sustained downturn" in commercial real estate and more bank defaults in 2008/2009 (*Dow Jones Financial Wire, 03/05/2008*)	– OCC releases statement urging all banks to follow new HOPE NOW disclosure feature to report on subprime losses (*Reuters News, 03/03/2008*)	
Q2/2008	– FDIC officially prepares for increasing bank defaults (*Reuters News, 04/07/2008*) – Additionally to increasing staff, FDIC hires crisis experts to deal with worsening of crisis (*Financial Times, 04/09/2008*) – Ms. Bair says markets are getting "over the hump" in the credit crisis, only concern is economic slowdown and credit defaults in other areas than real estate (*Dow Jones Newswires, 05/01/2008*) – FDIC issues "Financial Institutions Letter" reemphasizing the importance of strong capital and loan loss provisions (*Bank Auditing and Accounting Report, 05/01/2008*) – FDIC increases reserves for bank failures (*States News Service, 05/29/2008*) – Ms. Bair says markets are past the "worst of the turmoil" (*Seattle Post, 05/30/2008*)	– Mr. Dugan says that home equity loans could be the next victim of the ongoing housing turmoil, as falling home prices and lax underwriting are translating into accelerating losses (*Dow Jones Capital Markets Report, 05/22/2008*) – Mr. Dugan says banks need to tighten up on home equity loans in order to cut or avoid future losses (*American Banker, 05/23/2008*) – OCC expects more mortgage-related losses from banks for 2009 (*Dow Jones Capital Markets Report, 06/12/2009*)	– Fed and Department of Treasury discuss "Break the Glass Plan" on bank recapitalization, including the usage of 500 bn from Congress to buy mortgage securities from banks and securities firms including subprime loans to remove toxic assets in order to get capital flowing again (*04/15/2008*)

	– FDIC expects bigger and more bank failures (*Market Watch, 06/05/2008*) – FDIC urges federal regulators to tighten supervision of large investment banks (*Reuters News, 06/18/2008*)		
Q3/2008	– FDIC sets new rules: in case of bank failure, FDIC can settle existing accounts to avoid spillover effects in effect of failure (for large banks only) (*Reuters News, 07/18/2008*) – Ms. Bair says: "Based on the supervisory data and financial data I have, I would be very surprised if we had failures of large size institutions" (*Reuters News, 07/22/2008*) – FDIC is worried about peoples' trust in banking system as consequence of Indy Mac failure (*Reuters News, 08/12/2008*) – FDIC says they don't need money from US Treasury in case of increasing bank failures (*Reuters News, 08/27/2008*) – FDIC wants to increase insurance threshold beyond USD 100,000 to USD 250,000 (*Reuters News, 09/30/3008*)	– OCC urges banks to pay attention to liquidity risks and to submit comments to the Basel Committee on Banking Supervision about a draft guidance released the month of July intended to clamp down on liquidity risk. (*American Banker, 07/01/2008*) – OCC states that a few national banks have "significant" exposure to Fannie Mae and Freddie Mac preferred stock with respect to their capital. Some of the OCC staff provide the Treasury and the GSEs' regulator some help in examining the companies' risk management, financial and legal practices (*Reuters News, 08/09/2008*) – OCC expresses concern because too many banks are too heavily concentrated in commercial real estate (*Home Equity Report, 09/15/2008*)	– Chairman Bernanke and Secretary Paulson discuss with members of Congress that federal law should be changed so that the Fed could also deal with financial institutions other than large banks (Chairman Bernanke and Secretary Paulson already knew that big taxpayer money would be needed soon after) (*July 2008*) – Government takes over Fannie Mae and Freddie Mac *(09/04/2008)* – Lehman fails *(09/14/2008)* – OCC conditionally approves the conversion of Morgan Stanley to a commercial bank. Condition is sufficient capitalization (*09/22/2008*) – To reduce liquidity and other strains being experienced by money market mutual funds, the Federal Reserve adopts a special lending facility enabling banks to borrow from the Federal Reserve Bank of Boston on a nonrecourse basis if they use the proceeds of the loan to purchase certain types of asset-backed commercial paper (ABCP) from money market mutual funds (*09/26/2008*) – Secretary Paulson publicly announces that Fannie Mae and Freddie Mac need government support in terms of either governmental loans or purchases of equity in exchange for government money (*07/10/2008*)

Table A2. (*Continued*)

Quarter/Year	FDIC	OCC	Timeline of Events/Fed
Q4/2008	– FDIC is seeking temporary unlimited borrowing authority from the Treasury Department (*Reuters News, 10/01/2008*) – FDIC considering increasing deposit insurance premium to finance larger deposit coverage of USD 250,000 (*Congress Daily, 10/06/2008*) – Ms. Bair publicly acknowledges liquidity problems (*Dow Jones International News, 10/18/2008*) – Ms. Bair expects more bank failures over upcoming months (*Wall Street Journal, 10/29/2008*) – Ms. Bair urges small banks to apply for federal aid (*Dow Jones Capital Markets Report, 11/25/2008*) – FDIC board votes to increase the agency's 2009 budget to \$2.24 billion, an increase of \$1 billion compared with 2008, plans to beef up supervisory staff by more than 500 to 6,269 (*Wall Street Journal, 12/17/2008*) – FDIC "Supervisory Insights" Report features article about "liquidity crunch" and related problems (*FDIC Supervisory Insights, Q4 2008*)	– Mr. Dugan states there are some initial signs that the economy may be stabilizing, a good sign for banks, but warns that problems for U.S. banks are likely to lag any recovery (*Dow Jones International News, 10/14/2008*) – Mr. Dugan says the United States could benefit from consolidation of the bank supervision agencies, however downplays the importance of shared oversight as a cause of the banking system's problem. He also stops short of endorsing a proposal to unify those powers within one agency. He argues against removing the Fed from banking regulation altogether (*Dow Jones News Service, 11/05/2008*)	– Fed, FDIC, and OCC release joint statement saying the agencies are "assessing the exposures of banks to Fannie Mae and Freddie Mac." The number of institutions with holdings "that are significant compared to their capital" is expected to be limited. The agencies asserted a readiness "to work with these institutions to develop capital-restoration plans pursuant to the capital regulations (*10/01/2008*) – Fed, FDIC, and OCC are working on guidelines to set standards for bank examiners to restructure troubled commercial real estate and construction loans. The guidelines will be applied uniformly across the participating agencies (*10/30/2008*) – The Department of the Treasury, FDIC and Fed put into place several programs designed to promote financial stability and to mitigate procyclical effects of the current market conditions. These programs make new capital widely available to U.S. financial institutions, broaden and increase the guarantees on bank deposit accounts and certain liabilities, and provide backup liquidity to U.S. banking organizations (*11/12/2008*)

begins in Q1/2007 and ends in Q4/2008. A special focus is laid on the OCC as the regulator and supervisor for national banks and the FDIC as the main federal supervisor for state banks. To give additional guidance on the events during this time, a general timeline is given which also contains statements and/or press releases by the Federal Reserve.

Table A3a shows the bank assets and liabilities of the dataset and the liquidity classification I performed. As explained, I classify the balance sheet items in accordance with the Berger and Bouwman (2009a) method. Reported are assets, liabilities, and off-balance sheet items.

The following Table A3b and equation shows the calculation of the Liquidity Transformation (LT) Gap as proposed by Deep and Schaefer (2004). The table contains all balance sheet items which are used for the calculation of the liquid assets and the total deposits, the equation shows how to calculate the final ratio. The yielded values all lie within a range -1 and $+1$.

Table A4 shows the CAMEL indicators which are used in the chapter's analyses. The table lists all factors and explains how the factors contribute to bank instability. A (+) indicates that an increased CAMEL indicator value also increases bank fragility.

The following Table A5 contains descriptions of all observed and analyzed balance sheet items and ratios of the chapter's analyses. All data was collected from official Call Report data between 2005 and 2008, thus all balance sheet items were directly taken from this database. The necessary ratios were calculated using these items.

Table A6 shows the different characteristics of national and state banks as shown in the dataset. Reported are general size- and characteristics-related figures as well as fragility indicators. To obtain a direct comparison of "neutral" pre-crisis figures and the impact of the crisis on banks, all figures as of the fourth quarter of 2005 and the fourth quarter of 2008 are displayed. The bank characteristics numbers are reported in million USD, the further descriptive ratios are reported in percentage points. Reported are also a difference in means *t*-test and a Wilcoxon rank sum test (*z*-values in parentheses).

Table A7 shows the change in the development of the fragility figures over the pre-crisis and crisis period for national and state banks. Reported are the quarterly values as well as the full year values for each of the years 2005–2008. The full year values are the mean values of the respective year's quarterly values (as indicated by index [1)]). Mean, median, and standard deviation (SD) values are also reported. The "Change" indicator shows the change from the first quarter 2005 to the last quarter 2008.

Table A3a. Liquidity Calculation: Berger and Bouwman CAT methodology.

Illiquid Assets (Weight +0.5)	Semiliquid Assets (Weight 0)	Liquid Assets (Weight −0.5)
Assets		
Credit letters	Loans to banks	Cash
Commercial loans	Consumer loans	Due from banks
Investments	Government loans	Trading assets
Intangible assets		All securities
Premises and other assets		
Liabilities		
Transaction deposits	Savings deposits	Equity
Trading liabilities	Time deposits	Other liabilities
	Liabilities to banks	Bonds issued by the bank
		Debentures issued by the bank
Off balance sheet items		
Unused commitments	Net credit derivatives	Interest rate derivatives
Net standby letters of credit	Net securities lent	Foreign exchange derivatives
Commercial letters of credit		Equity and commodity derivatives
All other OBS liabilities		

Table A3b. Liquidity Calculation: Deep and Schaefer LT Gap methodology.

Liquid assets	Sum of cash, balances from depository institutions, government and nongovernment securities, federal funds sold, acceptances of other banks, and all loans with maturity of <3 months
Total deposits	Sum of the total amounts of savings, time, and checking accounts

$$\text{LT gap} = \frac{(\text{Total deposits} - \text{Liquid assets})}{\text{Total assets}}$$

Table A8 shows the change in banks' liquidity development over the pre-crisis and crisis period for national and state banks. Reported are the quarterly values as well as the full year values for each of the years 2005–2008. The full year values (as indicated by index [1)]) show the sum of total liquidity and total liquidity OBS as well as mean values for total liquidity/assets and LT Gap. Mean, median, and standard deviation (SD) values are also reported. The "Change" indicator shows the change from the first quarter 2005 to the last quarter 2008.

Table A4. CAMEL and Liquidity Indicators.

CAMEL/Liquidity Indicator	Influence on Fragility	Description
Total liquidity	(+)	A higher total liquidity figure indicates that a bank holds more illiquid items instead of the general public and thus provides the general public with more liquidity. The more liquidity a bank creates for the public, the higher is the illiquidity risk of a bank in case of a sudden liquidity demand by the public. Higher liquidity creation thus indicates a higher fragility and thus higher instability of a bank
Total liquidity OBS	(+)	The value for total liquidity OBS is calculated the same way as the total liquidity value, except that the liquidity created through off-balance sheet items is added to the liquidity calculation. The interpretation is the same as the total liquidity value: the higher the value, the more fragile is the bank
Total liquidity/ total assets	(+)	The total liquidity/total assets is calculated as the ratio of total liquidity to total assets. The ratio indicates the relative amount of the liquidity creation as compared to the size of the bank. The interpretation is thereby the same as for the total liquidity value. The higher the value, the more fragile is the bank
LT gap	(+)	The LT gap shows what portion of deposits a bank turns into illiquid assets. It therefore also indicates to which extent a bank withholds liquid items for itself and/or provides liquid items for the general public. The closer the LT gap is to +1, the more deposits are turned into illiquid assets. A higher LT gap thus indicates a higher risk for a bank by making the bank more fragile
Return on assets	(−)	The return on assets figure is an indicator of the profitability of the bank. The higher the indicator, the more assets are used for profitable business. The lower the number, the less profitable is the bank and fewer assets are thus used in a profitable way. The smaller the number, the more fragile is the bank
Cost efficiency	(−)	The cost efficiency is represented by the ratio of operating expenses to total revenues. This indicator is used to show the efficiency of management. The lower the ratio, the lower are the operating costs of the bank which indicates a higher stability

Table A4. (*Continued*)

CAMEL/Liquidity Indicator	Influence on Fragility	Description
Loan loss coverage	(–)	The loan loss coverage is the ratio of Tier-1 and Tier-2 capital plus excess loan loss reserves to the total amount of loans. The larger the ratio is, the more stable is the bank as it can cover a large portion of potential loan losses
Loan growth	(+)	The loan growth describes the quarterly growth of total loans. The larger the loan growth is the more risky are the banks' assets. First, a larger number of loans indicates a larger number of possible loan charge-offs. Second, a larger number of loans generally indicates that the loan portfolio contains loans which are of higher risk as the bank starts to accept loans from less creditworthy borrowers

Table A9 displays the results of the comparison of quarterly means analysis of national and state banks in the pre- and post-crisis periods. Reported are the mean values for each variable across all banks as well as the difference between these means (printed in bold). To indicate statistical significance, *t*-values are reported below the difference values in parentheses. The last column contains the difference-in-difference values, i.e. the difference between the differences during the crisis and the differences before the crisis.

Table A10 displays the results of the multivariate difference-in-difference analysis. Reported are the difference-in-difference estimates for the different CAMEL variables as dependent variables. The results are calculated using a dynamic panel regression with GMM estimator and heteroskedasticity robust standard errors. The coefficient of interest is the "Crisis*Treatment Dummy" interaction term, indicating the change of the treatment group compared to the control group from the pre-crisis to the crisis period. Further reported are a dummy variable for pre-crisis and crisis period ("Crisis Dummy") and a dummy indicating whether or not the bank is in the treatment or the control group, i.e. a state or national bank ("Treatment Dummy"). Bank specific and macroeconomic control variables just as bank fixed effects and year dummy variables are included in the regression (as indicated) but not reported. Values in brackets indicate *p*-values.

Table A11 displays the results of the multivariate difference-in-difference analysis. Reported are the difference-in-difference estimates for the different

Table A5. Description of Balance Sheet Indicators and Ratios.

Variable Name	Unit	Description
Assets	mn. USD	Amount of total assets as reported on balance sheet
Equity	mn. USD	Amount of total equity as reported on balance sheet
Deposit volume	mn. USD	Amount of total deposits, calculated as sum of transaction deposits, demand deposits, savings deposits and time deposits, as reported on balance sheet
Loan volume	mn. USD	Amount of total loans, calculated as sum of commercial loans, consumer loans, real estate loans, loans to depository institutions and agricultural loans, as reported on balance sheet
Loan charge-offs	mn. USD	Amount of total loan charge-offs as reported on balance sheet
Net income	mn. USD	Amount of net income as reported on bank P&L account
Return on equity	%	Ratio of net income (as reported on P&L account) to shareholders' equity (as reported on balance sheet)
Ratio short- to long-term deposits	%	Ratio of short- to long-term deposits. Short-term deposits are transaction and demand deposits, long-term deposits are savings and time deposits. All calculations use values as reported on balance sheet
Ratio private to institutional loans	%	Ratio of private to institutional loans. Private loans comprise all consumer loans and noncommercial real estate loans, institutional loans are commercial loans, loans to depository institutions and all commercial real estate and agricultural loans
Ratio trading assets to total assets	%	Ratio of all assets held for trading purposes to total assets
Ratio agricultural to total loans	%	Ratio of all loans for agricultural purposes, both private and commercial agricultural purposes (as reported on balance sheets)
Ratio real estate to total loans	%	Ratio of all real estate loans, both private and commercial, to total loans as reported on balance sheets
Short-term deposits	mn. USD	Total volume of all short-term deposits (transaction and demand deposits, as reported on balance sheets)
Trading assets	mn. USD	Total volume of all assets held for trading purposes as reported on balance sheets

Table A5. (*Continued*)

Variable Name	Unit	Description
BHC dummy	Dummy 0/1	Dummy variable indicating whether or not a bank is part of a bank holding company
Regulatory agent dummy	Dummy 0/1	Dummy variable indicating whether or not a bank is governed by the FDIC or the Fed/OCC as regulatory and supervisory agent
GDP	bn. USD	U.S. Gross Domestic Product (GDP)
Personal savings rate	%	Ratio of savings to total available income of private households in United States
Fed funds rate	%	Federal funds rate – the interest rate banks charge each other for loans (federal funds)
Yield curve spread	%	Spread between the yield curve of a 1-month U.S. Treasury Bond and a 10-year U.S. Treasury Bond
Crisis dummy	Dummy 0/1	Dummy variable indicating whether or not the observed period is before the crisis (before Q3/2007) or after the start of the crisis (Q3/2007–Q4/2008)
Treatment dummy	Dummy 0/1	Dummy variable indicating whether or not the observed bank is a national (treatment group) or a state (control group) bank
Crisis*Treatment dummy	Dummy 0/1	Interaction term of the crisis and treatment dummy, which is the relevant difference-in-difference estimator. The variable shows the change of the differences between the groups before the start of the crisis (Q3/2007) and the difference between the groups after the start of the crisis (after Q3/2007)

liquidity variables as dependent variables. The results are calculated using a dynamic panel regression with GMM estimator and heteroskedasticity robust standard errors. The coefficient of interest is the "Crisis*Treatment Dummy" interaction term, indicating the change of the treatment group compared to the control group from the pre-crisis to the crisis period. Further reported are a dummy variable for pre-crisis and crisis period ("Crisis Dummy") and a dummy indicating whether or not the bank is in the treatment or the control group, i.e. a state or national bank ("Treatment Dummy"). Bank-specific and macroeconomic control variables just as bank fixed effects and year dummy variables are included in the regression (as indicated) but not reported. Values in brackets indicate *p*-values.

Table A6. Descriptive Analysis of Data.

	As of Fourth Quarter 2005			As of Fourth Quarter 2008		
	National Banks	State Banks	*t*-Statistic	National Banks	State Banks	*t*-Statistic
Number of banks	1,238	4,222		1,238	4,222	
Bank characteristics						
Assets	3,699,636	545,090	−4.16*** [−7.69***]	5,698,421	745,800	−4.17*** [−7.22***]
Equity	352,694	56,684	−4.23*** [−7.47***]	498,054	74,150	−4.48*** [−7.52***]
Deposit volume	2,381,992	495,738	−4.24*** [−8.31***]	3,458,065	635,753	−4.36*** [−7.68***]
Loan volume	2,052,007	347,365	−4.44*** [−5.09***]	2,958,558	452,582	−4.65*** [−5.31***]
Loan charge-offs	25,776	4,259	−4.81*** [−5.40***]	71,003	8,179	−4.74*** [−5.53***]
Net income	44,510	6,966	−4.24*** [−6.57***]	18,414	47	−2.51** [−5.77***]
Further descriptive ratios						
Ratio short- to Long-term deposits	0.4715863	0.4455658	−3.85*** [−4.37***]	0.4092662	0.3957099	−1.91* [−2.07**]
Ratio private to Institutional loans	0.5517124	1.495633	0.55 [−0.59]	0.5128619	0.9502822	0.59 [−0.88]
Ratio trading assets to Total assets	0.0009235	0.0001021	−5.01*** [−5.44***]	0.0013356	0.0002654	−5.28*** [−5.69***]
Return on equity	0.1186551	0.115295	−1.37 [−1.27]	0.0486353	0.0571854	0.92 [−1.68*]

Note: Asterisks indicate significance levels at 99% level (***), 95% level (**), and 90% level (*).

Table A7. Fragility of US Banks – CAMEL Indicators.

	National				State			
	Loan Growth (%)	Loan Loss Coverage (%)	Cost Efficiency (%)	Return on Assets (%)	Loan Growth (%)	Loan Loss Coverage (%)	Cost Efficiency (%)	Return on Assets (%)
Q1 – 2005	−0.1	22.4	73.5	0.3	+0.6	26.1	73.4	0.3
Q2 – 2005	+6.3	22.4	73.4	0.6	+3.4	25.3	73.4	0.6
Q3 – 2005	+2.0	21.9	73.7	0.9	+1.9	25.4	73.4	0.9
Q4 – 2005	+0.4	21.7	74.4	1.2	+1.1	27.4	75.6	1.2
2005 Full Year[1)]	2.2	22.1	73.8	0.8	1.8	26.1	74.0	0.8
Q1 – 2006	−0.2	22.4	76.1	0.3	+0.8	27.9	76.4	0.3
Q2 – 2006	+2.2	21.6	76.2	0.6	+3.1	27.3	76.2	0.6
Q3 – 2006	+1.9	22.3	76.5	0.9	+1.5	28.1	76.5	0.9
Q4 – 2006	+0.7	22.2	77.3	1.2	+0.2	27.9	77.6	1.1
2006 Full Year[1)]	1.2	22.1	76.5	0.8	1.4	27.8	76.7	0.7
Q1 – 2007	+0.9	23.9	79.0	0.3	+0.5	27.7	79.2	0.2
Q2 – 2007	+2.6	22.1	78.8	0.6	+2.5	27.4	78.9	0.5
Q3 – 2007	+2.3	22.7	78.7	0.9	+2.2	27.9	79.0	0.8
Q4 – 2007	+0.9	22.8	79.3	1.2	+0.8	27.4	79.9	1.0
2007 Full Year[1)]	1.7	22.9	78.9	0.8	1.5	27.6	79.3	0.6
Q1 – 2008	+0.2	23.6	79.3	0.2	−0.3	27.9	80.0	0.2
Q2 – 2008	+2.2	22.6	79.0	0.5	+2.3	28.3	79.9	0.4
Q3 – 2008	+1.2	22.7	78.8	0.6	+1.7	28.0	79.5	0.6
Q4 – 2008	+0.3	23.1	79.4	0.7	+2.7	27.7	80.4	0.6
2008 Full Year[1)]	0.9	23.0	79.1	0.5	1.6	27.9	79.9	0.5
Mean	1.5	22.5	77.1	0.7	1.6	27.4	77.5	0.6
Change	+0.4	+0.7	+5.9	+0.4	+2.1	+1.6	+7.0	+0.3
Median	1.1	22.4	78.0	0.6	1.6	27.7	78.3	0.6
SD	0.016	0.006	0.023	0.003	0.011	0.009	0.025	0.003

Table A8. Fragility of US Banks – Liquidity Indicators.

	National				State			
	Total Liquidity	Total Liquidity OBS	Total Liquidity/ Assets (%)	LT Gap	Total Liquidity	Total Liquidity OBS	Total Liquidity/ Assets (%)	LT Gap
Q1 – 2005	193,387	983,579	26.6	0.334	201,413	598,418	26.7	0.317
Q2 – 2005	262,738	878,341	27.0	0.328	215,666	615,983	27.3	0.313
Q3 – 2005	264,703	1,063,777	27.6	0.329	225,224	628,485	27.9	0.309
Q4 – 2005	303,965	1,315,294	28.1	0.337	239,888	647,639	28.6	0.320
2005 Full Year[1)]	1,024,794	4,240,992	27.3	0.332	882,193	2,490,527	27.6	0.314
Q1 – 2006	270,764	1,376,580	27.9	0.331	247,923	662,920	28.4	0.312
Q2 – 2006	252,453	1,407,425	28.3	0.321	258,185	673,138	29.0	0.303
Q3 – 2006	253,770	1,621,299	27.8	0.309	248,938	670,506	28.7	0.291
Q4 – 2006	334,575	1,951,722	27.9	0.310	258,277	680,266	28.9	0.298
2006 Full Year[1)]	1,111,563	6,357,027	28.0	0.317	1,013,325	2,686,832	28.7	0.301
Q1 – 2007	331,215	2,038,664	27.7	0.301	264,161	693,373	28.5	0.288
Q2 – 2007	304,670	1,971,088	28.0	0.295	269,949	702,009	28.9	0.284
Q3 – 2007	307,285	2,076,135	27.6	0.286	267,735	695,764	28.5	0.275
Q4 – 2007	314,662	1,771,834	27.9	0.290	279,907	701,288	28.8	0.282
2007 Full Year[1)]	1,257,834	7,857,722	27.8	0.293	1,081,753	2,792,435	28.7	0.282
Q1 – 2008	251,173	1,297,908	27.1	0.278	277,991	692,669	28.1	0.270
Q2 – 2008	244,321	1,194,998	27.8	0.279	294,713	688,064	28.7	0.271
Q3 – 2008	280,416	1,284,813	27.9	0.273	303,215	689,165	29.0	0.266
Q4 – 2008	215,250	−1,811,324	27.4	0.269	283,966	649,205	28.6	0.265
2008 Full Year[1)]	991,162	1,966,395	27.5	0.274	1,159,887	2,719,105	28.6	0.268
Mean	274,084	1,276,383	27.7	0.304	258,572	668,056	28.4	0.292
Change	11.3%	−284.2%	0.8	−19.5	41.0%	8.5%	2.0	−16.4%
Median	267,733	1,345,937	27.8	0.305	261,219	676,702	28.6	0.290
SD	40,027	908,589	0.4	0.023	28,043	31,857	0.6	0.019

Table A9. Difference-in-Difference Univariate Analysis.

	Pre-Crisis Period Q1/2005–Q2/2007			Crisis Period Q3/2007–Q4/2008			Difference-in-Difference
	State Banks	National Banks	Difference	State Banks	National Banks	Difference	
Return on assets	0.60%	0.69%	+0.9% [2.34**]	0.64%	0.71%	+0.07% [3.98***]	−0.02% [−1.12]
Loan growth	1.4%	1.3%	−0.1% [−0.87]	1.6%	1.2%	−0.4% [−2.52***]	−0.3% [−2.35***]
Loan loss coverage	27.1%	22.3%	−4.8% [−2.13**]	27.9%	22.9%	−5% [−2.26**]	−0.2% [−0.87]
Cost efficiency	76.1%	75.9%	−0.2% [−0.83]	79.8%	79.0%	−0.8% [−1.06]	−0.6% [−1.16]
Total liquidity	83,780	173,808	90,028 [3.67***]	98,133	168,559	70,425 [1.72*]	−19,603 [1.31]
LT gap	0.304	0.320	+0.016 [9.79***]	0.271	0.279	+0.008 [3.38***]	−0.008 [−3.40***]
Total liquidity/assets	28.2%	27.6%	−0.6% [−3.32***]	28.6%	27.5%	−0.9% [−4.62***]	−0.3% [−3.03***]
OBS total liquidity	226,648	915,947	689,298 [5.49***]	236,549	607,678	371,128 [1.36]	−318,170 [−2.62**]

Note: Asterisks indicate significance levels at 99% level (***), 95% level (**), and 90% level (*).

Table A10. Difference-in-Difference – Multivariate Analysis of CAMEL Indicators (1/4).

Variables	Dynamic Panel-Data Estimation			
	Loan Growth	Loan Loss Coverage	Cost Efficiency	Return on Assets
Crisis*Treatment dummy	−0.4055 [0.023**]	0.0101 [0.126]	0.0059 [0.425]	−0.0001 [0.190]
Crisis dummy [0 = Pre-crisis, 1 = crisis]	−0.3866 [0.016**]	−0.0092 [0.120]	0.0104 [0.000***]	−0.0047 [0.000***]
Treatment Dummy [0 = State, 1 = national]	−0.3510 [0.050**]	0.0063 [0.817]	−0.0009 [0.777]	0.0002 [0.146]
Time dummies	Yes	Yes	Yes	Yes
Bank-specific control variables[a]	Yes	Yes	Yes	Yes
Macroeconomic control variables[b]	Yes	Yes	Yes	Yes
Banks	5,445	5,445	5,445	5,445
Number of observations	81,653	81,653	81,653	81,653
Arellano bond (2) (first diff.)	0.239	0.532	0.289	0.423
Sargan (p-value)	0.782	0.798	0.300	0.452

Note: Asterisks indicate significance levels at 99% level (***), 95% level (**), and 90% level (*).
[a]Included bank-specific control variables: capitalization, total assets, ratio of agricultural loans to total loans, ratio of transaction deposits to total deposits, ratio of private to institutional loans, net income, trading assets, and loan charge-offs.
[b]Included macroeconomic control variables: GDP, Federal Funds Rate, interest rate spread, and personal savings rate.

Table A12 displays the results of the multivariate difference-in-difference analysis. The reported regression follows the exact same methodology as the regression framework presented in Table A9. The difference is that the dummy variables representing the banking groups now distinguish between FDIC- and OCC-supervised banks. State member banks supervised by the Fed are thus excluded.

Table A13 displays the results of the multivariate difference-in-difference analysis. The reported regression follows the exact same methodology as the regression framework presented in Table A10. The difference is that the dummy variables representing the banking groups now distinguish between FDIC- and OCC-supervised banks. State member banks supervised by the Fed are thus excluded.

Table A11. Difference-in-Difference – Multivariate Analysis of Liquidity Indicators (2/4).

Variables	Dynamic Panel-Data Estimation			
	Total Liquidity	Total Liquidity OBS	Total Liquidity/ Assets	LT Gap
Crisis*Treatment dummy	−64,606 [0.632]	−137,488 [0.006***]	−0.00115 [0.000***]	−0.0073 [0.000***]
Crisis dummy [0 = Pre-crisis, 1 = crisis]	−41,614 [0.439]	−101,533 [0.002***]	−0.01175 [0.000***]	−0.0175 [0.000***]
Treatment dummy [0 = State, 1 = national]	36,942 [0.006***]	426,892 [0.000***]	−0.01138 [0.000***]	0.0060 [0.000***]
Time dummies	Yes	Yes	Yes	Yes
Bank-specific control variables[a]	Yes	Yes	Yes	Yes
Macroeconomic control variables[b]	Yes	Yes	Yes	Yes
Banks	5,445	5,445	5,445	5,445
Number of observations	81,653	81,653	81,653	81,653
Arellano bond (2) (first diff.)	0.380	0.209	0.401	0.284
Sargan (*p*-value)	0.605	0.190	0.428	0.442

Note: Asterisks indicate significance levels at 99% level (***), 95% level (**), and 90% level (*).
[a]Included bank specific control variables: capitalization, total assets, ratio of agricultural loans to total loans, ratio of transaction deposits to total deposits, ratio of private to institutional loans, net income, trading assets, and loan charge-offs.
[b]Included macroeconomic control variables: GDP, Federal Funds Rate, interest rate spread, and personal savings rate.

Table A14 displays the results of two probit regressions used in calculating the propensity scores. The dependent variable is a dummy indicating whether or not the respective bank is a state or national bank. All independent variables are either bank characteristic variables or fragility indicators. The fourth quarter of 2005 is used to calculate the propensity scores as this can be seen as the last truly "neutral" pre-crisis quarter which indicates "fair" propensity values. Reported are coefficients as well as *z*-statistics with standard errors in parentheses. The first regression uses all possible influence factors, the second regression uses only the significant influence factors to calculate the final propensity scores.

Table A15 displays the results of the multivariate difference-in-difference analysis. The reported regression framework is the same as reported in Tables A10–13 (using Eq. (1)), containing year dummies as well as bank

Table A12. Difference-in-Difference – Multivariate Analysis of CAMEL Indicators (3/4).

Variables	Dynamic Panel-Data E			
	Loan Growth	Loan Loss Coverage	Cost Efficiency	Return on Assets
Crisis*Treatment dummy	−0.2488 [0.041**]	0.3362 [0.120]	0.0504 [0.432]	0.0043 [0.150]
Crisis dummy [0 = Pre-crisis, 1 = crisis]	−1.148 [0.000***]	−0.2906 [0.066*]	−0.0146 [0.717]	0.0017 [0.197]
Treatment dummy [0 = FDIC, 1 = OCC]	−1.473 [0.000***]	0.1335 [0.510]	0.2669 [0.001***]	−0.0068 [0.310]
Time dummies	Yes	Yes	Yes	Yes
Bank-specific control variables[a]	Yes	Yes	Yes	Yes
Macroeconomic control variables[b]	Yes	Yes	Yes	Yes
Banks	5,445	5,445	5,445	5,445
Number of observations	81,653	81,653	81,653	81,653
Arellano bond (2) (first diff.)	0.465	0.270	0.172	0.344
Sargan (*p*-value)	0.890	0.562	0.284	0.683

Note: Asterisks indicate significance levels at 99% level (***), 95% level (**), and 90% level (*).
[a]Included bank specific control variables: capitalization, total assets, ratio of agricultural loans to total loans, ratio of transaction deposits to total deposits, ratio of private to institutional loans, net income, trading assets, and loan charge-offs.
[b]Included macroeconomic control variables: GDP, Federal Funds Rate, interest rate spread, and personal savings rate.

specific and macroeconomic control variables (not reported). The dependent variables are the four liquidity and CAMEL indicators. The regression is performed for the three subsamples obtained through the propensity score methodology (as reported in Table A14). The main variables for the analysis are reported: Crisis*Treatment Dummy, Crisis Dummy and Treatment Dummy. Just as in the prior regressions, the Crisis Dummy indicates whether or not the observed period was before the escalation of the crisis (0) or thereafter (1). The Treatment Dummy indicates which group the banks belong to (State = 0, National = 1). The Crisis*Treatment Dummy is the interaction term of Crisis and Treatment Dummy.

Table A13. Difference-in-Difference – Multivariate Analysis of Liquidity Indicators (4/4).

Variables	Dynamic Panel-Data Estimation			
	Total Liquidity	Total Liquidity OBS	Total Liquidity/ Assets	LT Gap
Crisis*Treatment dummy	101,940	−256,371	−0.0006	−0.0072
	[0.181]	[0.001***]	[0.007***]	[0.006***]
Crisis dummy	37,711	−443,148	0.05989	−0.0293
[0 = Pre-crisis, 1 = crisis]	[0.102]	[0.012**]	[0.000***]	[0.000***]
Treatment dummy	146,496	600,888	−0.0504	0.0154
[0 = FDIC, 1 = OCC]	[0.002***]	[0.010***]	[0.049**]	[0.001***]
Time dummies	Yes	Yes	Yes	Yes
Bank-specific control variables[a]	Yes	Yes	Yes	Yes
Macroeconomic control variables[b]	Yes	Yes	Yes	Yes
Banks	5,445	5,445	5,445	5,445
Number of observations	81,653	81,653	81,653	81,653
Arellano bond (2) (first diff.)	0.220	0.733	0.592	0.465
Sargan (*p*-value)	0.384	1.000	0.930	0.999

Note: Asterisks indicate significance levels at 99% level (***), 95% level (**), and 90% level (*).
[a]Included bank specific control variables: capitalization, total assets, ratio of agricultural loans to total loans, ratio of transaction deposits to total deposits, ratio of private to institutional loans, net income, trading assets and loan charge–offs.
[b]Included macroeconomic control variables: GDP, Federal Funds Rate, interest rate spread, and personal savings rate.

Table A14. Robustness Analyses-Probit Regression and Propensity Score Calculation.

Variables	Probit Regression (Preliminary)		Probit Regression (Significant Variables)	
Dependent Variable	Supervisor Dummy (1 = State, 0 = National)		Supervisor Dummy (1 = State, 0 = National)	
	Coefficient	*z*-Statistic	Coefficient	*z*-Statistic
Bank characteristics				
Total assets	−6.26e−08	0.29	Not included (no significance)	
Total equity	−8.14e−09	−0.06	Not included (no significance)	
Total loans	8.13e−08	1.33	Not included (no significance)	
Number of deposits	−3.04e−08	−1.92*	−2.30e−08	−3.77***
Ratio agricultural to total loans	1.023797	4.78***	1.011751	4.74***
Ratio private to institutional loans	0.4017233	1.64*	0.4286487	2.51**
Ratio real estate to total loans	0.0457573	0.24	Not included (no significance)	
Ratio trading assets to total assets	−63.81074	−2.82***	−57.65388	−2.89***
Ratio short- to long-term deposits	−1.00219	−4.05***	−1.024293	−4.20***
Operating income	−3.62e−07	−1.22	Not included (no significance)	
BHC dummy	0.3160805	5.87***	0.3184178	5.96***
Bank fragility indicators				
Total liquidity	−5.99e−08	−1.25	Not included (no significance)	
LT gap	0.7633535	2.54**	0.7816047	−2.62***
Return on assets	0.9523241	0.30	Not included (no significance)	
Loan growth	0.0002736	0.41	Not included (no significance)	
Loan loss coverage	0.0281257	2.72***	0.0421094	1.65*
Cost efficiency	0.1630364	0.82	Not included (no significance)	
Observations	5461		5461	
Log-likelihood	−3432.9588		−3434.9918	
Pseudo R^2	0.0256		0.0250	

Note: Asterisks indicate significance levels at 99% level (***), 95% level (**), and 90% level (*).

Table A15. Robustness Analyses-Multivariate Difference-in-Difference Analysis by Subsamples.

Prop. Score	Sample 1			Sample 2			Sample 3		
Banks	0.05765–0.3302			0.3302–0.60275			0.60275–0.8753		
	National: 30		State: 40	National: 361		State: 463	National: 1,494		State:3,076
	Crisis*Treatment Dummy	Crisis Dummy	Treatment Dummy	Crisis*Treatment Dummy	Crisis Dummy	Treatment Dummy	Crisis*Treatment Dummy	Crisis Dummy	Treatment Dummy
Total liquidity	1,531,791 [0.619]	2,490,000 [0.018**]	7,506,321 [0.211]	−78,201 [0.108]	−55,879 [0.208]	83,798 [0.002***]	−65,389 [0.103]	−23,301 [0.350]	44,210 [0.000***]
LT gap	0.0007 [0.044**]	−0.0966 [0.088*]	0.0116 [0.307]	−0.0055 [0.000***]	−0.0098 [0.000***]	0.0101 [0.021**]	−0.0083 [0.002***]	−0.0121 [0.000***]	0.0091 [0.044**]
Total liquidity/assets	0.0162 [0.050**]	0.1354 [0.013**]	0.0036 [0.554]	−0.0092 [0.000***]	−0.0298 [0.042**]	−0.0109 [0.001***]	−0.0124 [0.000***]	−0.0104 [0.004***]	−0.0231 [0.000***]
OBS total liquidity	−1,080,000 [0.830]	−1,010,000 [0.140]	939,661 [0.293]	−209,333 [0.012**]	−398,231 [0.035**]	492,003 [0.000***]	−114,879 [0.023**]	−177,984 [0.005***]	59,532 [0.000***]
Loan loss coverage	−0.0132 [0.661]	−0.0054 [0.382]	−0.0106 [0.063*]	0.5235 [0.306]	0.0030 [0.108]	0.0055 [0.489]	0.2450 [0.288]	−0.0041 [0.079*]	0.0042 [0.200]
Cost efficiency	0.0295 [0.706]	−0.1139 [0.621]	0.0290 [0.604]	0.0342 [0.326]	0.1154 [0.005***]	0.0032 [0.456]	0.0345 [0.987]	0.1345 [0.038**]	0.0324 [0.345]
Loan growth	171.6947 [0.375]	−87.2104 [0.330]	−88.3245 [0.433]	−0.1983 [0.020**]	−1.308 [0.000***]	−2.098 [0.038**]	−0.1800 [0.000***]	−1.028 [0.000***]	−1.924 [0.059*]
Return on assets	−0.0034 [0.337]	−0.0013 [0.834]	−0.0016 [0.697]	−0.0042 [0.432]	−0.0007 [0.032**]	−0.0013 [0.234]	−0.0032 [0.153]	−0.0021 [0.000***]	−0.0043 [0.434]

ASIA-PACIFIC PERSPECTIVES ON THE GLOBAL FINANCIAL CRISIS 2007–2009

Jonathan A. Batten, Warren P. Hogan and Peter G. Szilagyi

ABSTRACT

We consider recent events in financial markets and the subsequent responses by monetary and fiscal authorities, which are impressive for their scale, innovation and flexibility in the face of sharply deteriorating circumstances. Internationally, the economic malaise brought perverse responses not least being the apparent quest for higher capital adequacy requirements than was thought necessary before the downturn. Where possible the uniqueness of the responses by authorities in the Asia-Pacific region is highlighted. Other features impeding recovery cannot be dealt with immediately. Among these, the most important is the valuation procedures associated with accounting rules.

1. INTRODUCTION

Financial services across all major economies have borne witness beginning in the first half of 2007, to a general instability not experienced for more

International Banking in the New Era: Post-Crisis Challenges and Opportunities
International Finance Review, Volume 11, 87–117

ISSN: 1569-3767/doi:10.1108/S1569-3767(2010)0000011007

than 70 years. Balance sheets of banks, brokers and insurance groups have proved all too brittle. The lengthy credit expansion brought declines in the quality of risk assessments whether in banking or underwriting, neglect of effective oversight undertaken by ratings agencies and investors generally and an acceptance of modest rewards for taking risks. By the latter months of 2008, hopes that the severe dislocation would be confined to just a few sectors in major economies were dashed. Impacts bearing strong economic consequences rather than just financial sector adjustments proved inevitable. Real impacts displayed initially in residential building and property valuations were spread across economies worldwide with substantial implications for future levels of output, investment and employment. However, the declines in property valuations, though substantial, remained less in absolute terms than those experienced by the major Asia-Pacific economies following the 1997 Asian Financial Crisis. That housing and stock markets subsequently recovered offers some solace though the adjustment process has proven painful and protracted[1] as evidenced by the presence of high levels of unemployment, low levels of economic growth and the ongoing prospect of high fiscal deficits in all but a handful of economies.

Claims about the need to remedy the lack of measures to secure global co-ordination of economic policies or undertake significant revisions of the international financial architecture along the lines of those proposed by Eichengreen (2009) and others may be premature,[2] although there is certainly merit in the recapitalisation of key institutions such as the World Bank and the International Monetary Fund (IMF). Nonetheless, internationally-agreed standards for the conduct of banking and related activities have been in place since 1988. The Basel Accords were negotiated under the auspices of the Bank for International Settlements (BIS) and supervised by its affiliated Basel Committee on Banking Supervision (BCBS). The initial accord, referred to as Basel 1, had operated until 2008 when the revised Basel 2 agreement was being implemented. The initial accord and the revised one have been subject to criticism (Kaufman, 2004). Importantly key differences remain especially between the definitions of bank capital and accounting equity. However, the implementation of Basel 2 has come at a time to test against market experiences the scope for measuring risk in its various dimensions. It is noteworthy that stress testing of bank models of risk measurement in conjunction with the IMF did not envisage the scale of recent falls in equity prices or the volatility of exchange rates (Reserve Bank of Australia [RBA], 2006, pp. 46–48).

All these measures, whether relatively recent or new, have been found wanting; therefore, there is the immediate prospect for revisions to Basel 2, as a matter of some urgency (BCBS, 2008a, 2008c; Wellink, 2008; Allen & Carletti, 2010). Nevertheless, serious questions must be asked about the commitment of many national authorities to the implementation of these internationally-agreed standards. This feature rather than the lack of international agreements on co-ordination of most aspects of the workings of economic and financial markets may explain the frequency with which political leaderships across most substantial economies express the aim for effective international regulation.

Understanding the circumstances of this disturbance is critical to any assessment of future directions and developments in financial services activities as well as the monitoring and supervision of those activities.[3] No less important are the choices in policy responses to the dislocation besetting many economies around the world, but most of all the United States, many European ones, and those Asia-Pacific economies controlling significant international reserves, especially China and Japan. These features are not addressed here.

There is a focus to these deliberations in that the experiences and policy responses are treated with some emphasis on the efforts in the United States and those economies in the Asia-Pacific region. In the next section, a discussion of core issues is undertaken, and then, a perspective is provided on the impacts of events in key segments of the financial markets. The impediments to effective policy responses are then considered with the final section allowing for concluding remarks.

2. COURSE OF EVENTS

There have been a number of recent papers that map out the course of events as the financial crisis unfolded. Gorton (2009), Issing (2009), Filardo et al. (2009) and Allen and Carletti (2010) offer differing perspectives on the interlinked nature of counterparty and liquidity risk associated with derivatives – especially various credit derivatives. However, a most effective means to gain an understanding of the ways the gross market turbulence of recent months emerge from many years of monetary stability is to examine the behaviour of the United States dollar (US$) as traded in the market determining the London InterBank Offered Rate (otherwise known as LIBOR). This market sets the basis for international lending between banks throughout the world. For the purpose of this appraisal, attention will be directed to the three-month (90 days) and six-month rate. The yield spread between these two LIBOR rates and equivalent maturity US government

Treasury securities (90-day, 180-day Treasury bills or T-bills) will also be considered. This yield spread, termed the TED spread (Treasury-EuroDollar spread), has been widely presented by the financial market commentators as a combined measure of the premium demanded by investors as compensation for liquidity and credit risk.[4] One final measure, the spread between the 12-month T-bill and the 3-month bill, will also be presented as a measure of maturity differentiation.

The choice of the US$ rests upon its role as the central reserve currency for international trade and payments. This focus is heightened by the origins of the existing and continuing gross financial turbulence in the United States as well as the ways the bulk of financial claims and liabilities were measured in that currency. International attention has at times shifted to the foreign reserves built over the past decade in emerging and developing economies, especially China and other countries in the Asia-Pacific, and the location and form of these investments – especially in the Treasury securities of the United States. Nonetheless, it is important to note that notwithstanding the concentration of these investments, no other alternatives offer the same scale and scope of choice to these sovereign investors. This may eventually change, but certainly not immediately.[5]

The history of three-month and six-month LIBOR is reflected in the data shown in Fig. 1, with the two series labelled as BBUSD3M (British Bankers Association US dollar 3-month) and BBUSD6M (British Bankers Association US dollar 6-month). The coverage is for the period starting in January 1995 and ending in June 2009. A most notable feature of the series through the period before 2007 is the lack of differentiation in the rates for the two maturities embodied in this graph, with the difference in yields (recorded on the bottom of the graph) being slightly positive – consistent with an upward sloping yield curve – and averaging about nine basis points (or 0.09% p.a.) over the series. The interest rate for this earlier period reflected this modest premium above the funds rate determined by the Federal Reserve Board through the Federal Open Market Committee (FOMC). The lack of maturity differentiation reflected easy money conditions despite oscillations in the levels of yields, especially in recent years from the low levels of 1.0% in 2003.

Nevertheless, these opening months of 2007 held portents of the financial misfortunes soon to be visited upon market participants. The highly sensitive overnight Fed-funds rate showed some short-lived spikes initially in March–April, 2007, but then, a little more so in late June when problems with hedge funds drew much attention with the failure of two hedge funds associated with the Union Bank of Switzerland (UBS) through its Dean Witter subsidiary being noteworthy.

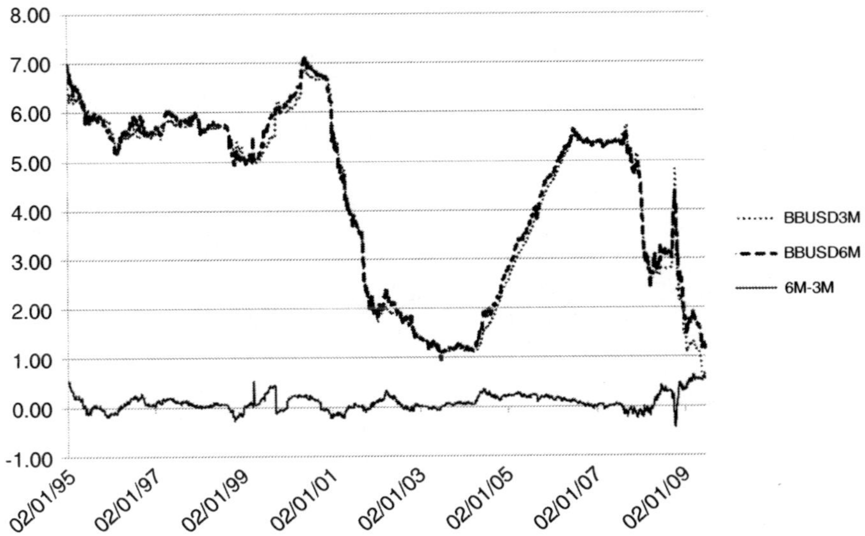

Fig. 1. Plot of three-month and six-month London Interbank Offered Rate (LIBOR) from January 1995 to June 2009. This figure plots the daily three-month and six-month British Bankers Association (BBA) US$ LIBOR. The solid line at the base is the difference between the six-month and the three-month rates. *Source*: Datastream.

The onset of what was even then recognised as a potentially dangerous systemic crisis came when the European Central Bank (ECB) announced a very large funding of about Euros 160 million – to support BNP Paribas. This was in August 2007. Overnight rates rose bringing 90-day rates even higher and both exceeding the 6-month and the 12-month rates for most days until April 2008. Under these conditions, the FOMC proceeded to reduce interest rates in response to the rapidly deteriorating market conditions reflected especially in the ever-tightening access to credit owing to the loss of liquidity. The frequency with which overnight rates spiked high through the remainder of 2007 is seen in Fig. 1 even though these seem mere pimples against what was to come with ever-increasing severity from March onwards during 2008.

A concern for the stability of Bear Stearns in March 2008 was the harbinger of the grave seizure of credit markets with the loss of liquidity in the months ahead. The folding of Bear Stearns into JPMorgan Chase was not seen in that light at the time though by then the Federal Reserve Board was fostering liquidity funding measures alongside interest rate reductions.

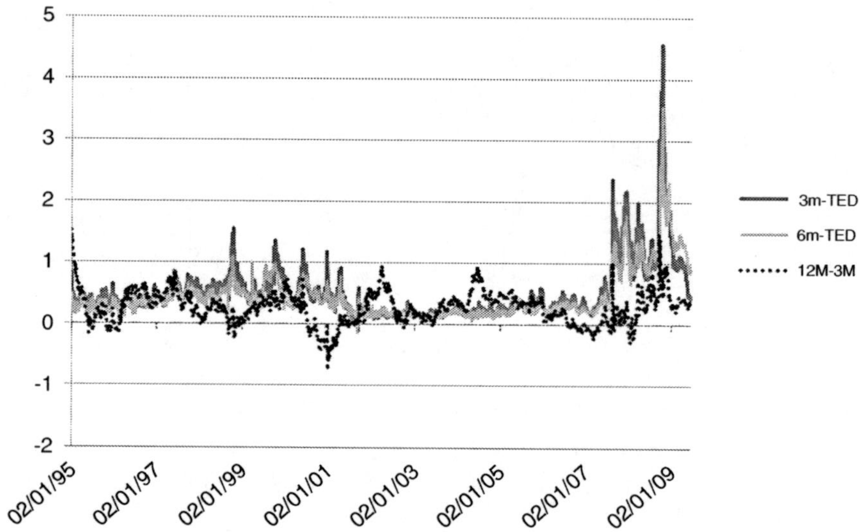

Fig. 2. The three-month and the six-month TED spread and the 12-month term premium from January 1995 to June 2009. This figure plots the yield spread between the three-month and the six-month British Bankers Association (BBA) US$ London Interbank Offered Rate (LIBOR) and the three-month and the six-month US Treasury Bill Rate, called the Treasury–Eurodollar (TED) Spread (blue and red lines respectively). Also shown is the premium between the 12-month and the 3-month Treasury Bill (Term premium) – green line. The US Treasury yields are based on nominal securities at a 'constant maturity' and are interpolated by the US Treasury from the daily yield curve for non-inflation-indexed Treasury securities. This curve, which relates the yield on a security to its time to maturity, is based on the closing market bid yields on actively traded Treasury securities in the over-the-counter market. *Source:* Federal Reserve Bank and Datastream.

By the latter part of April, LIBOR rates started to reveal a pricing of funding or credit risk, which related these risks and price to maturity. This is shown in Fig. 1 with a clear delineation between the three-month and the six-month series and especially so in Fig. 2 with the significant spikes in the three-month and the six-month TED spreads.

The emergence of a relatively stable yield structure in these different LIBOR maturities reflected the expected emergence of a new monetary environment with effective pricing of risk in contrast to the lax monetary conditions of previous years, which allowed a ready access to liquidity regardless of maturities. In part, this new phenomenon was an outcome from the increased co-operation in market intervention and responses between the major central banks, especially the Federal Reserve, the ECB and the Swiss National Bank. In fact as Filardo et al. (2009) demonstrate, the monetary and fiscal policy responses to the Crisis were very similar across countries,[6] with enhanced effort during the worsening of financial strains during September 2008. The most popular policy responses took the form of easing monetary conditions, providing fiscal stimulus, liquidity assistance and the expansion of deposit insurance. Within the Asia-Pacific region,[7] all countries eased monetary policy and provided fiscal stimulus, and all except China and India expanded deposit insurance, while restrictions on short sales (of stocks) were imposed in Australia, Hong Kong, Indonesia, Japan, Korea and Singapore.

The relative stability in the pricing of US dollar LIBOR maturities, at least as judged against immediately subsequent events, lasted until the early days of September 2008. Credit strains were heightened when the likely collapse of the two government-sponsored residential mortgage funding entities, Freddie Mac and Fannie Mae, brought direct government control and funding. Then the decision to let Lehmann Brothers fail brought further turmoil to financial markets unprecedented in experiences of recent decades. The very complicated array of transactions embracing various categories of securities and their derivatives brought seizure to credit markets and an unprecedented search for financial liquidity well beyond the already harsh experiences of the preceding 15 months. Twice in October, on the two Fridays of 10 and 24, the fabric of international financial markets appeared on the verge of collapse: for example, the TED spread reached a new high of 465 basis points on October 10, 2008. Importantly in response to the sharply deteriorating economic conditions in November 2008, China became the first government to announce a massive stimulatory package of 4 trillion yuan or US$570 billion for infrastructure spending (China View, 2008) to augment other budgetary initiatives proposed in the United States, Europe, Japan and Australia. In the United States, two key economic stimulus packages announced were for US$168 billion of tax cuts and rebates by the Bush administration in February 2008, then almost one year later, the Obama administration announced their widely disputed US$789 billion stimulus plan (February 10, 2009). Earlier, on October 30 2008, Japan announced a US$51 billion package and coinciding with the Obama plan Australia announced a US$26.5 billion package (Wassener & Folley, 2009; *New York Times*, 2009, June 8).

In addition to activities in money markets, amounts outstanding in derivatives markets also provide valuable insights into the behaviour and direction of markets during this period. Table 1, sourced from the Bank for International Settlements, International Financial Statistics (BIS, 2010,

Table 1. Amounts Outstanding of Over-the-Counter (OTC) Derivatives by Risk Category and Instrument.

	December 2006	December 2007	December 2008	December 2009	Change 2007–2008 (%)	Change 2008–2009 (%)
Total contracts	418,131.4	595,341.2	591,962.9	604,622	−0.6	2.1
Foreign exchange contracts	40,270.9	56,238.2	49,752.9	48,775	−11.5	−2.0
Forwards and forex swaps	19,882.4	29,143.7	24,562.5	23,107	−15.7	−5.9
Currency swaps	10,791.6	14,346.7	14,724.9	15,072	2.6	2.4
Options	9,596.9	12,747.9	10,465.6	10,596	−17.9	1.2
Interest rate contracts	291,581.5	393,138.1	418,678.1	437,198	6.5	4.4
Forward rate agreements	18,667.9	26,598.8	39,262.2	46,798	47.6	19.2
Interest rate swaps	229,693.1	309,588.3	328,114.5	341,886	6.0	4.2
Options	43,220.5	56,951.1	51,301.4	48,513	−9.9	−5.4
Equity-linked contracts	7,488.0	8,469.2	6,494.0	6,619	−23.3	1.9
Forwards and swaps	1,767.5	2,233.0	1,631.9	1,709	−26.9	4.7
Options	5,720.5	6,236.2	4,862.0	4,910	−22.0	1.0
Commodity contracts	7,115.0	8,455.5	4,427.1	3,729	-47.6	−15.8
Gold	639.9	594.8	394.9	425	−33.6	7.6
Other commodities	6,475.1	7,860.7	4,032.2	3,304	−48.7	−18.1
Credit default swaps	28,650.3	57,894.1	41,868.5	36,046	−27.7	−13.9
Single-name instruments	17,879.3	32,245.7	25,730.2	24,112	−20.2	−6.3
Multi-name instruments	10,771.0	25,648.4	16,138.3	11,934	−37.1	−26.1
Unallocated	43,025.8	71,146.1	70,742.3	72,255	−0.6	2.1

Source: BIS Quaterly Review, March 2010, Table 19. Amounts in US$ billions.

Table 12, p. A112), demonstrates that outstandings in over-the-counter (OTC) derivatives market declined rapidly in the latter part of 2008 in tandem with the deterioration in credit conditions, with outstandings recording an overall decrease of 0.6% from December 2007–December 2008 to US$591.2 trillion. The greatest annual declines in outstandings of specific products in this period occurred in OTC commodity markets (−47.6%), and importantly for credit risk management, there were declines of 27.7% in credit default swaps (CDSs). Interestingly, during this same period, there was a substantial increase in the use of Forward Rate Agreements (increase of 47.6%), and to a lesser extent, interest rate swaps (increase of 6.0%) as financial institutions tried to reduce interest rate risk in their balance sheets. The latest statistics provided by the BIS for the period to December 2009 suggest that foreign exchange, interest rate and equity-linked contracts outstandings have stabilised, although outstandings of commodity and credit linked products have continued to decline during 2009.

Focusing on developments in the CDS markets clarifies some of these concerns. In terms of notional amounts outstanding, the CDS market grew significantly (202%) from December 2006–2007 to US$41.8 trillion, then declined by 27.7% in the following year. This finding is consistent with reluctance by financial intermediaries to enter new contracts in the volatile market conditions evident in 2008, especially with non-bank financial institutions and hedge funds, which lacked the direct support and oversight of regulators. Note that there were significant reductions in outstandings with non-financial institutions and especially hedge funds, who were acting to hedge credit risk on their investments. This was especially the case with longer dated instruments, with evidence of a reluctance to issue CDS with maturities greater than five years (−35.3%). This may be compared with 91.6% in the previous year.

By year end 2008 and early 2009, Congressional approval was secured for massive funding support of financial markets in the United States. Thus, intervention by British and US authorities to prop up the capital of banks within their respective jurisdictions staved off this collapse. One criticism of these arrangements – as the data in Table 2 reveals – is that transactions were encouraged with other banks (reporting dealers) but not so with the non-bank financial sector. The rapid extension of access to the Federal Reserve funding window gave huge additional injections of liquidity to commercial paper and securities markets. International swap agreements between central banks, to which reference has already been made, brought a measure of stability to foreign exchange markets.

Nevertheless, the quest for cash was dominated by the need of many funds in the United States, not just the hedge variety, to meet redemptions

Table 2. Credit Default Swaps Market.

	December 2006	December 2007	December 2008	December 2007–December 2008 Change (%)
All counterparties (net)	28,650.3	57,894.1	41,868.5	−27.7
Reporting dealers (net)	16,292.5	32,030.0	25,021.9	−21.9
Other financial institutions	11,266.9	25,173.7	16,352.2	−35.0
Banks and security firms	5,322.2	14,005.9	11,345.3	−19.0
Insurance and financial guaranty firms	306.1	503.7	399.1	−20.8
Other including hedge funds, residual financial customers	5,638.6	10,664.1	4,607.8	−56.8
Non-financial institutions	1,090.9	690.4	494.4	−28.4
Maturity of one year or less	2,336.4	3,129.8	2,975.5	−4.9
Maturity over one year and up to five years	16,876.5	35,953.7	26,713.8	−25.7
Maturity over five years	9,437.4	18,810.6	12,179.1	−35.3

Source: BIS detailed tables on semi-annual over-the-counter derivatives statistics at end June 2009 (BIS, 2009). Amounts in US$ billions. At the time of writing, December 2009 data was not available.

requested by lenders at or before the end of 2008. This helps explain the upward surge in the US dollar against all other internationally traded currencies than the Japanese yen during the closing months of 2008. The collapse of commodity prices contributed to the market devaluation of many currencies including the Australian and Canadian dollars, which are perceived as ‘commodity currencies’ owing to the reliance on resource exports to maintain balance in trade.[8] Nonetheless, the quest for cash drove many US funds to close out foreign assets to secure cash to bolster balance sheet liquidity at home.

The reluctance by some financial institutions to lend to others in domestic markets encouraged the more credit worthy borrowers, or issuers, to seek funding internationally. Table 3 records a 23.3% increase to US$22.7 trillion in the issuance of international debt securities in the year to December 2007 and a more modest increase of 5.1% US$23.9 trillion in the year to December 2008, although this was largely due to increases in issuance from developed markets (24.1% increase in the year to 2007 and a 5.5% increase in the year to 2008). As financial markets stabilised in 2009, these trends continued with an overall increase of 13.2% in international

Table 3. International Debt Securities by Nationality of Issuer.

	December 2000	December 2005	December 2006	December 2007	December 2008	December 2009	December 2007–December 2008 Change (%)	December 2008–December 2009 Change (%)
All countries	6490.4	14600.9	18419.6	22714.7	23865.8	27,010.3	5.1	13.2
Developed countries	5444.0	13042.8	16630.9	20638.8	21781.4	24,619	5.5	13.0
Australia	110.2	293.3	398.6	491.2	468.1	556.9	−4.7	19.0
Hong Kong SAR	31.0	59.2	64.2	69.4	69.3	76.3	−0.1	10.1
Indonesia	11.2	14.1	18.2	20.0	24.4	32.7	22.0	34.0
Japan	284.8	273.3	316.7	358.0	402.2	397.7	12.3	−1.1
Malaysia	15.9	28.8	32.1	32.7	32.9	33.9	0.6	3.0
Philippines	18.7	29.6	32.2	32.4	32.0	36.2	−1.2	13.1
Singapore	14.2	39.7	44.9	51.2	52.8	53.5	3.1	1.3
South Korea	48.7	81.8	97.0	110.7	108.6	130.5	−1.9	20.2
Thailand	13.8	11.2	12.2	10.2	9.9	8.8	−2.9	−11.1
United Kingdom	546.7	1533.0	2061.9	2497.8	2773.4	3,173.5	11.0	14.4
United States	1727.7	3559.0	4429.9	5578.0	6033.6	6,712	8.2	11.2

Source: BIS Quarterly Review, March 2010, Table 12A. Amounts outstanding in US$ billions.

debt issuance to 27.0 trillion US$, with this increase due to issuance from developed countries and reduced issuance by developing countries. The major developed countries (especially the United Kingdom, United States and Japan) benefited from this funding with increases of a combined US$771.8 billion in the year to 2008, which represented 67.1% of the overall total increase. By 2009, issuance by these three countries had been reduced to 37.9% of new developed country issuance.

Attention should be drawn to the extensive issuance programmes by Australian borrowers, which totalled US$556.9 billion in outstandings in December 2009, which represented a small decline of 4.7% in 2008 and an increase of 19.0% in 2009. The Australian total has historically been driven by issuance from non-financial corporations, although the guarantee extended to financial firms in 2008 by the Australian Federal Government encouraged their issuance internationally (see Rudd, 2008; Swan, 2008). Of those countries exposed during the 1997 Asian Crisis, there were reductions in new issues by the Philippines, South Korea and Thailand, although there were increases from Malaysian and Indonesian borrowers during 2008, which was largely reversed in 2009. Thus, international investors were able to solace from the significant improvements in the balance of payments positions of these countries since the Asian crisis of 1997 (and especially the build up in foreign reserves), which reduced their vulnerability to external financing shocks, and the chance of default.

The deterioration in credit conditions in the US dollar LIBOR markets in 2007 and 2008 also flowed through to the syndicated lending of international banks. This was largely due to the difficulty in the pricing of these loans, which are typically LIBOR based, in the market conditions at the time. Table 4 reports new signed international syndicated loans in billions of US dollars, usually to the corporate sector. New issuance in this market largely collapsed after December 2007 with new issuance of just US$227.6 billion in December 2008 (34.3% of 2007 levels). Unlike lending in international securities markets, which reflected a flight to quality by international investors, syndicated bank lending in 2008 affected issuers from both developed and undeveloped countries with declines on new loans of 52.4% on the previous year. However, as LIBOR stabilised in 2009 and credit spreads (and the TED spread) declined, new syndicated lending increased by US$313 billion overall. Nonetheless, nearly half of this increase (43.5%) was US-based lending, with new UK-based lending continuing to decline.

Corporations in Asia and the Pacific region experienced collective declines in new syndicated lending in the one-year period to December 2008 to only

Table 4. New Signed International Syndicated Credit Facilities by Nationality of Borrower from December 1995 to December 2010.

	December 2006	December 2007	December 2008	December 2009	Change 2007–2008 (%)	Change 2008–2009 (%)
All Countries	601.674	662.739	227.621	313.115	−65.7	37.6
Developed Countries	503.851	540.959	188.453	232.308	−65.2	23.3
Australia	17.256	23.205	10.336	14.291	−55.5	38.3
Japan	18.68	11.148	4.167	7.131	−62.6	71.1
New Zealand	5.226	1.839	0.563	1.444	−69.4	156.5
United Kingdom	54.647	33.794	30.957	10.74	−8.4	−65.3
United States	205.17	255.063	73.304	101.161	−71.3	38.0
Hong Kong SAR	4.232	4.952	1.292	7.485	−73.9	479.3
China	1.305	3.552	0.873	2.52	−75.4	188.7
Chinese Taipei	1.738	2.452	2.843	3.834	15.9	34.9
Indonesia	0.72	1.18	1.077	1.659	−8.7	54.0
Malaysia	3.575	2.55	0.767	1.961	−69.9	155.7
South Korea	5.307	12.153	1.553	3.491	−87.2	124.8
Thailand	0.705	0.056	0	0.281		
Vietnam	0.515	0.46	0.294	0.692	−36.1%	135.4%

Source: BIS Quarterly Review, March 2010, Table 10. Amounts in US$ billions.

US$8.7 billion, compared with US$27.4 billion in 2007. Were it not for the presence of offshore securities markets that enabled alternate forms of financing for Asia-Pacific corporations, the liquidity effects of the reduction in syndicated lending may have been more pronounced. Thus, the impetus to develop regional and domestic bonds in the post 1997 Asian Crisis period bore fruit at this time.

3. CORE ISSUES

March 2007 might be viewed as the time when interest rates in direct funding markets, essentially the short-term wholesale markets, reflected concerns about the quality of assets being funded through asset-backed securities and bank lending. The initial worries were about the residential mortgage lending. Unlike provisions associated with residential mortgages in Britain, Australia and New Zealand, the legal obligation to repay the servicing charges tied to the house mortgage do not continue once the ownership of the house is abandoned by allowing foreclosure of the property. The ease, with which commitments tied to a residential mortgage may be abandoned, fosters an attitude that allows for the ready acceptance of housing loans in the knowledge the obligations entered into are not binding in all circumstances. In effect, the residential mortgage borrower in the United States has a free put option, which when exercised has significant destabilising effects to bank balance sheets. This came after a very long period of expansion in access to funding at low interest rates in the period January 2001 to 2005, themselves a reflection of an overly accommodating monetary policy, which brought substantial liquidity to financial markets and, as revealed in the preceding discussion, little discrimination across maturities.

3.1. Unloading Balance Sheet Obligations

The basic mechanism that had sustained this growth in financial liquidity was the development of off-balance sheet mechanisms by banks being special purpose entities. They have come to be known as Structured, or Special, Investment Vehicles (SIVs) or some similar name.

This technique had been devised in an earlier period to allow banks with relatively low ratings, say less than a Standard and Poors AA rating, to raise additional funding outside their balance sheet. This was achieved by creating independent entities supported by measures of credit enhancement to bring them to a higher rating than the sponsoring bank. This superior investment grade ensured access to funding in capital markets and participation in financing activities from which the originating bank would otherwise have been excluded. These entities were seen as independent of the sponsoring bank and without recourse to that bank.

Important in this original development was the complete separation of the independent entity from the bank; there could be no recourse to the sponsoring bank. The relationship was 'at arm's length'. This meant under Basel 1 capital provisions, the liabilities and assets held in the entity did not count when estimating a bank's capital requirements.

This technique has been transformed during the past decade. This SIV mechanism has been inverted from its origins. The SIV has become the instrument for shifting assets off the bank's balance sheet while funding comes from banks, some the sponsor of their SIV, and other financial intermediaries such as money market funds, hedge funds and property funds.[9] The explanation for this shift lies in the ways funding has been adapted to suit the provisions about maintenance of bank capital under the Basel Accords. Nonetheless, this process could not have been implemented had not the authorities set aside any concern for the ways in which these seemingly separate entities were fostered.

Whereas various categories of lending stipulate a minimum capital provision mainly between 4% and 8% of the sums lent, short-term lending with less than one year's duration does not attract any capital commitment. The effect has been to foster the growth of financial intermediaries funded on a short-term basis, all too often no more than 90 days, against which assets reflecting much longer maturities have been bought. This development rested upon a ready access to short-term funding, especially in LIBOR markets. Thus, the mechanism was open to seizure once liquidity fell away. That started, as noted earlier, in a modest way in March 2007 but accelerated from August 2007 onwards.

The rapid expansion in the numbers and size of SIVs has characterised the past five or six years. The scope for regulatory arbitrage, which is the process of evading capital requirements listed in the preceding paragraph, has been *the basic technique* to sustain a rapid expansion in the supply of funds to support demand in asset-based securities markets and the derivatives markets associated with them. The leverage gained in this way could be, and was, further extended by the ways these asset-backed securities formed the basis for distribution of derivative financial instruments. This expanded even more widely the means by which funds could be generated to ensure the further growth of asset portfolios.

Leverage allows the funding of assets to a much greater extent than appears possible for a given amount of bank capital comprising, at the core, equity and reserves.[10] At issue is the question about a plentiful supply of funds engendering laxity in standards of assets deemed suitable for financing. This result is contrary to a purpose of capital requirements being to contain leverage.

3.2. Leveraging and Deleveraging

Regulatory arbitrage has reflected badly on the effectiveness of the monitoring and supervision of banks and related entities during recent years, especially in the United States. In that country, the division of responsibilities for various parts of the banking system goes a long way to explain these regulatory failures. Not all internationally operating banks were subject to the scrutiny of the Federal Reserve Board. The so-called investment banks remained subject to the scrutiny of the Securities and Exchange Commission (SEC) with just co-operative links to the Federal Reserve Board. In practice, the legislation covering these investment banks meant they were treated as brokers for regulatory purposes. The commitment to risk assessment within the SEC was ineffectual being virtually non-existent.

However complicated the circumstances dictated by the multiplicity of supervisory authorities across financial markets, the failure to grasp the inherently destabilising possibilities of the SIV mechanism is surprising. The avoidance of capital requirements through that mechanism ensured the extension of leverage off a capital base thought to be contained by the provisions of the Basel 1 accord across central banks and banking supervisory authorities.

With commercial banks, the customary expectation for leverage off a capital base under Basel 1 would have been about 10 times, perhaps 12. The SIVs extended the leverage normally associated with commercial banks and thus enhanced their earning power. Leverage allowed the maintenance of, if not the increase in, returns on equity in face of declining margins as the various financial agents and intermediaries competed for business.[11]

However, the investment banks, with their essentially broker status, were not subject to funding restraints such as those arising from the Basel 1 provisions. Instead, leverage with these entities ran to 30 times or more. Additional leverage stemming from the workings of the SIV mechanism was not called upon to any substantial extent. The impact was to bring about a substantial increase in the velocity of circulation from a given monetary base or higher money supply series. These features, excessive leverage and the less than arm's length subsidiary but notionally independent, were the 'monkey wrenches' in this disorderly monetary setting.

The seizing up of the short-term funding markets with a lack of credit for the workings of money markets generally has brought about a reversal of the leverage processes associated with the growth of SIVs. This is clear in Table 2 with the decline in the CDS markets and especially the 'other financial institution' category, which includes SIV counterparties and hedge funds. This unwinding process is best described as 'deleveraging'. The inability to fund the requirements of the SIVs and related entities reflects in large measure the loss of real values in the asset holdings of these borrowers. Reliance on short-term funding brings a repetitive if not constant exposure to the vicissitudes of strained funding markets. Banks, having sponsored nominally independent SIVs, are placed in positions where to maintain the viability of those SIVs, they must re-absorb them onto the bank's balance sheet or let them fail with all the attendant risks to reputation and exposure to self-generated contagion, as witnessed with the failure of some investment banks and the folding into banks of some others.

This development in turn increases the need for capital by way of equity placements or retaining earnings as reserves. With money markets seized and capital markets little better placed, only with the funding through the US Treasury and the Federal Reserve of additional capital and other support into banks and the major insurer, AIG, was catastrophic failure across the financial system avoided. The steps taken by the United Kingdom at this time to recapitalise banks and the 'bad bank' special structure to treat the non-performing assets of the UBS were no less important to their respective national banking systems as well as significant for potential contagion impacts across national boundaries.

Deleveraging adds to the uncertainty about the scale of needs for funding as well as the duration of the adjustment process within real sectors of the economy quite apart from events within the financial services sector. What has been witnessed very recently has been the thrust to reach not just the minimum capital requirements as laid down by the Basel Accords, but to exceed them. Under existing arrangements, banks are required to have a minimum Tier 1capital of 4%. Tier 1 is shareholders' funds being equity and reserves. In recent months, banks have been seeking additional equity raisings to bring the Tier 1 ratio to about 8%. This has been evident in the Asia-Pacific region with new raisings to meet this new 'standard' by many major banks in the closing months of 2008 and early into 2009.[12]

Thus, the nominal 10 times associated with some commercial banks looks likely to reflect a new conservatism around 8 times thus adding to the duration of the adjustment from the past excesses in leverage.

4. FINANCIAL INSTRUMENTS

At any stage, a financial entity may choose to extend its funding horizons by creating collateralised debt obligations (CDOs) for selling on to some managed fund or other financial entity. The CDOs are a derivative instrument linked to some underlying security, most commonly a residential mortgage but also some other asset-backed security. The usual practice with the issue of these CDOs has been to divide them into tranches reflecting the different risk perceptions associated with the prospects for servicing the underlying security. By splitting the portfolio into different grades of quality, there would be a closer match to the risk appetites of the buyers. The sensitivity of the tranches to the ways they are 'sliced' against the underlying security tells much about the potential diversity of outcomes as well as the inherent risks (Fender, Tarashev, & Zhu, 2008). Recognition of the difficulties of pricing these derivatives using conventional models meant their use was fraught with risk.

Most reliance has been placed on residential mortgage-backed securities for the generation of CDOs. By 2006, they represented about 88% of the securities on which the issue of CDOs was based with about equal parts of those mortgage-backed securities in the ordinary and sub-prime categories (Fender et al., 2008). The deceleration in the rate of issuance of those CDOs in 2007 reflected uncertainty and concern from about March that year on the scope for maintaining earnings on the underlying securities, most of all with the servicing of sub-prime residential mortgages. This feature points firmly to the ways in which the characteristics of the securities underlying the CDOs had changed over the preceding four years.

As noted earlier, most challenging has been the proliferation of CDSs especially over the period 2006–2007 (where outstandings increased 202% as shown in Tables 1 and 2). The CDS was devised to provide a means whereby lending institutions could transfer the credit risk associated with a lending agreement or similar credit instrument. The seller of the CDS received a payment – a premium – for assuming the risk. The instrument is akin to an insurance product. Unlike the CDOs, the basis for pricing and using CDSs has been familiar for some years (Batten & Hogan, 2002). The worry had always been, from the outset of their use, the quite narrow funding base to support potentially substantial sums involved in these contracts. The entities involved in selling CDSs has comprised a relatively few very large financial intermediaries and agents being banks and insurance companies of various types.

The astonishing growth of CDSs traded in OTC markets reflects the use of this instrument not to gain insurance for an established credit risk associated with a loan or a corporate bond but to take a position in expectation that some lending activity or bond issuance would or should fail. The CDS in these circumstances was not to hedge the credit risk of a component of an asset portfolio but as a speculation about the likely course of prices for a specified tradable instrument. In short, the buying of a CDS by paying a premium was akin to naked short selling reflecting a stance taken without holding the instrument against which the CDS is written.

To place the significant turnover in the CDS markets in perspective, attention should be drawn to activity in exchange-traded derivatives markets. Table 5 provides information on the notional principal of various futures and options traded on organised exchanges from 1995 to 2009. From 1995 to 2007, there has been average annual growth of 21% in notional principal traded on futures markets and nearly 41% in options markets. The growth in notional outstandings though sizeable was significantly less than growth in outstandings of CDS. Importantly, from December 2007 to December 2008, there was a significant reduction (28.4%) in notional amounts outstanding of futures contracts. Reductions in interest rate, currency and equity index futures were 28.0%, 35.8% and 35.6% respectively. For the same period in options markets, there was a lesser reduction (20.6%) in notional amounts outstanding. Reductions in interest rate, currency and equity index options were 20.6%, 5.4% and 33.4% respectively. Thus of the potential risks of concern for markets, overwhelmingly credit risk was the major priority during this period. Note the subsequent increase in both options and futures outstanding in the period from 2008 to 2009 of 29.5% and 8.2% respectively returns options outstandings to pre-Crisis levels, although future volumes are only at levels seen in 2005.

Perhaps modestly less challenging than CDSs for market stability has been the role of ratings agencies in their assessments of financial instruments. They provided ratings recommendations about CDOs on the basis of expected loss or probability of default linked to the performance of corporate bonds. Thus, the underlying analysis was about credit risk measurements and specific appraisals of servicing probabilities for the underlying security. What brought about the miscalculations of quality and thus the values depicted in the ratings recommended is some combination of

Table 5. Derivative Financial Instruments Traded on Organised Exchanges.

	December 2005	December 2006	December 2007	December 2008	December 2009	December 2007–December 2008 Change (%)	December 2008–December 2009 Change (%)
Futures all markets	21600.4	25683.1	28059.7	20101.3	21,748.7	−28.4	8.2
Interest rate	20708.7	24476.2	26769.6	19271.1	20,622.6	−28.0	7.0
Currency	107.6	161.4	158.5	101.7	163.7	−35.8	61.0
Equity index	784.1	1045.4	1131.6	728.5	962.4	−35.6	32.1
Options All markets	35658.6	43722.1	51039.4	39696.0	51,388.3	−22.2	29.5
Interest rate	31588.2	38116.4	44281.7	35161.3	46,434.8	−20.6	32.1
Currency	66.1	78.6	132.7	125.6	146.8	−5.4	16.9
Equity index	4004.3	5527.0	6625.0	4409.1	1,991.8	−33.4	−54.8

Source: BIS Quarterly Review, 2010, Table 23A. Notional Principal in billions of US dollars.

a non-linear relationship between the CDO and the underlying security. Systemic risk plays more heavily on the derivative than the bond, but this seems to be about the way CDO tranches from the underlying security are determined, and the possibility for tranches associated with structured finance products to be even more prone to the impact of non-linearities in linkages. All told and subject to reservations due to complexities with assessments of potential loss distributions, these derivative instruments appear very troubling to value in any relatively straightforward way associated with underlying securities such as corporate bonds (Fender & Mitchell, 2005).

Little wonder then that revelations about mistakes in calculations have been proclaimed (Jones, Tett, & Davies, 2008). The worry is not so much with the mistakes arising from failure with financial modelling software but the decision not to reveal the event. In fairness, the many downgrades of ratings recommendations associated with CDOs took place all through 2007. But the willingness to offer ratings recommendations initially across a wide range of new instruments may have reflected all too easily the spirit of the times rather than awareness of the difficulties of calculation.

5. ACCOUNTING STANDARDS

Requirements for meeting accounting standards are based on internationally negotiated determinations. Central to all these deliberations has been the application of 'fair market' value concept and embodied in procedures for 'marking to market' the values of securities held by entities in the financial services sector. These difficulties have lead to the recent provision of further guidance requirements by the Basel Committee on Banking Supervision (BCBS, 2008b, 2008c). The application of this concept rests upon the unstated or implicit premise of there being operating markets, direct and indirect, for all the securities held on the balance sheets of banks and similar financial entities including all contingent claims linked to primary securities.

All the experiences since June 2007 point to markets that have closed down with few if any trades in any of the securities traded in normal times. Marking-to-market requirements have been discharged either with reference to the occasional 'fire sales' or with values reflecting duress and surrogate values derived from modelling markets based on historical values. The latter approach is of dubious merit in those cases where newly minted financial instruments have very little past experiences to support calculations.

Marking to market has *pro-cyclical* impacts. Any disturbance in financial markets generating downward revisions in values of financial instruments brings the need for provisioning against the perceived loss of value even though these instruments may not be defaulting on their interest payments or expected earnings associated with equities. The grave flaw in the procedure lies with the implicit assumption referred to in the preceding paragraph; namely, markets exist for all financial instruments being traded. Contemporary market experiences reveal a widespread shutting down of markets with only some revival of activity in short-term credit markets at the close of 2007.

An alternative procedure suited to effective risk management in banking and related activities would be to apply dynamic provisioning. This procedure means a proportion of each new loan is set aside based on historical experience with similar loans in the past. Annual allocations may be adjusted to reflect the usual outcomes as this type of loan matures as lessons from the recent past are absorbed.

This approach has been used by banks in the past though now frowned upon with the adoption of international accounting standards based on 'fair value' perceptions. The objection to dynamic provisioning has been the potential for 'smoothing' earnings flows because the setting aside of revenues providing for future losses meant understating actual earnings in any one specific period. In effect, the inherent losses in any portfolio of loans were not significant for contemporary accounting rules. The anti-cyclical characteristics inherent in dynamic provisioning had no place in the determination of accounting standards. Accounting perceptions and requirements laid down rules that were at odds with risk management approaches.

The 'fair value' concept maybe said to not necessarily imply the application of 'mark to market' valuations in all circumstances. Yet, there is every reason to argue otherwise once the accounting standard is specified. What audit team would certify accounts by some measure other than mark to market when shareholders and others might see a basis for litigation and recovery of monies in such a procedure? Accounting firms in their audit function are looked upon as having 'deep pockets' against which claims for restitution may be lodged. Unlike ratings agencies with their protection against claims for imperfect ratings of firms and instruments, accounting firms are not protected from litigation for exercising their judgement about accounting provisions. Inevitably, accounting firms as auditors will exercise caution in these circumstances.

6. POLICY RESPONSES

Most attention must be given to recent activities in the United States because of the dominant role of that economy on the world scene. However, the commonality of many problems based around the failures and weaknesses in the various national financial systems means policy measures may exhibit similarities of purpose from one country to another. Major differences in application arise from constitutional and institutional differences between countries.

6.1. Easing

The initial response in the United States to declining market conditions came in September 2007 with the easing of monetary policy revealed in the reduction of the federal funds rate. This approach was the dominant feature of policy through the balance of 2007 and into the first quarter of 2008. At the end of that period, the federal funds rate had been reduced by 325 basis points. These steps might be compared with the efforts of the ECB where policy easing was about providing additional liquidity to markets rather than interest rate reductions. The quantitative focus was present from the outset as witnessed by the initial injection of funds to BNP Paribas. The basis for lending was a very wide definition of acceptable collateral for these central bank loans so that access was immediate and extensive for most entities with access to the funding mechanisms. This stance is in contrast to the ways in which the Federal Reserve advanced a piecemeal approach to quantitative easing from the middle of 2008.[13]

The strategic focus of policy has been in sharp contrast between the ECB and the Federal Reserve. The former has from the outset been committed to quantitative easing with interest rate adjustments having a minor role. With the Federal Reserve, the initial focus was on interest rate reductions, massively so. Only when the pricing of credit had failed to ease the credit restraints did the emphasis turn to the quantitative thrust of the ECB. Worsening economic conditions emerged in the latter part of 2008 reflecting the transmission of financial instability to the real sectors of the economy well beyond the specific failures long apparent in the residential construction market. Although the easing of monetary policy had brought substantial reductions in some lending rates, the impact was limited by the loss of liquidity in most credit markets typified by the widening of spreads to which reference has been made at length earlier in this commentary. Credit markets were seizing up.

In these circumstances, the strategic focus of policy turned to matters of liquidity, a situation that has persisted to the present though some amelioration of conditions has been emerging with the coming of 2010. The impact has been most notable for the growth of the balance sheet of the Federal Reserve Board as it has purchased a variety of financial instruments.

6.2. Adaptation: Price to Quantity

The Federal Reserve expanded greatly its traditional activities providing short-term liquidity to viable financial entities. There has been quite an array of techniques employed but mostly directed to extending the terms of credit facilities made available.[14] Mention should also be made of the international co-operation in liquidity managements through the provision of bilateral currency swaps agreements between various central banks. In the Asia-Pacific region, these built on a number of earlier arrangements set in place in the post-Asian Crisis period between the Bank of Japan and the Peoples Bank of China among others.[15] The effect was to improve greatly liquidity in dollar funding markets.

However, these measures were insufficient to bring confidence back to credit markets generally. Funding through commercial paper and corporate bond activities had ground to a near halt requiring additional attention. Recognition of this plight saw the development of techniques for direct lending to participants in credit markets. Initially, this was a three-month facility for lending against highly rated commercial paper and accompanied by support facilities for money market mutual funds.[16] Separately, and very recently, the Federal Reserve and the US Treasury agreed on a joint provision whereby loans could be made against top-rated securities. The US Treasury backstopped this arrangement by providing US$20 billion as capital for the scheme.[17]

A different set of policy tools devised by the Federal Reserve appear to be in the offing. These proposals are directed to purchases of longer-dated securities linked to government-sponsored enterprises being their debt of their endorsed mortgage-backed securities. The aim with these measures is to further enhance funding conditions across private credit markets. That such steps, including the buying of Treasury securities, have had to be taken despite the extreme easing of conventional monetary policy through interest rate reductions reflected the chronic malaise besetting all credit markets.

The explanation for why this condition persists despite all the steps taken by the Federal Reserve lies in the illiquidity permeating balance sheets of many banks, brokers and insurance groups across the financial services sector in the United States. This remains probably the major general challenge for monetary and financial policies along with the specific challenges linked to the housing markets, now besetting the monetary and fiscal authorities in the United States.[18] All this remains despite the enormous injection of funds into these entities through the Troubled Assets Relief Program (TARP) and related programs in the United States and elsewhere.

These persistent failures to secure substantial relief across credit markets rather than some easing for the highest grade borrowers only explain the latest commitment to a new Financial Stability Plan (Geithner, Bernanke, Bair, & Dugan, 2009). This new commitment extends greatly the reach of previous efforts towards capital funding in banks and other financial institutions but incorporates efforts to improve the regulatory supervision of these entities. There is a partnership proposal designed to combine public and private funding to remove impaired assets – so-called legacy assets – on balance sheets as another means to improve the capital position in the relevant financial institutions. The expansion of the existing Term Asset-Backed Securities Lending Facility by up to $1 trillion aims to reduce credit spreads and foster securitised credit markets. Other segments support the efforts of the Federal Deposit Insurance Corporation (FDIC) in its liquidity guarantees. These steps are a comprehensive offering on a scale not previously invoked. The lessons from the earlier efforts would suggest relief may not come to credit markets for much of 2009.

6.3. Provisioning

The illiquid condition of many bank balance sheets explains the frustration expressed by the political leadership, officials and observers in the United States at the failure of banks to use the TARP funds to extend lending, especially with respect to business and residential mortgages. These capital injections have gone some way to enhance capital adequacy, provide means for writing down impaired assets and maintain existing loan portfolios. The strains have been exacerbated by the thrust for higher capital adequacy provisions than associated with the Basel Accords. That ratings agencies look to these efforts as positive is ironic in view of the ways these same requirements were ignored in the expansionary phases in the five years preceding 2007 and to which reference has been made in prior sections. Then the balance sheet valuation procedures resting upon flawed accounting practices reflected in notions of 'fair value' and 'mark to market' have generated the very circumstances whereby the harsh features of the secular deterioration in housing activities have been amplified through the financial system with repercussions on the real economy.

Setting aside the peculiar conditions of housing finance in the United States with its free put option feature available to borrowers, the extent to which legal and administrative requirements have imposed pro-cyclical consequences in deteriorating economic circumstances is extraordinary. Efforts to secure stabilisation of economic performance have been thwarted.

Foremost, there is a need to secure a realistic application of capital adequacy requirements reflecting Basel standards or something like them rather than the utterly inappropriate and therefore pro-cyclical push for capital adequacy provisions double those of the Basel commitment with respect to Tier 1 capital. Should regulators pursue this enhancement, then their efforts are contributing further to the strains hampering efforts to bring greater stability to banking conditions and lessening the scope for extending lending to business and households. The adjustment process gets stretched further.

Immediately, the problems remain with still excessive accumulation of impaired assets despite the huge commitment of funds to bolster capital in banks and insurance entities. One prospect would be the transfer of impaired assets to a separate entity being a 'bad bank'. The harsh issue is the values to be attached to the impaired assets on transfer. There must be some recourse, positive or negative, to the bank from which these impaired assets are withdrawn when they are sold off. Other possibilities may exist in partnership arrangements as witness with the arrangement between the Swiss national Bank and the UBS over the latter's impaired assets.

An operational example may be found in Switzerland. There the 'bad bank' example exists in the partnership arrangement as witness the special purpose vehicle negotiated between the Swiss National Bank and the UBS over the latter's impaired assets. (Jordan, 2008) The vehicle may acquire up to $60 billion of impaired assets from UBS. In a complicated set of provisions, the central bank contributes 90% of the funding of the acquisition at values either as shown in the book of UBS at 30 September, 2008, or valuation as determined by independent experts. Between the two values, the lower one applies to the acquisitions. UBS supplies 10% of funding in terms of equity capital. The primary aim of the fund is to hold to maturity. The loan from the central bank must be repaid before there is any distribution from the fund while the central also lays claim to 50% of any profits from the fund. Downside risk to the central bank is covered by a further provision whereby it has claim upon up to 100 million UBS shares. Another provision allows for the central bank to receive profits of $1 billion. The aim of this partnership/joint venture was to unburden UBS from the effects of volatile price movements and severe illiquidity of markets.

7. CLOSING COMMENTS

The measures taken during 2007–2009 by the monetary and fiscal authorities worldwide, but especially in the United States, have been impressive for their scale, innovation and flexibility in face of sharply deteriorating circumstances. The relatively limited success from all these endeavours points to the intractability of the issues not least their growing complexity. Undoubtedly past failures in the conduct of monetary policy, the complications arising from the structural arrangements with lending for residential mortgages combined with the proliferation of measures to aggregate residential mortgages into portfolios as asset-backed securities and then derivatives based on those portfolios, have added much to difficulties in devising measures for financing relief. Much with these failures can be attributed to the lack of an effective prudential monitoring and supervision mechanism across financial markets.

The economic malaise has brought perverse responses not least being the apparent quest for higher capital adequacy requirements than was thought necessary before the downturn. This aspect reflects the concerns about adequate provision for bad and doubtful loans. But the effect is to make the strains handicapping recovery all the more harsh. The opposite stance is required. However, current economic and financial circumstances make for difficulties with gaining broad acceptance for a revised stance.

Immediately this places the need for yet more comprehensive steps to relieve the burden of impaired assets on operating banks if those banks are to contribute additional funding to the real sectors of the economy. This is the motivation for the new Financial Stability Plan spelt out recently (Geithner et al., 2009). The precedent lies with the Swiss decision to shift the impaired assets of UBS into a separate unit, a partnership between the central bank and the commercial bank. How this is done elsewhere is likely to vary. The German authorities have funded developments such as the absorption of Dresdner Bank by Commerz Bank. The British experiences of funding and taking partial ownership of some major banks based in that country have not emerged as rewarding emulation.

Other features impeding recovery cannot be dealt with immediately. Among these, the most important is the valuation procedures associated with accounting rules. To secure a more cautious interpretation of 'fair value', an immediate solution would be to absolve auditors from legal challenge on their endorsement of accounts. Why not relieve auditors of legal challenge to their determinations, which would only be allowing them the privileges hitherto exclusively enjoyed by ratings agencies? Nevertheless the aim should be to bring an effective risk perspective to accounting rules rather than to sustain the simplifications of existing perceptions on measuring profits.

Bewilderment may best describe the ways in which prudential monitoring and supervision has been pursued in some countries, most of all the United States. This is in sharp contrast to the experiences in Australia where the supervisory body APRA has ensured adherence to the spirit as well as the perceived rules of the Basel Accords. There can be few other explanations for the relative achievements within the Australian banking system when compared to international experiences.

NOTES

1. Reinhart and Rogoff (2009) estimate that on a peak-to-trough basis, real housing price declines average 35% stretched out over six years, whereas equity price collapses average 55% over a downturn of about 3.5 years. For example, prices in Hong Kong, Philippines and Thailand fell 53%, 52% and 20% respectively after the 1997 Asian Crisis and declined over an average of 5 years (Table 1). House prices in the United States, United Kingdom and Ireland have so far fallen 27%, 17% and 20% respectively. Official unemployment levels in the United Kingdom and the United States of nearly 10% suggest a speedy recovery is unlikely.

2. Eichengreen (2009) calls for an (a) expansion of IMF quotas and the conduct of exchange rate surveillance; (b) expanded role for the Special Drawing Rights (SDR) in international transactions, which would require someone – like the IMF – to act as market maker; (c) reimposing Glass-Steagall-like restrictions on international commercial and investment banking; (d) require banks to purchase capital insurance; (e) establish a new agency or institution to deal with cross-border bank insolvencies; and (f) create a World Financial Organisation (WFO) with the power to sanction members whose national regulatory policies are not up to international standards. See also Issing (2009) and Allen and Carletti (2010) or discussion on lessons from the financial crisis.

3. Two impressive sources for information on policy developments as well as background data are the web sites for the Bank for International Settlements and the Board of Governors of the Federal Reserve System. Articles and speeches provide comprehensive assessments of events and circumstances. For example, the Stamp Lecture at the London School of Economics by the Chairman of the Board (Bernanke, 2009). There is an excellent summary of events from the BIS (Fender & Gyntelberg, 2008).

4. See the discussion available at www.tedspread.com/.

5. Refer Breuss, Werner, and Veldt (2008), who demonstrate that even with a significant redistribution of these US dollar assets into euro, the macroeconomic consequences will be minimal.

6. See Table I.1 in Filardo et al. (2009), which summarises the policy actions taken in North America, Europe, Asia and the Pacific.

7. The Asia-Pacific region is defined by Filardo et al. (2009) as Australia, China, Hong Kong, India, Indonesia, Japan, Korea, Malaysia, New Zealand, Philippines, Singapore and Thailand.

8. A most notable example is the successive devaluations of the Russian rouble in lockstep with the falling prices for crude oil.

9. Note each non-bank funding entity relies on some bank to have sufficient *financial liquidity* to fund the settlement of transactions.

10. Additional items include convertible bonds and various hybrid securities.

11. Plainly the promotion of SIVs was designed to increase earnings in relation to equity. This reflected competition of the intermediaries with direct financing agents such as private equity funds and other capital market entities including hedge funds.

12. For example, the ANZ bank raised A$2.85 billion in May 2009; South Korean banks raised US$22.3 billion (July 2008–March 2009), and notably, HSBC raised US$17.5 billion in March 2009.

13. The US scene is not comparable by substantial reason of the housing market in that country being so different in terms of ownership and structure from the European setting outside the United Kingdom, quite apart from the free put option characteristic in residential mortgage arrangements referred to much earlier.

14. Discount window loans extended from overnight to 90 days, the Term Auction Facility making credit for up to three months for deposit-taking institutions, and measures to support primary dealers in government securities through a securities lending facility and credit provision designed to enhance liquidity across these primary dealers.

15. See for example the swap arrangements set up between the Bank of Japan and its counterparty in Korea, Thailand, Philippines, Malaysia and China as part of the Chang Mai Initiative (http://www.mof.go.jp/jouhou/kokkin/cmi_030121e.htm).

16. Some of these measures relied for their authority on legal revisions requiring the Federal Reserve Board to declare market conditions were urgently needing relief in unusual circumstances.

17. The scheme is expected to come into operation towards the end of February, 2009.

18. Given the clogging of bank balance sheets in Germany, Switzerland and the United Kingdom, the same strictures apply in those countries, probably most of all in the last mentioned of the three.

REFERENCES

Allen, F., & Carletti, E. (2010). An overview of the crisis: Causes, consequences and solutions. *International Review of Finance*, *10*(1), 1–26.

Bank for International Settlements (BIS). (2010). International banking and financial market developments. *BIS Quarterly Review*, June, 1–139, Basle, Switzerland (Table 12, p. A112).

Basel Committee on Banking Supervision. (2008a). *Comprehensive strategy to address the lessons of the banking crisis announced by the Basel Committee*. Press release. Bank for International Settlements, 20 November, Basle, Switzerland.

Basel Committee on Banking Supervision. (2008b). *Assessing fair value practices: Basel Committee issues consultative paper*. Press release. Bank for International Settlements, 28 November, Basle, Switzerland.

Basel Committee on Banking Supervision. (2008c). *Supervisory guidance for assessing banks' financial instrument fair value practices*. Consultative Document. Bank for International Settlements, November, pp. 11, Basle, Switzerland.

Batten, J. A., & Hogan, W. P. (2002). A perspective on credit derivatives. *International Review of Financial Analysis*, *11*, 251–278.

Bernanke, B. S. (2009). *The crisis and the policy response*. The Stamp Lecture. London School of Economics, England, 13 January.

Breuss, F., Werner, R., & Veldt, J. (2008). *Global impact of a shift in foreign reserves to euros. European Economy*. Economic papers 345, November. European Commission, Brussels, Belgium.

China View. (2008). China's 4 trillion yuan stimulus to boost economy, domestic demand. Available at http://www.chinaview.cn (Retrieved on November 9, 2008) and http://news.xinhuanet.com/english/2008-11/09/content_10331324.htm

Eichengreen, B. (2009). *Out of the box thoughts about the international financial architecture*. WP/09/116, IMF Working Paper. Strategy, Policy, and Review Department, May 2009, pp. 1–36, Washington, DC, USA. Available at http://www.imf.org/external/pubs/ft/wp/2009/wp09116.pdf

Fender, I., & Gyntelberg, J. (2008). Overview: Global financial crisis spurs unprecedented policy actions. *Bank for International Settlements Quarterly Review*, December, 1–24.

Fender, I., & Mitchell, J. (2005). Structured finance: Complexity, risk and the use of ratings. *Bank for International Settlements Quarterly Review*, June, pp. 67–79.

Fender, I., Tarashev, N., & Zhu, H. (2008). Credit fundamentals, ratings and value-at-risk: CDOs versus corporate exposures. *Bank for International Settlements Quarterly Review*, March, 87–101.

Filardo, A., George, J., Loretan, M., Ma, G., Munro, A., Shim, I., Wooldridge, P., Yetman, J., & Zhu, H. (2009). The international financial crisis: Timeline, impact and policy responses in Asia and the Pacific. *The international financial crisis and policy challenges in Asia and the Pacific* Conference of the BIS Asian Research Programme, Shanghai, China, 6–8 August, 2009.

Geithner, T. F., Bernanke, B. S., Bair, S., & Dugan, J. C. (2009). *Financial stability plan, joint statement*. TG-21, US Treasury, 10 February.

Gorton, G. (2009). The subprime panic. *European Financial Management*, *15*(1), 10–46.

Issing, O. (2009). Some lessons from the financial market crisis. *International Finance*, *3*, 431–444.

Jones, S., Tett, G., & Davies, P. J. (2008). CPDOs expose ratings flaw at Moody's. *Financial Times*, Asia edition, Wednesday, May 21, pp. 1 and 25.

Jordan, T. (2008). Introductory remarks. *News Conference, Swiss National Bank*, Available at www.snb.ch. Retrieved on 11 December.

Kaufman, G. (2004). Basel II: The roar that moused. In: B. E. Gup (Eds), *The new basel capital accord*. New York: Thomson. pp. xi+462.

New York Times. (2009). Economic stimulus. *New York Times*, June 8. Available at http://topics.nytimes.com/topics/reference/timestopics/subjects/u/united_states_economy/economic_stimulus/

Reinhart, C., & Rogoff, K. (2009). *The aftermath of financial crises*. NBER Working Paper no. 14656, January. Available at http://www.nber.org/papers/w14656

Reserve Bank of Australia. (2006). The macroeconomic and financial environment. *Financial Stability Review*, September, 3–21.

Rudd, K. (2008). Global financial crisis. Prime Minister of Australia media release, 12 October.

Swan, W. (2008). Announces details of deposit and government wholesale funding guarantees. Treasurer, media release No. 117, 24 October.

Wassener, B., & Folley, M. (2009). Australia and Japan offer new stimulus plans. *The New York Times*, Available at http://www.nytimes.com/2009/02/04/business/worldbusiness/04australia.html. Retrieved on February 3.

Wellink, N. (2008). The importance of banking supervision in financial stability. The Role of Banking and Banking Supervision in Financial Stability, Beijing, 17 November.

BANKERS AND SCAPEGOATS☆

Sinclair Davidson

ABSTRACT

It is commonly believed that banks are in special need of regulation to prevent financial crises, and the recent sub-prime crisis would tend to support such views. Yet it is clear that a series of perverse incentives exist in the banking industry. Incentives for bankers to take on too much risk lead to financial crises, and then a lack of a bankruptcy process for large financial institutions lead to massive taxpayer bail-outs. This chapter canvasses the issues surrounding the sub-prime crisis and explores arguments relating to regulation and the political economy of the recent crisis. As long as the political cost-benefit of having inefficient banking regulation dominates an economic cost-benefit of having efficient regulation, we can expect that perverse incentives will remain and financial crises will be a regular feature of the economic landscape.

> And Aaron shall lay both his hands on the head of the live goat, and confess over it all the iniquities of the people of Israel, and all their transgressions, all their sins. (Leviticus 16: 21.)

☆An earlier version of this chapter was presented at the Australasian Public Choice Conference, December 2009. Jonathan Boymal and Richard Heaney provided valuable comments on an earlier version of the chapter.

International Banking in the New Era: Post-Crisis Challenges and Opportunities
International Finance Review, Volume 11, 119–134

ISSN: 1569-3767/doi:10.1108/S1569-3767(2010)0000011008

1. INTRODUCTION

Scapegoats are an ancient institution. They survive into the present, although it appears that a very important part of the process is now neglected. In biblical times, the sins of the people were transferred to the goat; it was guilty by proxy. Now, however, it seems the goat was guilty all along. Following the recent financial crisis, the banking system is being blamed for having taken on excessive risks and for being too greedy. Yet it is quite clear that in many instances bankers were responding to incentive structures that were established by the political process (this is especially the case in the United States). It is interesting to note that the same political process is now blaming bankers for the crisis – a clear case of scapegoating but without confession.

This chapter consists of four sections, which collectively canvas the issues surrounding the sub-prime crisis and explore the arguments relating to regulation and the political economy of the recent crisis. In Section 2 I round up some of the usual suspects, explaining why banks are said to be subject to systemic risks. Despite the recent crisis centring on the banking system and systemic risk, it is not clear that these sorts of argument explain the need for additional regulation of the banking system. I also examine some of the arguments that have been posited for the recent crisis. Those arguments that relate to bubbles, esoteric financial theory and sudden outbursts of greed, are particularly unsatisfactory. There may well be an argument about inappropriate regulation – poor incentive structures – that does go some way the explaining the crisis.

Section 3 examines modern theories of regulation. The economist's toolbox usually contains a public interest theory and a capture theory of regulation. Recent theoretical work undertaken by Andrei Shleifer and various co-authors provides a richer theory and understanding of regulation. This institutional framework provides a better understanding of the costs and benefits of regulation. Empirical analysis is consistent with this institutional theory of regulation.

Section 4 makes the argument that bankruptcy is the appropriate discipline measure for failed banks. Here the political economy of the response to the crisis is examined. Bailing out failed banks are fraught with financial peril and moral hazard. To be sure, the notion that financially distressed banks should be provided with liquidity is the traditional response to problems in the banking system, but economically distressed banks should be allowed to fail. By subscribing to either the 'too big to fail' or 'too big to discipline' philosophies of banking policy makers ensure that poor incentives remain in the banking system. Unfortunately, as policy makers derive political benefits from having inefficient banking regulations, it will be difficult to remove those inefficiencies from the system.

2. THE USUAL SUSPECTS

There appears to be a generalised view that banks and banking is somehow different from other sectors of the economy making it necessary for special attention. This view is difficult to justify; as Benson (2000, p. 188) indicates, 'Firms that do not affect people's health or safety or the defense (sic) of the nation rarely are regulated specifically. Why should banks be treated differently than these firms?' In this section, I discuss some of the bank-specific arguments for regulation while discussing the general argument (asymmetric information) in the next section.

Although banks perform a multitude of functions on behalf of their clients, the core business of banking consists of borrowing money to lend it. Banks earn their profit by managing the mismatch of risks arising from the different preferences of borrowers and lenders. Although this activity might be considered risky, the basic business model is similar to that of any market intermediary. Banks and the services they offer are ubiquitous. Banks serve all other firms in the economy, and most individuals will have, at least, one bank account. An ongoing relationship between a bank and a particular client is seen as providing information to observers regarding the quality of the client's income stream. Yet the same can be said for many other business relationships, and it is not clear that the kind of signalling that Fama (1985) emphasises is cause for public policy intervention.

The major argument that banks are somehow different is based on the notion that banks are subject to high levels of systemic risk. This is due to fractional reserve banking, high levels of leverage, and strong interrelationships between banks as they lend and borrow from each other. This leads to the view that a bank run could easily and quickly lead to a loss of confidence in the entire banking system. This, in turn, imposes very high costs on competitors, suppliers, consumers, and the economy as a whole. Benson (2000), however, suggests that these arguments are oversold. He divides those individuals and firms affected by a bank failure into two groups. First, those with a contractual relationship with the failed bank; Benson (2000, p. 190) makes the argument that these individuals should be well-placed to understand the risks of their relationship and should not get any greater protection than any other contractual relationship. Then there are those who may suffer an externality due to bank failure. Here Benson (2000, p. 191) argues that attempts to prevent this sort of externality has had the perverse effect of increasing the risk of failure.

There are, of course, the macroeconomic effects of a systemic crisis in banking. The macroeconomic issue at hand is due to the interaction between the banking system and the money supply. A run on the banking system can cause the money supply to contract quite sharply imposing huge costs on the real economy. The problem here is in differentiating between solvent and insolvent banks. There is a large theoretical literature dealing with this problem – yet the empirical evidence suggests less of a problem. Kaufman (1994) undertook a review of theory and evidence and reports that banks are only slightly different from non-bank firms with respect to failure. Kaufman (1994, p. 143) does provide some argument that is worth quoting in full.

> However, there is no evidence to support the widely held belief that, even in the absence of deposit insurance, bank contagion is a holocaust that can bring down solvent banks, the financial system, and even the entire macroeconomy in domino fashion. Indeed, losses to depositor creditors at failed banks, one of the major fears and causes of runs, are smaller on average than in nonbank industries. Even at its worst, as in the 1980s with deposit insurance, resolution of bank insolvencies appears far more efficient than resolution of nonbank firms through the bankruptcy process.

Benson (2000) concurs with Kaufman (1994) and suggests that even if banking crises could impact upon the macroeconomy, then the monetary authorities could quickly and easily intervene. He concludes (1994, p. 192) that protecting the macroeconomy is not a valid basis for regulating banks.

This sort of argument, however, would appear to be somewhat at odds with the events of the recent crisis period. It has been argued that financial markets and financial institutions are at the very centre of the recent financial crisis. Kaufman (1996, p. 41) has argued that bank failure can be associated with bubbles and that

> The best protection against widespread bank failures and systemic risk is macroeconomic policies that achieve stability and avoid price bubbles that leave banks highly vulnerable to failure.

The idea that there was a bubble in the United States is widespread – indeed it appears that Krugman (2002) encouraged the US government, and the Federal Reserve in particular, to generate a real estate bubble to keep the US economy strong. To the extent this occurred and Kaufman (1996) is correct, it is unsurprising that a financial crisis occurred. One problem with this type of argument is that, while the idea that asset markets are prone to bubbles is very common, it is also unsatisfactory. It is unclear what is meant by the term 'bubble' except that the user does not agree with or understand current asset pricing levels. As Eugene Fama said in an interview with John Cassidy (2010) of *The New Yorker*

> [Cassidy] I guess most people would define a bubble as an extended period during which asset prices depart quite significantly from economic fundamentals.
>
> [Fama] That's what I would think it is, but that means that somebody must have made a lot of money betting on that, if you could identify it. It's easy to say prices went down, it must have been a bubble, after the fact. I think most bubbles are twenty-twenty hindsight. Now after the fact you always find people who said before the fact that prices are too high. People are always saying that prices are too high. When they turn out to be right, we anoint them. When they turn out to be wrong, we ignore them. They are typically right and wrong about half the time.

A far more valuable exercise would be to examine fundamental factors within the market to understand how they may be influencing pricing.

Schneider and Kirchgassner (2009) suggest that economists were partly to blame for the financial crisis. Their argument is that financial economists had devised elegant and sophisticated models that masked their underlying assumptions and weaknesses. Users of those models, unaware of those assumptions and weaknesses, would have been taken by surprise when the models failed under real world conditions. According to Schneider and Kirchgassner (2009, p. 321)

> These new models, which were rigorous and promised to provide 'exact' information emboldened market participants to believe that the additional leverage was safe since participants now used scientific techniques and were convinced that they could manage it.

This is an argument that neglects any understanding of the efficient markets hypothesis. That theory suggests that mechanistic approaches to asset pricing and trading are bound to fail – the route to superior returns is by taking on additional risk (however defined). If any user of sophisticated modelling ever thought that they had found a riskless path to riches, they deserve to have lost their money.

Other economists seem to be arguing that the efficient markets hypothesis itself is partially to blame for the crisis. Quiggin (2010), for example, suggests that an understanding of the efficient market hypothesis lead to a change in regulatory philosophy.[1] Prior to the 1970s financial regulation had been restrictive, focusing on consumer protection and macroeconomic stability. Subsequently, however, regulation sought to facilitate innovation and be 'light-handed'. It is not clear that the efficient market hypothesis caused a change is regulatory approach or whether an improved understanding of regulation itself was the cause. Quiggin (2010), however, correctly argues that the term 'deregulation' when applied to the financial sector is misleading; no industry that ultimately is underwritten by the public purse can be described as being unregulated. The manner of the regulation may change over time, and it is those changes that may have perverse consequences.

It is clear, however, that US regulation played an important role in the sub-prime crisis. The usual argument along these lines is that inefficient deregulation occurred, but that view is difficult to sustain. Horwitz and Boettke (2009, p. 17), for example, indicate that over the period 1980–2009 there were four regulatory policies for every one deregulatory policy. Conversely, Schneider and Kirchgassner (2009, p. 320) argue that financial markets and innovation ran ahead of regulation, and there may be some merit to that story. But the real regulatory story must relate to the interaction between US housing policy and US banking regulation.

The US government has for decades followed policies that promote home-ownership. Although the United States is hardly unique in pursuing such policies, over the past 20 years or so, they expanded that policy dramatically. The US government pursued policies that effectively forced financial institutions to lend money to individuals that were poor credit risks. George Melloan (2010, pp. 365–366), former deputy editor of the *Wall Street Journal* describes the events leading up the sub-prime crisis as follows.[2]

> The relevant interference began over a decade ago when Congress and the Clinton administration began forcing banks to make highly risky loans to advance home ownership for Americans whose ability to afford homes and pay off mortgages was marginal. Two government sponsored lending and loan guarantee enterprises, Fannie Mae and Freddie Mac, became a receptacle for most of these dubious loans and folded them into mortgage-backed securities of equally dubious quality.
>
> The credit bubble created by the Federal Reserve Board in 2003–04 provided an environment for further irresponsible lending on a massive scale. Eventually it all came crashing down with a freeze-up in the $7.6 trillion mortgage-backed securities market that left several large players like Lehman Brothers and Bear Stearns insolvent.

If we agree that US government policy played an important role in contributing to the sub-prime crisis, then comments like this by Richard Salsman could be a good description of the situation.

> If there is anything more tragic than our current banking crisis, it is that the crisis is being blamed on the wrong group, on the bankers, instead of on the primary culprit, government intervention. The tragedy lies in failing to identify the fundamental cause of the problem, thereby ensuring its continuance. Bankers are not entirely innocent of wrongdoing in the present debacle, but to the extent that bankers have been irresponsible, it has been primarily government intervention that has encouraged them to

> be so. … Government has created these banking crises – by making it nearly impossible to practice prudent banking. Having done so, government has then pointed to bad banking practices as sufficient cause for still further interventions in the industry.

The only problem with this quote is that it does not apply to the sub-prime crisis. Salsman (1993, p. 81) wrote those words to describe the previous US banking crisis – the Savings and Loans (S&L) crisis of the late 1980s. In other words, it is very clear that the two crises have similar origins. Government intervention in the market – even for the very best of intentions – can have adverse consequences and very high costs associated with those consequences. As Ludwig von Mises (1980, p. 295) indicates, 'Imprudent granting of credit is bound to prove just as ruinous to a bank as to any other merchant'.

The political solution to the S&L crisis was, as now, to blame bankers for their greed and introduce regulation. A typical explanation along these lines was provided by the minority report in an Australian Senate Inquiry (Economic References Committee, 2009, pp. 49–50).

> From the middle of 2007, financial markets began showing signs of considerable turmoil as the realities of trade in exotic financial derivatives and the explosion in sub-prime lending that had characterised the finance market boom became clear.
>
> As subsequent events would reveal, inadequate regulation and greed on the part of financial market players would set in train a sequence of events in the United States, the United Kingdom and Europe that would culminate in the collapse, nationalisation or government bailout of major banks, insurers and credit providers. These included Citigroup, American International Group, Northern Rock, Fannie Mae, Freddie Mac, Bank of America, Goldman Sachs, Morgan Stanley, Royal Bank of Scotland, Lloyds TSB, HBOS and a number of major continental European financial institutions. The list of institutions involved reads like a veritable Who's Who of those who only months earlier would have considered themselves 'masters of the universe'. As we now know, these emperors had no clothes.

The idea that financial markets had become unusually greedy appeals to morality but is not a good economic explanation for the crisis. Regulations to limit greed and executive compensation have been proposed in the United States and in other jurisdictions such as Hong Kong. This notion, however, was rubbished in a *Wall Street Journal Asia* (2009) opinion piece.

> The idea that bankers caused the financial crisis is only credible with politicians and unaccountable bureaucrats. It's especially seductive in the U.S., where Wall Street firms leveraged up to their necks and then took taxpayer money when they were bailed out. But no such crisis happened in Hong Kong, where banks more prudently managed their balance sheets.

> The idea, too, that a public-sector bureaucrat can better align banker incentives than a competitive marketplace is laughable.

In addition to being 'laughable', the idea that bureaucrats can and should closely manage private institutions is inconsistent with the latest theory and evidence from regulatory and institutional economics.

3. AN INSTITUTIONAL THEORY OF REGULATION

The economics of regulation can be broken up into three strands. The first strand, generally associated with Arthur Cecil Pigou, is the 'public interest' theory and suggests that governments intervene to correct for externalities and other market failures. The second strand, associated with George Stigler (1972), suggests that industry seeks out regulation to create barriers to entry for new rivals and to maintain profitability. This strand of literature is known as the 'special interest' or 'capture theory' theory of regulation. The third strand, associated with Andrei Shleifer, sets out an institutional analysis of regulation that draws upon both the public interest and capture theories of regulation.

Shleifer (2005, p. 442) describes four broad general mechanisms to exert social control over organisations; 'market discipline, private litigation, public enforcement through regulation, and state ownership'. The trade-off in distinguishing between these mechanisms is between *disorder* and *dictatorship*. Djankov, Glaeser, La Porta, Lopez-de-Silanes, and Shleifer (2003, p. 598) have provided an excellent definition and discussion of *disorder* and *dictatorship*.

> The two central dangers that any society faces are disorder and dictatorship. Disorder refers to the risk to individuals and their property of private expropriation in such forms as banditry, murder, theft, violation of agreements, torts, or monopoly pricing. Disorder is also reflected in the private subversion of public institutions, such as courts, through bribes and threats, which allows private violators to escape penalties. Dictatorship refers to the risk to individuals and their property of expropriation by the state and its agents in such forms as murder, taxation, or violation of property. Dictatorship is also reflected in expropriation through, rather than just by, the state, such as occurs when state regulators help firms to restrict competitive entry. Some phenomena, such as corruption, reflect both disorder and dictatorship. When individuals pay bribes to avoid penalties for harmful conduct, corruption is a reflection of disorder. When officials create harmful rules to collect bribes from individuals seeking to circumvent them, corruption is a cost of dictatorship.

Market discipline is a very powerful force and should be considered as a regulatory default. It allows private decision making, consumer sovereignty and minimises the costs of dictatorship. Of course, it may well be the case that market discipline cannot control disorder. Shleifer (2005, p. 444) argues that the 'case for public intervention relies crucially on the presumptive failure of market discipline to control disorder'. At this point the control strategy becomes private litigation. The rules of contract and tort law administered by courts of law now control disorder; the state begins to play a role. Courts are institutions of the state and are staffed by bureaucrats and judges. Courts of law exist, at this level, to enforce private agreements and to adjudicate disputes between private parties.

Courts themselves, however, are imperfect institutions. Shleifer (2010) has argued that courts cannot always resolve disputes cheaply, predictably and impartially. When this occurs, courts and private litigation do not control disorder, and the scope for regulation opens up. Regulation occurs when the state not only provides a dispute resolution mechanism but also writes the rules that govern economic behaviour and transactions. There is substantial variation in how government can enforce its regulations. It can, for example, allow bureaucrats to engage in a regime of inspection and verification with fines being issued for non-compliance. Alternatively, the state can provide a set of rules that are privately litigated or publicly litigated. Public litigation can consist of either civil or criminal charges. Similarly the regulatory agency can initiate litigation itself for breeches of the regulations or act once a complaint has been received.

State ownership appears to be an efficient response to those situations where the disorder costs are likely to be very high. Shleifer (2005, p. 447) gives the examples of prisons, police force, and military where this is likely to be the case. The costs of disorder resulting from private ownership here are potentially so large that government needs to maintain control over these institutions.

It is one thing to have a generalised argument for regulation as an effective control mechanism, it is quite another to advocate regulation for a specific industry. The argument for regulating financial markets appears to be strong. Financial markets face what economists call an 'asymmetric information' problem. Of course security markets are hardly unique in this respect. Friedrich von Hayek (1945) has written that asymmetric information is *the* economic problem to be resolved. This represents a classic case of 'market failure' and gives rise to the need for regulation under public interest regulation theory.

La Porta, Lopez-de-Silanes, and Shleifer (2006) investigate the impact of security laws on financial markets across 49 economies. In particular they investigate how security laws operate to protect investors and whether regulators with public enforcement or rules with private enforcement lead to better outcomes. After exhaustive empirical analysis, La Porta et al. (2006, pp. 27–28) report,

> our findings suggest that securities laws matter because they facilitate private contracting rather than provide for public regulatory enforcement. Specifically, we find that several aspects of public enforcement, such as having an independent and/or focused regulator or criminal sanctions, do not matter, and others matter in only some regressions.

The upshot of this analysis is that legal rules matter, but that *regulators* do not always matter. So long as rules can be enforced in courts investors do not need to be protected by regulators. This is the very argument made by the *Wall Street Journal Asia* – investors do not need regulators to second-guess private decisions, they need a legal framework for decision making.

It would be easy to argue that the La Porta et al. (2006) is only generally true, but that banks and other financial institutions are different. Yet that is not the case. Barth, Caprio, and Levine (2004) find an analogous result in their investigation of bank regulation and supervision across 107 countries. They summarise their results as follows (Barth et al., 2004, pp. 245–246).

> In terms of broad implications, these findings raise a cautionary flag regarding reform strategies that place excessive reliance on countries adhering to an extensive checklist of regulations and supervisory practices that involve direct, government oversight of and restrictions on banks. Instead, our findings are consistent with the view that regulations and supervisory practices that
>
> (1) force accurate information disclosure,
> (2) empower private-sector corporate control of banks, and
> (3) foster incentives for private agents to exert corporate control,
>
> work best to promote bank development, performance and stability.

Barth et al. (2004) are not using the same law and finance approach to interpret their results as the La Porta et al. (2006) paper does; yet the conclusions are remarkably similar. Regulations involving prescriptive behaviour and powerful regulators using public enforcement mechanisms are not the better techniques to employ for the purpose of social control. These sorts of results raise the important question of why governments' pursue those types of regulation. Not only do they appear to be non-optimal from an economic perspective, they must be non-optimal at a personal and political level. Afterall, as the *Wall Street Journal Europe* (2009) points out,

'The bankruptcy of a systemically important bank is, necessarily, also a failure of the regulators who were overseeing it'.

4. BANKRUPTCY AS A REWARD FOR FAILURE

In Shleifer's regulatory framework, the important trade-off is between the costs of disorder and dictatorship. Banking regulators face that same trade-off with the costs of disorder being the 'too big to fail' problem and the costs of dictatorship being the 'too big to discipline' problem. This raises an acute problem for bank regulators because, as La Porta, Lopez-de-Silanes, and Shleifer (2002) show, government ownership of banks is particularly inefficient. In other words a suitable regulatory framework must be established. In most policy analysis a lot of attention is placed on the 'too big' aspect of the problem and not enough on the 'fail' and 'discipline' part of the problem. Congleton (2009, p. 315), for example, calls for greater antitrust enforcement in the financial system.

> The crisis in high finance also implies that some more aggressive application of antitrust law in the financial sector should be contemplated for the future. When a few large firms with poor management or mistaken theories can cause the world's entire financial system to become dysfunctional, it is prudent to diversify 'our' portfolio of managers by shrinking the average size and increasing the number of financial firms.

Deliberately retarding the size and scope of banking activity seems to be a very popular notion; yet Barth, Caprio, and Levine (2001) report restrictions on banking activities are associated with higher probabilities of banking crises and lower levels of efficiency. Ultimately, restricting the size of banks is a form of credit rationing and can have adverse economic consequences. It is not at all clear that bureaucrats are any better at making credit allocation decisions than are bankers. As the *Wall Street Journal Europe* (2009) opined

> But whether it's less leverage, more capital, or restrictions on banking activities, no one should be under any illusion that the same people who failed to detect the last bubble and crash will be able to design a system capable of catching the next one in time. The relative risks of being too lax or too restrictive may be hard to gauge, but either way the odds of getting it wrong are substantial if not overwhelming.
>
> This is why putting the risk of failure back into the system should be the sine qua non of any effort at reform. If regulators around the world get nothing else right, the final backstop has to be bankruptcy and/or dissolution for firms that have earned it.

The question to ask is why some commercial institutions are considered to be too big to fail or too big to discipline. Congleton (2009) has provided a public choice explanation of the political response to the crisis. He finds that a public choice explanation works reasonably well. He does not, however, seem to consider that calls for bank bailouts would themselves be part of a bankruptcy game. He makes the point that prior to September 2008 the United States seemed to be experiencing a standard recession and that many US financial institutions were actually bankrupt and not liquidity constrained.[3] He then argues (2009, pp. 305–306) that former Treasury Secretary Henry Paulson employed stronger rhetoric than circumstances indicated to promote his bailout package.

> There is some evidence that the 'Great Depression' rhetoric used to secure passage of the bailout bill exacerbated the credit problem and the recession. Because individual investors and firms naturally assume that Treasury experts have the very best data, the risk of another Great Depression apparently was 'new news' to many of them.

In the light of these arguments, it does seem puzzling that he does not give more weight to Stigler's capture argument saying that the evidence for capture is unclear. Perhaps so, yet the greatest beneficiary of an argument that some institutions are too big to fail would be those very institutions. Swan (2009, p. 130) has no doubt the capture hypothesis is at work.

> In effect, the U.S. government has now been captured by the recipients of hundreds of billions in taxpayer largess and must keep on upping the ante now that it has declared that all the banks with the one exception of Lehman's are 'too big to fail'.

Congleton (2009) finds in favour of the argument that bankruptcy procedures in 2008 were inadequate to deal with the financial crisis. That is, financial market innovation had outstripped regulators' ability to regulate the financial system and bring about an orderly process to manage failure. This view suggests that there are potentially very high costs associated with existing bankruptcy procedures. White (1996) has provided an important framework for understanding those costs and the various trade-off associated with bankruptcy procedures. She makes the important point that the incentive effects created by the bankruptcy process are more important than the impact of the bankruptcy process on those firms that are actually distressed. Unfortunately, it is here that our understanding of the bankruptcy process is particularly poor – a point also emphasised by Smith and Stromberg (2005, pp. 261–262). White (1996) makes the point that delay costs can be very high, and Congleton (2009) also makes the point that bankruptcy needs to be expedited in the financial sector.

Financial crises and bank failure, however, are not rare events. Perhaps the extent of the sub-prime crisis was unusual, yet it does seem strange that no expedited bankruptcy mechanism exists for large financial institutions. This does indicate a gap in the regulatory framework. This gap could exist by accident or by design.

The argument supporting a regulatory accident suggests that regulators did not foresee a financial crisis of sufficiently large magnitude to require expedited bankruptcy procedures. Conversely, it might be the case that regulators do not know how to design and implement an efficient bankruptcy procedure for large financial firms. It is an open question as to how plausible that argument might be. It is not at all clear that the market economy has exceeded the limits of bureaucratic control.

Alternatively, it is possible that a regulatory gap exists due to deliberate design. Kroszner (1994, p. 423) makes the argument, 'The demands of government finance have had a major impact on the financial regulations lawmakers adopt'. So why wouldn't regulators, or more likely politicians, want an efficient bankruptcy procedure? The most basic argument would be that it is not in their interests for such a mechanism to exist. So long as a political cost-benefit analysis for inefficient regulation dominates an economic cost-benefit analysis public choice theory suggests that inefficient regulation will occur. This simple analysis may be represented as:

$$\text{Political benefit} - \text{economic cost} > \text{political cost} - \text{economic benefit}$$

This framework begs the question as to the political benefits of inefficient regulation. Quite simply, inefficient regulation allows banks to take on too much risk. This could have, at least, two political benefits. First, it would allow politicians to pursue their social agendas, such as community housing, through the banking system. Second, by taking on too much risk, banks might become much more profitable than they otherwise would be, giving rise to high tax revenues to government that can be used to pursue other political objectives. An additional issue to consider is that misallocation of resources and waste can take many years to realise, and political horizons may be too short for those costs to be internalised by politicians. The absence of an efficient bankruptcy procedure in this instance could be a signalling device, indicating to financial institutions that they will be bailed out and not have to bear the full costs of failure as a consequence of their excessive risky behaviour.

The market system has a process for dealing with failure called bankruptcy. In the financial sector, this procedure works very differently than in most other parts of the economy. I have made the argument that this may well be due to the incentive structures within public choice. This does raise the additional question, however, of why regulators attempt to scapegoat bankers when a major financial crisis occurs. It seems the costs of failure are enforced through the political process rather than the market economy. The question becomes whether the costs of failure are better enforced in the political process or through the bankruptcy process. While this is an empirical question, it does seem more likely that the costs would be higher in the political process. In the first instance, the political process is more likely to be arbitrary, have higher deadweight costs associated with it, and lead to greater government involvement in the economy. On the contrary, a market-orientated bankruptcy process would create incentives to reduce unnecessary waste. After all an objective to the bankruptcy process is to maximise the value of the firm's assets despite failure. There is no such incentive in a political process.

5. CONCLUSION

Several scapegoats have been identified as having contributed to the sub-prime crisis: bubbles, financial economists, the efficient markets hypothesis, inefficient regulators, greedy bankers and the like. To be sure, there is enough blame to go around, yet the role that government and politicians play in establishing incentives for excessive risk-taking and the failure to provide an adequate bankruptcy mechanism has not yet been adequately understood. The efforts to create more prescriptive banking regulations and more powerful regulators is inconsistent with the latest research and understanding of effective regulation. Populist demands for greater regulation are almost certain to lead to poor policy implementation and perverse outcomes.

This chapter highlights the incentive that political decision makers face when designing a set of regulations to specifically ensure that banks take on too much as opposed to too little risk. The quid pro quo of such an incentive system is that government must stand ready to bail out those failed institutions that respond to those incentive structures. The cost of such a system is that the costs of failure are then enforced through a political process of scapegoating, as opposed to a market process of bankruptcy. The latter process includes the incentive to minimise those costs of failure, whereas the political process does not face those same incentives. For as long as politicians do not incur any failure costs as a consequence of policies they pursue in office, it is likely that these sorts of inefficiency will continue.

As Swan (2009, p. 131) asks, 'are politicians in what has become effectively, a socialised banking system, the best people to be setting bank lending policies and making investment decisions on citizens' behalf?' To reduce the incidence of failure, the costs of failure need to be privatised and enforce where they are incurred. That implies less government intervention and greater use of bankruptcy to dispose of failed firms, including banks.

NOTES

1. Quiggin's book is unpublished as yet, but a draft version can be found at http://zombiecon.wikidot.com/start
2. A more detailed discussion of US housing policy and its contribution to the sub-prime crisis can be found inter alia in Congleton (2009), Davidson (2010) and Wallison (2010). A recent special issue of *Critical Review* examines several arguments relating to the crisis. Stiglitz (2009) discusses irresponsible private behaviour, Jablecki and Machaj (2009) discuss the Basel accords, White (2009) investigates the role credit-rating agencies played, and Wallison discusses the contributions Fannie Mae and Freddie Mac and other features of the US housing market made to the crisis. At a more macroeconomic level Reinhart and Rogoff (2009) have provided an exhaustive history of boom and busts including the sub-prime crisis.
3. Strictly speaking those institutions should be described as being financially distressed, bankruptcy is a legal process.

REFERENCES

Barth, J., Caprio, G., Jr., & Levine, R. (2001). Banking systems around the globe: Do regulations and ownership affect performance and stability? In: F. Mishkin (Ed.), *Prudential supervision: What works and what doesn't*. Chicago: University of Chicago Press.

Barth, J., Caprio, G., Jr., & Levine, R. (2004). Bank regulation and supervision: What works best? *Journal of Financial Intermediation, 13*, 205–248.

Benson, G. (2000). Is government regulation of banks necessary? *Journal of Financial Services Research, 18*, 185–202.

Cassidy, J. (2010). Interview with Eugene Fama. Available at http://www.newyorker.com/online/blogs/johncassidy/2010/01/interview-with-eugene-fama.html

Congleton, R. (2009). On the political economy of the financial crisis and bailout of 2008–2009. *Public Choice, 140*, 287–317.

Davidson, S. (2010). Imprudent lending and the sub-prime crisis: An Austrian school perspective. *Griffith Law Review, 19*, 98–108.

Djankov, S., Glaeser, E., La Porta, R., Lopez-de-Silanes, F., & Shleifer, A. (2003). The new comparative economics. *Journal of Comparative Economics, 31*, 595–619.

Economic References Committee. (2009). *Government's economic stimulus initiatives*. Canberra: Senate Printing Unit.

Fama, E. (1985). What's different about banks? *Journal of Monetary Economics, 15*, 29–39.

Hayek, F. (1945). The use of knowledge in society. *American Economic Review, 35*(4), 519–530.
Horwitz, S., & Boettke, P. (2009). *The house that Uncle Sam built: The untold story of the great recession of 2008*. Irvington-on-Hudson: Foundation for Economic Education.
Jablecki, J., & Machaj, M. (2009). The regulated meltdown of 2008. *Critical Review, 21*, 2–3.
Kaufman, G. (1994). Bank contagion: A review of the theory and evidence. *Journal of Financial Services Research, 8*, 123–150.
Kaufman, G. (1996). Bank failures, systemic risk, and bank regulation. *Cato Journal, 16*, 17–45.
Kroszner, R. (1994). Financial regulation. In: P. Boettke (Ed.), *The Elgar companion to Austrian economics*. Cheltenham: Edward Elgar.
Krugman, P. (2002). Dubya's double dip. *The New York Times*, August 2, p. 21.
La Porta, R., Lopez-de-Silanes, F., & Shleifer, A. (2002). Government ownership of banks. *The Journal of Finance, 57*(1), 265–301.
La Porta, R., Lopez-de-Silanes, F., & Shleifer, A. (2006). What works in security laws? *The Journal of Finance, 61*(1), 1–32.
Melloan, G. (2010). Assessing the financial market damage. *The Cato Journal, 30*(2), 365–371.
Mises, L. von. (1980). *The theory of money and credit*. Indianapolis: Liberty Fund.
Quiggin, J. (2010). *Zombie economics: Six dead ideas that threaten the world economy* (Forthcoming). Princeton: Princeton University Press.
Reinhart, C., & Rogoff, K. (2009). *This time is different: Eight centuries of financial folly*. Princeton: Princeton University Press.
Salsman, R. (1993). Bankers as scapegoats for government-created banking crises in U.S. history. In: L. White (Ed.), *The crisis in American banking*. New York: New York University Press.
Schneider, F., & Kirchgassner, G. (2009). Financial and world economic crisis: What did economists contribute? *Public Choice, 140*, 319–327.
Shleifer, A. (2005). Understanding regulation. *European Financial Management, 11*(4), 439–451.
Shleifer, A. (2010). *Efficient regulation*. Unpublished Working Paper, Harvard University.
Smith, D., & Stromberg, P. (2005). Maximizing the value of distressed assets: Bankruptcy law and the efficient reorganization of firms. In: P. Honohan & L. Laeven (Eds), *Systemic financial crises: Containment and resolution*. Cambridge: Cambridge University Press.
Stigler, G. (1972). The theory of economic regulation. *Bell Journal of Economics and Management Science*, reproduced in Stigler, G. (1975). *The citizen and the state: Essays on regulation*. Chicago: The University of Chicago Press.
Stiglitz, J. (2009). The anatomy of a murder: Who killed America's economy? *Critical Review, 21*, 2–3.
Swan, P. (2009). The political economy of the subprime crisis: Why subprime was so attractive to its creators. *European Journal of Political Economy, 25*, 124–132.
Wall Street Journal Asia. (2009). Hong Kong regulatory lemmings. *Wall Street Journal Asia*. Available at http://online.wsj.com/article/SB10001424052748703740004574512732201171494.html. Retrieved on November 3, 2009.
Wall Street Journal Europe. (2009). When regulators fail. *Wall Street Journal Europe*. Available at http://online.wsj.com/article/SB10001424052748703740004574513413224061606.html. Retrieved on November 3, 2009.
Wallison, P. (2010). Government housing policy and the financial crisis. *The Cato Journal, 30*(2), 397–406.
White, L. (2009). The credit-rating agencies and the subprime debacle. *Critical Review, 21*, 2–3.
White, M. (1996). The corporate bankruptcy decisions. In: J. Bhandari & L. Weiss (Eds), *Corporate bankruptcy: Economic and legal perspectives*. Cambridge: Cambridge University Press.

THE LAWYERS AND THE MELTDOWN: THE ROLE OF LAWYERS IN THE CURRENT FINANCIAL CRISIS

William V. Rapp

ABSTRACT

This research chapter argues lawyers, not just bankers, for good and bad have been involved in all aspects of the current financial crisis. Indeed after examining and assessing various civil causes of action related to the "Mortgage Meltdown" and its aftermath, it appears if lawyers had been less involved or had raised warnings about legal risks as well as economic ones, whether the financial impact would have been so disastrous and widespread. Indeed by raising cautionary flags earlier, lawyers might have better served both the clients' and the public's long-term interests. This view thus complements issues related to criminally prosecuting mortgage fraud that has also seen explosive growth and where lawyers have again played central roles. Lawyers have been involved at the back end too in terms of legislation or resolving issues such as bankruptcies and foreclosures.

The chapter examines several causes of action the media have reported being raised by various parties and how they illustrate the role lawyers, regulations, and legislation have played in the origins and evolution of the current crisis. The cases explored involve individual parties and class

International Banking in the New Era: Post-Crisis Challenges and Opportunities
International Finance Review, Volume 11, 135–164

ISSN: 1569-3767/doi:10.1108/S1569-3767(2010)0000011009

actions. The chapter also analyzes in detail a case representing opposite ends of the origination and foreclosure closure spectrum by describing a derivative shareholder suit against corporate officers and directors actively involved in creating the subprime mess, who were then sued for covering up the inevitable results from failed loans in the reports to shareholders. It thus illustrates the legal complexities emerging from the abuse of complex financial and organizational structures impacting many investors. Finally the chapter concludes by arguing there is a public policy need not only for financial regulatory reform but also for a tightening in the professional standards and regulatory penalties imposed on lawyers involved in such transactions.

1. INTRODUCTION

This chapter describes the tip of a growing legal iceberg since the mortgage meltdown as numerous civil and criminal actions have been, and continue to be, initiated. It gives a glimpse of the scope of these actions and the role of lawyers, both positive and negative. Mortgage fraud in the United States, including Federal and state prosecution, is growing dramatically. This reflects the huge increase in the size of the US mortgage market and its complexity, both of which have opened many attractive opportunities for fraudsters across a range of financial activities and institutions. Yet plaintiffs seeking remedies often end up in civil court.

Within this complex financial and regulatory structure, lawyers have provided documentation and legal structures for every part and aspect of the mortgage generation process from origination and securitization to structuring complex mortgage-backed trust certificates on the upside to foreclosure mills on the downside. This is why it may be possible to assert that, without lawyers and their ability to structure and document complex transactions, the mortgage boom and bust might have been less severe. Lawyers have been heavily involved in dealing with the aftermath as well.

They are the ones pursuing or defending various civil actions on behalf of their clients or criminal prosecutions on behalf of the government and defendants. They are and continue to be involved in writing the laws and regulations designed to deal with the consequences flowing from the collapse such as massive foreclosures and a jump in bankruptcies. They have been called upon to draft laws and regulations seeking to prevent a future meltdown. However, they were also involved in drafting the legislation to repeal "inconvenient" laws such as Glass-Steagall or the NY "Bucket-Shop" law both of which had been passed in reaction to past crises as a way to prevent future ones and whose repeal helped to facilitate the current meltdown.

Unfortunately as is true with many booms and busts, everything happens in a rush on the upside and accelerates even faster on the downside. Therefore in many cases documentation was done at a rush and on the cheap due to the pressure on fees and the incentive to maximize revenues with lawyers perhaps telling themselves it was OK because US housing prices had always trended up. Thus, the stability of the supporting cash flows and the underlying value of the house as an asset guaranteed the documentation would never be tested. The underlying loans would just be rolled over or refinanced. But as the housing market began to collapse and more loans fell behind in terms of monthly payments or went into default, the chinks in the legal armor became apparent. As the *Financial Times* has reported "many deals suffer from poorly worded documentation and there are cases where the trustee does not know how to proceed." This has complicated various lawsuits as holders of different tranches with different rights fight about a decreasing cash pie.

Nevertheless it somehow seems ethically questionable that lawyers should benefit through litigation costs or foreclosure on the downside from their or other lawyers' errors or slipshod work on the upside where they were also compensated. Lawyers under Model Rule 1.3 Comment [2] in acting diligently on behalf of their clients are supposed to manage their time as part of their responsibilities to properly and diligently represent their clients.

Exposing clients to financial losses or litigation by not taking documentary precautions relative to what were certainly possible risks in the supporting cash flows for various structured assets probably does not meet the hurdle for malpractice, but it certainly raises questions the profession should be asking itself. Thus the ethical issues for the profession related to the financial meltdown along with many of the related cases should be with us for some time.

Indeed given the scope and complexity of the securities and contractual arrangements, the related legal actions are likely to persist even through the next boom and bust whatever that is. Therefore, the American Bar Association (ABA) should initiate a discussion on lawyers' proper role in facilitating and professionally exploiting such events on both sides of the bubble with the objective of tightening the standards on lawyers involved in structuring transactions they and their clients know are designed to fail and thus damage third-party investors. This would help rebalance the organizational role of lawyers back toward being the organizational cop as opposed to the facilitator of questionable transactions. Further to give teeth to these concerns as government regulators and central banks begin to explore approaches to controlling asset bubbles, a process already under way, holding involved lawyers responsible, should be part of the conversation and the final outcome.

In sum this chapter's basic thesis is that lawyers have been involved in all aspects of the subprime mortgage process, the resulting bubble, and the legal, economic, and political aftermath. Indeed when one examines and then assesses in more detail some of the civil causes of action related to the "Subprime Mortgage Meltdown" and its aftermath, the issue definitely arises as to if lawyers had been less involved or had raised early warnings about the inherent legal risks in addition to the economic ones whether the financial results and economic impact would have been reduced.

This conclusion is reflected in the direct causes of civil action different media have reported as being raised by various parties. These concern fraud, constructive fraud, misrepresentation, failure to disclose the actual risks, failure to disclose material information, ERISA violations, breach of duty of care or fiduciary responsibilities, public nuisance, and insider trading. They also include some class action suits making similar claims plus those unique to class actions such as shareholder derivative suits,[1] such as the case examined in more detail, *Accredited Lenders*, which represents the two ends of the origination and foreclosure closure spectrum, a derivative suit by shareholders against corporate officers and directors who permitted questionable lending practices on the upside and then covered up the results as the market collapsed. Furthermore, this case indicates the range of complexity in various complaints from abusing complex financial and organizational structures impacting many investors combined with irresponsible and predatory lending practices.

As already noted, the subprime mortgage meltdown and its aftermath have brought numerous actions both civil and criminal. Mortgage fraud in the United States, including Federal and state prosecution, has grown dramatically,[2] reflecting the US mortgage market's huge size and increased complexity. Yet while criminal prosecutions have grown with these developments, plaintiffs seeking remedies generally end up in civil court.[3] Furthermore, as explained later, plaintiffs' lawyers and their clients have been active in making other claims as well, trying to recover some of the billions of dollars in losses they have sustained. However, to fully grasp and understand these legal developments, one must first understand the critical changes that have occurred in the financial markets for mortgage-related securities and their legal underpinnings. The chapter then indicates how changes in US banking and security laws, many put forward by lawyers representing financial institutions, have greatly complicated the situation.

2. STRUCTURE AND EVOLUTION OF US MORTGAGE MARKET

2.1. Traditional Mortgage between Lender and Borrower

The US residential mortgage market is a multitrillion dollar market that dramatically increased over the real estate bubble period from 2002 to 2007. As of June 2007 residential and nonprofit mortgages outstanding amounted to $10.143 trillion up from $5.833 trillion in September 2002.[4] In turn, the number of firms and organizations participating in this huge market proliferated too. Twenty-five years ago, a local bank or local savings and loan (S&L) issued the typical home mortgage to a local borrower and the bank or S&L would hold that mortgage subject to local real estate laws and land registry regulations on its books to maturity or until the home was sold or the mortgage refinanced.

But starting in the 1980s and expanding into the 1990s and the first years of this century, that all changed. Banks and S&Ls discovered the benefits of securitization and balance sheet turnover. They realized mortgages and other regular payment credit instruments such as auto loans and credit cards had steady cash flows that if bundled would provide investors with a large steady income stream that could be capitalized and sold. That is, they were securitized.

This meant the banks and S&Ls rather than holding the loans in their investment portfolios[5] would bundle them and sell them to investors while retaining the servicing function for which they deducted fees.[6] This innovation meant the bank or S&L could now turn over their balance sheet on a rapid basis since they did not have to wait until a loan was repaid or their capital increased to make new loans and thus expand their revenues from the loan servicing and origination fees. This process increased their return on capital, earnings per share, and shareholder value[7] benefiting shareholders and corporate officers with stock options.

As this new system evolved, however, and became national or even international rather than local,[8] other financial intermediaries emerged that specialized in specific functions within the overall mortgage packaging and sale to investors' business chain. For example, mortgage brokers realized they could sell a New York mortgage to a California or Washington S&L that might price it more aggressively on rate and term than a local New York bank. This situation could arise due to the other lenders' lower funding costs, their desire to diversify their lending risks across more markets, or their interest in expanding their servicing portfolio where they had economies of scale. Indeed it could be a combination of all these factors. The broker could thus help a borrower find the best rate within an increasingly competitive and integrated national market for residential mortgages that ultimately squeezed out the small local bank or S&L.

Furthermore, as the market expanded, economies of scale in specialization at different points in the mortgage financing and investment chain emerged. The development of the Internet and personal computer power only increased such considerations as technological progress created significant cost improvements in sourcing and processing mortgage applications and approvals online. In the same way that a prospective home buyer could now virtually tour several houses in an afternoon without leaving home they could compare mortgage rates from several sources while the lenders could quickly scan a buyer's credit score and outstanding loans from all different sources. Similarly huge increases in computing power and telecommunications introduced economies of scale in servicing these mortgages (see Rapp, 2004).

Under this new and evolving structure, it was quite possible that no federally insured bank or S&L would ever be involved in the loan or that any one investor would even hold the actual mortgage as security. A mortgage broker could find a lender such as GMAC or GE Credit Services or Merrill Lynch instead of a traditional bank or S&L. These lenders in turn would bundle the mortgages into pools of cash flows usually in the form of a trust and either themselves or through investment banks such as Lehman Brothers or Bear Stearns[9] place them with investors. But rather than selling these pools as a whole or percentages of the pool to an insurance company, hedge fund, or structured investment vehicle (SIV), they sold pieces of the mortgage pool's cash flow tailored according to the investor's requirements. Thus long-term investors might only want the final monthly payments of the mortgage pool, whereas another, shorter-term investor, might desire only the first three years' interest payments.

The longer dated monthly payments would then be sold to a different investor group. Thus no one investor owned an entire mortgage, and none were involved in the loan administration or the handling of the security.[10] The power of large computer systems supported the servicing of these many different structures and favored those firms that could source and service in volume and so could spread the system costs over a large number of mortgages, customers, and structured investments. This led to a factory mentality in creating the pools including the supporting legal documentation, a practice that has apparently carried over to foreclosure activity in the current economic downturn and housing crisis (see Morgenson & Glater, 2008).

Because the initial lenders only expected to hold the mortgages[11] for a short period, they frequently funded the initial mortgage loan using commercial paper. In addition to GMAC and GE, several specialized mortgage lenders used this technique, including those that focused heavily on the subprime mortgage market.[12] The Countrywide Financial Corporation (CFC) perhaps the largest mortgage lender in the United States did this extensively with its commercial paper backed by its mortgages (Countrywide Financial Corporation, 2007). It did this even though a subsidiary was a federally insured S&L. It continued this funding practice up until 2006, probably to avoid the more stringent capital requirements the government had imposed on S&Ls in 1989 as part of The Resolution Corporation Trust Act.[13]

The collapse of the subprime market, though, forced Countrywide to change its business model. In 2006 it applied for changed status to a Federally Regulated Savings and Loan Holding Company,[14] although this shift did not save it from collapse, a takeover by Bank of America and subsequent suits of it and its officers by the several states and irate shareholders. However, this example is just one of many such situations.

The mortgage financing market's size, rapid growth, and increased complexity have combined with the current meltdown and the billions in losses by financial institutions and investors, to create many opportunities for legal actions covering both criminal prosecutions for mortgage and investor fraud and numerous civil actions seeking a legal remedy and some restitution of the lost billions.[15] Not surprisingly these points of legal altercation are often at intersections that represent handoffs of the loans and mortgages in some form between institutions such as the mortgage broker to the lender or between the lender and the packager or the packager and an investor since these points have usually been accompanied by contractual documentation representing the warranties and responsibilities of the party doing the handing off or the offering to the one receiving or accepting the securities. A very recent incident in this regard involves action by the SEC against Goldman Sachs for selling investors pools of mortgages designed to fail (see Story & Morgenson, 2010). These contractual obligations then become the basis for any recovery. However, the cookie cutter approach used to produce these securities on a mass production basis is now creating some problems (see Morgenson & Glater, 2008; and also Bajaj, 2008b).

2.2. Causes of Action

Litigation situations in fact exist at all points in the mortgage origination and investment chain as seen in the cases cited in this chapter. These points include origination, servicing, packaging, securitization, investment, hedging, and foreclosure. Although most of these actions are against or between financing institutions and especially packagers and investors, there are cases too where the people who influence or control the various points in the home sale to mortgage origination through foreclosure chain are being sued.[16]

However, the market developments described earlier have combined with changes in the legal regime regulating financial institutions to significantly complicate the steps a plaintiff's lawyer must take in developing a complaint or pursuing a particular course of action such as foreclosing on a loan or seizing collateral. This is because the slicing of loan pools into several tranches or pieces with varying rights to specific mortgage payments coupled with the multiplicity of documentation at each point in the chain have combined with the split between servicing and ownership to make it unclear who controls the pool or the underlying loan and mortgage and its payment stream.

Indeed in several cases the servicing agent holds the mortgage in trust for the pool, while the pool is controlled by the super senior tranche for a diverse group of investors with conflicting interests.[17]

3. CHANGES IN THE APPLICABLE LEGAL REGIME

Historically almost every financial boom and bust is followed by a series of scandals.[18] Since people are usually hurt by the collapse in asset values and especially the ones involving fraud, there is usually political pressure to punish those whose are perceived as having caused the problem as well as to prevent future abuses even though the real reason for the boom is generally the public's greed followed by panic as the bubble runs out of liquidity to further support much less inflate asset prices. Therefore, these episodes are frequently followed by "barn-door closing" legislation. The Federal

Reserve, the SEC, and Sarbanes-Oxley resulted from the financial crises of 1905, the crash of 1929, and the collapse of the Internet Bubble, respectively.

It is therefore not surprising the recent collapse of the US housing market and particularly the subprime mortgage market that was especially subject to broker and lender abuse has exposed similar bad practices such as predatory lending and no verification mortgages leading to subsequent Congressional action.[19] However, the new legislation builds on the prior intent of Congress in its 1989 legislation regarding loans secured by real estate needing to meet "standards as are consistent with safe and sound business practices."[20]

In fact it was this kind of response in 1989 and 1990 to the S&L crisis and the junk bond scandals[21] that resulted in Congress substantially increasing and broadening penalties for crimes impacting financial institutions by enacting FIRREA that included the establishment of the Resolution Trust Corporation and amendments that strengthened the penalties for mail, wire, and bank fraud.

To understand this in more detail, it is helpful to look at the 1989–1990 legislative history surrounding the FIRREA of 1989 that included legislation creating The Resolution Trust Corporation that was specifically designed to deal with that crisis and contained many of the revisions meant to address the set of problems the S&L crisis highlighted including irresponsible real estate lending. It is likely the current causes of action will be looking to these and related statutes for remedies.[22]

4. CIVIL CAUSES OF ACTION AND REPORTED CASES[23]

4.1. Misrepresentation

The City of Springfield Massachusetts sued Merrill Lynch for misrepresenting the quality of some subprime CDO investments and the associated risks. Merrill settled for $13.9 million, though that did not prevent the Massachusetts Attorney General from launching a fraud action against Merrill too.[24] A key issue in this and similar cases is "whether the lenders and securities underwriters fully disclosed the risks to borrowers who took out subprime loans or to investors [such as Springfield] who bought securities backed by them" (Hamilton, 2008). Therefore, a bank defendant's best defense is that these were sophisticated investors that understood the dangers, and they, just like the banks that sold the securities, failed to foresee the collapse of the housing market and the collateral damage it would spread to the financial markets (*ibid.*). So the amount of actual disclosure and the legally required disclosure will be critical elements in determining the strength of similar complaints. In this case Merrill apparently felt their position was weak but other suits will be case by case (Bajaj, 2008b).

Indeed such cases based on misrepresentation are still active two years later. On April 20, 2010, Charles Schwab agreed to a $200 million class action settlement relative to its YieldPlus Fund where plaintiffs argued it had represented the Fund as low risk even though as much 50% was invested in various mortgaged backed securities (*See* Reuters, 2010). In another misrepresentation suit MBIA the bond insurer filed suit against Countrywide financial in September 2008 for misrepresenting the quality of the mortgage backed bonds it was asked to insure but only received court approval for the case to proceed on April 30, 2010 (McCool, 2008).

4.2. Negligence and Misrepresentation

One of the largest US subprime lenders was New Century Financial. In 2007 it filed for bankruptcy, and the court appointed an examiner who concluded that its auditor KPMG had not been "skeptical enough" and the "lender's creditors could pursue negligence and misrepresentation claims against the auditors." However, he did not find any intentional fraud or wrong doing by KPMG regarding their audit or the handling of the reserves for the returned mortgage pools (Bajaj & Cresswell, 2008). Therefore, under the new Supreme Court standard, the lenders may face a tougher hurdle than previously in proving auditor liability since they would now have to show that KPMG was complicit or intentionally involved in the misrepresentation. See *Bell Atlantic v. Twombly*, 127S.Ct. 575 (2006) where the Supreme Court ruled a plaintiff needed to show misconduct was plausible not just possible. Also in *Tellabs v. Makor Issues and Rights*, 127S.Ct. 1511 (2007), the Court indicated that even prior to discovery the plaintiff needed to show a compelling argument that a corporate officer had the intent to defraud as opposed to any opposing explanation of nonfraudulent intent (Glater, 2008). Considering that KPMG withdrew and never completed the 2006 New Century audit, this may be a difficult legal bar to get over. This view is reinforced in a recent Supreme Court case, *Stone Ridge Investment Partners v. Scientific Atlanta*, WL 123801 (2008), where "the Court expressly rejected so-called 'scheme liability' under Section 10(b) of the 1934 Securities

Exchange Act and SEC Rule 10(b)-5, … and held that liability did not reach the respondents because they were secondary actors and did not make any statements or representations upon which investors relied" (Brejcha & Richmond, 2008).

4.3. Fraud[25]

The Australian Shire Council of Wingecarribee near Sydney sued Lehman Brothers arguing Lehman improperly sold them risky mortgages. According to the *Financial Times* the town claims Lehman had "failed to act in the council's best interest and engaged in misleading and deceptive conduct while serving as its financial adviser and investment manager by promoting the Lehman-originated Federation CDO, which was exposed to the US subprime market. Federation was last month marked down to 16 cents in the dollar" (Fry, 2007). The town's representative claims "it relied on Lehman's advice and representations in making its investments."

Although Lehman admitted that some of the CDOs breached the council's guidelines since the maturities were too long, a spokesman said, "We strongly deny the claims made in the [council's] press statement that we have not acted in their best interests or that we have engaged in any misleading or deceptive conduct." Furthermore, Lehman asserted the council were suitable investors because they were recognized as "sophisticated wholesale investors who have responsibility for their own investment decisions and due diligence" (*ibid.*). Thus, the case shows the two basic legal positions in these types of suits between "you did not inform us of the risk and complexity" and "you are a big boy and sophisticated enough to make your own judgments."

However, given the complexity of these instruments and that it is becoming more apparent given their big write-offs that the underwriters themselves did not always appreciate or understand the risks, investment banks that sold these securities may face some tough challenges in supporting their position, a point that is continuing in the SEC charge against Goldman Sachs noted earlier. As an independent risk consultant noted in the Lehman case, "CDOs were extremely complex and it was highly unlikely the councils were able to weigh independently the risks or value of the securities" (*ibid.*).

On the contrary, around the same time Lehman sued Fieldstone Investment Corporation for having sold them "dubious" loans. Lehman claimed the borrowers' income and the appraised home values were overstated and the conditions of the homes were poor. Lehman's requested remedy that Fieldstone resisted was to buy back the problem loans. Similarly PMI Group, a mortgage insurer, sued a subprime lender WMC in California to buy back the loans PMI insured claiming the latter "systematically" did not apply "sound underwriting practices" and indeed made the loans fraudulently or "in violation of the standards that the lender said it was using."[26] As evidence for its position the lawsuit stated that it hired a consultant to review the 5,000 loans in the mortgage pool and the consultant found 120 were defective of which WMC only offered to buy back fourteen.[27]

A complicating factor regarding such back-and-forth claims of fraud is whether material information was withheld and whether the underwriters or investors did their due diligence by providing or asking for detailed data about the mortgages underlying the pools. Clayton Holdings, a firm that provides such due diligence services, has claimed that over the mortgage boom period "it saw a significant deterioration of lending standards and a parallel jump in lending exceptions." Furthermore, "some investment banks directed Clayton to halve the sample of loans it evaluated in each portfolio" (Anderson & Bajaj, 2008). The outcome of these cases may thus turn on whether the courts see such due diligence reports and their credit evaluations of the underlying mortgages as material and whether there was a failure to provide investors with this data if required by law (*ibid.*).

Another problem facing some of the lenders and investment banks as defendants in these suits as opposed to when they are challenging or suing other knowledgeable financial institutions is whether they are considered very sophisticated and knowledgeable about the investments since they were the ones that developed and constructed them, decided when to cut corners when gathering and processing information about them, and used complex computer models to value them since there was no ready market for the securities. Furthermore they had much greater access to this information even if they chose not to gather it or to truncate their due diligence. So if the information they gave clients was false or materially misleading, they are going to have hard time arguing they were fooled too (Glater, 2008). Still the plaintiffs will need to show that 'but for" those misstatements they would not have made the investments and thus the misstatements were the proximate cause of their losses (*ibid.*).

4.4. Insider Trading

The SEC has filed a complaint against CFC's former CEO, Angelo Mozilo, for insider trading related his sales CFC stock sales between 2005 and 2007 prior to when Countrywide applied for Federal Holding Company status and started reporting a sharp increase in problem loans.[28] One defense he has asserted is that the sales were part of a preplanned selling program. However, the question then is when that program was actually put in place, whether there were any subsequent modification and the size difference between those plans and the prior ones (Morgenson, 2008b).[29] Under §16 of the Securities Exchange Act of 1934, all officers must report sales of securities and under 20A if it can be shown that this was done "while in possession of material, non-public information," the SEC can pursue civil penalties under §21A(2) that can amount to "three times the amount of the profit gained or loss avoided as a result of such unlawful, purchase, sale or communication."

The SEC has issued more detailed rules and regulations in terms of their administration of the 1934 Act regarding insider trading, which is covered primarily in Rules 10b5-1 and 10b5-2. Under these rules, it is an affirmative defense to an allegation of insider trading, 10b5-1(c)(1)(i)(A)(3), if the person had "adopted a written plan for trading securities." However, this must be done "before becoming aware of the information" and the plan "did not permit the person to exercise any subsequent influence over how, when, or whether to effect purchases or sales; provided, in addition, that any other person who, pursuant to the contract, instruction, or plan, did exercise such influence must not have been aware of the material nonpublic information when doing so." Any deviation or alteration in the plan including any subsequent hedging arrangements voids this defense. Thus, given the SEC complaint, Mr. Mozilo must show he did not know Countrywide's business model was in jeopardy when he established the plan and neither did the people who were implementing the plan know when they sold the stock. Furthermore, there should have been no change in the plan during the period.

This position is in question, however, given the basis of the SEC complaint combined with evidence presented in an earlier and separate derivative suit that shareholders in Countrywide have pursued against CFC and its officers and directors led by the Arkansas Teacher Retirement System also brought in Federal Court in Los Angeles claiming as in the SEC complaint that they turned a blind eye to deviations from mortgage underwriting standards (Morgenson, 2008a).[30] As part of their case the "plaintiffs contend that the officers and directors dumped shares even as the company spent $2.4 billion to repurchase its own stock in late 2006 and early 2007."

In his defense as one of those officers Mozilo did claim as noted earlier with respect to the SEC complaint that he had complied with the securities laws under a planned selling program. But the federal judge noted in denying the defendants motions to dismiss that Mozilo had revised the program several times, each time increasing the shares to be sold. Indeed in her opinion judge Pfaelzer wrote: "Mozilo's actions appear to defeat the very purpose of 10b5-1 plans". As the trial case proceeds,[31] the shareholders through discovery may find more smoking guns as seems to have been confirmed by the SEC complaint (Morgenson, 2008a). Given the SEC inquiry, Mozilo may thus face stiff penalties in addition to shareholder claims.[32]

5. IMPROPER DISCLOSURE OR NOT REPORT MATERIAL FACTS[33]

In a class action *Michael Atlas v. Accredited Home Lenders Holding Co.* (WL 80949 [2008]), the plaintiffs lead by the State of Arkansas's Teacher Retirement Plan alleged that accredited and certain directors concealed the firm's "true financial condition and made materially false and misleading statements regarding the company's operations and income" (Brejcha & Richmond, 2008). Particularly they cited the firm's assertions that underwriting standards for subprime borrowers were especially conservative and reserve policies for possible delinquent loans or repurchase obligations were more than adequate. Furthermore, the plaintiffs alleged that Accredited did not write down to fair value properties gained by foreclosure. Since Accredited's statements seem to have erroneously and artificially inflated its income, the plaintiffs asserted they had a course of action. In turn the Federal Court in Southern California agreed and denied Accredited's motion to dismiss noting a "prior auditor's refusal during the class period to approve the company's 2006 financial statements before the deadline for filing its form 10-K, and the new auditor requiring the company to restate to increase its allowance for loan losses by over $30 million."[34]

Nevertheless these cases do not fall all one way. Although in *Atlas* the court agreed with the plaintiffs that they had met their burden of showing a cause of action and thus the case could proceed, in 2007 another class action suit, *Claude A. Reese v. IndyMac Bancorp*, No. 07-CV-01635, where the plaintiffs also claimed the company had overly touted its business prospects, "the court dismissed the case without prejudice, finding among other things – absent significant insider sales during the class period – that the complaint did not satisfy the heightened scienter requirements of *Tellabs.*"[35]

Although many actions remain in early stages, some have made it through a court adjudication and settlement process. *Atlas v. Accredited Home*

Lenders Holding, which is a derivative class action suit, is one and it did involve a large sophisticated financial loan originator and packager as well as some large sophisticated investors.[36] Accredited is a mortgage banking company originating, servicing and selling pools of primarily subprime mortgage loans that rode the US housing and mortgage securitization boom. In turn it established a Real Estate Investment Trust (REIT) subsidiary that bought mortgage backed securities. The REIT in turn sold and publicly listed its preferred shares with Accredited owning all the common stock. The company's officers and directors as well as the officers and directors of the REIT were sued in Federal Court in Southern California in a derivative action by their shareholders with the lead plaintiff being the Arkansas Teacher Retirement System. The defendants in turn made a motion to dismiss which was not granted.

The Court, however, did divide the case into two by finding that while the officers and directors of the parent company whose stock was listed in 2003 may have made false statements, there is not sufficient evidence that the directors of the REIT made any false statements. Therefore, the derivative suit against the REIT directors by the REIT preferred shareholders was dismissed. However, the court found the following allegations against particularly the officers of parent were persuasive enough to survive the motion to dismiss and thus the derivative class action case could still proceed. These claims included allegations very similar to those made in other shareholder actions against corporate participants in the great subprime mortgage meltdown that have had their balance sheets, income statement, and stock prices hammered. Thus, this case may represent somewhat of a template for those that are coming or in process.[37]

1. The plaintiffs alleged the defendants intentionally made false statements to conceal Accredited's real financial condition and made materially false and misleading statements regarding the company's operations and income, the purpose being to artificially inflate the firm's stock price. Once the real situation was apparent the stock price plummeted. A major problem was that Accredited borrowed funds in the wholesale financial markets to fund their mortgage loans unlike the traditional S&Ls that used retail saving's deposits. These loans were in turn supported by securitized pools of subprime mortgages where Accredited had agreed as part of their financing arrangements to buy back loans and mortgages that became impaired. Therefore, just as a bank will provide reserves on its balance sheet for expected loan losses it was an important aspect of Accredited's business model to take reserves against such possible

buybacks. But accounting rules require such increases in reserves to be charged against earnings. This would naturally affect the stock price.

2. As part of the securitization process and their funding arrangements, the company had to make certain representations and warranties concerning the underwriting standards they were using in making the loans. The suit alleged as these standards deteriorated the firm continued to make the same representations and warranties implying that there would be no need to change the size of the reserves for returned mortgages. These warranties were also false and thus misleading as to the company's real financial condition.
3. When a mortgage lender forecloses on a property, the lender now owns the property and must carry it as an asset while trying to sell it. But frequently it will not be able to sell it for the amount of the original mortgage. There are also carrying costs in terms of property taxes, insurance, and utilities while the firm looks for a buyer. There are also brokers' fees to be paid. All these considerations imply that a reserve be established for such owned real estate reflecting the amount of impairment in asset values. In this case the plaintiffs argue the defendants intentionally underreserved.

After considering these arguments and the supporting evidence, the court found the plaintiffs had shown enough that their claims could not be dismissed except against the nonofficer directors of the REIT and the case could proceed.[38]

5.1. Public Nuisance

The City of Cleveland has sued 21 Ohio banks under Ohio's Public Nuisance Law accusing them of reckless lending that is now placing a financial and administrative burden on the city due to the high number of foreclosures (Hamilton, 2008).

5.2. Breach of Contract and Failure to Disclose Risk

Investors in two hedge funds organized in the Cayman Islands that were feeder funds for a Bear Stearns' master fund successfully seized control of those feeder funds in a Cayman court by having their own liquidator appointed instead of KPMG as Bear Stearns had requested. The court saw

KPMG as having a conflict since it was the liquidator for the master fund. The investors hoped their control of the feeder funds would give them standing to sue. The investors argued "that [Bear] generated and relied upon erroneous net asset value calculations and that [Bear] 'warehoused' or 'dumped' unrealizable … subprime debt in the feeder funds in contravention of the offering memorandum." Furthermore, the judge ruled Bear should share some of the costs as "the bank was behind the decision to put the funds into liquidation ahead of a petition by investors to take control by electing their own directors" (Mackintosh, 2008).

In another breach of contract case, Merrill Lynch sued XL Capital Assurance, a Security Capital Assurance owned subsidiary, for failing to meet its obligations regarding $3.1 billion in credit default swaps (CDSs). Merrill said, "We filed suit to make clear that XL Capital Insurance Inc. is required to meets its contractual obligations for credit default swaps it agreed to" (Charles Schwab On-Line Market Comments, 2008).

5.3. Breach Fiduciary Duty or Duty of Care

Barclays Bank believed itself to be the victim of a hedge fund managed by Bear Stearns that irresponsibly invested its investors' money in complex subprime securities. But Barclays ultimately had to withdraw its case showing the difficulty of winning when one is "sophisticated" (Larsen & Murphy, 2007).

HSH Nordbank, a state-controlled German bank, sued UBS in US Federal court under New York law. It contended UBS improperly sold it complex collateralized debt obligations (CDOs) that it mismanaged. HSH asserted its claims based on "the manner in which the investments were sold to HSH Nordbank and UBS's subsequent management of the assets [being] clearly contrary to [its] interests." HSH claims UBS was supposed to manage the investment conservatively and prudently but did not (Werdigier, 2008).

5.4. Improper Sale of Securities to Pension Funds

One area where such claims for prudence seem to have more clear authority is where pensions are involved. Under ERISA managers of pension funds have a fiduciary responsibility to act in the their clients' interests. State Street Global Advisors, a subsidiary of State Street bank, has set aside more than $600 million to "settle claims that the firm invested in risky mortgage-related securities" including those brought by five pension plans.[39] The pension clients claim State Street told them the funds "would be invested in risk-free debt securities (e.g. Treasuries) but were used instead to acquire 'high risk' investments and mortgage-backed securities."[40] The applicable law here seems to be 29 U.S.C.A. §1104, covering the fiduciary duties of plan administrators. Here the act requires under subsection (a) a prudent man standard of care where "subject to sections 1103(c) and (d), 1342, and 1344 of this title, a fiduciary shall discharge his duties with respect to a plan solely in the interest of the participants and beneficiaries and (A) for the exclusive purpose of: (i) providing benefits to participants and their beneficiaries; and (ii) defraying reasonable expenses of administering the plan; (B) with the care, skill, prudence, and diligence under the circumstances then prevailing that a prudent man acting in a like capacity and familiar with such matters would use in the conduct of an enterprise of a like character and with like aims; (C) by diversifying the investments of the plan so as to minimize the risk of large losses, unless under the circumstances it is clearly prudent not to do so; and (D) in accordance with the documents and instruments governing the plan insofar as such documents and instruments are consistent with the provisions of this subchapter and subchapter III of this chapter." It appears State Street recognizes CDOs backed by subprime mortgages did not meet this test.

5.5. Breach of Fiduciary Duty to Homebuyer by Withholding Material Information

A couple in California is suing their buyer's broker for not disclosing that other similar houses in the immediate neighborhood were available for much lower prices. It used to be that brokers only worked for sellers and therefore had no obligation to the buyers unless they actually lied about the property's condition. But during the housing boom, buyers engaged their own brokers to work with them to find a suitable property and look "after their interests." Sometimes this involved a contract but often did not because the buyer's broker still received payment out of the seller's commission. Nevertheless in this particular case even though there was no contract the buyers are suing their agent as having breached his duty of care by withholding the information of prices for comparable houses for sale in the same neighborhood that were substantially lower than what they paid for theirs while at the same time stating the house they bought was a "very good buy." They argue he was just trying to close the sale and did not look after their interests as he was supposed to do. This position may resonate with a jury since as one real estate lawyer noted, "Agents have a lot of fiduciary duties, but they don't make money unless they close the sale ... In an inflated market, there are built-in temptations to cut corners" (Streitfeld, 2008).

6. SUMMARY AND CONCLUSIONS

6.1. Causes of Action

This chapter has examined some of the legal causes of action related to the subprime mortgage meltdown. Since the related securities were sold globally, some of these suits have involved foreign parties suing in both US and foreign courts. In this way the US housing bubble fueled by the aggressive securitization of mortgages organized and distributed by a number of large financial institutions has created its own corresponding legal bubble in both class action and direct party claims as various claimants look for their share of the remaining cash flow or restitution by others not in bankruptcy and with deep pockets.

Yet it is clear many of the large financial firms that created the problem have taken huge hits and in many respects did not fully understand the risks they were assuming or selling to others. Therefore, from a legal point of view in terms of a defense against potential plaintiffs, this "honest belief" in a security's value and the absence of intent to defraud may prove their best defense in various actions and in cases such as *Barclays v. Bear Stearns* has seemed to work. The higher defendant intent and participation requirement bar the Supreme Court has set in recent cases for plaintiffs to hurdle also argues for this legal strategy. Thus most suits are being decided case by case. What is clear from all this, however, is lawyers have been and continue to be involved in every step of the subprime crisis and its related fallout.

6.2. Lawyer Involvement

Even traditional direct mortgage lending involved extensive documentation in terms of land records, building certificates, zoning, easements, loans, recordings, and mortgages. The securitization boom then added several more complex contractual layers to this basic legal structure for real estate, particularly residential, to bundle the mortgages and then slice and dice the cash flows. Furthermore, to get the assets and attendant liabilities off their balance sheets or to offset default risk, the financial institutions created new vehicles and financial instruments such as CDOs, SIVs, and CDSs. All these financial innovations required extensive legal documentation that lawyers supplied. This work generated millions in fees even when the deals were designed to fail and to profit those that bet against them.[41]

In sum lawyers provided documentation and legal structures for every part of the subprime paper generation process from origination and securitization to structuring complex mortgage backed trust certificates on the upside to foreclosure mills on the downside. Indeed it seems possible to assert that without lawyers and their ability to structure and document complex transactions the subprime mortgage boom and bust might not have been possible or would have been attenuated. It is clear too lawyers are heavily involved in dealing with the aftermath.

As described earlier, lawyers are the ones pursuing or defending various civil actions on behalf of their clients or criminal prosecutions on behalf of the government and defendants.[42] They are and will continue to be involved in writing the laws and regulations designed to deal with the consequences flowing from the subprime collapse such as massive foreclosures and a jump in bankruptcies. They will also be called upon to draft laws and regulations that will seek to prevent a similar future meltdown.

Unfortunately as is true with many booms and busts, everything happens in a rush on the upside and accelerates even faster on the downside. Therefore in many cases the documentation was done at a rush and on the cheap due to the pressure on fees and the incentive to maximize revenues with lawyers perhaps telling themselves it was OK because US housing prices had always trended up. Thus the stability of the supporting cash flows and the underlying value of the house as an asset guaranteed the documentation would never be tested. The underlying loans would just be rolled over or refinanced. However, as the housing market began to collapse and more loans fell behind in terms of monthly payments or went into default, the chinks in the legal armor became apparent. As the *Financial Times* recently reported "many deals suffer from poorly worded documentation and there are cases where the trustee does not know how to proceed." This has complicated various lawsuits as holders of different tranches with different rights fight about a decreasing cash pie.[43]

However, some trustees have moved to protect cash flows. Deutsche Bank and Wells Fargo have already sued to ensure payments to credit holders of trusts they administer (van Duyn & Mackenzie, 2008). In addition, as explained in Morgenson and Glater (2008), some lawyers representing lenders in foreclosure actions have come up short in front of judges demanding documentation that shows their clients actually hold registered mortgages on the properties for which they seek foreclosure.

Yet it somehow seems wrong that lawyers should benefit through the cost of litigation or foreclosure on the downside from their or other lawyers' errors or slipshod work on the upside where they were also compensated. Lawyers under Model Rule 1.3 Comment [2] to act diligently on behalf of their clients are supposed to manage their time as part of their responsibilities to properly and diligently represent their clients.

Furthermore, it seems like a total waste of valuable legal and judicial resources that one group of lawyers is devoting thousands of hours of pro bono assistance to distressed homeowners to keep them in their houses while another group of lawyers working for many of the same financial institutions that created the mess are trying to get them out while also putting tremendous additional pressure on an already overstretched judicial system. Hopefully some of this can be avoided in the future through changes in how lawyers regulate themselves and how governments hold them responsible when the next bubble arises and the lawyers are once again involved.

Exposing clients to financial losses or litigation by not taking documentary precautions relative to what were certainly possible risks in the supporting cash flows for various structured assets probably does not meet the hurdle for malpractice but it certainly raises the questions the profession should be asking itself. This is why the ethical issues for the profession related to this mess along with many of the related cases will be with us for years to come.

Indeed given the scope and complexity of the underlying securities and contractual arrangements, the related legal actions are likely to persist even through the next boom and bust whatever that is. Therefore the ABA and similar institutions in other countries as part of the reform movement to manage future bubbles should initiate a discussion regarding the proper role for lawyers in facilitating and professionally exploiting such events on both sides of a bubble. Further from a public policy standpoint it is also the responsibility of governments and central banks as they explore regulatory approaches to controlling asset bubbles to hold lawyers involved in the process, whether as outside or inside counsel, accountable as responsible actors and not just see them as the facilitators of actions by the financial institutions that employ them. In this manner the lawyer as policeman versus the lawyer as facilitator should be rebalanced as a public policy objective.

NOTES

1. Although a large and growing number of class action suits related to the mortgage meltdown have been filed, such suits are a distinct type of civil legal action from those involving individual complaints since they require a two-step process of having the class certified before a complaint can move forward. Thus many such complaints related to the subprime mortgage crisis are still in the early stages of the litigation process. However, some that have been adjudicated or settled are examined later in the chapter

2. A former federal prosecutor notes suspicious activity reports (SARs) related to mortgage fraud increased over 1,000% between 1997 and 2005, and pending FBI mortgage fraud investigations rose from 436 in fiscal 2002 to 1,210 in fiscal 2007 (*see* Grant, 2008). Furthermore, the FBI in its 2008 Mortgage Fraud report notes that SARs for "mortgage fraud filings from financial institutions increased 36 percent to 63,713 during Fiscal Year (FY) 2008 compared to 46,717 filings in FY2007" (available at www.fbi.gov/publications/fraud/mortgage_fraud08.htm). Although estimated losses are in the billions of dollars, only a small number of SARs lead to prosecutions by Federal or state law enforcement. Thus many result in civil claims instead or in conjunction with criminal cases. *See* Pierson (2007) and Gibeaut (2007) where it is cited that US mortgage fraud reports have really jumped since the 1990s along with the housing boom. The most common types of fraud involve "property flipping" or other illegal schemes to get the proceeds from mortgages or property sales through misleading appraisals or false documentation. The SEC is also looking at insider trading related to unexpected write-downs by publicly traded companies with assets tied to mortgage-backed securities (see Grant, 2008). The SEC also filed a complaint against Cioffi and Tannin in an action related to the *Barclays v. Bear Sterns* case available at www.sec.gov.

3. The number of fraud reports in 1996 were 1,318; 1997 – 1,720; 1998 – 2,269; 1999 – 2,934; 2000 – 3,515; 2001 – 4,696; 2002 – 5,387; 2003 – 9,539; 2004 – 18,391; and 2005 – 25,989. It rose again in 2006 with the FBI reporting on a fiscal year basis a rise to 35,700 from 22,000 in fiscal 2005 and from 7,000 in fiscal 2003 and to 63,713 in 2008 indicating an exploding trend (see Bajaj, 2008a). Comparing these growing number of reports with the number of investigations, much less the actual prosecutions, indicates the growth potential in various civil actions. Furthermore, there are many possible causes of action other than fraud that plaintiffs seeking financial recovery and other remedies can pursue. Opportunities for mortgage fraud and misrepresentation leading to civil action on these and other legal grounds exist in the commercial real estate sector too as some cases show. But residential mortgages are where the market, technical changes, and number of players is largest and the players are both sophisticated and unsophisticated ranging from large financial institutions to public entities to individual homeowners and investors.

4. *Source*: Federal Reserve Bank (2008), available at https://www.federalreserve.gov/datadownload/Review.aspx?rel = Z1&series = dd6e0a09170055cee26a1e11b50710fc&lastObs = 10&from = &to = &filetype = csv&label = include&layout = seriesrow&type = package. This compares with $2.3 trillion in single family mortgage debt in 1989 and $3.5 trillion in that year for all mortgage debt. See Korngold and Goldstein (2002).

5. Any statistically steady stream of payments can be discounted to determine a present value that then sets the price of an obligation that can be sold to investors who receive the future cash flows. This process is called asset securitization. Home mortgages are attractive to securitize due to the long payment periods and underlying assets.

6. See for example the business model description of Countrywide Financial Corporation (2007).

7. In the 1980s under the Basle agreements and The Resolution Trust Corporation Act, banks and S&Ls became subject to more stringent capital requirements relative to the loans on their books. This gave them an incentive to no longer hold loans to maturity or payoff. Rather it made sense to package and sell these loans to long-term investors such as insurance companies. See the chapter on Citibank in Rapp (2004).

8. See Countrywide Financial Corporation (2007), relative to their UK operations.

9. A client study during the crisis by Yoshinobu Yamada, a bank analyst at Merrill Lynch, indicated Bear Stearns and Lehman Brothers were the number 1 and 2 underwriters respectively of subprime mortgage-backed securities (see Yamada & Kubo, 2008).

10. For a deal based view of this process, see Sloan (2007).

11. See Countrywide's 10K for description of their business model, Note 6.

12. In their 2005 annual reports GM (General Motors, 2006) and GE indicate this kind of activity. Indeed GM indicated $4 billion in mortgage servicing rights on its balance sheet. Examples of GMAC's mortgage activities are available at http://www.gmacmortgage.com/index.html. The *ABA Journal* has published articles on the subprime mortgage meltdown and the related collapse in the US housing market. Some are available at http://www.abajournal.com/topics/real+estate+property+-law. They include discussions of mortgage fraud, *see* Gibeaut (2007) or Neil (2007b). However they also note the increase in related litigation and the fact some law firms are setting up special practices to sue banks or to pursue owner claims. See for example Weiss (2007a, 2007b) or Neil (2007a), More Law Firms Seek to Sue Banks. *ABA Journal*.

13. Financial Institutions Reform, Recovery, and Enforcement Act of 1989, P.L. 101-73 or FIRREA.

14. *Ibid.*, pp. 17–24.

15. See Note 1.

16. "A wave of lawsuits is beginning to wash over the troubled mortgage market and the rest of the financial world. Homeowners are suing mortgage lenders. Mortgage lenders are suing Wall Street banks. Wall Street banks are suing loan specialists. And investors are suing everyone" (Bajaj, 2008b). This article also notes two important legal issues underpinning these cases. Whether lenders and packagers alerted borrowers and investors to the risks involved and how much they were legally required to disclose.

17. The mortgages are bundled into pools and then the cash flows from the pool are separated into tiered tranches each with its own documentation and rights to the cash flow including proceeds from the sale of the property after foreclosure. The super senior sit on top and as recently reported can force liquidation wiping out the more junior tranches (see van Duyn & Mackenzie, 2008; Mackenzie, 2008).

18. The classic study in this regard is Kindleberger and Aliber (2005). See Chap. 9 on "Frauds, Swindles, and the Credit Cycle."

19. In the House Conference Report No. 101-222, August 4, 1989, the committee noted that "Although the Conferees deleted from statutory language the loan to value requirements enacted by the Senate, the appropriate Federal banking agencies are to ensure that general limits or loan to value ratios, for both banks and thrifts are implemented. The appropriate Federal banking agencies shall consider specifically the standards in the Senate bill for loans secured by residential property, loans secured by developed commercial real estate and loans secured by raw land and implement such standards as are consistent with safe and sound business practices." Thus Congress intended mortgage lending to be conducted in a prudent manner relative to a bank's or S&L's capital. However, this is precisely what the current mortgage origination and placement chain has avoided, creating the boom and subsequent bust. Countrywide's defensive initiative to subject itself to these regulations is very instructive. For recently passed legislation by the House dealing with perceived predatory lending practices in the current crisis, see the *Financial Times*' dedicated website www.ft.com/subprime. Similarly the *ABA Journal* reported on December 6, 2007, that "The New York attorney general has subpoenaed major Wall Street banks in an investigation of whether they turned a blind eye as mortgages were issued to unqualified buyers and then repackaged for sale in large bundles to investors."…"At the same time, the FBI is launching a new Washington, D.C.-based task force today to investigate such potential fraud, according to the Washington Post. 'Investigators are seeking to uncover evidence of overvalued home appraisals, shoddy lending practices and alleged irregularities in the packaging and sale of groups of loans that were marketed to ordinary investors, state investment funds and big Wall Street banks" (Available at www.abajournal.com/news/mortgage_mess_gets_messier/).

20. See Note 19.

21. For an excellent and very readable assessment of this period, see Bruck (1989).

22. See Notes 14 and 19.

23. See Hamilton (2008). The author notes, "First came the subprime mortgage boom. Next was the bust. Now, surely as day follows night, come the lawsuits. All large-scale financial scandals spawn mountains of lawsuits, but the subprime financial stands out because of the complexity of the system that funneled more than $1 trillion from investors around the world through Wall Street and mortgage lenders to borrowers with dicey credits. As losses mount on those loans, the scene of the blame game is shifting to the courts. Subprime borrowers are suing loan brokers and lenders accusing them of deceptive practices. Wall Street companies that bought now delinquent subprime loans are trying to force lenders to buy them back. Investment bank shareholders are going after those companies' managers, saying they took excessive risks by loading up on bonds backed by subprime mortgages. And investors are suing managers whose subprime laden funds have suffered hefty losses." Already observers are expecting the number of suits to exceed those filed during the 1980s' S&L crisis.

24. See Davis and Wighton (2008). In the same article, the authors quote a former head of a Wall Street concerning the potential litigation as stating "This is going to go on for years" (see Anderson, 2008). One reason the Attorney General sued Merrill

Lynch despite its settlement with Springfield is because the case was "part of a larger investigation into Merrill's sales of similar investments to other Massachusetts towns and cities" (*ibid.*). Attorney General Gavin in his complaint "argued that the city had not been properly warned of the risks associated with the investments. By the end of 2007, the $13.9 million of securities was worth $1.2 million" (*ibid.*). Merrill Lynch trying to limit any wider legal damage from the settlement claimed the Springfield situation was unusual "because the central issue was the firm's sales practices, not whether the city was a suitable buyer for the securities" (*ibid.*). However, this distinction between not having responsibility for a security's market performance and not properly advising of the inherent risks may still open a wide line of attack for certain plaintiffs since upon review Merrill found no one in Springfield had ever authorized the specific purchase of CDOs but only triple-A-rated investments. Thus the fact the securities were triple-A rated may not help Merrill in similar suits if the risky chinks in those ratings were not fully explained to the various investors.

25. At first some lawyers thought class action lawsuits would be limited in number "because mortgage securities tend to vary in composition and disclosure". Related complaints are thus more complicated to prove, forcing plaintiffs to argue case-by-case (see Bajaj, 2008b). However, as the crisis has shifted, expanded and incorporated other issues and as lenders and underwriters have lost billions and their stock values have collapsed, the opportunities for class action suits has expanded. For example in February plaintiff shareholders filed suit in Federal court in Los Angeles against Morgan Stanley's chief legal officer claiming the firm had "knowingly and recklessly" delayed disclosing its exposure to mortgage-backed securities to conceal this material information from the investing public. "The day after the $3.7 billion charge was announced the stock dropped 6%" (see Glater, 2008). Many of these cases involve claims of fraud but also include inadequate disclosure to borrowers in terms of pricing, temporary inflation of a firm's stock price due to inaccurate or incomplete disclosure, claims demanding repurchase because of violations of representations and warranties to investors at the time of purchase, claims related to employment contracts and finally those involving bankruptcy claims. According to a study by Nielsen (2008), Navigant Consulting, there were 278 class actions filed in 2007 with the number filed in the second half, 181, almost double the 97 in the first half. He further notes that "virtually every party along the mortgage origination and securitization chain is being sued, including: mortgage brokers, lenders, appraisers, title companies, homebuilders, servicers, issuers, underwriting firms, securitization trustees, bond issuers, rating agencies, money managers, public accounting firms and company directors and officers." To this list we could also add real estate brokers and bond insurance companies. The following subprime originators have been named in one or more of these actions: HSBC Financial, New Century Financial, Countrywide Financial, CB Mortgage, WMC Mortgage, Fremont Investment and Loan, Ameriquest Mortgage, H&R Block's Option One Mortgage, Wells Fargo Home Mortgage, and Merrill Lynch's First Franklin Financial Corp with 73% of the suits class actions brought by borrowers, investors or employees (*ibid.*).

26. See Bajaj (2008b). The article notes however these cases will be difficult since the plaintiffs have to prove intent to defraud. This why it notes some lawyers are using the pension laws.

27. *Ibid.*

28. "Securities and Exchange Commission today [June 4. 2009] charged former Countrywide Financial CEO Angelo Mozilo and two other former executives with securities fraud for deliberately misleading investors about the significant credit risks being taken in efforts to build and maintain the company's market share. Mozilo was additionally charged with insider trading for selling his Countrywide stock based on non-public information for nearly $140 million in profits" (available at www.sec.gov/news/press/2009/2009-129.htm). Furthermore, "[t]he SEC alleges that Mozilo along with former chief operating officer and president David Sambol and former chief financial officer Eric Sieracki misled the market by falsely assuring investors that Countrywide was primarily a prime quality mortgage lender that had avoided the excesses of its competitors." This complaint was filed in Federal Court in Los Angeles. "The SEC's complaint alleges that each of the defendants violated Section 17(a) of the Securities Act of 1933, Section 10(b) of the Securities Exchange Act of 1934 and Rule 10b-5 thereunder, and aided and abetted violations of Sections 13(a) of the Exchange Act and Rules 12b-20, 13a-1, and 13a-13 thereunder. The complaint further alleges that Mozilo and Sieracki violated Rule 13a-1413,14 under the Exchange Act."

29. Also see relative to suspected securities fraud Hernandez (2008).

30. The total amount of Mozilo's stock sales during the relevant three-year period was $474 million.

31. On December 9, 2009, the federal judge certified all classes in the suit. See securities.stanford.edu/1038/CFC_01/.

32. Complicating the matter is another derivative suit pursued in Delaware Chancery Court where an agreed settlement on class certification was initially postponed due to issues related to claims of common fraud but then approved August 2009. See delawarelitigation.com/2009/08/articles/chancery-court-updates/chancery-court-approves-class-action-settlement-involving-countrywide-and-attorneys-fees-for-plaintiffs-attorneys-based-on-therapeutic-disclosures/

33. Several mortgage lenders and underwriters have been accused of taking inadequate reserves or not properly accounting for returned mortgages pools or those held in portfolio even while delinquencies and foreclosures have been rising and could reach epidemic proportions nationwide. See article on New Century by Bajaj and Cresswell (2008). This is particularly troublesome because some legal obstacles are starting to emerge to the foreclosure mills that certain law firms have organized to deal with these problems. One Federal District Court ruled "that the plaintiff-lenders failed to show Article III standing because they did not prove that each was the holder of the note and mortgage on each property when the foreclosures were filed. The court refused to accept documents showing an intent to convey the rights in the mortgages – as opposed to proof of ownership." Furthermore, the FTC may bring "unfair and deceptive marketing actions" against some lenders that marketed "non-traditional" mortgages and the Department of Justice's Civil Rights Division could bring enforcement actions against lenders who aimed higher cost and riskier products at a protected class (Mintz, 2008). Furthermore, the US Trustee Program that is a unit of the Justice Department overseeing the integrity of the bankruptcy system is bringing cases against lenders and indirectly their law firms for abusing the bankruptcy system. In one case in

Georgia they are specifically suing Countrywide. These abuses arise from legal "foreclosure mills" that get "paid by number of motions filed in foreclosure cases." Volume and speed are their metrics. However, some judges have begun to sanction firms for filing faulty motions (see Morgenson & Glater, 2008). Revenues come from eviction and appraisal charges, late fees, title search costs, recording fees, certified mailing costs, document retrieval fees, and legal fees. Fidelity National Default Solutions is one of the biggest foreclosure service companies with revenues of $448 million in 2007. Two smaller law firms Wilson Castle Daffin & Frappier in Houston and McCalla, Raymer, Padrick, Cobb, Nichols & Clark in Atlanta are actively pursuing this business. The former had estimated 2007 foreclosure related fees of roughly $11 million and the latter had over $10 million from Countrywide alone (*ibid.*). However, some possible improper fee sharing arrangements between some law firms and the foreclosure-servicing firms have come to light (*ibid.*). Such situations bring into question whether lenders and underwriters have correctly estimated the time and effort needed to handle foreclosures and have adequately accounted for the likely recoveries or related costs.

34. WL 80949 (2008).

35. *Ibid.*

36. *Ibid.*

37. See, for example, report on New Century and its accounting for reserves (Bajaj & Cresswell, 2008).

38. There were also claims related to an acquisition and alleged violation of US securities laws. However, these claims appear on the whole to be particular to this case, whereas the allegations related to failure to disclose material information or the disclosure of deliberately misleading information related to appropriately accounting for reserves are quite similar to those arising in other derivative class action suits involving mortgage lenders and underwriters. So the reserve issue and its impact on income, net equity, and the stock price are likely to be at the center of many such suits. Therefore, the court's treatment of these allegations in this case could be an indicator of how this and other courts will treat defendants' motions to dismiss or for summary judgment in the cases to come.

39. See Bajaj (2008b). The article notes however these cases will be difficult since the plaintiffs have to prove intent to defraud. See also Brejcha and Richmond (2008).

40. *Ibid.*

41. An excellent description of these deals designed to die, their complex structures and those who bet against them is found in Lewis (2010).

42. For the expanding scope of criminal actions see Note 2.

43. See Mackenzie (2008). He quotes Janet Tavakoli of Tavakoli Structured Finance as opining that "[a] lot of senior note holders did not do their job and ask for clarity on the documentation of deals."

REFERENCES

Anderson, J. (2008). Massachusetts accuses Merrill of fraud. *New York Times*, February 2. Available at www.nytimes.com/2008/02/02/.../02legal.html

Anderson, J., & Bajaj, V. (2008). Reviewer of subprime loans agrees to aid inquiry. *New York Times*, January 27. Available at www.nytimes.com/2008/01/27/business/27subprime.html

Bajaj, V. (2008a). F.B.I. opens subprime inquiry. *New York Times*, January 30. Available at www.nytimes.com/2008/01/30/business/30fbi.html

Bajaj, V. (2008b). If everyone's finger-pointing, who's to blame? *New York Times*, January 22. Available at www.nytimes.com/2008/01/22/.../22legal.html

Bajaj, V., & Cresswell, J. (2008). A lender failed. Did its auditor? *New York Times*, April 14. Available at www.nytimes.com/2008/04/13/.../13audit.htm

Brejcha, B., & Richmond, K. (2008). The subprime crisis: Investigating and defending disputes. *Securities Litigation Journal, 18*(2). American Bar Association, Chicago, IL.

Bruck, C. (1989). *The predators' ball: The inside story of Drexel Burnham and the rise of the Junk Bond Raiders*. New York, NY: Penguin Books.

Charles Schwab On-Line Market Comments. (2008). March 19. Available at www.schwab.com

Countrywide Financial Corporation. (2007). *2006 10K*. Available at http://about.countrywide.com/SECFilings/Form10K.aspx

Davis, P., & Wighton, D. (2008). CDO case may not be foretaste of suits to come. *Financial Times*, February 26. Available at www.ft.com/cms/s/0/3d9ebeb4-e40c-11dc-8799-0000779fd2ac.html

FBI. (2008). Suspicious activity reports. Available at www.fbi.gov/publications/fraud/mortgage_fraud08.htm

Federal Reserve Bank. (2008). Mortgage statistics. Available at www.federalreserve.gov/datadownload/Review.aspx?rel = Z1&series = dd6e0a09170055cee26a1e11b50710fc&lastObs = 10&from = &to = &filetype = csv&label = include&layout = seriesrow&type = package

Financial Institutions Reform, Recovery, and Enforcement Act. (1989). P.L. 101-73, 103 STAT 183. Available at http://thomas.loc.gov/

Fry, E. (2007). Lehman faces lawsuit over CDO losses. *Financial Times*, December 20. Available at www.ft.com/cms/s/0/70a21802-af27-11dc-880f-0000779fd2ac.html

General Motors. (2006). *10K*. Available at http://www.gmacmortgage.com/index.html

Gibeaut, J. (2007). Mortgage fraud mess. *ABA Journal*, July. Available at http://www.abajournal.com/magazine/mortgage_fraud_mess

Glater, J. (2008). Wave of lawsuits over losses could hit a wall. *New York Times*, May 8. Available at www.nytimes.com/2008/05/08/business/08legal.html

Grant, J. (2008). FBI opens subprime fraud inquiries. *Financial Times*, January 30. Available at www.ft.com/cms/s/0/8a10f7d6-ced5-11dc-877a-000077b07658.html

Hamilton, W. (2008). Lawyers smell opportunity as subprime suits start to boom. *Los Angeles Times*, March 3. Available at pqasb.pqarchiver.com/latimes/access/1438365601.html?FMT=ABS&FMTS = ABS:FT&type = current&date = Mar + 3%2C + 2008&author=Walter + Hamilton&pub = Los + Angeles + Times&edition = &startpage = C.1&desc=MORTGAGES%3B + Loan + blame + game + now + in + court%3B + The + sub-prime + debacle + is + spurring + a + big-money + litigation + free-for-all

Hernandez, R. (2008). Countrywide said to be subject of federal criminal inquiry. *New York Times*, March 9. Available at www.nytimes.com/2008/03/09/business/09lend.html

House Conference Report No. 101-222. (1989). Congressional Record 135, Washington, DC (part of legislative background and support for the Financial Institutions Reform, Recovery, and Enforcement Act of 1989 under H.R. 1278).

Kindleberger, C., & Aliber, R. (2005). *Manias, panics and crashes*. Hoboken, NJ: Wiley.

Korngold, G., & Goldstein, P. (2002). *Real estate transactions* (p. 359). New York, NY: Foundation Press.

Larsen, P., & Murphy, M. (2007). Barclay's ready for subprime fight. *Financial Times*, December 21. Available at www.ft.com/cms/s/0/5baf519c-af38-11dc-880f-0000779fd2ac.html

Lewis, M. (2010). *The Big short, inside the doomsday machine*. New York, NY: W. W. Norton.

Mackenzie, M. (2008). Super-senior CDO investors begin to flex their muscles. *Financial Times*, April 14. Available at www.ft.com/cms/s/0/b2bcd0ee-0a5b-11dd-b5b1-0000779fd2ac.html

Mackintosh, J. (2008). Rebel investors seize Bear Stearns hedge funds. *Financial Times*, February 28. Available at www.ft.com/cms/s/0/d2526862-e641-11dc-8398-0000779fd2ac.html

McCool, G. (2008). NY judge approves MBIA suit over Countrywide loans. *Reuters*. Available at www.Reuters.com

Mintz, S. (2008). Subprime mortgage meltdown spurs wave of litigation. *Litigation News*, March. Available at www.abanet.org/litigation/litigationnews/.../0308_article_mortgage.html

Morgenson, G. (2008a). Judge says countrywide officers must face suit by shareholders. *New York Times*, May 15. Available at www.nytimes.com/2008/05/15/.../15countrywide.html

Morgenson, G. (2008b). Lenders who sold and left. *New York Times*, February 3. Available at www.nytimes.com/2008/02/03/business/03gret.html

Morgenson, G., & Glater, J. (2008). The foreclosure machine. *New York Times*, March 30. Available at www.nytimes.com/2008/03/30/business/30mills.html

Neil, M. (2007a). More law firms seek to sue banks. *ABA Journal Daily News*, November 14. Available at www.abajournal.com

Neil, M. (2007b). N.Y. Lawyer stole $24M, gets 10 years. *ABA Journal Daily News*, November 14. Available at www.abajournal.com

Nielsen, J. (2008). *Subprime mortgage and related litigation 2007: Looking back at what's ahead.* Chicago, IL: Navigant Consulting.

Pierson, H. (2007). Mortgage fraud boot camp: Basic training of defending a criminal mortgage fraud case. *The Champion*, National Association of Criminal Defense Lawyers, September/October, p. 14.

Rapp, W. (2004). *Information technology strategies*. New York, NY: Oxford University Press.

Reuters. (2010). Schwab legal settlement nearly wipes out Q1 profit. Available at www.reuters.com/article/idUSN2025626320100420

Securities and Exchange Commission. (2009). SEC charges Mozilo. Available at www.sec.gov/news/press/2009/2009-129.htm

Sloan, A. (2007). House of junk. *Fortune*, October 16. Available at money.cnn.com/2007/10/15/markets/junk_mortgages.fortune/index.htm?postversion=2007101609

Story, L., & Morgenson, G. (2010). For Goldman, a bet's stakes keep growing. *New York Times*, April 17.

Streitfeld, D. (2008). Feeling misled on home prices, buyers sue agent. *New York Times*, January 22. Available at www.nytimes.com/2008/01/22/.../22agent.html

van Duyn, A., & Mackenzie, M. (2008). Tranche warfare breaks out over CDOs. *Financial Times*, April 14. Available at www.ft.com/cms/s/0/ae3ce724-0a48-11dd-b5b1-0000779fd2ac.html

Weiss, D. C. (2007a). Judges crack down on law firm "Foreclosure Mills". *ABA Journal Daily News*, November 30. Available at www.abajournal.com

Weiss, D. C. (2007b). Suits follow mortgage meltdown. *ABA Journal Daily News*, September 11. Available at www.abajournal.com/search/results/79786010f223bfa9d1a6a784dba2ab36/

Werdigier, J. (2008). Faulting UBS for its losses in bad debt, a client is to sue. *New York Times*, February 25. Available at www.nytimes.com/2008/02/25/.../25bank.html

Yamada, Y., & Kubo, T. (2008). *Japanese major banks*. Tokyo, Japan: Merrill Lynch Japan Securities.

PART III
POST-CRISIS FINANCIAL REGULATION

THE GLOBAL FINANCIAL CRISIS: CAUSES, EFFECTS AND ISSUES TO CONSIDER IN THE REFORM OF FINANCIAL REGULATION[☆]

Folarin Akinbami

ABSTRACT

Purpose – *The global financial crisis of 2007–2009 has highlighted the need for reform of financial regulation in several jurisdictions across the globe, including the United Kingdom and the United States. This chapter argues that the reforms need to be comprehensive and will therefore have to cover several aspects of financial regulation.*

Design/methodology/approach – *The chapter critically examines some of the areas where reforms are most needed. This involves consideration of the merits and demerits of multi-functional or universal banking. It also involves consideration of the systemic and other problems that arise as a result of the increasingly international nature of banking and other*

[☆]This chapter is an edited version of one of the chapters of my PhD thesis. I would like to thank my PhD supervisors, Professor Andrew McGee and Mr. Andrew Griffiths, for their feedback and comments on the earlier draft. I would also like to thank my PhD examiners, Professor Joanna Gray and Professor Emilios Avgouleas, for their thorough critique and examination of my PhD thesis. All errors and omissions are my own.

International Banking in the New Era: Post-Crisis Challenges and Opportunities
International Finance Review, Volume 11, 167–190

ISSN: 1569-3767/doi:10.1108/S1569-3767(2010)0000011010

financial services. Moreover, it examines the need for regulators to understand and keep pace with financial innovation. Furthermore, it involves discussion on the need to improve corporate governance and remuneration policies in banks and other financial services providers as well as the need for adequate arrangements for dealing with bank insolvencies and collapses.

Findings – *Market fundamentalism and over-reliance on the alleged self-correcting powers of the market have led to excessive deregulation and liberalisation in world financial markets. Financial regulatory reforms will therefore have to be substantial and comprehensive to properly address the problems caused by excessive financial liberalisation.*

Originality/value – *The chapter examines significant issues that academics, regulators and policy makers should consider when devising or implementing reforms designed to prevent, or reduce the impact of, financial crises in the future.*

INTRODUCTION

The financial system is inherently prone to crisis, for example, the multitude of financial crises from the Great Crash of 1929 in the United States, which led to the Great Depression up to the recent financial crisis which, arguably, exposed several economies, including the United States and the United Kingdom to recession. This tendency to crisis conflicts with the view that market-based finance, and its innovations, provide an efficient, cost-effective form of financial intermediation (Picciotto, 2009). Many of the market-based financial innovations created in recent years have actually led to enormous losses and increased the risk of systemic collapse, rather than helping to manage financial risk (Avgouleas, 2009; Picciotto & Haines, 1999; Soros, 2008). This suggests the need for tighter regulation to ensure the stability of the financial system. The global financial crisis has highlighted the need for significant changes in domestic and global financial regulation to prevent future financial crises (Arner, 2009; G20, 2009; Hubbard, 2009; Litan, 2009). This chapter looks at the current financial crisis and identifies some of its causes. It also analyses some of the issues that must be considered, with regard to financial regulation, to prevent such crises occurring again in the future.

THE AIMS OF FINANCIAL REGULATION

The three most significant aims of financial services regulation are, arguably, systemic stability, consumer protection and the maintenance of the integrity of the financial markets (Avgouleas, 2005; IOSCO, 2008). Systemic stability is, arguably, a more important aim in banking than in non-banking financial services (Goodhart, 1998). Consumer protection is more important to non-banking financial services, such as investment business and insurance, but of less importance to banking (Goodhart, 1998). A good understanding of these three reasons for regulation is essential to any discussion on how to improve financial regulation.

THE CAUSES AND EFFECTS OF THE FINANCIAL CRISIS

The Effects of the Financial Crisis

The public cost of the crisis is significant. It can be witnessed by the global economic recession that occurred, which includes reduction of production in most sectors of the economy, significant job losses and an increase in unemployment (Kollewe & Wearden, 2009), as well as the closures of several businesses (Kollewe, 2009). The UK bank bailouts cost £131 billion, while total public sector support for the UK financial services industry (including guarantees and liquidity support from the Bank of England, as well as savings depositor protection) have cost the UK taxpayer £850 billion to date (NAO, 2009; Seager, 2009).

In the United States, the unemployment rate reached levels not seen since 1983 and remained at 10% as at January 2010 (BLS, 2010). The Troubled Assets Relief Program (TARP), used to bail out US financial institutions, cost $700 billion (Emergency Economic Stabilisation Act, 2008) (USGAO, 2009), and a further economic stimulus package, aimed at reviving the entire US economy, cost $787 billion (American Recovery and Reinvestment Act, 2009). These costs are substantial and will, more than likely, impose significant constraints on government finances in the future.

The Origins of the Crisis

Deregulatory measures (e.g. the opening up of capital markets), benign macro-economic conditions, financial innovation, excessive liquidity and easy availability of credit led to a significant deterioration of risk controls for the extension of credit and subsequently the creation of an asset price bubble in the US and UK housing markets (Jagger, 2008). This deterioration in risk controls for the extension of credit led to excessive lowering of underwriting standards for sub-prime mortgages (Avgouleas, 2009). The banks, furthermore, adopted an 'originate-to-distribute' model and began to repackage those loans into marketable securities (Residential Mortgage-Backed Securities (RMBS) and Collateralised Debt Obligations (CDOs)), which were then traded on global capital markets (Avgouleas, 2009). The funding for the sub-prime mortgages under the originate-to-distribute model was therefore ultimately provided by investors on the capital markets such as hedge funds, banks, pension funds and other financial institutions.

When the asset price bubble burst and sub-prime borrowers saw the values of their houses begin to fall, coupled with increases in their monthly mortgage repayments due to initial 'teaser' rates coming to an end and being re-priced, the numbers of defaults on sub-prime mortgages soared (PWGFM, 2008). As these sub-prime mortgages were part of the structured credit products under the originate-to-distribute model (RMBS and CDOs), the losses associated with the US defaults spread to the hedge funds, banks and other capital market investors who were the main buyers of RMBS, CDOs and other such Asset Backed Commercial Paper (ABCP) (PWGFM, 2008). This practically removed all demand for these structured credit products in the capital markets, because the fear of hidden RMBS and CDO liabilities led to investors becoming wary of purchasing such products (PWGFM, 2008).

The shortage of liquidity caused by the closing up of the capital markets has had a very significant impact globally, not just on the financial markets but also on the wider community in general – it triggered a credit crunch and a subsequent financial crisis, the cost of which has been in the region of $1 trillion in money terms, and even more in terms of its impact on the global economy (Avgouleas, 2009). Banks and insurance companies across the globe made huge losses and subsequently saw their market capitalisations fall dramatically as their share prices tumbled – one estimate puts these losses at about $1.1 trillion (Wilmarth, 2009).

The Run on Northern Rock

The drying up of funds in the capital markets led to a run on Northern Rock plc, a bank that specialised in providing residential mortgages in the

United Kingdom. This was the first run on a bank in the United Kingdom since Victorian times (Brown, 2008). Northern Rock was particularly affected by the drying up of funds in the wholesale markets because its business model was fundamentally flawed – it over-relied on funding from the wholesale markets.

In August 2007, conditions in the global credit markets deteriorated markedly, and Northern Rock experienced chronic difficulty in securing wholesale funding (FSA, 2008b). The bank had failed to adequately diversify its funding sources and had also failed to take out adequate insurance for the problems it faced (HC, 2008). Its over-reliance on the wholesale capital markets for its funding meant that it suffered liquidity problems when those markets dried up (HC, 2008). It was this liquidity crisis, rather than solvency issues, that led to the run on the bank, and its subsequent nationalisation.

The UK regulator, the Financial Services Authority (FSA) failed to properly address the weaknesses in the bank's funding model and did nothing to prevent the problems that came to the fore from August 2007 onwards (HC, 2008). This has been described as a significant regulatory failure (HC, 2008). The near-collapse of Northern Rock also brought to light serious weaknesses in the regulation of the liquidity of banks. The Sterling Stock liquidity regulatory regime under which Northern Rock operated was designed to cater for 'shock' or short-term liquidity issues (i.e. for one week or less) – it was not designed to deal with 'chronic' or long-term liquidity stresses (FSA, 2007). The FSA has subsequently been criticised for not being as concerned with liquidity issues as it is with capital adequacy and solvency issues (HC, 2008). The regime for regulating liquidity was flawed, and it therefore failed to adequately identify or address the risks that Northern Rock was running with regard to its liquidity position.

The Rescues of Bear Sterns, Fannie Mae and Freddie Mac

The next significant event in the build-up to the financial crisis was the failure of Bear Sterns, which was the fifth largest US investment bank at the time, and the one with the greatest direct involvement in the debt capital markets (Arner, 2009; Pruzan, 2008). It faced severe liquidity problems, which ultimately led to the need for it to be rescued through a takeover by JP Morgan, with financing support from the Federal Reserve Bank of New York (Arner, 2009).

The loss of confidence that led to the collapse of Bear Sterns then spread to the two central institutions in the US mortgage market, Fannie Mae and Freddie Mac. These two Government-Sponsored Enterprises (GSEs) were the largest participants in the US markets, by way of guarantees, purchases and securitisation of 'conforming loans' (Arner, 2009). It therefore made sense for market participants to be concerned about them. Despite the fact that these two institutions enjoyed an implicit guarantee (against failure or financial collapse) by the US Government, this was not sufficient to restore confidence in them, and they subsequently had to be nationalised (at significant financial cost to the US taxpayer) (Arner, 2009).

The Collapse and Insolvency of Lehman Brothers

The next stage in the run-up to the financial crisis was the collapse of Lehman Brothers, the fourth largest US investment bank at the time. Although the US authorities had organised rescues for Bear Sterns, Fannie Mae and Freddie Mac, they decided not to rescue Lehman Brothers. The decision to allow Lehman to fail was based on the conclusion that Lehman did not pose any systemic risk to the financial system (Arner, 2009). The decision has been roundly criticised as incorrect (Arner, 2009; Posner, 2009b). It has been argued that allowing Lehman to fail was the event that actually triggered the systemic financial crisis, that is, the event that transformed a credit crunch and loss of confidence in some financial firms into a full-blown systemic financial crisis (Arner, 2009; Samuel & Wallop, 2008; Tett, 2009). The collapse of Lehman is significant for this reason, and because it showed that the US authorities had neither a consistent nor a coordinated approach for dealing with the insolvency of large financial institutions.

The Problems at American Insurance Group

The same weekend that Lehman Brothers failed, it became clear that American Insurance Group (AIG), the world's largest insurer at the time, would need a substantial financial bailout from the US Federal Reserve (Arner, 2009). This was because AIG had become one of the largest counterparties in the global market for credit default swaps (CDS), which exposed it to default, thus potentially triggering the insolvencies of many of the world's largest financial institutions (Arner, 2009).

Underlying Causes of the Financial Crisis

The finger of blame for the financial crisis has been pointed at the financial services industry and the behaviour of participants in the industry (Akerlof & Shiller, 2009; Wilmarth, 2009). It has also been pointed at the regulators and the monetary policy of governments in the years leading to the financial crisis (Posner, 2009a, 2009b).

In truth, there were several separate factors that, when combined, led to the financial crisis. These factors must all be noted and duly reflected upon. Some of the most significant of these factors are monetary policy, financial innovation, the proliferation of shadow banking activities, multi-functional banking, the international (global) nature of banking, capital adequacy, liquidity, the remuneration and corporate governance structures of financial firms, insufficient clarity on how to deal with bank failures and insolvencies, flawed credit ratings and regulatory failure (Avgouleas, 2009).

ISSUES FOR CONSIDERATION IN THE REFORM OF FINANCIAL SERVICES REGULATION

There are a range of issues that must be considered when regulating financial services, and any attempts to reform financial services regulation will be more likely to succeed if the reformers make a genuine attempt to tackle them. They include the growth and proliferation of multi-functional banks, the problem of how to adequately respond to the increasingly international nature of banking and other financial services, the growth in the use of complex financial innovations and instruments, arrangements for dealing with insolvent banks and the role that corporate governance and pay structures can play in improving the quality of regulation.

The Rise of the Multi-Functional Bank

A multi-functional bank is a financial institution that engages in the provision of more than one type of financial service, for example, core banking combined with securities or derivatives trading (Cranston, 2002). The rise of multi-functional banking raises the serious question of whether it is desirable for core banking to be combined with riskier activities such as dealing, underwriting and investing in securities (Cranston, 2002). The financial crisis has re-focused attention on this question of whether or not there should be greater institutional separation between classic bank services to the real economy ('narrow' banking) and risky proprietary trading activities ('investment' banking) (FSA, 2009). Answering this question requires a look at the merits and demerits of such a separation, as well as a look at the history of multi-functional banking.

The arguments in favour of multi-functional banking are based on the fact that it leads to economic efficiency, greater competition and customer convenience (Cranston, 2002). It has been argued that allowing banks to perform multiple types of financial services presents several advantages such as economies of scale and scope in gathering and processing information about firms, risk diversification, a diverse base of activities for banks (which leads to a more stable source of income for banks, thus making them more stable) and increasing the franchise value of banks (which creates added incentives for them to behave prudently) (Barth, Brumbaugh, & Wilcox, 2000; Claessens & Klingebiel, 2000). There are, therefore, some very strong arguments in favour of preserving the multi-functional bank.

The arguments against having multi-functional banks are largely based on the risks inherent in securities and other trading activity (Dale, 1992a). The first of these is the potential for contagion to arise if core banking is mixed with securities business, that is, the possibility that losses incurred by the securities or trading arm of the business will also affect the banking arm (Cranston, 2002). The second argument against having multi-functional banks is the fact that the risk arising from securities and trading (market risk) is different from the risk arising from core banking (credit risk), thus making risk mitigation more difficult in multi-functional banks (Dale, 1995). Moreover, there is a significant distinction between the key issue in bank regulation (which is stability) and the key issue in securities regulation (which is transparency) (Padoa-Schioppa, 2004). Another argument against having multi-functional banks is based on the argument that access to retail deposit insurance, and to lender of last resort facilities, should not be allowed for firms that conduct risky trading services or engage in risky trading activities (FSA, 2009). These arguments are all strong arguments, which present a solid case for separating retail or 'narrow' banking from proprietary securities trading and investment banking.

A brief look at the history of bank regulation in the United States will buttress the arguments for separating narrow banking from investment banking. The separation of investment banking from core banking was first done under the National Bank Act 1864, but in 1913, the Federal Reserve Act effectively nullified the distinction, thus allowing banks to engage in underwriting, distributing and facilitating the issue of securities on a large scale (Carosso, Sears, & Katz, 1970; Cranston, 2002). This removal of the separation between core banking and investment banking contributed significantly to the Great Crash of 1929, which led to the Great Depression (Cranston, 2002). In response to the crash, the Glass-Steagal Act 1933 was enacted to once again separate core banking from securities and investment banking (Cranston, 2002). The Glass-Steagal Act later came under pressure from some who were in favour of multi-functional banks and was eventually repealed by the Gramm-Leach-Bliley Act 1999 (Cranston, 2002). The current financial crisis has occurred against the backdrop of this abolition of the distinction between core banking and investment banking, and this has led some to conclude that allowing multi-functional banks to undertake both core banking and investment banking has contributed, in no small part, to the current financial crisis (Avgouleas, 2009). It is interesting that on the two occasions when the separation between core banking and investment banking was removed, it was followed by financial crises, and this should surely provide considerable support for the argument that the separation between core banking and investment banking should be reinstated.

There is a growing consensus that some sort of separation between core banking and investment banking is necessary (Avgouleas, 2010; Griffiths, 2009; Wilmarth, 2009), and there have been a number of different proposals on how to do this. The Turner Review has suggested combining significantly increased capital requirements with a gross leverage ratio rule, which constrains balance sheet size, intensifying the supervision of liquidity risks and improving remuneration policies within multi-functional banks and financial services firms (FSA, 2009). A slight variation on this is one which suggests imposing much higher capital requirements on high-risk activities such as large scale proprietary trading carried out by banks that also take retail deposits, in the hope that it would prevent banks that take retail deposits from engaging in many high-risk activities, by making them more expensive (Conservatives, 2009). These proposals are in line with the proposals of the Group of Thirty (G30) Report that similarly seeks to constrain risk-taking within multi-functional banks rather than separating core banks from investment banks and other types of financial services firms (G30, 2009). Such proposals, however, do not go far enough and are unlikely to be sufficient to address the problems created by multi-functional banks.

There are, however, other proposals that go further in the direction of separating core banking from investment banking. One of these is the Obama Administration's proposed 'Volcker Rule', which forbids any bank that holds deposits guaranteed by the government from trading on its own book or operating hedge funds or private equity funds (Avgouleas, 2010;

Barker & Braithwaite, 2010; Clark, 2010). Another is the proposal by Professor Kay that there should be an extreme form of 'narrow banking' whereby retail deposits are invested in risk-free government assets (Kay, 2009). A third and more comprehensive approach is that proposed by Professor Avgouleas, which advocates the separation of bank activities along business lines, into three types or tiers of institutions – savings and loans institutions that do not take part in investment banking activities (and can therefore be backed by substantial deposit insurance and lender of last resort facilities), banks that are allowed to take part in proprietary trading and securitisation only to a certain extent (and can therefore be backed by limited deposit insurance and lender of last resort facilities) and investment firms allowed to engage in the full range of capital market activities and proprietary trading (but having no access to deposit insurance and limited liquidity insurance at market rates) (Avgouleas, 2010). This proposal has the advantage that it would substantially strengthen the stability of individual institutions and could be more appealing to the industry because the three-tier model would leave multi-functional banks ample room to restructure their different business lines and readjust their business models and sources of funding without having to shut down entire business units (Avgouleas, 2010).

The significant role that multi-functional banks played in the financial crisis has fuelled debate on multi-functional banks. If we accept that some sort of separation between core banking and investment banking is necessary, then we must also accept that the proposals for clearer institutional separation, for example, the 'Volcker Rule', the Kay proposal and the Avgouleas proposal, are all much better proposals than the proposals that merely require banks to hold increased capital or liquidity reserves for riskier activities.

Regulating International Banks and Financial Institutions

The increasingly international nature of banking and other financial services activities raises two major concerns for regulators. The first of these is the problem of regulatory arbitrage, whereby regulated firms intentionally set up in jurisdictions with lax regulation to avoid having to fulfil regulatory requirements (Cranston, 2002). The second concern is the growing interconnectedness between world financial markets, which means that crises or problems in one jurisdiction or financial market can spread to other jurisdictions or financial markets (FSA, 2009). To fully understand the difficulties that international banking raises, these two concerns must be looked at in some detail.

The first concern (of regulatory arbitrage) arises largely because of varied levels of stringency in the regulation in different jurisdictions. This occurs despite the fact that firms are often allowed to provide services in jurisdictions other than the one in which they are domiciled. The collapse of BCCI, an international bank, highlighted the limitations of cross-border bank regulation when international banks are able to take advantage of inadequate banking regulation in some jurisdictions (Cranston, 2002; Dale, 1992b, 1993). The Basel Committee on Banking Supervision has put in place a host of different measures aimed at improving the level of cooperation and coordination between home and host country regulators in charge of regulating firms domiciled in one country but providing financial services in other countries or jurisdictions (Cranston, 2002). Such consolidated supervision is, however, only one aspect of the regulation of international financial services firms, and international standards are another aspect (Cranston, 2002). Such international standards are desirable because they can help to counter the temptation for home jurisdictions to impose less burdensome regulation on their financial services firms (Cranston, 2002).

Other suggestions for improving the regulation of international firms include centralisation, for example, the creation of a European-wide regulator for banking (Louis, 1995) or securities regulation (Thieffrey, 2001), or alternatively a global or international regulator with extensive regulatory powers (Eatwell & Taylor, 2000). Regardless of which option is chosen, it is clear that international firms pose a problem that needs to be addressed, and this problem must be properly dealt with.

The second problem (of the growing interconnectedness of world financial markets) arises as a result of the increasingly global nature of financial markets. The significant effects, on global financial markets, of the failure of Lehman Brothers, for example, show this inherent interconnectedness – the decision of the US authorities to allow Lehman to fail clearly had huge financial and economic implications, not just in the United States, but across the globe (FSA, 2009). This global interconnectedness of world financial markets raises the question of how to adapt international regulation and supervision so as to reduce the likelihood and severity of future global financial crises (FSA, 2009).

In response to this question, the Financial Stability Board (formerly the Financial Stability Forum (FSF)) has proposed the creation of a 'college of supervisors' from different countries, to oversee each of the largest global financial institutions (FSF, 2009), and this proposal has been endorsed by the Summit of Leaders of the Group of Twenty (G20). The problem with this proposal, however, is that it lacks detail (Avgouleas, 2009). The FSF has also proposed increasing international coordination of measures designed to mitigate financial crises, such as the extension of lender of last resort facilities or fiscal support (FSF, 2009).

Other measures that have been proposed, by others, include suggestions that hedge funds be made to provide regulators with a list of their exposures (Bernanke, 2006), although even this would be insufficient unless an international regime for dealing with the systemic risks posed by international funds is also established (Avgouleas, 2009). There is the need for such a global approach to regulation, as part of a combined approach, which also includes the tightening up of regulation at the national level (FSA, 2009). Moreover, it is also possible to improve regulation at the European level. This involves increasing the powers of host country supervisors to monitor European firms operating in their country, and the possibility of greater cross-European coordination of supervision and regulation (FSA, 2009).

In sum, the increasingly international nature of financial services raises issues that must be addressed at the European and the global levels, and financial services regulation has to take this into account. Going forward, efforts to improve the supervision and regulation of financial services cannot be carried out solely at the national level, but must also be carried out at both the global and the European levels.

The Need for Regulators to Understand and Keep Pace with Financial Innovation

Innovation has been defined as the implementation and taking to market of new inventions or finding new and more efficient ways of doing things (Chesbrough, 2003). Financial innovation is therefore the implementation of new products, processes or services in the financial services industry. The ability to innovate is seen by many as an essential characteristic if a particular industry is to evolve and survive through time, and this, it has been argued, is particularly the case with regard to the financial services industry (Bernanke, 2009).

There have been many innovations in the financial industry in recent years, but the ones that are most relevant to any discussion on the financial crisis are structured finance products and credit derivatives. Structured finance involves the pooling together of economic assets such as bonds, loans and mortgages, and their repackaging into a privatised capital structure of claims, known as tranches, against the returns on the assets or their cash flows (Coval, Jurek, & Stafford, 2009). Securitisation is the name given to the process through which structured finance products are created. It is the process of converting illiquid assets into liquid securities and is the method through which banks sell loans, owed to them, to other investors (Keys, Mukherjee, Seru, & Vig, 2008). An example of a structured finance product is a CDO, which was the main form of structured finance that contributed to the financial crisis.

Credit derivatives are financial instruments whose payoffs are linked in some way to a change in the credit quality of an issuer or issuers (Partnoy & Skeel, 2007). The two types of credit derivatives that are relevant to the financial crisis are CDS and CDOs. A CDS is a private contract in which private parties bet on a debt issuers bankruptcy, default or restructuring (Partnoy & Skeel, 2007). The party betting 'yes' is effectively buying protection like an individual buying insurance, whereas the party betting 'no' is effectively selling protection like an insurance company (Partnoy, 2003). A major source of AIG's problems was its involvement in such bets using CDS.

Advantages of Structured Finance

A significant advantage of structured finance products, such as CDOs, is they allow investors to diversify their portfolios of fixed income instruments. The pooling together of different assets allows for broad diversification, which means that the end product (e.g. the CDO) is more reflective of the wider economy or a stock market index (Coval, et al., 2009). To this extent, structured finance allows investors to protect themselves against large declines in the aggregate economy (Coval, et al., 2009).

A second advantage of structured finance is the creation of structured finance products such as CDOs involves the use of financial engineering to complete financial markets, because they create investment opportunities that would not otherwise be available (Partnoy & Skeel, 2007). In addition, synthetic CDOs also provide arbitrage opportunities for investors (Partnoy & Skeel, 2007).

The third advantage of structured finance is the re-packaging of mortgages into mortgage-backed securities to be resold in the capital markets provides a good way of financial intermediation, because the funds raised from the capital markets could be used to issue new mortgages, thus making mortgage finance cheaper and more readily available – this is, in fact, the major function of Fannie Mae and Freddie Mac

(Coval, et al., 2009). In addition, structured finance reduces financing costs as it affords greater access to capital to small-sized and medium-sized borrowers (Avgouleas, 2009; Bernanke, 2008). These are significant advantages, which have contributed to the popularity and proliferation of structured finance.

Disadvantages of Structured Finance

A major disadvantage of structured finance is that it reduces the incentive for banks to play their traditional monitoring function of vetting borrowers (Partnoy & Skeel, 2007). Weak incentives to operate strict credit controls and provide information on the quality and performance of the assets (loans) that were repackaged through the originate-to-distribute process contributed to the financial crisis (Avgouleas, 2009). This is particularly problematic if we bear in mind the fact that banks are the institutions that are best-placed to carry out such vetting and monitoring of borrowers.

Another disadvantage of structured finance is that it magnifies systemic risk and leads to systemic problems. CDOs for example, pose the risk that a default on one or more bonds could generate a ripple effect of defaults in CDOs (Partnoy & Skeel, 2007). This was the case with regard to the financial crisis – by selling CDOs created out of mortgages and loans that were not properly underwritten, the banks were able to transfer the risk of loan or mortgage defaults to the wider capital markets, thus creating panic within the entire financial system, because it was unclear who would ultimately have to bear the losses if the mortgages and loans went into default.

The third disadvantage of structured finance is the difficulty inherent in rating or pricing structured finance products. Rating a structured finance product that has multiple components or tranches is difficult and complex. This is because minor or insignificant mistakes made when rating each underlying security or asset can become magnified when the underlying assets are pooled together to form a structured finance product such as a CDO (Coval, et al., 2009). Moreover, where the risks or likelihood of default are co-related across the underlying assets, even the senior (safer) tranches will default, thereby making even a AAA-rated tranche likely to default (Coval, et al., 2009). This raises issues regarding the suitability of these products for any investors other than the most sophisticated financial firms – there is evidence that even some of the most sophisticated financial firms sometimes do not understand the risks associated with structured finance products such as CDOs, for example, American Express, a sophisticated financial institution, suffered an $826 million loss on its investments in CDOs in 2001 and had to admit that it failed to fully comprehend the risk on these investments (Partnoy, 2003). The use of structured finance is clearly problematic if even the most sophisticated investors and credit rating agencies struggle to rate, price or even to understand such products.

Advantages of Credit Derivatives

The first advantage of credit derivatives is that they provide a simple device for banks and lenders to hedge the risks associated with a particular company (borrower) or group of companies (Partnoy & Skeel, 2007). It is arguable that the reason why large corporate bankruptcies such as Enron and Worldcom did not, in turn, lead to huge financial losses for the banks they owed money to was that those banks had managed to hedge the risks associated with those defaults by using credit derivatives (Partnoy, 2003). This led Alan Greenspan, the former Chairman of the US Federal Reserve, to describe them as being essential to the stability and flexibility of the US economy (Greenspan, 2005). The use of credit derivatives can, thus, clearly be advantageous.

The second advantage of credit derivatives is that they increase liquidity and access to capital – CDS enable banks pass on default risk to other parties such as insurance companies and pension funds, thus making the banks willing to lend much more money to many more businesses (Partnoy & Skeel, 2007). They therefore significantly expand companies' access to capital from bank lending. If handled properly, this can be a good thing for the economy.

Another advantage of credit derivatives is that they provide information to market participants – the pricing of CDS provides a valuable source of market-based information about a company's financial health (Partnoy & Skeel, 2007). This can be an advantage, although the often opaque nature of credit derivatives reduces the strength of any argument as to the 'illuminative' qualities of credit derivatives.

Disadvantages of Credit Derivatives

Both forms of credit derivatives (CDOs and CDS) can undermine the amount or quality of monitoring and oversight, because they reduce the incentives for banks to carry out such monitoring and oversight (Partnoy & Skeel, 2007). This is because the ability to offset or hedge default risk by using CDS reduces the bank's potential losses if a borrower defaults, thus reducing the bank's incentive to monitor the borrower. To this extent, it can be argued that the use of CDS can lead to moral hazard on the part of borrowers subject to less financial discipline from their lenders (Partnoy & Skeel, 2007).

Credit derivatives contribute to or exacerbate systemic risk (Partnoy & Skeel, 2007). CDS, for example, allow banks to pass on their risks to others (Partnoy, 2003), while at the same time reducing their incentives to monitor their borrowers, and this makes them a major source of systemic risk. This unbundling of credit risk is potentially problematic because it shifts risks away from the banks, which are best placed to understand such risks, to other people and institutions who might not fully understand the nature of those risks (Partnoy, 2003). In essence, credit derivatives shift risks from regulated banks to less regulated insurers (Partnoy, 2003), thereby creating, rather than reducing, market instability (Westlake, 2002). This potential to create systemic financial crisis is what led Warren Buffett to refer to credit derivatives as 'financial weapons of mass destruction' (Buffett, 2003).

Conclusion on Financial Innovation

The role that financial innovations, such as structured finance and credit derivatives, played in the run-up to the financial crisis sharply contrasts with the view that market-based finance and its innovations greatly enhance financial intermediation (Picciotto, 2009). This shows that regulators have to take a more comprehensive approach to dealing with financial innovation and should not allow the use of financial innovations that they do not fully understand.

Remuneration and Corporate Governance

The financial crisis has shown that while shareholders enjoy limited liability, the taxpayers face potentially unlimited liability with regard to the failures of systemically important banks and financial institutions (Walker, 2009). This suggests the need for measures to encourage the shareholders and boards of such companies to maintain robust corporate governance.

The Walker Review proposes increased time commitment from Non-Executive Directors (NEDs) and the Chairman and requirements for NEDs to have financial industry experience and independence of mind (Walker, 2009). The aim is to promote effective boardroom challenge of the executive before decision-making on major risk and strategic issues (Walker, 2009). The Review also proposes increased board-level engagement in risk oversight, to be achieved through board risk committees supported by a

Chief Risk Officer (CRO) with enterprise-wide authority and independence (Walker, 2009).

In addition to controls imposed by the board, the Review also recommends controls imposed by shareholders. To this extent, it proposes better engagement between fund managers, acting on behalf of their clients as beneficial owners, and the boards of the companies in which they invest their clients' funds (Walker, 2009). Asking shareholders to take a stronger role in monitoring their investments (and therefore their self-interest) appears on the face of it to be an effective proposal, but this will not necessarily be the case, due to investors' cognitive limitations and their focus on short-term profits (Avgouleas, 2009), as well as the fact that their liability is limited.

Remuneration policy is another area of corporate governance that the Walker Review considered. A large portion of financial practitioners' pay is often derived from performance-related bonuses or commissions, rather than salaries or wages in the more traditional sense. The problem with this is that it increases the pressure, on practitioners, to perform, thus increasing the potential for problems such as mis-selling (Black & Nobles, 1998) or rogue-trading (Krawiec, 2000) by employees, or over-emphasis, by executives and management, on short-term profit, to the detriment of the long-term profitability or viability of the firm or company (FSA, 2009).

The Walker Review therefore proposes alignment of remuneration structures with the medium- and longer-term risk appetite and strategy of the company, as well as mandatory disclosure of 'senior' or 'high-end' remuneration on a banded basis (Walker, 2009). Other suggestions include trying to make remuneration policies take account of risk management, so that such policies do not become catalysts for excessive risk-taking (FSA, 2009), and that investors (shareholders) take the lead in demanding compensation structures that are more aligned with their interests (Carney, 2008). Investors' cognitive limitations and focus on short-term profits will again limit the ability and willingness of shareholders to effectively control executives' and employees' pay structures (Avgouleas, 2009).

Another suggestion is the use of capital requirements as a kind of 'tax' on risky bonus structures that incentivise employees to seek short-term profits at the expense of longer term stability (Conservatives, 2009). The problem with this, however, is that although regulators ought to consider the incentive impact of remuneration arrangements when assessing firms' risk management and internal control systems, attempting to directly regulate pay or remuneration within private institutions is viewed, in some quarters, as highly inappropriate (Carney, 2008). Plans for direct regulation of pay or remuneration structures in such firms would, therefore, be difficult to implement.

Regulatory Arrangements for Dealing with Bank Insolvencies and Collapses

The issues discussed so far are those that arise while the bank is still solvent. They are therefore precautionary measures designed to prevent bank failures. The probability of bank failures, however, cannot be reduced to zero, and the bank regulation regime must contain arrangements for dealing with bank insolvencies and crises, in addition to the measures for trying to avoid them (FSA, 2009). There are two main arrangements for dealing with bank failures. The first is deposit insurance and the second is the orderly resolution of bank insolvencies.

Deposit Insurance

Deposit insurance refers to arrangements designed to safeguard the funds of depositors should the bank that they have deposited money into become insolvent. It is used in both the United States and the United Kingdom, although the rationale for it differs slightly in the two countries – in the United States, the rationale of deposit insurance is to prevent instability in the system by preventing bank runs, whereas in the United Kingdom, the rationale of deposit insurance is the protection of unsophisticated depositors who are at an informational disadvantage in judging the soundness of banks (Cranston, 2002). The difference is, however, a very subtle one, and it is fair to say that deposit protection is ultimately always concerned with ring-fencing or safeguarding funds to return them to depositors should their banks become insolvent.

A particularly memorable moment in the run-up to the financial crisis was the run on Northern Rock, and two contributors to this run on Northern Rock were the inadequacy of the deposit insurance arrangements to prevent a retail deposit run and a dearth of consumer understanding of the coverage of the deposit insurance arrangements (FSA, 2009). The FSA has made attempts to address this by increasing the coverage of the scheme so that it now covers the first £50,000 of each person's deposit with a bank (FSA, 2008a). Although there were calls for the coverage to be unlimited, which have gone unheeded, the recent increase coupled with efforts to educate depositors on the existence and coverage of the scheme should go some way towards preventing bank runs in the future.

There is an argument that deposit insurance gives rise to moral hazard because it undermines the incentive for depositors to monitor excessive risk-taking by banks (Cranston, 2002; Padoa-Schioppa, 2004). The argument is that deposit insurance and other safety nets for banks have perverse effects, by giving rise to moral hazard and encouraging risk-prone behaviour, thereby imposing excessive costs on the financial system and, in the worst cases, on taxpayers as well (Padoa-Schioppa, 2004). The Turner Review acknowledges this and is of the opinion that although deposit insurance is a good thing, it must be designed to ensure that the benefits (of such deposit insurance) are not used to cross-subsidise risky activities (FSA, 2009). There are, however, those who argue that moral hazard is not a significant issue at all – Cranston, for example, has argued that analyses of moral hazard as a significant disadvantage of deposit insurance are 'somewhat removed from the real world', because unsophisticated depositors are in no position to be vigilant and would, in any case, lack the expertise required to interpret or analyse the relevant information on banks' solvency and risk-taking (Cranston, 2002). Clearly deposit insurance does raise some issues regarding moral hazard, but the inability of regulation to completely eliminate the possibility of bank failures, coupled with the need to protect depositors and to avoid bank runs and further systemic instability, demonstrates a convincing, if not overwhelming, case, for deposit insurance.

Orderly Resolution of Bank Insolvencies

Deposit insurance is not the only arrangement for dealing with bank insolvencies. If a bank fails or becomes insolvent, it will have to either be rescued (in the form of an injection of funds into it so that it can carry on trading) or be wound up in a suitable manner so as to minimise systemic instability and losses to depositors and investors (Cranston, 2002). The decision on whether to rescue a struggling bank or to wind it up will require systemic, economic and even political considerations, for example, rescues that involve the use of taxpayer funds can be controversial (Giles, 2008; Hamnett, 2008).

Moral hazard is once again a significant concern and is arguably even more significant with regard to bank rescues than it is to deposit insurance. The argument is that the existence of rescue mechanisms such as taxpayer-funded bailouts can encourage banks to take excessive risks safe in the knowledge that should they suffer significant losses the state will come to their rescue, and this has led to suggestions that banks should be allowed to fail to prevent moral hazard (Benston & Kaufman, 1995). There is some sense in this argument, but in most cases, bank regulators cannot afford to take chances with regard to systemic risk and will therefore intervene to rescue struggling banks (Goodhart, 1988). The solution is therefore to stop banks from becoming too big to fail (Avgouleas, 2010; Clark, 2010) or to devise a regime for dealing with the insolvency of systemically important financial institutions (Avgouleas, Goodhart, & Schoenmaker, 2010).

CONCLUSION

Over the past two decades, market fundamentalism and the belief in the self-correcting powers of the market have been the dominant view. As a consequence, the volume of deregulation and liberalisation in world financial markets has been substantial. The consequences of financial liberalisation are that banks pursue more aggressive marketing and take greater risks, and the appropriate response to financial liberalisation is, therefore, a tightening of regulation (Cranston, 2002). The fact that there has been so much liberalisation in global financial markets in the recent past means that regulatory reforms will have to be substantial and comprehensive to address the problems caused by financial liberalisation.

Such regulatory reforms do not necessarily involve creating more regulatory rules, but can be achieved by improved supervision of the financial services industry, as well as the acceptance that market fundamentalism has its shortcomings. To improve the supervision of the financial industry, governments and regulators will have to thoroughly consider all of the issues outlined in this chapter, namely whether or not to separate 'narrow banking' from risky investment banking, the best way to supervise international banks, the dangers associated with the excessive use of financial innovation, the best way to tackle the problem of misaligned incentives for bank managements and the way banks manage their finances both when they are solvent and when they become insolvent.

Addressing these issues will help regulators to better monitor the way in which banks and other financial firms structure themselves, what they do, how they do it and their financial health. Improved supervision in all of these areas will go a long way towards preventing the re-occurrence of financial crises in the future.

REFERENCES

Akerlof, G. A., & Shiller, R. J. (2009). *Animal spirits: How human psychology drives the economy, and why it matters for global capitalism.* Princeton; Oxford: Princeton University Press.

Arner, D. W. (2009). The global credit crisis of 2008: Causes and consequences. *International Lawyer, 43*, 91–136.

Avgouleas, E. (2005). *The mechanics and regulation of market abuse: A legal and economic analysis.* Oxford; New York: Oxford University Press.

Avgouleas, E. (2009). The global financial crisis, behavioural finance and financial regulation: In search of a new orthodoxy. *Journal of Corporate Law Studies, 9*(1), 23–59.

Avgouleas, E. (2010). *The reform of 'Too-Big-To-Fail' banks: A new regulatory model for the institutional separation of 'casino' from 'utility' banking.* Working Paper. Available at http://ssrn.com/abstract=1552970

Avgouleas, E., Goodhart, C. A., & Schoenmaker, D. (2010). *Living wills as a catalyst for action.* DSF Policy Paper No. 4. Duisenberg School of Finance. Available at http://ssrn.com/paper=1533808

Barker, A., & Braithwaite, T. (2010). Mandelson knocks 'Volcker Rule' as too difficult. *Financial Times*, March 3. Available at www.ft.com/cms/s/78ce471c-2707-11df-8c08-00144feabcd0,dwp-uuid=fe95602e-e821-11db-b2c3-000b5df10621

Barth, J. R., Brumbaugh, R. D., & Wilcox, J. A. (2000). The repeal of Glass-Steagal and the advent of broad banking. *Journal of Economic Perspectives, 14*(2), 191–204.

Benston, G. J., & Kaufman, G. G. (1995). Is the banking and payments system fragile? *Journal of Financial Services Research, 9*(3), 209–240.

Bernanke, B. (2006). Hedge funds and systemic risk. Paper presented at the Federal Reserve Bank of Atlanta 2006 Financial Markets Conference. Available at http://www.federalreserve.gov/newsevents/speech/bernanke20060516a.htm

Bernanke, B. (2008). Addressing weaknesses in the global financial markets: The report of the President's Working Group on Financial Markets. Paper presented at the World Affairs Council. Available at http://www.federalreserve.gov/newsevents/speech/bernanke20080410a.htm

Bernanke, B. (2009). Financial innovation and consumer protection. Paper presented at the Federal Reserve's Sixth Biennial Community Affairs Research Conference. Available at http://www.federalreserve.gov/newsevents/speech/bernanke20090417a.htm

Black, J., & Nobles, R. (1998). Personal pensions misselling: The causes and lessons of regulatory failure. *Modern Law Review, 61*(6), 789–820.

BLS. (2010). Employment situation summary. Available at http://www.bls.gov/news.release/empsit.nr0.htm

Brown, C. (2008). MP's blame regulator's failures for run on Northern Rock. *The Independent*, January 26. Available at http://www.independent.co.uk/news/uk/politics/mps-blame-regulators-failures-for-run-on-northern-rock-bank-774296.html

Buffett, W. (2003). Letter to Berkshire Hathaway shareholders. Available at www.berkshirehathaway.com

Carney, M. (2008). Addressing financial market turbulence. Paper presented at the Toronto Board of Trade. Available at http://www.bankofcanada.ca/en/speeches/2008/sp08-3.html

Carosso, V. P., Sears, M. V., & Katz, I. (1970). *Investment banking in America: A history.* Cambridge, MA: Harvard University Press.

Chesbrough, H. W. (2003). *Open innovation: The new imperative for creating and profiting from technology*. Boston, MA: Harvard Business School Press.

Claessens, S., & Klingebiel, D. (2000). *Competition and scope of activities in financial services*. Mimeo, World Bank.

Clark, A. (2010). Obama takes on banking industry. *The Guardian*, January 21. Available at www.guardian.co.uk/business/2010/jan/21/obama-banking-restrictions-reform-wall-street

Conservatives. (2009). *From crisis to confidence: Plan for sound banking*. Policy White Paper. Available at www.conservatives.com/news/news-stories/2009/07/~/media/files/downloadable%20files/planforsoundbanking.ashx

Coval, J., Jurek, J., & Stafford, E. (2009). The economics of structured finance. *Journal of Economic Perspectives, 23*(1), 3–25.

Cranston, R. (2002). *Principles of banking law*. Oxford: Oxford University Press.

Dale, R. (1992a). *International banking deregulation: The great banking experiment*. Oxford: Blackwell.

Dale, R. (1992b). Reflections on the BCCI affair. *International Lawyer*, *26*(4), 949–961.

Dale, R. (1993). Bank regulation after BCCI. *Journal of International Banking Law*, *8*(1), 8–17.

Dale, R. (1995). The regulation of investment firms in the European Union. In: G. Ferrarini (Ed.), *Prudential regulation of banks and securities firms: European and international aspects*. London: Kluwer Law International.

Eatwell, J., & Taylor, L. (2000). *Global finance at risk: The case for international regulation*. Cambridge: Polity Press.

FSA. (2007). *Review of the liquidity requirements for banks and building societies*. London: FSA.

FSA. (2008a). Handbook, Compensation Sourcebook (Amendment No. 8) Instrument 2008, Comp 10.2 C.F.R.

FSA. (2008b). *Internal audit review of the supervision of Northern Rock*. London: FSA.

FSA. (2009). *The Turner review: A regulatory response to the global banking crisis*. London: FSA.

FSF. (2009). Report of the financial stability forum on enhancing market and institutional resilience: Update on implementation. Available at http://www.financialstabilityboard.org/publications/r_0904d.pdf

G20. (2009). The global plan for recovery and reform. Available at http://www.g20.org/documents/final-communique.pdf

G30. (2009). Financial reform: A framework for financial stability. Available at www.group30.org/pubs/recommendations.pdf

Giles, C. (2008). Rescue's impact on public finances. *Financial Times*, October 8. Available at http://www.ft.com/cms/s/0/fb5dc486-9523-11dd-aedd-000077b07658,s01 = 1.html?nclick_check = 1

Goodhart, C. A. E. (1988). *The evolution of central banks*. Cambridge, MA; London: MIT Press.

Goodhart, C. A. E. (1998). *Financial regulation: Why, how, and where now?* London: Routledge.

Greenspan, A. (2005). Risk transfer and financial stability. Paper presented at the Federal Reserve Bank of Chicago 41st Annual Conference on Bank Structure. Available at http://www.federalreserve.gov/boarddocs/speeches/2005/20050505/default.htm

Griffiths, K. (2009). Mervyn King presses his case to limit size of banks. *The Times*, June 18. Available at http://business.timesonline.co.uk/tol/business/industry_sectors/banking_and_finance/article6523514.ece

Hamnett, C. (2008). Stop rewarding greedy failures. *The Guardian*, October 2. Available at www.guardian.co.uk/commentisfree/2008/oct/02/creditcrunch.marketturmoil1

HC. (2008). *The run on the rock*. Treasury Select Committee, Fifth Report of Session 2007–08.

Hubbard, G. R. (2009). Finding the sweet spot for effective regulation. *The Economists' Voice*, *6*(11). doi: 10.2202/1553-3832.1661.

IOSCO. (2008). Objectives and principles of securities regulation. Available at www.iosco.org/library/pubdocs/pdf/IOSCOPD265.pdf

Jagger, S. (2008). Sub-prime and banking crisis: Who caused this nightmare? The blame spreads. *The Times*, *1*(March 19). Available at http://business.timesonline.co.uk/tol/business/industry_sectors/banking_and_finance/article3579171.ece

Kay, J. A. (2009). *Narrow banking: The reform of banking regulation*. London: Centre for the Study of Financial Innovation.

Keys, B. J., Mukherjee, T. K., Seru, A., & Vig, V. (2008). *Did securitisation lead to lax screening? Evidence from sub-prime loans*. EFA 2008 Athens Meetings Papers. Working Paper. Available at http://papers.ssrn.com/sol3/papers.cfm?abstract_id=1093137

Kollewe, J. (2009). Timeline: High street casualties. *The Guardian*, January 15. Available at http://www.guardian.co.uk/business/2008/dec/29/high-street-retailers-administration

Kollewe, J., & Wearden, G. (2009). Timeline: Britain's mounting job losses. *The Guardian*, January 16. Available at http://www.guardian.co.uk/business/2009/jan/13/recession-retail

Krawiec, K. D. (2000). Accounting for greed: Unravelling the rogue trader mystery. *Oregon Law Review*, *79*(2), 301–338.

Litan, R. E. (2009). Whither financial reform? *The Economists' Voice*, *6*(11). doi: 10.2202/1553-3832.1654.

Louis, J. V. (1995). *Banking supervision and the European Community*. Brussels: Editions de l'Universite de Bruxelles.

NAO. (2009). Maintaining financial stability across the UK's banking system. Available at www.nao.org.uk/publications/0910/uk_banking_system.aspx

Padoa-Schioppa, T. (2004). *Regulating finance: Balancing freedom and risk*. Oxford: Oxford University Press.

Partnoy, F. (2003). *Infectious greed: How deceit and risk corrupted the financial markets*. London: Profile.

Partnoy, F., & Skeel, D. A. (2007). The promise and perils of credit derivatives. *Cincinnati Law Review*, *75*(3), 1019–1051.

Picciotto, S. (2009). *Disembedding and regulation: The paradox of international finance*. The Social Embeddedness of Transnational Markets (Unpublished). Available at http://eprints.lancs.ac.uk/23551/1/Regulation_and_International_Finance.pdf

Picciotto, S., & Haines, J. (1999). Regulating global financial markets. *Journal of Law and Society*, *26*(3), 351–368.

Posner, R. A. (2009a). *A failure of capitalism: The crisis of '08 and the descent into depression*. Cambridge, MA; London: Harvard University Press.

Posner, R. A. (2009b). Financial regulatory reform: The politics of denial. *The Economists' Voice*, *6*(11). doi: 10.2202/1553-3832.1664.

Pruzan, J. (2008). Timeline: Bear Sterns' year of turmoil. *Financial Times*, March 14. Available at http://us.ft.com/ftgateway/superpage.ft?news_id=fto031720081327004236

PWGFM. (2008). Policy statement on financial market developments. Available at http://www.ustreas.gov/press/releases/reports/pwgpolicystatemktturmoil_03122008.pdf

Samuel, H., & Wallop, H. (2008). Financial crisis: Christine Lagarde warned Hank Paulson to bail out Lehman Brothers. *Daily Telegraph*, October 16. Available at http://www.telegraph.co.uk/finance/financetopics/financialcrisis/3212182/financial-crisis-Christine-Lagarde-warned-Hank-Paulson-to-bail-out-Lehman-Brothers.html

Seager, A. (2009). Banks bailout to cost tax-payer 131 billion pounds. *The Guardian*, December 4. Available at www.guardian.co.uk/business/2009/dec/04/bailout-bank-national-audit-office-report

Soros, G. (2008). *The new paradigm for financial markets: The credit crisis of 2008 and what it means*. New York: Public Affairs.

Tett, G. (2009). *Fool's gold: How unrestrained greed corrupted a dream, shattered global markets and unleashed a catastrophe*. London: Little Brown.

Thieffrey, G. (2001). The case for a European Securities Commission. In: E. Ferran & C. A. E. Goodhart (Eds), *Regulating financial services and markets in the 21st century*. Oxford: Hart.

USGAO. (2009). Troubled asset relief program, status and efforts to address transparency and accountability issues. Available at www.gao.gov/new.items/d091048t.pdf

Walker, D. (2009). A review of corporate governance in UK banks and other financial industry entities: Final recommendations. Available at http://www.ecgi.org/codes/documents/walker_review_261109.pdf

Westlake, M. (2002). Surviving the credit crisis. *The Banker*, *152*(915), 109–112.

Wilmarth, A. E. (2009). The dark side of universal banking: Financial conglomerates and the origins of the subprime financial crisis. *Connecticut Law Review*, *41*(4), 963–1050.

REFORMING INTERNATIONAL STANDARDS FOR BANK CAPITAL REQUIREMENTS: A PERSPECTIVE FROM THE DEVELOPING WORLD ☆

Pierre-Richard Agénor and Luiz A. Pereira da Silva

ABSTRACT

Purpose – *To discuss, from the perspective of developing countries, recent proposals for reforming international standards for bank capital requirements.*

Methodology/approach – *After evaluating, from the viewpoint of developing countries, the effectiveness of capital requirements reforms and progress in implementing existing regulatory accords, the chapter discusses the procyclical effects of Basel regimes, and suggests a reform proposal.*

☆This chapter dwells in part on some of our previous papers, including joint work with Koray Alper (Central Bank of Turkey). We have benefited from comments in seminars at the Bank for International Settlements, the Banque de France, the European Central Bank, the OECD, the Center for Monetary and Banking Studies, the University of Manchester, the University of Clermont-Ferrand, and the World Bank, as well as from Andrew Berg and Fabian Valencia at the International Monetary Fund. Financial support from the World Bank is gratefully acknowledged. The views expressed in this chapter are our own.

International Banking in the New Era: Post-Crisis Challenges and Opportunities
International Finance Review, Volume 11, 191–254

ISSN: 1569-3767/doi:10.1108/S1569-3767(2010)0000011011

Findings – *Minimum bank capital requirements proposals in developing countries should be complemented by the adoption of an incremental, size-based leverage ratio.*

Originality/value of chapter – *This chapter contributes to enlarge the academic and policy debate related to bank capital regulation, with a particular focus on the situation of developing countries.*

> To restrain private people from receiving in payment the promissory notes of a banker, for any sum whether great or small, when they themselves are willing to receive them, or to restrain a banker from issuing such notes, when all his neighbors' are willing to accept of them, is a manifest violation of that natural liberty which it is the proper business of law not to infringe, but to support. Such regulations may, no doubt, be considered as in some respects a violation of natural liberty. But those exertions of the natural liberty of a few individuals, which might endanger the security of the whole society, are, and ought to be, restrained by the laws of all governments, of the most free as well as of the most despotical.
>
> Adam Smith, An Inquiry into the Nature and Causes of the Wealth of Nations (Book II, Chapter ii, §94).

INTRODUCTION

The global financial crisis that began with the collapse of the subprime mortgage market in mid-2007 in the United States, and evolved after September 2008 into a severe global credit crunch and the worst global recession since the 1930s, had a two-stage impact on developing countries. At first, the direct impact was quite modest, essentially because, in these countries, exposure to "toxic assets" was limited, domestic credit could substitute external funding as a greater proportion of loans tends to be funded with (domestic) deposits and, in some cases, accumulated international reserves were used to finance trade credit. However, after the collapse of Lehman Brothers and around October–November 2008, the rapidly deteriorating situation in the financial system and the real economy in the United States, Europe, and Japan had major (and more severe than expected) adverse effects on a number of middle-income countries.[1] Box 1 summarizes the transmission channels of the crisis to developing countries.

At the global level, the amplitude and severity of the crisis vindicated the camp of "pessimists" who warned against "exuberance" and "leniency" vis-à-vis growing global imbalances and associated credit bubbles. It has shaken the financial sector's aura and naturally led to a reassessment of the policies

Box 1. Transmission of the US Crisis to Developing Countries: Alternative Channels and lessons of Brazil and China for regulatory reforms

The transmission of the US financial crisis to developing countries took place through an initial financial contagion channel that was later compounded by a real channel. It should be noted that most developing countries' banking sectors had little or no direct exposure to the US subprime market and/or its associated financial products; and in most developing countries, a significant proportion of loans are funded by local deposits. Thus, the direct balance sheet effect of the subprime meltdown did not occur.

For many emerging markets, the financial contagion channel followed market developments in the United States but accelerated sharply after, the bankruptcy of Lehman Bros. by mid-September 2008. The main vehicle was the tightening of external lines of credit from foreign to domestic banks. This "sudden stop" of external funding affected even exporters. The global credit crunch resulted in higher spreads and more costly credit for domestic firms. The dollar funding shortage, especially during the gridlock in major interbank money markets at the end of 2008, triggered significant capital outflows from developing countries, including profit-taking by investors with consequent repatriation. In some countries, outflows were compounded by lower remittances from abroad. The high level of uncertainty over the depth and duration of the global crisis at the end of 2008 caused a paradoxical liquidity flight to quality into US Treasuries. All these concurred to produce a dramatic fall in many emerging markets' equity markets, with impressive losses of market capitalization that worsened the credit crunch in these countries.

For countries with floating exchange rates and/or limited room for maneuver (e.g., unwilling or incapable of using international reserves), the dollar liquidity shortage weakened temporarily the currency and resulted in more volatility in local foreign exchange markets. The crisis also prompted a reversal of expectations in many developing countries about the robustness of their external position in the short and medium term: current accounts would weaken with lower global demand for commodities and this would translate into falls of export quantities and prices. Although this would help to control inflation (and offset the food and commodity price bubble of early 2008), it indeed increased developing countries' financing risks and led to higher depreciation and greater volatility in foreign exchange markets, weaker prospects for capital accounts (FDI, portfolio flows, etc), and expectations of weaker external demand, possibly fueled by anticipations of a global recession.

Domestic banking sectors were affected by these developments in several ways: first, by the global credit crunch, e.g., the tightening of their external lines of credit and higher spreads; second, by the balance sheet effects of the sudden currency depreciation and dramatic falls in domestic equity prices; and third, in some cases, by exposure to Over The Counter (OTC) local derivative products that had been constructed on the assumption a continuous appreciation of local currencies and were now posting huge potential losses.

The impact on the domestic economy and the real contagion channel began later. A trade channel of transmission was particularly strong given weaker export prospects. Expectations changed dramatically by the end of 2008 and prompted a sudden revision in production plans. Domestic producers reduced activity considerably and relied on existing stocks, while waiting for an improvement in the global outlook. Exporters, in particular, were adversely affected by the dramatic turnaround in the availability of external lines of credit – despite significant exchange rate depreciation. The tightening of credit conditions also affected access to short-term loans for working capital needs and contributed to lower investment. That in turn translated into increased layoffs, higher unemployment, and weaker prospect for domestic consumption.

The transmission of the US crisis to countries like Brazil and China occurred more rapidly than envisaged but the policy reactions were large and swift. Countercyclical fiscal measures were implemented: Brazil relied on tax reductions while China used direct public investment in infrastructure. In Brazil the banking sector's liquidity problems were addressed by a significant reduction in reserve requirements, larger than usual cuts in the policy rate and additional liquidity injections, including through public sector financial institutions and reserve-backed external credit lines for exports. In China, the dependence on external credit was less pronounced given the massive amount of external reserves, but quantitative restrictions on credit growth were eased together with aggressive cuts in policy rates.

Brazil and China also intervened in foreign exchange markets. Brazil, which operates a highly flexible exchange rate regime in normal times, used foreign exchange reserves to provide export financing and to reduce volatility in spot and futures foreign exchange markets but could not prevent a significant depreciation of the Real. China, with tougher capital controls and a closely managed regime, succeeded in keeping the Renminbi stable against the US Dollar at the end of 2008 while the domestic credit market expanded.

In both Brazil and China there was no need for any direct public intervention in domestic banks: first, because their financial health was never questioned by markets given their very limited exposure to global toxic assets; and second, because there were large public sector financial institutions already operating whose activities could be expanded. Therefore, there were no changes in regulatory frameworks to facilitate sailing through the financial crisis.

The trade channel was especially strong in Asian countries (and China) and China used the crisis as an opportunity to increase its inventories of imported commodities, purchasing significant volumes at relatively low prices.

The lessons of the crisis and its transmission for both Brazil and China are that an immediate provision of liquidity for trade financing and working capital, targeted and timely interventions in foreign exchange markets, and extension of sizeable amounts of working capital through public sector banks proved crucial to avoid major disruptions. Despite the quick drop in the level of activity in both countries, the recovery in both of them has been among the fastest on record in 2009. These lessons are important for regulatory purposes, as discussed in the text.

and rules that have allowed – and inadvertently even promoted – the buildup of financial fragilities in industrial countries. The regulatory framework, and the distortions in bank behavior and the financial intermediation process that it has engendered, have come under renewed scrutiny.[2]

During the most acute phase of the crisis, there was significant international consensus, expressed in many meetings of the G20 leaders, finance ministers and governors of central banks (see: www.g20.org/pub_communiques.aspx), for stronger regulation, aimed in particular at reducing systemic risk, preventing future crises, and "developing by end of 2010 internationally agreed rules to improve both the quantity and quality of bank capital and to discourage excessive leverage." At the beginning, the dominant sentiment in policy circles was not whether to regulate, but rather when to do it – rules could be phased in as financial conditions improve and economic recovery is assured – and how best to do it, without unduly constraining financial innovation and the functioning of the financial system, which in turn could adversely affect economic growth. Now, as the system recovers, it seems that the leverage and political willingness to reform financial regulation is moving away from the center stage (e.g., the G20) to more technical and quieter discussion forums.

In any event, because the crisis triggered a bank balance sheet meltdown with an erosion of asset values, skyrocketing liabilities and an ensuing credit crunch, one of the most debated issues has been that of bank capital requirements regimes and their implications for lending cycles. In this respect, there have been several proposals to amend existing regimes; among them, the most popular one advocates the accumulation of higher capital buffers (capital in excess of regulatory capital) in booms, to mitigate the procyclical effects of bank lending during downturns. However, what appears to be missing in the ongoing debate is a systematic analysis of how these proposals would operate in the context of developing countries. It is only very recently, with the increasing role of the BRICs in the G20 and others that the traditional "hubs" of regulatory reform began including representatives from these countries. Basel rules, which were primarily designed for industrialized countries with mature financial markets and internationally active large banks, are a case in point. The pervasiveness of credit market imperfections in developing countries, coupled with their greater vulnerability to shocks, suggests that a specific analysis of how Basel II rules operate in these countries, and whether they should be implemented as such or amended to reflect their characteristics, is warranted.

Indeed, while a better regulatory regime is certainly necessary and while reforms need to contemplate capital requirements, how should they be applied to developing countries, given the nature of their financial systems? Should new Basel rules be applied uniformly to both industrialized and developing countries alike? Or alternatively should more specific financial regulations be adapted to stages of financial development and/or phases of credit growth in an explicit or merely implicit way, differentiating industrialized and developing countries (i.e., leaving the local regulator to make the best use of its own discretion)? Can an excessively uniform reform, tightening standards considerably, decided essentially by industrialized countries, given the G10's prominent role in the Basel Committee on Banking Supervision (BCBS), be ill-adapted to developing countries?[3] Is this an important issue for the prevention of future banking crises in the developing world? With non-G7 members of the G20 now incorporated in the Financial Stability Board (which succeeded the Financial Stability

Forum) (see www.financialstabilityboard.org/press/pr_090402b.pdf), it is becoming more urgent to address these questions and to indicate which direction regulatory efforts should prioritize and whether the same policy recommendations can apply to both industrialized and developing (especially middle-income) economies.

Accordingly, the purpose of this chapter is to discuss how to amend the global capital requirement rules embedded in Basel II, and ways to supplement them if necessary, to mitigate the procyclicality effect of regulatory regimes, with a particular emphasis on developing countries. We also examine the role of monetary policy in that context. The remainder of the chapter is organized as follows. The second section reviews the financial characteristics of developing countries, particularly with regard to the credit market. The third section assesses the stage of implementation of existing accords and reasons that have hampered progress toward their adoption. The procyclical nature of bank capital requirements is discussed in fourth section, with a focus on the existing Basel regimes. The fifth section provides a critical review of some existing reform proposals, whereas sixth section presents our own proposal, which suggests complementing capital adequacy requirements under Pillar 2 of Basel II (with centralized risk weights) by an incremental, size-based leverage ratio. In seventh section we also discuss some complementary reforms (including accounting standards and international cooperation) that would help strengthen the role of capital requirements, as well as the role of monetary policy in mitigating financial instability. The last section offers some concluding remarks.

BACKGROUND: FINANCIAL FEATURES OF DEVELOPING COUNTRIES AND THEIR REGULATORY ENVIRONMENT

Financial market imperfections are pervasive in developing countries and it is therefore quite surprising to find only limited thinking on how these imperfections are taken into account under the global regulatory environment defined by international institutions (and especially the Bank for International Settlements, BIS). Although there is an extensive literature on these issues per se, in what follows we briefly summarize the main features that we believe are relevant to address the issue at hand; they relate to the central role of banks and the credit market, and weaknesses in the regulatory environment.

The Central Role of Bank Credit

In most developing countries, commercial banks tend to dominate the financial system. Equity issues are limited or inexistent, as firms are often family-owned. Although, privatization and cross-border acquisitions have improved in recent years the degree of banking sophistication in many countries,[4] financial systems in developing countries have lagged behind development in industrial markets – namely, the rapid development of nonbank financial intermediaries, the shift toward the "originate and distribute" model of banking, and the development of opaque, off-balance sheet instruments.

At the same time, however, financial market imperfections remain pervasive in most of these countries. These imperfections cover a broad spectrum:

- underdeveloped capital markets, as aforementioned, which imply limited alternatives (such as corporate bonds and commercial paper) to bank credit, to finance either short-term working capital needs or longer-term investment projects;
- limited competition among banks, which leads to monopolistic or oligopolistic market structure and pricing practices, and segmentation of credit markets;
- more severe asymmetric information problems (compared to industrial countries), which make screening out good credit risks from bad ones difficult, and foster collateralized lending and short-maturity loans;
- a more pervasive role of government, directly or indirectly, in banking (despite recent trends toward privatization), and uncertain public guarantees, particularly with respect to the financial safety net;
- inadequate disclosure and transparency requirements on corporate firms.[5] With poor regulation of corporate governance and weak financial accounting transparency, firms have limited incentives to consider equity issuance as an alternative source of funding – preferring instead either to rely on internal funds or to borrow from banks with which they have established close links;
- weak property rights and an inefficient legal system, which makes contract enforcement difficult and also encourages collateralized lending. In particular, bankruptcy procedures for liquidating the assets of firms in default are weak and inefficient in many developing countries.[6] Bankruptcy law typically provides little creditor protection. This in turn results in weak intermediation, a high cost of capital, high collateralization rates, and low recovery rates for creditors.

Another characteristic of developing countries that may magnify the financial distortions described above is a highly volatile economic environment, due to a high incidence (compared to industrial countries) of domestic and external shocks.[7] Such shocks, which include large foreign capital inflows, followed by abrupt withdrawals or "sudden stops," may fuel unsustainable lending booms, as for instance in East Asia in the early 1990s or, in a different stage of economic development, in Eastern Europe and Central Asia in the 2000s. In turn, increased exposure to adverse shocks magnifies the possibility of default and the risk of bankruptcy by borrowers and lenders alike – which, again, tends to foster collateralized lending.

A first implication of the credit market imperfections described earlier is that a large majority of small and medium-size firms (often operating mostly in the informal sector) are simply squeezed out of the credit market, whereas those who do have access to it – well-established firms, with "traditional" connections with specific banks – face an elastic supply of loans and borrow at terms that depend on their ability to pledge collateral. Even with "connected" lending, actual collateral ratios may be quite high; as illustrated in Fig. 1, which shows average collateral values in percent of loans in the manufacturing sector for a group of developing countries, these ratios are well above 100 percent for many of them – reflecting perhaps a weak judiciary environment and high recovery costs, as noted earlier. Equally important, credit rationing (which results fundamentally from the

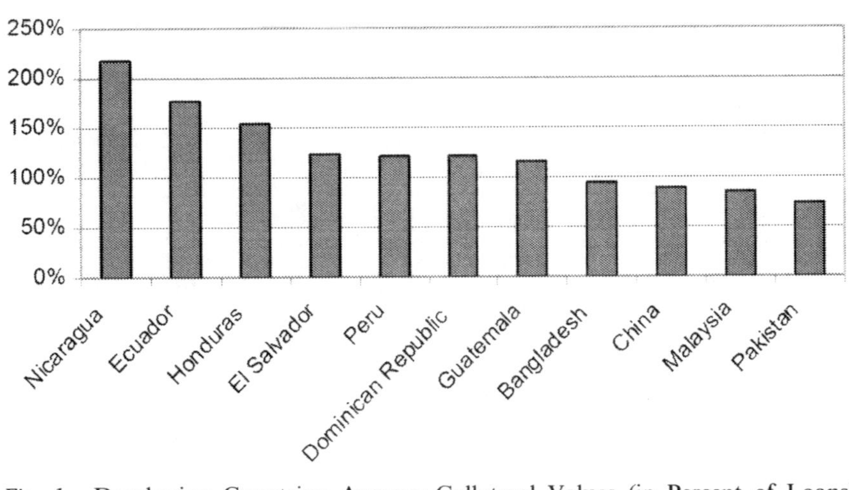

Fig. 1. Developing Countries: Average Collateral Values (in Percent of Loans) Manufacturing Sector only. *Source:* World Bank.

fact that inadequate collateral would have led to prohibitive rates) is largely exogenous. A second implication is the importance of the cost channel (short-term loans to finance working capital needs), which becomes a key part of the monetary transmission mechanism.[8]

The Regulatory Environment

Another important feature of the financial system in developing countries is that it is often subject to weak supervision and a limited ability to enforce prudential regulations. In some cases, inadequate supervision and porous regulations is the legacy of heavy public sector involvement in the banking system (which weakens enforcement incentives) and an inadequate pay structure (which makes it difficult to lure well-qualified individuals away from more lucrative private activities). Fig. 2 indicates that the overall compliance index with the so-called Basel Core Principles for Effective Bank Supervision (which include 10 recommendations on prudential regulations

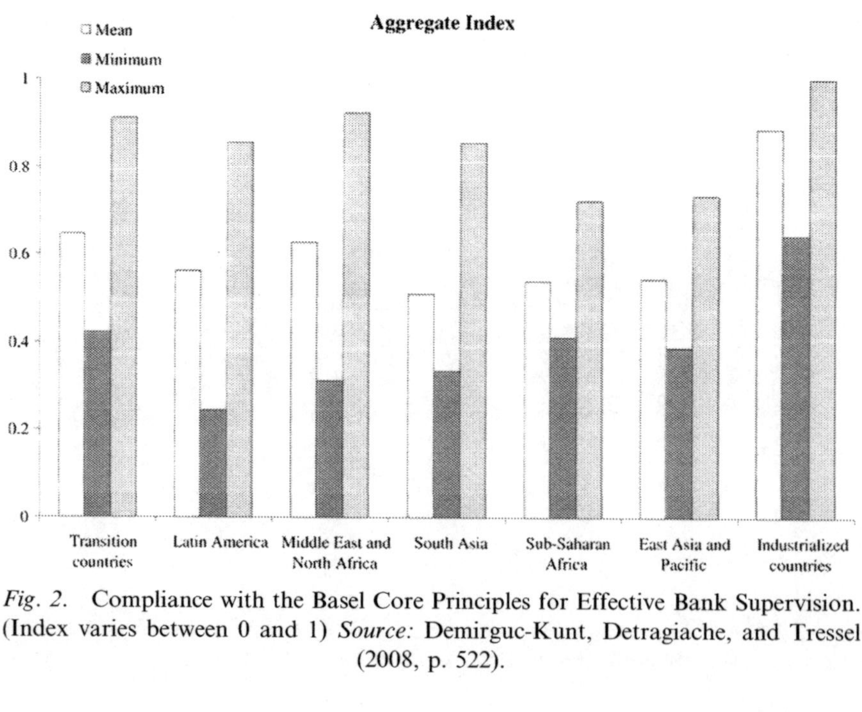

Fig. 2. Compliance with the Basel Core Principles for Effective Bank Supervision. (Index varies between 0 and 1) *Source:* Demirguc-Kunt, Detragiache, and Tressel (2008, p. 522).

and requirements) tend to be much lower for developing countries – especially those of Latin America.

In turn, as documented in various studies, a weak regulatory environment may lead to regulatory capture and create perverse incentives for banks to engage in risky activities.[9] The impact of capital regulation on bank risk may depend also on each bank's ownership structure – possibly in complex, ambiguous ways.[10] This ambiguity may help to explain why, as documented in some studies, capital requirements appear to be associated with a lower share of nonperforming loans (often a manifestation of excessive risk-taking behavior), but do not appear to be robustly related to banking sector stability.[11]

The thrust of the foregoing discussion is thus that, when thinking about financial regulation in a developing-country context, there are two key features to keep in mind. First, banks play a dominant role in the financial system; because developing countries' credit market is often highly distorted – this may affect the effectiveness (both at the micro and macro levels) of a regulatory capital regime. Second, developing countries have limited ability to enforce financial regulation, and this should have important implications for the design, and effectiveness, of bank capital standards.

IMPLEMENTATION OF BASEL ACCORDS IN DEVELOPING COUNTRIES

The 1988 Basel I Accord and the 2004 Basel II Accord represent, respectively, the past and current international agreements on bank capital standards that should be used to guard against financial and operational risks faced by banks. As we shall see, although the accords correspond to an evolving perception of risk and how (some) developing countries interact with it, they were originally conceived essentially by and for the regulators and the banks of the developed and industrialized countries. After reviewing the basic principles of these accords, their implementation in developing countries is discussed.

Principles of the Basel Accords

The 1988 Basel I Capital Accord (see www.bis.org/publ/bcbsc111.htm) was the first international agreement on the implementation of a credit risk measurement framework that required the establishment of uniform bank capital standards. The approach followed was to divide bank assets into broad risk categories (e.g., cash, claims on central governments, claims on OECD banks, on non-OECD banks, etc.), each with a specific weight (from 0 up to 100 percent), and to establish an 8 percent minimum capital requirement to be held against all on-balance-sheet assets weighted accordingly, by end of 1992. Since 1988, the Basel Capital Accord has been progressively introduced not only in BCBS countries but also in virtually all other countries with internationally active banks.

In addition to capital standards, over the past few years, the BCBS or the Committee has moved more aggressively to promote sound supervisory standards worldwide. In close collaboration with many jurisdictions which are not members of the Committee (see endnote 3 above), in 1997 it developed a set of "Core Principles for Effective Banking Supervision," which provides a comprehensive blueprint for an effective supervisory system. To facilitate implementation and assessment, the Committee in October 1999 developed the "Core Principles Methodology." The Core Principles and the Methodology were revised recently and released in October 2006.

However, as bank risk management became more sophisticated and as the possibilities for transforming asset risk grew, the potential distortions created by these simple rules and the opportunities for arbitraging across them expanded. Critics were quick to point out that banks willing to expand their business had incentives to exploit differences in origin of claims (OECD or non-OECD) to securitize assets for which capital requirements bind to reduce their weight and move assets when requirements would bind off their balance sheets. In this way, banks would transform the risk on their balance sheets to ensure compliance with minimum capital requirements. In June 1999, the BCBS issued a proposal for a revised Capital Adequacy Framework, in response to these perceived weaknesses of the Basel I Accord and the increased sophistication of banking practices and risk-management techniques and following extensive interaction with banks, industry groups and both BCBS and non-BSCBS supervisory authorities, a revised framework (a New Basel Accord) was issued on June 2004, as a basis for national rule-making and for banks to complete their preparations for the new framework's implementation.

The 2004 Basel II Capital Accord aimed to introduce a more risk-sensitive approach to setting capital requirements and to reduce regulatory arbitrage (see www.bis.org/publ/bcbs107.htm and Box 2 for details). Just as in Basel I, the total capital ratio must be no lower than 8 percent and is calculated using the definition of regulatory capital and risk-weighted assets.

Box 2. The Three Pillars of the Basel II Accord

The Basel II Accord (see www.bis.org/publ/bcbs128.htm) uses a "three pillar" framework: (1) minimum capital requirements; (2) supervisory review; and (3) market discipline.

Pillar 1 enforces the maintenance of minimum regulatory capital calculated for three major components of risk that a bank faces: credit risk, operational risk and market risk. As in Basel I, the minimum regulatory capital or the capital adequacy ratio (CAR) = 8 percent of risk-weighted assets. Total risk-weighted assets equal the capital requirements for market risk and operational risk multiplied by 12.5 (the maximum leverage ratio or the reciprocal of the CAR of 8 percent) and adding the resulting figures to the sum of risk-weighted assets for credit risk.

The risk weights for assessing the credit risk component can be calculated in three different ways, of varying degree of sophistication:

- Standardized approach relies on external ratings from External Credit Rating Agencies, by category of assets (adding for some types of assets a new 150 percent weight for borrowers with poor credit ratings, higher than the Basel I maximum risk weight).
- Foundation Internal Rating-Based (F-IRB) approach. The F-IRB allows banks to use their models to estimate the probability of default (PD) of assets but subject to approval by their local regulators. Then banks are required to use regulator's prescribed LGD (Loss Given Default) and other parameters (EAD, Exposure at Default), etc., required for calculating their Risk Weighted Assets which will determine (fixed percentage) their total required capital.
- Advanced IRB (A-IRB). Under the A-IRB, banks are allowed to use all their own parameters, subject to an ex post validation by their local regulator.

For operational risk, there are three different approaches – a basic indicator approach or BIA, a standardized approach, and an advanced measurement approach or AMA. For market risk the preferred approach is VaR (value at risk).

Pillar 2 refers to the regulatory response of the first pillar, giving regulators more tools vis-à-vis those available under Basel I, including raising capital requirements discretionarily to reflect their own perception of systemic risk. It also provides a framework for dealing with all the other risks a bank may face (pension risk, concentration risk, strategic risk, reputation risk, liquidity risk, and legal risk), which the Accord combines under the title of residual risk. It gives regulators the power to review banks' risk management systems.

Pillar 3 increases the disclosures that banks are required to make. This is designed to allow markets to have a better picture of the overall risk position of each bank and therefore create incentives for the counterparties of the bank to price and deal appropriately.

The Committee allows banks to choose between two basic approaches to calculate minimum capital requirements (Pillar 1) for credit risk:

- the Standardized Approach, which uses external credit rating agencies together with a reference table – which includes a greater array of risk classes than in Basel I – that maps those ratings directly into capital requirements (an approach that is very similar to that of Basel I but cannot avoid the issue of the role of local rating agencies and the comparability of their ratings with that of large, global rating agencies) and
- the Internal Ratings-Based (IRB) approach, in which the banks themselves estimate their customers' default probability – without relying on external rating agencies – and then use a particular formula specified in Basel II to determine capital requirements as a function of the estimated default probability and other parameters.

The Standardized Approach (where risk weights are those of external ratings) is simpler and less costly to implement than the IRB approaches. In addition, because there is a fixed weight for each type of risk exposure, it does not provide the same potential for dramatic fluctuations in capital requirements. If the objective is to establish a risk-sensitive approach to setting bank capital, it has been argued that only the IRB approach provides an adequate incentive for strengthening risk measurement systems at our largest banks by making their capital requirements vary with risk.

Under a more risk-sensitive approach an important question is also the homogeneity and comparability of the risk-weighting methodologies being used for the "first pillar" of Basel II and, if an IRB approach were to be used by local banks (advanced or foundation), the technical capacity to adequately implement it. In any event, the regulatory authorities have to define and sanction any risk evaluation method used by their banks and the BCBS set up an Accord Implementation Group (AIG) to promote consistency in the Framework's application and encourage supervisors to exchange information on how they intended to implement Basel II.

Implementation of the Basel Accords

The Basel I Accord was enforced by law in the Group of Ten (G10) countries in 1992.[12] Other countries –among them developing countries – started to implement its main provisions progressively, on a voluntary basis and without a pre-defined time schedule for full implementation. The database of Barth, Caprio, and Levine (2008), constructed using surveys up to June 2008, shows that of 143 countries surveyed, 138 (96.5 percent) reported their compliance with Basel I's 8 percent minimum capital requirement ratio, whereas 108 countries (78.3 percent) reported banks holding capital requirement ratio above the minimum. Fig. 3 shows indeed that bank capital buffers (defined as excess bank capital over required capital) were significant. The ratio of total capital (including buffers) over required capital substantially exceeded unity in most countries in Asia and Latin America, with average ratios of 1.8 and 1.6, respectively.

Because of the complexity of Pillar 1, implementation of the Basel II Accord has followed a more haphazard process – even in developed countries, where extensions were granted for using the standardized approach for some institutions while making IRB approaches compulsory. The Barth et al. (2008) database shows that, by June 2008, only about 20 percent of the 143 reporting countries had initiated risk valuation processes of banks' assets toward the direction of Basel II, that is, taking into account some form of market risk in the calculation of risk weights (18 developed and 10 developing countries). This number is striking because in response to a 2006 questionnaire conducted by the Financial Stability Institute (FSI), 82 nonmember national regulators of 98 respondents indicated that they intended to implement Basel II, in some form or another, by 2015.[13] Among those, were 30 non-BCBS European members, 16 Asian countries, 17 African, 21 from Latin America and the Caribbean, and 8 from the Middle East.

Among the developed countries that took steps toward implementing the Basel II Accord, there were delays and uneven progress before the summer of 2007.[14] Among middle-income countries and countries that are non-BCBS members, situations vary significantly. Asia and Brazil are cases in point. In Thailand, for example, the adoption of Basel II was gradual to benefit from international best practices and reduce the fallouts of the

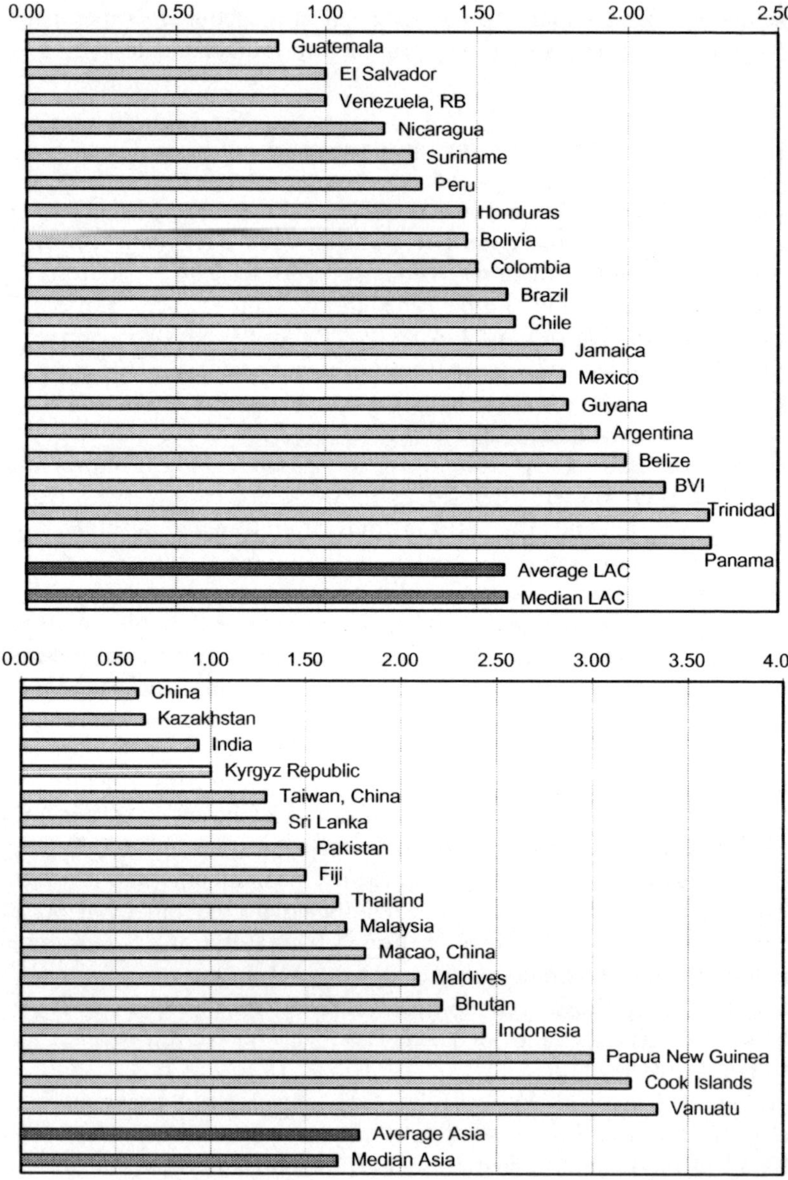

Fig. 3. Bank Capital Buffers, Latin America and Asia. Note Capital buffers are pictured here as total (including excess) bank capital over required capital. *Source:* Barth et al. (2008).

Asian crisis. In China, Basel II will be required for large banks by 2010–2012 but the rest of local banks, including foreign subsidiaries will have extensions. The cautious approach in many non-BCBS countries seems to be motivated essentially by the goal of making *pari pasu* progress in enhancing regulation together with a strengthening of their own monitoring and supervision capabilities.

Korea is introducing since 2006 the standardized approach of Basel II and is concerned by the quality of its own agencies' rating system. In Brazil (Communiqué No. 12.746, December 2004) the central bank combined (Pillar 1) the standardized approach for most banks – but with greater reliance on the central bank's own risk weights and not external ratings – and an Advanced IRB approach for large banks. The standardized approach had a 2005 deadline for compliance and the Advanced IRB approach would be gradually tested and adopted by 2011 (the timeframe was subsequently extended by one year; Communiqué No. 16.137, December 2007). Hence, among many developing countries, there were some commitments, declared intentions to proceed along the process but hardly a widespread and homogeneous dissemination of BCBS standards.

Overall, in middle-income countries, there are two issues: (a) many countries have a different pace and timeframe for implementing financial sector regulatory frameworks vis-à-vis industrialized economies and (b) a reported compliance with Basel rules does not guarantee full comparability of the different accounting measures of capital and risk-weighting methodologies across countries and different classes of assets. Put differently, with idiosyncrasies associated with local ratings, and the use of individual bank-generated ratings and default probability estimations, two countries with the same reported percentage of bank assets at risk under Basel II may have banking systems facing very different degrees of vulnerability.[15]

At the individual country level, there are also two major problems in implementing the risk-weighting mechanisms that form part of the Basel II Accord in developing countries. First, there are few (if any) rating agencies in most of these countries; the standardized approach would therefore have little effect in linking regulatory capital to risk.[16] More importantly, the IRB approach may not be calibrated appropriately for many of these countries, because they face default probabilities that are significantly higher than in advanced industrialized countries. By recalibrating default probabilities, Majnoni and Powell (2005) found that to achieve a 99 percent level of protection (i.e., to ensure that capital covers an unexpected loss to 99 percent of the distribution), capital requirements would need to be significantly higher than the 8 percent level recommended in Basel I and closer to 15 percent of total risk-weighted assets.

Second, the complexity of the IRB approach means that it may stretch scarce supervisory resources in many countries. This has led some observers to argue that, in these countries, there may be little choice but to remain on Basel I for a substantial period of time, or to adopt Basel II only for a subset of (major) banks. Moving too quickly to rules that are too complex may be counterproductive if the ability to enforce them is weak. At the same time, however, the issue of how to supplement Basel I rules to enhance financial stability remains intact. Indeed, as discussed in the later section, both Basel I and Basel II regimes may magnify cyclical effects and potentially exacerbate the impact of financial crises.

CYCLICAL EFFECTS OF BANK CAPITAL REGIMES

As noted earlier, the 1988 Basel I Accord prescribed that banks hold capital of at least 8 percent of their risk-weighted assets. Critics noted early on that it treated, for instance, all corporate credits alike and thereby invited regulatory arbitrage, and that it failed to take account of the distortions induced by capital regulation. It is now well recognized that the Basel I regulatory capital regime US banks were subject to, gave them strong incentives to reduce required capital by shifting loans off their balance sheets. As aforementioned, banks turned to an "originate and distribute" lending model, in which standardized loans, mostly high-risk mortgages – could be bundled and sold as securities, thereby leaving the originating bank free to use its capital elsewhere. As the housing market deteriorated, and uncertainty about the underlying value of subprime mortgage-backed securities mounted, efforts to maintain capital adequacy led to massive deleveraging, capital hoarding, liquidity shortages, and contractions in credit supply, with adverse consequences for the functioning of both real and financial markets.

Since consultations on the Basel II accord started, and since the release of the BCBS main position document in 2004,[17] there has been a broader debate on the procyclicality effect of prudential and regulatory rules. As noted earlier, Basel II allows banks to use their internal models to assess the riskiness of their portfolios and to determine their required capital cushion. Capital requirements are based on asset quality rather than only on asset type, and banks must use "marking to market" to price assets, rather than book value.[18] As the rules make bank capital requirements more sensitive to changes in the banks' risk exposure and as the riskiness of loan books changes over the business cycle, the required regulatory capital varies with the business cycle. For instance, when asset prices start declining, banks may be forced to undertake continuous write-downs (accompanied by increased provisioning), and this raises their need for capital. Capital requirements may therefore increase in a cyclical downturn. If banks are highly leveraged, to maintain their capital ratio during a recession, they must either raise capital (which is difficult and/or costly in bad times) or cut back their lending, which in turn tends to amplify the downturn. Thus, the introduction of risk-sensitive capital charges may not only unduly increase the volatility of regulatory capital; it may also (by limiting banks' ability to lend and/or calling for deleveraging) exacerbate an economic downturn given an inherent procyclicality.

If this is true, it would be ironic: Basel II was conceived and negotiated with the goal of improving risk-sensitivity, thus reduce regulatory arbitrage and financial instability; the claim is now that it ended up increasing macrofinancial procyclicality and actually compounding financial instability. Is that an indisputable result? There are nuances: most existing studies of the procyclicality of risk-sensitive capital regulatory regimes, be they theoretical or empirical, are based mainly on industrialized countries and have been conducted in partial equilibrium (e.g., focusing on banks' lending determinants and the role of capital in the supply of credit) without exploring a more rigorous modeling analytical framework. Other determinants, price and risk factors, behind the demand for credit, inherent to a general equilibrium analysis were not fully captured.

In this section we show how to remedy that and examine the various channels through which capital requirements may exacerbate or mitigate cyclical fluctuations, with particular attention to the role of credit markets, especially in the context of developing countries. We begin with a partial equilibrium analysis, and then consider a variety of general equilibrium effects.

Bank Capital and Procyclicality in Partial Equilibrium Analysis

To illustrate the procyclical effect of regulatory regimes in a developing-country context, it is useful to consider the basic analytical framework developed in Agénor and Pereira da Silva (2009). To fix ideas, consider an economy where exposure to idiosyncratic shocks makes borrowers' ability to repay uncertain, and (as discussed earlier) weak bankruptcy laws and inefficient judicial systems hamper the ability of financial intermediaries to enforce the terms of loan contracts in case of default. As a result, lending is collateralized, and the value of collateral (net of bank borrowing) affects the terms of credit – specifically, the risk premium that banks demand from their customers. Suppose also that collateral is a fraction of realized output, so that the higher real output is, the lower the premium. At the (premium-inclusive) prevailing lending rate, banks provide all the liquidity that firms need; the economy therefore operates in a regime where credit rationing is only exogenous and the supply of credit is perfectly elastic.

Consider two regulatory regimes, both of which characterized by a zero risk weight on "safe" assets: a Basel I-type regime (or Basel I, for short), where the risk weight on risky assets (say, longer-term loans for investment purpose) is fixed, and a Basel II-type regime (or Basel II, for short), where the risk weight is endogenous and inversely related to loan quality, which in turn is inversely related to the risk premium imposed by the bank. Thus, under Basel II, the bank is assumed to use an IRB-type approach, or its own default risk assessment, in calculating the appropriate risk weight – and by implication required regulatory capital.[19]

Suppose then that there is a negative output shock. In a partial equilibrium perspective, if lending to firms is considered riskier under Basel II because the value of collateral (the fraction of output that can be seized in case of default) falls, the bank will be required to hold more capital – or, failing that, to reduce lending (indirectly in the present case, by increasing the risk premium). In turn, the ensuing credit crunch will exacerbate the economic downturn, making capital requirements procyclical. Put differently, by lowering effective collateral and raising the premium on risky loans, capital requirements increase by more under Basel II (than under fixed Basel I weights), because the risk weight associated with these loans goes up as well; thus, if the capital constraint is binding (because banks find it difficult to issue equity during a downturn), bank lending must fall by more under Basel II than under Basel I. This simple framework captures therefore the general concern about Basel II alluded to above.[20]

However, the framework upon which this procyclicality result is drawn is of a partial equilibrium nature. In a general equilibrium setting, there are a number of other (endogenous) factors that will affect the risk premium. The fall in lending that may result from a binding capital constraint, following an increase in risk, tends not only to reduce output but also the collateral required by the bank to lend; the fall in borrowing dampens the initial increase in the premium. In addition, changes in lending and aggregate supply will affect prices, which in turn will affect the equilibrium values of output and the premium as well. These interactions imply that the net effect of shocks, hence the pro- or counter-cyclicality of Basel I and II capital requirements, can be fully assessed only through a general equilibrium analysis, to which we now turn.

Bank Capital Channels in General Equilibrium

As noted earlier, the mechanisms through which regulatory regimes affect any economy depend crucially on its financial market characteristics. This section examines several channels through which these regimes, and capital buffers in particular, may induce procyclical effects through general equilibrium interactions.

Signaling Effect of Capital Buffers in a Volatile Environment

Banks in most developing countries maintain a capital buffer that is substantially higher than required by regulation. One possible explanation is that in a volatile environment, with no (or imperfectly credible) deposit insurance scheme or uncertain public guarantees in general, banks hold more capital for precautionary purposes, because the risk of default on their loans is higher and depositors know it. This is consistent with the data displayed in Fig. 4, which suggest a positive (albeit loose) relationship between capital buffers and output volatility.

An alternative, but related, explanation is that there is a signaling role to capital buffers in a developing-country context: higher buffers may increase incentives for banks to screen and monitor their borrowers (given that they have more at stake); if households internalize this effect in their portfolio allocation decisions, it may induce them to demand a lower (assuming that well-capitalized banks are safer) interest rate on their deposits. Banks are therefore able to fund their lending operations at a lower cost.[21,22] This is consistent with the data displayed in Fig. 5, which suggest a negative (albeit loose) relationship between capital buffers, measured as in Fig. 3, and bank deposit rates.

More direct support is provided by Fonseca, González, and Pereira da Silva (2010), in a study of pricing behavior by more than 2,300 banks in 92 countries over the period 1990–2007. They found that capital buffers are negatively and significantly associated with deposit rate spreads, regardless of the regulatory regime. Moreover, this association appears to be stronger for developing countries (where deposit insurance schemes either do not exist or are not credible), compared to industrial countries.

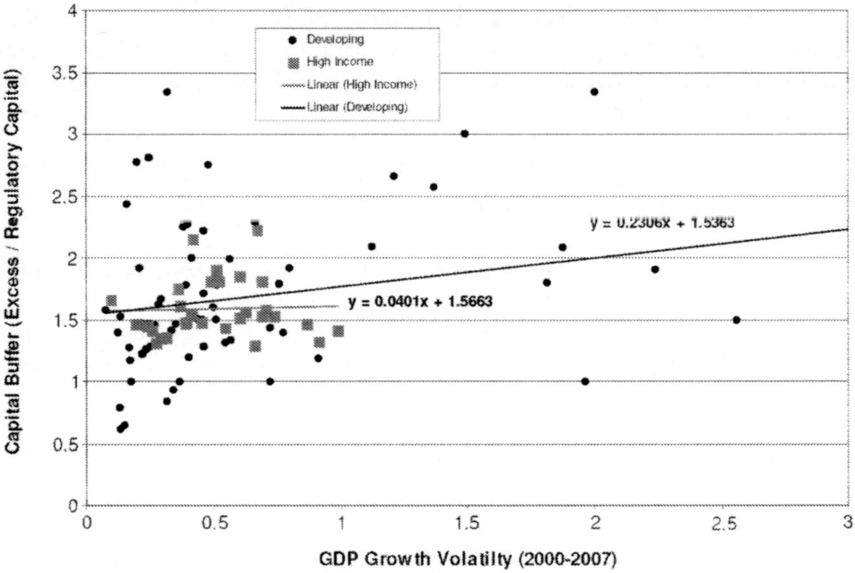

Fig. 4. Capital Buffers and Output Volatility. *Source:* Authors' own calculations.

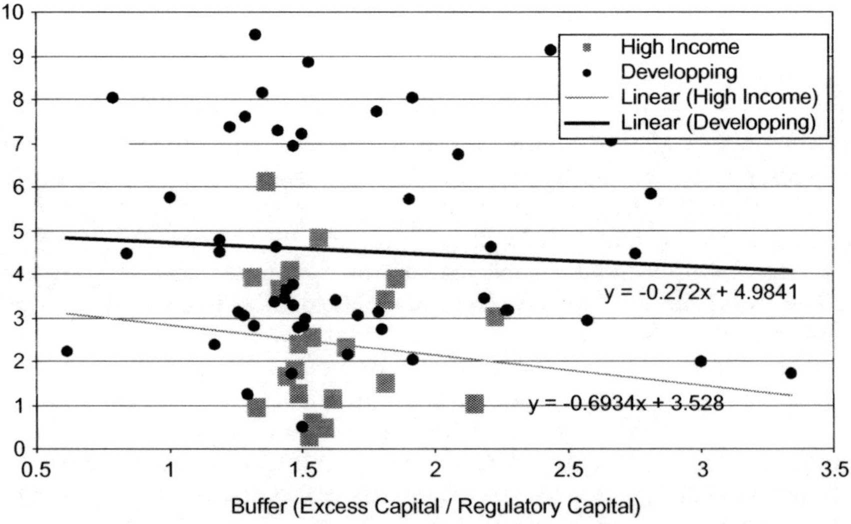

Fig. 5. Capital Buffers and Deposit Rates. *Source:* Authors' own calculations.

A negative link between capital buffers and deposit rates could result from other factors as well. First, it may reduce the regulator's incentives to monitor banks; if this is perceived as a sign of confidence in the health of banks, it may also induce depositors to accept a lower rate of return. Second, well-capitalized banks may face lower expected bankruptcy costs (i.e., lower ex post monitoring costs in case of default) and this may also lead to lower funding costs ex ante from households. Both of these mechanisms are consistent with greater market discipline.[23] Whatever the interpretation, the general point is that in a volatile economic environment, where the risk of adverse shocks is high, signals about a bank's solvency can have a significant effect on depositors' behavior – particularly when government deposit guarantees (in the form of a deposit insurance system) do not exist or are not reliable.[24]

Suppose, then, that banks set deposit rates not only on the basis of the marginal cost of liquidity (the official policy interest rate, if the supply of liquidity by the central bank is perfectly elastic), but also on the basis of their capital position. The extent to which this signaling effect generates general equilibrium interactions depends on how changes in deposit rates affect private income and spending – which in turn depends on the strength of intertemporal substitution effects (the opportunity cost of saving versus consuming).

A formal analysis of these general equilibrium effects are provided in Agénor and Pereira da Silva (2009), in the framework described earlier. Consider a negative output shock in that model; there are two key results.

The first finding is that both bank capital regimes (Basel I and Basel II) magnify the procyclical effect of a negative supply shock (i.e., the increase in the risk premium is magnified). To set a benchmark for comparison, consider first the case where there is no bank capital regulatory regime. A drop in output reduces the value of collateral, so the risk premium goes up. At the same time, it creates excess demand in the goods market. At initial prices, the risk premium must increase to lower investment and restore equilibrium. However, the initial increase in the premium is not sufficient to eliminate excess demand through a drop in investment only; prices must therefore increase, and this lowers consumption through a negative wealth effect. Because the increase in prices also lowers real wages, the initial drop in output (and thus the increase in the premium) is dampened; but in general, the behavior of the premium remains procyclical.

Consider next what happens in the presence of a bank capital regulatory regime, of either type (Basel I and Basel II), under the assumption that capital requirements are not binding (banks hold excess capital) – a more relevant case in practice, given the evidence mentioned in the previous section. The drop in investment alluded to earlier (induced by the initial rise in both the risk premium and the lending rate) lowers capital requirements under both regimes; thus, because actual bank capital does not adjust immediately, the capital buffer increases. Under the model's assumptions, the signaling effect allows a lower deposit rate, which stimulates consumption through an intertemporal effect. There are thus forces (investment and consumption) pulling in opposite directions: given the expansionary consumption effect, at initial prices, reducing demand to the lower level of output requires a bigger drop in investment and thus a larger increase in the premium. Because this effect operates under both Basel I and Basel II, both regimes are procyclical, in the sense that they magnify the procyclicality inherent to the functioning of (imperfect) credit markets.

The second, and somewhat counterintuitive, result is that Basel II may be less procyclical than Basel I. Under Basel II, the initial increase in the risk premium also raises the risk weight; this limits the downward effect on (higher) capital requirements resulting from the fall in investment loans discussed earlier. The increase in the capital buffer is thus less significant, the deposit rate falls by less, and the stimulus to consumption induced by the intertemporal effect is thus mitigated. By implication, the rise in the risk premium required to restore equilibrium to the goods market is of a smaller magnitude. As discussed in more detail in Agénor and Pereira da Silva (2009), if capital requirements are binding (i.e., banks hold just the minimum regulatory level of capital), it cannot be determined a priori whether Basel II is more procyclical than Basel I; but the same counter-intuitive result is also possible.

The thrust of this general equilibrium analysis therefore is that, regardless of whether bank capital requirements are binding or not, regulatory regimes have important real effects; outcomes of supply or demand shocks will depend on the overall macro-effects (through changes in risk premia, prices, aggregate demand, and supply adjustments), which in turn are conditioned by the structural features of the economy (such as the degree of imperfections in the credit market and the strength of intertemporal substitution) and not simply the regulatory regime. In particular, once general equilibrium interactions are taken into account, it cannot be determined a priori whether a particular regulatory regime (say, Basel II) is always more procyclical than another regime.

"Monb Itoring Incentive" Effect and Risk Premia

An alternative channel through which the general equilibrium effects associated with change in regulatory regimes may affect their procyclicality is through the risk premium that banks charge their customers. If bank capital induces banks to screen and monitor borrowers more carefully, the risk premium that they charge will be lower – assuming of course that screening and monitoring costs are not prohibitive.[25] This monitoring incentive effect is consistent with the evidence for the United States reported in Hubbard, Kuttner, and Palia (2002), which suggests that (controlling for information costs, loan contract terms, and borrower risk) the capital position of individual US banks affects negatively the interest rate at which their clients borrow. Coleman, Esho, and Sharpe (2002), also found that capital-constrained banks charge higher spreads on their loans. Unfortunately, there is no direct empirical evidence of this sort (yet) for developing countries; however, it is worth noting that this effect is consistent with the evidence in Barth, Caprio, and Levine (2004), based on cross-country regressions for 107 industrial and developing countries, which suggests that all else equal, capital requirements are associated with a lower share of nonperforming loans in total assets (which could reflect better screening and monitoring of loan applicants).[26] It is also consistent with the results of Pasiouras, Tanna, and Zopounidis (2009), based on data for 615 publicly listed commercial banks operating in 74 countries, which indicate that stricter capital requirements tend to lower management costs. Direct support for this effect is also provided by Fonseca et al. (2010), in the study referred to earlier; they found that capital buffers (irrespective of the regulatory regime) are negatively and significantly associated with lending rate spreads, with a stronger effect in developing countries.

Through this channel, bank capital may also play a significant cyclical role. The higher bank capital (in proportion of risky loans) is, the lower the lending rate, and the greater the expansionary effect on activity. At the same time, during a recession, if capital requirements increase and banks are unable to increase actual capital, the cost of borrowing will go up, thereby exacerbating the downturn. In this situation, the partial equilibrium view described earlier calls for the accumulated bank capital to be used precisely to mitigate the downturn. However, in a general equilibrium setting, there are other factors affecting the premium – including the cyclical position of the economy itself. In many developing countries, there seems to be a significant correlation between cyclical output and bank interest rate spreads (an implicit measure of the risk premium). This relationship, which

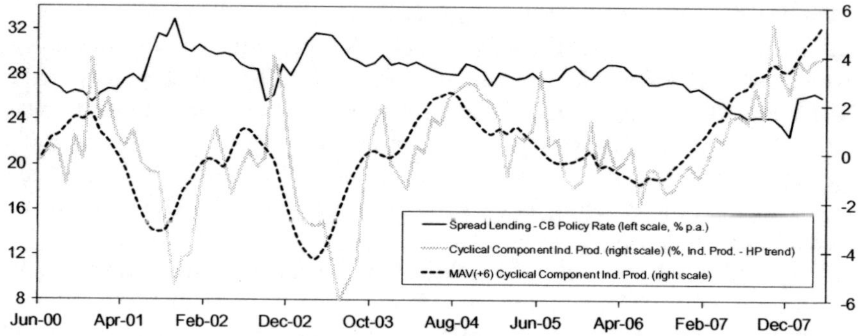

Fig. 6. Brazil: Interest Rate Spread and Output Gap, 2000–2008. *Source:* Authors' own calculations.

is illustrated in Fig. 6 for Brazil, may capture the fact that, during downturns for instance, default rates tend to rise because of an economy-wide adverse effect on cash flows, or expectations about the capacity to repay loans turn highly pessimistic.

Suppose then that the repayment probability on bank loans – which affects directly the premium – depends positively on three variables: the bank capital–loan ratio (because holding more capital induces banks to screen and monitor borrowers more carefully), the cyclical position of the economy (which affects cash flows and profitability); and the effective collateral–loan ratio (which mitigates moral hazard).[27] The numerical simulations performed by Agénor, Alper, and Pereira da Silva (2009a) show that, contrary to intuition, a Basel II-type regime may be *less* procyclical than a Basel I-type regime, once general equilibrium effects are accounted for.[28]

Following, say, a negative shock to output, a fall in the demand for production-related loans tends to raise initially the effective collateral–loan ratio, which tends to increase the repayment probability of loans and thus to lower the premium and then the lending rate. By contrast, this negative shock produces a fall in cyclical output which tends to lower the repayment probability and thus to increase the premium and the lending rate. Both of these (conflicting) effects operate in the same manner under either regulatory regime.

If the cyclical output effect dominates the collateral–loan effect on the repayment probability, and if the fall in that probability is sufficiently large, then, the Basel I-type regime mitigates the procyclicality inherent in the behavior of the repayment probability: with only fixed, risk-insensitive capital requirements – the cost of issuing bank equity falls as required capital falls; this in turn lowers the lending rate. In addition, while the bank capital–loan ratio does not change under a Basel I-type regime (given that risk-weights are fixed), it may either increase or fall under a Basel II-type regime, because the risk-weight is now directly related to the repayment probability.

If again the cyclical output effect dominates the collateral–loan effect, so that the repayment probability falls, then, the Basel II-type regime will lead to a higher risk weight and hence larger capital requirements – which will in turn tend to mitigate the initial drop in the repayment probability. If this (alternative) "bank capital channel" is sufficiently strong, the Basel II-type regime may be less procyclical than the Basel I-type regime, depending in particular on the sensitivity of the repayment probability to the bank capital–loan ratio.[29]

It is worth noting that although both of the transmission mechanisms of bank capital onto the business cycle described earlier imply that a switch to a more risk-sensitive regime may make the financial system *less*, rather than *more*, procyclical (contrary to the current conventional wisdom), their policy implications are substantially different. In the first case, which is in our view mostly relevant for developing countries, if indeed capital buffers play a signaling role because of uncertain public guarantees, a switch to a Basel II-type regime should be accompanied by measures aimed at increasing confidence in the deposit insurance system. Indeed, if high uncertainty associated with public guarantees tends to induce suboptimal behavior by depositors and foster instability (as discussed previously), then the key problem is to instill greater confidence in the financial safety net – while at the same time taking appropriate measures to avoid exacerbating moral hazard problems in bank behavior (see for instance Pennacchi, 2005). Capital buffers would then play their role without any destabilizing, expansionary effect on consumption.

In the second case, which in our view applies equally well to developed and developing countries, the policy implications are quite different. If the switch to a Basel II-type regime induces less procyclicality, then there is no need for complementary policies. If, on the contrary, the regime switch makes the financial system more procyclical (as in the conventional view), then there may be a need to implement additional measures simultaneously – in the form of either a supplementary regulatory tool, or a monetary policy rule that responds more aggressively to indicators associated with financial instability, as discussed in the next section. Which outcome dominates depends very much on country-specific elasticities relating risk premia and interest rates to their underlying determinants. The key implication, nevertheless, is that the greater procyclicality of Basel II cannot be established unambiguously once general equilibrium effects are accounted for; thus, global requirements on bank capital buffers are either not desirable or should be tailored to groups of countries, depending on their respective financial market structure.

Other Channels and Their Relevance for Developing Countries

There are several other transmission mechanisms that could explain how bank capital could influence the propagation of economic shocks to lending and thus induce more procyclicality. Most of them are based on the assumption that banks cannot easily issue new equity, especially in a downturn.[30] In addition, this literature makes clear that there could be important differences in the transmission effects of adverse supply shocks if there is heterogeneity in the capital position of individual banks. However, because these issues are not directly related to our main point, a full discussion is omitted. Indeed, either one of the two channels described earlier is sufficient to make our main claim: in a "typical" developing country context, once general equilibrium effects are accounted for, there is no clear presumption that a more risk-sensitive regulatory regime is always more procyclical. This has important implications for the design and implementation of international reforms to bank capital standards, as discussed in the next section. Although at this stage the compelling empirical evidence to back the channels that we have identified is partial (with some of it pertaining to developed countries), at the very least what this suggests is that caution should be exercised in (a) considering some of the reforms (especially the mandatory higher minimum capital requirements and higher capital buffers) that have been proposed to mitigate the procyclicality of regulatory regimes and (b) imposing these reforms across the board for both developed and developing countries.

Empirical Evidence and Implications

There are many empirical studies on the cyclical effects of capital requirements covering industrial countries, but only a limited literature on developing countries. In the latter countries, empirical work has only recently begun. The analysis of cyclicality is being almost always derived from simple co-movements of bank capital vis-à-vis loans and/or output in partial equilibrium. The empirical work usually uses cross-sectional or panel approaches, using both macro- and microdata (bank databases, either at a global or country level), across time periods that mixes the implementation periods for Basel I (after 1988 till 2004) and/or Basel II (after 2004) as well as booms and busts.

Some of the recent literature is summarized in Box 3.[31] The main conclusion that may be derived from this review is that overall it appears that this empirical work does not provide a clear cut answer to the issue of pro- or contra-cyclicality of capital buffers under Basel I and/or Basel II. A first strand of the literature, regarding the determinants and role of buffers, provides ambiguous results on the significance of the cycle and risk. Many results do not confirm that Basel II rules are procyclical and the significance and the signs of coefficients depend on the method considered and the type of data being used. However, although focusing only on developed countries, a second strand of the literature does bring some empirical confirmation of the role of a bank capital channel. It suggests that higher levels of bank capital (and thus, capital buffers) tend to allow banks to lower-lending rates, controlling for risk and information costs of monitoring firms' quality.

PROPOSALS FOR REFORMING INTERNATIONAL BANK CAPITAL STANDARDS: AN ASSESSMENT

As noted in the introduction, the global financial crisis has led to a reassessment of the policies and rules that have contributed to the buildup of financial fragilities. In the United States, in addition to a number of other macro- and microproblems (e.g., multiplicity of regulatory and supervisory agencies, "shadow" banking system, etc.), it has been argued that the capital rules in place at the inception of the financial crisis did not require banks to hold enough capital in light of the risks they really faced. But some banks that failed during this crisis were considered well-capitalized just before their failure. Capital rules did not require banks to hold sufficient capital against implicit exposures to off-balance sheet vehicles (structured investment vehicles, asset-backed commercial paper programs, etc.) and did not provide sufficient coverage for the risks of trading assets and certain structured credit products (US Treasury (2009)). In addition, many of the capital instruments that comprised the capital base of banks and bank holding companies (BHCs) did not have the loss-absorption capacity expected of them.

The state of profound distress of the US (and global) banking sector in the first quarters of the crisis (end of 2008 and early 2009) seemed initially to indicate that the huge liquidity rescue facilities would be accompanied by

Box 3. Determinants of Capital Buffers: Some Recent Empirical Evidence

The determinants of capital buffers (the difference or the ratio of observed capital and minimum regulatory capital requirements) are mainly empirically studied for banks in developed countries in the context of the Basel Accords in a vast literature. There is limited work specifically on developing countries banks' buffers. The existing literature covers many issues. First, the contribution of buffers to pro- or contra-cyclicality in bank lending is analyzed purely through the significance *and sign of* the relationship between capital buffers and cycle-dependent variables (e.g., loans and/or output), controlling for other effects including risk and lending rates. Related to this first issue is assessing whether Basel I rules are more or less pro- or contra-cyclical than Basel II. Second, the role of buffers in the transmission of monetary policy is analyzed, given a monetary policy stance, looking at whether banks do modify (and how) their deposit and/or lending rates in the presence of buffers.

Hence, a first strand in this empirical literature looks precisely at banks' holding of buffers, comparing the opportunity cost of remunerating this additional capital vis-à-vis penalties and reputational costs of banks' inability to pursue lending due to binding minimum capital requirements. As stated in the text, the rationale for holding a buffer above minimum legal requirements depends on banks' lending strategy: a "precautionary" behavior to prevent excessive deleveraging in downturns given legally binding minimum requirements, an insurance against falling below the required minimum capital ratios during a negative shock, etc. all that could entail using buffers in downturns (and accumulating them in upswings) to smooth lending. However, the empirical evidence is mixed, supporting both a negative and positive relationship between capital buffers and cyclical variables (output and loans). It is also interesting to note that the same empirical ambiguity is found for the relationship between buffers and risk (measured ex post in this literature by nonperforming loans).

In parallel, other empirical tests look at the specific dates of changes in deposits and loans of emerging markets' banks due to changes in capital regulations positing that the "enforcement" of new or tougher capital requirements (increasing capital requirements) reduces the supply of credit. The tests derive from differentiating balance sheet identities and separate situations where (a) banks are capital constrained or not and (b) changes in capital requirements are driven by new regulation and/or crisis. The results indicate that for less-well capitalized or capital constrained banks, tougher capital requirements trims down the supply of credit especially during crisis. Both deposit and loans changes are strongly significant and positively correlated with the observed changes in capital requirements. Hence, a negative shock to capital (a crisis or a regulatory change) causes a reduction in deposits and in leverage, the consequence being a reduction in loans.

A second and different strand in the literature looks at banks' holding of buffers, in relation to the pricing of both their deposit and lending rates. The issue in this literature is to examine a bank capital channel of monetary transmission. On the banks' side, the rationale for being openly well-capitalized (that is, above minimum requirements) could be either to attract deposits at lower remuneration rates and/or to enable pricing loans at lower rates (as aforementioned in the text).

Although there is an extensive examination of the role of deposit insurance on deposit rates, essentially in developed countries, there is some evidence of a (negative) relationship between buffers and deposit rates coming from cross-country examination of data including developing and developed countries. In addition, there is empirical work using microdata on firms, loans, and banks (in developed countries) that examines the role of banks' financial health (measured by their level of capital) in setting loan rates. The relationship seems to confirm that, controlling for firms' risk and information costs, less well-capitalized banks tend to charge a higher premium on loans or that stronger banks charge lower lending rates.

significant regulatory reforms, some of them announced by the G20 meetings, even if only in general terms.

Many official reports and academic proposals were published by the end of 2008 and early 2009 calling for a strengthening of prudential regulation, a more accurate evaluation of risk, and a tightening of accounting standards.[32] There was a widespread consensus that – irrespective of divergent weights that economists might put on the macro- and microfactors behind the financial crisis – it was imperative for a reformed regulatory framework to reduce the perceived perverse macroprudential procyclicality that markets and the general public witnessed in the critical months of the unfolding of the crisis and that brought the global economy on the brink of a Great Depression type of event.

At the time of this writing (December 2009), the enthusiasm for regulatory reform, expressed earlier in many G20 Communiqués and in FSB workshops, is fading with the lesser leverage power over major financial institutions. But with a global recovery still uncertain (and plagued with possible new unpredictable events, e.g., Dubai World investment fund, further bankruptcies of banks in Eastern Europe, weaker partners in the Eurozone, etc.), the issues examined above are likely to haunt us for quite some time. An issue that has received particular attention is the extent to which capital standards must be adjusted to mitigate the alleged procyclical effects of Basel II.[33] In this section we examine, again from the perspective of their applicability in developing countries, the following proposals: higher minimum regulatory capital requirements and improved methods for calculating risk weights; countercyclical provisions and capital buffers; and insurance schemes. The next section dwells on this discussion to put forward our own proposal for reforming capital standards.

Minimum Capital Requirements and Risk Weights

The reform that addresses the issue of the excessive leverage in the financial system, insufficient coverage of off-balance sheet activities and/or of loss-absorption capacity is an increase in regulatory minimum capital requirement:

First, among the proposals for reforming the Basel II framework are those of the BCBS, published in January 16, 2009. There are two main suggestions:

- Strengthen Pillar 1 by focusing on the risk measurement of the framework for collateralized debt obligations comprised of asset-backed securities. Those seems to be more highly correlated with systematic risk than are traditional securitizations and therefore, call for a higher capital charge.
- Provide additional Pillar 2 guidance to address the flaws in risk management practices revealed by the crisis.

Second, in addition and following its March 10–11, 2009 meeting, the BCBS announced that the level of capital in the banking system needs to be strengthened to raise its resilience to future episodes of economic and financial stress. The envisaged measures include introducing standards to promote the accumulation of capital buffers (which we discuss later), and improving the risk coverage of the capital framework and introducing a nonrisk-based supplementary measure. The BCBS is also planning to issue guidelines to harmonize the definition of capital by the end of 2009, to review the regulatory minimum level of capital in 2010, and to develop (higher) recommendations on minimum capital levels by next year.

Regarding risk weights, there is broad recognition of the need to revise models and to ensure that risk weights and parameters in the capital framework are calculated "through-the-cycle" (that is, using the length of a complete business cycle to determine asset values and risks and not only a point in time calculation nor a specific period that could be an upswing) and that tail risks (that is, extreme events) are accounted for.[34] Specifically, the BCBS is planning to refine the risk weights applicable to the trading book and securitized products, while improving the definition of capital by the end of 2009.

Moreover, the Group of Central Bank Governors and Heads of Supervision, the oversight body of the BCBS, met on September 6, 2009 to review a comprehensive set of measures to strengthen the regulation, supervision and risk management of the banking sector with measures aiming at substantially reducing the probability and severity of economic and financial crises. They reached agreement on the following key measures to strengthen the regulation of the banking sector (some of which are examined below):

- "Raise the quality, consistency and transparency of the Tier 1 capital base. The predominant form of Tier 1 capital must be common shares and retained earnings.
- Introduce a leverage ratio as a supplementary measure to the Basel II risk-based framework with a view to migrating to a Pillar 1 treatment based on appropriate review and calibration. To ensure comparability, the details of the leverage ratio will be harmonized internationally, fully adjusting for differences in accounting.
- Introduce a minimum global standard for funding liquidity that includes a stressed liquidity coverage ratio requirement, underpinned by a longer-term structural liquidity ratio.
- Introduce a framework for countercyclical capital buffers above the minimum requirement. The framework will include capital conservation measures such as constraints on capital distributions. The Basel Committee will review an appropriate set of indicators, such as earnings and credit-based variables, as a way to condition the buildup and release of capital buffers. In addition, the Committee will promote more forward-looking provisions based on expected losses."

The BCBS issued concrete proposals on some of these measures in December 2009 (see BCBS, 2009a) and will carry out an impact assessment in 2010, with calibration of the new requirements to be completed by the end of 2010.

In sum, the proposals aforementioned go in a direction of a more capital-intensive Basel II regulatory framework with better estimated (higher) risk-weights. Before or concomitantly to the BCBS, all the reports cited (see endnote 33 above) called for higher minimum regulatory capital requirements (i.e. increasing the minimum CAR from 8 percent of all risk-weighted assets to a bigger number). The only apparent difference resided in the speed of this change, some (e.g., De Larosière, 2009) being prudent in recommending that the CARs should only be increased gradually to allow banks to absorb the cost of the new regulation. Indeed, the BCBS confirmed the need for a stronger capital base when it issued on October 16, 2009 the results of its recent trading book quantitative impact study, about the revisions to the 1996 rules governing trading book capital. The study concludes that the changes should increase average trading book capital requirements by two to three times their current levels, with significant dispersion around this average.

Finally, these proposals are mostly referring to a developed-country context. How should they be analyzed in a developing-country context? As noted earlier, a weak supervisory capacity has been one of the key factors that hampered progress toward the early adoption of the Basel II rules in these countries. Even under the standardized approach of Pillar 1, for instance, the evidence shows that there is a limited capability to adequately weigh risks (in local banks) and to evaluate risk models (by regulators). It is therefore difficult to see how a strengthening of these rules, which are likely to put additional pressure on limited human resources, could be an adequate response. In addition, making capital requirements too onerous may end up pushing lending activities to unregulated parts of the financial system. This dis-intermediation effect may have adverse effects on growth in the longer run.[35]

In our view, before adopting even more complex rules, there must be a consolidation of the existing efforts to implement Pillar 1 and complement capital requirements by another instrument, as discussed in the next section.

Countercyclical Provisions

The reform that addresses the issue of the procyclical behavior of bank lending is that of creating countercyclical provisions: there have been two mechanisms proposed to implement counter-cyclical bank regulation, either through banks' provisions or through their capital. Essentially, under a dynamic provisioning system, in boom years banks would make provisions against profits which would then remain on the balance sheets as reserves against (unspecified) potential losses. In bad years they draw down on these reserves. This smoothes banks' profits over the cycle and makes their capital positions countercyclical.[36]

Introducing counter-cyclical bank provisions has already been successfully done for some time in Spain and Portugal; and Switzerland recently introduced countercyclical regulations. The Spanish system requires higher general provisions when credit grows more than the historical average (or what we may call the "credit gap"), linking provisioning to the credit and business cycle.[37] These both discourages – albeit without eliminating – excessive lending in booms and strengthens the banks' ability to cope in bad times, when they can draw on the general provisions. An advantage of this method (e.g., working with simple historical averages) is that it does not require precise estimates of the length of the cycle, or predictions when the cycle will turn; it can also be capped, to avoid very large growth of reserves in a long expansion phase. It has been argued that as a result of this system of provisioning, Spanish banks were better placed than their counterparts in other countries to absorb losses related to the recent global financial crisis, without eating their core capital.

The introduction of counter-cyclical provisions in Spain was facilitated by a crucial fact – the design of accounting rules was under the authority of the Bank of Spain. This helped to overcome the issue that accountants do not readily accept the concept of "latent" or expected losses, on which the Spanish system of counter-cyclical provisions is based, but instead prefer to focus on actual losses. Nevertheless, the Bank of Spain was obliged to make some changes to its dynamic provisioning system when the European Union adopted in 2005 standards issued by the International Accounting Standards Board (IASB). These points to a key problem for countries considering the adoption of dynamic provisioning rules: they may not comply with standard "incurred loss" accounting rules. More generally, even though countercyclical capital rules are deemed desirable, dynamic provisioning may not a good way to achieve them. Instead of smoothing profits, it may be better to require banks directly to hold higher capital ratios, as discussed next.

Countercyclical Buffer Requirements

An alternative approach for counter-cyclical bank regulation is through capital. Several official reports have argued in favor of countercyclical capital buffers; in the BIS 79th Annual Report of June 2009, the BCBS for instance explicitly suggests rules to build capital buffers above the regulatory minimum and how they should be designed to absorb losses during downturns.[38]

A similar proposal that has received much attention in this regard is by Goodhart and Persaud (GP, 2008) also present in Brunnermeier, Crockett, Goodhart, Persaud, and Shin (2009). Their proposal is to increase Basle II capital requirements by a ratio linked to recent growth of total banks' assets. In this proposal, each bank would have a basic allowance of asset growth, linked to macroeconomic variables, such as inflation and the long-run economic growth rate, hence, relating credit growth to that of trend real economic growth. The proposal would compute actual growth of bank assets as a weighted average of annual economic growth (with higher weights for recent growth). Essentially, raising bank capital requirements (above and beyond a base level) in a procyclical way will help to "choke off" asset price bubbles. This would imply, for instance, linking the capital adequacy requirement on mortgage lending not only to the rise in mortgage lending but also to the growth rate of house prices.[39]

The GP proposal, in a sense, proposes to apply CARs to growth rates, rather than levels. In doing so it provides a clear and simple rule for introducing counter-cyclicality into regulation of banks. Another useful aspect of this proposal is that it could be fairly easily implemented, in that it builds on Basle II. Finally, it has the advantage that having fairly similar effects, it does not face the accounting difficulties aforementioned regarding dynamic provisioning. At the same time, however, there are a number of technical problems associated with the GP and related proposals. For instance, over what periods should growth rates in asset prices be calculated? Should the focus just be on increase in total bank assets, or should there also be some weighting for excessive growth of bank lending in specific sectors that have grown particularly rapidly (such as real estate during the recent financial crisis)? Crises in both industrial and developing countries have often arisen due to excessive lending during boom times to particular sectors or countries. Finally, such a simple nonrisk-based rule could potentially penalize banks that increase their assets through lending to less risky borrowers than their competitors do (see Bank of England, 2008).

There are also two important additional problems with these proposals for "endogenous regulatory rules." The first is the implicit assumption that capital buffers would operate in a countercyclical fashion. As discussed at length in the previous section, there are good reasons to believe that in a typical developing-country context, general equilibrium effects can make increases in capital requirements (or, more specifically, capital buffers) more, rather than less, procyclical. Indeed, a general equilibrium perspective suggests that the transmission mechanism from buffers to the business cycle is far more complex than suggested by a partial equilibrium view. Even though more empirical work is needed to support the particular bank capital channels that we highlighted earlier, our analysis suggests, at the very least, that one needs to be careful and avoid assuming that the same policy recommendations necessarily apply to both industrialized and developing countries. The second problem with these regulatory rules aimed at fostering *financial* stability is that little is known regarding their impact on *macroeconomic* stability, and the extent to which they need to be *complemented* by a monetary policy rule that "leans against bubbles" to achieve both outcomes. This issue is further discussed in the next section.

Insurance-Based Contingent Buffers

There are two recent proposals for implementing contingent, insurance-type capital buffers. The first, by Kashyap, Rajan, and Stein (2009), proposes a choice between the higher fixed CAR suggested above and the purchase of an insurance policy. Their major concern is to avoid banks freezing costly excess capital to protect themselves against a very unlikely event. This type of insurance would, during a crisis, avoid fire-sale and excessive deleveraging to meet capital requirements. The insurance pays off in the form of additional capital available to banks only when a systemic event occurs (e.g., write-offs of the whole financial system exceed a given threshold). The insurance would work like a "contingent buffer." The idea is advocated especially for large systemic institutions, or Too Big To Fail (TBTF) banks or financial institutions.[40] The underlying assumption is that their size makes them inherently too interconnected with all other banks and almost by definition posing a systemic risk to any financial sector.[41] With all these caveats, the regulator-defined systemic bank would pay a specific premium to say nonbanks selling this insurance (investors, pension funds, SWFs, etc.) to ensure the availability of sufficient capital (buffer) during a downturn.

The second proposal, by Caballero and Kurlat (2009), provides a different market mechanism for the same idea of an insurance policy that substitutes for capital buffers. They propose a Tradable Insurance Credit or TIC framework to be issued by governments (e.g., the central bank). Their departure point is that the main ingredient of this crisis has been "fear" and "panic," that is, irrational behavior by investors triggering a fire sale of assets. The TIC is a simple government/central bank-backed, insurance against extreme financial events that investors fear and is proposed as an ex ante alternative to massive ex post fiscally expensive bailouts by governments and/or central banks. The authorities determine a threshold which triggers the convertibility of the TICs into insurance. The TIC can be thus considered a government-backed, asset-specific, event-determined, credit default swap (CDS). Before the trigger the TICs can be traded but are not convertible. Once a crisis provides a high level of financial stress, TICs can be attached to assets, in order to guarantee a more orderly pricing and to protect assets and liabilities when systemic panic destroys the value of otherwise worthy securities. The government does not need to provide direct capital resources during the crisis, as it would with an asset purchase or capital injection program. TICs are thus capable of stopping a vicious feedback loop between the financial and the real sector that occurs when banks are left to absorb losses due to macroeconomic shocks (similarly to what a capital injection does). The TIC framework also addresses the issue of timely intervention that we know is key during severe financial crises. Because TICs are issued before a crisis, and traded among institutions (without being convertible), it becomes an analog of conventional monetary policy, but directly targeted at offsetting the damaging effect of uncertainty-spikes on balance sheets and credit markets once, with the crisis, it becomes convertible.

The appeal of these proposals should be weighed against the capability of developing an effective market for this type of TICs in most developing countries. In particular, it is difficult to see how developing countries would be able to develop their own new market for this type of insurance, price this adequately, and define properly the triggering thresholds for these instruments.

A PROPOSAL FOR DEVELOPING COUNTRIES

Based on the preceding review for international reform of bank capital standards, we offer in this section our own proposal for developing countries. Our concern is to take into account: (a) the characteristics of credit market imperfections in developing countries; (b) differences between partial and general equilibrium effects of capital buffers; and (c) the implementation capability of most regulatory authorities in developing countries. We "make our case" in two steps: the need for a transitional regime between Basel I and Basel II; and the implementation of an incremental, size-based leverage ratio.

Minimum Capital Requirements and Modified IRB Ratings

Regarding capital requirements, we recommend increases to higher level than the current Basel minimum (8 percent), but at the discretion of local regulators in Pillar 2, to take into account local circumstances, not to penalize the funding cost, and foster fair competition of local banks and stronger international banks. Our preference for a higher capital requirement explicitly in Pillar 2 derives from our analytical work that has established the ambiguity – depending on the elasticity that relates the repayment probability to the capital–loan ratio – of the procyclicality of Basel II vis-à-vis Basel I. Since this elasticity is country-specific, and since general equilibrium effects of higher capital requirements might result in more procyclicality, we recommend that regulators conduct the adequate country-specific research and establish their additional levels of capital, not the global regulator.

Regarding risk weights, given the complexity of Basel II rules, many developing countries may have no choice but to remain for an extended period of time under a Basel I regime. For other countries with better supervisory capacity (mostly middle income), it is desirable to continue strengthening the implementation of Pillar 1 with respect to the development of sound practices and capabilities to assess and weigh risk, starting from standardized approaches (controlled and approved by local regulators) up to IRB approaches.

Regulators in middle-income countries need to define homogeneous standards for risk measurement and test the impact of various methodologies on banks' portfolio. Risk-assessment capabilities in local banking systems need to be evaluated by regulators to identify trade-off between most accurate risk-weighting and local technical capabilities; local banking technical infrastructure needs to be strengthened. Accounting standards and provisioning rules can also be enhanced and worked "through-the-cycle," even if they are not integrated with capital buffers or special reserve accounts.

During the transition to a full IRB approach, we believe that the simplification proposal by Majnoni and Powell (2005) is the most suitable for developing countries. This centralized ratings-based (CRB) approach involves banks rating their clients, but with local regulators determining the rating scale and the way in which the banks' ratings map into default probabilities. The use of a centralized scale would facilitate comparison across banks and ease the monitoring of banks' ratings. Those requirements would also be easier to monitor, since the regulator would determine how banks' ratings would feed into capital requirements. As argued by Majnoni and Powell, the CRB approach could be used to set forward-looking provisioning requirements only. A country could then adopt the Basel II standardized approach, set provisions using the CRB methodology to cover the value at risk minus the standardized approach's capital, and thereby ensure that banks' total reserves (provisions plus capital) covered the entire value at risk up to the desired level of protection.

The CRB approach may still require significant improvements in risk-assessment capabilities in local banks; their technical infrastructure may therefore need to be significantly strengthened. The approach may also impose significant demands on local regulators. We therefore suggest that the CRB approach be used only for the most important banks, whereas smaller or less important banks be maintained under a set of Basel I rules for evaluating risk weights.

Leverage Ratio: General Considerations

In a weak regulatory environment, a simple leverage ratio is an appealing complement to capital requirements to prevent excessive credit growth and mitigate procyclicality. This is not only a relevant issue for developing countries; in the United States, for instance, the Federal Deposit Insurance Corporation (FDIC) maintains an additional risk-independent capital requirement that is proportional to the size of banks' assets, a so-called leverage ratio restriction.[42] The main reason is the rising concern about the ability of supervisors to validate the banks' risk assessments, and hence the fundamental problem of whether Basel II can be implemented effectively. Canada, which has a single regulatory regime for commercial and investment banks, applies a maximum gross leverage ratio (Asset to Capital Multiple, ACM) of 20:1 and Switzerland has introduced one to encourage rapid downsizing of the large trading books of its major universal banks.[43] Several recent reports (BCBS, 2009a; FSA, 2009; Andritzky et al., 2009) have also advocated the systematic adoption of a leverage ratio.[44]

Conceptually, there are solid arguments for imposing a leverage ratio as a complement to capital requirements – despite the common criticism that it is a blunt instrument, and usually attracts strong resistance from banks. In general, regulators can audit banks ex post and determine the success probability of the projects that they finance. But because the supervisor has only limited information about the banks' risk ex ante (i.e., before any uncertainty about banks' investments has been revealed by their performance), he has to rely on banks' risk reports. But because banks know that reporting a high level of risk translates into a higher level of required capital, they have an incentive to understate the "true" degree of risk. In order to induce truthful revelation of banks' risks, it is necessary for the regulator to sanction dishonest banks whenever such banks are detected ex post, that is, after the return on banks' investments has been realized. If the supervisor's ability to detect or to sanction dishonest banks is limited, however, risky banks still have an incentive to understate their risk. In that case, an additional leverage ratio restriction helps to align risky banks' incentives and induce truthful revelation of their risk by reducing the risky banks' gains through understating their risk. There are two reasons for that (Blum, 2008): (a) a leverage ratio puts a ceiling on the potential loss of limited liability. As banks have more of their own money invested, they bear a larger part of the downside risks themselves and (b) supervisors have more options when it comes to imposing sanctions on dishonest banks.

Indeed, given limited liability, the size of the fine that can be imposed on banks is restricted by the level of their capital. Hence, setting a capital floor ensures a minimum level of potential fines for banks. Both effects reduce the expected profits of banks that understate their risk. If a sufficiently high leverage ratio is imposed, it is then in the risky banks' own interest to report their risk truthfully. The better the supervisor's ability to detect and to punish untruthful banks, the lower is the necessary maximum leverage ratio. If the supervisor's ability is very high, a leverage ratio may even become superfluous. At the other extreme, if the supervisor has no ability to detect or to punish banks, the second-best capital regulation reduces to a simple leverage ratio without any additional risk-sensitive requirements. Because the actual situation in many developing countries is somewhere in between, the thrust of this discussion is that it is optimal to supplement risk-sensitive capital requirements with a leverage ratio.

A practical issue in implementing a leverage ratio of the sort envisaged here is whether to express it as assets to Tier 1 capital or assets to Core Tier 1 capital,[45] and how to identify sustainable trends in credit, by smoothing or averaging.

Introduction of an Incremental, Size-Based Ratio

Given these general considerations, the second element of our proposal is the introduction of an incremental, size-based leverage ratio. This scheme would involve imposing a minimum across-the-board leverage ratio on all banks; in addition, beyond a certain size (measured by the proportion of total assets of the banking sector), banks would be subject to an incremental adjustment in the minimum ratio. To maximize the scheme's effectiveness, increments in the leverage ratio should themselves be increasing with bank size. The minimum ratio could be set as a common international standard, but to give maximum flexibility to local regulators, the choice of the number and size of the incremental steps involved in the scheme should be implemented under Pillar 2 of Basel II.[46]

The key advantage of the incremental component of the scheme that we propose is that it would implicitly recognize, ex ante rather than ex post, the "too big to fail" problem in banking. By imposing more stringent regulatory measures on bigger banks, incentives to take excessive risk taking by these institutions would also be curbed. Moreover, to the extent that banks that are too big to fail are also too interconnected to fail (a difficult notion to measure, as noted earlier), it would also reduce systemic risk. This is especially important, given that at the moment there is no consensus on how to measure interconnectedness and how to mitigate its potential implications for financial stability. To some extent, the scheme may also end up penalizing dynamic, yet prudent and well-managed, banks and therefore hamper competition; however, given the oligopolistic nature of banking systems in many developing countries, it is not clear that adverse effects on competition are likely to be large. In fact, given that (too much) competition itself may be a source of banking instability, this is not necessarily an undesirable outcome (Box 4).[49]

A summary of our views and how they compare with the current conventional wisdom and consensus from several reports is provided in Table 1.

COMPLEMENTARY REFORMS TO IMPROVE THE EFFECTIVENESS OF BANK CAPITAL STANDARDS AND THE ROLE OF MONETARY POLICY

Many proposals to reform capital standards (including ours) require some complementary reforms to make them more effective, both within and

Box 4. A Maturity-Based Leverage Ratio?

A relevant question in the present context is whether to introduce a maturity-based leverage ratio, as an alternative or complement to the size-based ratio discussed in the text. As noted earlier, bank credit and working capital loans are essential in many developing countries to maintain activity. Therefore, there could be merit to define the leverage ratio so as to focus more narrowly on loans to the private sector, and to exclude from it short-term loans to firms. Banks in developing countries play a critical role in financing, in the short-term, macroeconomic activity. Such lending therefore is, by definition, procyclical and curtailing it through a leverage ratio could be very costly economically and socially. The key issue then, is how to avoid distortions in credit allocation, and specifically to avoid encouraging banks to lend short term instead of medium to long term – a problem that many developing countries continue to face, in part because of a highly volatile environment and limited enforceability of contracts (as discussed earlier).[47]

To avoid the distortions in credit allocation that a maturity-based (and/or sector based) leverage ratio would entail, it would be necessary to impose a cost to ensure that expected returns on short- and longer-term lending are not affected by the regulatory regime.[48] This could take the form of ex post penalties.

Indeed, regulators could detect ex post the true risk of a portfolio or project as well as ensure that there is no arbitrage regarding the maturity of proposed loans. As stated previously, to be credible authorities must have adequate instruments at their disposable to enforce regulatory rules. In that sense, ex post penalties can increase the incentives for a better assessment of risk by banks as well as preventing the regulatory arbitrage that weakened Basel I. However, given the limitations in the regulatory and supervisory capacity in developing countries, the practical implementation of this type of penalties may be very difficult.

across countries. These reforms include a strengthening of accounting standards, improvements in transparency and market discipline, and improved international cooperation to mitigate regulatory arbitrage. In addition, we discuss the potential role of monetary policy in mitigating financial instability.[50]

Table 1. Capital Standard Reform Proposals.

	Current Conventional Consensus and Wisdom from Various Reports	A Proposal for Developing Countries
Minimum regulatory capital requirement	Increase to higher level than current Basel minimum (8%), mandatory in Pillar 1; raise the quality, consistency and transparency of the Tier 1 capital base. The predominant form of Tier 1 capital must be common shares and retained earnings	Recommend increases to higher level than current Basel minimum (8%), but at discretion of local regulator in Pillar 2; avoid penalizing funding cost, competition of local banks vis-à-vis international banks
Risk-weight methodology	Revise models, "through-the-cycle" valuations, account for extreme "tail" events; Move to advanced approaches quickly to strengthen risk assessments	Improve Basel I regime first; when better supervisory capacity emerges continue strengthening the implementation of Pillar 1 to assess and weight risk, starting from standardized approaches (controlled and approved by local regulators) up to IRB approaches starting with a centralized ratings-based (CRB) approach
Counter-cyclical buffer requirement	Introduce a framework for countercyclical capital buffers above the minimum requirement. The framework will include capital conservation measures such as constraints on capital distributions. Many reports (including the Basel Committee) are reviewing an appropriate set of indicators, such as macro, earnings and credit-based variables, as a way to condition the buildup and release of capital buffers	Avoid using buffers until more work is done on their possible counter-intuitive procyclicality, opposite to the intended policy; (a) introduce measures aimed at increasing confidence in the deposit insurance system; (b) conduct country-based research across a variety of cases to identify ranges and patterns across countries and financial market structures. One eventual conclusion might be that the procyclicality of Basel II can not be established analytically a priori and that uniform, global, BIS-BCBS-based bank capital regulations on buffers are either not be desirable or at least have to be tailored to groups of countries and their respective financial market structures

Leverage ratio	Introduce a leverage ratio as a supplementary measure to the Basel II risk-based framework with a view to migrating to a Pillar 1 treatment based on appropriate review and calibration. To ensure comparability, the details of the leverage ratio will be harmonized internationally, fully adjusting for differences in accounting	
Size-based leverage ratio		Introduction of an incremental, size-based leverage ratio. This scheme would involve imposing a minimum across-the-board leverage ratio on all banks; in addition, beyond a certain size (measured by the proportion of total assets of the banking sector), banks would be subject to an incremental adjustment in the minimum ratio

Strengthening Accounting Standards

There is substantial consensus that accounting standards need to be improved, and that the new standards should be global in nature. In its April 2009 statement addressing procyclicality in the financial system, the Financial Stability Board or FSB (then still the Financial Stability Forum or FSF) determined that earlier recognition of loan losses by financial firms could have reduced the procyclical effect of write-downs in the ongoing financial crisis. It recommended that the accounting standard setters issue a statement that the current incurred loss approach to loan loss provisions allows for more judgment than banks in industrial countries currently exercise.[51] It also recommended that the accounting standard setters give consideration to alternative conceptual approaches to loan loss recognition, such as a fair value model, an expected loss model, and dynamic provisioning (as discussed earlier), to replace eventually the current incurred loss model.

The International Accounting Standards Board (IASB) aims to develop by the end of 2009 a new financial measurement standard that would replace International Accounting Standard (IAS) 39, *Financial Instruments: Recognition and Measurement*, the fair value measurement standard under International Financial Reporting Standards (IFRS), and reduce the complexity of accounting standards. Recommendations were issued in August 2009 (see www.iasb.org/Home.htm).

In addition, the Financial Accounting Standards Board (FASB) and IASB have provided additional guidance on fair value measurement. The standard setters are also evaluating the recommendations provided by the Financial Crisis Advisory Group (FCAG), a high level advisory group that standard setters established in December 2008.

From the perspective of developing countries, the risk is that the new accounting standards, to the extent that they become global, may impose additional constraints not only on domestic banks but also on supervisors.

Improving Transparency and Market Discipline

There has been much emphasis since the onset of the global financial crisis on the need for significant improvements in transparency in financial transactions in general, and bank operations in particular. It has been argued, for instance, that over-the-counter (OTC) derivatives must all be brought on exchanges, whereas off-balance sheets instruments, such as structured investment vehicles, should be brought into balance sheets.[52] The argument is often that even though some of these measures may entail microeconomic costs, they would help considerably in limiting systemic risk.

From the perspective of many developing countries, improved transparency in bank operations is essential. But again, even where the type of sophisticated financial products aforementioned exist, increasing regulatory oversight may be unfeasible due to severe constraints on capacity. To monitor OTC transactions and assess their systemic implications, local regulators may need to evaluate exposure of their financial institutions in a consolidated balance sheet; this, in turn, may require expanding on-site inspection of banks and other financial institutions, improved monitoring of cross-border operations, and so on. At least in the short term, this may put a considerable strain on existing resources. Our view is that in these countries a more realistic approach would be to adopt a gradual agenda, focusing first on improving and enforcing "basic" disclosure requirements. However, some countries might be ready to enforce a central "clearing system" for all OTC derivatives and rely on international cooperation to get a truly consolidated balance sheet of financial institutions operating within their jurisdiction. It is in the interest of all members of the G20 to go in this direction for its members.[53]

To some extent, greater transparency may improve private monitoring and market discipline on banks. This may in turn improve their functioning and consequently their efficiency. However, requirements for increased disclosures can also have a negative impact on efficiency due to direct costs of making additional disclosures, maintaining investor relations departments, additional time and efforts to prepare formal disclosure documents, and the release of sensitive information to competitors.[54]

Regulatory Arbitrage and International Coordination

The rapid propagation of the financial crisis that started in the United States has made abundantly clear that outcomes in developing countries are considerably influenced by outcomes in industrial countries. As noted earlier (Box 1), one of the most direct transmission channels of the crisis was the abrupt fall in cross-border lending by the US and European banks. Thus, it is well recognized that developing countries need to maintain a keen interest in proposed changes to bank regulation in developed countries, as problems in these countries' financial markets can spill over quickly to them – especially during crisis times.

Indeed, some of the least regulated parts of the financial system in developed counties may have some of the strongest procyclical impacts, including on emerging economies. One such example is the role that hedge funds and derivatives play in carry trade; there is increasing empirical evidence that such carry trade has very procyclical effects (on over or undershooting) of exchange rates of both developed and developing economies, with negative effects often on the real economy.

Several initiatives are now under way to put in place ongoing mechanisms for cross-border information sharing and collaboration among international regulators of significant global financial institutions. The EU, for instance, is planning to create a European System of Financial Supervisors, a committee of regulators; regional systems of this sort may also be important for developing regions. At a more global level, at the London Summit of April 2009, the G20 Leaders called for the reconstitution of the FSF, originally created in 1999. The FSF, now called the FSB, expanded its membership to include all G20 members, and the FSB's mandate to promote global financial stability was strengthened. Under its new mandate, the FSB will assess financial system vulnerabilities, promote coordination and information exchange among authorities, advise and monitor best practices to meet regulatory standards, set guidelines for and support the establishment of supervisory colleges, and support cross-border crisis management and contingency planning. It is essential for developing countries to play an active role in this forum, to ensure that (as discussed earlier) new regulatory rules that are discussed take properly into account their specific features.

International cooperation will also entail establishing the basis for financial crisis resolution frameworks with some form of cross-border agreements. In its absence, national authorities are unlikely to move toward accepting more global supervision. There is a need to create loss-sharing arrangements for cross-border losses to create more concrete incentives for regional supervisors to cooperate, otherwise it is likely that insulated behavior will continue. Although, as aforementioned, the EU is moving toward cross-border supervision (see De Larosière, 2008), there are institutional and incentive problems. Pooling supervision is theoretically wise but without an agreement on burden sharing, it is going to be difficult to implement in practice.[55] The incentive, coordination and information structure might also be a problem. There are many banks with foreign subsidiaries. But how would a "college of supervisors" be effective? Without a clear loss-sharing agreement, complete transparency between two national supervisors is unlikely. In addition, sharing fully balance sheet information might be difficult because if transparency is complete, there might be perverse incentives for one national supervisor to preventive ring-fencing – based on its foreign colleague's information – the assets of a foreign bank or a subsidiary. That might even trigger a self-fulfilling financial crisis instead of contributing to prevent systemic risk and an overall coordinated improvement of the financial systems of the two countries.

Finally, to reinforce supervision at an international level, the BCBS has also focused on further elevating the resilience of internationally active banks vis-à-vis global liquidity criteria. This implies as well increasing international harmonization of liquidity risk supervision. The BCBS has recently developed internationally consistent regulatory standards for liquidity risk supervision, responding to recommendations of the G20 (see BCBS, 2009b).

Financial Stability, Macroeconomic Stability, and Monetary Policy

Over the past few years, in developed and developing countries alike, there has been a tendency to view monetary policy's "principal" objective as being price stability, although in practice most developing countries that have adopted an inflation targeting regime have done so in the context of poststabilization macroeconomic frameworks with many other objectives pursued under an agenda for structural reforms. In a number of developing countries, inflation targeting policies have been met with significant success.[56] In achieving positive outcomes, most developing countries benefited also from the period of "Great Moderation" in world inflation. However, since the onset of the financial crisis, an issue that has come under renewed attention is the role that monetary policy might be able to play in mitigating financial instability.[57] Specifically, instead of adding a countercyclical component to macroprudential regulation, should policymakers use monetary policy to achieve financial stability?

To answer this question, the first step is to define financial stability. Surprisingly enough, the definition of financial stability has remained elusive; financial stability is usually perceived as a negative concept, involving the absence of something unwanted. Indeed, two common definitions are "financial stability is the absence of an adverse impact on the real economy from dysfunction in the financial system, or risk thereof," or "financial stability is the absence of financial crises, and a financial crisis is defined as a sequence of events, or the risk thereof, that impairs credit intermediation or capital allocation."[58] From an operational perspective, financial stability may therefore be captured by focusing on the behavior of some macroeconomic variables that are believed to be strongly correlated with (future) crises – such as credit growth, nonperforming loans, or asset prices, all three of which have been shown in some empirical studies to rise significantly before a banking crisis.[59]

Assuming, then, that an operational measure of financial stability is defined, should monetary policy reaction functions (Taylor-type rules) be modified to incorporate financial stability concerns? Pre-dating the crisis, a number of contributions had already discussed the extent to which monetary policy should respond to perceived misalignments in asset prices (such as real estate and equity prices) or credit growth, and whether the central bank's policy loss function (and therefore interest rate response) should account explicitly for an objective of financial stability.[60]

Quantitative studies of these issues must consider several factors. First, although there is little doubt that financial stability affects the effectiveness of monetary policy, the issue is whether the policy instrument typically used to affect prices and output (a short-term interest rate) is also effective in dealing with financial stability issues. More importantly, there may be a *dynamic trade-off* between price stability (which may require higher interest rates, following an adverse supply shock) and financial stability (because the risk of default may increase if interest rates go up, thereby raising the share of nonperforming loans and weakening the banking system).[61] Second, monetary policy's effectiveness is based largely on the central bank's commitment to achieve price stability. If, markets perceive changes in preferences, during periods of financial stress in particular, a shift in expectations may lead to higher long-term interest rates – and help to precipitate the very crisis that the central bank was trying to avoid in the first place.

In sum, there is no strong argument at this stage to argue that monetary policy alone can be effective in "leaning against bubbles" and prevent financial crises. The inherent trade-off between financial stability and price stability is such that an inappropriate policy response may lead to suboptimal outcomes with respect to *both* objectives. Although further research is needed to examine the quantitative importance of these trade-offs, it would appear that monetary policy is not a substitute to a strengthening of the regulatory framework. At the same time, because financial stability matters for the transmission of monetary policy (possibly because of heterogeneity among banks regarding their capital position), increased collaboration between central bankers and regulators is essential. Indeed, a key issue that needs to be addressed is the possible need for the *joint determination* of monetary and regulatory policies (the latter taking the form of cyclical adjustments in capital requirements, either through our maturity-based leverage ratio, or a country-specific, cycle-dependent component of capital requirements), to achieve the twin objectives of macroeconomic stability and financial stability. Agénor, Alper, and Pereira da Silva (2010) have proposed a framework to conduct such analysis. In their model, the capital adequacy ratio is decomposed into a deterministic component (corresponding to the minimum capital requirement under Pillar 1 of Basel II) and a cyclical component (which could be established by the local regulator under Pillar 2), related to changes in credit growth.[62] Macroeconomic stability is defined in terms of the variability of nominal income (thereby implicitly imposing equal weights on output and price stability), whereas financial stability is defined in terms of the variability of real house prices. Preliminary results suggest that if monetary policy cannot respond with sufficient strength to changes in credit growth, it may need to be supplemented by cyclical adjustment in capital adequacy ratios in order to achieve economic stability.

CONCLUDING REMARKS

In this chapter we discussed how to reform capital requirement rules embedded in Basel II, and ways to supplement them if necessary, in order to mitigate the procyclicality effects of regulatory regimes. In contrast to most of the recent contributions to this debate, we focused our analysis squarely on the case of developing countries and developed our arguments with a systematic account of their financial characteristics – particularly with regard to the multiple imperfections of their credit markets – and their weaknesses in regulatory oversight. We reviewed the implementation of the existing Basel accords and the differences in progress between developed and developing countries toward their adoption. We also documented the ambiguous empirical findings regarding the procyclical nature of bank capital requirements under the two Basel regimes, and conducted a critical review – again from the perspective of their relevance for, and implementability in, developing countries of some of the existing reform proposals of Basel rules.

The current consensus that seems to be emerging from the G20 meetings, backed by other technical meetings at the BCBS and the FSB, is in a nutshell to: (1) raise mandatory minimum capital requirements, focusing on "high quality" Tier 1 capital, as opposed to "hybrid" securities; (2) introduce a maximum leverage ratio, as a supplementary measure to the Basel II risk-based framework with a view to migrating to a Pillar 1 treatment, based on appropriate review and calibration. To ensure global comparability, the leverage ratio would be harmonized internationally; and (3) introduce countercyclical capital buffers above the minimum requirement, with capital conservation measures such as constraints on capital distributions and with an appropriate set of indicators, such as earnings and credit-based variables, as a way to condition the buildup and draw down of capital buffers.

Although we concur with the general philosophy of (1) and (2) – albeit with specific views on the details, as summarized in Table 1 – we are cautious about (3) in the context of our general equilibrium analysis of the transmission mechanisms of capital buffers in developing countries. In our view, in the absence of detailed empirical work, a more cautious approach is needed regarding countercyclical buffers; there are some good reasons (some of them specific to developing countries) to believe that, in practice, capital buffers may operate in the opposite direction. In particular, we argued that if there is no deposit insurance, and depositors are unable to assess the relative riskiness of bank balance sheets, capital buffers may play an important signaling role and may affect bank deposit pricing conditions – which in turn may affect macroeconomic equilibrium and lead to counter-intuitive results about the procyclicality of a Basel II-type regime compared to a Basel I-type regime. Thus, the "bank capital channel," the way banks react to output shocks, and the response of the economy, are closely related to the amount of capital held in excess of regulatory requirements.

Based on this analysis, we presented in our own proposal a less ambitious, but perhaps more pragmatic, direction for reforms. Regarding (1), we agree that developing countries need to increase mandatory minimum capital requirements but we suggest that human capacity constraints might force many developing countries to first consolidate the implementation of Basel I, second move progressively toward Basel II by strengthening their assessment of risk, including through adopting a central bank-backed system for risk weighting, along the lines proposed by Majnoni and Powell (2005). Regarding (2), we also suggest complementing capital adequacy requirements by a leverage ratio – but we argue that there is a need for an incremental, size-based ratio. We believe that the scheme that we proposed (which involved a minimum ratio, set as an international standard, and incremental, size-based adjustments in the minimum ratio under Pillar 2 of Basel II) can be implemented without unduly taxing regulatory capacity in developing countries, although a phased introduction could be required in some cases. Finally, like others we also believe in the merits of complementary reforms (including accounting standards and international cooperation) that would help strengthen the role of capital requirements. We are cautious, however, on the proposal to impose identical floors and ceilings on capital requirements under Pillar 1 of Basel II in both developed and developing countries.

We have tried to lay out our proposal from the perspective of a broad range of developing countries. But these countries will have to work step by step to define their own contribution in the G20, the FSB and the BCBS working groups,[63] in the forthcoming negotiations for a new financial sector regulatory framework; first, by constructing a "minimalist common denominator" proposal; second, by identifying the key reforms that are needed in *developed* countries' financial regulations to ensure more collective security; and third, weighing carefully the pros and cons of accepting all the binding new rules being proposed at a global level by the BCBS if it appears that these rules might have different results in developed and developing countries.

As in any other negotiated framework, developing countries will also have to look at their own differences to assess their relative strength in the reform process, as a group but also as individual countries: these differences exist in the quality of their regulatory and supervisory capabilities, even within the smaller group of middle-income economies represented in the G20: some middle-income countries might wish for specific points (e.g., vis-à-vis global "clearing" for OTC derivatives, or burden sharing rules in the resolution of cross-border defaults, etc.); some may be able already to implement an IRB approach while others still need to improve a standardized approach. Finally, developing countries have different exposure to global financial and capital markets and might view differently the need to adopt rapidly new rules that could influence postcrisis cross-border flows. They have, nevertheless, also in common the need to ensure that financial stability prevails in the coming years in order to promote growth and sustainable development.

NOTES

1. See Dooley and Hutchison (2009) and Eichengreen, Mody, Nedeljkovic, and Sarno (2009) for a formal statistical analysis based on a large group of middle-income countries, and Fidrmuc and Korhonen (2009) for a focus on China and India. Bartram and Bodnar (2009) focus on global equity markets, whereas Fratzscher (2009) focuses on global exchange rate movements.
2. After the collapse of Lehman Bros. on September 15, 2008, and with the benefit of hindsight, the causes of the crisis became clearer: excessive leverage related to incentives to bypass required capital regulations by shifting loans off banks' balance

sheets (geographical and regulatory arbitrage); the switch to an "originate and distribute" lending model, in which loans, mostly high-risk mortgages could be bundled and sold as securities, thereby leaving the originating bank free to use its capital elsewhere and increase its leverage; large, complex, too big to fail (TBTF) financial institutions, with global, extensive and opaque set of operations, difficult to disentangle, making any divestiture plan too complex to be worked out expeditiously, and forcing de facto public interventions; risk models that did not take into account "extreme events," the "Black Swan" hypothesis and thus mispriced risk; regulatory gray areas (e.g., some financial products were not regulated), multiplicity of regulators (by function, industry, by state in federations); lax corporate governance in financial sector industry (e.g. subprime lending with no money down, interest payments only or less as the initial payment, with no documentation on borrowers' capacity to pay and initial "teaser" interest rates that would adjust upward even if market rates remained constant); perverse financial sector industry's compensation rules (e.g., "bonus-based," short-term results-based compensation schemes in the financial industry); large and persistent US current account imbalances, which fueled capital inflows and helped to maintain interest rates low – thereby encouraging excessive lending. See Calomiris (2009), Kashyap et al. (2009), Steil (2009), and Warnock and Warnock (2009).

3. The BCBS was created originally by the central bank Governors of the group of ten nations in 1974 and meets regularly four times a year. It has four main working groups. Its membership is composed of senior representatives of bank supervisory authorities and central banks and usually meets at the Bank for International Settlements (BIS) in Basel, where its permanent Secretariat is located. The Committee's members nowadays are from Argentina, Australia, Belgium, Brazil, Canada, China, France, Germany, Hong Kong SAR, India, Indonesia, Italy, Japan, Korea, Luxembourg, Mexico, the Netherlands, Russia, Saudi Arabia, Singapore, South Africa, Spain, Sweden, Switzerland, Turkey, the United Kingdom, and the United States but came originally only from the group of seven industrialized countries (G7) plus Belgium, Switzerland, the Netherlands, and Sweden. Countries are represented by their central bank and also by the authority with formal responsibility for the prudential supervision of banking business where not the central bank. The BCBS formulates broad supervisory standards and guidelines and recommends statements of best practice in banking supervision with the expectation that member authorities and other nations' authorities will take steps to implement them through their own national systems, whether in statutory form or otherwise. It has no founding treaty, and it does not issue binding regulation.

4. In some specific circumstances (e.g., very high inflation in Brazil in the 1990s) banks had to develop sophisticated financial management techniques.

5. See for instance Black, de Carvalho, and Gorga (2010) for Brazil, and Balasubramanian, Black, and Khanna (2009) for India. The "Asian funding model," where bank credit dominates and subsidiaries are financially dependent of the established relationship between their parent offices and their own bank, can be interpreted in a similar way.

6. See Araujo and Funchal (2005) for the case of Latin America and Djankov, Hart, McLiesh, and Shleifer (2008) for a general review of debt insolvency procedures in developing countries.

7. See Agénor and Montiel (2008a, Chapter 2) and the references therein. See also Malik and Temple (2009) for some recent analysis.

8. A direct effect of bank lending rates on firms' marginal production costs is a common feature of developing economies, and there is evidence that it may be important also in industrial countries. See the references in Agénor and Alper (2009) for more details.

9. See Barth et al. (2004) and references therein. Morrison and White (2005) analyze the role of capital requirements in the presence of this type of moral hazard problems when the regulator has a weak screening reputation.

10. As documented by Laeven and Levine (2009), using data for 270 banks from 48 developed and developing countries, owners seek to compensate for the utility loss from capital regulations by increasing bank risk. Stricter capital regulations are associated with greater risk when the bank has a sufficiently powerful owner, but stricter capital regulations have the opposite effect in widely held banks. Ignoring bank governance may therefore lead to erroneous conclusions about the risk-taking effects of banking regulations.

11. See Barth et al. (2004). They also find that capital requirements are not robustly associated with banking sector development or bank performance (as measured by overhead and margin ratios), even after controlling for other supervisory-regulatory policies.

12. The member countries of the original G-10 currently comprise Belgium, Canada, France, Germany, Italy, Japan, Luxemburg, Netherlands, Spain, Sweden, Switzerland, United Kingdom and the United States of America. Japanese banks were granted an extended transition period for implementation of Basel II.

13. The FSI was established in 1999 by the BIS and the BCBS, to improve the coordination between regulators. It was set up in response to the East Asian financial crisis of 1997, as a result of a perceived weakness in coordination between national regulators mostly from developing countries. Hence, its activities are concentrated on non-G10 nations.

14. In developed countries, a key implementation difficulty was the need for negotiations within unions (e.g., the EU) or federations (e.g., the United States), as well as agreeing on a division of labor between sometimes different regulators for the various segments of the financial industry (e.g., the United States). For example, the Capital Requirement Directive (CRD) was only approved in the European Parliament in June 2006. In the United taes, the Notice of Proposed Rulemaking (NPR), after extensive consultations between various agencies was finally approved by the Federal Reserve Board in November 2007. Most of Japan's largest banks adopted the FIRB approach by 2007 and the Advanced IRB approach by 2008 (see (Harada, 2006). The same occurred in the EU while the United States allowed the possibility for smaller banks to use a standardized approach. For a more detailed review, see CEPS Task Force (2008) and US Treasury (2009) for the case of the United States.

15. As discussed later, this creates major problems for cross-country empirical work in this area.

16. See SEC (2008) for a discussion of the role of credit rating agencies in providing inputs to risk models, and how they improperly managed conflicts of interest in the US subprime crisis. Weber and Darbellay (2008) offer a more general criticism of the regulatory use of credit ratings.

17. The BCBS released on June 26, 2004 the *International Convergence of Capital Measurement and Capital Standards: A Revised Framework - Comprehensive Version*, a compilation of the June 2004 Basel II Framework, the elements of the 1988 Accord that were not revised during the Basel II process, the 1996 Amendment to the Capital Accord to Incorporate Market Risks, and the 2005 paper on the Application of Basel II to Trading Activities.

18. In the comprehensive approach, when taking collateral, banks will need to calculate their adjusted exposure to a counterparty for capital adequacy purposes to take account of the effects of that collateral. Using haircuts, banks are required to adjust both the amount of the exposure to the counterparty and the value of any collateral received in support of that counterparty to take account of possible future fluctuations in the value of either, occasioned by market movements." BCBS, *International Convergence of Capital Measurement and Capital Standards: A Revised Framework - Comprehensive Version*, June 2006.

19. In the Agénor–Pereira da Silva framework, the standardized approach in Basel II (see Box 2) can be modeled by making the risk weight a function of the output gap (in a manner similar to Zicchino (2006) for instance), under the assumption that ratings are procyclical.

20. There are other factors, at the microlevel, that determine the procyclical effect of Basel II relative to Basel I; as discussed by Jacques (2008) for instance, these include the degree of competition in lending and deposit markets, and the degree to which banks hold a buffer stock of securities. Relationship lending and costly access to the equity market may also matter (see Repullo & Suarez, 2009). We abstract from these considerations, given that they are not central to our argument.

21. This argument is consistent with the view, discussed by Calomiris and Wilson (2004), that depositors have a low preference for high-risk deposits and may demand a "lemons premium" (or penalty interest rate) as a result of a perceived increase in bank debt risk. To limit this risk (and therefore reduce deposit rates), banks may respond by accumulating capital. Interestingly enough, in the empirical part of their study, Calomiris and Wilson (2004) focus on the behavior of New York City banks during the 1920s and 1930s. They argue that doing so is important because during that time the US deposit insurance system either did not exist or did not have much impact on the risk choices of these banks – therefore allowing them to better assess the link between deposit default risk and bank capital.

22. In the same vein, Allen, Carletti, and Marquez (2009) have argued that market forces lead banks to keep capital buffers, even when capital is relatively costly, as bank capital commits the bank to monitor and, without deposit insurance, allows the bank to raise deposits more cheaply.

23. See Rochet (2008).

24. The relationship between deposit insurance and capital buffers may also be nonlinear. In their cross-country regressions, Angkinand and Wihlborg (2010) found that the relationship between deposit insurance coverage and the capital-total asset ratio is U-shaped; high explicit coverage as well as low explicit coverage induces greater risk-taking through relatively low capital ratios.

25. This channel is discussed in more detail in Agénor et al. (2009a). Standard results suggest that a bank's incentive to monitor does not depend on its capital if it

can completely diversify the risk in its loan portfolio; see Freixas and Rochet (1997). However, the inability to fully diversify risk away is one of the key constraints on banking activity in developing countries.

26. Pasiouras et al. offer an alternative explanation – the possibility that higher capital requirements reduce the likelihood of financial distress and thus lower the need for costly risk management activities.

27. Thus, the model exhibits a "double moral hazard" problem, as in Meh and Moran (2010) for instance. In their model, however, bank capital arises endogenously, whereas in the present setting it results from government regulation.

28. Agénor et al. (2009a) extend the New Keynesian model with credit market imperfections developed in Agénor and Alper (2009) to compare bank regulatory regimes. In their framework, capital markets are not perfect; issuing capital is costly. Thus, the Modigliani–Miller theorem does not apply.

29. Note that in the foregoing discussion we abstracted from any independent effect of bank capitalization on the repayment probability through changes in risk-taking behavior. As is well-known, the theoretical literature on the link between bank capital and risk taking by banks is ambiguous. On the one hand, if capital is viewed as a cushion against contingencies, this relationship can be positive (see for instance Dewatripont & Tirole, 1994). On the other, if capital being more costly compared to other sources of funds leads to a moral hazard problem, high capital ratios can lead to less risk aversion – the so-called "gambling for resurrection" problem (see Rochet, 1992). In the first case, the repayment probability is likely to increase in response to higher bank capital, whereas in the second it is likely to fall – thereby raising the probability of bank failure.

30. See Van den Heuvel (2007) and Meh and Moran (2010). More generally, the "bank capital channel," as commonly defined, relies on three assumptions. First, there is an imperfect market for bank equity: banks cannot easily issue new equity because of the presence of agency costs and tax disadvantages. Second, banks are subject to interest rate risk because their assets typically have a longer maturity than liabilities. Third, banks have to meet regulatory capital requirements linked to credit supply. Our approach dwells only on the last one.

31. Box 3 dwells on Pereira da Silva (2009), who provides a more detailed review of the literature related to financial procyclicality and its various econometric testing.

32. See Financial Services Authority (2009), International Monetary Fund (2009a), Brunnermeier et al. (2009), the EU High Level Group or De Larosière Report (2008), US Treasury (2009), OECD (2009), and several BIS-BCBS Consultative Documents (2009). Some academics have proposed more sophisticated crisis-triggered insurance payment schemes (see below). Dowd (2009) offers a more radical view on the Basel II regime.

33. A different proposal to reduce procyclicality involves strengthening risk-based deposit insurance; see for instance Pennacchi (2005). We will return to this issue later.

34. Some proposals include more complex methods to ensure that the aforementioned multiplier(s) factor(s) for systemic risk are estimated using calculations of the conditional VaR of all bank's counterparties or even the whole system. Conditional Value at Risk is meant to be an extension of Value at Risk (VaR). The VaR model does allow managers to limit the likelihood of incurring losses caused by certain types of risk – but not all risks. The problem with relying solely on the VaR model is

that the scope of risk assessed is limited, since the tail end of the distribution of loss is not typically assessed. See, for instance, Benford and Nier (2007).

35. In the same vein, the Squam Lake Working Group (2009) has argued, in the context of the United States, that capital requirements that are too onerous may lead to a migration of activities from banks to other less regulated financial institutions either at home or offshore, making it harder to identify and control systemic risks to the financial system.

36. There is some controversy as to the performance of Spanish banks under this system.

37. See Lis, Martínez Pagés, and Saurina (2000).

38. See BIS Annual Report 2009 (p. 133), Box VII7.B ("Alternative rules for countercyclical capital buffers – an illustration").

39. Buiter (2008) extended the Goodhart–Persaud proposal by suggesting that capital and liquidity requirements be applied to all highly leveraged financial institutions, not only banks. Jokivuolle, Kiema, and Vesala (2009) offer some analytical support for the argument of state-contingent capital requirements – but they abstract from the type of macroconsiderations that we focus on here. See also Andritzky et al. (2009).

40. There has been a significant amount of discussion about large, Too Big Too Fail (TBTF) financial institutions and their systemic role. Some reports call for an ad hoc additional capital requirement linked to the size of the institution, to account for its "systemic" risk. Others would use the aforementioned insurance buffer for the same purpose. Recently, radical views have emerged; Mervyn King, Governor of the Bank of England, called on October 20, 2009 for "banks to be split into separate utility companies and risky ventures," saying it was "a delusion" to think tougher regulation would prevent future financial crises. The G20 devoted workshops to the issue. It seems that one should be cautious – whatever the obvious issues of political leverage of TBTFs – about creating funding cost distortions in financial markets without necessarily knowing whether this type of penalty does foster financial stability.

41. Systemic risk is often defined as the possibility of large losses to other financial institutions induced by the failure of a particular institution due to its interconnectedness. Measuring the degree of interconnectedness in financial systems has proved difficult (see International Monetary Fund (2009b, 2010)). There are various methods to assess systemic linkages but it does not necessarily translate into a clear and practical measure of systemic risk except that it appears highly correlated with the asset-size of such institutions. See Acharya (2009) for a formal analysis of the implications of systemic risk for capital adequacy requirements.

42. See S. Bair, www.fdic.gov/news/news/speeches/archives/2006/chairman/spoct0606.html and her Statement www.fdic.gov/news/news/speeches/chairman/spjan1410.html to the Financial Crisis Inquiry Commission on January 14, 2010.

43. See Ratnovski and Huang (2009) for a more detailed discussion of the Canadian case. The United States have traditionally applied a gross leverage ratio to the GAAP assets of bank holding companies, but exempted investment banks from its coverage. This was the root cause for the major increase in investment bank leverage that occurred between 2003 and the inception of the financial crisis.

44. The FSA Report (or Turner Review), for instance, advocates a maximum gross leverage ratio should be introduced as a backstop discipline against excessive

growth in absolute balance sheet size. In their view, capital requirements calculated on the basis of internal models will always entail significant judgment, and there are dangers that debates between bank management and regulators might result in pressure for too lenient a treatment. Andritzky et al. (2009) propose a countercyclical leverage ratio (rather than a maximal leverage limit) based on the equity/asset ratio but with enhanced sensitivity to off-balance sheet exposures to constrain excessive growth in upswings.

45. See www.bis.org/publ/bcbsc111.pdf?noframes = 1. The BCBS defines capital, for supervisory purposes, in two tiers in a way which will have the effect of requiring at least 50 percent of a bank's capital base to consist of a core element comprised of equity capital and published reserves from post-tax retained earnings (core tier 1) but may also include nonredeemable noncumulative preferred stock. The other elements of capital (supplementary capital) will be admitted into tier 2 up to an amount equal to that of the core capital. Each of these elements may be included or not included by national authorities at their discretion in the light of their national accounting and supervisory regulations. According to the Financial Times (September 7, 2009), European banks face pressure to issue far more shares to meet a tough new global regulatory framework outlined by finance ministers of the G20 group of nations, which calls for much bigger and better capital buffers against shocks. The request follows criticism that some banks have relied too heavily on complex securities. Some banks have met up to more than half the existing regulatory requirements on capital buffers through the issuance of "hybrid" securities which are more like debt than equity. Accordingly, data from the International Monetary Fund show that the average ratio of equity made up of issued ordinary shares to assets at the end of 2008 was 2.5 percent for European banks against 3.7 percent for US banks.

46. Of course, this should not prevent the BCBS and the FSB from elaborating "general guidelines" that local regulators could use to design country-specific schemes.

47. Another issue is whether the leverage ratio should be extended to nonbank institutions. The reason is that if this type of countercyclical regulation were only implemented for banks, this would – by increasing the cost of their lending operations in booms – create incentives for the growth of intermediation outside the regulated banking system.

48. One of the problems faced by some Asian countries (especially Korea) during the Asian crisis was the effect of financial sector regulations that had created incentives for banks to move from longer-term project lending toward short-term, for capital adequacy reasons, in addition to issues of risks related to exchange rate and cross-border lending.

49. See for instance Degryse and Ongena (2008) for a general review of the evidence on the link between competition and bank stability, and Ariss (2010) for some recent evidence for developing countries. Another possibility is to implement a maturity-based leverage ratio; however, as discussed in Box 4, this is unlikely to be feasible in practice, due to incentives for regulatory arbitrage.

50. The issue of systemic risk associated with too-big-to-fail institutions (TBTF) and the resolution of cross-border banks has been fully identified by both academia and policymakers. For instance, the BCBS in its September 6 communiqué stresses that it "will also assess the need for a capital surcharge to mitigate the risk of

systemic banks." It is still unclear how this would be practically implemented without creating distortions between groups of banks, how one could specifically request a TBTF firm to raise additional capital without triggering legal action, etc. Although the issue is very important, we do not pretend to have the proper analytical tools to treat it satisfactorily yet.

51. "Consistent guidance has been issued by the International Accounting Standards Board (IASB) and the US Financial Accounting Standards Board (FASB) for fair valuation when markets are illiquid, and for the transfer of assets between valuation categories in rare circumstances. The IASB has also proposed revised standards for the consolidation and disclosure of off-balance sheet entities and related exposures. The IASB finalized in March 2009 an amendment to IFRS 7 setting forth enhancements to required risk and valuation disclosures for financial activities, including for complex financial instruments" (see Financial Stability Forum, 2009).

52. See Ackermann (2008) and Institute of International Finance (2009).

53. The ongoing global financial crisis has revealed some paradoxes that need to be taken into account by the various approaches toward regulatory reform. For example bank supervision in some developing countries (e.g., Brazil and China) was most likely stronger than that of many developed countries (e.g., the United States, the United Kingdom, the PIGS in the Euro zone, Eastern Europe, etc.).

54. See Levine (2005) for a discussion of the empirical evidence on this issue.

55. For instance, in the Baltic countries, there is burden sharing, but it happened only ex post, after the crisis. See Acharya, Wachtel, and Walter (2009) for an analytical discussion.

56. See Gonçalves and Salles (2008) and Lin and Ye (2009) for an evaluation of the performance of inflation targeting in developing countries.

57. Ironically, low interest rates under Greenspan's tenure are increasingly blamed for the buildup of the US subprime real estate bubble.

58. See Goodhart (2006).

59. See Demirguc-Kunt et Detragiache (2005) and Agénor and Montiel (2008b, Chapter 16).

60. See Wadhwani (2008) for an overview of this chapter. Cúrdia and Woodford (2009) is one of the few contributions based on the New Keynesian framework.

61. Actually, in developing countries, this inflation-financial stability trade-off may not be too different from the "standard" output-inflation trade-off, if financial stability is defined in terms of moderate credit growth. The reason is that if short-term credit tends to be highly elastic in response to working capital needs (as in the analytical framework discussed in Agénor and Pereira da Silva (2009), for instance), changes in credit growth will be highly correlated with changes in output.

62. Other regulatory rules, as proposed in the literature, would involve linking the cyclical component of capital requirements to an alternative indicator of cyclical pressure, such as the deviation between actual and potential output.

63. Developing countries as a whole are unevenly represented in the various forums (e.g., the FSB and the working groups of the BCBS) where the discussions on regulatory reform are conducted and might not have identical views, given the different stages of development of their own financial systems.

REFERENCES

Acharya, V. V. (2009). A theory of systemic risk and design of prudential bank regulation. *Journal of Financial Stability*, *5*, 224–255.

Acharya, V. V., Wachtel, P., & Walter, I. (2009). International alignment of financial sector regulation. In: V. V. Acharya, M. Richarson, & J. Wiley, (Eds), *Restoring Financial Stability: How to Repair a Failed System*. New York: Wiley.

Ackermann, J. (2008). The subprime crisis and its consequences. *Journal of Financial Stability*, *4*, 329–337.

Agénor, P., & Alper, K. (2009). *Monetary shocks and central bank liquidity with credit market imperfections*. Working Paper No. 120, Centre for Growth and Business Cycle Research.

Agénor, P., Alper, K., & Pereira da Silva, L. (2009). *Capital requirements and business cycles with credit market imperfections*. Working Paper No. 120. Centre for Growth and Business Cycle Research.

Agénor, P., Alper, K., & Pereira da Silva, L. (2010). *Capital regulation, monetary policy, and financial stability*. Unpublished. University of Manchester, Central Bank of Turkey, and World Bank.

Agénor, P., & Montiel, P. J. (2008a). Monetary policy analysis in a small open credit-based economy. *Open Economies Review*, *19*, 423–455.

Agénor, P., & Montiel, P. J. (2008b). *Development macroeconomics* (3rd ed.). Princeton, NJ: Princeton University Press.

Agénor, P., & Pereira, S. L. (2009). *Cyclical effects of bank capital requirements with imperfect credit markets. Policy Research*. Working Paper No. 5067, World Bank. Forthcoming, *Journal of Financial Stability*.

Allen, F., Carletti, E., & Marquez, R. (2009). *Credit market competition and capital*. Working Paper No. ECO 2009/08, European University Institute. Regulation.

Andritzky, J., et al. (2009). *Policies to mitigate procyclicality*. International Monetary Fund. IMF Staff Position Note No. 09/09.

Angkinand, A., & Wihlborg, C. (2010). Deposit insurance coverage, ownership, and banks' risk-taking in emerging markets. *Journal of International Money and Finance*, *29*, 252–274.

Araujo, A., & Funchal, B. (2005). Bankruptcy law in latin America: Past and future. *Economia*, *6*, 149–216.

Ariss, R. T. (2010). On the implications of market power in banking: Evidence from developing countries. *Journal of Banking and Finance*, *34*, 765–775.

Balasubramanian, N., Black, B. S., & Khanna, V. (2009). *Firm-level corporate governance in emerging markets: A case study of India*. Working Paper No. 119, European Corporate Government Institute.

Bank of England. (2008). *Box 6-countercyclical measures*. Financial Stability Report.

Barth, J., Caprio, G., & Levine, R. (2004). Bank regulation and supervision: What works best. *Journal of Financial Intermediation*, *12*, 205–248.

Barth, J., Caprio, G., & Levine, R. (2008). *Bank regulations are changing: For better or worse?* Policy Research Working Paper No. 4646, World Bank.

Bartram, S. M., & Bodnar, G. M. (2009). No place to hide: The global crisis in equity markets in 2008/09. *Journal of International Money and Finance*, *28*, 1246–1292.

BCBS (Basel Committee on Banking Supervision). (2009a). Strengthening the Resilience of the Banking Sector-Consultative Document. Geneva.

BCBS (Basel Committee on Banking Supervision). (2009b). International Framework for Liquidity Risk Measurement, Standards and Monitoring-Consultative Document. Geneva.

Benford, J., & Nier, E. (2007). *Monitoring cyclicality of Basel II capital requirements*. Bank of England. Financial Stability Paper No. 3.

Black, B. S., de Carvalho, A. G., & Gorga, E. (2010). Corporate Governance in Brazil. *Emerging Markets Review*, *11*, 21–38.

Blum, J. M. (2008). Why 'basel II' may need a leverage ratio restriction. *Journal of Banking & Finance*, *32*, 1699–1707.

Brunnermeier, M., Crockett, A., Goodhart, C., Persaud, A. D., & Shin, H. (2009). *The fundamental principles of financial regulation*. Geneva: International Center for Monetary and Banking Studies.

Buiter, W. H. (2008). *Central banks and financial crises*. Financial Markets Group, London School of Economics. Discussion Paper No. 619.

Caballero, R., & Kurlat, P. (2009). *The 'surprising' origin and nature of financial crises: A macroeconomic policy proposal*. Working Paper No. 09-24, MIT Department of Economics.

Calomiris, C. W. (2009). The subprime turmoil: What's old, what's new and what's next. *Journal of Structured Finance*, *15*, 6–52.

Calomiris, C. W., & Wilson, B. (2004). Bank capital and portfolio management: The 1930s 'capital crunch' and the scramble to shed risk. *Journal of Business*, *77*, 421–455.

CEPS Task Force. (2008). *Basel II implementation in the midst of turbulence*. Brussels: Centre for European Policy Studies.

Coleman, A. D. F., Esho, N., & Sharpe, I. G. (2002). *Do bank characteristics influence loan contract terms?* Working Paper No. 2002-2001, Australian Prudential Regulation Authority.

Cúrdia, V., & Woodford, M. (2009). *Credit frictions and optimal monetary policy*. Working Paper No. 278, Bank for International Settlements.

De Larosière, J. (2009). Chair, *The high-level group of financial supervision in the EU*. European Union, Brussels.

Degryse, H., & Ongena, S. (2008). Competition and regulation in the banking sector: A review of the empirical evidence on the sources of Bank Rents. In: A. V. Thakor & A. W. A. Boot (Eds), *Handbook of financial intermediation and banking*. Amsterdam: Elsevier.

Demirguc-Kunt, A., & Detragiache, E. (2005). Cross-Country empirical studies of systemic bank distress: A survey. *National Institute Economic Review*, *192*, 68–83.

Demirguc-Kunt, A., Detragiache, E., & Tressel, T. (2008). Banking on the principles: Compliance with basel core principles and bank soundness. *Journal of Financial Intermediation*, *17*, 511–542.

Dewatripont, M., & Tirole, J. (1994). *The prudential regulation of banks*. Cambridge, MA: MIT Press.

Djankov, S., Hart, O., McLiesh, C., & Shleifer, A. (2008). Debt enforcement around the world. *Journal of Political Economy*, *116*, 1105–1149.

Dooley, M., & Hutchison, M. (2009). Transmission of the U.S. Subprime crisis to emerging markets: Evidence on the decoupling-recoupling hypothesis. *Journal of International Money and Finance*, *28*, 1331–1349.

Dowd, K. (2009). The failure of capital adequacy regulation. In: P. Booth (Ed.), *Verdict on the Crash: Causes and Policy Implications*. London: Institute of Economic Affairs.

Eichengreen, B., Mody, A., Nedeljkovic, M., & Sarno, L. (2009). *How the subprime crisis went global: Evidence from bank credit default swaps*. Working Paper No. 14904, National Bureau of Economic Research.

Fidrmuc, J., & Korhonen, I. (2009). *The impact of the global financial crisis on business cycles in Asian emerging economies*. BOFIT Discussion Paper No. 11.

Financial Services Authority. (2009). The turner review – A regulatory response to the global banking crisis, FSA.

Financial Stability Forum. (2009). Improving financial regulation: Report of the financial stability board to G0 leaders, Basel.

Fonseca, A. R., González, F., & Pereira da Silva, L. (2010). *Cyclical effects of bank capital buffers with imperfect credit markets: International evidence*. Unpublished, University of Oviedo and World Bank.

Fratzscher, M. (2009). What explains global exchange rate movements during the financial crisis? *Journal of International Money and Finance*, *28*, 1390–1407.

Freixas, X., & Rochet, J. (1997). *Microeconomics of banking*. Cambridge, MA: MIT Press.

Gonçalves, C. E. S., & Salles, J. M. (2008). Inflation targeting in emerging economies: What do the data say? *Journal of Development Economics*, *85*, 312–318.

Goodhart, C. E. (2006). A framework for assessing financial stability? *Journal of Banking and Finance*, *30*, 3415–3422.

Goodhart, C. E., & Persaud, A. (2008). A proposal for how to avoid the next crash. *The Financial Times*.

Harada, K. (2006). Macroeconomic implications of the New Basel Accord for Japan. In: H.-W. Kim & H. S. Shin (Eds), *Adapting the New Basel accord: Impact and policy responses of Asia-Pacific Developing Countries*. Seoul, Korea: Korea Development Institute.

Hubbard, R. G., Kuttner, K. N., & Palia, D. N. (2002). Are there Bank effects in borrowers' costs of funds? Evidence from a matched sample of borrowers and banks. *Journal of Business*, *75*, 559–581.

Institute of International Finance. (2009). *Restoring confidence, creating resilience: An industry perspective on the future of international financial regulation and the search for stability*.

International Monetary Fund. (2009). Lessons of the financial crisis for future regulation of financial institutions and markets and for liquidity management. Monetary and Capital Markets Department, International Monetary Fund.

International Monetary Fund. (2009). *Global financial stability report*, April 2009. International Monetary Fund. Washington DC.

International Monetary Fund. (2010). *Global financial stability report*, April 2010. International Monetary Fund. Washington DC.

Jacques, K. T. (2008). Capital shocks, bank asset allocation, and the revised basel accord. *Review of Financial Economics*, *17*, 79–91.

Jokivuolle, E., Kiema, I., & Vesala, T. (2009). *Credit allocation, capital requirements and procyclicality*. Unpublished. Bank of Finland.

Kashyap, A. K., Rajan, R. G., & Stein, J. C. (2009). *Rethinking capital regulation*. Unpublished. University of Chicago.

Laeven, L., & Levine, R. (2009). Bank governance, regulation and risk taking. *Journal of Financial Economics*, *93*, 259–275.

Levine, R. (2005). Law, endowments and property rights. *Journal of Economic Perspectives*, *19*(June), 61–88.

Lin, S., & Ye, H. (2009). Does inflation targeting make a difference in developing countries? *Journal of Development Economics*, *89*, 118–123.

Lis, S. F., de Martínez Pagés, J., & Saurina, J. (2000). *Credit growth, problem loans and credit risk provisioning in Spain*. Working Paper No. 18, Bank of Spain.

Majnoni, G., & Powell, A. P. (2005). Reforming bank capital requirements: Implications of basel II for Latin American countries. *Economia*, *5*, 105–149.

Malik, A., & Temple, J. R. W. (2009). The geography of output volatility. *Journal of Development Economics*, *90*, 163–178.

Meh, C., & Moran, K. (2010). The role of Bank capital in the propagation of shocks. *Journal of Economic Dynamics and Control*, *34*, 555–576.

Morrison, A. D., & White, L. (2005). Crises and capital requirements in banking. *American Economic Review*, *95*, 1548–1572.

OECD. (2009). *The financial crisis: Reform and exit strategies*. Paris: OECD.

Pasiouras, F., Tanna, S., & Zopounidis, C. (2009). The impact of banking regulations on banks' cost and profit efficiency: Cross-country evidence. *International Review of Financial Analysis*, *18*, 294–302.

Pennacchi, G. G. (2005). Risk-based capital standards, deposit insurance, and procyclicality. *Journal of Financial Intermediation*, *14*, 432–465.

Pereira da Silva, L. A. (2009). Cyclical effects of bank capital requirements: A review of methods, evidence, and policy implications. Unpublished. World Bank.

Ratnovski, L., & Huang, R. (2009). *Why are Canadian banks more resilient?* Working Paper No. 09/152, International Monetary Fund.

Repullo, R., & Suarez, J. (2009). *The procyclical effects of bank capital regulation*. Discussion Paper No. 2010-05S, European Banking Center.

Rochet, J. (1992). Capital requirements and the behaviour of commercial banks. *European Economic Review*, *36*, 1137–1170.

Rochet, J. (2008). Procyclicality of financial systems: Is there a need to modify current accounting and regulatory rules? *Financial Stability Review*, *12*, 101–114.

SEC. (2008). *Summary report of issues identified in the commission staff's examinations of select credit rating agencies*. Unpublished. Securities and Exchange Commission July.

Squam Lake Working Group. (2009). *Reforming capital requirements for financial institutions*. Working Paper, Council on Foreign Relations.

Steil, B. (2009). *Lessons of the financial crisis*. Special Report No. 45, Council on Foreign Relations.

U.S. Treasury. (2009). *Financial regulatory reform. A new foundation: Rebuilding financial supervision and regulation*. Washington DC: Department of Treasury.

Van den Heuvel, S. J. (2007). *The bank capital channel of monetary policy*. unpublished. University of Pennsylvania, Pennsylvania, June.

Wadhwani, S. (2008). Should monetary policy respond to asset price bubbles? Revisiting the debate. *National Institute Economic Review*, *206*, 25–34.

Warnock, F. E., & Warnock, V. C. (2009). International capital flows and U.S. Interest rates. *Journal of International Money and Finance*, *28*, 903–919.

Weber, R. H., & Darbellay, A. (2008). The regulatory use of credit ratings in bank capital requirement regulations. *Journal of banking regulation*, *10*, 1–16.

Zicchino, L. (2006). A model of bank capital, lending and the macroeconomy: Basel I versus Basel II. *Manchester School*, *74*, 50–77.

FINANCIAL FRAGILITY AND SECURITISATION: THE DISCUSSIONS WITH AUSTRALIAN REGULATORS AND BANK RISK MANAGERS

Siqiwen Li

ABSTRACT

Among divergent approaches to understand the global financial crisis, Minsky's Financial Instability Hypothesis has gained increased attention. In part, the chapter draws upon Minsky's notion that the seeds of instability are sown when banks, households, and firms move from hedge to speculative and then into Ponzi financial positions. Financial innovations such as securitisation contribute to this transformation. In addition, the paper will discuss the findings arising from an analysis of interviews that focus on securitisation related issues after the sub-prime crisis with practitioners who were closely involved in regulation and risk-management. The paper highlights the need for fundamental reform in the financial sector with a more consistent regulatory platform and enhanced supervision, to facilitate rapid healing from the damage arising from the financial crisis in Australia.

International Banking in the New Era: Post-Crisis Challenges and Opportunities
International Finance Review, Volume 11, 255–269

ISSN: 1569-3767/doi:10.1108/S1569-3767(2010)0000011012

INTRODUCTION

Hyman Minsky's work has enjoyed unprecedented interest, during the recent global financial crisis, which has subsequently been dubbed an exemplary 'Minsky Moment' by some commentators (Magnus, 2007). According to Minsky's Financial Instability Hypothesis (FIH), a slow transformation occurs within financial markets as they move away from robust positions towards those characterised by increasing fragility, until this fragility issues into a systemic and global crisis. During this recent period of crisis, financial institutions changed both their appetite for risk and their risk-taking behaviour as perceived, and actual safety margins began to evaporate.

In the heartland of US capitalism, the unsustainable growth in consumption has spawned a mountain of 'dodgy' IOU's. Once securitised by financial institutions, they have spread to the far corners of the globe. The compromised position of global ratings resulted in a dramatic underpricing of the risk associated with these securitised assets, while the on-sale of insurance risk in the form of credit default swaps has led to an avalanche of highly leveraged speculative investments, most notably those dispensed by the London office of AIG. This process has been assisted by the fact that banks have strayed far from their traditional role as intermediaries between short-term household depositors and long-term corporate borrowers to become brokers between hedge funds, investors, providers of securitised assets as collateral, ratings agencies, and erstwhile borrowers.

It was in this political context that Australian banks began to implement the Basel II reforms to banking practice and prudential control. Australia has suffered less than many other countries is partly a result of the two overly modest stimulus packages introduced by the Rudd government, although it is also due to both the lower level of low-doc loans issued by Australia's big banks, and the magnitude and duration of the global commodity boom.

Grounded in Minsky's FIH, the development of financial fragility can be displayed with a focus on two determinants of the financial system fragility: the degree of liquidity in the financial system and the increasing reliance on external finance with which to support discretionary expenditure.

MINSKY'S FINANCIAL INSTABILITY HYPOTHESIS

Following Keynes, Minsky (1982, 1986) proposed his FIH to illustrate how financial crises can occur as an endogenous outcome of decision making within economic units that rely upon the sale, purchase, or creation of financial assets. He focused on the relationship between the banking system and investors, highlighting the possibility of financial fragility developing during upturns in the business cycle (also see Kindleberger, 1978). His approach postulated a cyclical process, relating continuing economic expansion to a decline in uncertainty, rising optimism, and an increasing preference for externally financed expenditure. He saw that over time, both an increasing reliance on external finance, a loss of diversification, and the increasing deferment of (present value) 'break-even' times, would transform what was a relatively 'sound' financial structure into a more 'fragile' one.

Hedge, Speculative and Ponzi Positions

The FIH sets out two fundamental propositions. The first is that the economy has financing regimes under which it is stable and financing regimes under which it is unstable. The second proposition is that over periods of prolonged prosperity, the economy transits from financial relations that make for a stable system to financial relations that make for an unstable system.

The articulation between these expected cash inflows and the contractual payment commitments are termed 'financial regimes'. Minsky classified financial regime into three financial positions: hedge, speculative and Ponzi, with each financing regime characterised by different relations between cash payment commitments on debt and expected cash inflows due to the quasi-rents earned by capital assets.

Hedge positions are the most financially prudent positions, because they are able to clear outstanding debt, in full, out of the current receipts. Hedge units expect the cash flow from operating assets to be more than sufficient to meet contractual payment commitments now and into the future, with expected cash flows always exceeding both financing costs and operating expenses (including dividend payments to shareholders), by a pre-determined, desired level.

Agents, who adopt speculative positions, expect to experience occasional cash shortfalls in the short run, but in the long run they are presumed to be able to generate cash inflows that more than cover their outgoing cash commitments. A speculative financing unit may experience a period, typically near term, when its cash payment commitment is greater than the expected quasi-rents for these periods. This characteristic differs from a hedge-financial unit, which expects its quasi-rents to exceed its contractual commitments in each and every time period. The speculative unit will continually require re-financing. Accordingly, speculative units have lower margins of safety as they are more exposed to economic shocks.

Ponzi positions are the most fragile in the system. The cash flows from operations are not sufficient to fulfil either the repayment of principal or the interest due on outstanding debts, thus Ponzi agents always increase their outstanding debt to meet their financial commitments, cover their existing debt and generate profit (Darity, 1992, p. 75). During an economic boom, expectations about the expected future returns become increasingly optimistic. Firms undertake riskier investment projects and therefore increase their debts. Banks also participate in this expectation by supplying the loans required to undertake such investments. In fact, banks as profit-seeking institutions are willing to provide loans to more risky customers at a higher price. At this point, most of the firms, as well as banks, move from hedge financial positions to more speculative and Ponzi ones, as they overestimate their expected returns. Since Ponzi units have no margins of safety, any abnormal functioning of the financial system could result in an inability to meet contractual payment commitments so that the debt–equity ratio would have to increase at an accelerating rate.

Consequently, as the admixture of Ponzi and Speculative units increases relative to those that are hedge units, the economy will slowly become unstable. The system is inherently unstable because of the overly optimistic behaviour of financial units. Although units that engage in hedge finance are vulnerable only to what happens in the market for their product, units that engage in speculative and Ponzi finance are also vulnerable to shocks originating in financial markets. This is because of the elimination of the margins of safety that are built-in to the hedge-financing regime.

According to Minsky, the fragility of the financial system depends on the number of factors that can amplify initial disturbances. Hedge-, speculative- and Ponzi-financing units are all vulnerable to events that reduce the cash flows from assets. Not only are speculative and Ponzi units vulnerable to shocks that are originated in financial markets such as an unanticipated rise in interest rates etc. (as they must continually refinance their positions), they are also vulnerable to financial market disruptions such as market stress or market breaks.

Liquidity and Reliance of Debt as Other Determinants of Financial System Fragility

Apart from the relative weight of financial regimes, there are two other determinants of the fragility of the financial system: the degree of liquidity in the system and the reliance on debt and other forms of external finance to support investment and other forms of discretionary expenditure.

The analysis of the endogenous process of increasing fragility usually begins during the aftermath of a recession. Even if they managed to avoid bankruptcy, many units would face significant difficulty in meeting their contractual commitments, thus being obliged to make the judgement that their margins of safety were too low. Accordingly, the units would endeavour to restore these margins to adequately reflect the current economic climate. Such a period is usually referred to as one of 'balance sheet restructuring'.

In taking some time to restore receipts to pre-recession levels, the stabilising effect of any economic recovery heightens confidence about the sustainability of current levels of receipts. Cash flow is further enhanced by the return of consumer and investor confidence, boosting gross national expenditure. Firms may begin to see retained profits rising, increasing the equity of the units. More firms will become hedge-financing units as the quasi-rents earned come to exceed outgoing cash payment commitments.

If the above sequence is an accurate depiction of the financial structure of a majority of existing units, the recovery phase has brought about liability structures conducive to a stable economic system. The economy is heavily weighted towards hedge-financing arrangements that feature sufficient margins of safety. However, the imprint of the recession on the collective psyche of borrowers and lenders has a dampening effect on their willingness to undertake profitable investment projects, especially if they have long gestation periods. If the economy does not dip back into recession, the recovery gives way to a period of economic tranquillity. If the business cycle consists of nine stages (Mitchell, 1951, p. 14): trough; early, mid and late expansion; peak; early, mid and late contraction; trough, then a period of economic tranquillity encompasses the stages: early, mid and the early part of the late expansion.

During this period of economic tranquillity, the cash flow, capital value and balance sheet characteristics of borrowers and lenders continue to improve. As this period of economic tranquillity lengthens, investing units observe that realised quasi-rents on capital assets begin to exceed expectations. In hindsight, it appears that margins of safety incorporated into liability structures were too pessimistic. Effective demand for the goods and services of business exceed ex ante aggregate supply. For a time, firms may be able to accommodate the excess through higher capacity utilisation rates. However, in the continuing presence of a revival in effective demand, units will have to increase the level of their investment expenditures.

As the period of tranquillity continues, the expectation of future cash flows, formed by extrapolations of current economic conditions, require increasing levels of investment expenditure for expected demand to be fulfilled. Internal finance is no longer sufficient; external finance must be tapped. In the case of debt financing, the units must emit new liabilities. In order for units to emit liabilities, there must be willing lenders. The FIH asserts that bankers live in the same climate of expectation as the managers of capital assets. The extent to which layering, or leveraging of retained earnings, that is, debt-financing, takes place in the financing of investment depends not only on the expectation of investing firms, but also on the willingness of bankers to go along with, if not to urge such layering.

Thus, not only are borrowers willing to assume liability structures that are less cautious, but so are lenders. Once a change in expectations occurs, borrowers, with liability structures that previously, from the point of view of the lender, would have carried the possibility of bringing them credit risk, now become quite acceptable. Financial intermediaries (particularly banks) also accept more risk in their own liability structures, which, in a more pessimistic expectation climate, they would have rejected. Therefore, as the period of economic tranquillity continues, investing units discover that their current liability structure is compatible with a previous state of confidence, which incorporated an unused margin of 'borrowing power'. Units are able to increase their debt levels as views about an 'appropriate' liability structure have changed (Minsky, 1977).

What has been sketched out is a loop of positive feedback. The negative feedback of the recession period resulted in a reappraisal of borrowers and lenders positions in assets and liabilities. The revival of profits due to economic recovery operating through increased private sector confidence encourages more optimistic expectations about the future, manifesting in increased investment expenditure. The realisation of cash flows that equal or exceed expenditures transforms expectations about future cash flows, again resulting in a reappraisal of position. In the presence of economic tranquillity, this loop of positive feedback reinforces itself creating an investment boom, that is, new investment leads to increases in income that stimulate further investment and further income increases (Minsky, 1986).

As the dynamic described earlier becomes more advanced, expectations about the future begin to incorporate views consistent with the prospect that the existing tranquil economic conditions will continue indefinitely. Success breeds a disregard for the possibility of failure. Rather than an extended period of economic tranquillity being regarded as an aberration, it becomes the norm. Thus, expectation of a normal business cycle is replaced by the expectation of steady economic growth – a 'new era' has arrived. The 'economics of euphoria' is a phrase that has been coined to describe an economy infected with such a change of state (Kindleberger, 1978). In other words, the reluctance to hold illiquid assets in a portfolio declines as a direct result of 'euphoria'; this is particularly the case for financial institutions. The shift to euphoria increases the willingness of financial institutions to acquire assets by engaging in liquidity-decreasing portfolio transformations. Thus, the increased incidence of positive feedback trading and the emergence of 'bubbles' in the asset market are consequences of 'euphoria'.

Another feature of the euphoric economy is that the short-term financing of long positions becomes a way of life for many organisations such as the favour of securitisation. If the term structure of interest rates corresponds to a normal yield curve, the carrying costs of debt can be made less burdensome, by converting long-term debt into short-term debt. With the economy characterised by expensive long-lived capital assets, such a financing method seems irrational. In the realm of normal economic conditions, where the memory of past instability impinges on current behaviour, such a deduction would be correct (Kindleberger, 1978). However, the operation of euphoric economic conditions means that the distant memories of instability results in the short-term financing of long-lived capital assets being perceived as rational. Borrowers and lenders discount the likelihood that difficulty will be encountered in the rolling over of maturing short-term debt. The future promises perpetual expansion and the smooth functioning of factor, product and financial markets. This is one route whereby an economy experiencing a period of prolonged prosperity endogenously progresses from one characterised by robust financial structures to one dominated by fragile financial structures. The pyramiding of liquidity together with the increased use of debt leads to increasing leverage in the financial structure (Minsky, 1982). The three determinants of systemic fragility are in operation, and the economy is exposed to shocks. Thus, the successful normal functioning of the economy has endogenously generated a fragile financial structure.

Financial institutions and banks, in particular, play an important role in the transformation from a robust to a fragile financial structure, especially one in which banks increasingly act as brokers instead of intermediaries. The following discussions, which focus on the issue of securitisation, arise from an analysis of interviews undertaken after the sub-prime crisis, foreshadow such a transformation and reflect the consequent evolution of instability in the financial market. In general, the responses of interviewees reflect a reasonable level of awareness about the 'deceptive' nature of asset securitisation processes, the dubious quality of external ratings and the potentially problematic nature of credit enhancement through such means as 'buy-back' guarantees. The interview material also indicates awareness of the transformation that has occurred to financial systems in Australia due to the adoption of emerging innovations.

FINANCIAL INNOVATIONS FUEL FINANCIAL MARKET BOOM AND TRIGGER REGULATORY ARBITRAGE

The past few decades have seen a considerable concentration of financial power due to the long-term regulatory transition from more heavily regulated banking towards more 'market-based' regulation. Under the new policy regime, regulators have eased controls over markets to let banks pursue higher profit returns associated with riskier activities (Wray, 1994; Black, 2005). During the profit-chasing process, there is increasing use of financial instruments whose value derives from underlying collateral assets, and these financial instruments have, it has been argued, contributed to conditions that have made the recent crisis possible.

Among 'off-balance-sheet' types of financial innovations, securitisation has played a vital role in fuelling the prosperity of financial market, through dispersal of risk and by enhancing the liquidity of underlying assets. As Minsky (1987) argued, securitisation has been important for the globalisation of finance, as it allows assets to escape from being embedded in national markets. Securitisation is also a response to efforts to reduce the cost structure of banks. In this role securitised assets operate as a form of collateral reducing capital requirements. Bank participation in securitisation is part of the drive to supplement fund income with fee income. Simultaneously it has spread bank risk more broadly to whoever presumes to handle it.

In serving the purpose of 'optimising' the management of capital, securitisation directly delivers 'tangible' benefit to banks – in the form of lower regulatory capital-holdings – principally by enabling them to arbitrage and, thus, evade regulatory capital burdens (regulatory arbitrage arises when a regulated institution takes advantage of the difference between its real or economic risk and the risk calculated in regard to regulatory requirements). The following comments from bank risk managers confirm these functions of securitisation under both the previous and the current Basel International Capital Adequacy regulatory framework:

> It happened all the time. That's what securitisation was, so it was pure regulatory arbitrage. (Interview No. 13)

> Previously the arbitrage opportunities arose through the banks taking their assets off their balance sheet. As an example of these, there are ones that were securitised so we didn't have to hold capital for them. (Interview No. 12)

For some aggressive market practitioners, the reduction of regulatory capital holdings through securitisation during the upturn period was of obvious benefit for capital management:

> You know, you securitise loans so that, obviously, you don't pay as much in capital by passing the risk off to someone else. (Interview No. 7)

As noted by one of the risk managers, securitisation satisfies the banks' objectives of 'moving' risks off their balance sheets through risk dispersion, but also exposes investors to new forms of risks when they lack sufficient understanding and knowledge about the resulting complex financial instruments:

> I mean securitisation serves a purpose. If a bank wants to move its risk, and there are people out there who want to take the risk for a price, there'll be a market for it. (Interview No. 15)

For a business like banking, which, no less than other firms, is driven by 'animal spirits', securitisation serves a multiplicity of 'desirable' functions as shown by the following response:

> If they find it *easy to sell the loan*, they *get better spreads* and *easier approval*, so that's the impetus for banks to want to do that. (Interview No. 7)

Owing to various positive feedbacks, and arcane forms of complexity, the securitisation market, while stimulating the growth of other markets, such as commercial paper and property, has helped to cover up the underlying fragility of the system until conditions for the subsequent crisis were firmly entrenched.

Thus, securitisation is actually a double-edged sword, when used effectively during an upturn; it can assist investors to enhance the liquidity of underlying assets. However, the problematic nature of the securitisation process, especially its complexity, along with the increased reliance on external ratings agencies, has put banks and other players in great danger, not least through the prospect of rapidly eroding balance sheets.

'DECEPTIVE' NATURE OF SECURITISATION

In many cases, the complexity of underlying financial instruments and their derivatives made the whole securitisation process hard to understand for both top management within banks and their regulators. Furthermore, specialised risk experts in banks created and priced these new financial instruments using highly complex models, in part, kept secret to prevent competitors from copying the innovations in banking practice. As one interviewee observed – 'It gets more complicated, due to the sophistication of the models and so on' (Interview No. 6).

As revealed by the following comment, the increasing complexity of securitisation arises not only from the adopted techniques of risk-management but also from associated securitisation clauses:

> Some of the clauses under securitisation are not clear ... especially under a stressed environment ... it is an issue, because it is deceptive. (Interview No. 14)

The existence of a disconnection between banks acting as brokers, those offering securitised assets, the actual originators of the assets that are going to be securitised, and those providing hedging and insurance services in relation to the assets, result in a vulnerable and fragile market environment. Final buyers of securities could be 'trapped' by the underlying risks that have been either concealed by complicated quantitative risk techniques or hidden by unclear clauses that will be uncovered and become harmful during downturn. Banks as brokers in this process are exposed to threats as well.

> Securitisation is a *deceptive* thing ... and it's a *dynamic* thing as well, because you know, it could be normal in the market, assuming nothing comes up. But when you are in the stressed environment, it can *come back to bite you*. So everything is fine when you have low securitisation happening as in the last few years, but if things go bad, the banks, for reputation reasons, have to take the risks back. (Interview No.14)

Furthermore, external risk ratings have been widely criticised, after the 2008 financial crisis, as being the accomplice of securitisation of a 'deceptive' nature.

Risk ratings produced by economic models serve a purpose of credit enhancement that gives securities the investment-grade rating required. Among various forms of credit enhancement, a buy-back guarantee that offers buyers a 'warranty' in the case of capital losses due to unexpected high defaults brings potential threats to banks because risks will come back to them once default occurs. Therefore, as one of those types of financial instruments whose value is driven by the underlying collateral assets, the quality of underlying assets as collateral is a vital issue for the players involved in the securitisation process. The occurrence of the 2008 crisis obviously gives a lesson to all market participants especially banks, and they are more alert about the quality of collaterals that is reflected by their attitudes towards this aspect in the following comment:

> So, yeah, *most of the market was expecting the securitisation of low quality assets to potentially dry up, even to die, but it significantly increased when it came to high quality assets.* (Interview No. 1)

However, although they realise the potential problems associated with over-valued collateral, there is still ignorance of a more profound issue relating to the disconnection between various players within the securitisation process, as pointed out by a regulatory supervisor:

> The independence principle in APS 120, will work (to solve some of the problems related to securitisation), but the point is that it will create *problems* as well, for example, the problems derived from management of operational process of ADIs are independent with securitisation vehicle. (Interview No. 4)

Apart from these issues, the involvement of external ratings in the problems arising from securitisation with over-valued collaterals, particularly after credit enhancement, was also raised and discussed by bank risk managers and supervisors.

THE THREAT FROM POOR QUALITY EXTERNAL RATINGS AND 'FAVOURABLE' CREDIT ENHANCEMENT IN SECURITISING PROCESS

The profit-driven nature of external rating agencies has been exposed heavily by the 2008 financial crisis. As Minsky (1987) argued investment banks would pay ratings agencies to enhance the liquidity of securities. At the same time, the economic models banks developed assisted them to convince regulators and rating agencies that interest earned was able to cover or exceed the compensate for risks. Hence, as one regulatory supervisor commented:

> Well it's more volatile. Now with the Sub-prime crisis, there are actually a lot of *question* marks about the rating agencies. *How effective* they are; *how far back with price corrections* they were ... ; *how lagging* they were in re-rating things they should have re-rated much earlier. (Interview No. 15)

One instance noted by one of the bank managers indicates that the profit that external rating agencies receive from offering 'favourable' ratings to their customers raises doubts about the quality of the ratings applied to business products:

> *I think most of the benefit is in the investment grade corporates.* Where previously as an Australian bank, or ourselves lending to BHP Petroleum, or one of the BHP entities, we had to hold 100% of the risk weighted asset, (of course now we now are left with a lot of the underlying collateral), they can apply to get any loans they want, as well as a strong credit rating. So with a risk weighted asset, for BHP, it is now likely to weigh in under 10%. (Interview No. 2)

As the customers of those agencies, another bank risk manager also criticised the quality of external ratings they relied on (although arguably, banks were overly confident about their internal modellings and underlying risk methodologies that has been proved to be flawed, but this is not the concern of this chapter). The following comment uncovers the 'story' behind the external ratings:

> We use external data for some modelling, but we assign our own credit rates to companies. So companies that might have high credit ratings we might not necessarily want to lend money to. (Interview No. 12)

It has been witnessed through sub-prime crisis that banks hold almost worst securities especially with 'buy-back' guarantee for credit enhancement purpose. But banks under prudential control guided by Basel accord are required by regulators to hold certain regulatory capital as buffer against risks, although that number is not risk-sensitive enough as the existence of regulatory arbitrage partially make evident. On the contrary, as pointed out by an interviewee from the banking sector, other less regulated market players – Non-Bank Financial Institutions (NBFIs) are more vulnerable to the shocks related to securitisation. And the failure of those players will broadly impact on the entire financial market:

> When banks were holding it (securitised assets), there were regulatory rules applied to it in terms of how much capital you are holding. But if unrelated private investors were going to hold it, they got their own views on essentially how leveraged they could be in their own position, what kind of risk premium that's required. (Interview No. 6)

The inconsistency of the regulatory framework of financial market is also apparent in the lack of regulation on external rating agencies. As one of being blamed and criticised components of the financial market, rating agencies are still kept sway from prudential controls by regulators due to the so-called independence principle that acts as a guarantee to ensure the trustworthiness of their 'products'. Unfortunately, the quality of their ratings has been demonstrated to be doubtful:

> The ratings agency just runs without the regulators at the moment. (Interview No. 10)

> In general, against those same risks, it is a bit tricky, because there's no framework which extends to cover the banks, the insurers, and everybody under the same methodology. (Interview No. 7)

In that sense, as advocated by bank risk managers, despite the 'independence principle', rating agencies should be covered under the regulatory framework with other market participants. Otherwise, external rating-related problems will not disappear and will soon come to affect the stability of the financial market again:

> But I think that's (regulating external rating agencies) the only solution. As long as the issue of regulating the ratings agencies isn't solved, there's always this problem. (Interview No. 10)

And,

> There is a lot of pressure especially in Europe, to bring in regulation of the ratings agencies. (Interview No.11)

However, when the actual regulatory requirements have been put on the table for regulators to deal with, things become quite difficult. Furthermore, as raised by bank risk managers, there is a necessity for regulators to put more effort on prudential supervision, especially to scrutinise modelling aspect. It could be argued that this should be applied to the entire process of securitisation and include all major players under regulations:

> I think maybe the review and scrutiny of the models by APRA needs to be a lot heavier, because there are so many more inputs now that go into them. You can't just move the exposure around, and play regulatory capital games. (Interview No. 7)

The above discussion of securitisation and issues of external ratings and credit enhancement drawn from the interview material reveal just the tip of the iceberg, in regard to how speculation, fuelled by financial innovations, has driven the transformation of financial positions. The relevant issues exposed heavily by the recent global financial crisis, raise the alarm and, most importantly, recall the attention of market practitioners, and policy makers, to the behavioural transformation of financial institutions in terms of the growth of innovations. In that sense, there is a necessity for policy makers to put more effort into building a consistent regulatory platform for various market participants including the banks, NBFIs, and external rating agencies, both domestically and across borders, and this regulatory consistency is able to further promote effective communication and collaboration among practitioners and regulators, which could create more transparent, robust and stable market environment.

CONCLUSION

In general, with the help of credit enhancement and 'favourable' external ratings, the growth of the securitisation market led to a tremendous increase of leverage ratios. A virtuous cycle was consequently created: loose credit issued triggered the increase of asset prices, which consequently encouraged the development of financial innovations and also competition to further increase leverage. Financial innovations such as securitisation enhanced the liquidity of bundled securities that, with hindsight, incorporated substantial portions of over-valued underlying assets. While this lead to an expanded supply of loans. It also fuelled further rounds of home buying driving up the value of real estate and simultaneously increasing the size of loans required. This cycle was responsible for transforming the financial system into one that was more vulnerable to external shocks.

From the findings revealed in this chapter, policy makers need to return to a financial structure that promotes stability rather than speculation. The enhanced supervision of financial institutions based on effective communication and consistent regulatory platform must be seen as vital to the overall goal of controlling and ameliorating future periods of financial instability. Although the occurrence of market turmoil is hardly avoidable, the extent of turbulence can be managed, through a fundamental reform of the financial system, beyond the focus on quantitative risk management. On-going studies of this aspect need to be conducted.

REFERENCES

Black, W. (2005). *The bets way to rob a bank is to own one*. Austin, TX: University of Texas at Austin.

Darity, W., Jr. (1992). Financial instability hypothesis. In: P. M. Newman & J. Eatwell (Eds), *The new Palgrave: Dictionary of money and finance* (Vol. 3, pp. 75–76). London: Macmillan.

Kindleberger, C. P. (1978). *Manias, panics, and crashes: A history of financial crises*. New York: Basic Books.

Magnus, G. (2007). What this Minsky moment means for business. *Financial Times, 23*, 11.

Minsky, H. P. (1977). A theory of systemic fragility. In: E. I. Altman & A. W. Sametz (Eds), *Financial crisis: Institutions and markets in a fragile environment* (pp. 138–152). New York: Wiley.

Minsky, H. P. (1982). The financial-instability hypothesis: Capitalist processes and the behaviour of the economy. In: P. K. Charles & P. L. Jean (Eds), *Financial crises: Theory, history and policy* (pp. 13–38). New York: Cambridge University Press.

Minsky, H. P. (1986). *Stabilizing an unstable economy*. New Heaven: Yale University Press.

Minsky, H. P. (1987). *Securitization. Handout Econ 335A (Fall)*. Mimeo, in Levy archives, published as Levy Economics Institute Policy 2008 Note.

Mitchell, W. C. (1951). *What happens during business cycles: A progress report*. National Bureau of Economic Research, Studies in Business Cycles No. 5.

Wray, R. (1994). The political economy of the current US financial crisis. *International Papers in Political Economy*, *1*(3), 1–51.

PART IV
FINANCIAL MARKETS AND BANKING

THE EFFECTS OF UNDERWRITING PRACTICES ON LOAN LOSSES: EVIDENCE FROM THE FDIC SURVEY OF BANK LENDING PRACTICES☆

John O'Keefe

ABSTRACT

Purpose – *This chapter investigates the influence of bank loan underwriting practices on loan losses and identifies potential determinants of lending practices for five categories of loans: business, consumer, commercial real estate, home equity, and construction and land development loans.*

Methodology/approach – *Using data on the riskiness of lending practices obtained from the U.S. Federal Deposit Insurance Corporation (FDIC) bank examiner surveys from January 1996 to March 2009, I fit a two-step treatment effects model to measure the effects of underwriting practices on loan losses, controlling for the potential endogeneity of lending practices.*

☆The views and opinions expressed here are those of the author and do not necessarily reflect those of the Federal Deposit Insurance Corporation.

International Banking in the New Era: Post-Crisis Challenges and Opportunities
International Finance Review, Volume 11, 273–314

ISSN: 1569-3767/doi:10.1108/S1569-3767(2010)0000011013

Findings – *In the selection step, I find that for business loans, the likelihood that bank management will adopt low-risk lending practices increases with bank financial performance and management quality hierarchical complexity and decreases with market competition. Results for the selection of lending practices for consumer loans and three categories of real estate loans are similar to those found for business loans but show weaker statistical relationships to all explanatory variables. In the loss determination step, I find that lower (higher) risk underwriting practices are generally associated with lower (higher) gross loan charge-offs (as percentage of gross loans and leases) for five categories of loans: business, consumer, commercial real estate, home equity, and construction and land development loans.*

Originality/value of chapter – *This is the first study to model the determinants of loan underwriting practices with the practices being characterized in terms of their risk to the bank. In addition, this is the first study to consider the effects of the riskiness of lending practices on loan losses, controlling for the endogeneity of practices.*

The proximate cause of the current U.S. financial crisis is the collapse of the housing market (International Monetary Fund [IMF], 2009b). That collapse followed a classic boom-bust cycle in residential real estate prices, fueled by the rapid expansion and subsequent contraction of credit made available to potential homebuyers. In the boom phase, low interest rates and strong economic growth increased the affordability of housing in the United States to historic levels. Lenders dramatically increased mortgage originations, supported by strong market demand for mortgage-backed securities that, in turn, fueled securitization activities at banks. Decreases in lending standards for residential mortgages, coupled with increases in household leverage, played a significant role in the crisis (Dell'Ariccia, Igan, & Laeven, 2008). Had the expansion of credit been constrained by prudent lending standards or adequate financial transparency and due diligence on the part of investors in mortgage-related loan securitizations, it is possible that real estate price volatility would have been similarly constrained.[1]

The expectation that lending standards vary with macroeconomic conditions is central to many theoretical models of credit cycles: lenders relax lending standards during periods of macroeconomic expansion and tighten standards during periods of macroeconomic contraction, smoothing the overall risk profile of their institutions (Weinberg, 1995).

The risk smoothing hypothesis suggests that the effects of variations in lending standards on loan portfolios can be offset, to some degree, by countervailing macroeconomic conditions. Rapid expansion of credit can lead to banking crises, however, if the boom in credit availability is accompanied by substantial reductions in lending standards and increases in borrower and lender leverage (Dell'Ariccia & Marquez, 2006).

Whereas changes in lending standards play an important role in theoretical models of credit cycles and financial crises, there is little direct evidence of the effects of lending standards on loan portfolio performance. This is because direct measures on lending criteria are, in general, not publically available. Direct measures of the lending standards include the criteria used to approve loans, loan pricing, repayment terms, sources of repayment, collateral requirements, loan portfolio management and administration, written lending policies, and adherence to polices. As these data are typically only available from lenders or their supervisors, empirical studies rely on indirect measures of lending criteria such as loan growth, loan denial rates, and loan-to-income ratios.

The primary objective of this chapter is to assess whether bank lending standards are statistically and economically significant determinants of loan portfolio performance for business, consumer, commercial real estate, home equity, and construction and land development loans. Although there is ample evidence of the role that lax lending standards played, in recent years, in subprime mortgage markets (Dell'Ariccia et al., 2008), I am unaware of any published empirical studies on the importance of lending standards for the performance of other types of loans.[2] A second objective of this chapter is to learn the determinants of bank lending standards. In response to the global financial crisis, the Group of Twenty (G20) Leaders called on bank supervisors to be more forward looking and, to the extent possible, dampen the procyclicality of bank regulation (e.g., capital adequacy requirements, loan-loss reserving, and deposit insurance pricing).[3] Supervisors must understand the factors influencing bank lending standards if they are to anticipate and correct behaviors countercyclically.

BACKGROUND AND FINDINGS

In 1995, the U.S. Federal Deposit Insurance Corporation (FDIC) developed an Examination Supplement on Current Underwriting Standards – a survey that is completed by the examiner in charge at the conclusion of each FDIC safety-and-soundness examination. The survey contains over 50 questions on bank lending practices overall and on practices in specific loan categories. FDIC bank examiners assess both the risk of lending practices and the frequency of certain practices that regulators determined had contributed to the banking crises of the 1980s and early 1990s. Using these unique examination data, I investigate possible determinants of loan underwriting practices and the influence of these practices on loan losses. Specifically, I fit a treatment effects model using a two-step Heckman consistent estimator to consider the effects of an endogenously chosen binary variable (low-risk underwriting practices) on loan losses. In the selection step, I find that for business loans, the selection of low-risk underwriting practices is positively related to strong prior period bank financial performance, management quality, and hierarchical complexity, and negatively related to market competition. Results for the selection of lending practices for consumer loans and three categories of real estate loans are similar to those found for business loans but show weaker statistical relationships to all explanatory variables. In the loss determination step, I find that lower (higher) risk underwriting practices are generally associated with lower (higher) loan losses for five categories of loans: business, consumer, commercial real estate, home equity, and construction and land development loans. The results support the commonly held view that credit standards vary cyclically with banking market conditions and demonstrate the important influence lending standards have on loan portfolio performance. I believe this is the first study to model the determinants of loan underwriting practices with the practices being characterized in terms of their risk to the bank. In addition, I believe this is the first study to consider the effects of the riskiness of lending practices on loan losses, controlling for the endogeneity of practices.

I next discuss the previous literature on the determinants of banks' loan underwriting practices as well as the determinants of loan losses. Subsequent sections of the chapter discuss the FDIC underwriting survey, the methodology I use to investigate the determinants of loan underwriting practices and loan losses, the empirical results, and conclusions.

PREVIOUS LITERATURE

Loan underwriting practices are an amalgam of a number of things: the criteria used to approve loans, loan pricing, repayment terms, sources of repayment, collateral requirements, loan portfolio management and administration (including decisions about loan growth and concentrations), written lending policies, and adherence to polices. Given the breadth of loan underwriting practices and their effects on bank performance and credit availability, there is a vast literature that bears either directly or indirectly on loan underwriting practices. This literature can be divided into studies of the relationship between organizational form and firms' decision making (Stein, 2000), studies that deal directly with the determinants of loan underwriting practices for small-business finance (Cole, Goldberg, & White, 2004; Berger, Miller, Peterson, Rajan, & Stein, 2002), studies of the effects of loan underwriting practices on credit cycles (Berger & Udell, 2002; Rajan, 1994; Weinberg, 1995), as well as the effects of loan underwriting practices on the risk of bank failure (Office of the Comptroller of the Currency [OCC], 1988; FDIC, 1997).

Cole et al. (2004) – who are primarily concerned with differences between large and small banks in their small-business lending practices – model both banks' decisions to approve loan applications and borrowers' selections of lenders (banks). Using data obtained from the 1993 Federal Reserve National Survey of Small Business Finance and bank financial reports, the authors estimate the lender and borrower choices using full information maximum likelihood estimation of two simultaneous probit equations, with controls for selection. They find that small businesses prefer to borrow from small banks and that small banks, in turn, approve small-business loan applications more often than large banks do. The authors also conclude that small banks prefer to lend to small businesses that are relatively informationally opaque, whereas large banks prefer to lend to larger businesses that are able to provide hard data on their financial condition. The Cole et al. (2004) study is particularly relevant to this study because their results suggest that smaller banks adopt small-business loan underwriting practices that are riskier than those of larger banks, riskier in that small banks prefer to lend to small firms that lack hard financial data to support the lending decision and riskier to the extent that the failure rates of small businesses are higher than those of larger, established firms.

Berger et al. (2002) use the 1993 Federal Reserve National Survey of Small Business Finance to analyze businesses' choices of lenders. Their results indicate among other things that small businesses tend to form long-term banking relationships with local, small banks. They argue that this occurs partly because small banks are more willing to make business loans to borrowers whose finances are relatively opaque. Their results agree with those of Cole et al. (2004); however, Berger et al. do not study banks' lending decisions directly.

Berger and Udell (2002) develop an institutional-memory hypothesis as a partial explanation of two common observations about banking cycles. The first observation is that bank lending appears to be procyclical, expanding during economic booms and contracting during economic recessions. The second is that bank loan performance, as indicated by past due and nonaccrual loans and loan losses, is also procyclical, with performance generally declining as economic conditions worsen and improving with the economy. They attribute both observations about banking cycles to changes in loan underwriting practices. Berger and Udell (2002) suggest that when bank loan officers make lending decisions, they tend to rely on past experience. Berger and Udell (2002) hypothesize that with the passage of time between problem-loan periods, loan officers' memories fade. This loss of knowledge, combined with bank employee turnover, weakens banks' institutional memory, with loan officers then repeating past mistakes. Berger and Udell (2002) suggest that the result is a relaxation of loan underwriting standards as time passes since the last problem-loan period. Conversely, they suggest that standards are tightened as bankers gain experience during a banking crisis. Berger and Udell (2002) infer lending standards from three sources: (1) measures of growth in both commercial and industrial loans and in commercial real estate loans, (2) loan-level data on interest-rate premiums from the Federal Reserve's Survey of the Terms of Bank Lending, and (3) data on overall credit standards and bank-level loan spreads from the Federal Reserve's Senior Loan Officer Opinion Survey on Bank Lending Practices. In the senior loan officer survey, bank loan officers voluntarily report whether credit terms have tightened or loosened since the previous quarter for four major loan categories.[4] Among their sample of banks, Berger and Udell (2002) find support for the institutional-memory hypothesis when they use loan growth proxies for lending standards, but generally they do not find support for their hypothesis when they use lending-standard measures from either the Survey of the Terms of Bank Lending or the Senior Loan Officer Survey.[5] Berger and Udell's (2002) hypothesis does not suggest other reasons that lending standards might change over the business cycle. Under the institutional-memory hypothesis, the relationship between lending standards and business cycles is based solely on the suggested atrophy of loan officers' knowledge and abilities.[6]

Most academic researchers do not have access to the types of confidential survey data used by Cole et al. (2004) and Berger and Udell (2002). Consequently, most academic studies try to infer underwriting practices from banks' public financial reports. Rapid growth in bank loans, changes in loan concentrations, and changes in loan interest rates are commonly interpreted as reflecting underlying changes in bankers' risk acceptance and, by inference, in loan underwriting standards. Supply-side explanations of the expansion of bank loans frequently suggest a relaxation of underwriting standards, whereas loan contractions are said to suggest a tightening of standards. Aside from the obvious need to control for loan demand, the extent to which changes in loan levels reflect changes in standards or in bankers' risk acceptance or in both is open to question. Loan performance is influenced by underlying economic conditions: booming economies can mitigate the risks of lowered lending standards, whereas contracting economies can aggravate risks. For this reason, theoretical studies (Rajan, 1994; Weinberg, 1995) have suggested that loan underwriting practices follow a cycle associated with that of the underlying economy. Rajan (1994) hypothesizes that bank managers have short-term decision horizons because their reputations are strongly influenced by public perceptions of their performance, as evidenced by short-term earnings. Managers' reputations suffer if they fail to expand credit when the economy is expanding and bank earnings are improving. This herd behavior will result in some loans going to customers with higher default risk than would occur otherwise. Weinberg (1995) suggests that bank managers adjust lending standards as market conditions change, seeking to smooth overall lending risk. Weinberg (1995) hypothesizes that risk-neutral lenders increase lending during periods of economic expansion because the expected returns from investment projects improve, and therefore, the expected returns from all loan customers rise. Weinberg (1995) uses data on the growth rate of total loans and loan charge-offs in the United States from 1950 to 1992 to show a pattern of increases in lending preceding increases in loan losses and argues that these patterns are consistent with the notion of underwriting cycles.

U.S. bank regulators have relied on confidential supervisory information from bank examinations and from interviews with examiners to understand how bank management and underwriting practices shape bank performance. The Office of the Comptroller of the Currency (OCC, 1988) concludes that the dominant reason for bank failure in the early 1980s was poor bank management, which encompasses lax lending standards. An FDIC study of the causes of the banking crises of the 1980s and early 1990s (FDIC, 1997) finds that a combination of factors – economic, legislative, managerial, and regulatory – led to the banking crises. Importantly, the FDIC study finds that bank managers adjusted lending practices as economic conditions changed, increasing lending into economic and sectoral booms and reducing lending during economic contractions. In addition, the FDIC study suggests that bank managers reacted to competition from other bankers and that this competition might have encouraged weaker lending standards.

The previously discussed studies are important because they identify several possible determinants of banks' loan underwriting practices. The determinants are both internal to the bank and external: (1) bank organizational form, as indicated by size and complexity; (2) bank management quality; (3) bank financial performance; (4) local economic conditions; and (5) competition from other lenders. These studies also suggest that loan losses are determined by some of these same factors (bank financial performance and local economic conditions) and by underwriting practices. The empirical methodology used in this chapter is designed to take account of these interrelationships. I next discuss the FDIC underwriting survey and the sample, followed by a discussion of the empirical methodology.

DATA AND SAMPLE

My sample consists of observations from the FDIC underwriting survey (completed by the examiner in charge at the conclusion of all examinations of FDIC-supervised banks) between January 1996 and March 2009. The survey covers FDIC-supervised commercial and savings banks, the vast majority of which are smaller, community banks.[7] As Tables 1 and 2 indicate, the number of survey responses differs across loan types and practices, varying between approximately 20,000 and 9,000 observations.[8] There are several reasons for this variation in responses. Examiners report survey results only if the loan category is reviewed during the examination and if the practice is relevant, given the bank's activities. A missing response for a loan category would typically occur if a bank was not actively lending in that category. Additionally, the number and frequency of survey responses are determined by congressional statute and supervisory policy on examination frequency. The Federal Deposit Insurance Corporation Improvement Act (FDICIA) of 1991 established minimum examination frequencies of between 12 and 18 months for all banks, and current requirements call for annual examinations for all banks except those with composite safety-and-soundness ratings (CAMELS ratings) of 1 or 2 and assets under $250 million. The FDIC shares examination responsibilities with state bank supervisors and typically alternates examinations with state supervisors unless a bank's performance is poor. As a result, one typically observes underwriting survey responses every two to three years for FDIC-supervised banks.

Table 1. Survey Responses for Underwriting Practices by Loan Type (January 1996–March 2009).

Question	Responses[a]	*N*	Percent
Business loans			
To what extent does the institution make business loans without a clear and reasonably predictable source of repayment?	Infrequently	20,348	85.3
	Noticeably	3,122	13.1
	Commonly	390	1.6
To what extent does the institution make business loans to borrowers who lack documented financial strength to support such lending?	Infrequently	18,972	79.5
	Noticeably	4,411	18.5
	Commonly	467	2.0
With respect to asset-based business loans, to what extent does the institution fail to monitor collateral?	Infrequently	11,437	79.5
	Noticeably	2,537	17.6
	Commonly	419	2.9
Construction loans			
To what extent is the institution funding construction projects on a speculative basis (e.g., without presale or prelease commitments)	Infrequently	4,196	73.1
	Noticeably	1,252	21.8
	Commonly	292	5.1
To what extent are residential or commercial real estate development loans made without consideration of repayment sources other than the project being funded?	Infrequently	13,258	84.4
	Noticeably	2,036	13.0
	Commonly	413	2.6
When alternative repayment sources are required, to what extent does the institution fail to take appropriate steps to verify the quality of these sources?	Infrequently	13,218	84.2
	Noticeably	2,087	13.3
	Commonly	388	2.5
To what extent does the institution fail to use realistic appraisal values relative to the current economic environment or performance of similar credits?	Infrequently	13,621	86.7
	Noticeably	1,852	11.8
	Commonly	231	1.5
To what extent does the institution fund, or defer, interest payments during the term of its residential or commercial real estate development loans?	Infrequently	10,570	75.9
	Noticeably	2,050	14.7
	Commonly	1,312	9.4
To what extent does the institution fund 100% of the cost of construction and land, with no cash equity on the part of the borrower/developer?	Infrequently	11,511	85.5
	Noticeably	1,621	12.0
	Commonly	334	2.5

[a]The responses have been edited for brevity. The full responses are never or infrequently, frequent enough to warrant notice, and commonly or standard procedure.

Table 2. Survey Responses for Underwriting Practices by Loan Type (January 1996–March 2009).

Question	Responses[a]	*N*	Percent
Commercial real estate loans			
To what extent are commercial real estate loans made without consideration of repayment sources other than the project being funded?	Infrequently	17,809	88.0
	Noticeably	2,146	10.6
	Commonly	284	1.4
To what extent does the institution make interest-only, extended amortization, or negative amortization permanent commercial real estate loans?	Infrequently	18,355	90.7
	Noticeably	1,672	8.3
	Commonly	221	1.1
To what extent does the institution make short-term commercial real estate loans ("mini-perms") with minimal amortization terms and large "balloon" payments at maturity?	Infrequently	16,307	80.5
	Noticeably	3,190	15.8
	Commonly	752	3.7
To what extent does the institution fail to use realistic appraisal values relative to the current economic environment or performance observed on similar credits?	Infrequently	18,253	90.1
	Noticeably	1,861	9.2
	Commonly	148	0.7
Consumer loans			
To what extent does the institution make "secured" consumer loans without adequate collateral protection?	Infrequently	15,803	84.8
	Noticeably	2,437	13.1
	Commonly	399	2.1
To what extent does the institution make consumer loans to borrowers who lack demonstrable ability to repay?	Infrequently	15,220	81.7
	Noticeably	2,937	15.8
	Commonly	463	2.5
Home equity loans			
To what extent does the institution make home equity loans that push mortgage indebtedness above 90 percent of collateral value?	Infrequently	7,942	87.8
	Noticeably	943	10.4
	Commonly	157	1.7
To what extent does the institution qualify borrowers for home equity credit on the basis of loan rates that are initially discounted ("teaser rates")?	Infrequently	8,875	98.3
	Noticeably	113	1.3
	Commonly	38	0.4

[a]The responses have been edited for brevity. The full responses are never or infrequently, frequent enough to warrant notice, and commonly or standard procedure.

METHODOLOGY

The literature discussed above suggests factors that influence both loan underwriting practices and loan losses. As noted, I address this possibility econometrically by fitting a treatment effects model using a two-step Heckman consistent estimator to consider the effects of an endogenously chosen binary variable (low-risk underwriting practices) on loan losses. More generally, the empirical methodology is designed to test the hypothesis that there are important, unobservable factors that influence both underwriting practices and loan losses. One such unobservable factor is the state of the economy. Others factors are the states of banking market competition and regulation. Failure to control for such unobserved factors can result in overestimation of the effects of underwriting practices on loan losses.[9]

Selection of Lending Practices

The FDIC underwriting survey asks respondents to rank the relative frequency of specific risky lending practices for a loan category, using three mutually exclusive levels of frequency: never or infrequently, frequently enough to warrant notice, and commonly or standard practice (Tables 1 and 2).[10] Given the relatively low number of "commonly" responses, I combine responses of "commonly" and "frequently" into one category to simplify the estimations. There is also a high degree of similarity in examiner rankings of the riskiness of different lending practices within a loan category.[11] As a result, I measure the dependent variable in my model of the selection of lending practices using a binomial (0, 1) variable, where a value of 1 indicates a response of "never or infrequently" for any surveyed risky lending practice within a loan category and a value of 0 indicates a response of "commonly" or "frequently" for the same summary risk practice measure. That is, the response variable for lending practices aggregates responses across all surveyed risk practices within a loan category for a specific survey date-bank observation. As such, a value of 1 for the binomial variable is interpreted as indicating the selection of low-risk lending practices and a value of 0 is interpreted as indicating the selection of high-risk lending practices.[12] For brevity, in the discussion, I treat responses of "never or infrequently" as synonymous with the occurrence of low-risk lending practices, and responses of "frequently" or "commonly" as synonymous with the occurrence of high-risk lending practices.

Drawing upon the previous literature, I hypothesize that underwriting practices are related to lagged measures of banks' financial performance, local economic conditions, bank management quality, hierarchical complexity, and local market competition. I now discuss the motivation for each of these explanatory variables and each variable's expected influence on the selection of loan underwriting practices.

A bank's financial performance should reflect the cumulative effect of loan underwriting practices the bank chose in the recent past (OCC, 1988; FDIC, 1997). If a bank adopted high-risk lending practices in the past, I anticipate higher loan concentrations, as well as higher nonperforming loans and loan losses, all other things being equal. Additionally, high-risk practices will also mean high allowances for loan losses and high-equity capitalization to absorb potential loan losses, assuming management properly anticipated lending risks. Accordingly, I measure financial performance using lagged values for performing loans and nonperforming loans for the loan category relevant to the lending practice. The loan categories I use are business, consumer, commercial real estate, home equity, and construction and land development.[13] Nonperforming loans consist of all loans past due 90 days or more and nonaccrual loans for the particular loan category. I normalize each loan category of performing and nonperforming loans by gross loans and leases. In addition, I also include lagged equity and allowances for loan and lease losses (both normalized by bank assets) as measures of financial performance. I do not use lagged measures of loan losses (gross loan charge-offs) as measures of financial performance in the lending practice selection model because of timing considerations and potential seasonality in loan losses.[14]

The relationship between lagged financial performance and current lending practices should depend on the amount of time between lagged financial performance and practices. There are two possible scenarios. In the first scenario, if the time interval between lagged financial performance and current lending practices is sufficiently long, bank management may have chosen to reduce the frequency of risky practices to offset previous adverse outcomes (or alternatively, to accept more risk if previous outcomes were beneficial). In the first scenario, if the time interval is sufficiently long, weak prior-period financial performance – as indicated by high levels of nonperforming loans, high allowances for loan losses, and low equity capitalization – would be positively related to the selection of a low-risk practice today. In contrast, if prior-period financial performance is strong, the reverse would occur.

In the second scenario, if the time interval between lagged financial performance and current lending practices is sufficiently short, bank management may not have had enough time to alter their lending practices. In the second scenario, lagged financial performance serves as an indicator of ongoing lending practices. In this situation, I anticipate relationships the exact opposite of those I hypothesized under the first scenario. That is, I anticipate that weak (strong) prior-period financial performance will be negatively (positively) related to the selection of low-risk practices today.

The amount of time required to alter lending practices will depend on loan type and terms, especially maturity. In the selection model, the time interval between lagged financial performance and current lending practices is short (one quarter), however, so I anticipate that lagged financial performance will serve as an indicator of ongoing practices.

Local economic conditions also have a bearing on lending practices (Rajan, 1994; Weinberg, 1995; FDIC, 1997). I anticipate that strong (weak) local economies give banks an incentive to loosen (tighten) lending standards, allowing banks to smooth fluctuations in credit risk over the business cycle. I tested alternative measures of state economic conditions to find those measures that best explain selection of lending practices and loan losses. Specifically, using quarterly data on state economic conditions, I tested the growth rate in state unemployment rates, growth rate in real per capita income, personal loan delinquency rates, and mortgage foreclosures as a percentage of mortgage loans and chose those measures exhibiting the strongest statistical significance. For the business loan model, I measure local economic conditions using the growth rate in state unemployment rates. For all other loan categories, I measure state economic conditions using mortgage loan foreclosure rates.

The overall quality of bank management, as indicated by examiner assignments of the CAMELS component rating for management quality, should also influence the choice of lending practice in much the same way that financial performance does. Management quality ratings vary from "1" (strongest) to "5" (weakest) under the U.S. Uniform Financial Institutions Rating System. If bank management has recently been determined to be of poor quality, I anticipate that ongoing lending practices will be relatively riskier than if bank management had been well rated. I measure management quality using two dummy variables for management quality ratings of "1" and "2".[15]

Studies have suggested that the extent of organizational hierarchy present in a bank influences the bank's decision-making processes, including its lending practices (Berger et al., 2002; Cole et al., 2004). The general notion is that large, complex banking organizations need hard data on loan applicants to approve loans. This need is largely due to the fact that in large banking organizations, second-level management reviews loan officers' work. Conversely, smaller, simpler banking organizations – where the same individual serves as both the loan officer and the loan approver – can focus on developing relationships with more informationally opaque borrowers. If a small-bank loan officer is adept at assessing the credit risk of informationally opaque customers, he or she will be rewarded. But if the person had worked in a larger, more hierarchical organization, he or she would not have been able to demonstrate this ability to higher management in the absence of hard financial data from the loan applicant. To capture the degree of hierarchy, I use three measures: the natural logarithm of bank assets (bank size), the number of bank employees, and a dummy variable indicating whether the bank is a member of a multibank holding company. On the basis of the previous literature, I anticipate that bank size, the number of employees, and multibank holding company membership will be positively related to the selection of low-risk lending practices. Whereas the aforementioned literature does not suggest benchmarks for what constitutes large or complex banking organizations, I anticipate that most of the FDIC-supervised banks that comprise the sample are not large or complex. This characteristic of the sample might limit the significance of my measures of the degree of hierarchy in the lending practice selection model.

The degree of competition from other lenders in a market is also expected to influence the selection of lending practices. Previous studies suggest that competitive pressures encourage banks to loosen lending standards to maintain market share (FDIC, 1997). To measure banking market competition, I use a Herfindahl–Hirschman Index (HHI) of county deposit concentrations, measured using bank branch deposit data contained in the Summary of Deposit (SOD) reports that banks file with their primary federal regulator each June. For other quarters of the year, I compute the HHI by using the most recent lagged value of the SOD data.

Eq. (1) presents the selection model in general form. The dependent variable, $D^k_{j,t-4}$ is a dummy variable used to indicate the selection of low-risk lending practices for loan type k by bank j at quarter $t-4$, $\boldsymbol{\theta}$ is a vector of unknown parameters, $\boldsymbol{Z}^k_{j,t-5}$ is a vector of the previously discussed explanatory variables as of the previous quarter ($t-5$), and $\mu_{j,t}$ is the disturbance term.[16] Eq. (1) is estimated by probit regression in the first step of a two-step treatment model.

$$D^k_{j,t-4} = \boldsymbol{\theta}' \boldsymbol{Z}^k_{j,t-5} + \mu_{j,t} \tag{1}$$

Loan Losses

In the second stage of the estimation, I model loan losses for a loan category as being determined by lagged measures of banks' financial performance, local economic conditions, and lending practices, controlling for the endogeneity of practices. I measure loan losses by the four quarter sum of gross loan charge-offs for a loan category, expressed as a percentage of gross loans and leases as of the fourth quarter. The loan categories – business, consumer, commercial real estate, home equity, and construction and land development – correspond to those used by the FDIC loan underwriting survey. The explanatory variables overlap with the corresponding variables in the selection model and are defined identically. I now discuss the motivation for these explanatory variables and each variable's expected relationship with loan losses.

Following Dahl, O'Keefe, and Hanweck (1998), I assume that loan losses for each loan category are determined by the bank's previous financial performance as measured by lagged performing loans, nonperforming loans, equity, and the allowance for loan and lease losses. Nonperforming loans are expected to be the primary source of loan losses, whereas performing loans are included to account for general lending risk. Performing and nonperforming loans are measured as a percentage of gross loans and leases. Using this normalization, I can measure the effect of increases in loan concentrations on loan losses, holding constant the relative shares of performing and nonperforming loans, by the sum of the regression coefficients for the performing and nonperforming loans. Equity capital (as a percentage of bank assets) might influence management's ability and willingness to recognize loan losses (especially if regulatory capital standards might become binding). I anticipate a positive relationship between equity capitalization and subsequent loan losses. Similarly, the allowance for loan losses (as a percentage of bank assets) is expected to be related to management's expectations of future loans losses and therefore to be positively related to subsequent loan losses. Local economic conditions affect borrowers' ability to make loan payments. To control for local economic conditions, I include lagged values of state unemployment growth rates in the business loan-loss model and lagged values of mortgage default rates in the consumer, commercial real estate, home equity, and construction and land development loan-loss models. To control for the effects of lending practices on loan losses, I include a dummy variable for indicating the riskiness of the bank's chosen lending practices in the relevant loan category. This explanatory dummy variable is defined exactly like the dependent variable in Eq. (1). I anticipate that the use of lower-risk lending practices reduces subsequent loan losses. Finally, following Greene (2003), I control for the effect of a potentially endogenously determined dummy explanatory variable (low-risk lending practices) by including the estimated hazard rate (inverse Mills ratio) obtained from Eq. (1) in the loss determination model (Eq. (2)). This control treats the unobserved variable as a missing explanatory variable and corrects the estimated coefficient for lending practices for any endogeneity.

Eq. (2) shows the loan-loss determination model in general form: Where $L^k_{j,t \text{ to } t-4}$ represents gross loan charge-offs by bank j for loan type k summed for four quarters (from end of quarters $t-4$ to t) and normalized by gross loans and leases at period t, $\boldsymbol{\beta}$ is a vector of unknown parameters, $\boldsymbol{X}^k_{j,t-5}$ is a vector of the previously discussed determinants of gross loan charge-offs, $D^k_{j,t-4}$ is a dummy variable indicating whether bank j uses low-risk lending practices for loan type k (as defined in Eq. (1)), $H^k_{j,t-4}$ is the hazard rate obtained from estimation of Eq. (1) and $\varepsilon_{j,t}$ is the disturbance term.

$$L^k_{j,t \text{ to } t-4} = \boldsymbol{\beta}'\boldsymbol{X}^k_{j,t-5} + \delta D^k_{j,t-4} + \lambda H^k_{j,t-4} + \varepsilon_{j,t} \tag{2}$$

EMPIRICAL RESULTS

In this section I present the results of univariate and multivariate statistical analyses of the causes and consequences of lending practices. As indicated in Tables 1 and 2, the FDIC underwriting survey includes several questions for each loan category. I study the effects of lending practices on each of five loan categories separately over the June 1996–March 2009 period.[17] To allow for potential variation in the effects of lending practices on loan losses over time, I estimate the treatment effects models biannually.[18] I first describe univariate statistics and then move on to the multivariate analysis.

Univariate Results

Table 3 presents univariate statistics for both the continuous dependent variables and the explanatory variables used in the treatment effects models. The univariate statistics indicate that the highest loss rates occur for business and consumer loans, with mean four quarter gross charge-off rates of 0.23 and 0.13 percent of gross loans and leases, respectively. The mean four quarter gross charge-off rates for the remaining loan categories are

Table 3. Sample Characteristics (March 1996–March 2009).

Variable	M	Mdn	SD	Min	Max	P1	P99
Performing business loans	37.28	37.13	19.85	0.00	100.00	0.00	88.10
Nonperforming business loans	0.72	0.33	2.17	0.00	89.52	0.00	5.62
Business loan gross charge-offs (annual)	0.23	0.08	0.83	−0.96	82.23	0.00	2.43
Performing commercial real estate loans	17.53	15.99	12.64	0.00	100.00	0.00	59.30
Nonperforming commercial real estate loans	0.34	0.09	0.77	0.00	22.23	0.00	3.49
Commercial real estate loan gross charge-offs (annual)	0.06	0.00	0.25	−0.81	25.89	0.00	0.96
Performing construction and land development loans	4.31	2.73	5.14	0.00	60.75	0.00	24.56
Nonperforming construction and land development loans	0.13	0.00	1.14	0.00	100.00	0.00	2.05
Construction and land development loan gross charge-offs (annual)	0.02	0.00	0.14	−0.27	9.03	0.00	0.45
Performing consumer loans	11.73	8.43	12.03	0.00	100.00	0.00	53.06
Nonperforming consumer loans	0.07	0.02	0.52	0.00	91.94	0.00	0.64
Consumer loan gross charge-offs (annual)	0.13	0.06	0.43	−0.48	30.48	0.00	0.94
Performing home equity loans	31.73	27.99	22.63	0.00	100.00	0.00	94.33
Nonperforming home equity loans	0.03	0.00	0.13	0.00	4.83	0.00	0.52
Home equity loan gross charge-offs (annual)	0.01	0.00	0.15	−0.38	25.89	0.00	0.17
Herfindahl–Hirschman Index	1,954	1,726	1,145	405	10,000	580	6,622
Natural logarithm of bank assets	13.79	13.32	1.45	7.69	21.00	11.27	18.40
Equity-to-assets	9.36	8.30	5.14	0.41	99.08	4.93	30.65
Allowance for loan losses-to-assets	1.10	0.92	0.89	0.00	28.88	0.04	4.71

Notes: M, mean; Mdn, median; SD, standard deviation; Min, minimum; Max, maximum; P1, first percentile; P99, 99th percentile. All financial variables are expressed as percentages of gross loans and leases, unless otherwise stated. $N = 43{,}568$.

lower: commercial real estate (0.06 percent), construction and land development loans (0.02 percent), and home equity loans (0.01 percent). These average loss rates reflect the benign economic conditions banks faced over much of the time period used in this chapter. These banking market conditions are very important in that my statistical analysis tests for the relationships between underwriting practices and loan losses under both benign banking market conditions (1996–2006) and the recent period of financial market stress (2007 to the first quarter of 2009). I believe that these banking market conditions provide a robust test of the influence of underwriting practices on loan losses across a range of economic conditions. Table 3 also indicates there are many outliers in my initial sample, where some reported loss rates and performing loan levels appear to be misstated. To control for bank reporting error, I eliminate these outliers from the final sample.[19]

Multivariate Results

The results for the selection of business lending practices (Table 4) are for the most part consistent with my prior expectations and in agreement with previous studies. The selection of low-risk business lending practices is positively related to the prior quarter's performing business loans and negatively related to nonperforming business loans. Bank equity capitalization is statistically significant in four of seven model estimations; however, there is inconsistency in the coefficient sign. Allowances for loan losses are negatively related to the selection of low-risk practices, in agreement with my prior expectations. Similarly, management ratings indicating well-rated management (ratings of 1 or 2) are consistently statistically significant and positively related to selection of low-risk business lending practices. As predicted by the literature on small-business lending practices, I find that two of my proxies for hierarchical banking organizations – the dummy variable indicating membership in a multibank holding company and the number of bank employees – are positively related to the selection of low-risk business lending practices. My measure of bank size, the natural logarithm of bank assets, is generally not statistically significant. One possible explanation for the asset size results is that bank asset size may be too crude a measure for organizational complexity, especially among FDIC-supervised banks, the vast majority of which are small community-based organizations. I find that my measure of market competition, the deposit market HHI, is in general negatively related to the selection of low-risk

Table 4. Selection of Low-Risk Business Lending Practices by Estimation Period.

Variable	b (SE)						
	1996–1997	1998–1999	2000–2001	2002–2003	2004–2005	2006–2007	2008–2009
Constant	3.695***	1.355**	0.492	1.386**	0.602	0.857	0.322
	(1.424)	(0.652)	(0.599)	(0.560)	(0.623)	(0.653)	(0.755)
Performing business loans/gross loans ($t-5$)	0.000	0.010	0.003	0.007	0.005	0.008	0.000
	(0.005)	(0.002)***	(0.002)	(0.002)***	(0.002)**	(0.002)***	(0.003)
Nonperforming business loans/gross loans ($t-5$)	−0.035	−0.049*	−0.134***	−0.113***	−0.059*	−0.138***	−0.131***
	(0.038)	(0.026)	(0.025)	(0.032)	(0.031)	(0.034)	(0.044)
Equity/assets ($t-5$)	0.002	−0.017**	−0.007	−0.008	0.025**	0.015*	0.033***
	(0.022)	(0.008)	(0.008)	(0.008)	(0.011)	(0.009)	(0.012)
Allowance for loan losses/assets ($t-5$)	0.157	−0.040	−0.054	−0.137*	−0.245***	−0.307***	−0.342***
	(0.168)	(0.068)	(0.063)	(0.073)	(0.066)	(0.076)	(0.085)
State unemployment growth rate ($t-5$)	0.014	−0.003	0.005	−0.006	−0.016	−0.013**	−0.009
	(0.024)	(0.008)	(0.008)	(0.006)	(0.010)	(0.006)	(0.010)
Management rating = 1 dummy ($t-5$)	1.131***	1.084***	1.042***	1.042***	1.138***	0.910***	0.884***
	(0.268)	(0.123)	(0.115)	(0.110)	(0.120)	(0.124)	(0.139)

Table 4. *(Continued)*

Variable	b (SE)						
	1996–1997	1998–1999	2000–2001	2002–2003	2004–2005	2006–2007	2008–2009
Management rating = 2 dummy (t–5)	0.712***	0.542***	0.497***	0.496***	0.506***	0.397***	0.537***
	(0.166)	(0.097)	(0.097)	(0.091)	(0.090)	(0.097)	(0.116)
Member multibank holding co. dummy (t–5)	0.371*	0.020	0.253***	0.258***	0.302***	0.127	0.371***
	(0.208)	(0.085)	(0.091)	(0.090)	(0.101)	(0.101)	(0.137)
log_e (assets) (t–5)	–0.244*	–0.070	0.034	–0.053	–0.008	–0.017	0.033
	(0.135)	(0.061)	(0.054)	(0.049)	(0.055)	(0.057)	(0.065)
Number of employees (t–5)	0.005*	0.003***	0.001*	0.002**	0.002**	0.002**	0.002*
	(0.003)	(0.001)	(0.001)	(0.001)	(0.001)	(0.001)	(0.001)
Herfindahl–Hirschman Index/1000, (t–5)	–0.088**	–0.059***	–0.049**	–0.060***	–0.023	0.002	–0.025
	(0.038)	(0.021)	(0.020)	(0.020)	(0.021)	(0.021)	(0.025)
n	1,380	2,746	3,138	3,246	3,187	3,070	1,818
Pseudo R^2	.12	.10	.12	.10	.13	.11	.12
χ^2	36.2***	99.9***	118.6***	127.2***	121.9***	75.6***	64.6***

*$p<.10$, **$p<.05$, ***$p<.01$.

business lending practices. This result agrees with many previous studies that suggest that competition among banks can result in the relaxation of lending standards. Finally, I find that my measure of state-level macroeconomic conditions, the quarterly growth rate in the state unemployment rate as of period $t-5$, is not a statistically significant determinant of business lending practices.[20] In addition to the coefficient estimations, Table 4 also reports the pseudo R^2 for the overall fit of the probit model.[21] The Pseudo R^2 statistics range in value between 10 percent and 13 percent and is in order with summary fit statistics reported in other studies on lending practices.[22] As a robustness check, I also estimate the χ^2 statistic for a joint test of the significance of the identifying terms in the lending practice selection equation (i.e., all explanatory variables included in lending practice selection equation but excluded from the loan-loss determination equation). The χ^2 values indicate that one can reject the null hypothesis that the coefficients on the identifying terms are all zero (where $p < .001$).

The results for business loan-loss determination also agree with my prior expectations. Gross charge-offs on business loans are positively related to both performing and nonperforming loans. As expected, nonperforming loans have a much larger influence on loan losses than do performing loans. For example, in Table 5 we see that for the 1996–1997 period estimates, a 1 percent increase in performing business loans will increase annual loan charge-off rates 0.003 percent; however, the same increase in nonperforming loans will increase the charge-off rate 0.10 percent. As was the case for business lending-practice selection, equity capitalization is generally not statistically significant. The allowance for loan losses, however, is positively related to business loan losses. As was the case for the selection of business lending practices, I find that measures of state economic conditions are not statistically significant in the loss determination model.

I now come to the main result of this study, the influence of lending practices on loan losses. Table 5 summarizes that low-risk business lending practices reduce business loan charge-offs rates. The economic significance of lending practices is large. To see this, I return to the results in Table 5 for 1996–1997. If a bank exhibited low-risk business lending practices as of time $t-4$, the business loan charge-off rate (as a percentage of gross loans and leases) would fall approximately 0.20 percent. To appreciate the magnitude of this decline, one should recall that the mean business loan charge-off rate for the March 1996–March 2009 period is 0.23 percent (Table 3). Finally, the coefficient for the hazard rate is, in general, not statistically significant in Table 5 indicating that the correction for the endogeneity of business lending practices does not appear to be necessary.

Table 5. Business Loan-Loss Determination by Estimation Period.

Variable	b (SE)						
	1996–1997	1998–1999	2000–2001	2002–2003	2004–2005	2006–2007	2008–2009
Performing business loans/gross loans ($t-5$)	0.003*** (0.001)	0.003*** (0.001)	0.003*** (0.001)	0.002*** (0.000)	0.002*** (0.000)	0.002*** (0.000)	0.004*** (0.001)
Nonperforming business loans/gross loans ($t-5$)	0.105*** (0.006)	0.125*** (0.008)	0.113*** (0.008)	0.090*** (0.008)	0.091*** (0.007)	0.096*** (0.008)	0.121*** (0.012)
Equity/assets ($t-5$)	0.004 (0.003)	0.001 (0.002)	0.002 (0.002)	−0.002 (0.002)	0.003* (0.002)	−0.002 (0.001)	−0.004** (0.002)
Allowance for loan losses/assets ($t-5$)	0.151*** (0.020)	0.102*** (0.018)	0.142*** (0.016)	0.214*** (0.016)	0.210*** (0.014)	0.085*** (0.014)	0.143*** (0.021)
State unemployment growth rate ($t-5$)	−0.011*** (0.003)	0.002 (0.002)	−0.001 (0.002)	0.000 (0.001)	0.001 (0.002)	0.000 (0.001)	0.003 (0.002)
Low-risk business lending practices ($t-4$)	−0.198*** (0.040)	−0.135*** (0.037)	−0.170*** (0.031)	−0.153*** (0.031)	−0.234*** (0.030)	−0.093*** (0.026)	−0.160*** (0.040)
Hazard	0.015 (0.029)	0.034 (0.025)	0.013 (0.022)	−0.001 (0.020)	0.068 (0.020)	0.005 (0.017)	0.0056 (0.027)
n	1,380	2,746	3,138	3,246	3,187	3,070	1,818

*$p<.10$, **$p<.05$, ***$p<.01$.

Tables 6 and 7 present the results of estimation of the treatment effects model for consumer loans. The results for consumer loans are very similar to those obtained for business loans. (In the interest of brevity, I will henceforth point out only important differences and other interesting results.) In contrast to the results for business loans, I find that performing consumer loans are negatively related to the selection of low-risk consumer lending practices. One possible explanation for this result is that higher concentrations of consumer loans pose greater generic lending risk than do concentration of business loans. The effect of concentrations of consumer loans on practice selection (holding the mix of performing and nonperforming consumer loans constant) is measured by the sum of the coefficients on performing and nonperforming consumer loans. The results for my measures of hierarchical banking organizations indicate that the hypothesized relationships between organization form and lending practices do not extend to consumer lending. Finally, banking market competition, as measured by the HHI for deposit market share, is not related to the selection of low-risk consumer lending practices.

The results for consumer loan-loss determination agree with my prior expectations. Gross charge-offs on consumer loans are positively related to both performing and nonperforming loans. As expected, nonperforming loans have a much larger influence on loan losses than do performing loans. For example, in Table 7, we see that in the 1996–1997 period, a 1 percent increase in performing consumer loans will increase annual loan charge-off rates 0.009 percent; however, the same increase in nonperforming loans will increase the charge-off rate 0.60 percent. Table 7 also summarizes that consumer loan losses are, in general, positively related to mortgage foreclosure rates. Importantly, as for business loans, I find a strong negative relationship between the selection of low-risk consumer lending practices and subsequent loan losses. The economic significance of lending practices is also very large for consumer loans. For example, Table 7 summarizes that for the 1996–1997 period, banks that exhibited low-risk consumer lending practices reduced consumer loan charge-off rates by approximately 0.26 percent. To gauge the magnitude of this decline, one should recall that the mean consumer loan charge-off rate for the March 1996–March 2009 period is 0.13 percent (Table 3).

Tables 8–13 present the results of estimation of the treatment effects model for three categories of real estate loans: construction and land development loans, commercial real estate loans, and home equity loans. Although the results are generally consistent with my prior expectations, the overall significance of the explanatory variables of the treatment effects

Table 6. Selection of Low-Risk Consumer Lending Practices by Estimation Period.

Variable	b (SE)						
	1996–1097	1998–1999	2000–2001	2002–2003	2004–2005	2006–2007	2008–2009
Constant	2.289***	0.963**	0.598	1.147**	0.474	−0.544	−1.363*
	(0.863)	(0.449)	(0.449)	(0.510)	(0.630)	(0.530)	(0.719)
Performing consumer loans/gross loans ($t-5$)	−0.012**	−0.014***	−0.008***	−0.018***	−0.021***	−0.009**	−0.014***
	(0.005)	(0.003)	(0.003)	(0.003)	(0.004)	(0.004)	(0.005)
Nonperforming consumer loans/gross loans ($t-5$)	−0.477***	−0.418***	−0.858***	−0.403***	−0.191**	−0.514***	−0.953***
	(0.151)	(0.076)	(0.114)	(0.098)	(0.088)	(0.163)	(0.248)
Equity/assets ($t-5$)	−0.001	0.018*	0.015	−0.003	0.014	0.010	0.048***
	(0.016)	(0.010)	(0.009)	(0.008)	(0.011)	(0.009)	(0.015)
Allowance for loan losses/assets ($t-5$)	−0.065	−0.121*	−0.109*	−0.194***	−0.242***	−0.256***	−0.320***
	(0.106)	(0.069)	(0.064)	(0.069)	(0.062)	(0.070)	(0.095)
Mortgage foreclosures as % of loans ($t-5$)	0.549	0.865**	−0.135	−0.730***	0.140	0.354	−0.050
	(0.568)	(0.405)	(0.308)	(0.227)	(0.263)	(0.280)	(0.266)
Management rating = 1 dummy ($t-5$)	1.010***	0.760***	0.833***	0.866***	0.980***	0.950***	1.060***
	(0.204)	(0.127)	(0.119)	(0.111)	(0.123)	(0.134)	(0.184)

Management rating = 2 dummy ($t-5$)	0.569***	0.416***	0.419***	0.324***	0.475***	0.450***	0.398***
	(0.142)	(0.106)	(0.102)	(0.095)	(0.098)	(0.109)	(0.142)
Member multibank holding co. dummy ($t-5$)	0.325**	0.092	0.192**	0.090	0.105	−0.015	−0.004
	(0.154)	(0.090)	(0.092)	(0.090)	(0.101)	(0.109)	(0.155)
log_e (assets) ($t-5$)	−0.101	−0.020	0.048	0.044	0.051	0.138***	0.193***
	(0.075)	(0.038)	(0.038)	(0.042)	(0.055)	(0.041)	(0.059)
Number of employees ($t-5$)	0.001	0.000	0.000	0.000	0.001	0.000	0.000
	(0.001)	(0.000)	(0.000)	(0.000)	(0.001)	(0.000)	(0.000)
Herfindahl–Hirschman Index/1000 ($t-5$)	−0.080**	0.002	−0.038*	−0.027	−0.019	−0.016	0.009
	(0.032)	(0.024)	(0.021)	(0.020)	(0.022)	(0.023)	(0.031)
n	1,286	2,247	2,838	2,751	2,511	2,202	1,283
Pseudo R^2	.12	.09	.14	.13	.14	.13	.18
χ^2	41.2***	40.1***	68.4***	87.3***	84.7***	71.8***	47.9***

*$p<.10$, **$p<.05$, ***$p<.01$.

Table 7. Consumer Loan-Loss Determination by Estimation Period.

Variable	b (SE)						
	1996–1997	1998–1999	2000–2001	2002–2003	2004–2005	2006–2007	2008–2009
Performing consumer loans/gross loans ($t-5$)	0.009*** (0.001)	0.015*** (0.001)	0.012*** (0.001)	0.011*** (0.001)	0.010*** (0.001)	0.016*** (0.001)	0.020*** (0.001)
Nonperforming consumer loans/gross loans ($t-5$)	0.604*** (0.034)	0.368*** (0.033)	0.203*** (0.031)	0.294*** (0.023)	0.382*** (0.017)	0.060** (0.026)	0.176*** (0.057)
Equity/assets ($t-5$)	0.001 (0.002)	0.009*** (0.003)	0.001 (0.002)	−0.001 (0.002)	−0.003** (0.001)	−0.001 (0.001)	0.001 (0.002)
Allowance for loan losses/assets ($t-5$)	0.091*** (0.016)	0.305*** (0.023)	0.301*** (0.014)	0.120*** (0.014)	0.091*** (0.009)	0.123*** (0.010)	0.105*** (0.018)
Mortgage foreclosures as % of loans ($t-5$)	0.316*** (0.081)	0.324** (0.127)	0.162*** (0.061)	0.032 (0.042)	0.057* (0.033)	−0.015 (0.038)	−0.006 (0.044)
Low-risk consumer lending practices ($t-4$)	−0.258*** (0.036)	−0.680*** (0.056)	−0.416*** (0.031)	−0.170*** (0.026)	−0.131*** (0.021)	−0.160*** (0.024)	−0.195*** (0.040)
Hazard	0.061*** (0.024)	0.3374*** (0.035)	0.1775*** (0.020)	0.023 (0.018)	0.048*** (0.014)	0.055*** (0.016)	0.0804*** (0.027)
n	1,286	2,247	2,838	2,751	2,511	2,202	1,283

*$p<.10$, **$p<.05$, ***$p<.01$.

Table 8. Selection of Low-Risk Construction and Land Development Lending Practices by Estimation Period.

Variable	b (SE)						
	1996–1997	1998–1999	2000–2001	2002–2003	2004–2005	2006–2007	2008–2009
Constant	8.457** (3.699)	3.299** (1.418)	4.250*** (1.430)	3.195*** (1.150)	6.312*** (2.141)	2.718** (1.355)	2.074* (1.102)
Performing construction loans/gross loans ($t-5$)	0.004 (0.021)	−0.011 (0.009)	−0.018** (0.008)	−0.006 (0.007)	0.002 (0.010)	−0.012** (0.005)	−0.011** (0.005)
Nonperforming construction loans/gross loans ($t-5$)	−0.394** (0.195)	−0.132 (0.212)	−0.375*** (0.128)	−0.274** (0.138)	−0.039 (0.131)	−0.175 (0.196)	−0.173*** (0.061)
Equity/assets ($t-5$)	−0.023 (0.046)	0.049 (0.033)	−0.017 (0.026)	−0.027 (0.017)	−0.009 (0.030)	0.064** (0.030)	0.027 (0.020)
Allowance for loan losses/assets ($t-5$)	−0.317 (0.304)	−0.166 (0.198)	0.018 (0.209)	−0.087 (0.181)	−0.372** (0.173)	−0.667*** (0.167)	−0.412** (0.162)
Mortgage foreclosures as % of loans ($t-5$)	−1.012 (1.102)	−0.477 (0.768)	0.585 (0.850)	−0.150 (0.554)	−0.152 (0.641)	−0.039 (0.459)	0.685** (0.337)
Management rating = 1 dummy ($t-5$)	0.577 (0.490)	0.537* (0.287)	0.544** (0.256)	0.738*** (0.242)	0.928*** (0.296)	0.250 (0.265)	0.383* (0.215)

Table 8. *(Continued)*

Variable	b (SE)						
	1996–1997	1998–1999	2000–2001	2002–2003	2004–2005	2006–2007	2008–2009
Management rating = 2 dummy ($t-5$)	0.641*	0.305	0.782***	0.490**	0.851***	0.133	0.264
	(0.371)	(0.232)	(0.252)	(0.203)	(0.248)	(0.231)	(0.190)
Member multibank holding co. dummy ($t-5$)	0.500	0.058	−0.215	0.108	6.962	−0.033	0.297
	(0.502)	(0.198)	(0.191)	(0.210)	0.000	(0.186)	(0.214)
log_e (assets) ($t-5$)	−0.536	−0.128	−0.176	−0.092	−0.370	−0.046	−0.067
	(0.343)	(0.127)	(0.120)	(0.091)	(0.177)	(0.107)	(0.083)
Number of employees ($t-5$)	0.009	0.001	0.001	0.000	0.002	0.000	0.000
	(0.006)	(0.001)	(0.001)	(0.001)	(0.002)	(0.001)	(0.000)
Herfindahl–Hirschman Index/1000 ($t-5$)	−0.067	−0.111**	−0.129***	0.025	0.034	0.045	0.083
	(0.082)	(0.044)	(0.044)	(0.056)	(0.071)	(0.051)	(0.053)
n	859	1,310	1,860	2,056	2,032	2,257	1,403
Pseudo R^2	.20	.07	.15	.07	.17	.10	.13
χ^2	6.0	10.2	19.8***	11.3*	14.8**	2.0	9.0

*$p<.10$, **$p<.05$, ***$p<.01$.

Table 9. Construction and Land Development Loan-Loss Determination by Estimation Period.

Variable	b (SE)						
	1996–1997	1998–1999	2000–2001	2002–2003	2004–2005	2006–2007	2008–2009
Performing construction loans/gross loans ($t-5$)	0.001 (0.000)	0.000*** (0.000)	0.000 (0.000)	0.001* (0.000)	0.000 (0.000)	0.001*** (0.000)	0.020*** (0.003)
Nonperforming construction loans/gross loans ($t-5$)	0.045*** (0.009)	0.005 (0.004)	0.072*** (0.006)	0.126*** (0.008)	0.066*** (0.006)	0.030*** (0.007)	0.341*** (0.056)
Equity/assets ($t-5$)	0.000 (0.001)	0.000 (0.000)	0.000 (0.001)	0.001** (0.001)	−0.001 (0.001)	0.001* (0.000)	−0.002 (0.008)
Allowance for loan losses/assets ($t-5$)	0.021*** (0.006)	0.006*** (0.002)	0.009** (0.004)	0.000 (0.006)	0.055*** (0.006)	0.017*** (0.005)	0.021 (0.105)
Mortgage foreclosures as % of loans ($t-5$)	0.066*** (0.023)	0.006 (0.009)	0.038** (0.016)	0.013 (0.017)	−0.001 (0.018)	0.022** (0.011)	0.489*** (0.188)
Low-risk construction lending practices ($t-4$)	−0.034*** (0.013)	−0.002 (0.004)	−0.015* (0.008)	−0.020* (0.011)	−0.038*** (0.013)	−0.033*** (0.008)	−0.507*** (0.180)
Hazard	0.045*** (0.011)	−0.002 (0.004)	−0.010 (0.007)	−0.010 (0.009)	−0.046*** (0.012)	−0.005 (0.007)	0.146 (0.129)
n	859	1,310	1,860	2,056	2,032	2,257	1,403

*$p < .10$, **$p < .05$, ***$p < .01$.

Table 10. Selection of Low-Risk Commercial Real Estate Lending Practices by Estimation Period.

Variable	b (SE)						
	1996–1997	1998–1999	2000–2001	2002–2003	2004–2005	2006–2007	2008–2009
Constant	11.292***	2.221	3.580***	5.424***	4.508***	4.439***	1.409
	(4.233)	(1.922)	(1.122)	(1.124)	(1.341)	(1.381)	(1.486)
Performing commercial real estate loans/gross loans ($t-5$)	0.010	0.015	−0.004	−0.003	0.001	0.000	−0.003
	(0.015)	(0.009)	(0.005)	(0.006)	(0.005)	(0.005)	(0.006)
Nonperforming commercial real estate loans/gross loans ($t-5$)	−0.121	−0.179*	−0.282**	−0.190**	−0.072	−0.236***	0.117
	(0.135)	(0.107)	(0.124)	(0.089)	(0.092)	(0.075)	(0.128)
Equity/assets ($t-5$)	0.005	0.055	0.018	0.023	−0.007	0.004	0.076**
	(0.049)	(0.038)	(0.024)	(0.030)	(0.018)	(0.017)	(0.030)
Allowance for loan losses/assets ($t-5$)	−0.192	0.195	0.047	−0.294**	−0.200*	−0.438***	−0.547***
	(0.372)	(0.242)	(0.183)	(0.126)	(0.120)	(0.121)	(0.163)
Mortgage foreclosures as % of loans ($t-5$)	−0.747	−0.671	−0.802	−0.813	0.223	−0.454	−0.038
	(1.327)	(0.932)	(0.550)	(0.591)	(0.450)	(0.398)	(0.340)
Management rating = 1 dummy ($t-5$)	5.051	1.128***	0.590**	1.504***	1.510***	0.237	0.512**
	0.000	(0.319)	(0.230)	(0.377)	(0.349)	(0.216)	(0.238)

Management rating = 2 dummy ($t-5$)	0.680	0.798***	0.367*	0.500**	0.513***	0.209	0.337*
	(0.451)	(0.221)	(0.199)	(0.200)	(0.164)	(0.186)	(0.197)
Member multibank holding co. dummy ($t-5$)	−0.372	−0.266	0.100	0.010	0.390	0.448**	0.177
	(0.446)	(0.207)	(0.177)	(0.213)	(0.236)	(0.221)	(0.220)
log_e (assets) ($t-5$)	−0.776**	−0.114	−0.115	−0.235***	−0.245**	−0.175	−0.004
	(0.385)	(0.181)	(0.096)	(0.087)	(0.117)	(0.118)	(0.126)
Number of employees ($t-5$)	0.006	0.005	0.000	0.000	0.002	0.003	0.001
	(0.004)	(0.004)	(0.001)	(0.000)	(0.001)	(0.002)	(0.002)
Herfindahl–Hirschman Index/1000 ($t-5$)	−0.100	−0.060	−0.110***	−0.123***	−0.014	−0.002	0.014
	(0.100)	(0.054)	(0.035)	(0.042)	(0.040)	(0.040)	(0.052)
n	1,113	2,076	2,474	2,758	2,737	2,706	1,627
Pseudo R^2	.27	.14	.08	.20	.13	.09	.10
χ^2	7.6	20.5**	16.8**	27.7***	25.9***	8.7	8.6

*$p < .10$, **$p < .05$, ***$p < .01$.

Table 11. Commercial Real Estate Loan-Loss Determination by Estimation Period.

Variable	b (SE)						
	1996–1997	1998–1999	2000–2001	2002–2003	2004–2005	2006–2007	2008–2009
Performing commercial real estate loans/gross loans ($t-5$)	0.000 (0.000)	0.000 (0.000)	0.000* (0.000)	0.000 (0.000)	0.000 (0.000)	0.001* (0.000)	0.000 (0.000)
Nonperforming commercial real estate loans/gross loans ($t-5$)	0.030*** (0.006)	0.065*** (0.004)	0.040*** (0.005)	0.049*** (0.005)	0.059*** (0.005)	0.045*** (0.008)	0.115*** (0.008)
Equity/assets ($t-5$)	−0.001 (0.001)	−0.002** (0.001)	0.000 (0.001)	0.000 (0.001)	−0.001 (0.001)	0.000 (0.001)	−0.001 (0.001)
Allowance for loan losses/assets ($t-5$)	0.077*** (0.009)	0.016*** (0.005)	0.007 (0.004)	0.053*** (0.007)	0.061*** (0.006)	0.017* (0.009)	0.055*** (0.012)
Mortgage foreclosures as % of loans ($t-5$)	0.207*** (0.035)	0.030 (0.020)	0.015 (0.015)	0.021 (0.020)	0.041** (0.017)	0.036 (0.022)	0.055** (0.022)
Low-risk commercial real estate lending practices ($t-4$)	−0.099*** (0.016)	0.000 (0.010)	−0.004 (0.008)	−0.042*** (0.014)	−0.053*** (0.013)	−0.028 (0.017)	−0.054** (0.021)
Hazard	0.019 (0.025)	−0.002 (0.010)	−0.001 (0.007)	0.000 (0.013)	0.009 (0.010)	−0.004 (0.014)	0.007 (0.017)
n	1,113	2,076	2,474	2,758	2,737	2,706	1,627

*$p<.10$, **$p<.05$, ***$p<.01$.

Table 12. Selection of Low-Risk Home Equity Lending Practices by Estimation Period.

Variable	b (SE)						
	1996–1997	1998–1999	2000–2001	2002–2003	2004–2005	2006–2007	2008–2009
Constant	2.968 (5.458)	5.100 (0.000)	2.666 (2.116)	5.850*** (2.037)	1.284 (1.823)	2.536 (1.961)	1.845 (3.127)
Performing home equity loans/gross loans ($t-5$)	−0.018 (0.015)	0.009 (0.011)	0.008 (0.009)	−0.004 (0.008)	−0.007 (0.006)	−0.002 (0.008)	−0.007 (0.009)
Nonperforming home equity loans/gross loans ($t-5$)	1190.715 (0.000)	7.152 (14.772)	−1.655 (1.136)	1.088 (1.188)	0.143 (0.355)	−0.186 (0.178)	−0.199 (0.270)
Equity/assets ($t-5$)	0.059 (0.102)	0.214 (0.149)	0.024 (0.061)	0.039 (0.065)	0.116* (0.067)	0.041 (0.060)	0.224** (0.097)
Allowance for loan losses/assets ($t-5$)	0.382 (0.936)	0.476 (0.759)	0.217 (0.524)	0.031 (0.377)	−0.183 (0.244)	−0.199 (0.391)	−0.590 (0.376)
Mortgage foreclosures as % of loans ($t-5$)	1.823 (3.107)	0.417 (1.652)	0.558 (1.665)	1.267 (1.279)	−0.791 (0.787)	0.371 (0.916)	1.243 (1.008)
Management rating = 1 dummy ($t-5$)	5.586 (0.000)	0.747 (0.000)	0.635 (0.583)	1.191*** (0.438)	0.154 (0.413)	0.401 (0.476)	−1.119 (0.996)

Table 12. *(Continued)*

Variable	b (SE)						
	1996–1997	1998–1999	2000–2001	2002–2003	2004–2005	2006–2007	2008–2009
Management rating = 2 dummy ($t-5$)	0.750 (0.615)	−4.380 (3.944)	0.175 (0.485)	6.402 (0.000)	0.271 (0.383)	0.257 (0.425)	−0.903 (0.949)
Member multibank holding co. dummy ($t-5$)	4.862 (0.000)	−0.383 (0.459)	0.155 (0.433)	0.107 (0.453)	0.337 (0.396)	0.170 (0.395)	5.257 0.000
log_e (assets) ($t-5$)	−0.145 (0.518)	−0.168 (0.343)	−0.128 (0.153)	−0.428*** (0.154)	0.006 (0.125)	−0.062 (0.136)	−0.099 (0.226)
Number of employees ($t-5$)	0.000 (0.009)	0.001 (0.003)	0.000 (0.000)	0.000 (0.000)	0.000 (0.000)	0.000*** (0.000)	0.001 (0.002)
Herfindahl–Hirschman Index/1000 ($t-5$)	−0.024 (0.200)	0.391 (0.314)	0.210 (0.211)	0.098 (0.140)	0.239 (0.150)	0.082 (0.111)	0.196 (0.165)
n	531	614	1,253	1,299	1,218	1,212	744
Pseudo R^2	.27	.26	.18	.39	.11	.21	.23
χ^2	1.51	17.07***	9.14	15.22**	5.41	8.53	2.93

*$p<.10$, **$p<.05$, ***$p<.01$.

Table 13. Home Equity Loan-Loss Determination by Estimation Period.

Variable	b (SE)						
	1996–1997	1998–1999	2000–2001	2002–2003	2004–2005	2006–2007	2008–2009
Performing home equity loans/gross loans ($t-5$)	0.000 (0.000)	0.001** (0.000)	0.000 (0.000)	0.000** (0.000)	0.000* (0.000)	0.000 (0.000)	0.001* (0.000)
Nonperforming home equity loans/gross loans ($t-5$)	0.114*** (0.013)	0.086 (0.095)	0.033 (0.023)	0.060*** (0.007)	0.059*** (0.006)	0.015*** (0.004)	0.089*** (0.012)
Equity/assets ($t-5$)	−0.001* (0.000)	−0.004 (0.002)	0.001*** (0.000)	−0.001*** (0.000)	−0.001* (0.001)	0.001 (0.000)	−0.002* (0.001)
Allowance for loan losses/assets ($t-5$)	0.011*** (0.003)	−0.011 (0.020)	−0.006 (0.004)	0.037*** (0.005)	0.042*** (0.005)	0.046*** (0.006)	0.133*** (0.018)
Mortgage foreclosures as % of loans ($t-5$)	0.030*** (0.011)	−0.062 (0.082)	0.022* (0.013)	0.046*** (0.013)	0.047*** (0.015)	0.066*** (0.012)	0.150*** (0.028)
Low-risk home equity lending practices ($t-4$)	−0.010 (0.006)	0.037 (0.044)	−0.009 (0.007)	−0.031*** (0.009)	−0.039*** (0.012)	−0.058*** (0.010)	−0.163*** (0.033)
Hazard	0.005 (0.008)	−0.017 (0.049)	−0.008 (0.008)	0.001 (0.011)	0.014 (0.010)	0.016* (0.010)	0.084*** (0.029)
n	531	614	1,253	1,299	1,218	1,212	744

*$p<.10$, **$p<.05$, ***$p<.01$.

models is weaker than is seen for business and consumer loans. I do find, however, that lending practices are important determinants of real estate loan-loss rates, particularly in the post-2002 period. I believe the weak results for real estate loans are largely due to the very low loss rates experienced during most of the sample period (Table 3).

Consistency of Multivariate Results

The biannual estimations of the treatment effects models can be used to assess the stability of the results over the March 1996–March 2009 period. The results for loan-loss determination show the consistent importance of lending practices for business, consumer, and commercial real estate loans. Low-risk lending practices are, in general, negatively related to gross loan charge-offs (as a percentage of gross loans and leases) for these three categories of loans, and there do not appear to be systematic changes in the effects of lending practices on loan losses over time. For construction and home equity loans, however, there does appear to be systematic variation in the influence of lending practices on loan losses. Specifically, the reduction in loan charge-offs associated with low-risk lending practices for construction and home equity loans is substantially greater in the 2008–2009 period than in prior periods. One possible reason for this latter result might be a larger qualitative difference in lending standards between my measures of "high-risk" and "low-risk" construction and home equity lenders in the 2008–2009 estimation than occurs in prior periods. Alternatively, the unprecedented severity of commercial and residential property market prices declines in 2008 and 2009 may have exposed high-risk lenders to greater losses than in prior periods.

Relevance to Non-U.S. Banks

To judge the applicability of these results to non-U.S. banking markets, I begin with a review of the chapter's sample and data. This chapter examines the determinants of lending practices and the influence of those practices on credit risk for FDIC-supervised banks over the period June 1996–March 2009. FDIC-supervised banks comprise the majority of U.S banks, averaging 58 percent of all FDIC-insured banks for the study period. The five categories of lending included in the FDIC loan underwriting survey comprise all major business and consumer loan categories for U.S.

banks, except residential mortgages. Importantly, the FDIC survey assesses lending practices in terms of their riskiness, focusing on those basic practices known to have contributed to the 1980s and early 1990s U.S. banking crises. On the basis of these features of the data, the chapter's scope in terms of lending practices, loan types, time periods, and coverage of U.S. banking markets is quite broad. A significant limitation of the sample, however, is its focus on smaller, community banks. I next discuss this limitation and its relevance to my findings.

As discussed previously, the vast majority of FDIC-supervised banks are small, community banks. Whereas the FDIC supervised 58 percent of banks on average for the study period, these banks only held 19 percent of industry assets. Large, complex, multinational banking organizations differ from community banks in many fundamental ways, most notably in their risk exposures (e.g., foreign exchange rates, off-balance-sheet commitments, and financial derivatives) and in their risk management practices. The current financial crisis has shown, however, that weaknesses in basic lending standards, combined with risky credit concentrations, stress in underlying collateral markets, and declines in borrower income can result in financial distress for any banking organization. For these reasons, I believe my results are broadly applicable to European and many other non-U.S. banking markets. For those non-U.S. economies that differ significantly from the United States in terms of the level of financial market competition, bank supervision, and closure policies, the results might be less applicable, however. For example, government support programs for borrowers will mitigate the adverse effects of weak lending practices on loan losses.[23]

CONCLUSIONS

I find that loan losses for business, consumer and three categories of real estate loans are strongly influenced by loan underwriting practices, as characterized by the frequency of specific risky practices. I also find evidence that lending practices for business loans are determined by banks' prior-period financial performance, management quality, hierarchical complexity, and market competition, but these factors are not strongly related to consumer and real estate lending practices. I base these conclusions on estimates of two-step treatment effects models that control for the endogeneity of dummy explanatory variables for lending practices.

These findings add to the literature on loan-loss determination in two important ways. First, this is the first study to present evidence of lending practice selection for specific types of loans, with the practices being characterized by their risk to the bank. I believe that the dependent variables in the practice selection models (FDIC-underwriting-survey data on practices) are direct measures of actual lending practices rather than proxies for practices. Importantly, FDIC-underwriting-survey data on lending practices are defined in terms of the risk of practices known to have led to bank and thrift failures. Second, I find that lending practices have statistically significant and economically large effects on loan portfolio losses. I believe these findings reinforce the usefulness of bank supervisors' monitoring of bank loan underwriting practices and show that underwriting practices are altered as market conditions change. This latter result is a useful explanation of the need for frequent on-site examinations, as required by FDICIA (1991) and explains previous research showing that the informational content of bank examination ratings deteriorates quickly.[24]

These findings also underscore the important influence of lending practices for the stability of individual banks and the financial system as a whole. In response to the current financial crisis, the United States and other Group of Twenty (G20) nations developed proposals for strengthening financial market supervision and regulation.[25] To achieve this goal, the G20 countries have undertaken a number of initiatives, four of which are related to lending practices: (1) enhance financial market regulation, (2) strengthen financial transparency, (3) reduce procyclicality in the financial system, and (4) improve macro-prudential supervision. With regard to enhancing financial market regulation, the United States and other G20 nations seek to strengthen adherence to international regulatory and prudential standards and to expand the scale and scope of regulation to ensure that significant gaps in financial market regulation are eliminated. For example, a contributing factor to the U.S. subprime real estate crisis was the growth of mortgage brokers and nonbank mortgage lenders, many of whom engaged in high-risk lending practices. U.S. bank regulators have also admitted to lapses in bank supervision, such as ineffective or slow responses to risky lending practices, as a contributing factor in the recent wave of U.S. bank failures. With regard to financial transparency, many U.S. banks and financial institutions effectively outsourced credit analysis of mortgage-backed securities and related products to credit rating agencies (CRAs) during the years preceding the current crisis. CRAs were later found to have been overly lenient when assigning credit risk ratings to mortgage-backed securities and their issuers, in part due to conflicts of interests resulting from multiple business relationships with securities issuers. Regulatory reform of financial transparency is intended to allow investors in asset-backed securities and related products to better understand the risks of the underlying assets (loans). Similarly, improvement in the financial transparency of banks, securities issuers, and financial conglomerates will improve market discipline. While current initiatives for reducing the procyclicality of financial markets do not specifically address lending standards, the findings of this chapter suggest that risk measures based on lending standards can serve as leading indicators of risk and, therefore, could be applied by counter-cyclical supervisory strategies. Finally, macro-prudential assessments of financial sector vulnerability to stress would benefit greatly from a thorough understanding of bank lending practices and their inherent risks.

NOTES

1. According to International Monetary Fund (IMF) (2009a), CRAs pursuing security issuers' fees "diluted risk assessments" of the mortgage loans that served as collateral for securities. Hedge funds and other investors, also failed to conduct due diligence, accepted CRA risk assessments, overestimated the protection of credit enhancements and underestimated liquidity risk.
2. O'Keefe, Olin, and Richardson (2003) find a relationship between the riskiness of general lending practices and total nonperforming assets but do not investigate the importance of lending standards for specific types of loan portfolios. Their study uses supervisory assessments of lending standards obtained from the FDIC Examination Supplement on Current [Loan] Underwriting Standards.
3. Group of Twenty Finance Ministers and Central Bank Governors (2009, April 2).
4. To measure credit standards using the senior loan officer survey, Berger and Udell (2002) use a single question taken from the survey: "over the past three months, how have your bank's credit standards for approving loan applications for C&I loans or credit lines changed?" Respondents can pick one of five possible answers: tightened considerably, tightened somewhat, remained basically unchanged, eased somewhat, and eased considerably.
5. Berger and Udell (2002) state that in the paper their main indicator of lending standards is commercial loan growth.
6. Berger and Udell (2002, p. 2) state, "Although the institutional memory hypothesis is rooted in the bank's own loan performance problems rather than the aggregate business cycle, this hypothesis may help explain the stylized facts about bank lending over the aggregate cycle because banks tend to experience problem loans simultaneously."
7. As of March 31, 2009, the number and total assets of FDIC-supervised banks (industry shares in parentheses) were 4,660 (57 percent) and $1,996 billion (15 percent), respectively.
8. In this study, I focus on the loan-level survey questions for all categories of loans covered in the survey except agricultural loans and credit card loans. The reasons for the two exclusions are the relatively low risk currently in agricultural

loans and the very small number of credit card lenders in the sample. The survey does not include questions on residential mortgage loans.

9. See Greene (2003, pp. 787–789) for a discussion of treatment effects models.

10. The survey definitions for these frequency categories are (1) never or infrequently: the institution does not engage in the practice, or does so only to an extent that does not warrant notice by bank supervisors; (2) frequently enough to warrant notice: the institution engages in the practice often enough for it to be brought to the attention of bank supervisors; there may or may not be factors that offset the risks the practice imposes on the institution; and (3) commonly or as standard procedure: the practice is either common or standard at the institution and therefore should be brought to the attention of bank supervisors; there may or may not be factors that offset the risks the practice imposes on the institution.

11. I find that for individual lending practices that there is about an 80–90 percent correspondence in ratings of low risk across lending practices within a loan category.

12. I also estimated the selection model for each surveyed lending practice within loan categories separately using a binary dependent variable to indicate low- and high-risk lending practice selection. As before, survey responses of "never or infrequently" for individual practices are interpreted as low risk and all other responses interpreted as high risk. The results of estimations of the selection model using individual practices were very similar to those based on my summary risk practice measure for each loan category.

13. The FDIC underwriting survey provides detailed descriptions of the loan categories. Using those descriptions, I relate the survey loan categories to loans reported in quarterly financial statements banks are required to file with their supervisors (Call Reports) as follows: "business loans" include traditional commercial and industrial loans and business loans collateralized by real estate (commercial and agricultural real estate, excluding commercial real estate development loans); "construction loans" are construction and land development loans, including both commercial and residential real estate development; "permanent commercial (nonresidential) real estate loans" are a Call Report loan category; and "consumer loans" are all installment loans to households and individuals for personal (nonbusiness) use, except credit card loans. Finally, home equity loans are a Call Report loan category. Loan charge-offs are those for the corresponding loan categories. Note that as defined the loan categories overlap where business loans are secured by real estate.

14. In sum, for the lending practice selection model, I relate lending practices selected in one quarter to bank financial performance in the prior quarter as well as to other nonfinancial variables in the prior quarter. Quarterly loan losses tend to exhibit seasonality, however. To avoid the seasonality problem, I exclude loan losses from the practice selection model and use annual loan losses in the loss determination model.

15. I chose not to include dummy variables to indicate for management ratings of "3", "4," and "5" due to the relatively low number of ratings of "3" or worse over my sample period.

16. Specifically, lending practices are observations from an FDIC examination that took place between 365 and 455 days before the end date used for loss measurement in Eq. (2).

17. The beginning and ending dates for the empirical analysis are based on those dates for which the treatment effects model could be estimated.

18. All estimations of the treatment effects model use full biannual periods except the 1996–1997 and 2008–2009 periods. Due to data limitations, the 1996–1997 model estimations begin in June 1996 and end in December 1997. The 2008–2009 model estimations begin in March 2008 and end in March 2009.

19. I eliminate all observations in which reported performing and nonperforming loans for a loan category exceed 100 percent of gross loans and leases or are less than zero. Similarly, observations where loss rates are less than –1 percent or greater than 100 percent of gross loans and leases are eliminated.

20. As robustness checks, I tested alternative measures of state-level macroeconomic conditions, including the growth rate in real per capita income, growth in the rate of personal loan delinquencies, and the mortgage foreclosure rate. The results for these macroeconomic control variables are very similar to those for the growth in state unemployment rates.

21. The pseudo R^2 is defined here as one minus the ratio of the log likelihood function maximized with all the explanatory variables in the model to the value of the log likelihood function maximized with none of the explanatory variables (intercept only) in the model. Thus, this pseudo R^2 statistic does not control for the number of parameters estimated and should not be used to compare models when the number of explanatory variables is significantly different.

22. See, for example, Berger and Udell (2002).

23. For example, U.S. government support programs for farmers no doubt lessen the impact of weak lending standards on agricultural banks' performance.

24. Hirtle and Lopez (1999) estimate that the private supervisory information contained in CAMELS ratings decays within 6–12 quarters of an examination. They state that the decay occurs more quickly for banks with composite CAMELS ratings of 3, 4, or 5 than for well-rated banks.

25. See Group of Twenty Finance Ministers and Central Bank Governors (2009, April 2) and Financial Stability Board (2010, April).

REFERENCES

Berger, A. N., Miller, N. H., Peterson, M. A., Rajan, R. G., & Stein, J. C. (2002). *Does function follow organizational form? Evidence from the lending practices of large and small banks*. Discussion Paper no. 1976. Harvard University, Harvard Institute of Economic Research, Cambridge, MA.

Berger, A. N., & Udell, G. F. (2002). *The institutional memory hypothesis and the procyclicality of bank lending behavior*. Finance and Economics Discussion Series no. 2003-02. Board of Governors of the Federal Reserve System, Washington, DC.

Cole, R. A., Goldberg, L. G., & White, L. J. (2004). Cookie cutter vs. character: The micro structure of small business lending by large and small banks. *Journal of Financial and Quantitative Analysis*, *39*(2), 227–251.

Dahl, D., O'Keefe, J., & Hanweck, G. A. (1998). The influence of examiners and auditors on loan-loss recognition. *FDIC Banking Review*, *11*(4), 10–25.

Dell'Ariccia, G., Igan, D., & Laeven, L. (2008). *Credit booms and lending standards: Evidence from the subprime mortgage market.* IMF Working Paper 08/106. International Monetary Fund, Washington, DC.

Dell'Ariccia, G., & Marquez, R. (2006). Lending booms and lending standards. *The Journal of Finance, 51*(5), 2511–2546.

Federal Deposit Insurance Corporation. (1997). *History of the eighties, lessons for the future, vol. 1: An examination of the banking crises of the 1980s and early 1990s.* Washington, DC: Federal Deposit Insurance Corporation.

Financial Stability Board. (2010). *Progress since the St Andrews meeting in implementing the G20 recommendations for strengthening financial stability*, April. Report of the Financial Stability Board to G20 Finance Ministers and Governors. Available at http://www.financialstabilityboard.org/publications/r_100419.pdf. Retrieved from Financial Stability Board.

Greene, W. H. (2003). *Econometric analysis.* Upper Saddle River, NJ: Prentice Hall.

Group of Twenty Finance Ministers and Central Bank Governors. (2009). Leaders statement – the global plan for recovery and reform, April 2. Available at http://www.g20.org/Documents/final-communique.pdf

Hirtle, B. J., & Lopez, J. A. (1999). Supervisory information and the frequency of bank examinations. *Economic Policy Review, Federal Reserve Bank of New York*, *5*(1), 1–19.

International Monetary Fund. (2009a). *Initial lessons of the crisis.* IMF Staff Paper 09/37. International Monetary Fund, Washington, DC.

International Monetary Fund. (2009b). *Lessons of the global crisis for macroeconomic policy.* IMF Staff Paper 09/37. International Monetary Fund, Washington, DC.

Office of the Comptroller of the Currency. (1988). *Bank failure: An evaluation of the factors contributing to the failure of national banks.* Washington, DC: Office of the Comptroller of the Currency.

O'Keefe, J., Olin, V., & Richardson, C. (2003). *Bank loan underwriting practices: Can supervisory assessments contribute to early warning systems*? FDIC Working Paper 2003-06. Federal Deposit Insurance Corporation, Washington, DC.

Rajan, R. G. (1994). Why bank credit policies fluctuate: A theory and some evidence. *Quarterly Journal of Economics, 109*(2), 399–441.

Stein, J.C. (2000). *Information production and capital allocation: Decentralized vs. hierarchical firms.* Working Paper 7705. National Bureau of Economic Research, Cambridge, MA.

Weinberg, J. A. (1995). Cycles in lending standards? *Economic Quarterly, Federal Reserve Bank of Richmond, 81*(3), 1–18.

BANKS, ABS'S AND CDS'S: INFORMATION PRODUCTION, RISK BEARING, AND INCENTIVE COMPATIBILITY

Thi Ngoc Tuan Bui, Thi Tuong Van Nguyen and Piet Sercu

ABSTRACT

Purpose – *We discuss the microeconomic pros and cons of bankloan-backed securities and credit default swaps, that is, the passing on of bank loans or their default risk from originator to the general investor. By 'micro' we mean that our focus is on comparative advantages for banks versus other holders of the loans or risks, not the macro pros and cons of higher credit volumes.*

Methodology/approach – *We apply standard ideas from the corporate finance literature on the choice between loans versus public debt, related to information asymmetries and signaling at the time of origination. We also add new arguments related the possibly unhappy end of the loan.*

Findings – *Quite apart of the by now familiar quality-preservation incentive issue we think that securitization and CDS destroy value because*

International Banking in the New Era: Post-Crisis Challenges and Opportunities
International Finance Review, Volume 11, 315–333

ISSN: 1569-3767/doi:10.1108/S1569-3767(2010)0000011014

they move loans and risks away from the party best informed about the risk and best placed to deal with default toward worse-placed parties. Limitations – *The analysis takes the volume of loans as given.*

Practical/social implications – *ABS and CDS should be confined to the highest-quality type of chapter where no information asymmetries exist, like in Europe where the traditional MBS have not caused problems for centuries.*

Originality/value of the paper – *To the best of our knowledge, the literature on bank loans versus public debt has not been applied to ABS/CDS before, whereas the issue of who is best placed to bear the risks has not even been raised elsewhere.*

INTRODUCTION

The subprime crisis and the ensuing credit crunch had many roots and causes. This text focuses on a subset: the bankers' incentives, the information asymmetries, and the ensuing conflicts of interest and agency problems that arise when flawed instruments are being introduced. The macrocircumstances, which are familiar enough, we will not discuss again. At our chosen microlevel we bring up the bonuses etc. only tangentially – not because we think they were unimportant but because it's again a familiar issue; in our view, there are more stories going on, and more subtle stories, than bonuses. And, to end this preamble, we recognize that most individual bankers all over the world did avoid the excesses we describe below and continued to do a good job at traditional Main Street banking; the problem was that enough of them did not do a good job from any point of view but their own monetary interests.

Our main arguments can be summarized as follows. For borrowers, about whom there is a substantial information asymmetry, bank loans have long been accepted as the more rational solution relative to public debt: compared to dispersed individual investors, banks often have better incentives to produce information, they get more information, they are typically better at using it, and they are also better placed to deal with default, both ex ante and ex post. Given that banks are superior at assessing and bearing risk, it makes no economic sense, from a social perspective, to shift those risks to other parties via ABS and CDS contracts, thus undoing all comparative advantages of bank debt. In addition, new incentive issues crop up, beside the now universally recognized problem of the issuer's care about the quality of the underlying loans. The issuer's information advantage means that buyers are likely to be overcharged, and rating agencies have been found to be more part of this adverse-selection problem than part of its solution. In the case of CDS contracts, in addition, the product is likely – and perhaps even designed – to attract relatively more overconfident noise traders than do standard corporate bonds. Lastly, in the event of financial distress, incentives to find a rational solution are absent or even reversed. These problems are not solved by forcing banks to retain a segment of each ABS issue: one also needs the ABS to be default free in the first place. This rule may look hard to enforce given the bankers' personal incentives, but banks in Denmark and Germany have pulled this off for centuries. For CDS contracts, the problems in remediation seem insurmountable, involving moral hazard, adverse selection, and inefficient renegotiations or reorganizations when the borrower does get into financial distress.

Our economic analysis starts with a description of how bankers' incentives started shifting, in the 1980s, toward the volume of dealmaking, both in the fields and at headquarters. For our purposes, the main shift in headquarters' incentives came from securitization of debt, the conversion of private bank loans into publicly traded instruments, and from Basle I, Basle I-bis, and the thirst for AAA instruments. Securitization brings us to a discussion of the role of banks and the pros and cons of bank loans versus public debt. The hunt for AAA instruments helped to promote the emergence of CDS contracts, which brings us again to the pros and cons of debt insurance in general and to CDS in particular.

INCENTIVE SHIFTS IN THE FIELDS AND AT HQS

Traditionally, commercial bankers were not too far from their then caricature: pinstriped, conservative nine-to-fivers who worked in their local branch for decades and received a modest share in their agency's net contribution to the bank's overall (and equally modest) corporate profits. As of the 1980s – in Europe, the change must have come earlier in the United States – the incentives started shifting, and local managers' compensations became based on the deal's putative NPV rather than on the gradually realized profits, or even on the gross turnover.[1] As intended, the faster remuneration meant greater incentives to initiate deals, especially since bankers no longer staid put in one place for ages. The concomitant risk, of course, was that loan officers and branch managers might myopically focus on turnover, or on accounting profits – maximizing the difference between interest received and interest paid, which often means maximizing risk – at the cost of ignoring the too-distant-looking and hard-to-model default issues. This long-run perspective was supposedly taken care of by the credit committees at HQ, the internal vetters. But even at HQs the incentives started shifting when loans were no longer carried till maturity by the bank, as they always had been. Instead, as we all know, loans were increasingly often put into a portfolio, and claims against that portfolio were then flogged to the public. Familiarly, when this started in New York in the 1980s, these portfolios contained prime mortgage loans (mortgage-backed securities or mortgage-backed obligations), following long-standing practice in Denmark and Germany (Pfandbriefe) and the example of Fanny Mae and Freddy Mac. Equally familiarly, later on also student, car, and credit card loans and, in the end, anything and everything was repackaged and resold as collateralized debt obligations (CDOs) or ABS, including, crucially, low-quality loans.

Tables 1 and 2 summarize the evolution of the total ABS market and its subsections (like mortgages, car loans, etc.), showing, respectively, annual net issues and cumulative net outstanding values. In the 10 years, 1996–2005, the total volume issued rose almost fivefold, i.e. by 16 percent compound per year. The big items were, familiarly, home loans, followed at a great distance by credit card, car, and student loans. Home loans were already biggest in 1996; but also in terms of growth rates they were the best performer, with a compound growth of almost 30% p.a. Outstanding volumes rose, of course, correspondingly, except that the marked drop in issuing volumes as of 2007 and especially 2008 is, of course, absent in the outstanding volumes. Fig. 1 pictures the evolutions of the total issuance and outstanding volumes. This growth resulted from fast-rising volumes of loans granted by banks, compounded by an increasing tendency to flog these loans via ABS. Worryingly, especially dubious loans were packaged and sold. Over 2000–2006, *The Economist* reports, the fraction of noninvestment-grade loans that banks kept themselves fell from 90% to 60% in Europe, and from 60% to a mind-boggling 20% in the United States. This way, bankers became too focused on deal-making and the bonuses it brought, shrugging off default issues: these were supposed to be the concern of the buyer (*caveat emptor* – let the buyer beware) and of the rating agencies that vetted the ABS.

Let us now briefly digress about what roles banks are meant to play, in financial markets, and then judge how well ABS do in that framework.

Table 1. US Asset-Backed Securities Issuance by Major Types of Credit.

	Auto	Credit Cards	Equipment	Home	Manufactured Housing	Student Loans	Other	Total
1996	33	49	12	36	8	8	20	167
1997	36	41	8	66	10	13	29	202
1998	40	43	10	84	12	10	48	247
1999	43	41	13	75	15	11	39	236
2000	67	57	11	74	11	19	41	281
2001	70	69	8	112	7	15	45	326
2002	89	70	6	151	5	28	25	374
2003	76	67	9	229	0	43	37	462
2004	67	54	8	425	0	48	49	652
2005	85	68	10	460	0	63	66	754
2006	82	67	9	484	0	67	45	754
2007	74	100	6	217	0	61	52	510
2008	36	59	3	4	0	28	9	139
2009	63	46	8	2	0	22	10	151
$\frac{2005}{1996}$	2.58	1.39	0.48	12.78	0.00	7.88	3.30	4.51
id, ppa	10	3	−7	29	–	23	13	16

Notes:

1. Home equity contains both 1st and junior lien home equity loans and lines of credit, subprime, small balance issues, and servicing rights; these numbers do not overlap with mortgage-related issuance in other SIFMA statistics.
2. Auto includes truck loans and wholesale auto receivables, and as of 2008 include floorplans, motorcycles, rentals, and recreational vehicles. Prior years have not been revised to include these categories yet.
3. Equipment does not include aircraft leases.
4. Credit cards include charge cards.
5. Data in prior quarters may be subject to revision.
6. Numbers are in USD millions.

Source: Thomson Financial, Bloomberg, SIFMA (Securities Industry and Financial Markets Association).

THE ORTHODOX LOGIC OF BANKING

Why don't lenders (households, insurance companies, pension funds, etc.) directly deal with borrowers (mostly other households, companies, and governments)? Actually, sometimes they do: family and close friends do lend to each other, occasionally; and on an economically more meaningful scale, especially big corporations and governments have been selling their bonds directly to savers for centuries. But smaller firms and households almost

Table 2. US Asset-Backed Securities Outstanding by Major Types of Credit.

	Auto	Credit Cards	Home	Manufactured Housing	Student Loans	Other	Total
1996	71	181	52	15	10	76	404
1997	77	215	90	19	18	117	536
1998	87	237	124	25	25	234	732
1999	114	258	142	34	36	317	901
2000	133	306	152	37	41	403	1,072
2001	188	362	185	43	60	443	1,281
2002	222	398	287	45	74	518	1,543
2003	235	402	346	44	99	568	1,694
2004	232	391	454	42	115	594	1,828
2005	220	357	551	35	153	640	1,955
2006	202	340	581	29	184	795	2,130
2007	199	348	586	27	244	1,070	2,472
2008	138	314	396	20	240	1,565	2,672

Notes:
1. Data in prior quarters may be subject to revision.
2. Numbers are in USD millions.

Source: Thomson Financial, Bloomberg, SIFMA (Securities Industry and Financial Markets Association).

always work via banks that then collect the funds from savers. So what do banks add?[2]

There are some obvious functions. One is providing a place where (parts of) supply and demand meet. Also, banks offer diversification: they borrow from many and lend to many, so that each depositor's income is tied to a portfolio of many loans rather than to one or a few of them. But these functions are also offered by peer-to-peer lending websites, which are now being touted as the great alternative to the now-unloved traditional banks. We think these internet ventures are condemned to, at best, a marginal existence: a bank worth its salt offers far more. Macro textbooks like to emphasize maturity transformation, for instance: banks borrow short term (as lenders prefer to stay liquid) and lend long term, which entails an interest risk to the bank or, more precisely, its stakeholders. Lastly, and most crucially for our story, banks traditionally gather and process information and bear default risk.

Relative to average retail investors, traditional credit analysts are masters at reading balance sheets and interpreting them, taking into account what they already know of the sector and the economy. They also have access to

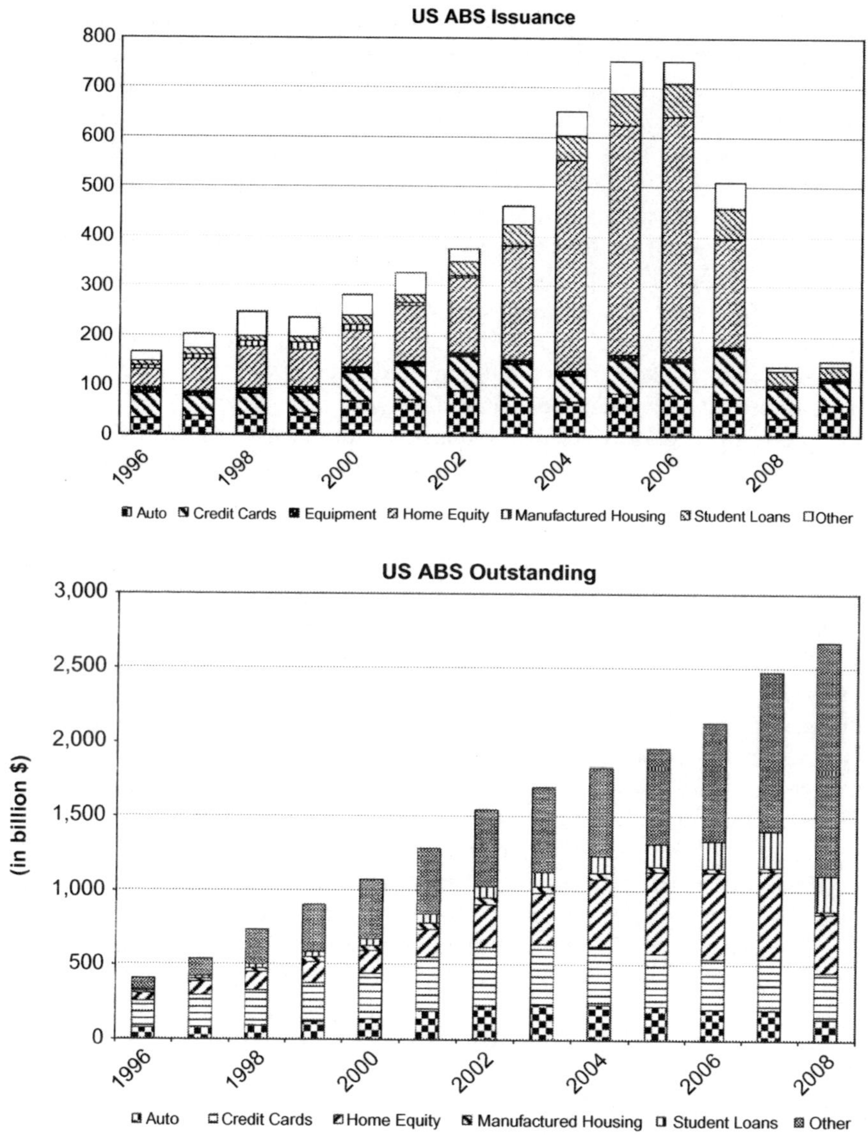

Fig. 1. US ABS Issuance and Outstanding Volumes. *Source:* See Tables 1 and 2.

private information that the borrower would never divulge to the public at large by, for instance, putting it into a prospectus. Similarly, banks often have long-standing relations with the borrower, they work with clients from the same sector and the same region, they can see the daily financial in- and outflows, and so on. In short, a bank knows so much more, and knows so much better what all that stuff means; Fama (1985) calls them quasi-insiders. They are motivated to make the effort of information gathering because the amount at stake is usually sizable. For a small investor who also wants diversification, it would never pay to personally investigate the soundness of, say, 100 separate borrowers: the amount lent by one saver to one borrower simply would be too small to justify the effort, and the costs of ever acquiring as much information even about just one borrower would be substantially higher than the cost to the bank.

A bank's comparative advantage in loan initiation and credit evaluation is a standard insight from the theory of corporate finance or financial intermediation. Less often one hears about banks also being much better at debt collection; yet this is an argument that, for our purpose, is at least as important as the standard one. Again the crucial ideas are incentives and costs. In case there is a problem, the bank again has a big amount at stake, so it will do an effort; a small, diversified lender will rarely bother. Banks also know exactly what to do in case of default, and what the legal nitty-gritty is. In addition, banks are in a stronger position: for a financially distressed household or firm, defaulting toward the house bank is costly because the borrower will probably have to come back for more loans later and because anyway the bank would add the defaulter's name to a blacklist which is then passed on to other banks. Lastly, a bank loan is easy to renegotiate, compared to, for instance, a bond issue: just two parties are involved rather than an array of investors with conflicting points of view and low incentices to actually show up at the negotiation table. This flexibility can be used to both the lender's and the borrower's advantage.

THE PROBLEMS WITH ABS

Why is all this relevant? Let's see how investors should have reacted when offered a ABS. They should have smelled a rat, or perhaps several of them.

The most glaring problem, universally recognized now but studiously ignored then, is that bankers who immediately pass on their loans to other investors no longer have an incentive to vet the original borrowers properly. At the time it was thought that banks would never take the risk of losing their reputation and, at one and the same stroke, also their huge market value by selling overpriced low-quality products. Let us return to that argument later. Our contention at this stage is that even for a given pool of loans, a ABS is intrinsically worth less than the very same loans would have been if kept by the bank.

Think of debt collection, for instance. The trust that issued the bonds on the strength of the pool of loans has no incentive to make an effort because its equity is small and easily wiped out. Actually, a trust is not even set up to make decisions and take action. ABS holders do have an incentive, in principle, but the amounts at stake do not warrant big efforts or costs; also, there is a free-riding issue: why should one investors spend time and money at debt collection if the fellow ABS-holders that shirk are benefiting equally?[3]

Also the bank's erstwhile option to renegotiate when a borrower is in dire streets has been effectively killed off by the securitization: given the difficulties of getting a dispersed set of ABS holders around the table and making them agree, revising the loan rates or principals has been unheard of, thus far. Courts or governments might be able to change the terms of the contracts, but thus far they have not done so either. Borrowers, lastly, know that banks no longer care and ABS holders are powerless, all of which should not do wonders for their willingness to tighten belts or work harder or sell the family silver so as to stave off default.

Not only is the product worth less, after securitization: the new buyer is being overcharged for it. Remember, indeed, that the bank that originates the ABS still has an information advantage over any other party bar the borrowers themselves. The buyers of ABS should have been familiar with the agency issues and adverse-selection problems that arise when a well-informed party (the bank that grants the loan) passes-on a product to a less-informed one. After all, issuers of ABS are like used-car dealers: they know the problems of the car, but they obviously will never tell this to prospective customers. So prospective buyers of used cars should be (and usually are) very suspicious. For ABS, however, the buyers did not have this reaction; they happily bought cats in bags. Also overseers should have lifted eyebrows sky-high, on seeing the wrong information balance and the conflict of interest: this was a system that let the risks end not in the hands of the party best placed to asses and bear the risk, but in the hands of the biggest fools, as Arnaud Boot nicely puts it. But instead of viewing this ABS fashion as the Sodom & Gomorrah of banking, as they should have, overseers regarded this innovation as a zenith of efficiency, a blessing to humanity ("the pollinating bees of Wall Street"). Actually, many of the unbewaring buyers were non-U.S. banks that wanted to join the party, and hedge/pension/mutual funds – institutions where the incentives were often as distorted as at the banks that issued the ABS in the first place. Even though these buyers often were banks themselves, they did not have the same advantages the original lender/bank has with respect to information acquisition and default-risk handling.

Let us contrast this with a very sensible traditional banking product, the Letter of Credit (L/C). Familiarly, perhaps, an L/C is an endorsement of an importer's trade debt by the importer's house bank and is often used in international trade between parties that do not know each other well. This risk shifting is economically useful because the importer's house bank knows far more about the importer than does the exporter, and is also better placed to get the money and even to bear the loss if outright default would be the eventual outcome. "Confirmation" of an L/C (an endorsement of the L/C by a second bank that is well known to the exporter) is, likewise, a useful function because the confirming bank knows more about the L/C-issuing bank's reliability, the transfer risk, etc., than does the exporter, and is in a better position to get the money and to bear a possible loss. In short, risk is being re-allocated to parties that are better placed to both asses and bear it. What ABS achieve is exactly the opposite. The ABS holder is no good at estimating risk (and thus, gauging the fair value) and at dealing with default.

Combining an inefficient reallocation of risk analysis/bearing with adverse selection, it's hard to see why anyone ever would be willing to buy a ABS at the price that makes also the bank happy. But many did, because rating agencies or insurance companies told them the product was fine. The raters were viewed as the ultimate guardians of the game. Their reputation would never be put at risk, academics gushed, because the destruction of the present value of their income from rating would be too high a cost. The argument was, interestingly, the same as the one advanced to explain why banks themselves would never sell bad investment products, and why audit firms – and especially large ones, like Arthur Anderson – would never consent to sloppy or dishonest work. Even after Enron, raters remained above all suspicion.

HOW CDS CONTRACTS GOT INTO THE GAME

The insurers and raters got in via Basle I. As is well known, under Basle I every $100 of unsecured loans granted needs $8 in bank capital (equity, reserved earnings, and some types of long-term subordinated or hybrid debt), of which $4 in equity and retained earnings. But the risk weighting was much reduced for loans to financial institutions, for loans that were insured against default risk or, as of the mid-1990s, loans that received top ratings.

In one splendid illustration of The Law of Unintended Consequences, this made banks channel their loans and hide their risks in conduits or SIVs. These were not banks, so Basle did not apply, but this effect is tangential to our story. Also in response to Basle I, banks started buying massive credit insurance contracts, partly from standard insurers and partly from the general public, via Credit Default Swaps (CDS contracts). Technically, the buyer of CDS protection pays an insurance fee, say 3% p.a., to the seller of protection as long as the insured debt is not in default or has not expired; in case of default, however, either the insured party cedes the claim to the insuror, who has to pay the full principal value for it,[4] or the insured party receives the difference between face value and market value of the impaired obligation. Any seller of protection can later buy protection, in turn, from another party, at a premium that reflects the revised default risk. Such a transfer brings in cash if the insured debt has gone up in quality, meanwhile, so that the original 3% amounts to more than is now needed to buy protection. Obviously, however, the transfer may also require a cash outlay – notably if the original 3% is no longer viewed as sufficient and the new insuror, therefore, needs to be bribed by an additional payment.

CDS started very small-scale and ad hoc in the 1990s, but as of 2001 the amounts (and the standardization) made the product interesting enough to be tracked by ISDA. The outstanding volumes, measured by ensured amounts, are shown in Fig. 2. They are impressive. ISDA does not show the market value of the underlying bonds, but a commonly cited figure is that the CDS-ensured volume amounts to three times the volume of the underlying loans themselves. Since the ISDA now reports numbers that are claimed to be net of double-counting – this was and still is an OTC product without central clearing house[5] – this means that the average loan was ensured more than once and/or or that outsiders started gambling on default. In the Harrah case discussed below it surely was a problem. In a more notorious case, when Lehman Brothers filed for bankruptcy, it had approximately $155 billion of outstanding debt, whereas the notional value of CDS protection bought in reference to that debt amounted to around $400 billion.[6]

This protection was provided by unrelated parties which, unhindered by expertise or good information, thought the insurance income was irresistibly high. The over-insurance phenomenon should actually have been viewed as

2001	I	0.6
	II	0.9
2002	I	1.6
	II	2.2
2003	I	2.7
	II	3.8
2004	I	5.4
	II	8.4
2005	I	12.4
	II	17.1
2006	I	26
	II	34.4
2007	I	45.5
	II	62.2
2008	I	54.6
	II	38.6
2009	I	31.2

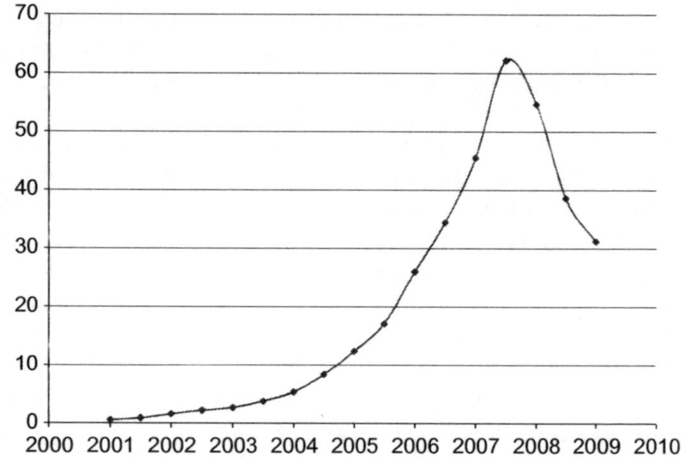

Fig. 2. Credit Default Swap Outstanding (Semi-Annual). *Source:* ISDA; Notional amounts in trillions of US dollars, adjusted for double-counting.

a signal of "underpricing of risk", meaning underpricing of insurance. But, once more, the unbewaring buyers did not smell a rat. Are there any reasons to believe the insurors were being ripped off, and, if so, why did they not see it? Adverse selection following from information asymmetry offer one possible explanation.

CDS MISPRICING FROM ADVERSE SELECTION?

One of the rats that might have been smellable is the natural mispricing that arises when experts play against amateurs. The amateurs should have seen red lights flashing (asymmetric information + asymmetric expertise + divergent incentives = adverse selection = I lose). But they just saw golden profit opportunities – a stream of insurance premium income in return for piffling-looking risks.

One objection to the above view may be that in reality adverse selection is unlikely to be a serious problem, or at least unlikely to be a new problem, because CDS contracts are typically written for publicly traded corporate bonds or for debt of companies with a similar stature. Thus, the objection is, pricing CDS is no more difficult than pricing corporate bonds; if we object to CDS contracts being sold to amateurs, we should also object to corporate bonds being issued to the general public. We do not buy this: a CDS *is* harder to price than a corporate bond. For instance, next to default risk also interest-risk arises because, at default, the insurer pays the face value regardless of the underlying loan's remaining time to maturity and the then prevailing term structure. Thus, a CDS is a messy type of option, not a swap. The modeling of both risk-free bonds and corporate default events are controversial; there is no premier model that, like Black-Scholes for European puts and calls, is universally accepted as a reasonable starting point. In addition, a traditional academic valuation model would typically take the law and the contracts literally, thus ignoring the moral-hazard games that can be played at times of financial distress (see next section); that is, in reality the payoff function is rather fuzzy, unlike that of a call.

Less technically, and more in line with our main line of thought, CDS contracts may also be attracting a far less critical clientele than do corporate bonds. Having to fork out a full value, as one does when buying a corporate bond, has a wonderfully sobering effect on the investor's mind. Buying a CDS, in contrast, requires no cash outlay: instead, there just is the prospect of "easy money", the premium income, with at the back an 'unlikely' loss if default would ever occur. (The historical rate of default for investment-grade debt is 0.2%.[7]) Such a product may attract fools like candles attract moths. It might also especially appeal to low-risk-aversion players or gamblers, who are naturally keen on leverage and are, therefore, enthralled by the low or sometimes even negative initial investment offered by a CDS.

The above view is not just an unverified and unverifiable opinion; the moths-and-candles phenomenon is actually observed in studies of the now-defunct "forward" markets for stocks, in Paris and Brussels. In a forward market, one can buy without any immediate cash outlay, and one can even entirely avoid paying the main amount by closing out before the contract expires; likewise, one can sell short without any questions asked and without having to borrow shares. In Brussels, the forward market actually co-existed with a standard "spot" market (with $t+3$ settlement) for the same stocks, but the forward tier had lower costs, much higher volumes, and, at least during the last decade of its life, a continuous electronic trading system; the spot section, dowdily, still worked with manually kept order books, floor trading, and blackboard-and-chalk information systems. In the traditional efficient-markets view, there can be no doubt that the forward tier should be more efficient than the spot tier. Bui and Sercu (2009a, 2009b) however find that the spot market is faster at price discovery and contains far less noise, regardless of what model or measure they use. Bui and Sercu (2009c) also find that forward investors not only tend to price slowly and noisily, but also tend to overpay: relative to excessive forward discounts, excessive forward premiums are four times as prevalent, are typically larger, and tend to persist while discounts tend to vanish overnight. The conclusion that Bui and Sercu make is that the smooth organisation of the forward market attracted not so much a higher number of informed, rational players but, instead, mainly more noise traders. Similar conclusions are obtained for Paris by Foucault, Sraer, and Thesmar (2008), even though the situation is somewhat different from that in Brussels. If easier access and automatic leverage appeals to fools even more than it appeals to informed traders in stock markets, the same is likely in debt markets.

ECONOMIC DRAWBACKS OF CDS CONTRACTS

Actually, mispricing of risk in the CDS market is not the sole issue, and probably not the main one either. As in the case of ABSs, the adverse-selection problem that causes mispricing (underpricing of risk) comes hand-in-hand with a drop in the intrinsic value, an economic inefficiency. Again, it has to do with debt collection issues and moral hazard. To get the full picture it is useful to highlight some features that make the difference between CDSs and standard credit-insurance. One such feature is that the CDS protection buyer does not need an "insurable interest". In fire insurance, for instance, the insuree needs to be the owner or leaseholder, etc. of the house that is being insured; imagine, indeed, the perverse incentives one would get if Mr A could claim an amount of money if ever the house of an unconnected Mrs B burns down. Also, unlike in standard insurance, with a CDS one can effectively over-insure. Imagine the incentives if Mr A can insure his house three times over, and gets compensated three times if the house does burn down.

Of course, with CDS the risk is not that the protection buyer would set fire to the company's main plant; that least, that's what one would hope. Rather, the problem is that the CDS creates a perfectly legal substitute of committing arson, as it were: an insured lender has no incentive whatsoever to renegotiate when they can get the full amount from the insurers. Actually, in case of financial distress, CDS-insured lenders have every incentive to go for default and immediately get their full pound rather than negotiate and maybe get part of the money back later. *The Economist* mentions that games of this type may even be one of the reasons why CDS contracts are so much in demand: hedge funds, etc. buy a material amount of debt, just enough to be at the Chapter 11 table, and then buy a CDS hedge for a much larger notional. This gives them tremendous gains in case of default.

Examples cited where this game was played were AbitibiBowater, a paper manufacturer, and General Growth Properties, a property investor, in mid-April 2009. Some even suspect that CDS contracts also played a role in the GM filing, June 2009 (*The Economist*, June 20–26, 2009, p. 71). The same names are cited in *The Financial Times*, July 23, 2009, which adds GMAC and also describes the Harrah and Unisys cases. Harrah Entertainment, a Vegas gaming company had $20 bn of debt outstanding which it wanted to reorganize via an exchange offer. There were CDS contracts outstanding for a total notional of $30 bn. If all of these had been held by bondholders, then the gains on the value of the debt after the exchange offer would have been more than wiped out by the loss in value of the CDS contracts. Clearly, however (and luckily for Harrah), enough CDS contracts were held by third parties: Harrah could eventually revise its debt, albeit with a narrow voting margin. Unisys was not that fortunate. At the time of writing, the company was also trying to exchange some of its debt for other paper. Unluckily for Unisys, about two thirds of its debt holders was estimated to have bought CDS protection. After a failed first exchange offer the company figured that, to sway the bondholders with CDS protection, it needed to offer more than 100 cent on the dollar. Its second offer consisted of 20 cents in cash, and new senior secured debt for a face value of 95 cents on the dollar, enough to lift the value of the bonds in themselves above par. Thus, Unisys paid almost 120 cents.

In short, CDS contracts allow debtholders to totally turn the tables, at the Chapter 11 negotiations. CDS-protected holders of subordinated debt could even go home with more money than senior claimholders, if the latter did not buy protection themselves. Obviously, the entire Chapter 11 or *concordat* or financial reorganization legislation is not yet taking into account CDS. Proposals that debtholders should lose the votes attached to their claims to the extent that these claims are insured make some sense, but this rule would easily be sidestepped by placing the CDS protection with a third party that acts in concert with the debtholder. Another issue with the proposed solution is that the voting rights taken away from covered debtholders should logically revert to the protection sellers. The CDS protection *sellers* themselves, of course, would have every incentive to talk and bargain, and should receive the right since they bear the related risk.[8] But there is no clear bilateral link between seller and buyer: the sellers as a group offer protection to the buyers as a group, and since 80 percent of CDSs are rumored to be naked contracts (held without insurable interest), each unit of debt might be replaced by four units of protection sellers. There are ways out, but they are unelegant: one could think of two classes of

CDSs – with versus without contingent voting rights – or one could randomly select the CDS sellers that get to vote in case of a reorganization (in the same way as an option clearing house randomly picks one of the writers when an American option is exercised early). Even more radically, one could require an insurable interest, and steer speculators to the standard ways of punting on a catastrophe, like selling calls or buying puts or shorting stock or corporate bonds.

Even if CDS writers do eventually obtain a seat at the table, there is the usual coordination and free-riding problem. The insurance comes not from a single regular company, but from an unorganized assortment of CDS writers which are as hard to coordinate as for a bunch of bond- or ABS-holders. There were 4,000 protection writers in Harrah's case. True, the average CDS writer still had a stake of millions of dollars, but a free-riding issue or a coordination issue still arises: one's motivation is still low if it is known that there are 3,999 shirkers out there. That is, even if the legal issues about who votes in case of reorganization get sorted out, a CDS-insured bank loan would still have become as inconvenient and unwieldy as a public debt issue.

Summing up: also CDS contracts shifts risk to a party that is not well informed about that risk and is very badly placed to deal with the bad events if and when they do happen. At first blush, the seller of CDS protection who buys risk-free debt with the same face value as the insured debt should get the same income as the original holder of the loan, apart from term structure risk. In reality, CDS insurance destroys value because debt collection is much worse. This is similar to what we noted about ABS.

CONCLUDING COMMENTS

We have described ABS and CDS contracts as products that give perverse incentive to banks and other lenders, reduce the value of loans, and shift risks to parties that cannot evaluate them and deal with them as competently and safely as banks themselves. Is there any merit in them?

Banks' standard reply is that securitization and default-risk protection disperse risks that used to be concentrated in banks, reducing their default risk and systemic threats. This would have been fine if there had not been the unintended or ignored drawbacks or moral hazard and adverse selection. Proposals to make banks hang on to a seizable portion of any ABS they launch are only part of the solution. It is hoped that banks would pay more attention to the quality of the pool, this way, but "banks" are not persons; the true decision-makers are individuals, and a lot of thinking needs to be done about re-aligning individuals' objectives with those of the bank. Stock options and employee participation plans are not the solution. It's not that bankers do not like to receive shares and see their prices rise: rather, the problem is that very few people, in a big bank, really see any connection between their own decisions and the stock price. The price is set by a load of exogenous market-wide factors and by the bank's profits, but the impact of virtually every single employee on profits is negligible. Being "price takers", these bankers' decisions cannot logically be motivated by the stock price. What they think of is their bonus.

Anyway, loan quality is but one issue. The inefficiencies introduced wrt debt collection are not solved by making banks retain 10 percent of a mortgage loan: for the bank, the amount at stake is still piffling, and there still is the issue of the loss of renegotiation as a way to solve unexpected financial distress issues. Only in the case of very safe loans, say mortgages with a very healthy haircut, are these flaws less important. For that reason, ABS should be confined to such loans.

CDS contracts, if they are tolerated at all, should be regulated the same way as corporate bonds (apart from practical issues of standardization, novation via clearing houses, etc.).

NOTES

1. At Dexia, a Belgian-French bank, bonuses were notoriously linked to just the volume of one product, which was not even making any profits to the bank.
2. The (vast) literature includes Berger and Udell (1995), Biais and Gollier (1997), Campbell (1979), Campbell and Kracaw (1980), Chemmanur and Fulghieri (1994), Detragiache (1994), Diamond (1984, 1991), Easterbrook (1984), Fama (1985), Franks and Sussman (2005), Houston and James (1996), James (1987), Jensen and Meckling (1976), Leland and Pyle (1977), Lummer and McConnell (1989), Myers (1977), Myers and Majluf (1984), Petersen and Rajan (1994, 1997), Rajan (1992), Sharpe (1990), Shleifer and Vishny (1997), Opler and Titman (1994) and Yosha (1995). In our discussion we ignore a literature on the indirect benefits of relationship banking, like monitoring, less adverse selection in the lender–borrower relation, implicit certification toward third parties. There is s flipside too: banks may also exploit their information advantage (and the resulting barrier to entry for other banks) by extracting rent from their clients; easy lending may mean soft budgets and debt overhang; lending dries up when the bank gets in dire streets, etc.
3. Standard economic analysis would predict that individuals would not mind the others free-riding as long as the agent himself still gains. In reality, the $100-game phenomenon often arises. (In this game, two players receive $100 to share; one player can propose a division, say 50/50 or 99/1, and the second says Yes or No; if the

verdict is No, the game is over and the $100 is lost. Contradicting standard economic thinking, the second player often says No when the proposal deviates far from the "fair" outcome, 50/50.) *The Economist* (March 15, 2008, p. 78) describes how at the Chapter-11 negotiations of American Remanufacturers, a car-parts firm, the junior claimholders asked for more than they were contractually entitled to. Rather than reluctantly agreeing as economists would predict, the senior claimholders blew up all talks even though that meant that both parties were left with nothing. "The two groups of lien holders 'just shot each other,' one lawyer said." Unusually (and disappointingly for the lawyers) the whole thing took just 11 days. Thus, issues of fairness magnify the standard free-riding problem.

4. This is the "swap" part of the story, the "s" in CDS. The word insurance was studiously avoided, not only for marketing purposes but also for legal and regulatory reasons, but we have no such qualms; so for brevity we often speak of insurer and insured, etc.

5. The lack of clearing also creates a default-risk issue: when a credit event arises, the holder addresses the last seller, who then has recourse to the preceding seller, etc.

6. Wikipedia/CDS/Settlement, which refers to http://seekingalpha.com/article/99286-settlement-auction-for-lehman-cds-surprises-ahead

7. http://www.efalken.com/banking/html's/defaultcurves.htm

8. Currently, CDS protection sellers do not have a seat at the renegotiation table. Of course, after default has occurred the CDS writers probably end up with some of the debt; but that's too late, of course: negotiations are meant to avoid default.

ACKNOWLEDGMENTS

We thank Nancy Huyghebaert, Patrick Van Cayseele, and Lambert Vanthienen for useful comments on this chapter or related presentations; all remaining shortcomings remain ours.

REFERENCES

Berger, A. N., & Udell, G. F. (1995). Relationship lending and lines of credit in small firm finance. *Journal of Business*, *68*, 351–381.

Biais, B., & Gollier, C. (1997). Trade credit and credit rationing. *Review of Financial Studies*, *10*(4), 903–937.

Bui, T., & Sercu, P. (2009a). More friction, less noise? Relative efficiency in a two-tier stock exchange. K. U. Leuven, Faculty of Business and Economics, AFI working paper series.

Bui, T., & Sercu, P. (2009b). Trading systems efficiency and noise: Price-discovery dynamics in the two-tier brussels exchange. K. U. Leuven, Faculty of Business and Economics, AFI working paper series.

Bui, T., & Sercu, P. (2009c). Spot and forward prices in the Brussels SE: Time value v convenience premiums. K. U. Leuven, Faculty of Business and Economics, AFI working paper series.

Campbell, T. S. (1979). Optimal investment financing decisions and the value of confidentiality. *Journal of Financial and Quantitative Analysis, 14*, 913–924.

Campbell, T. S., & Kracaw, W. A. (1980). Information production, market signalling, and the theory of financial intermediation. *Journal of Finance, 35*, 863–882.

Chemmanur, T., & Fulghieri, P. (1994). Reputation, renegotiation, and the choice between bank loans and publicly traded debt. *Review of Financial Studies, 7*, 475–506.

Detragiache, E. (1994). Public versus private borrowing: A theory with implications for bankruptcy reform. *Journal of Financial Intermediation, 3*, 327–354.

Diamond, D. (1984). Financial intermediation and delegated monitoring. *Review of Economic Studies, 51*, 393–414.

Diamond, D. (1991). Monitoring and reputation: The choice between bank loans and directly placed debt. *Journal of Political Economy, 99*, 689–720.

Easterbrook, F. H. (1984). Two agency cost explanations of dividends. *American Economic Review, 74*, 650–659.

Fama, E. (1985). Whats different about banks. *Journal of Monetary Economics, 15*, 29–39.

Foucault, T., Sraer, D., & Thesmar, D., (2008). Individual investors and volatility. AFFI conference, December.

Franks, J., & Sussman, O. (2005). Financial distress and bank restructuring of small to medium size UK companies. *Review of Finance, 9*(1), 65–96.

Houston, J., & James, C. (1996). Bank information monopolies and the mix of public and private debt claims. *Journal of Finance, 51*, 1863–1889.

James, C. (1987). Some evidence on the uniqueness of bank loans. *Journal of Financial Economics, 19*, 217–235.

Jensen, M. C., & Meckling, W. H. (1976). Theory of the firm: Managerial behavior, agency costs and ownership structure. *Journal of Financial Economics, 3*, 305–360.

Leland, H. E., & Pyle, D. H. (1977). Informational asymmetries, financial structure, and financial intermediation. *Journal of Finance, 32*, 371–387.

Lummer, S. L., & McConnell, J. J. (1989). Further evidence on the bank lending process and the capital market response to bank loan agreements. *Journal of Financial Economics, 25*, 99–122.

Myers, S. C., & Majluf, N. C. (1984). Corporate financing and investment decisions when firms have information the investors do not have. *Journal of Financial Economics, 13*, 187–221.

Myers, S. C. (1977). The determinants of corporate borrowing. *Journal of Financial Economics, 5*, 147–175.

Opler, T. C., & Titman, S. (1994). Financial distress and corporate performance. *Journal of Finance, 49*(3), Papers and Proceedings Fifty-Fourth Annual Meeting of the American Finance Association, Boston, Massachusetts, January 3–5, 1994 (July, 1994), 1015–1040.

Petersen, M. A., & Rajan, R. G. (1994). The benefits of lending relationships: Evidence from small business data. *Journal of Finance, 49*(1), 3–37.

Rajan, R. G. (1992). Insiders and outsiders: The choice between relationship and arm's length debt. *Journal of Finance, 47*, 1367–1400.

Sharpe, S. (1990). Asymmetric information, bank lending, and implicit contracts: A stylized model of customer relationships. *Journal of Finance, 45*, 1069–1087.

Shleifer, A., & Vishny, R. W. (1997). A survey of corporate governance. *Journal of Finance, 52*, 737–783.

Yosha, O. (1995). Information disclosure costs and the choice of financing source. *Journal of Financial Intermediation, 4*, 3–20.

DISTRESS RESOLUTION STRATEGIES IN THE BANKING SECTOR: IMPLICATIONS FOR GLOBAL FINANCIAL CRISES[☆]

Maria Carapeto, Scott Moeller, Anna Faelten, Valeriya Vitkova and Leonardo Bortolotto

ABSTRACT

This chapter investigates the effectiveness and the motivation behind the choice of different types of distress resolution strategies in the banking sector. This is a global study that analyzes key financial characteristics of distressed banks that were either acquired by other banks, divested assets, or were subject to government intervention, as well as the change in the financial profile of those distressed institutions from one year pre-deal to three years post-deal. The results show that governments intervene in the (relatively) best performers that only underperform in liquidity ratios, an indication of critical short-term flow problems. Distressed sellers, the underperformers of the three groups, enjoy much improved performance,

[☆]The contents of this chapter reflect the views of the M&A Research Centre and do not necessarily reflect the views of the sponsors of the Centre. The M&A Research Centre would like to express grateful thanks to its sponsors, Allen & Overy, Credit Suisse, and Mergermarket, for their support and practical guidance.

International Banking in the New Era: Post-Crisis Challenges and Opportunities
International Finance Review, Volume 11, 335–360

ISSN: 1569-3767/doi:10.1108/S1569-3767(2010)0000011015

in particular in cross-border deals. There is some evidence of foreign acquirers "cherry picking" the least distressed banks, though no significant differences in target performance remain post-deal between cross-border and domestic deals. These findings provide some useful guidance for policy makers globally and for future financial crises that impact the banking sector.

INTRODUCTION

The 2007–2009 global financial crisis has had a major impact in the banking sector leading to the need to identify the most effective strategies that can be adopted by banks and government agencies to resolve corporate distress in the industry. Worldwide, governments have been forced to step in and orchestrate massive bailouts to prevent the financial world from collapsing (e.g., Northern Rock, Fannie Mae, and Freddie Mac) as shown in the timeline of events illustrated in Fig. 1.

In just the United States, it has been estimated that the asset relief program, which was implemented to prevent a collapse of the entire banking system in 2008, amounted to $700 billion (Guerrera & Guha, 2010). In the context of the high costs associated with government bailout programs and the need to recover the funds provided to financial institutions by the government, many academics and practitioners have questioned the effectiveness of government intervention as a distress resolution strategy. Consequently, the ability to identify viable alternatives to government intervention in the banking sector such as acquisitions (e.g., Wells Fargo's acquisition of Wachovia) and divestitures (e.g., Barclays' announced sale of iShares and Banco Popolare's divestiture of 33 branches to Credit Emiliano), including cross-border deals (e.g., Banco Santander's acquisition of Sovereign Bancorp), is an issue of particular interest and importance for academics and practitioners alike. In fact, Tschoegl (2004) argues that "foreign banks can act as rehabilitators of weak or failed banks" with their most obvious role being that of recapitalizing and restructuring the distressed banks. However, they are more likely to take over banks in relatively better shape. Note as well that this phenomenon is not new, as healthy banks have been involved in the purchase of weak or failing banks for many decades, often with the support or encouragement of governments. Deutsche Bank's cross-border acquisition of Bankers Trust in 1999 is just one such example. This chapter will, however, focus on the implications of

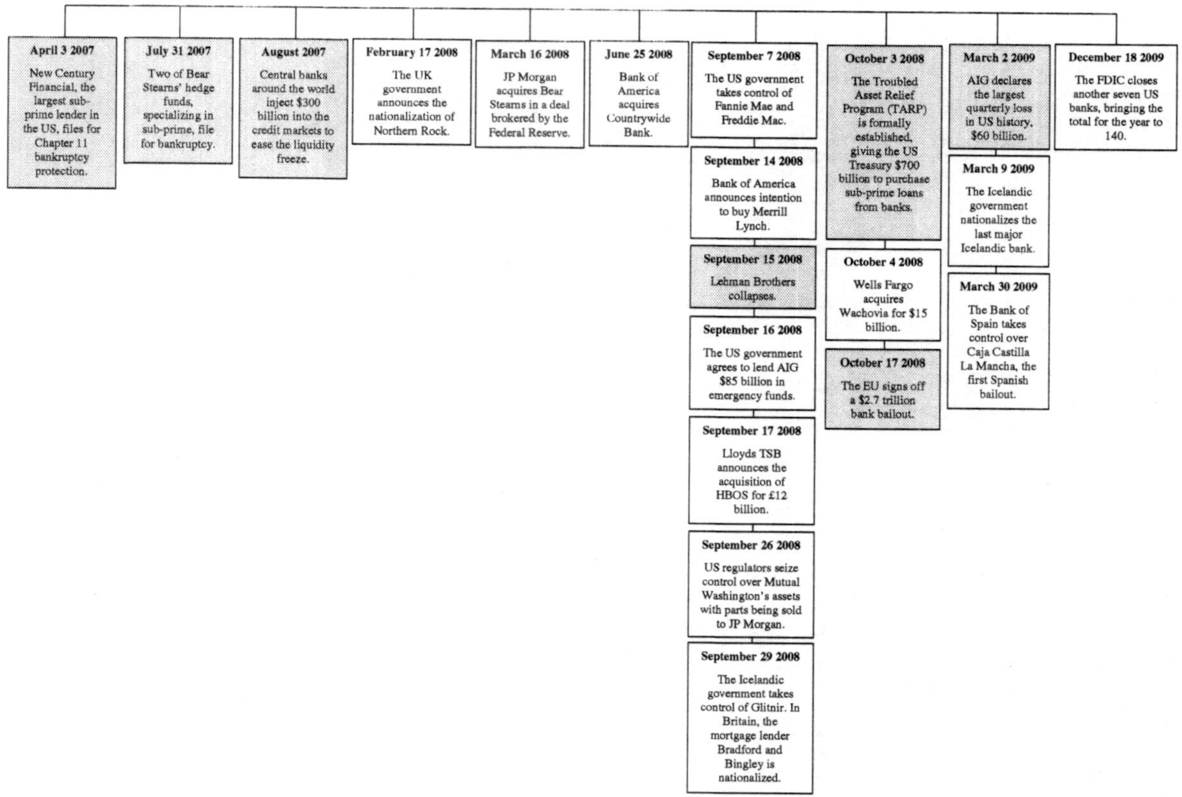

Fig. 1. 2007–2009 Global Financial Crisis – Chronology of Events and Bank Rescues. *Note:* "Events" are described in gray boxes and "Bank Rescues" in white boxes. *Sources:* This schedule references "Welcome to the Museum of Natural Credit Crunch," *Financial Times*, April 2009, and "Timeline: Credit Crunch to Downturn," *BBC News Online*, August 2009.

these deals in today's market, although building on a database of such deals going back to 1994, and utilize a global database covering targets from 20 different countries. Approximately 60% of the deals are cross-border (excluding government deals).

There are different restructuring methods that a financial institution at risk of default can use for the purpose of resolving distress: (i) the distressed bank may be acquired by another bank and thereby rescued through an injection of fresh capital; (ii) the distressed bank may be the acquirer in a merger and acquisition (M&A) deal as a survival strategy via the acquisition of assets or even an entire financial institution; this deal type can be structured as a merger of equals or a reverse takeover, where the payment structure is such that the target transforms into the acquirer; (iii) the distressed bank may divest assets to increase cash levels and improve capital adequacy; often, the assets that are divested are profitable and represent the "crown jewels" of the business of the distressed seller; (iv) survival M&A deals may be orchestrated by the government when banks that are of great significance to a national banking system (due to reputation, size, or interbank connections) are at risk of default; in these cases it is not unusual for the government to step in and "encourage" a deal; and (v) the government may act as the lender of last resort, rescuing the bank by using taxpayers' money or nationalizing the bank. The first three of these methods are most often structured as domestic deals, but can also be cross-border.

So far, there has been no methodical and comprehensive analysis of the different restructuring types that can be employed as distress resolution methods in the banking sector and the way these deals may be a function of or impact on the financial characteristics of banks involved in such deals, as noted by Elsas (2007). Studies of deals involving distressed banks are very few and limited in scope, focusing on the probability of bank failure through liquidation or acquisition by another bank (Wheelock & Wilson, 2000), or the comparison of M&A deals involving distressed and non-distressed banks (Elsas, 2007; Koetter et al., 2007). In what concerns cross-border deals, only the following three papers focus on the target banks, and their findings are somehow mixed: while there is generally some consensus that target banks are poor performers prior to the acquisition, the first study finds increases in profit efficiency but not in cost efficiency or profitability (Vander & Vennet, 2002), another shows no performance improvements (Correa, 2008), and the most recent study finds subsequent improvements in profitability and efficiency (Fraser & Zhang, 2009). The aim of this chapter is thus to bring these different research papers together by analyzing distressed banks involved in M&A deals through acquisitions, divestitures, or government intervention.

The ability to resolve distress in banks in an efficient manner is of crucial importance to the sound functioning of national and global financial systems. In fact, the financial system of any particular country plays a pivotal role owing to three key characteristics of banks and the banking system which render them different from the rest of the economy. Firstly, banks transfer financial capital from economic agents with surplus funds to those with a deficit. Secondly, the sound functioning of any banking system is founded on the basis of confidence in the financial stability of the banking institutions themselves. Thirdly, due to the nature of the banking system, the bankruptcy of one bank may trigger contagion effects within the financial sector and result in the collapse of the entire system. These three characteristics of the financial system imply that the inability to resolve effectively distress in the sector could lead to severe loss of welfare for society and significant value erosion for the economy as a whole.

In order to analyze the different methods of eliminating distress that have been adopted by financial institutions at risk of default, this chapter examines a unique dataset of 59 representative deals that involved distressed banks over the period 1994–2005. Since information about banks that are at risk of default is most often confidential, this study uses the ratio of non-performing loans to total loans (based on a three-year industry moving average) in order to identify the banks that were distressed within the examined sample (see Carapeto, Moeller, Faelten, Vitkova, & Bortolotto, 2010). In addition, it is assumed that those banks which were the subject of government intervention (i.e., majority acquisition) were distressed. Following Tschoegl's (2004) observation of the rehabilitation role that foreign banks can play as acquirers of distressed banks, the analysis considers a cross-section of domestic and cross-border deals. Specifically, the sample comprises 14 cases of government intervention, 18 divestitures of major assets (including six cross-border deals), and 20 cases where the distressed bank was acquired (including 14 cross-border acquisitions); note that there were no cases of distressed banks acquiring other banks, although in theory this option would exist as mentioned above. It should be noted as well that, in order to analyze the effectiveness and efficiency of different types of restructuring deals as distress resolution techniques, it is necessary to take into account all the different costs that are foregone by avoiding the bankruptcy of financial institutions. This type of analysis requires, however, the ability to measure the foregone social costs associated with the bankruptcy of financial institutions, as well as the indirect financial and economic costs that could result from the contagion effects associated with the bankruptcy of banks. Since it is very difficult to capture these types of foregone costs associated with bank bankruptcy, this study instead considers the perspective of the investors in financial institutions when analyzing the effectiveness of different distress resolution techniques, and therefore their interest in the financial performance of the banks in which they own shares as that financial performance will have a direct impact on shareholder value. As a result, the analysis performed in this chapter is focused entirely on the financial profile of banks and how this financial profile is impacted by the different distress resolution methods. Although this study analyzes a period of one year prior to three years post-deal, results of distress resolution strategies may require longer to take full effect, yet it is clear that the first three years post-deal will certainly provide a strong indication of the likely direction of that long-term performance.

Using financial ratios one year prior to the deals, the results show that distressed banks with government intervention are the best performers to start with. This finding is true for all the financial performance factors except for the issue of liquidity, where these deals underperform the other methods of intervention. This result is because critical short-term liquidity problems constitute the main reason for the government intervention. Strategies involving the sale of divisions in distressed banks especially to foreign banks are associated with much improved performance post-deal, in particular because, prior to the deal, distressed sellers are the under-performers of the three groups. Distressed targets are somewhere in the middle when it comes to performance, with some evidence of "cherry picking" by foreign acquirers of the least distressed banks. Three years later no differences persist in performance between targets of cross-border and domestic acquisitions, as the distressed targets involved in domestic deals catch up with those acquired in cross-border transactions.

As the study uses three-year performance post-deal to determine success, it has not been possible to include the more recent distressed banking deals, for example, Bank of America's acquisition in late 2008 of Merrill Lynch or Lloyds TSB's purchase of HBOS in the same period. Nevertheless, the analysis of a recent global sample of distressed banks over 2007–2009 reveals that the motivation behind their choice of resolution strategies in terms of one-year performance prior to deal announcement is consistent for most factors with the results outlined here for deals from the earlier years. As such, the findings of this research may therefore be extended to the recent financial crisis.

The remainder of the chapter is organized as follows: "Literature Review" section provides a review of the literature on distressed and non-distressed M&A deals within the financial services sector as well as the role and consequences of government intervention in the sector. The "Data and Methodology" section describes the sample and methodology used in the study. The "Results" section discusses the empirical results, and the "Conclusion" section concludes.

LITERATURE REVIEW

The existing literature on mergers and acquisitions within the financial services sector is vast, and the majority of empirical studies are based on US data. The results on post-M&A performance are typically quite mixed. Findings range from improvements in cost efficiency (Beccalli & Frantz, 2009) and profitability (Cornett & Tehranian, 1992) to no improvements in operating efficiency (Chamberlain, 1998), profit efficiency, or profitability (Linder & Crane, 1992; Beccalli & Frantz, 2009). On the international side, Correa (2008) finds that, compared to domestic deals, target banks involved in cross-border deals are typically larger, poor performers, and fail to enjoy improvements in performance post-deal, with routine decreases in net interest margin to gain market share in developed markets or increased overhead costs in emerging markets. Fraser and Zhang (2009) corroborate the poor operating performance of targets involved in cross-border acquisitions in the years leading up to the deals, but find subsequent improvements in profitability and efficiency. However, Vander and Vennet (2002) show that target banks enjoy increases in profit efficiency but not in cost efficiency or profitability in cross-border deals. Beccalli and Frantz (2009) find improvements in cost efficiency but a slight deterioration in profitability and profit efficiency for the combined entity following cross-border deals.

Since the objective of this chapter is to analyze the choice of deal as a distress resolution technique, this literature review is focused on those studies that examine the performance characteristics of targets and acquirers before and after the completion of distressed M&A deals. The review starts with the key studies on distressed deals and is followed by those studies that analyze the effects of government intervention within the financial services sector.

Distressed Deals

Wheelock and Wilson (2000) relate the probability of bank failure (including acquisition by another bank) in the United States to various bank characteristics, with a special emphasis on managerial quality as reflected in alternative measures of productive efficiency. The sample of banks included in the study comprises 231 failed banks and 2,380 banks that were acquired over a period from 1984 to 1993. The results of the study suggest that small banks with low leverage and high asset quality, profitability, liquidity, and efficiency are more likely to be acquired.

Elsas (2007) examines the consequences of the use of M&A deals to resolve financial distress of 266 distressed banks from a total of 2,480 banks in Germany over the period 1993–2001. The results of the study show that if a bank is distressed, then there is an increased probability that it will participate in an M&A deal. In addition, the asset quality of the combined entity increases substantially for several years after a distressed deal. The findings also indicate that there is a temporary decrease in profitability and no significant change in the degree of default risk or cost efficiency. Altogether, there is evidence of diversification gains for the combined entity relative to non-distressed M&A deals.

Koetter et al. (2007) use undisclosed information to compare the characteristics of acquirers and targets that participated in about 1,000 M&A deals in Germany over the period 1995–2001, including 141 distressed targets. According to the results of the study, distressed participants in M&A deals have in general bad financial profiles, defined by lower capital reserve ratios, lower exposure to securities business, higher net loan loss provisions, and below average efficiency, relative to banks that do not participate in M&A deals.

Government Intervention

Since the financial sector is prone to periods of instability and is also highly regulated, it is important to analyze the role of the regulatory environment and regulatory intervention when examining financial institutions. The major role of regulators and, more specifically, government agencies as the principal actors in the regulatory framework is to monitor the financial soundness of banks and the financial stability of the entire banking system. This role is particularly important when a bank is at risk of default. In the majority of cases, government bodies have to step in and act as intermediaries to prevent individual bank failures and systemic banking crises. According to Laeven and Valencia (2008), there are three methods that government agencies can adopt to prevent firm-specific and systemic failures: (i) the government can encourage a healthy bank to acquire the distressed one; (ii) the distressed bank can be recapitalized via the injection of fresh capital by the government; and (iii) the government can establish an asset management company to buy all the non-performing bank assets (the so-called "bad bank" solution). The review of the literature on government intervention within the financial services sector shows that there is little agreement on what constitutes best practice or even good practice when considering the possible policies to prevent the bankruptcy of financial institutions and avoid or resolve systemic financial crises.

Laeven and Valencia (2008) compare the above-mentioned methods of government intervention in order to determine which type of policy works most effectively under different economic circumstances. According to the results of the study, the fiscal costs and output losses associated with policies to resolve systemic financial crises can be considerable. The study also indicates that emergency liquidity support and the provision of government guarantees have been the most frequently used policy tools for managing financial crises by governments in the past. Bank recapitalization programs can be successful if they are selective with regard to the institutions which they entitle to assistance, if they specify quantifiable rules that determine access to preferred stock assistance and if they implement capital regulation requirements which establish meaningful standards for risk-based capital. The formation of government-owned asset management firms appears least effective in terms of resolving distress, owing to legal and political constraints. In order to resolve the financial distress of companies and households, intervention via the implementation of targeted debt relief programs to distressed borrowers and corporate restructuring programs appear most successful.

The issue of the effectiveness of government intervention in resolving distress is of particular importance in the context of the US government rescue plan developed in 2009 in order to acquire the non-performing assets of a large number of distressed financial institutions. The so-called "Geithner–Summers Plan" involved a public–private investment program (PPIP) that was set up to absorb the impaired assets of distressed banks which was intended to enable those distressed institutions to resume lending. This government rescue strategy has certainly been criticized by many academics and economists for creating an overbid of assets at the expense of taxpayers. Wilson (2009) argues that shareholders of banks that face insolvency will sell impaired assets at a price equal to their expected future value plus the value of the put option that shareholders hold, owing to their limited liability. Consequently, according to that author, the government is not able to acquire the non-performing assets of distressed banks without simultaneously providing the banks that voluntarily participate in the asset sell-off with substantial taxpayers' subsidy.

In addition, Sachs (2009) argues that the rescue plan devised by the US Treasury is inefficient due to the fact that the PPIPs will be purchasing the nonperforming assets of distressed banks at a premium. Using an analysis of the capital structure of the purchase deal, the author shows how the price that will be paid in order to acquire the impaired assets includes a subsidy to the shareholders of the distressed bank. The Federal Deposit Insurance Corporation finances 85.7% of the asset purchase through a non-recourse loan, and the US Treasury and private investors each commit 7.15%, respectively. As a result of this capital structure of the deal, it is expected that private investors will be willing to offer a higher price than the expected future value of the non-performing assets that should equal the maximum price under which they can still break even.

Ayotte and Skeel (2009) analyze the effectiveness of government bailouts as a method to resolve bank distress and avoid systemic banking crises. The authors suggest that government rescue loans could increase uncertainty and the costs of moral hazard, and dampen the incentive of financial institutions to attempt and prevent or resolve distress without the provision of government aid. Consequently, the study concludes that government rescue schemes are likely to create costs over and above the direct costs to the taxpayer of the rescue funding. Although there are considerable costs associated with resolving distress via filing for bankruptcy using Chapter 11 of the United States Bankruptcy Code, the authors argue that the firm-specific costs related to bankruptcy tend to be overstated and may not be sufficient to justify government intervention.

In summary, the review of the literature on distressed M&A within the banking sector shows that there is no systematic and comprehensive analysis of the motivation behind the use of the different distressed M&A deal structures that banks participate in and their post-merger performance. More specifically, no studies compare the motivation behind using government intervention, outright M&A, or divestitures as strategies to resolve financial distress. In addition, there are no empirical studies that examine the effectiveness of the different strategies to deal with financial distress in terms of the changes in the key financial characteristics of the financial institutions that adopt and/or become the subject of these distress resolution techniques. Consequently, the primary objective of this chapter is to eliminate this existing deficiency within the literature on M&A deals within the banking sector.

DATA AND METHODOLOGY

This study analyzes the characteristics of distressed banks with respect to their size, asset quality, capital adequacy, efficiency, profitability, and liquidity one year prior to the announcement of restructuring deals, and how these characteristics change afterwards. Table 1 presents the specific accounting ratios that have been used to proxy for these financial characteristics.

In order to perform the above-mentioned type of analysis, it is necessary to have a reliable, accurate, and simple measure of distress to be able to distinguish between the distressed and non-distressed deals. Following Carapeto et al. (2010), this study uses the ratio of non-performing loans to total loans based on a three-year industry moving average to distinguish between distressed and healthy financial institutions. In addition, those banks in the sample which are targets of government agencies are assumed to be distressed since the only feasible motivation behind government agencies acquiring banks is to resolve distress. This study investigates the direct financial effects of different distress resolution techniques and, as a result, takes the perspective of the investors of the financial institutions that participate in distressed deals. This approach is adopted due to the fact that the indirect costs that are foregone by avoiding the bankruptcy of financial institutions (e.g., social costs and the economic and financial costs that could result from the contagion effects of the failure of banks) are difficult to capture with the use of financial ratios or other company-specific data. As noted earlier, this study analyzes performance over a period of one year before to three years after the announcement of the deals, despite the recognition of the fact that the results of the implemented strategies to resolve distress may require much longer to materialize.

This study uses data on mergers, acquisitions, and divestiture deals in the banking sector acquired from the Bloomberg database. The sample is global and comprises all 1,930 announced and completed banking deals over the period 1987–2005, including 1,216 acquisitions, 695 divestitures, and 19 government interventions (majority purchases). As three-year performance is then analyzed for each deal, the sample period extends to 2008. The search criteria for relevant deals did not include any specific constraints, apart from limiting the observations of targets and sellers to public companies within the banking industry and the need to analyze the performance of the distressed banks one year prior to the deal and three years afterwards. In this initial sample, there are 25 distressed targets and 28 distressed sellers using the definition of distress from Carapeto et al. (2010). Issues of data

Table 1. Definitions of Financial Ratios.

Type	Ratio	Definition
Size	Total assets	The value of a bank's total assets is used as a proxy for size.
Asset quality	Loan loss provision to net interest revenue	This ratio represents the relationship between provisions of expected future losses in a bank's income statement and the interest income generated over the same period. In a well-run bank, if the lending policy is higher risk, then the approach should be compensated by higher interest margins. Therefore, this ratio should be as low as possible.
Capital adequacy	Total equity to total assets	This ratio represents bank equity capital functions as a cushion against unexpected losses in asset value. Consequently, this ratio measures the degree to which a bank is protected against a sudden fall in asset value and the higher the ratio, the less vulnerable a bank is.
Efficiency	Cost to income ratio	This ratio equals total overhead costs of a bank divided by the income generated before accounting for any provisions. The lower the ratio, the more efficient a bank is.
Profitability	Return on average assets	This ratio equals the net income generated by the bank before any interest and dividend payments divided by the average of the total assets of the bank of the year before and the year in which the income was earned. This ratio is used to compare the efficiency and operational performance between different banks. The higher the ratio the better.
	Net interest margin	This ratio equals the net interest income a bank generates as a percentage of its operating assets. A higher ratio indicates that a bank is charging a high interest margin or that it can acquire cheap funding. Higher profitability and interest margins are desirable as long as they do not result in a deterioration of the quality of bank assets.
Liquidity	Interbank ratio	This ratio is equal to the funds lent to other banks divided by the funds borrowed from other banks. A ratio higher than 100% indicates that a bank is a net lender and vice versa. A higher ratio indicates a better liquidity position.
	Net loans to total assets	This ratio equals net loans divided by total assets and indicates what proportion of a bank's assets are tied up in loans. A lower ratio indicates a better liquidity position.

availability restrict the final sample to 59 deals (down from 72, hence still quite representative), which comprises 14 cases of government intervention, 25 divestitures, and 20 acquisitions, within the period from 1994 to 2005. Of these, almost half (27) are cross-border deals (14 acquisitions and 13 divestitures). Table 2 shows the time-series distribution of the sample of distressed banks as well as type of deals and country of target in the final sample.

Financial ratios are collected for each bank over a period of one year prior to three years after the announcement of the deal from the Bureau van Dijk BankScope database. Information from the BankScope database has also been used to estimate industry medians. In order to ensure consistency when calculating the industry medians, certain categories of banks ("clearing institutions" and "other non-banking credit institutions") were excluded from the dataset due to the fact that these groupings were not represented in the sample of deals that is examined in this study. Each accounting ratio is adjusted for industry effects by subtracting the industry median for the corresponding year. This procedure ensures that financial institutions are analyzed relative to their peers and thereby strengthens the validity of the findings of the study, consistent with, for example, Fraser and Zhang (2009). The analysis of the characteristics of participants in distressed M&A deals involves tests of equality of medians between different groups of targets and sellers, and the performance analysis comprises tests of the changes in the accounting measures examined in this study from the above-mentioned one year prior to the deal to three years post-deal outcomes.

RESULTS

Motivation behind the Choice of Distress Resolution Methods

Table 3 shows the analysis of the different financial characteristics of distressed targets and sellers one year prior to the announcement of M&A, divestiture, or government intervention, in order to identify motivational differences with regard to the resolution strategy that the distressed banks adopt and/or to which they become subject.

According to the results of the tests, distressed banks involved in the three types of restructuring deals are typically less profitable and display lower asset quality than their peers, as expected. In general, distressed targets and sellers have significantly unfavorable median-adjusted indicators. Distressed sellers are much larger than those banks in the other two categories and are

Table 2. Sample Description.

Year	Acquisition	Divestiture	Government	Total
Panel A: Time-series distribution				
1994			1	1
1996			1	1
1997		1		1
1998		1	2	3
1999	4	1		5
2000	5	5	4	14
2001	3	1	3	7
2002	1	3	1	5
2003	3	7	1	11
2004	4	1		5
2005		5	1	6
Total	20	25	14	59

Restructuring Type	Cross-Border	Domestic	Total
Panel B: Cross-border/domestic distribution			
Acquisition	14	6	20
Divestiture	13	12	25
Government			14
Total	27	18	59

Country	Acquisition	Divestiture	Government	Total
Panel C: Country distribution				
Canada		1		1
China	1		1	2
Croatia	3			3
Denmark			1	1
Germany		2	1	3
India			1	1
Indonesia	1		1	2
Israel		1		1
Italy	7	8	2	17
Japan	1	1	1	3
Lithuania			1	1
Malaysia		1		1
Norway			1	1
Philippines	1	3		4
Poland	6	3	2	11
Portugal		1		1
Romania			1	1
United Kingdom		1		1
United States		3		3
Venezuela			1	1
Total	20	25	14	59

Table 3. Bank Performance Pre-restructuring.

Ratios	Acquisitions	Test[a]	Divestitures	Test[b]	Government	Test[c]	Total
Size	20		25		14		59
Median	8,358.25	***	41,036.10	**	10,336.40		18,884.50
Loan loss provision to net interest revenue	20		25		12		57
Median	27.49		35.58	***	11.82		27.38
Industry-median adjusted	26.14***		34.17***	***	10.21**		26.03***
Total equity to total assets	20		25		13		58
Median	7.51	*	5.48	***	16.61	***	7.31
Industry-median adjusted	−1.00	*	−2.91**	***	15.74***	***	−0.62
Cost to income ratio	20		25		14		59
Median	65.67		70.72	***	1.48	***	64.28
Industry-median adjusted	0.28		5.18	**	0.84		0.87
Return on average assets	20		25		14		59
Median	0.35		0.21	***	8.10	***	0.57
Industry-median adjusted	−0.34**		−0.61***	***	7.41***	***	−0.20*
Net interest margin	20		25		14		59
Median	3.37	**	2.33		3.15		3.03
Industry-median adjusted	−0.27	**	−1.30***	***	1.91**	**	−0.35
Interbank ratio	15		20		14		49
Median	69.80		70.34	***	44.61	***	58.61
Industry-median adjusted	−7.18	*	−19.84***		37.09		−14.95
Net loans to total assets	20		24		14		58
Median	56.26		59.10		53.64		57.34
Industry-median adjusted	−4.08***		−0.07	***	46.49*	***	−0.85

*Significant at the 10% level and refers to the sign test on the significance of industry median-adjusted indicators.
**Significant at the 5% level and refers to the sign test on the significance of industry median-adjusted indicators.
***Significant at the 1% level and refers to the sign test on the significance of industry median-adjusted indicators.
[a]Sign test on comparison of medians between "acquisition" and "divestiture."
[b]Sign test on comparison of medians between "divestiture" and "government."
[c]Sign test on comparison of medians between "acquisition" and "government."

the worst in terms of all indicators except for efficiency, where they are not significantly different from targets of distressed acquisitions. Distressed targets are in the middle, though their performance is not good using median-adjusted ratios as they underperform their peers in terms of asset quality and profitability, but their liquidity levels are better. Distressed banks in which the government intervened enjoy better asset quality, capital adequacy, efficiency, and profitability when compared to banks involved in the other deals. The problem of government-intervened banks lies in their poor liquidity, which emphasizes the flow-based insolvency of these banks as opposed to stock-based insolvency (see Wruck, 1990). Thus, these banks are "fair performers" with short-term cash-flow issues. The fact that these banks are not relatively larger does not support the argument that they are "too big to fail."

Effectiveness of the Different Distress Resolution Methods

In order to identify the most efficient distress resolution methods, it is necessary to examine the changes in the financial characteristics of the distressed banks that adopt these different techniques. The results of this analysis are presented in Table 4.

For the restructuring deals, all banks have significantly increased in size over the four-year span. The banks with government intervention are still the best performers but there are now no significant changes between distressed targets and distressed sellers except for profitability, with evidence of distressed targets enjoying a larger net interest margin. The winners are the distressed sellers, showing significant improvements in capital adequacy, profitability, and liquidity. While the performance indicators for distressed targets have not significantly changed, there is evidence of liquidity deterioration for those banks in which the government intervened.

These findings should however be interpreted with caution since the sample size is not very large, and the focus is on the performance one year prior to the M&A deal or divestiture announcement to three years afterwards. As noted earlier, some of the effects associated with the implemented distress resolution strategies may take longer to manifest.

Cross-Border Deals

Table 5 provides a comparison of the financial characteristics of cross-border and domestic deals in the different types of restructuring methods

Table 4. Bank Performance Post-restructuring.

Ratios	Acquisitions	Test[a]	Divestitures	Test[b]	Government	Test[c]	Total
Size	20		25		14		59
Median	13,627.40	***	67,703.70		15,437.90		24,913.00
Year −1 to year +3	Up***		Up**		Up***		Up***
Loan loss provision to net interest revenue	20		25		12		57
Median	17.93		16.95		11.52		16.01
Year −1 to year +3							
Industry-median adjusted	16.58***		15.61***		10.13**		15.61***
Year −1 to year +3							
Total equity to total assets	20		25		13		58
Median	8.15		7.87	***	12.60	***	8.68
Year −1 to year +3			Up***				Up***
Industry-median adjusted	−1.17***		−1.77	***	11.13***	***	−0.58
Year −1 to year +3			Up***				
Cost to income ratio	20		25		14		59
Median	66.45		62.70	***	1.68	***	60.87
Year −1 to year +3							
Industry-median adjusted	1.42		−3.43	***	−63.19	***	−1.67
Year −1 to year +3							
Return on average assets	20		25		14		59
Median	0.98		0.92	***	12.60	***	1.05
Year −1 to year +3			Up**				Up***
Industry-median adjusted	0.10		−0.02	***	12.16***	***	0.21
Year −1 to year +3			Up*				Up**

Table 4. (*Continued*)

Ratios	Acquisitions	Test[a]	Divestitures	Test[b]	Government	Test[c]	Total
Net interest margin	20		25		14		59
Median	3.18	**	2.42		3.00		2.73
Year −1 to year +3							
Industry-median adjusted	−0.49	**	−1.18***	***	0.46		−0.62***
Year −1 to year +3							
Interbank ratio	15		20		14		49
Median	99.18		110.79	***	58.12	***	75.58
Year −1 to year +3			Up***				Up***
Industry-median adjusted	0.42		17.08	*	−22.99		5.10
Year −1 to year +3							
Net loans to total assets	20		24		14		58
Median	57.22		61.33	***	75.28	**	60.54
Year −1 to year +3					Up*		Up**
Industry-median adjusted	−3.78**		−3.06	***	29.76*	***	−0.68
Year −1 to year +3							

*Significant at the 10% level and refers to the sign test on the significance of industry median-adjusted indicators
**Significant at the 5% level and refers to the sign test on the significance of industry median-adjusted indicators
***Significant at the 1% level and refers to the sign test on the significance of industry median-adjusted indicators.
[a]Sign test on comparison of medians between "acquisition" and "divestiture."
[b]Sign test on comparison of medians between "divestiture" and "government."
[c]Sign test on comparison of medians between "acquisition" and "government."

Table 5. Bank Performance Pre-restructuring – Cross-Border vs. Domestic Deals.

Ratios	Acquisitions			Divestitures			Total		
	Cross-border	Test[a]	Domestic	Cross-border	Test[b]	Domestic	Cross-border	Test[c]	Domestic
Size	14		6	13		12	27		18
Median	13,184.00	***	1,491.95	41,036.10		77,678.80	24,691.00		10,525.00
Loan loss provision to net interest revenue	14		6	13		12	27		18
Median	27.10		30.19	37.01		29.37	31.18		29.37
Industry-median adjusted	25.74***		28.82**	35.60***		27.99***	29.81***		27.99***
Total equity to total assets	14		6	13		12	27		18
Median	7.08		7.64	5.48		5.26	6.35		7.14
Industry-median adjusted	−1.08		−1.00	−2.91**		−2.54	−2.56**		−1.49
Cost to income ratio	14		6	13		12	27		18
Median	63.81	**	87.79	66.28		70.72	65.98	**	71.38
Industry-median adjusted	−3.34	**	22.60	2.27		5.37	0.36	**	6.21
Return on average assets	14		6	13		12	27		18
Median	0.59	**	0.10	0.21		0.22	0.53		0.20
Industry-median adjusted	−0.16	*	−0.66**	−0.38***		−0.62	−0.30***		−0.62***
Net interest margin	14		6	13		12	27		18
Median	3.42		3.31	2.37		2.33	3.03		2.96
Industry-median adjusted	0.10		−0.41	−1.24***		−1.39	−0.64**		−0.72*
Interbank ratio	12		3	11		9	23		12
Median	64.46		192.96	70.34		70.34	69.80		70.34
Industry-median adjusted	−11.07		112.80	−19.84**		−19.84	−16.04*		−19.84
Net loans to total assets	14		6	13		11	27		17
Median	52.40	***	60.10	57.92		60.28	56.65	*	60.28
Industry-median adjusted	−9.22***	***	−0.06	−0.07		−0.07	−3.82***	*	−0.07

*Significant at the 10% level and refers to the sign test on the significance of industry median-adjusted indicators.
**Significant at the 5% level and refers to the sign test on the significance of industry median-adjusted indicators.
***Significant at the 1% level and refers to the sign test on the significance of industry median-adjusted indicators.
[a]Sign test on comparison of medians between "cross-border" and "domestic" for "acquisition."
[b]Sign test on comparison of medians between "cross-border" and "domestic" for "divestiture."
[c]Sign test on comparison of medians between "cross-border" and "domestic" for "total."

one year prior to the announcement of M&A deal or divestiture. As before, the aim is to identify motivational differences regarding the resolution strategy that the distressed banks adopt or to which they become subject.

According to the results of the tests, distressed banks involved in cross-border deals are typically more liquid and efficient than those engaged in domestic deals. Distressed sellers in cross-border deals are underperformers compared to their peers except for the efficiency ratio, where there is no significant difference. Still, there are no significant differences between distressed sellers involved in domestic and cross-border deals. The situation is, however, the reverse when it comes to acquisitions as foreign acquirers seem to "cherry pick" the relatively largest and least distressed banks; that is, these targets are more profitable, efficient, and liquid compared to distressed targets in domestic deals. This evidence thus supports Tschoegl's (2004) argument that foreign banks are more likely to take over banks in relatively better shape yet still they underperform their peers, in line with Correa (2008) and Fraser and Zhang (2009).

Regarding the analysis of the changes in the financial characteristics of the distressed banks following the restructuring, Table 6 presents the results classified by type of deal.

Following the restructuring deals, banks in all cross-border deals have significantly increased in size over the four-year span while those in domestic deals have improved their efficiency. Three years after the deals, the performance of the distressed banks is very different. If before the deals, distressed targets in cross-border deals were in better shape than those in domestic deals, three years later there are no significant differences in performance, mainly as a result of significant improvements in capital adequacy and profitability in the latter banks. Conversely, the distressed sellers involved in cross-border deals enjoy significant improvements in profitability, liquidity, and capital adequacy, with distressed sellers in domestic deals also displaying increases in the latter indicator.

The results support Correa (2008) and Vander and Vennet (2002) as they confirm that targets involved in cross-border acquisitions are larger than those in domestic deals and fail to enjoy improvements in performance post-deal. However, the results do not support Correa's (2008) finding that targets in cross-border deals are poor performers compared to those acquired in domestic deals. Nor do they support Fraser and Zhang's (2009) observation of improvements in profitability and efficiency post-deal.

Table 6. Bank Performance Post-restructuring – Cross-Border vs. Domestic Deals.

	Acquisitions			Divestitures			Total		
Ratios	Cross-border	Test[a]	Domestic	Cross-border	Test[b]	Domestic	Cross-border	Test[c]	Domestic
Size	14		6	13		12	27		18
Median	20,179.30	***	1,399.50	67,703.70		52,665.40	39,061.20	*	14,717.50
Year −1 to year +3	Up**			Up*			Up***		
Loan loss provision to net interest revenue	14		6	13		12	27		18
Median	16.65		21.99	16.95		15.47	16.95		20.22
Year −1 to year +3									
Industry-median adjusted	15.27**		20.67	15.61**		14.14**	15.61***		18.96***
Year −1 to year +3									
Total equity to total assets	14		6	13		12	27		18
Median	8.15		8.33	7.28		8.67	7.87	*	8.57
Year −1 to year +3			Up**	Up**		Up***			Up***
Industry-median adjusted	−1.17**		−1.15	−2.06*		−0.62	−1.77***	*	−0.87
Year −1 to year +3				Up**					Up*
Cost to income ratio	14		6	13		12	27		18
Median	66.34		66.87	65.89		60.87	65.89		61.79
Year −1 to year +3									Down*
Industry-median adjusted	1.42		1.71	−0.67		−3.43	0.62		−3.00
Year −1 to year +3									Down*
Return on average assets	14		6	13		12	27		18
Median	1.03		0.60	0.92		0.92	0.94		0.90
Year −1 to year +3			Up**	Up*					Up**
Industry-median adjusted	0.12		−0.30	−0.02		0.01	0.05		−0.02
Year −1 to year +3				Up*					

Table 6. (*Continued*)

Ratios	Acquisitions			Divestitures			Total		
	Cross-border	Test[a]	Domestic	Cross-border	Test[b]	Domestic	Cross-border	Test[c]	Domestic
Net interest margin	14		6	13		12	27		18
Median	3.18		2.85	2.32		2.58	2.73		2.59
Year −1 to year +3				Down*					
Industry-median adjusted	−0.49		−0.76	−1.21**		−1.05**	−0.97**		−1.04**
Year −1 to year +3									
Interbank ratio	12		3	11		9	23		12
Median	94.61		229.73	120.74		96.15	100.84		108.45
Year −1 to year +3				Up*					
Industry-median adjusted	0.14		143.97	38.62		5.98	5.10		17.08
Year −1 to year +3									
Net loans to total assets	14		6	13		11	27		17
Median	54.56		61.43	61.39		61.27	56.97		61.27
Year −1 to year +3									
Industry-median adjusted	−7.96*		−0.68	−4.58		0.92	−7.06**		−0.51
Year −1 to year +3									

*Significant at the 10% level and refers to the sign test on the significance of industry median-adjusted indicators.
**Significant at the 5% level and refers to the sign test on the significance of industry median-adjusted indicators.
***Significant at the 1% level and refers to the sign test on the significance of industry median-adjusted indicators.
[a]Sign test on comparison of medians between "cross-border" and "domestic" for "acquisition."
[b]Sign test on comparison of medians between "cross-border" and "domestic" for "divestiture."
[c]Sign test on comparison of medians between "cross-border" and "domestic" for "total."

Evidence from Recent Bank Failures

In order to see whether the results of the study can be extended to recent bank failures, the financial characteristics of a global sample of 129 distressed targets and sellers were analyzed one year prior to the announcement of an acquisition, divestiture, or government intervention during the period 2007–2009. Overall, the motivation behind the different distress resolution strategies appears to have been similar during the recent financial crisis to the 1994–2005 main sample, as outlined in Table 7.

As before, distressed banks involved in the three types of restructuring deal are less profitable and display lower asset quality than their peers. In addition, their capital adequacy and efficiency ratios are worse. Distressed targets are still the worst performers prior to the restructuring deals, while banks which have had government intervention suffer from the same liquidity issues as in the main sample (this time proxied by another liquidity ratio). Surprisingly, the evidence points toward governments intervening in the smallest banks during the recent financial crisis, despite the massive bailouts.

It is too early to provide empirical evidence on post-performance following these different restructuring strategies during the recent financial crisis as the methodology used in this research requires three years of data post-deal. However, the fact that the findings with regard to motivation are confirmed by this more recent group of distressed banks suggests that the post-performance results presented in this study may be extended to the recent crisis and used as a reliable predictor of future post-performance outcomes.

CONCLUSION

The recent financial crisis has highlighted the need to assess the efficiency and financial consequences of existing methods to deal with distress and to identify the most effective distress resolution technique(s). Governments around the world have struggled with the decision of whether to rescue failing financial institutions or to allow (or encourage) private sector solutions. The existing literature includes no studies that analyze the motivation behind the different distress resolution techniques that have been adopted in the past or how the financial characteristics of the banks that participate in distressed M&A deals change over time. The chapter's objective is to eliminate this deficiency in the existing literature.

Table 7. Bank Performance Pre-restructuring (Recent Financial Crisis).

Ratios	Acquisitions	Test[a]	Divestitures	Test[b]	Government	Test[c]	Total
Size	30		67		32		129
Median	10,129.40	**	60,909.50	***	1,535.21	***	6,709.10
Loan loss provision to net interest revenue	30		67		32		129
Median	16.07	***	50.01	***	8.07	***	23.89
Industry-median adjusted	5.63***	***	40.48***		31.80***	**	19.38***
Total equity to total assets	30		67		32		129
Median	6.69		6.02	***	9.16	**	7.07
Industry-median adjusted	−2.89**		−3.63***	***	−0.48	**	−2.55***
Cost to income ratio	28		67		32		127
Median	63.89	***	72.28	*	68.28		70.91
Industry-median adjusted	−3.34	***	3.79**	*	1.89		2.29**
Return on average assets	30		67		32		129
Median	0.61	***	−0.41	***	0.72		0.34
Industry-median adjusted	−0.18	***	−1.05***	***	−0.15		−0.42***
Net interest margin	30		67		32		129
Median	3.50	**	2.92	***	3.84		3.02
Industry-median adjusted	0.04	**	−0.73***	***	0.38**		−0.52***
Interbank ratio	17		28		3		48
Median	40.17	*	87.67		143.15		68.71
Industry-median adjusted	−58.64		−9.61		47.40		−29.50
Net loans to total assets	30		67		32		129
Median	56.45		62.12	***	77.55	***	66.76
Industry-median adjusted	−7.55		−4.57	***	12.12***	***	0.97

*Significant at the 10% level and refers to the sign test on the significance of industry median-adjusted indicators.
**Significant at the 5% level and refers to the sign test on the significance of industry median-adjusted indicators.
***Significant at the 1% level and refers to the sign test on the significance of industry median-adjusted indicators.
[a]Sign test on comparison of medians between "acquisition" and "divestiture."
[b]Sign test on comparison of medians between "divestiture" and "government."
[c]Sign test on comparison of medians between "acquisition" and "government."

The findings of this study show that distressed banks that choose to divest divisions are the worst performers one year prior to the deal but the most improved three years later. Distressed banks which have government intervention are the best performers over the four-year span, though their persistent major challenge is liquidity. Distressed targets are in between those two groups.

Prior to the deal, while there are no significant differences in performance between distressed sellers involved in domestic and cross-border deals, there is evidence that foreign acquirers seem to "cherry pick" the least distressed banks. Interestingly, three years later distressed targets involved in domestic deals have managed to catch up with improvements in capital adequacy and profitability, and, as such, no significant differences remain in performance between distressed targets in cross-border and domestic deals. Conversely, the distressed sellers involved in cross-border deals seem to enjoy an improved performance compared to those involved in domestic deals.

The findings presented in this study should be viewed with caution since they are based on the analysis of the direct financial costs associated with different distress resolution techniques. As a result, the effectiveness of distressed M&A is evaluated from the perspective of the investors of the financial institutions that participate in these types of deals. Further research and analysis is necessary in order to determine the strategy that could resolve financial distress most effectively and efficiently for all stakeholders directly or indirectly affected by it. Also, although the study has examined more recent deals in terms of motivation, in a few years it would be useful to apply this chapter's post-deal performance methodology to these deals to determine whether the findings and conclusions do still apply.

There are interesting policy implications for governments and regulators globally. The results from this study provide guidance to governments and regulators throughout the world, which may be faced with decisions in a future banking crisis. There is clear evidence from this work that distressed banks with government intervention were the best performers over the period studied, despite the challenges with the long-term liquidity issues in those banks noted above, although the private sector does have better capacity to implement effective distress resolution strategies relative to the public sector in cases of very poor performers (perhaps implying that in these extreme cases, government policy should encourage a private sector solution). This study therefore does provide support for regulations and policies that allow, if not even encourage, bank mergers, acquisitions, and divestitures as a mechanism to resolve distress involving both domestic and foreign banks.

REFERENCES

Ayotte, K., & Skeel, D. (2009). *Bankruptcy or bailouts*. Working Paper.

Beccalli, E., & Frantz, P. (2009). M&A operations and performance in banking. *Journal of Financial Services Research*, *36*, 203–226.

Carapeto, M., Moeller, S., Faelten, A., Vitkova, V., & Bortolotto, L. (2010). *Distress classification measures in the banking sector*. Working Paper.

Chamberlain, S. L. (1998). The effect of bank ownership changes on subsidiary-level earnings In: Y. Amihud & G. Miller (Eds), *Bank mergers and acquisitions* (pp. 132–172). Boston: Kluwer Academic Publishers.

Cornett, M., & Tehranian, H. (1992). Changes in corporate performance associated with bank performance. *Journal of Financial Economics*, *31*, 211–234.

Correa, R. (2008). *Cross-border bank acquisitions: Is there a performance effect*? Board of Governors of the Federal Reserve System (International Finance Discussion Papers).

Elsas, R. (2007). *Preemptive distress resolution through bank mergers*. Working Paper.

Fraser, D. R., & Zhang, H. (2009). Mergers and long-term corporate performance: Evidence from cross-border bank acquisitions. *Journal of Money, Credit and Banking*, *41*(7), 1503–1513.

Guerrera, F., & Guha, K. (2010). Outcry on Wall St. at 'absurd' levy plan. *Financial Times*, January 10. Available at http://www.ft.com/cms/s/0/6074a644-ffa1-11de-921f-00144feabdc0.html. Accessed on 14 September 2009.

Koetter, M., Bos, B., Heid, F., Kool, C., Kolari, J., & Porath, D. (2007). Accounting for distress in bank mergers. *Journal of Banking and Finance*, *31*(10), 3200–3217.

Laeven, L., & Valencia, F. (2008). *Systemic banking crises: A new database*. International Monetary Fund Working Paper. Available at http://imf.org/external/pubs/ft/wp/2008/wp08224.pdf

Linder, J. C., & Crane, D. B. (1992). Bank mergers: Integration and profitability. *Journal of Financial Service Research*, *7*, 35–55.

Sachs, J. (2009). The Geithner-Summers plan is even worse than we thought. *The Guardian*, April 8. Available at http://www.huffingtonpost.com/jeffrey-sachs/the-geithner-summers-plan_b_183499.html. Accessed on 14 September 2009.

Tschoegl, A. E. (2004). *Financial crises and the presence of foreign banks*. International Finance 0405016, Economics Working Paper.

Vander, M., & Vennet, R. (2002). Cross-border mergers in European banking and bank efficiency. In: H. Herrmann & R. Lipsey (Eds), *Foreign direct investment in the real and financial sector of industrial countries* (pp. 295–315). Berlin, Heidelberg, New York: Springer Verlag.

Wheelock, D., & Wilson, P. (2000). Why do banks disappear? The determinants of U.S. bank failures and acquisitions. *The Review of Economics and Statistics*, *82*(1), 127–138.

Wilson, L. (2009). The put problem with buying toxic assets. *Journal of Applied Financial Economics*, *20*, 31–35.

Wruck, K. H. (1990). Financial distress, reorganization, and organizational efficiency. *Journal of Financial Economics*, *27*, 419–444.

COMPARISON OF BANKING EFFICIENCY IN EUROPE: ISLAMIC VERSUS CONVENTIONAL BANKS

Wahida Ahmad and Robin H. Luo

ABSTRACT

Many banking efficiency studies have focused on conventional banks. Recently, Islamic banks have opened in many countries and operated in similar fashion to traditional banks. This chapter measures and compares Islamic banking efficiency to conventional banking efficiency represented by three European countries – Germany, Turkey and the United Kingdom. The study covers the period from 2005 to 2008 in measuring the X-efficiency using the non-parametric method, known as Data Envelopment Analysis (DEA). It reveals that Islamic banks are technically more efficient than conventional banks but are beset by lower allocative efficiency. This results in lower cost efficiency for Islamic banks in comparison to the more conventional banks in Europe.

1. INTRODUCTION

Before the emergence of the Islamic financial system, Muslims worldwide have only had a conventional financial system to fulfil their financial needs. The Islamic resurgence in the late 1960s and 1970s initiated the call for a

International Banking in the New Era: Post-Crisis Challenges and Opportunities
International Finance Review, Volume 11, 361–389

ISSN: 1569-3767/doi:10.1108/S1569-3767(2010)0000011016

financial system that allowed Muslims to transact in a system that is consistent with their religious beliefs. Islamic banking and financial institutions exist on the basis of their compliance to Shari'ah law. The major distinction it has from the traditional banking system is in the issue of prohibition of riba'.[1]

The desire to fulfil the financial needs of Muslims led to the establishment of the Islamic Development Bank in 1974, followed in 1975 by the Islamic Bank of Dubai, the world's first Islamic commercial bank. As the years passed numbers of Islamic banks were established, concentrated mainly in the Middle East, including the Islamic Bank of Faisal in Egypt and Jordan (1977 and 1978, respectively), Bank of Islamic Finance and Investment in Jordan (1978), and the Islamic Investment Company Ltd. in UAE (1979).

The substantial growth in Islamic banks that began in the Middle East was later followed by expansion in South East Asian countries. Malaysia is now on its way to become the world's centre for Islamic banking. In Malaysia, Islamic finance traces its roots back to 1963, with the establishment of the Pilgrims Fund Board or Lembaga Tabung Haji (LTH) as the first Islamic saving institution and followed by the creation of full-fledged Islamic banking and non-banking institutions. The legal basis for the establishment of Islamic banks was the Islamic Banking Act (IBA) which took effect on 7 April 1983. Bank Islam Malaysia Berhad (BIMB), the first Islamic bank in Malaysia began its operation in July 1983. It is now generally agreed that Bahrain and Malaysia represent the premier hubs of Islamic banking operations.

The Islamic financial system's growth and development were further developed by many countries issuing licenses to foreign banks, allowing them to offer Islamic products in an effort to improve Islamic financial operations. For instance, one of the early pioneers, the Central Bank of Kuwait (CBK) and later the Bank Negara Malaysia (BNM), started granting licenses to foreign players.[2] This new financial structure not only widened the network of Islamic banking within a country but also increased the effectiveness and performance of Islamic financial instruments.

Islamic banking later branched out so that the potential market did not solely concentrate on Muslim countries. The system has broadened the horizon from Muslim countries to the Western markets. This chapter discusses the existence of Islamic banking in three European countries, Germany (Western Europe), Turkey (Southern Europe) and the United Kingdom (Northern Europe) and how it compares to conventional banking. It also analyses and compares the efficiency of banking as represented by Islamic banks on one hand and conventional European banks on the other.

2. ISLAMIC BANKING AND THE EUROPEAN BANKING MARKET

2.1. European Banking and Financial Markets

European financial markets have diversified practices that are increasingly deregulated. The distinction between each country's financial systems is becoming increasingly blurred particularly in the recent endeavour to create a single market. The shift to a single European market in banking started at the end of the 1970s with the First Banking Directive, which aimed to remove obstacles to establishing branches in European Union (EU) member states. This ambition to create a single market became evident with Basel I, Capital Adequacy Regulation (1988) and Basel II, Capital Requirement Directive (2008). The creation of the European Monetary Union in 1999 and the implementation of the Financial Service Action Plan (FSAP) between 1999 and 2005 reinforced this desire (Dermine, 2005).

The literature on this subject has highlighted the problems in realising a thorough integration of the European banking markets. Challenges include national economic conditions, culture, language and important differences in the fiscal and legal systems (Goddard, Molyneux, Wilson, & Tavakoli, 2007). Integrating Europe's banks has been complicated by the establishment of many subsidiaries rather than branches in another European country. The establishment of subsidiaries limits the operations where subsidiary banks owned by a foreign parent bank are bound by a country's banking legislation and regulations.

The process of creating a single market has led to structural change in the European market. Market openness has also been influenced by the drive to globalisation, deregulation, technological change, harmonisation, market integration and liberalisation. Thus the banking market operates in a highly competitive environment where foreign banks compete for business in European financial markets. In order to succeed in the European market, growth is important for banks and success is built either on internally generated growth or through market expansion. Increased cross-border activities or geographic diversification lead to sustain growth (Goddard et al., 2007). Banks are willing to offer non-interest income products that generate income in the form of fees and commissions such as off-balance sheet business. This growth will allow banks to realise scale and scope economies, reduce their variable costs and thus reduce operational inefficiencies.

2.2. Competition, Efficiency and Islamic Banking in the European Market

A single market programme and deregulation in Europe have resulted in a significant decline in the number of banks but overall the growth in total assets has still been remarkable (Goddard et al., 2007). Single market or European financial market integration will at least gradually have an impact on market concentration and existing financial institutions' market power. With loosen power on market concentration, competition draw closer to take place. Maudos, Pastor, Pérez, and Quesada (2002) analyse the cost and profit efficiency of 832 banks in 10 European Union countries and find that market concentration is positively related to profit efficiency and negatively related to cost efficiency. Generally banks that have been more involved in more concentrated market normally have less pressure to control cost expenditures.

Maudos and de Guevara (2007) study the market power and efficiency of the loan and deposit market in the European Union (EU15) countries from 1993 to 2003 and concludes that there is a positive relationship between market power and cost efficiency, leading to rejection of the quiet life hypothesis. Staikouras, Mamatzakis, and Koutsomanoli-Filippaki (2008) in their cost efficiency study of six South Eastern European (SEE) countries find a negative correlation of cost inefficiency with bank capitalisation and market share. The results highlight low levels of cost efficiency and the authors promote the idea of foreign banks entering a SEE country's financial system to improve banking efficiency. Indeed many studies agree that foreign ownership is the most efficient form of banking ownership in comparison to all other types (Berger, Hasan, & Zhou, 2009; Bonin, Hasan, & Wachtel, 2005; Fries & Taci, 2005). Jaap and James (2005) further point out that there are possible potential efficiency gains by large European and US banks expanding geographically.

Koutsomanoli-Filippaki, Margaritis, and Staikouras (2009) document that competition and concentration are strongly linked to bank efficiency in their study of efficiency and productivity growth in the Central and Eastern European banking industry. The harmonisation of regulations and macroeconomic convergence in the European Union (EU15) signifies that there is a trade-off between competition and stability (De Jonghe & Vennet, 2008). It is a fact that banks in Europe are feeling the pressure in a very competitive environment, and banks have to develop solutions such as considering vertical product differentiation, diversification and consolidation. Such strategies are deemed to guarantee that banks will remain competitive and survive well into the future.

Horizontal product differentiation refer to banks offering other than its main retail product such as loans and deposits by introducing or focusing more on non-interest earning activities such as assets management, mutual funds and private banking. These products will generate income in the form of fees and commissions. Currently, non-interest earning products are becoming more popular in the banking industry because they represent a major source of income for banks, and they have increased off-balance sheet activities. Although the Basel Committee of Banking Supervision focused on capital adequacy regulation, it should have reflected on risk management, off-balance sheets and disclosure standards for the European financial market (Welfens & Wolf, 1997).

Vertical product differentiation promotes the idea of improved service quality to customers and the ability to be different from their rivals allow for less competition. For instance, some financial institutions offer remote access for their customers to enhance their services. Lozano-Vivas (2009) measures and explains the impact of vertical product differentiation on banking efficiency and from the production point of view, it encourages banks to operate efficiently. Degryse (1996) classifies financial products as embodying both characteristics – horizontal and vertical product differentiation – which means in effect multi-dimensional product differentiation. Thus Islamic banks in Europe have taken the opportunity to expand there through product innovation precisely through multi-dimensional product differentiation. The existence of Islamic products in the European banking industry may well lead to improved banking efficiency and competitiveness.

In order to succeed in Europe's competitive financial market, it is very critical for banks to ensure they remain efficient so that they are economically viable. The single market programme has removed many obstacles for foreign entry and this includes recognising Islamic banking activities. Although the efficiency level of Islamic banking is very much a topic of debate,[3] it is important to analyse and compare whether the establishment of Islamic banking in Europe could enhance its banking industry's efficiency. There are only small numbers of Islamic banks in Europe compared to the conventional banks, and as our concern no studies have been done to evaluate the performance of these market players. De Jonghe and Vennet (2008) and many other studies have argued that country-specific macroeconomic variables have a significant impact on banking performance, and the efficiency of Islamic banking raises interesting points with respect to the European banking market.

2.3. Islamic Banking and Financial Crisis

Islamic and conventional banks operate according to their own rules and principles yet they are exposed to similar market risks. It is worthwhile comparing these two bank groups' persistence in managing financial sector crisis, since the failure of either one may cause systemic risk to the entire financial system. Nevertheless, a mild level financial crisis may provide long-run advantages in improving banking efficiency by eliminating inefficient banks in the industry. Although Islamic banks remain loyal to Shari'ah principles and operate under profit and loss sharing (PLS) mechanisms, they are expected to be more stable and less likely to be affected by a financial crisis.

The basis of Islamic finance is to uphold business ethics and the value of investment should depend on the actual business. The PLS principle promotes equity participation which in turn encourages due diligence in managing investment and active monitoring. A financial crisis results from excessive risk-taking activities and the use of innovative yet complex products. Then again, Islamic banking prohibits interest and speculation which may lead to risky investments. For instance, Bank Islam Malaysia Berhad (BIMB), the first Islamic bank in Malaysia, bears comparatively lower risks than conventional banks in Malaysia because it has more investment in government securities. Furthermore, BIMB has lower leverage and solvency risks than conventional banks. For these reasons, BIMB was not severely affected by the Asian financial crisis of 1997. In addition, Malaysia's Islamic banks, particularly BIMB, were not compromised by the Global Financial Crisis because they remained compliant to Shari'ah finance regulations. Currently, with the dual banking systems framework, Malaysian Islamic banks are required to meet all standards applicable to conventional banks such as the capital reserves requirement, risk management and financial disclosure. In order to segregate Islamic banking division from their conventional banking, they are governed by the Shari'ah Advisory Board under National Shari'ah Advisory Council of Bank Negara Malaysia.

In general, Islamic banks are experiencing excess liquidity in their accounts. In contrast to conventional banks, Islamic banks are not permitted to become involved in conventional money market instruments. Thus in avoiding liquidity risk, Islamic banks hold more cash or very low return assets as their liquid assets. Despite the fact that many banks suffered losses during the Global Financial Crisis, most Islamic banks remained untouched by the credit crunch because they enjoyed a cushion liquidity position. Islamic banks, however, have to understand that there is a trade-off between profitability and liquidity in their operations. Samad and Hassan (1999) in their study find an insignificant difference in the profitability performance of BIMB compared to other conventional banks in Malaysia. However, they conclude that BIMB has a higher liquidity position than conventional banks. Furthermore BIMB has maintained a high liquidity level since it began and thus it is more stable and flexible in managing customers' deposits.

Many liquidity management instruments have recently been adopted by Islamic banks in line with Shari'ah principles such as Commodity Murabaha, Sukuk al-Salam, Islamic Inter-bank Money Market, Islamic Debt Security and Musharakah Certificates.[4] The motivation of the Islamic liquidity market is similar to that of conventional markets in wanting to promote growth and efficiency of fund transmission in the marketplace. Partnership sukuk (Islamic bond), the hybrid of debt and equity-based sukuk has become one of the most popular Islamic instruments for avoiding a financial crisis. This is one way of replying to the recent criticism against sukuk as it becomes a more recognisable form of conventional debt. The true sukuk under Shari'ah principle must be attached to real tangible assets rather than cash flows and there should be no promissory returns since it is linked closely to the PLS principle (Khan, Iliasu, & Chowdhry, 2009). Unlike conventional mortgage-backed securities (MBS), periodic return and capital gains of partnership sukuk is based on the actual underlying assets. In order to ensure the implementation of true Islamic instruments in accordance with Shari'ah, the existence of a proper regulatory framework is essential. In 2008, the Accounting and Auditing Organisation for Islamic Financial Institutions (AAOIFI) outlined that borrowers in sukuk mudaraba and musharaka should not promise upfront to pay back their face value at maturity. Though the growth of sukuk markets is promising, currently the size is still far behind their conventional counterparts. Consequently the investors who support sukuk markets are extended beyond the conventional debt markets, which are forced to violate the Shari'ah principle of PLS by having a fixed-income cash flow.

Islamic banks are dealing with unique products in accordance with Shari'ah compliance and thus they face risks that distinguish them from those of conventional banks. Under Islamic laws and concepts, Islamic banks should be less affected by a financial and banking crisis. The participation of Shari'ah scholars in regulating and supervising the industry is critical to ensure Islamic banks do not behave like conventional banks and stay close to their traditional rules. Furthermore, with the collaboration of AAOIFI and IFSB, Basel II compliance would assist in the international recognition of Islamic banks and ensure their standardization (Hassan & Dicle, 2005).

3. LITERATURE REVIEW

3.1. Comparative Studies on Banking Efficiency across European Countries

Cross-country studies provide valuable information regarding the competitiveness of banks in different countries, especially considering the internationalisation of finance and its much more globalised character now and in the future. Research studies that have measured the efficiency of banking systems in many countries have varied findings.

The European banking system varies across countries but there are evidences of insignificant differences among European countries. Carbó Valverde, Humphrey, and López del Paso (2007) study 153 large banks across 10 European countries with certain control variables and find the average efficiency among banks in each country is almost identical. In a similar study of 5,000 large commercial banks from 15 major European banking market, Bos and Schmiedel (2007) document a single European banking market characterised by cost and profit meta-frontier. The authors, however, find relatively pooled frontier estimations tend to underestimate efficiency levels and have poor correlation with country-specific frontier efficiency ranks. Weill (2009) verifies the financial integration of European banking on the basis of convergence in banking efficiency for some countries.

Other studies have produced conflicting results on cross-country banking efficiency themes. Pastor, Pérez, and Quesada (1997) use a non-parametric approach with the Malmquist index to compare US and European commercial banks' efficiency, productivity and technology. Their study classifies the banking systems into two categories with Austria, Italy, Germany and Belgium being more productive than the United States, the United Kingdom, France and Spain. Dietsch and Lozano-Vivas (2000) investigate the impact of environment on determining the banking efficiency of the French and Spanish banking industries. They demonstrate that environmental variables contribute significantly to the difference in these two countries' efficiency scores. Staikouras et al. (2008) study six South Eastern European countries and discovered that in general there are low levels of cost efficiency for selected banks. They also discovered significant banking inefficiencies among these countries.

Mixed efficiency results in cross-country studies may be due to different regulatory and economic environments, levels and quality of service for deposits and loans, the specification of common frontier across countries (Berger & Humphrey, 1997), choice of methodology and other factors. The authors suggest the need for proper specification of country-specific environmental influences for realistic cross-country comparison. The environmental or control variables are classified into macroeconomic or country-specific factors, bank structure and regulations, bank-specific factors, banks' internal productivity, accessibility of banking services and institutionalisation, which later depending on the research issues of each study.

A number of studies identify specific environmental variables when estimating cross-country differences by controlling these factors (see Altunbas & Chakravarty, 1998; Beccalli, 2004; Carbó Valverde et al., 2007; Dietsch & Lozano-Vivas, 2000; Weill, 2009). One aspect of environmental factors is the macroeconomic variables or country-specific factors. Popular control variables consist of market or industry concentration, per capita GDP, nominal market interest rate, intermediation ratio, population density and demand density. Other factors taken into consideration are International Monetary Fund (IMF) support (Thoraneenitiyan & Avkiran, 2009), average wage rate and banking openness index (Kwan, 2003), European Bank for Reconstruction and Development (EBRD) index of banking reform (Koutsomanoli-Filippaki et al., 2009), population per ATM and population per branch (Carbó Valverde et al., 2007).

Environmental factors are also marked by bank-specific data or bank structure and regulations. Among the variables used in the literature that has evaluated cross-country differences are bank size, equity level or capitalization, product differentiation, variation in risk taking, the ratio of state-owned banks' assets to total banking assets, the ratio of foreign-owned banks assets to total banking assets, output quality and the ratio of retail deposits to total deposits (e.g. Fries & Taci, 2005; Kwan, 2003; Staikouras et al., 2008).

Carbó Valverde et al. (2007) incorporate internal productivity measures as part of the control variables in their research on determining 'national champions' of banking efficiency in Europe. The measures include the ratio of ATM to branch, deposits per worker, workers per branch, deposits per branch and number of large banks. Dietsch and Lozano-Vivas (2000) focus on the number of branches per square kilometre to proxy accessibility of banking services when comparing the efficiency of commercial banks and savings banks in France and Spain. Beccalli (2004) controls the institutional environment with six variables consisting of market performance, number of domestic listed companies, legal reserve, ownership, accounting standards and inwards and outwards business transactions. The results show that controlling environmental factors for cross-country comparison do significantly influence cost efficiency and profitability.

Other studies integrate the ownership structure and bank size in cross-country banking efficiency studies. For instance, Hensel (2003) discovers that larger banks are more likely to extensively utilise bank branches which are exposed to less cost efficiencies because there are more branches. Ownership studies on banking efficiency across countries have suggested that foreign-owned banks or banks subject to majority foreign ownership perform better with greater efficiency scores, especially in the European market (e.g. Fries & Taci, 2005; Koutsomanoli-Filippaki et al., 2009; Staikouras et al., 2008).

Cross-country results might be influenced by the selection and specification of a common frontier or country-specific frontier. Berger (2007) reviews and critiques over 100 studies that compare banking efficiency across several countries. The author classifies the studies into three categories: (i) comparisons of banking efficiency across nations with a common frontier; (ii) comparisons of banking efficiency across nations against their own nation-specific frontier and (iii) comparisons of banking efficiencies of foreign-owned versus domestically owned banks within the same nation against its nation-specific frontier.

Comparing efficiency with global frontier permits a more accurate study to be made across nations, as the same standard is being compared. However, the specification of a common frontier where best-performing banks are the benchmark may not indicate the best efficiency score for each bank in a different country. The use of a common frontier, however, is widespread with improved econometric methods by controlling environmental variables. Bos and Schmiedel (2007) analyse the possibility of a common benchmark using cost and profit frontier in European banking markets. The results led directly to a single European banking market characterised by a cost and profit meta-frontier. Dietsch and Lozano-Vivas (2000) attempt to specify the common frontier of different countries and took environmental variables into consideration.

Hence comparing the efficiency of a country's own measured best-practice frontier may provide a better comparison rather than comparing it with the global frontier. A bank's efficiency measured relative to its own country frontier represents a similar level of service, regulatory treatment and economic environment. Berger (2007) brings up the problem with a specific-nation frontier that is not suitable for comparing different banks in other countries.

3.2. Islamic Banking Efficiency

Most studies on banking efficiency for conventional banks have focused on the United States and Europe. However, a limited numbers of studies have been undertaken on measuring the efficiency of Islamic banking. It is generally contended that Islamic banks are totally different in their practices to conventional banks, but it is notable that Islamic banking offers products and services similar to commercial and investment banks. Available studies on Islamic banking focus on conceptual issues (e.g. Ahmed, 1989; Memon, 2007) rather than empirical analysis. This is particularly due to the small number of Islamic banks relative to conventional banks. The tremendous growth in Islamic banking worldwide has necessitated research on efficiency in Islamic banking operations.

In order to fully understand the Islamic banking system, it is important to note the existing structure and regulations. El-Hawary, Grais, and Iqbal (2007) point out that the regulatory regime for Islamic Financial Institutions varies across countries. Their study discusses the set of standards and harmonising prudential regulations such as the Accounting and Auditing Organization for Islamic Financial Institutions (AAOIFI), International Islamic Rating Agency (IIRA), Liquidity Management Center (LMC) and Islamic Financial Services Board (IFSB). The first three are based in Bahrain and the latter is based in Malaysia. However, Karim (2001) discovers lack of appreciation by the relevant agencies to acknowledge the set standards for the accounting harmonization and Islamic banking regulation.

It is notorious that, in many countries, Islamic banking emerges from the traditional banking and thus in essence it works in the existing conventional banking framework. It is obviously a shortfall for Islamic banks as they have to perform their operations in accordance to Shari'ah law within traditional framework. This has subsequently become a hurdle for Islamic banks wanting to achieve their optimum efficiency level. Sarker (1999) documents that Islamic banks cannot fully achieve great efficiency when operating within the confines of a conventional banking system. However, the evidence from Bangladesh Islamic banks reveals that these banks can still survive in the existing market structure and framework and function according to Islamic principles. Islamic products have different risk characteristics and consequently different prudential regulations should be erected.

It is also essential to make a distinction between the terms and variables concerning accounting data when measuring Islamic banks' efficiency.

Islamic banking operations prohibit interest earnings and interest charges, while interest is the main income for conventional banks. Analogous to conventional banking, Islamic banks offer deposit accounts and loans to their customers, but Islamic banks reinstate interest with the principle of profit and loss sharing. Islamic deposits include current account, savings deposit, investment deposits and special investment accounts. In Islamic banking, the deposit holder is acknowledged as the equity holder. This is referred to as the Mudarabah concept and it refers to a special passive partnership between capital owner (*rabb al-mal*) and investment manager (*mudarib*). They share the profits but the financial loss is borne by the capital owner (up to the contributed capital) where the investment manager bears the opportunity cost for the time and effort (Iqbal & Molyneux, 2005). As for the loan to the customer, Islamic banks consider this to be a form of capital participation and it is called a financing plan instead of borrowing. It includes housing finance, consumer finance and business finance which comply with Shari'ah law. The main principles followed are Mudarabah, Musharakah (joint venture) and Ijarah (leasing) (Iqbal & Llewellyn, 2002).

As aforementioned, only a few studies have been undertaken on Islamic banking efficiency compared to the many studies done on traditional or Western banking. Sufian and Noor (2009) study a comparative analysis on the performance of 16 Middle East North Africa (MENA) and Asian countries. Their study report that MENA are technically more efficient and banks from this region do dominate the efficiency frontier. The authors also noted that banks with smaller market share and lower non-performing loans ratio are technically more efficient. Hussein (2003) measures the operational efficiency of 17 Sudanese (Islamic) banks and finds major efficiency differences across banks. Sudanese banks are notorious in that they do not fully utilise the Mudarabah and Musharakah. This attitude contributes partly to their inefficiency. Other than that, the author suggests that human capital should be seriously invested in so that inefficiency is reduced.

Bader, Mohamad, Ariff, and Hassan (2008) measure and compare the cost, revenue and profit efficiency of Islamic and conventional banks using Data Envelopment Analysis (DEA) in 21 Organisation of the Islamic Conference (OIC) member countries. They discover insignificant differences between the overall efficiency for the two groups of banks. Olson and Zoubi (2008) use accounting ratios from five categories (profitability, efficiency, asset quality, liquidity and risk) to distinguish between Islamic and conventional banks in the Gulf Cooperation Council (GCC) region. The authors find that although several means for the ratio are similar between Islamic and conventional banks, measuring bank characteristics is a good way of finding differences between them. Further findings confirm Islamic banks are more profitable than conventional banks with regards to the six profitability ratios in the study.

Iqbal and Molyneux (2005) review the empirical evidence regarding efficiency in Islamic banks in various countries via a series of methods and approaches. They conclude that Islamic banks are at least as efficient as European or conventional banks, and in Qatar, GCC countries and some Middle East countries, Islamic banks are certainly more efficient.

Although there is no concrete agreement that Islamic banks outperform conventional banks, many studies relate efficiency to profitability. Cost efficiency would improve the profitability of financial institutions and enhance their ability to operate in a deregulated and competitive market (Iqbal & Molyneux, 2005). Sufian and Noor (2009) support this idea in their discovery of a positive relationship between bank efficiency and loan intensity, size, capitalization and profitability.

Further studies are required on Islamic banking efficiency and performance in comparison to the more recognised traditional banking system. There is no available literature on comparing the efficiency of Islamic banking in European countries. Dalla Pellegrina (2006) uses a comparative experiment to measure the impact of capitalisation on efficiency between Islamic banks for 15 European banks but not to compare on the efficiency.

4. DATA AND VARIABLES

4.1. Data Description

Our aim is to study the comparison on banking operating efficiency, the cost efficiency between conventional banks with the Islamic banks. Our study consists of 167 observations obtained from 9 Islamic banks and 33 conventional banks[5] between 2005 and 2008. The sample banks are selected from 3 countries: Germany, Turkey and the United Kingdom. Owing to the recent development of Islamic banking in Europe our analysis is limited to these three countries where Islamic banking operations are practiced.[6] The data were obtained from the financial statements of individual banks documented on the International Bank Credit Analysis Bankscope database. Consolidated statements are used only if the unconsolidated statement is unavailable or data is insufficient. Table 1 illustrates a comparison of the major profit and cost ratios between Islamic banks and conventional banks between 2005 and 2008.

Table 1. Comparisons of Major Ratios.

	Financial Cost (%)							
	2005		2006		2007		2008	
	IB	CB	IB	CB	IB	CB	IB	CB
Germany	1.91	2.36	2.94	2.77	4.04	3.01	3.64	2.99
Turkey	5.56	4.98	5.59	6.00	5.82	6.59	6.29	7.29
The United Kingdom	1.06	2.65	2.01	3.12	4.61	3.61	2.75	3.68
	Operating Cost (%)							
	2005		2006		2007		2008	
	IB	CB	IB	CB	IB	CB	IB	CB
Germany	1.34	2.20	0.94	2.01	1.11	1.82	1.03	1.78
Turkey	4.38	4.48	4.05	4.12	3.76	4.06	3.83	4.78
The United Kingdom	3.00	2.37	3.37	2.14	2.83	2.07	3.10	1.95
	Average Total Cost (%)							
	2005		2006		2007		2008	
	IB	CB	IB	CB	IB	CB	IB	CB
Germany	3.26	4.56	3.88	4.78	5.16	4.83	4.67	4.77
Turkey	9.94	9.47	9.65	10.12	9.58	10.66	10.12	12.08
The United Kingdom	4.06	5.02	5.39	5.26	7.44	5.68	5.84	5.63
	ROAA (%)							
	2005		2006		2007		2008	
	IB	CB	IB	CB	IB	CB	IB	CB
Germany	0.79	0.50	1.09	0.49	1.18	0.45	2.07	0.20
Turkey	2.25	2.50	3.27	2.45	2.86	2.58	2.69	2.07
The United Kingdom	−0.94	0.93	−1.33	1.10	−0.67	1.16	−0.90	0.62
	ROAE (%)							
	2005		2006		2007		2008	
	IB	CB	IB	CB	IB	CB	IB	CB
Germany	7.82	11.44	14.66	12.43	16.14	13.45	26.26	4.83
Turkey	23.18	16.46	29.18	16.16	23.65	18.56	19.79	13.24
The United Kingdom	0.66	10.84	−0.82	13.54	−0.62	15.21	−4.36	4.74

Note: ISLAMIC BANKS (IB): GERMANY (1), TURKEY (4), UK (4) CONVENTIONAL BANKS (CB): GERMANY (4), TURKEY (16), UK (13)

Table 2. Total Cost and Profit as a Share of Assets: Mean Values 2006–2008 (%).

	Islamic Banks		Conventional Banks	
	TC/TA	PAT/TA	TC/TA	PAT/TA
Germany	4.24	1.19	4.73	0.39
Turkey	9.81	2.47	10.58	2.25
The United Kingdom	5.68	−0.75	5.40	0.88
Mean	6.58	0.97	6.90	1.17
Standard deviation	2.89	1.62	3.20	0.96

Referring to Table 2, the mean value of total costs and profit as a share of assets for Germany, Turkey and the United Kingdom, the statistics reveal that Islamic banks perform better in controlling costs. However, from the perspective of profitability, conventional banks earn slightly more profits. The statistics do confirm previous findings (Berger & Mester, 1997) on the relationship between cost and profit efficiency – it is not positively correlated. In addition, Mahesh and Bhide (2008) find cost and profit efficiencies display varying trends for different bank groups. Comparing the two groups of banks, it is clear that conventional banks have larger variability in terms of costs than Islamic banks. On the contrary, the profit dispersion for Islamic banks is larger than that of conventional banks.

In general, Islamic banks' financial costs are lower than those of conventional banks in the three countries particularly where Turkish and UK Islamic banks operate. The operating costs for Islamic banks in the United Kingdom are higher where conventional banks are better in managing their operating costs. Islamic banks in Turkey and Germany, however, manage to control their operating costs. More specifically, Turkish Islamic banks had lower average total costs for the period 2006–2008. For the United Kingdom, conventional banks performed better throughout these 3 years in regard to average total costs except for 2005. Banks in Germany demonstrated mixed results for 2005–2008 with Islamic banks performing better in 2005, 2006 and 2008 but not 2007.

The 4 years' trend concerning the return on average assets (ROAA) and return on average equity (ROAE) for Germany, Turkey and the United Kingdom are quite similar; Islamic banks operating in Germany and Turkey illustrated an outstanding performance when compared to conventional banks. Islamic banks in the United Kingdom, however, experienced low and negative returns during the 4 years. Without regard for the small sample size and arbitrary selection of conventional banks in the three countries, it is notable that Islamic banks performed better than conventional banks in Germany and Turkey but not in the United Kingdom. This might be attributable to different banking structure and country-specific factors, which may influence Islamic banking operations in each country. For instance, in their study of the French and Spanish banking industries, Dietsch and Lozano-Vivas (2000) reveal environmental variables contribute significantly to the differences in the two countries' efficiency scores. Furthermore Islamic banks in Turkey are more mature than those operating in the United Kingdom, indicating that the legal framework for banking activities in the United Kingdom may not suit for the operating principles of Islamic banks.

Conventional banks are much larger than Islamic banks in terms of Euro dollar value. The mean value of total loans and total assets for Islamic banks are 55 times and 70 times smaller than conventional banks in Europe, respectively. This statistic could have some influence on comparing the efficiency of these two different sized entities as claim by Debasish (2006). Smaller banks in his study were characterised as being globally efficient, yet large banks emerged as operating in a locally efficient way. It is important to note that the number of Islamic banks in Europe is limited with smaller assets size. Taking this into consideration, it is expected that Islamic banks are not able to become more efficient through economies of scale.

4.2. Variables

The variables were chosen according to their explanatory power of efficiency based on previous banking efficiency studies. Our analysis will cover the cost functions with the dependent variables of total cost. Numerous studies analysed efficiency using cost function but in many studies, profit efficiency score is mostly lower and varies more than the cost efficiency score. Berger and Mester (1997) find there is no significant positive correlation between profit efficiency and cost efficiency. Furthermore, Mahesh and Bhide (2008) indicate the varying trend of cost and profit efficiency for different groups of bank. Considering exogenous and endogenous factors, profit and cost efficiency may vary in many ways. Chatterjee (2006) suggests joint analysis of cost and profit efficiency for better insight of this matter.

Cost efficiency consists of two elements: technical efficiency and allocative efficiency. Technical efficiency measures the proportional decrease in input usage which can be attained if a bank operates on the efficiency frontier.

It is used when only quantity data are available. In comparison allocative efficiency measures the proportional decline in cost if a bank chooses the right mix of input and takes price into consideration. Given both the quantity and price available, overall cost efficiency can be computed. This is also referred to as economic efficiency or x-efficiency. Isik and Hassan (2002) note that the inefficiency of Turkish banks is due to technical inefficiency rather than allocative inefficiency. Hence, price plays an important part in determining bank efficiency as it relates to economies of scale.

4.2.1. The Inputs and Outputs Variable

The selection of inputs and outputs variable is essential when measuring banking efficiency. Two distinct concepts known as intermediation approach and production approach can vary the selection of inputs and outputs variable when measuring efficiency. In the production approach (also known as value-added or user cost approach), banks produce loans and deposits accounts using labour and capital as inputs. In the intermediation approach (also known as the asset approach), banks are deemed financial intermediaries that collect purchased funds using labour and capital to transform these funds into loans and other assets. Depending on how we define the concept of efficiency itself, deposits can represent either input or output because they share both characteristics. The production approach allows deposits to act as an output variable while it is classifies as input from the intermediaries perspective.

Pasiouras (2008) employs variation of the inputs and outputs variable in five DEA models with four of them based on the intermediation approach. One is based on the production approach and it revealed mixed results. The author finds variation in terms of overall mean efficiency score between the production and intermediation approaches. Thus the selection of inputs/outputs set may lead to efficiency measurements measuring different aspects of the banking sector. Our selection of variables is based on the intermediation approach where banks are considered to be intermediaries that collect deposits and transform them into loans and other assets. Berger and Humphrey (1997) in their international study on banking efficiency concluded that the intermediation approach is more relevant in measuring bank level efficiency. The production approach proved to be more suitable for branch level efficiency. Thus the four (4) inputs in the study are labour, fixed assets, total funds and loan loss provisions while the three (3) output variables are total loans, other earning assets and off-balance sheet items.

The definitions of the inputs and outputs in this chapter are indicated below:

Inputs

There are four input factors

X_1 = Labour. This is defined as the total expenditure on employees (personnel expenses)
X_2 = Fixed assets. The fixed assets are defined as the sum of physical capital and premises
X_3 = Total funds. The total funds are defined as total deposits plus total borrowed funds
X_4 = Loan loss provision. The loan loss provision is defined as the loan loss reserves

Input prices

PI_1 = Price of labour. This is the ratio of personnel expenses to total funds
PI_2 = Price of fixed assets. The price of fixed assets is equal to other non-interest expenses divided by fixed assets
PI_3 = Price of funds. The price of funds is derived by dividing total costs from total funds
PI_4 = Price of credit risk. This price is measured as loan loss reserves per unit of total loans.

Outputs

There are three measures of outputs

Y_1 = Total loans. This is defined as the total of short- and long-term loans
Y_2 = Other earning assets. This is the sum of investment securities, inter-bank funds sold and loan to special sectors (directed lending)
Y_3 = Off-balance sheet items. This is the sum of guarantees, acceptances, committed credit lines and other contingent liabilities reported off-balance sheet

Loan loss provisions are included in this study with regard to the soaring impact that credit risk issues have on banking efficiency. Hensel (2003) and Pasiouras (2008) specify loan loss provision as the input variables in measuring banking efficiency. Pasiouras (2008) indicates that loan loss provision has a greater impact on the efficiency score rather than off-balance sheet items.

Off-balance sheet items refer to credits, other guarantees and acceptances which are not reported on a balance sheet. These activities contribute to similar risk levels associated on-balance sheet activities. Berger and Mester (1997) in explaining the efficiency of financial institutions, denote the off-balance sheet transaction as an effective substitute for directly issued loans. Hence the inclusion of these items when measuring banking efficiency is necessary with regard to the banks' solvency and survival. Furthermore Islamic banking principle of riba' prohibition leads to the creation of many products include as off-balance sheet items and other earnings assets.

5. METHODOLOGY

In measuring efficiency, financial institution should be close to a 'best-practice' frontier, where it relies on many accounting measures such as costs, outputs, inputs, revenues and profits. There are various approaches in evaluating efficiency in financial institutions but there is no consensus method in determining the best practice frontier. Major differences between these methods are in terms of assumptions which may later become shortfalls in the method itself. The assumption differs in: (i) determining the functional form of the best-practice frontier; (ii) the treatment of its random error and (iii) whether random error (if any), the probability distribution assumed for the efficiencies.

Non-parametric frontiers such as DEA and Free Disposal Hull (FDH) have relatively little structure on the specification of the best-practice frontier. DEA is a linear programming technique where the set of best practices or frontier observations are those for which no other decision-making unit (DMU) or linear combination of units with given inputs has more of every output or with given outputs has less of every input. The FDH production possibilities set is composed only of the DEA vertices and FDH points interior to these vertices. Thus, FDH will typically generate larger estimates of average efficiency than DEA. These non-parametric approaches assume that there is no random error where it is assumed that there is no measurement error in developing frontier, no luck in decision-making unit would be a better measure and no inaccuracy in inputs/outputs measurement from the accounting distortion.

Among others (Casu & Girardone, 2009; Pastor et al., 1997; Resti, 1997) DEA method were utilised in the empirical banking efficiency studies. Pastor et al. (1997) compute the production frontier and used the Malmquist index to analyse relative productivity between two firms belonging to different banking systems. The advantage with this index is that it does not need the estimation of technology but instead focuses on the estimation of inputs, outputs, prices and production function. Casu and Girardone (2009) provide two alternative methods in measuring bank cost efficiency, the DEA and parametric approach, Stochastic Frontier Analysis (SFA). Their estimation is based on Granger-type causality test.

This chapter applies frontier analysis or X-efficiency using DEA to compare the technical efficiency and cost efficiency in Islamic banks and conventional banks in Europe. X-efficiency measures how well a bank performs relative to the predicted performance of the 'best' one in the industry and is suited to small sample sizes. Based on the concept of technological efficiency, DEA evaluates the performance of each bank by relating its input and output combinations to a common efficient frontier. DEA has the advantage of being able to handle multiple inputs and outputs stated in different measurement units. It also focuses on a best-practice frontier rather than population central tendencies and does not require a functional form to be imposed relating inputs to outputs (Charnes, Cooper, Lewin, & Seiford, 1995).

The analysis of the efficiency of the operations of commercial banks often begins with an estimation of its cost or profit function. In general, a cost function could be expressed as:

$$C = C(p, y, u, v, \varepsilon) \tag{1}$$

where C is bank cost, p the vector of input prices, y the vector of outputs, u the vector of fixed bank parameters (bank capital, fixed assets), v the inefficiency term that captures the difference between the efficient level of cost for a given output level and input prices and the actual level of cost and lastly, ε the random error term.

The constant returns to scale (CRS) assumption is only valid when all decision-making units (DMUs) are operating at an optimal scale (Banker, Charnes, & Cooper, 1984). This chapter adopts the variable returns to scale (VRS) DEA model because European Islamic banking markets are not fully developed and therefore perfect competition is unlikely. The CRS linear programming problem is given as:

$$\min_{\theta,\lambda}\theta, \text{ subject to} : -y_i + Y\lambda \geq 0, \ \ \theta x_i - X\lambda \geq 0, \ \ \lambda \geq 0 \tag{2}$$

where θ is a scalar and λ an $N \times 1$ vector of constants, Y represents all input and output data for N firms, x_i the individual inputs and y_i the outputs for the ith firm (Coelli, Rao, & Battese, 1998). The efficiency score for each DMU is given by θ, and will have a value between 0 and 1, which indicates the efficiency level.

With VRS cost minimisation, technical efficiency (TE) can be obtained by running the input-orientated DEA shown in Eq. (2). The cost efficiency will be estimated by running the following cost minimisation DEA:

$$\min_{\lambda,xi} w_i' x_i^*, \text{ subject to}: -y_i + Y\lambda \geq 0,\ x_i^* - X\lambda \geq 0,\ N1'\lambda = 1,\ \lambda \geq 0 \tag{3}$$

where w_i is a vector of input for the ith DMU and x_i^* the cost-minimising vector of input quantities for the ith DMU, given the input prices w_i and the output levels y_i (Coelli et al., 1998). The total cost efficiency (CE) for the ith DMU would be calculated as:

$$\text{CE} = \frac{w_i' x_i^*}{w_i^* x_i} \tag{4}$$

This is the ratio of minimum cost to observed cost. The allocative efficiency (AE) can be calculated as:

$$\text{AE} = \frac{\text{CE}}{\text{TE}} \tag{5}$$

The intermediation approach for inputs and outputs is taken rather than the production approach, since the latter is suited to branch evaluation. Banks are viewed as financial intermediaries that accumulate deposits and purchase funds and then intermediate these funds (Sealey & Lindley, 1977).

6. EMPIRICAL RESULTS

The efficiency scores for the Islamic and conventional banks are measured in terms of technical efficiency (TE), allocative efficiency (AE) and overall cost efficiency (CE). The study reveals that the TE for Islamic and conventional banks had improved from 2005 to 2008 (see Tables 3 and 4).

It is worth noting that the Islamic banks outperformed the conventional banks in TE for all the years except 2005. In the Islamic banks' efficiency frontier, there are two Islamic banks classified as technically inefficient while the remaining seven banks are technically efficient. However, as indicated in Table 5, results obtained from the common frontier of Islamic and conventional banks lead to another three Islamic banks (efficient in the Islamic frontier) becoming inefficient. In this common frontier, the efficiency of conventional banks persists.

In general, overall efficiency, the CE is mostly supplied by the TE as the results for all banks (Islamic and conventional) for all years represents TE

Table 3. Technical Efficiency in Islamic Frontier (2005–2008).

Islamic Banks	2005	2006	2007	2008
1	1.000	1.000	1.000	1.000
2	1.000	1.000	1.000	1.000
3	1.000	1.000	1.000	1.000
4	0.945	0.930	0.936	1.000
5	1.000	1.000	1.000	1.000
6	1.000	1.000	1.000	1.000
7	1.000	1.000	1.000	1.000
8	0.338	0.840	0.955	1.000
Mean	0.910	0.971	0.986	1.000

dominates AE (refer to Table 6). Out of all, TE does better than AE for the 4 years, which reflects that the banks inefficiency is contributed by the choices of the inputs price mix rather than managerial inefficiencies. Although Islamic banks have higher scores on TE, but their CE are lower than those of conventional banks except for 2007. This is mainly due to relative low AE that drag the overall efficiency of Islamic banks in years 2005, 2006 and 2008.

The mean efficiency score for conventional banks improved steadily throughout the year as all TE and AE increased each year. It can be seen from the individual scores of 33 conventional banks that the number of banks with 1.000 efficiency score increased from 2006 to 2008. Of all the conventional banks, 9, 10, 11 and 12 conventional banks operated at the efficient frontier for 2005, 2006, 2007 and 2008, respectively. The Islamic banks also showed improvement in CE from 2005 to 2007 but as the mean AE declined in 2008, mean CE for Islamic banks declined. There are 2 Islamic banks at the efficient frontier 2005 and 2006 and the number increased to 4 banks in 2007. However, it declined to only 3 banks of a total of 9 banks with a CE score of 1.000 in 2008.

The highest mean for CE score for the sample periods is 91.1% for conventional banks in 2008. For Islamic banks the highest mean for CE score is slightly lower than conventional banks with 90.1% achieved in 2007. It seems likely that Islamic banks in Europe took advantage of trading opportunities in favourable economic conditions in 2007. Yet, perhaps due to internal factors, these banks were unable to sustain the mean efficiency score in 2008. As reported in the European Financial Integration Report 2007 (European Commission, 2007), banking sector efficiency was bolstered by favourable economic conditions as well as banking sector product

Table 4. Technical Efficiency in Conventional Frontier (2005 – 2008).

Conventional Banks	2005	2006	2007	2008
1	1.000	0.972	1.000	1.000
2	1.000	0.951	0.979	1.000
3	1.000	1.000	1.000	1.000
4	1.000	1.000	1.000	1.000
5	0.812	0.920	0.958	0.998
6	0.827	0.917	0.872	0.950
7	0.855	0.900	0.878	0.954
8	1.000	0.985	1.000	1.000
9	0.929	0.889	0.936	0.970
10	0.979	0.906	0.972	0.986
11	1.000	1.000	1.000	1.000
12	1.000	1.000	1.000	0.987
13	0.894	0.945	0.985	1.000
14	0.936	0.990	1.000	1.000
15	1.000	1.000	1.000	1.000
16	0.958	1.000	0.952	0.930
17	1.000	1.000	0.927	0.967
18	1.000	1.000	0.920	0.928
19	0.967	0.982	1.000	0.950
20	1.000	0.968	1.000	1.000
21	1.000	1.000	1.000	1.000
22	1.000	1.000	1.000	1.000
23	0.803	0.885	1.000	1.000
24	0.789	0.891	0.908	0.946
25	1.000	1.000	1.000	1.000
26	1.000	1.000	1.000	1.000
27	1.000	1.000	1.000	1.000
28	1.000	1.000	1.000	1.000
29	1.000	1.000	1.000	1.000
30	1.000	1.000	1.000	1.000
31	1.000	1.000	1.000	1.000
32	0.861	0.984	1.000	1.000
33	0.896	0.913	1.000	1.000
Mean	0.955	0.970	0.978	0.987

innovation. Innovations allow for transaction costs to fall and promote competition in the market. Apart from IT development in Europe that improved distribution channels and market practices, new products in the sector can improve bank stability and lead to better cost efficiency. Islamic banking products that obey Shari'ah principles are considered to be new innovative products in European markets since traditional banking relies on

Table 5. Technical Efficiency in Common Frontier (2005–2008).

Islamic and Conventional	2005	2006	2007	2008
1	1.000	1.000	1.000	1.000
2	0.869	0.951	0.971	1.000
3	1.000	1.000	1.000	1.000
4	0.813	0.900	0.889	0.876
5	1.000	1.000	0.939	1.000
6	1.000	1.000	0.651	1.000
7	1.000	1.000	1.000	1.000
8	0.335	0.500	0.555	0.992
9	1.000	0.972	1.000	1.000
10	1.000	0.951	0.979	1.000
11	1.000	1.000	1.000	1.000
12	1.000	1.000	1.000	1.000
13	0.786	0.913	0.958	0.998
14	0.812	0.907	0.863	0.941
15	0.854	0.900	0.875	0.953
16	1.000	0.984	1.000	1.000
17	0.918	0.877	0.917	0.969
18	0.975	0.905	0.970	0.985
19	1.000	1.000	1.000	1.000
20	1.000	1.000	1.000	0.968
21	0.761	0.870	0.968	1.000
22	0.900	0.928	1.000	1.000
23	1.000	1.000	1.000	1.000
24	0.952	0.993	0.949	0.897
25	0.760	0.825	0.868	0.912
26	0.886	0.829	0.880	0.842
27	0.894	0.951	1.000	0.913
28	0.481	0.659	0.729	1.000
29	1.000	1.000	1.000	1.000
30	1.000	1.000	1.000	1.000
31	0.784	0.817	1.000	0.928
32	0.780	0.856	0.885	0.936
33	1.000	1.000	1.000	1.000
34	1.000	1.000	1.000	1.000
35	1.000	1.000	1.000	1.000
36	1.000	1.000	1.000	1.000
37	1.000	1.000	1.000	1.000
38	1.000	1.000	1.000	1.000
39	1.000	1.000	1.000	1.000
40	0.715	0.807	0.843	1.000
41	0.499	0.725	1.000	0.985
Mean	0.897	0.927	0.944	0.978

Note: The first eight banks are representing Islamic banks in the common frontier.

Table 6. Mean Efficiency (2005–2008).

	Panel A: Islamic Frontier				Panel B: Conventional Frontier				Panel C: Common Frontier			
	2005	2006	2007	2008	2005	2006	2007	2008	2005	2006	2007	2008
Technical efficiency	0.910	0.971	0.986	1.000	0.955	0.970	0.978	0.987	0.897	0.927	0.944	0.978
Allocative efficiency	0.853	0.854	0.911	0.860	0.875	0.903	0.915	0.923	0.841	0.859	0.896	0.894
Cost efficiency	0.830	0.841	0.901	0.860	0.838	0.876	0.895	0.911	0.773	0.808	0.852	0.874

conventional products. This could be a good omen for Islamic banks in Europe taking advantage of innovation and making them more competitive.

7. CONCLUSION

Islamic banking is a comparatively recent phenomenon in the European banking system. Measuring their efficiency is vital when trying to understand the significance of Islamic banks in Europe when compared to conventional banks. This chapter makes a contribution to the knowledge of how Islamic banks operate by focusing on inputs/outputs selection, which plays an important role in assessing their efficiency. This chapter employs the intermediation approach to determine the efficiency frontier of Islamic banks and conventional banks in Germany, Turkey and the United Kingdom.

Although Islamic banks have less values of asset than conventional banks, these banks continue to be efficient especially in terms of cost. In general, Islamic banks are better at controlling costs comparing to conventional banks. Statistically, their operations have less financial costs to worry about. In the three European countries, Islamic banks are more technically efficient than conventional banks. Yet, Islamic banks do experience high allocative inefficiency which leads to low-cost efficiency especially in regard to common frontier. It indicates that Islamic banks experience problems with choice of input price mix as the sources of inefficiency do not arise from managerial issues.

Conventional banks are practicing close to its frontier and the means efficiency score are steady along the 3 years. The variation in the efficiency score (especially the AE) among Islamic banks and conventional banks is perhaps caused by internal factors rather than economic and environmental factors. Furthermore Islamic banks seem to take advantage of the competitive environment created by the integrated banking market in Europe. They exploited favourable economic conditions and banking innovations during 2007 and this supports the hypothesis of market power and efficiency, the quiet life hypothesis where in more integrated market Islamic banks improve management effort to maximise operating efficiency. More competition in the European market has increased the pressures of cost control in Islamic banks.

NOTES

1. Iqbal and Molyneux (2005) in their book clarify riba' as anything pecuniary or non-pecuniary, in excess of the principal in a loan that must be paid by the borrower to the lender along with the principal as a condition of the loan or for an extension in its maturity. According to Islamic jurists, it is comparable to the modern concept of interest.
2. Bank Negara Malaysia (BNM) announced in September 2003 that it would issue three licenses to foreign players to operate full-fledged Islamic banks in Malaysia. BNM issued an Islamic banking license to Kuwait Finance House (KFH) in 2004.
3. Iqbal and Molyneux (2005) in their book compare and analyse the development and efficiency of Islamic banking over a 30-year period.
4. Majid (2003) discusses further the challenges and opportunities of the development of liquidity management instruments.
5. Conventional banks are randomly selected commercial banks to be compared with nine Islamic banks in the three countries.
6. Islamic banks in Russia and Denmark are excluded from this study due to the unavailability of relevant data.

ACKNOWLEDGMENT

We appreciate helpful comments from Sisira Jayasuriya, Paul Kim, Jan Libich, Damien Eldridge, Daisy Chou and other participants in workshop at La Trobe University. We also thank Suk-Joong Kim (editor), Michael D. McKenzie (editor) and an anonymous referee, whose suggestions have led to substantial improvements of the chapter.

REFERENCES

Ahmed, S. (1989). Islamic banking and finance: A review essay. *Journal of Monetary Economics*, *24*(1), 157–167.

Altunbas, Y., & Chakravarty, S. P. (1998). Efficiency measures and the banking structure in Europe. *Economics Letters*, *60*(2), 205–208.

Bader, M. K. I., Mohamad, S., Ariff, M., & Hassan, T. (2008). Cost, revenue, and profit efficiency of Islamic versus conventional banks: International evidence using data envelopment analysis. *Islamic Research & Training Institute*, *15*(2), 23–76.

Banker, R. D., Charnes, A., & Cooper, W. W. (1984). Some models for estimating technical and scale inefficiencies in data envelopment analysis. *Management Science*, *30*(9), 1078–1092.

Beccalli, E. (2004). Cross-country comparisons of efficiency: Evidence from the UK and Italian investment firms. *Journal of Banking & Finance*, *28*(6), 1363–1383.

Berger, A. N. (2007). International comparisons of banking efficiency. *Financial Markets, Institutions & Instruments*, *16*(3), 119–144.

Berger, A. N., Hasan, I., & Zhou, M. (2009). Bank ownership and efficiency in China: What will happen in the world's largest nation? *Journal of Banking & Finance*, *33*(1), 113–130.

Berger, A. N., & Humphrey, D. B. (1997). Efficiency of financial institutions: International survey and directions for future research. *European Journal of Operational Research*, *98*(2), 175–212.

Berger, A. N., & Mester, L. J. (1997). Inside the black box: What explains differences in the efficiencies of financial institutions? *Journal of Banking & Finance*, *21*(7), 895–947.

Bonin, J. P., Hasan, I., & Wachtel, P. (2005). Bank performance, efficiency and ownership in transition countries. *Journal of Banking & Finance*, *29*(1), 31–53.

Bos, J. W. B., & Schmiedel, H. (2007). Is there a single frontier in a single European banking market? *Journal of Banking & Finance*, *31*(7), 2081–2102.

Carbó Valverde, S., Humphrey, D. B., & López del Paso, R. (2007). Do cross-country differences in bank efficiency support a policy of "national champions"? *Journal of Banking & Finance*, *31*(7), 2173–2188.

Casu, B., & Girardone, C. (2009). Testing the relationship between competition and efficiency in banking: A panel data analysis. *Economics Letters*, *105*(1), 134–137.

Charnes, A., Cooper, W. W., Lewin, A. Y., & Seiford, L. M. (1995). *Data envelopment analysis, theory, methodology and applications*. Boston: Kluwer Academic Publishers.

Chatterjee, G. (2006). Is inefficiency of banks in India a cause for concern? Evidence from the post-reforms era. *Journal of Emerging Market Finance*, *5*(2), 151–182.

Coelli, T. S., Rao, P., & Battese, G. E. (1998). *An introduction to efficiency and productivity analysis*. Boston: Kluwer Academic Publishers.

Dalla Pellegrina, L. (2006). Capitalization requirements, efficiency and governance: A comparative experiment on Islamic and Western Banks. *SSRN eLibrary*.

Debasish, S. S. (2006). Efficiency performance in Indian banking-use of data envelopment analysis. *Global Business Review*, *7*(2), 325–333.

Degryse, H. (1996). On the interaction between vertical and horizontal product differentiation: An application to banking. *Journal of Industrial Economics*, *44*(2), 169–186.

Dermine, J. (2005). European banking integration: Don't put the cart before the horse. *SSRN eLibrary*.

Dietsch, M., & Lozano-Vivas, A. (2000). How the environment determines banking efficiency: A comparison between French and Spanish industries. *Journal of Banking & Finance*, *24*(6), 985–1004.

El-Hawary, D., Grais, W., & Iqbal, Z. (2007). Diversity in the regulation of Islamic Financial Institutions. *Quarterly Review of Economics and Finance*, *46*(5), 778–800.

European Commission. (2007). European Financial Integration Report.

Fries, S., & Taci, A. (2005). Cost efficiency of banks in transition: Evidence from 289 banks in 15 post-communist countries. *Journal of Banking & Finance*, *29*(1), 55–81.

Goddard, J., Molyneux, P., Wilson, J. O. S., & Tavakoli, M. (2007). European banking: An overview. *Journal of Banking & Finance*, *31*(7), 1911–1935.

Hassan, M. K., & Dicle, M. F. (2005). Basel II and regulatory framework for Islamic banks. *Islamic Economics, Banking and Finance: Islami Bank Training and Research Academy (IBTRA)*, *1*(1), 1–16.

Hensel, N. D. (2003). Strategic management of cost efficiencies in networks: Cross-country evidence on European branch banking. *European Financial Management*, *9*(3), 333–360.

Hussein, K. A. (2003). *Operational efficiency in Islamic banking: The sudanese experience*. Working papers, Islamic Research & Training Institute (IRTI).

Iqbal, M., & Llewellyn, D. T. (2002). *Islamic banking and finance: New perspectives on profit-sharing and risk*. Cheltenhem, UK: Edward Elgar.

Iqbal, M., & Molyneux, P. (2005). *Thirty years of Islamic banking: History, performance and prospects*. Hampshire, NY: Palgrave Macmillan.

Isik, I., & Hassan, M. K. (2002). Technical, scale and allocative efficiencies of Turkish banking industry. *Journal of Banking & Finance*, *26*(4), 719–766.

Jaap, W. B. J. B., & James, W. J. K. (2005). Large bank efficiency in Europe and the United States: Are there economic motivations for geographic expansion in financial services? *Journal of Business*, *78*(4), 1555–1592.

De Jonghe, O., & Vennet, R. V. (2008). Competition versus efficiency: What drives franchise values in European banking? *Journal of Banking & Finance*, *32*(9), 1820–1835.

Karim, R. A. A. (2001). International accounting harmonization, banking regulation, and Islamic banks. *International Journal of Accounting*, *36*(2), 169–193.

Khan, W., Iliasu, F. B., & Chowdhry, S. (2009). Preventing residential mortgage crises: An Islamic finance perspective. *SSRN eLibrary*.

Koutsomanoli-Filippaki, A., Margaritis, D., & Staikouras, C. (2009). Efficiency and productivity growth in the banking industry of Central and Eastern Europe. *Journal of Banking & Finance*, *33*(3), 557–567.

Kwan, S. H. (2003). Operating performance of banks among Asian economies: An international and time series comparison. *Journal of Banking & Finance*, *27*(3), 471–489.

Lozano-Vivas, A. (2009). Measuring and explaining the impact of vertical product differentiation on banking efficiency. *Managerial Finance*, *35*(3), 246–259.

Mahesh, H. P., & Bhide, S. (2008). Do financial sector reforms make commercial banks more efficient? A parametric exploration of the Indian case. Margin. *Journal of Applied Economic Research*, *2*(4), 415–441.

Majid, A. R. A. (2003). Development of liquidity management instruments: Challenges and opportunities. Paper presented at the International Conference on Islamic Banking: Risk Mangement, Regulation and Supervision.

Maudos, J., & de Guevara, J. F. (2007). The cost of market power in banking: Social welfare loss vs. cost inefficiency. *Journal of Banking & Finance*, *31*(7), 2103–2125.

Maudos, J., Pastor, J. M., Pérez, F., & Quesada, J. (2002). Cost and profit efficiency in European banks. *Journal of International Financial Markets, Institutions and Money*, *12*(1), 33–58.

Memon, N. A. (2007). Islamic banking: Present and future challenges. *Journal of Management and Social Sciences*, *3*(1), 1–10.

Olson, D., & Zoubi, T. A. (2008). Using accounting ratios to distinguish between Islamic and conventional banks in the GCC region. *International Journal of Accounting*, *43*(1), 45–65.

Pasiouras, F. (2008). Estimating the technical and scale efficiency of Greek commercial banks: The impact of credit risk, off-balance sheet activities, and international operations. *Research in International Business and Finance*, *22*(3), 301–318.

Pastor, J., Pérez, F., & Quesada, J. (1997). Efficiency analysis in banking firms: An international comparison. *European Journal of Operational Research*, *98*(2), 395–407.

Resti, A. (1997). Evaluating the cost-efficiency of the Italian banking system: What can be learned from the joint application of parametric and non-parametric techniques. *Journal of Banking & Finance*, *21*(2), 221–250.

Samad, A., & Hassan, M. K. (1999). The performance of Malaysian Islamic bank during 1984–1997: An exploratory study. *International Journal of Islamic Financial Services*, *1*(3), 1–14.

Sarker, M. A. A. (1999). Islamic banking in Bangladesh: Performance, problems & prospects. *International Journal of Islamic Financial Services*, *1*(3), 15–36.

Sealey, C. W., Jr., & Lindley, J. T. (1977). Inputs, outputs, and a theory of production and cost at depository financial institutions. *Journal of Finance*, *32*(4), 1251–1266.

Staikouras, C., Mamatzakis, E., & Koutsomanoli-Filippaki, A. (2008). Cost efficiency of the banking industry in the South Eastern European region. *Journal of International Financial Markets, Institutions and Money*, *18*(5), 483–497.

Sufian, F., & Noor, M. A. M. (2009). The determinants of Islamic banks' efficiency changes: Empirical evidence from the MENA and Asian banking sectors. *International Journal of Islamic and Middle Eastern Finance and Management*, *2*(2), 120–138.

Thoraneenitiyan, N., & Avkiran, N. K. (2009). Measuring the impact of restructuring and country-specific factors on the efficiency of post-crisis East Asian banking systems: Integrating DEA with SFA. *Socio-Economic Planning Sciences*, *43*(4), 240–252.

Weill, L. (2009). Convergence in banking efficiency across European countries. *Journal of International Financial Markets, Institutions and Money*, *19*(5), 818–833.

Welfens, P. J. J., & Wolf, H. C. (1997). *Banking, international capital flows and growth in Europe: Financial markets, savings and monetary integration in a world with uncertain convergence*. Berlin: Springer.

PART V
LOCATION AND DETERMINANTS OF INTERNATIONAL BANKING

THE ECONOMIC DETERMINANTS AND BEHAVIOR OF FOREIGN BANKS IN EMERGING COUNTRIES DURING A PERIOD OF GLOBAL ECONOMIC DOWNTURN☆

Aneta Hryckiewicz and Oskar Kowalewski

ABSTRACT

In recent years, foreign banks have significantly expanded their presence in many emerging countries. In our study, we use panel data to examine the economic determinants of foreign banks' entry modes into emerging European countries during the period from 1994 to 2008. Our results suggest that a parent bank's choice of an organizational structure is a function of its strategic plans in the region and the countries'

☆The authors thank Franklin Allen, Thorsten Beck, Iftekhar Hasan, Reinhard Schmidt, Celso Brunetti, Sheng Huang, and Editor Jonathan Batten for their helpful comments and suggestions. The chapter has also benefited from comments from the participants of the 2008 European Financial Management Association, the 2008 Financial Intermediation Research Society Conference, the Midwest Finance Association's 57th Annual Meeting and the XVI International "Tor Vergata" Conference on Banking and Finance. Oskar Kowalewski was supported by a fellowship from the Program Support for International Mobility of Scientists from the Polish Ministry of Science and Higher Education.

International Banking in the New Era: Post-Crisis Challenges and Opportunities
International Finance Review, Volume 11, 393–429

ISSN: 1569-3767/doi:10.1108/S1569-3767(2010)0000011017

characteristics. After further consideration of the financial crisis of 2007–2010, we find that as a result, parent banks tend to behave differently toward their foreign affiliates depending on its organizational structure. Our findings suggest that these differences are especially observable during periods of economic expansion and home financial distress.

1. INTRODUCTION

The literature on financial development has shown that a good financial system is an essential ingredient for sustainable economic growth (Beck, Levine, & Loayza, 2000). It has also shown that foreign banking participation can help develop a more efficient and robust financial system (Claessens, Demirgüç-Kunt, & Huizinga, 2001). In particular, studies that focus on developing countries find evidence that increased foreign bank participation is associated with improvements in the domestic banking sector efficiency and can help strengthen the national financial system. Following these studies, many developing countries decided to liberalize their banking sectors to encourage foreign bank entry. However, the existing research on the determinants of the specific entry choice into the emerging economies is very limited. Also, little attention has been paid to the behavior of foreign banks and their parents with respect to their organizational form. From the perspective of policy makers and supervisory authorities, these issues become highly relevant for several reasons.

First, there is still a group of emerging countries that would like to invite in foreign institutions. Claessens, Van Hooren, Gurcanlar, and Mercado Sapiain (2008) show that despite the strong efforts of governments to attract foreign banks into the lower-middle-income emerging countries, the participation of foreign institutions in this region is still very scarce. In 2006, this type of investment only accounted for 7.5% of the regional banking sector. Second, the supervisory authorities should pay more attention to how the foreign banks operate in the host country. Several emerging economies promote one entry mode while putting restrictions on other forms. For example, India has very strictly regulated foreign entry and promotes entries only through greenfield operations. Some Asian economies allow foreign institutions to enter only via offshore lending or a branch of a parent bank. Ukraine is considering allowing foreign banks to open branches. Such restrictions might influence the decision of a foreign bank to enter a particular location. Also, different organizational forms might have different effects on the financial stability of an emerging country. This issue might become especially relevant during a period of economic downturn or a domestic financial distress of a banking institution when the role of a parent bank might become crucial in weakening or strengthening the financial performance of its foreign affiliate. Therefore, the policy authorities should understand how to create a favorable environment that encourages cross-border activity, thereby minimizing the instability risk associated with the functioning of foreign institutions.

With our study we fill this gap and raise the aforementioned issues, with a particular consideration of the current crisis. Our contribution to the international banking literature is twofold. First, we discuss the factors that affect the particular choice of a bank's entry mode in the emerging countries. We do this by sampling several European emerging countries, which in recent decades have experienced the most rapid pace of foreign bank entries in the world (Claessens et al., 2008).

The results of our empirical study shows that parent institutions have different motivations for establishing a greenfield operation as an entry through acquisition of a local institution. Thus, the economic determinants promoting the particular organizational structures vary significantly between the entry modes and the time periods. Consistent with other studies, we find that the foreign banks tend to use the host country's economic distortions to enter the new markets. However, this occurs mostly by acquiring distressed entities in the emerging economies. The result is in line with the trend observed during the current crisis, where some Western European banks decided to enter the emerging region. For example, AIB entered the Baltic region by acquiring AmCredit's mortgage finance business from the Baltic-American Enterprise Fund, KBC increased its stakes in Slovakia by taking over the illiquid Istrobanka, and Spanish BBVA decided to use the global economic downturn and signed an agreement with China Citic Bank to set up a 20% of private-banking joint venture. The last deal has placed BBVA as second-biggest European bank in Asia after HSBC. Our results also show that at the beginning customer relationship is of lesser relevance for parent banks because they are likely to support their greenfield operations. However, we also find that this is true only during periods of global economic expansion. The parent banks, mostly stemming from the developed countries, do this by reallocating their capital from countries with low net interest margins into the emerging countries with high net interest margins. Therefore, we also observe a more aggressively behavior of these institutions on the credit market than other types of entrants. On the contrary, during the period of economic downturn, the parent banks tend to enter more developed markets, which are less risky, due to the uncertainty of their own home market conditions. We also find that the banking restrictions are important impediments for choosing a preferred entry mode and in countries where these restrictions are high parent banks tend to enter by acquisition of a local bank to overcome it.

Second, in our study we also examine the behavior of parent banks toward their foreign affiliates during the period of their economic expansion as well as their financial distress. The results from our first empirical study indicate that because the parent banks have different motivations for establishing a specific organizational structure, their behavior toward their foreign affiliates may also vary. This behavior is observable especially during a time of financial distress for a foreign affiliate or an economic downturn in a home market. Whereas some empirical evidence on the behavior of parent banks toward their foreign affiliates during a period of host country economic downturn have been provided by the academic literature, there are almost no research studies on the behavior of parent banks during their own financial distress. The current worldwide economic downturn has shown that financial crises are not only the phenomena of emerging countries, but their occurrence is also likely in developed countries. Furthermore, the economic consequences seem to be even more severe than that of the crises in emerging countries.

The results from our analysis suggest that parent banks behave differently toward their foreign operations depending on their organizational structure. Specifically, our results provide evidence that foreign greenfield operations more rapidly extend their credit growth than other banks during periods of economic growth because they are heavily supported by their parent banks. However, their reliance on parent bank's capital suggests that they have more exposure to the financial vulnerabilities stemming from parent home markets. Hence, in the time of their parent's financial distress, their performance deteriorates more quickly than in other domestic institutions. In addition, we find strong evidence that parent banks feel to a lesser extent responsible for their greenfield operations because they operate on a stand-alone basis and are not affiliated with a one-bank holding company, as compared to the local institutions in which they have ownership. Accordingly, our findings suggest that parent banks are more willing to inject capital into these institutions, provided that the institution is of strategic importance for the parent bank. We also find that, during the time of their financial distress, parent banks are more likely to draw on the funds of their foreign affiliates. Because the parent local banks are less exposed to home country vulnerabilities, the parent banks are more likely to reallocate the capital from their financially stronger affiliated institutions instead of their stand-alone subsidiaries.

2. BACKGROUND

In the past 15 years, there has been a significant increase in the activity of foreign banks in the transition economies of Central Europe as a consequence of European governments deciding to build a more effective financial system following the political changes of 1989. The aim was to implement a market-oriented economy, and fundamental changes were needed in the financial system. As part of the process of creating a two-tier banking system, commercial operations were divested from central bank activities. Depending on the country, this divestment resulted in the creation of three to nine state-owned commercial banks within each nation. However, the banking system remained concentrated, with three to four state-owned specialist banks continuing to dominate the marketplace. Therefore, at the beginning, the central banks set up a very lenient licensing procedure for establishing new banks. The principal motivation was to increase competition in the banking sector, as the state-owned banks were considered ineffective. As a result, an impressive number of new banks were established in short order. In 1990, 6 new banks began operations in Hungary, 40 in Poland, and 13 in Czechoslovakia. Of these, three of Hungary's new banks were foreign-owned, as were five in Poland and four in Czechoslovakia. Hence, the features of the banking system before the transformation included structural segmentation, a high concentration of assets consistent with the existence of a few large- and medium-sized state-owned banks, and an increasing number of small domestic and foreign commercial banks.[1] Today, however, the banking sectors of all Central European countries feature some of the highest foreign banking participation rates in the world. Shares range from 70% in Poland to almost 100% in Slovakia (Allen, Bartiloro, & Kowalewski, 2006). Table 1 provides an overview of the development of foreign banks' participation in European emerging countries.

Table 1 shows that among the transition countries in our survey, Poland had the highest number of foreign bank entries, which can be attributed to the size of the country. However, the relative importance of foreign banks ultimately became greater in the Czech Republic and Slovakia than in Hungary or Poland. Table 1 shows that in the Czech Republic and Slovakia, more than 90% of total banking assets are controlled by foreign banks,

Table 1. The Origin of Foreign Banks, Their Entry Routes, and Share of Total Banking Assets.

Host Home	Czech Republic	Hungary	Poland	Slovakia	Total
Austria	2	7	2	7	18
Belgium	2	3	3	2	10
Czech Republic	–	0	3	1	4
Denmark	0	0	2	0	2
France	1	4	3	0	8
Germany	4	9	15	3	31
Hungary	0	–	0	1	1
Ireland	0	0	1	0	1
Italy	3	4	4	2	13
Japan	0	0	2	0	2
The Netherlands	1	2	7	1	11
Portugal	0	0	2	0	2
South Korea	0	4	1	0	5
Spain	0	0	1	0	1
Sweden	0	0	3	0	3
United Kingdom	1	0	2	0	3
United States	1	3	7	1	12
Slovakia	1	0	0	–	1
Total	16	36	58	18	128

	1994	1995	1996	1997	1998	1999	2000	2001	2002	2003	2004	2005	2006	2007	2008	Total
Poland																
Acquisition	1	2	4	2	4	8	9	3	6	1	1	0	0	1	1	43
Branch	0	0	0	0	0	0	0	0	0	0	2	0	0	0	0	2
Subsidiaries	0	2	2	3	0	0	1	2	1	0	0	0	0	0	2	13
Share of total assets (%)	3	4	14	15	17	47	70	69	67	68	67	70	68	68	67	–
Hungary																
Acquisition	2	2	3	6	3	1	2	2	0	0	0	0	0	3	0	24
Branch	0	0	0	0	0	0	0	0	0	0	0	0	1	0	0	0
Subsidiaries	1	1	3	1	0	0	1	2	0	1	0	0	0	1	0	11
Share of total assets (%)	N/A	42	46	53	64	66	68	70	91	83	77	83	81	83	89	–
Czech Republic																
Acquisition	0	0	0	0	3	1	3	1	1	0	0	0	0	1	0	10
Branch	1	0	1	0	0	0	0	0	0	0	0	0	1	0	0	3
Subsidiaries	0	0	1	0	0	0	0	0	0	0	0	0	0	2	0	3
Share of total assets (%)	N/A	16	20	24	26	39	75	93	94	96	92	93	97	96	97	–
Slovakia																
Acquisition	0	0	0	0	0	1	2	2	2	1	1	0	0	0	1	10
Branch	0	0	0	0	0	0	0	0	0	0	2	0	0	0	0	2
Subsidiaries	1	4	1	0	0	0	0	0	0	0	0	0	0	0	0	6
Share of total assets (%)	N/A	19	23	30	30	31	43	91	96	96	97	98	99	97	96	–

Source: National Central Banks and Commissions for Banking Supervision.

whereas in Hungary and Poland, foreign-owned banks represent close to 70% of the total banking assets.

Table 1 also shows that the pattern of banking internationalization in the European emerging countries was not uniform. Before the transformation, foreign banks entered the region mainly as de novo operations. Encouraged by the swift pace of economical and political reform, the pressure to enter attractive European emerging markets has increased. With the intention of rapidly gaining local market share, most of the foreign banks pursued mergers and acquisitions (M&As) instead of commencing de novo operations abroad. Note that the acquisitions and subsidiaries have been foreign banks' preferred modes of entry into European emerging markets. The unfavorable attitudes of host regulators toward branches explain the relatively small number in our sample. Before the 2004 EU accession, regulators often refused foreign banks' applications to open branches, doing so based on a wider set of criteria than when banks sought to use subsidiaries (Cerutti, Ariccia, & Martinez Peria, 2007).

In terms of the number of foreign bank entries, German (31), Austrian (18), and US banks (12) dominate the 128 data points in our sample. However, in 2008, the largest foreign investors in Central and Eastern Europe in terms of banking assets were Italian, Austrian, and Belgian banks. Banks from those countries accounted for 18%, 15%, and 11%, respectively, of total banking assets in the Central and Eastern European (CEE) region (UniCredit Group Research, 2008).

3. DATA

We used annual data over the period 1995–2008, covering all foreign bank entries from OECD countries. Our primary sources of information were BankScope and annual reports from national banks. Our final sample contained 129 cross-border entries into one of the four host countries by a foreign bank from one of the OECD member countries.

Following the definition generally applied in the literature on foreign banking (Clarke, Cull, Martinez Peria, & Sanchez, 2003; Claessens et al., 2001; Claeys & Hainz, 2006), we consider a bank to be foreign-owned if foreigners own 50% or more of its shares. A foreign bank entry is determined as the outcome of an acquisition of a domestic bank (acquired bank) or the establishment of either a subsidiary or a branch in a host country. When an entry occurs by establishing one of the two latter forms, we refer to the entry as a greenfield operation. Whereas the determination of a foreign bank entry through subsidiaries or branches is straightforward, entry through acquisition requires a more precise explanation. In our study, we define an acquisition as a percentage change of shares held by the largest foreign investors relative to the previous year. We were interested only in horizontal foreign bank engagements, which are assumed to offer a broad potential for cost and profit efficiency improvements. As a consequence, other types of transactions such as state-owned banks or other financial institutions acquiring a domestic bank are excluded from our study. Moreover, our analysis does not include domestic M&As. We define a foreign subsidiary or branch as an organization that has received a license or approval from a domestic bank supervisory institution. The transformations of operating subsidiaries into branches or vice versa are not considered in our study.

4. EMPIRICAL METHODOLOGY

4.1. Model

In our study, we are interested in the relationship between economic determinants and the entry modes adopted by foreign banks. In particular, we are interested in changes in the determinants that impact a bank's choice of organizational structure. To analyze foreign bank entry decisions, we consider the number of entries at year t into Poland, Hungary, the Czech Republic, and Slovakia segmented by country of origin, conditioned on specific groups of regressors such as the host country's characteristics, the physical relationship between the host country and the home country, and other potential determinants of entry. We use the Poisson regression of the following specification:

$$Pr(Y_{iht} = y)\frac{\exp^{-\lambda_{iht}}\lambda_{iht}^{y_{iht}}}{y_{iht}!} \tag{1}$$

where i indexes home countries (i.e., OECD countries), h indexes host countries (Hungary, Poland, Czech Republic, and Slovakia), t indexes time in years, and y equals one when an acquisition, branch opening, or subsidiary formation by a foreign bank from country i in country h occurs at year t versus when an engagement through another operation mode from country i into country h occurs at year t, in which case it is zero. We also specify that λ_{iht}'s are log-linearly dependent on the explanatory variables as follows:

$$\ln \lambda_{iht} = \beta_0 + \beta_1 K_{ht} + \beta_2 H_{hit} + \beta_3 B_{it} + \varepsilon_{iht} \tag{2}$$

In addition, the randomness in the model arises from the Poisson specification for y_{iht}. The moment-generating function of the Poisson distribution is $m(t) = m(t) = e^{-\lambda}e^{\lambda e^{t}}$, where the first two moments are $E(y_{iht}) = \lambda_{iht}$ and $V(y_{iht}) = \lambda_{iht}$. Moreover, K_{ht} is a vector of variables that is specific to the host country at time t. Consistent with the eclectic theory of Dunning (1977) that identifies ownership and location-specific factors responsible for foreign bank entry, we use *income per capita* to control for the potential of the emerging markets, *net interest margin* proxies for sophistication of the banking industry in a host country. Claessens et al. (2001) show that higher net interest margin is associated with higher profitability and less-developed banking sector. We also employ *CR-5* to proxy for the degree of concentration of a host banking market. We assume that higher concentration will encourage foreign banks to enter by greenfield operations but discourage the acquisitions. This organizational form will allow the foreign banks to easily gain a market share in a country. Also, branches of foreign institutions might not require further authorization, provided that parent bank has a license in the European Union (EU) (Dermine, 2006). Furthermore, we also employ a *stock market capitalization* as a percentage of GDP, as we assume that the level of development of capital markets may impact competition in the financial services industry. Aliber (1984) and Hultman and McGee (1989) have documented that a host country's regulatory environment influences foreign banking operations. Therefore, we include into our regression an index developed by European Bank for Reconstruction and Development (EBRD) (2009), which captures the quality of banking regulations in a host country. The index ranges from 1 to 4.5 with the higher values referring to the standards and performance norms of industrial countries. The index is available for all CEE countries and all periods. Overseas bank expansion is frequently attributed to variations in the tax treatment of banks in different countries, which may influence decisions to enter a new market with a certain organizational structure. Indeed, we expect high taxes to favor branches, since they allow for easier cross-border shifting (Cerruti et al., 2007). Therefore, we control for the corporate income tax in our regression. Finally, foreign banks may use economic crises to enter new markets. We control for economic distortions by employing the *country risk index* and *exchange rate*. The depreciation of currency and higher risk might positively affect foreign bank entry. The country index has been taken from *International Country Risk Guide* and is available for all sample countries and periods. It ranges from 0–49.5 points high country risk to 80–100 points low country's risk. We assume that lower country index should discourage the entry through a branch operation but favor entry through acquisition. Branches, as opposed to other form of operations, are integral part of a parent bank. Therefore, they are also more risky for a parent bank as crisis in the host market can spillover from a branch to the parent bank. We also control for the macroeconomic environment by including the *inflation rate* in logs. Consistent with Claessens et al. (2001), we assume that higher inflation rate is associated with higher interest rate margins, which might encourage the foreign bank entries. H_{iht} is a vector of variables that are specific to the relationship between the host country and the home country at time t. We use a difference in the *economic growth rates* between the host and the origin country. Scher and Weller (2001) claim that higher economic growth in a host country but lower in a home market positively affects the foreign banks' presence in a host location. Finally, B_{it} is a vector of variables specific to the home countries at time t. We include a distance from the home country into a host market that is used as a proxy for the *degree of economic integration and cultural proximity* (Ball & Tschoegl, 1982). Given the importance of information regarding the host markets and their customers, we expect that this variable will have a negative relationship with foreign entry. We also control for the legal origin of a home country. Claessens and Van Horen (2008) show that foreign banks tend to enter countries that have legal origin and institutional structure similar to their home markets to best exploit their competitive advantage. Consistent with La Porta, Lopez-de-Silanes, Shleifer, and Vishny (1997), we distinguish between English, German, French, and Scandinavian legal origin of home economies. We expect that countries with the German and French legal origin are more likely to enter the European emerging economies, whose legal systems are based on these types of law families.

Finally, following Magri, Mori, and Rossi (2005), we also introduce a dummy variable to identify home countries that belong to the EU, which should be an advantage for foreign banks due to lower entry barriers and less regulation.

4.2. Descriptive Statistics and Correlation

Table 2 presents descriptive statistics for our regression model. We note that the data exhibit wide variation, both cross-sectionally and as a time series. For example, the average corporate tax rate ranges from 18% in Poland to 41% in Slovakia over the period 1995–2008. Considerable variation also exists among the location-specific factors. The ratio of GDP per capita ranges from 9,494 euros in Poland to 14,187 euros in the Czech Republic in

Table 2. Descriptive Statistics.

Variable	Number of Observations	Mean	Minimum	Maximum	Standard Deviation
Exchange rate	1,624	78.50	3.10	264.26	94.50
Inflation rate	1,624	1.77	−2.30	3.34	0.88
Country risk	1,624	76.05	71.50	83.50	2.53
Bank regulations index	1,624	3.48	2.67	4.00	0.44
Net interest margin	1,624	3.89	2.00	7.40	1.34
Stock market capitalization	1,624	10.17	0.05	51.10	12.68
Concentration ratio	1,624	61.86	43.00	91.00	9.58
Differences in GDP growth rates	1,624	−1.19	−13.00	12.00	3.18
Distance	1,624	7.51	5.24	9.81	1.11
Trade	1,508	1.15	0.50	1.74	0.35
Income per capita	1,624	8.67	7.94	9.56	0.41
Corporate tax rate	1,624	27.00	16.00	41.00	8.46

Note: This table shows summary statistics when the dependent variable is equal to the number of foreign bank entries from one of the OECD countries into one of the host countries over the years 1995–2008.

2008. The variation is even greater when one considers the variation across both countries and time-series. For example, among the macroeconomic variables, the inflation ratio ranges from −2.30% in the Czech Republic to 3.34% in Hungary between 1995 and 2008. Among the home and the host country characteristics, the difference in economic growth rates varies from −13% in Poland to 12% in the Czech Republic over the same period.

Regarding the correlation shown in Table 3, we are aware of the multicollinearity problem that might exist in regressions featuring a considerable number of control variables. A large number of econometrics studies indicate how serious this problem might be when the independent variables are highly correlated with one other. In general, factor analyses suggest reducing collinearity by eliminating from analysis one or more highly-correlated variables using ridge regression or by combining two or more variables into a single matrix. In fact, this approach creates more severe problems than it eliminates due to the omission of information (Greene, 2000). O'Brien (2007) showed that as long as a regression coefficient is statistically significant, multicollinearity does not negatively impact the results, even in the case of high correlations between the independent variables. Therefore, the choice of the set of control variables included in our regression specification is based not only on our statistical assessments but also on the econometrics literature.[2] We also observe that some of the

Table 4. The Determinants of Foreign Bank Entry Using Acquisition as an Entry Mode.

	(1)	(2)	(3)	(4)
Exchange rate	−0.001	0.000	−0.001	−0.001
	(0.004)	(0.004)	(0.004)	(0.004)
Exchange rate rate × crisis dummy			0.040***	0.039***
			(0.010)	(0.010)
Inflation	0.179	0.185	0.167	0.167
	(0.156)	(0.142)	(0.142)	(0.142)
Inflation × crisis dummy			5.626***	5.601***
			(1.913)	(1.938)
Country risk	−0.204***	−0.206***	−0.201***	−0.200***
	(0.060)	(0.057)	(0.058)	(0.058)
Country risk × crisis dummy			2.211***	2.195***
			(0.778)	(0.781)
Net interest margin	0.174	0.103	0.098	0.098
	(0.215)	(0.176)	(0.258)	(0.257)
Bank regulations	2.416***	2.179***	2.164***	2.164***
	(0.480)	(0.489)	(0.516)	(0.519)
Stock market capital	−0.068***	−0.073***	−0.057**	−0.057**
	(0.022)	(0.015)	(0.026)	(0.026)
Concentration ratio	0.038**	0.008	0.026	0.026
	(0.018)	(0.013)	(0.016)	(0.016)
Difference in growth rates	−0.020	−0.031	−0.043	−0.043
	(0.067)	(0.061)	(0.069)	(0.069)
Difference in growth rates × dummy crisis				0.001
				(0.000)
English legal origin	1.221	1.418	1.435*	1.434
	(0.849)	(0.868)	(0.867)	(0.867)
German legal origin	2.222***	2.368***	2.354***	2.354***
	(0.556)	(0.610)	(0.612)	(0.612)
French legal origin	1.208**	1.557**	1.553**	1.553**
	(0.572)	(0.651)	(0.646)	(0.646)
Distance	−0.265	−0.283	−0.285	−0.285
	(0.219)	(0.223)	(0.229)	(0.247)
Distance × dummy crisis				0.004
				(0.387)
Trade	−2.006**	−1.704**	−1.983**	−1.982**
	(0.935)	(0.888)	(0.965)	(0.965)
Income per capita	−0.001***	−0.001***	−0.001***	−0.001***
	(0.000)	(0.000)	(0.000)	(0.000)
Tax rate	−0.004	0.000	−0.001	−0.001
	(0.037)	(0.037)	(0.037)	(0.037)
Tax rate × dummy crisis			−0.122	−0.122
			(0.323)	(0.320)

Table 4. (*Continued*)

	(1)	(2)	(3)	(4)
EU dummy	1.183***	1.176***	1.175***	1.176***
	(0.382)	(0.391)	(0.389)	(0.396)
Crisis dummy		3.236***	−174.17***	−172.94***
		(0.803)	(57.41)	(58.88)
Log likelihood	−202.33	−229.38	−229.13	−227.65
Number of observations	1,276	1,508	1,508	1,508

Notes: The dependent variable is equal to the number of foreign banks' entries using acquisition by country of origin. Specification (1) includes observations only for the period 1995–2006, whereas specifications (2–4) also include the period 2007–2008. *Crisis dummy* is 1 for the years 2007–2008. The *t*-statistics based on robust standard errors appear in brackets
***, **, and * denote statistical significance at the 1%, 5%, and 10% levels, respectively.

exchange rate and the crisis dummy, which suggest the appreciation of the foreign bank's home currency relative to the host country's currency. The depreciation of host country currency creates an opportunity for the banks to acquire assets at a discount, which is the result of increased risk aversion during the financial crisis. We also note a positive and statistically significant coefficient of bank regulations on the number of entries into the emerging countries. The results confirm that foreign banks choose an acquisition of a local bank as an entry mode when there are high barriers of entering the region. Such an acquisition enables a foreign institution to step in the region and quickly gain the market share. According to our expectations, we find that it is more likely that the foreign bank using acquisition originates in a country with the same legal origin as the emerging market. The results should not be a surprise when considering the legal and cultural complexity of bank acquisitions. Therefore, we also find that EU membership of both the host and the home countries is a significant determinant for foreign bank entry, while distance is negatively related to foreign banking.

Table 5 shows the results of specifications (1)–(4) as determinants of foreign bank entry modes using a subsidiary condition on the global business cycle. They differ significantly in comparison with the previous results. The positive and statistically significant coefficient of the exchange rate suggests that foreign banks tend to use the economic downturn in the host market to enter it. On the contrary, the results of specifications (3) and (4) show that during the global financial crisis, when a local currency appreciated, the subsidiary was the preferable entry mode for foreign banks. Consequently, we find that the exchange rate is an important factor

Table 5. The Determinants of Foreign Bank Entry Using Subsidiary as an Entry Mode.

	(1)	(2)	(3)	(4)
Exchange rate	0.021***	0.027***	0.020***	0.020***
	(0.005)	(0.008)	(0.005)	(0.005)
Exchange rate × crisis dummy			−0.045**	−0.045**
			(0.022)	(0.023)
Inflation rate	0.149	0.251	0.012	0.023
	(0.215)	(0.209)	(0.218)	(0.221)
Inflation × crisis dummy			4.909*	−2.935
			(2.763)	(0.833)
Country risk	−0.115	−0.036	−0.042	−0.057
	(0.143)	(0.104)	(0.172)	(0.183)
Country risk × crisis dummy			−2.906***	−2.935***
			(0.816)	(0.833)
Net interest margin	0.043	−0.606**	−0.163	−0.175
	(0.246)	(0.255)	(0.355)	(0.363)
Bank regulations	0.209	−0.840	−0.532	−0.549
	(0.713)	(0.732)	(0.826)	(0.817)
Stock market capital	−0.117***	−0.053***	−0.079***	−0.083***
	(0.024)	(0.015)	(0.032)	(0.034)
Concentration ratio	0.084	0.007	−0.009	−0.005
	(0.059)	(0.033)	(0.043)	(0.045)
Difference in growth rates	−0.255***	−0.207***	−0.181***	−0.204***
	(0.041)	(0.069)	(0.065)	(0.058)
Difference in growth rates × dummy crisis				0.002**
				(0.001)
English legal origin	0.853	1.071	1.062	1.097
	(1.242)	(1.335)	(1.333)	(1.315)
German legal origin	2.464***	3.161***	3.173***	3.102***
	(0.832)	(0.963)	(0.961)	(0.975)
French legal origin	0.496	1.135	1.146	1.135
	(0.911)	(0.958)	(0.968)	(0.970)
Distance	0.525*	0.408	0.401	0.596**
	(0.290)	(0.293)	(0.294)	(0.309)
Distance × dummy crisis				−0.898**
				(0.400)
Trade	−5.533**	−7.065***	−4.291***	−4.450
	(2.241)	(2.397)	2.191	(2.241)
Income per capita	0.000	0.000	0.000	0.000
	(0.000)	(0.000)	0.000	(0.000)
Tax rate	0.065	0.118	0.056	0.058
	(0.045)	(0.074)	0.047	(0.048)
Tax rate × dummy crisis			1.223***	1.157***
			0.207	(0.213)

Table 5. *(Continued)*

	(1)	(2)	(3)	(4)
EU dummy	2.377***	2.511***	2.454***	2.583***
	(0.905)	(0.939)	0.934	(0.982)
Crisis dummy		3.552***	194.87***	205.43***
		(0.921)	63.658	65.088
Log likelihood	−67.419	−88.698	−85.700	−84.590
Number of observations	1,276	1,508	1,508	1,508

Notes: The dependent variable is equal to the number of foreign banks' entries using subsidiary by country of origin. Specification (1) includes observations only for the period 1995–2006, whereas specifications (2–4) also include the period 2007–2008. *Crisis dummy* is 1 for the years 2007–2008. The *t*-statistics based on robust standard errors appear in brackets.
***, **, and * denote statistical significance at the 1%, 5%, and 10% levels, respectively.

determining the mode of foreign bank entry through either acquisition or subsidiary. The results of specifications (3) and (4) also reveal that foreign banks tend to use a subsidiary as an entry mode instead of acquisition in riskier economies, which can be the result of inefficient market knowledge. Using a theoretical model, Lehner (2009) demonstrated that foreign banks choose their entry mode according to their efficiency in screening potential borrowers. In markets where foreign banks are not very efficient in screening, they will opt for de novo investment. As the knowledge that foreign owned banks have about the local market increases, they will favor the acquisition of a domestic bank, and the price of the domestic bank will decrease as the efficiency increases. Inversely, as the market knowledge of foreign banks and their screening efficiency decrease, entry may no longer be profitable. Therefore, the results confirm Lehner's theory, as they show that the relationship between country risk and the crisis dummy has a negative sign and is statistically significant.

In specification (1), the coefficient for the differences in the growth rates between the host and home economies is negative and significant. This means that in a period of global expansion, foreign banks tend to reallocate capital to emerging markets with higher economic growth rates than the home market. The results confirm the previous finding of de Haas and van Lelyvald (2010), who showed that foreign bank subsidiary lending grows when economic growth in their home country decreases. Those authors also found that high host country growth stimulates credit growth, although its effect is mainly limited to greenfield investment. Moreover,

Table 6. The Determinants of Foreign Bank Entry Using Branches as an Entry Mode.

	(1)	(2)	(3)	(4)
Exchange rate	0.024***	0.024***	0.024***	0.024***
	(0.005)	(0.005)	(0.005)	(0.005)
Exchange rate × crisis dummy			0.048***	0.052***
			(0.017)	(0.017)
Inflation	−0.142	−0.120	−0.120	−0.120
	(0.164)	(0.149)	(0.149)	(0.149)
Inflation × crisis dummy			−4.566*	−5.900**
			(2.709)	(2.844)
Country risk	0.067	0.065	0.065	0.065
	(0.581)	(0.581)	(0.581)	(0.581)
Country risk × crisis dummy			0.352	0.466
			(1.222)	(1.175)
Net interest margin	−0.776***	−0.777***	−0.777***	−0.777***
	(0.231)	(0.217)	(0.217)	(0.217)
Bank regulations	−10.510***	−10.488***	−10.488***	−10.488***
	(4.086)	(4.074)	(4.074)	(4.074)
Stock market capital	−0.001	−0.001	−0.001	−0.001
	(0.027)	(0.026)	(0.026)	(0.026)
Concentration ratio	0.006	0.007	0.007	0.007
	(0.130)	(0.129)	(0.129)	(0.129)
Difference in growth rates	−0.632***	−0.627***	−0.627***	−0.627***
	(0.246)	(0.244)	(0.244)	(0.244)
Difference in growth rates × dummy crisis				0.000
				(0.001)
English legal origin	0.944	1.268*	1.268*	1.268*
	(0.793)	(0.748)	(0.748)	(0.748)
German legal of origin	−19.186***	−19.017***	−19.224***	−18.444***
	(1.518)	(1.720)	(1.721)	(1.721)
French legal origin	−0.688	−0.408	−0.408	−0.408
	(1.064)	(1.206)	(1.206)	(1.206)
Distance	−1.530	−1.606	−1.606	−1.606**
	(1.129)	(1.204)	(1.204)	(1.204)
Distance × dummy crisis				4.376
				(1.721)
Trade	−8.679***	−8.706***	−8.707***	−8.707***
	(3.236)	(3.220)	(3.221)	(3.221)
Income per capita	0.002***	0.002***	0.002***	0.002***
	(0.000)	(0.000)	(0.000)	(0.000)
Tax rate	−0.128**	−0.126**	−0.126**	−0.126**
	(0.069)	(0.067)	(0.067)	(0.067)
Tax rate × dummy crisis			0.431	0.616
			(0.357)	(0.417)

Table 6. *(Continued)*

	(1)	(2)	(3)	(4)
EU dummy	17.564***	17.454***	17.435***	16.795***
	(0.867)	(0.962)	(0.960)	(1.090)
Crisis dummy		−25.429***	−55.957	−97.657
		(1.398)	(93.391)	(86.117)
Log likelihood	−21.748	−22.035	22.035	−22.035
Number of observations	1276	1508	1508	1508

Notes: The dependent variable is equal to the number of foreign banks' entries using acquisition by country of origin. Specification (1) includes observations only for the period 1995–2006, whereas specifications (2–4) also include the period 2007–2008. *Crisis dummy* is 1 for the years 2007–2008.The *t*-statistics based on robust standard errors appear in brackets
***, **, and * denote statistical significance at the 1%, 5%, and 10% levels, respectively.

our results show that during the financial crisis, foreign bank entry was more likely from countries less affected by it, as the interactive term of differences in the growth rates variable with the dummy crisis is positive and significant.

Similarly to the previous results, we find that foreign banks with the same legal origin and institutional framework as the host country are more likely to enter the host country. However, in specification (4), both coefficients of the distance variable and the interactive term with the crisis dummy are statistically different from zero. The latter also shows a negative sign, which suggests that distance becomes an extremely important decision factor for the foreign banks during an economic downturn. Again, the results can be driven by monitoring and information efficiency, which might be higher in foreign subsidiaries that are closer to the home country of the parent bank. In specifications (3) and (4), the corporate tax and the interactive coefficients with the crisis is positive and statistically significant. This could mean that in times of financial crisis, higher taxes did not have a negative impact on the entry decision, as other factors such as risk and the country's economic stability are seen as more important determinants for foreign banks.

Table 6 present the results for the determinants of a foreign bank's choice to enter an emerging market by opening a branch. We employ the same set of the regressors as in the previous two regressions, but the dependent variable this time is the number of branches opened in the sample countries. In the table, all the specifications show that the determinants of choosing a branch as an entry mode by a foreign bank are in line with our main results. In addition, the results seem to be independent of the global business cycle. However, in Table 1, we show that during the financial crisis, none of the foreign banks decided to use branches as a mode of expansion into emerging markets. This means that during a global financial crisis, using branches to expand into emerging markets can be too risky for the parent bank. The reasoning behind this may relate to the increased risk of investment in emerging markets, the deterioration of the economic situation in the home country or both factors at the same time.

We find, however, that foreign banks decided to enter the emerging markets using branches during periods of global economic expansion. The results also reveal that branches were used as an entry mode in more developed emerging markets, which are often seen as less risky countries, confirming our previous assumptions. Therefore, the coefficient of income per capita is positive and statistically significant. In addition, we report a negative and statistically significant coefficient of the net interest margin. Claessens et al. (2001) showed that net interest margins decline as a result of a foreign bank's entry and increased competition. We may therefore assume that branches are used in more developed and saturated markets. We find also that foreign banks choose branches as an entry mode during a period of host currency depreciation. The coefficient of exchange rate is positive and statistically significant in all specifications. However, contrary to our expectations, we find negative coefficients for the tax rate and the banking sector's regulations in all specifications. The negative sign of the tax rate might indicate that it may have lower relevance than country risk or growth potential. Indeed, we find again that the coefficient of a variable controlling for the differences in the growth rates between the home and the host countries is negative and statistically significant. This would mean that branches are preferred in those countries that exhibit faster economic growth than the home market. This is not surprising, as using branches allows the foreign bank to operate on a larger scale then using a subsidiary abroad.

In contrast to our previous findings, we find that the German legal origin dummy is negative and significant. This means that branches were chosen mostly by foreign banks from countries with a British or Scandinavian legal origin, whereas those banks with a German legal origin preferred to use acquisition or subsidiary as an entry mode into emerging markets. Finally, our results confirm that EU membership was an important factor that has facilitated the use of branches as an entry mode in Central European emerging markets.

5. THE BEHAVIOR OF FOREIGN INSTITUTIONS DEPENDING ON THE MODE OF ENTRY

5.1. The Behavior of Foreign Institutions Depending on the Mode of Entry in the Period before Their Economic Downturn

The analysis of determinants of entry modes suggests that foreign banks have different motivations when choosing their specific organizational form and therefore react differently to the same economic factors. This behavior, in turn, implies that the greenfield entrants versus acquired banks and their parent banks might significantly differ from each other. As a consequence, the choice of a particular entry mode by a foreign institution will have different implications on their financial stability, especially during a time of distress. For example, Schmidt (2009) claims that foreign banks, which enter through greenfield operations, face greater exposure to higher competition in a host country, and therefore, they experience lower profit margins. As a result, they have fewer incentives to undertake costly monitoring, which in turn has an adverse impact on the credit quality of these institutions as compared to the acquired banks. The author claims that these banks create a higher risk for an economy. On the contrary, Schmidt (2009) finds that higher competition in the emerging banking markets reduces the interest rate margins and thus requires the foreign greenfield institutions to extend more credit than the acquired banks. Therefore, these institutions have to extend credits in the emerging countries more rapidly. Kraft (2002) and de Haas and van Lelyvald (2006) reached the same conclusion. Fig. 1 presents the evolution of credit growth to the bank's asset, and Figs. 2 and 3 show the loan-to-deposit ratio by entry mode in European emerging countries between the years 2005 through 2008.

Consistent with the academic studies, we find that greenfield entrants extend more credit than acquirers. However, they are also more likely to squeeze the credit extension during the economic distress. The average ratio of net loans to the bank's assets increased in the greenfield entrants by more than 15% between 2005 and 2008; however, the increase in the acquired banks amounted to only 9% during the same period. The highest credit growth is noted in the foreign greenfield banks between 2006 and 2007, shortly before the parent banks started revealing their huge financial losses. On the contrary, the data seem to suggest that foreign banks, which entered by acquiring the local institutions, are less affected by economic turbulence. In fact, their credit growth increases more rapidly as compared to their

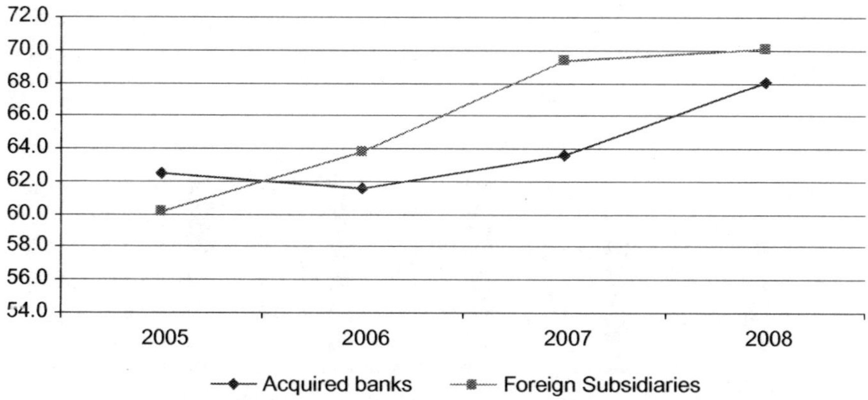

Fig. 1. Net Loans to Assets by Entry Modes of Foreign Banks. *Note:* The average of seven European emerging countries: Poland, Hungary, Czech Republic, Slovakia, Latvia, Lithuania, and Estonia.

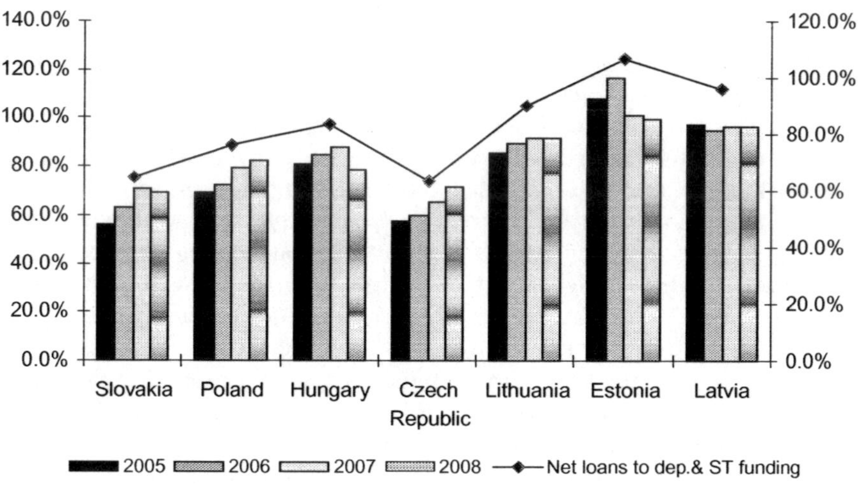

Fig. 2. Ratio of Loans-to-Deposit of the Acquired Banks.

greenfield competitors and to previous periods. This result might suggest that parent banks reallocate their capital from their home countries by setting up subsidiaries that are more exposed to the economic distortions, especially in the home country. This observation is consistent with our empirical results from the previous section where the difference in growth

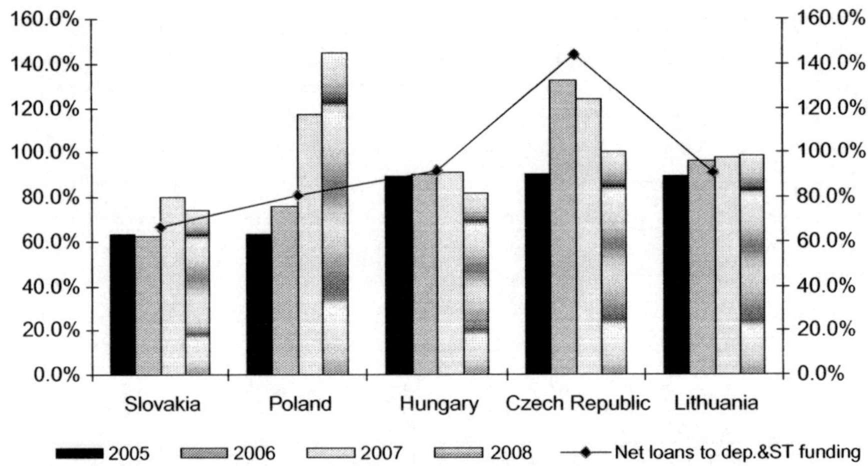

Fig. 3. Ratio of Loans-to-Deposit of the Foreign Greenfield Operations.

rates between the parent country and host country is statistically negative and significant only for the subsidiary operation. Similar results have been also found by de Haas and van Lelyvald (2006).

The table data also reveal that the loan-to-deposit (LTD) ratio was very high in most of the European emerging countries between 2005 and 2007. In some of these countries, it exceeded 120%, although significant differences between these economies are observable. Specifically, the data show that the LTD ratio varies between banks' organizational structures. It is considerably higher for the foreign greenfield banks than for the acquired banks. The average ratio for the former organizational form exceeded 100% in 2007, whereas for the latter it was only 84%. The credit changes in the greenfield banks were significantly higher than the deposit development, suggesting that deposit growth has not been able to keep up with the rapid credit growth in recent years at these banks.

Although credit growth has important implications for economic growth, from the financial stability perspective, it is important to know how foreign banks finance their credit extension. The recent crises have revealed that heavy reliance on external financing might have severe consequences for the performance of financial institutions, especially if the credit growth has been funded abroad by easy access to the cheap funds of parent banks. The spillover effects from the home into the host country could spread very quickly and result in the sudden shortfall of or costly access to funds available to the local banks, which in turn would make further extension of credit difficult. In addition, liquidity or solvency problems experienced by a parent bank could be transferred to its subsidiaries or branches in other countries and negatively affect confidence in the banking sector. Figs. 4 and 5 show the level of reliance of foreign banks in the European

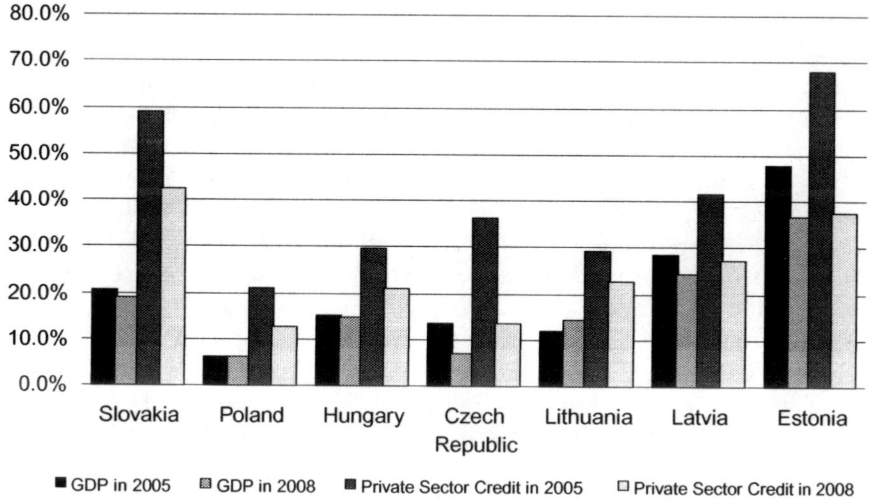

Fig. 4. Outstanding Consolidated Claims of the Reporting Banks on European Emerging Banking Systems (in Percent).

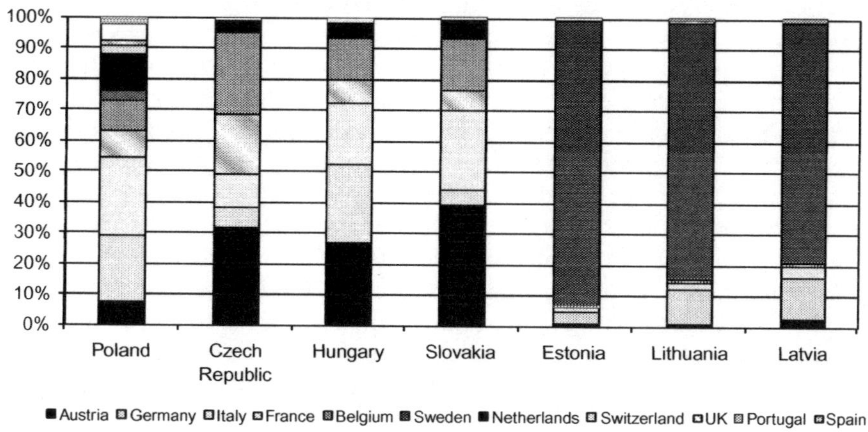

Fig. 5. Concentration of Funding Dependence of CEE Banks on BIS Reporting Banks in Western Europe, End 2008. *Note:* Foreign claims owed by a CEE country to a Western European countries' banks as a share of the CEE country's GDP, in percent.

emerging countries on the Western banks and the concentration of funding dependence according to the country of origin. The data present foreign claims reported in the BIS international banking statistics and include outstanding consolidated claims of the reporting banks on both European emerging local banking systems and on the nonbanking sector (i.e., direct lending). From the borrowers' perspective, the data give an idea of the magnitude and distribution of the dependence of banking institutions in the emerging markets on Western European banks and illustrate the magnitude of control over a country's assets and liabilities by foreign banks.

The analyses of foreign claims show that most foreign institutions in emerging countries were heavily dependent on foreign external funds to support the rapid expansion of lending to the private sector. The dependence ratio is significant, both in relation to the domestic GDP and to the size of the European banking sectors. The highest dependence ratio was in the Baltic States and Slovakia, where it ranged between 50% and 70% of all the banks' credit volume. Most European emerging banking institutions have concentrated exposure, in particular in such countries as Austria, Italy, and Germany. Additionally, the Baltic States had large exposure in Sweden.

Concerning the financing patterns of foreign banks in European emerging countries, depending on the entry mode, our empirical results from the previous section suggest that the probability of an entry through a greenfield operation is more likely when the deposit base is lower and the difference in the economic growth rates between the home and host country is higher. Given our analyses, these results suggest that foreign subsidiaries are more likely to be critically dependent on the borrowed funds; parent banks reallocate their funds into countries with high return projects. Therefore, foreign subsidiaries seem to be more dependent on parent banks in financing their operations in emerging markets than the acquired local banks, and hence, they might face greater exposure to the financial vulnerabilities of the home country. Fig. 6 presents the level of dependency of foreign subsidiaries and acquired local institutions on the interbank market based on the specific entry modes. The interbank dependency ratio is defined as the ratio of deposits from credit institutions to a bank's total assets.

The data suggest that acquired banks finance their activities to a greater extent through internal funds, whereas the greenfield operations rely more on borrowed funds. The difference between the entry modes is significant because it suggests that foreign greenfield banks were almost twice as dependent on borrowed funds as were the acquired local banks. In addition, the graph also suggests two opposite directions of the ratio development, supporting our previous observations. It clearly suggests that during a

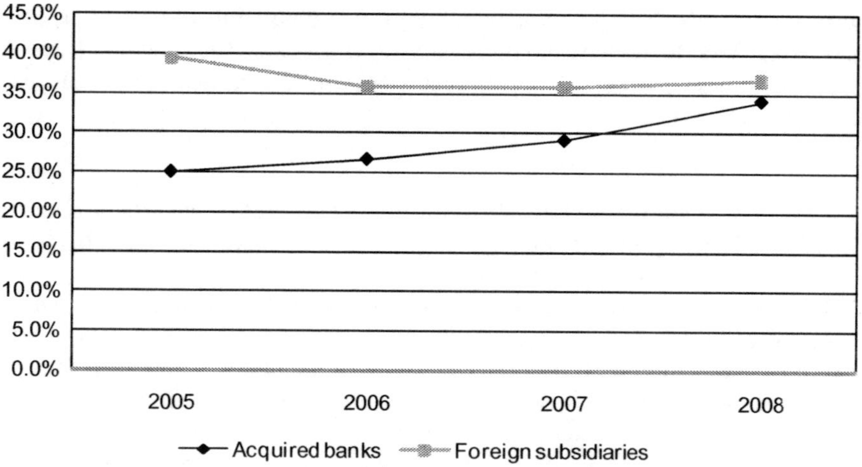

Fig. 6. Interbank Dependency Ratio of Foreign Banks in European Emerging Countries by Entry Mode. *Note:* The average of seven European emerging countries: Poland, Hungary, Czech Republic, Slovakia, Latvia, Lithuania, and Estonia.

period of economic growth, the greenfield operations extend the credits more rapidly than do the acquired local banks being supported by the parent banks. However, during periods of financial distress, especially in the home country, the parent banks tighten the credit line for their foreign subsidiaries, which negatively affects the credit extension in these banks. Conversely, for the acquired local banks, the credit growth during times of financial turbulence seems to be buttressed by the parent banks. The highest dependency ratio occurred in 2008, the year in which banks in European emerging countries started to first report financial losses. This analysis has important implications on liquidity shock transmission, in particular during times of financial stress in the home market. Namely, it suggests that greenfield operations are exposed to financial vulnerabilities in the home market to a greater extent, whereas the acquired local banks seem to be aided by their parents. Our observation seems to be consistent with empirical studies examining the linkage between foreign greenfield operations and parent banks. For example, de Haas and van Lelyvald (2010) find that parent banks support their foreign subsidiaries with high net interest margins or low loan loss provisioning, but this mostly occurs during the good times of a business cycle. However, in another study the authors (2005) show that credit growth of greenfield foreign banks depends to a greater extent on the financial position of the Western European banks. Also in line with our results, de Haas and van Lelyvald (2006) find that the acquired banks are less dependent on their parent banks than the greenfield operations are, and Ashcraft (2008) shows that, therefore, they are safer than other foreign affiliates.

5.2. The Behavior of Parent Banks toward Their Foreign Operations Depending on Entry Mode in a Period of Global Economic Downturn

Until now, our analysis has identified various patterns of foreign banks' operations in the European emerging countries, varying by entry mode. From the policy makers' perspective, it is also interesting to look at the role of parent banks toward their foreign operations by organizational structure during a period of financial shock, either in a host country or in a home country. In the academic literature this topic has not been widely researched although it has important policy implications. For example, the parent banks during a period of economic extension might reallocate capital from their home country into countries with higher profit opportunities, whereas in a period of economic distress they might withdraw their funds from these institutions to increase their own capital. Such behavior has important financial stability implications because it may lead to a shock transmission from one country into another, that is, bank runs, and as a result it may severely endanger the financial stability of a host country. Furthermore, the role of a parent bank as a lender of last resort, depending on the entry mode, has not been widely investigated in academic studies although such research might discover important implications for the supervisory authorities. Therefore, in this section, we try to review, for the first time, the behavior of parent banks toward their foreign affiliates by their organizational structure during a time of financial distress, with particular attention to the current crisis.

Hryckiewicz and Kowalewski (2010) show that parent banks are more likely to sell their stakes in local banks instead of closing their foreign greenfield operations. The authors document that the probability of selling stakes is higher when a parent bank experiences financial problems. The parent banks decide to do this to increase their own profitability or capital. Not surprisingly, the authors report that the likelihood of disposing of parent banks' stakes increases during a crisis in the home market. In addition, Tschoegl (2005) claims that the reason why parent banks decide to sell their stakes and not close their subsidiaries is due to fear of tarnishing their reputation. Also, subsidiaries cost parent banks more than do other

Table 7. Number of Operations' Divestment in the Host Country.

Countries	1998	1999	2000	2001	2002	2003	2004	2005	2006	2007	2008	2009	Total
Czech Republic					1-A	1-S	1-A		1-A		1-A		5
Hungary	1-S		1-A	1-A, 1-S		1-A			1-A				6
Latvia				1-S									1
Poland					2-S	1-A							3
Slovakia						1-A	1-S			1-A			3

Source: Hryckiewicz and Kowalewski (2010).
Note: "A" stands for acquisition and "S" for subsidiary.

organizational forms. Table 7 lists the identified divestment of foreign operations in the European emerging countries for the years 1997 through 2009.

Not surprisingly most of the closures of foreign operations occurred in these countries between the years 2002 and 2004. This was a period of time when most industrialized countries went into a mild recession caused by the crash of the Internet bubble and the bankruptcy of Internet and technology companies across the world. As a consequence, the profitability of the parent banks shrank – an event that may have prompted the divestment of international operations. Note that in most cases the parent banks decided to withdraw their operations from the European emerging economies by selling their stakes in the local banks. Only in 6 of 18 cases did the parent banks decide to close their foreign subsidiaries.

On the contrary, if a foreign operation is of high strategic importance for a parent bank, Gilbert (1991) and Ashcraft (2008) empirically show that a parent bank will not sell such an institution. Instead, it is willing to provide a capital injection, even when it suffers liquidity problems of its own. The authors show that capital injection is more likely for the distressed acquired institutions than for the stand-alone banks. This probability increases with parent bank's ownership in such an institution. The assistance of parent banks in the recovery of distressed local institutions also occurred during the current financial crisis. Owing to the high strategic relevance of most European emerging markets' operations and continued high potential of this region, most of the parent banks decided to sustain their operations in this region. Hence, there were almost no bank disposals despite several rumors to this effect. In fact, many parent banks finally decided to support their foreign operations in this area. Such a capital injection was received by Romanian BRD, which has been supported by its French parent bank

Societé Generale, whereas Austrian *Erste Bank* decided to support, through minor capital increases, its operations in Croatia, Serbia, and Hungary. Greek *Alpha Bank* supported the financial base in its Romanian bank. Note that most of these banks operate as multibank holding companies. The reason why an entry mode might matter is that the greenfield operations function on a stand-alone basis, whereas the acquired local banks are incorporated into a parent bank's balance sheet.

The behavior of a parent bank toward its foreign operations might also vary if a parent bank faces liquidity problems itself, whereas its foreign operation remains profitable. In such a case, a parent bank might decide to sell its affiliate to increase or strengthen its capital. However, such a scenario is less likely when a foreign operation is of high strategic importance for a parent bank. A parent bank might also try to allocate funds from its foreign affiliate into its home market. There are several reasons for such a behavior. First, the foreign affiliate can pay out dividends on behalf of its parent bank; however, this solution is expensive because the parent banks will have to pay income tax. Second, the parent bank might lend from its foreign affiliates at a low interest rate. A third possibility is to reallocate funds from a foreign affiliate to a parent bank through interbank deposits. This method is very difficult to examine because parent banks do not have an obligation to publish such as data. Desai, Foley, and Hines (2007) document that parent companies are more likely to draw on the resources of their foreign affiliates through repatriations when a parent institution is in need of cash.

For a long time in European emerging countries, parent banks tried to passively keep their foreign subsidiaries by setting low dividend payout ratios. This approach leaves the subsidiaries with more than sufficient capital to support their credit expansion (de Haas & Naaborg, 2006) However, an event such as a financial crisis in the home market, as we have experienced recently, may increase the probability of drawing on the funds of foreign affiliates, especially if the crisis has first hit the parent bank. Fig. 7 presents the development of the interbank ratio of foreign institutions by entry mode. This ratio is defined as money lent to other banks divided by money borrowed from other banks. Figs. 8–11 show the dividend payouts of the main players in the European emerging countries.

Fig. 7 shows that with the beginning of the crisis in the parent bank's home market, the ratio of greenfield operations started decreasing at a more rapid pace than that of the acquired local banks. Only in Poland did the ratio substantially increase between 2005 and 2007, exceeding 150% in 2007, with a 45% change during this period. This fact might suggest that parent banks tried to borrow funds from their still very profitable Polish foreign

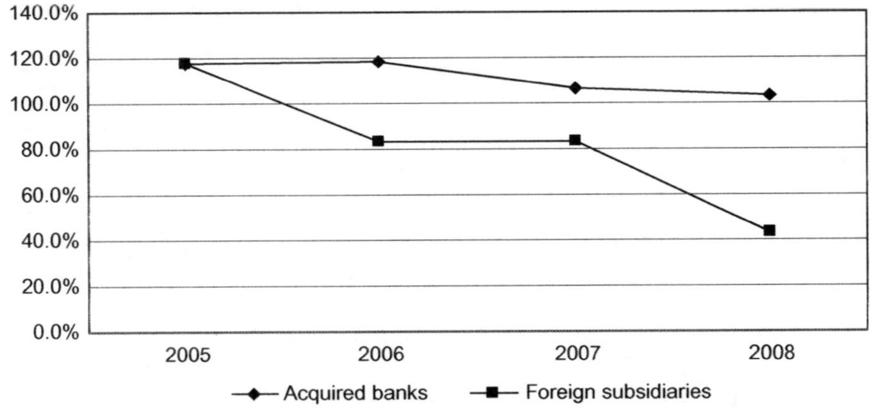

Fig. 7. Interbank Ratio of Foreign Banks in European Emerging Countries by Entry Mode. *Note:* The average of seven European emerging countries: Poland, Hungary, Czech Republic, Slovakia, Latvia, Lithuania, and Estonia.

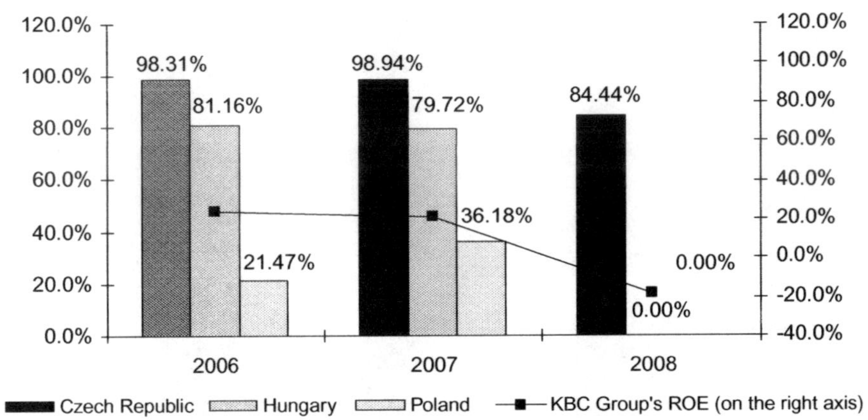

Fig. 8. Dividend Payouts of KBC Banks in European Emerging Countries.

subsidiaries. In all other European emerging countries, the interbank ratio for foreign subsidiaries showed a downturn trend. Note that the banking sector in emerging Europe started to report high financial losses in 2008. The years 2006 and 2007 saw record profits among banking institutions in this region. The decreasing interbank ratio might suggest that greenfield banks had to start searching for more costly funding as a result of the poor performance of their parent banks and heavy reliance on their funding

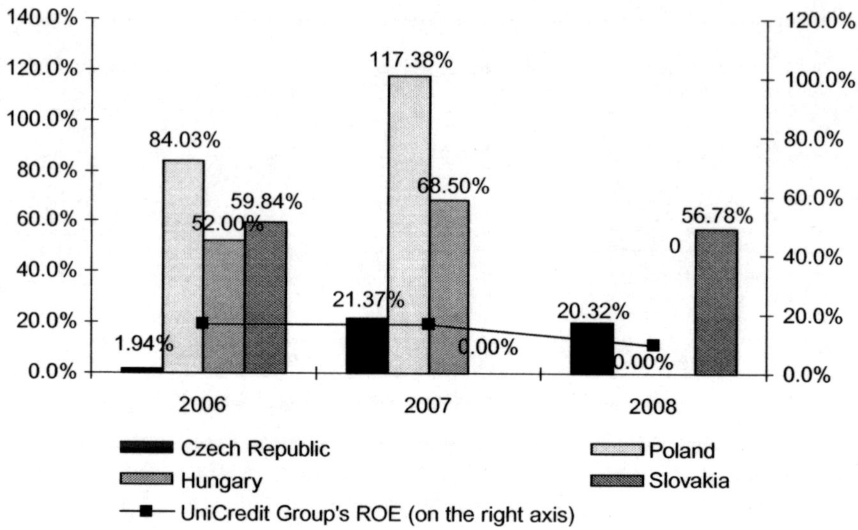

Fig. 9. Dividend Payouts of UniCredit Group's Banks in European Emerging Countries.

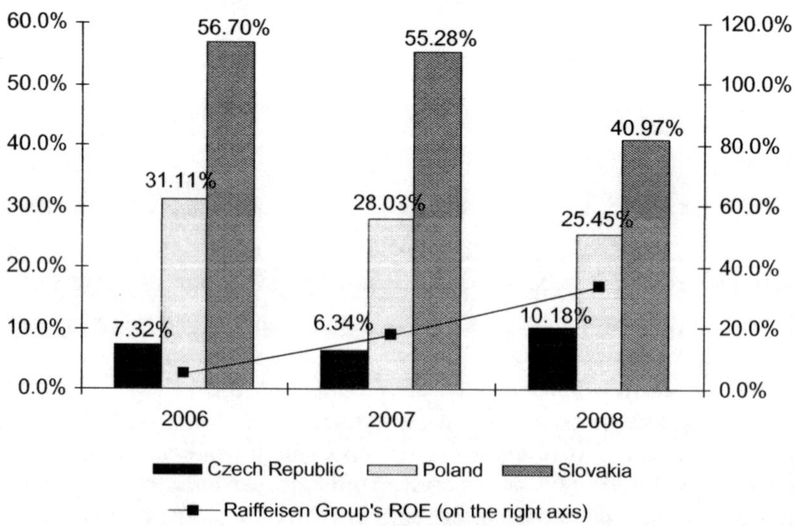

Fig. 10. Dividend Payouts of Raiffeisen Group's Banks in European Emerging Countries.

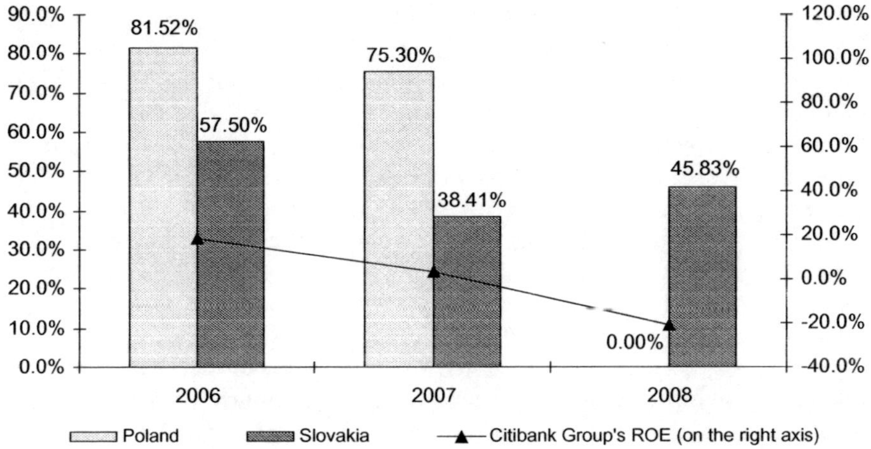

Fig. 11. Dividend Payouts of Citibank Group's Banks in European Emerging Countries.

during fruitful times. This reasoning might also explain why the financial performance of foreign greenfield banks deteriorates more rapidly than other banking institutions (Schmidt, 2009). This observation is also consistent with previous findings that show that foreign subsidiaries are more dependent on their parent banks and hence more exposed to the financial vulnerabilities of their home markets. The situation was not as dramatic in the acquired local banks. Although the interbank ratio also decreased as a result of deterioration of financial results of parent banks and as a result, their foreign operations, in most of the countries it exceeded 100%. In addition, the ratio increased between the years 2005 and 2006, and in several countries there was also a high upward change in 2007. For example, in Lithuania, the interbank ratio increased from 65% to 142%, suggesting that Lithuanian foreign banks started to become net lenders, most likely supporting their parent institutions. The similar situation occurred in Slovakia, Poland, and Hungary between 2005 and 2006. Figs. 8–11, presenting the dividend payouts of the main players in the European emerging banking markets, indicate that the highest payout ratio occurred in the periods when the banking institutions in this region reported great financial results (throughout 2006 and 2007). In most cases, the purpose of the dividend was to support the parent banks, whose financial performance started deteriorating in this time.

6. CONCLUSION

The widely established international banking literature has identified several arguments for increased participation of foreign banks in the emerging countries. Following these studies, many emerging economies decided to attract foreign banking institutions. However, the entry of foreign banks has also brought some risk into these regions. In our study, we identified the economic determinants of a parent bank's choice of organizational structure in an emerging economy and investigated from a host country's perspective the risk associated with the functioning of entry models.

The results of our study indicate important policy implications. They suggest that a parent bank's choice of an organizational structure is a function of its strategic plans in the region and the countries' characteristics. We find that parent banks are more likely to use greenfield operations in countries with high growth potential and where they can achieve high returns on invested capital. In these cases, they also tend to reallocate capital from the home markets into the host countries, supporting their operations during times of economic expansion. Dages, Goldberg, and Kinney (2000) and Montgomery (2009) also find that parent banks are likely to support their foreign subsidiaries during periods of the host country's economic distress, making the credit supply in the region less volatile than that of other domestic banks. However, our findings suggest that foreign greenfield banks operate more aggressively in the host markets and are also riskier for these economies than other organizational forms. This finding is strengthened by the fact that they rely more heavily on external funds. The deterioration of an interbank market's condition or the financial performance of a parent bank has severe consequences on the liquidity position of these institutions. The spillover effects spread very quickly, resulting in a sudden shortage of funds in their foreign subsidiaries. Specifically, we find that parent banks during periods of home market distress feel more responsible for their affiliated banks than for their stand-alone institutions, provided an institution is highly strategic for its parent institution. In such a case, a parent bank is even willing to provide a capital injection for its distressed local institution, despite its own liquidity problems. We also find that parent banks are more likely to draw on the funds of their foreign banks during times of a parent bank's financial distress. Because the parent local banks are less exposed to home country vulnerabilities, the parent banks are more likely to reallocate the capital from their financially stronger affiliated institutions instead of their stand-alone subsidiaries.

NOTES

1. A detailed overview of banking system development in transition economies may be found in Bonin and Wachtel (2003) and in Hryckiewicz and Kowalewski (2008).

2. Because it is not possible to estimate the variance inflation factor for the nonlinear models, which is used as a common measure of collinearity by many researchers, we instead estimate the variance–covariance matrix as an indicator of correlations between the independent variables. Our results are available upon request.

REFERENCES:

Aliber, R. (1984). International banking: A survey. *Journal of Money Credit and Banking, 16*, 661–712.

Allen, F., Bartiloro, L., & Kowalewski, O. (2006). The financial system of the EU 25. In: K. Liebscher, J. Christl & P. Mooslechner (Eds), *Financial development, integration and stability: Evidence from central, Eastern and South-Eastern Europe* (pp. 80–105). Cheltenham: Edward Elgar.

Ashcraft, A. (2008). Are bank holding companies source of strength to their banking subsidiaries? *Journal of Money, Banking and Credit, 40*, 273–294.

Ball, C. A., & Tschoegl, A. E. (1982). The decision to establish a foreign bank: Branch or subsidiary. An application of binary classification procedures. *Journal of Financial and Quantitative Analysis, 17*, 411–424.

Beck, T. H. L., Levine, R., & Loayza, N. (2000). Finance and the sources of growth. *Journal of Financial Economics, 58*, 261–300.

Bonin, J. K., & Wachtel, P. (2003). Financial sector development in transition economies: Lessons from the first decade. *Financial Markets, Institutions and Instruments, 12*, 1–66.

Cerutti, E., Ariccia, G. D., & Martinez Peria, M. S. (2007). How banks go abroad: Branches or subsidiaries? *Journal of Banking and Finance, 31*, 1669–1692.

Claessens, S., Demirgüç-Kunt, A., & Huizinga, H. (2001). How does foreign entry affect the domestic banking market? *Journal of Banking and Finance, 5*, 891–911.

Claessens, S., Van Hooren, N., Gurcanlar, T., & Mercado Sapiain, J. (2008). *Foreign bank presence in developing countries 1995–2006: Data and trends.* Working Paper. World Bank, Washington.

Claessens, S., & Van Horen, N. (2008). *Location decisions of foreign banks and institutional competitive advantage.* Working Paper. Netherlands Central Bank, Netherlands.

Claeys, S., & Hainz, Ch. (2006). *Acquisition versus greenfield – The impact of the mode of foreign bank entry on information and bank lending rates.* Working Paper. European Central Bank.

Clarke, G., Cull, R., Martinez Peria, M. S., & Sanchez, S. M. (2003). Foreign bank entry: Experience, implications for developing economies and agenda for future research. *The World Bank Research Observer, 18*, 25–59.

Dages, B. G., Goldberg, L., & Kinney, D. (2000). Foreign and domestic bank participation in emerging markets: Lessons from Mexico and Argentina. *Federal Reserve Bank of New York Economic Policy Review* (September), 17–36.

de Haas, R., & van Lelyvald, I. (2006). Foreign banks and credit stability in central and Eastern Europe. A panel data analysis. *Journal of Banking and Finance*, *30*, 1927–1952.

de Haas, R., & van Lelyvald, I. (2010). Internal capital markets and lending by multinational bank subsidiaries. *Journal of Financial Intermediation*, *19*, 1–25.

de Haas, R., & Naaborg, I. J. (2006). Foreign banks in transition countries: To whom do they lend and how are they financed? *Financial Markets, Institutions and Instruments*, *15*, 159–199.

Dermine, J. (2006). European banking integration: Don't put the cart before the horse. *Financial Institutions, Markets and Money*, *15*, 57–106.

Desai, M. A., Foley, C. F., Jr., & Hines, J. R. (2007). Dividend policy inside the multinational firm. *Financial Management*, *36*, 5–26.

Dunning, J. H. (1977). Trade, location of economic activity and the MNE: A search for an eclectic approach. In: B. Ohlin, P. O. Hesselborn & P. K. Wijkman (Eds), *The international allocation of economic activity* (pp. 395–418). London: Macmillan.

European Bank for Reconstruction and Development (EBRD). (2009). Transition Report 2009, London.

Gilbert, R. A. (1991). Do bank holding companies act as source of strength for their bank subsidiaries? *Economic Review*, Federal Reserve Bank St. Louis, pp. 3–18.

Greene, W. H. (2000). *Econometric analysis* (4th ed.). New Jersey, NJ: Prentice Hall.

Hryckiewicz, A., & Kowalewski, K. (2010). Why do foreign banks withdraw from other nations? *CAREFIN Research Paper*, 6/09, Bocconi University.

Hryckiewicz, A., & Kowalewski, O. (2008). *The economic determinants and engagement modes of foreign banks in Central Europe*. Working Paper. National Bank of Poland.

Hultman, C. W., & McGee, R. L. (1989). Factors affecting the foreign banking presence in the US. *Journal of Banking and Finance*, *13*, 383–396.

Kraft, E. (2002). *Foreign banks in Croatia: Another look*. Working Paper. Croatian National Bank.

La Porta, R., Lopez-de-Silanes, F., Shleifer, A., & Vishny, R. W. (1997). Legal determinants of external finance. *Journal of Finance*, *52*, 1131–1150.

Lehner, H. (2009). Entry mode choice of multinational banks. *Journal of Banking and Finance*, *33*, 1781–1792.

Magri, S., Mori, A., & Rossi, P. (2005). The entry and the activity level of foreign banks in Italy: An analysis of the determinants. *Journal of Banking and Finance*, *29*, 1295–1310.

Montgomery, H. (2009). *The role of foreign banks in post-crisis Asia: The importance of method of entry*. ADB Institute Research Paper No. 51.

O'Brien, R. M. (2007). A caution regarding rules of thumb for variance inflation factors. *Quality and Quantity*, *41*, 673–690.

Peek, J., & Rosengren, E. (2000). Implications of the globalization of the banking sector: The Latin American experience. *New England Economic Review* (September/October), 45–62.

Scher, M., & Weller, C. E. (2001). Multinational bank credit in less industrialized economies. *Journal of International Business Studies*, *32*, 833–851.

Schmidt, N. F. (2009). *Foreign bank entry: The stability implications of greenfield entry vs. acquisition*. Working Paper. London School of Economics.

Tschoegl, A. (2005). Financial crises and the presence of foreign banks. In: P. Honohan & L. Laeven (Eds), *Systemic financial distress: Containment and resolution*. Cambridge: Cambridge University Press.

UniCredit Group. (2008). CEE banking study 2009: Banking in CEE – Adequate risk appetite crucial to win the upside. *CEE Strategic Analysis*, November.

DOES DISTANCE AFFECT THE PERFORMANCE OF FOREIGN BANKS? EVIDENCE FROM MULTINATIONAL BANKING IN DEVELOPING COUNTRIES☆

Ji Wu, Bang Nam Jeon and Alina C. Luca

ABSTRACT

This chapter examines whether the geographic distance between subsidiaries of multinational banks and their headquarters is an important factor in determining the performance of the subsidiaries. Using various performance indicators of 340 subsidiaries in 54 emerging and developing economies from 69 global banks during the years 1994–2008, we find evidence that first, the distance constraint adversely affects loan growth, profitability, and performance of foreign bank subsidiaries, and second, the unfavorable information asymmetry faced by foreign banks, due to the distance constraint, in financing foreign clients cannot be fully overcome

☆The views expressed herein are those of the authors and should not be attributed to the IMF, its Executive Board, or its management. We thank Suk-Joong Kim, the Volume Editor of the *International Banking in the New Era: Post-Crisis Challenges and Opportunities*, for very useful suggestions.

International Banking in the New Era: Post-Crisis Challenges and Opportunities
International Finance Review, Volume 11, 431–474

ISSN: 1569-3767/doi:10.1108/S1569-3767(2010)0000011018

by establishing their presence abroad such as setting up their foreign subsidiaries. We further examine if the effect of distance is symmetric across different banks and countries and find the following various economic, financial, and institutional factors to affect the strength of distance constraints in the multinational banking activities: the entry mode of foreign banks, the history of presence in local markets, the existence of credit information institutions, the cultural similarity between the home and host markets, financial depth, financial crisis periods, the stock market development, the banking market structure in host markets, and the hierarchy of the subsidiary in the multinational banking conglomerate.

1. INTRODUCTION

This chapter examines the economic implications of distance in the realm of multinational banking, particularly the effect of the geographical distance between foreign bank subsidiaries and their headquarters on the performance of the foreign bank subsidiaries in emerging and developing countries. In the gravity model literature of international trade, it has been intensively studied and supported by numerous empirical studies that, after controlling for other factors, the exporter–importer distance imposes an important adverse effect on the bilateral trade links. In international finance, there have been several studies examining how the cross-border lending and portfolio investment activities are affected by geographical distance. For example, empirical papers, such as Portes, Rey, and Oh (2001), Portes and Rey (2005), and Buch (2005), found evidence that a longer distance in international banking have an adverse effect on cross-border lending or foreign asset holding, which is ascribed to higher informational costs as distance increases.

Banks depend on information to identify good borrowers and determine their loan supply. Credible information is especially essential to provide larger loans (Degryse & Ongena, 2005). However, banks' access to information (or ability to analyze and evaluate information) varies, thus affecting banks' performance. Compared to domestic banks, foreign banks especially face more adverse information constraints when they provide cross-border credit, because they might be thousands miles away from their customers. The constraints faced by foreign banks include higher costs to either identify potentially good borrowers or monitor borrowers. Banks can only obtain less precise information for more distant loan applicants (e.g., Almanza, 2002; Hauswald & Marquez, 2006; Carling & Lundberg, 2005).

The information disadvantages become more conspicuous and challenging in multinational banking operations.

Since the early 1990s, multinational banks have established a large number of subsidiaries outside their border. Foreign ownership in the banking system has increased significantly in a number of emerging economies. For example, as of end 2007, the share of foreign bank assets in banking sector total assets has reached 80% in Mexico and exceeded the 90% level in several Central and Eastern European countries such as Estonia, Romania, and the Czech Republic (see Bank for International Settlement [BIS], 2009, p. 85). If a longer distance between the lender and the borrower really captures an adverse effect of information asymmetry associated with screening and monitoring, it is natural to ask if this "distance constraint" will stay the same or lose its edge when cross-border credit is substituted with local claims. In other words, we ask whether or not foreign banks are able to fully overcome the constraints of information asymmetry by shortening the geographical distance to customers through the establishment of their affiliates in borrowers' country. In the extant literature, however, only very few studies have examined if distance still plays any significant role in determining foreign banks' performance in terms of lending, pricing, and their profits in host markets. To our best knowledge, our study is the first to examine a role of distance in multinational banking using bank-level data of headquarters and their foreign subsidiaries and the geographical and cultural distance between the two.

This chapter addresses how the distance constraints faced by foreign banks affect their banking performance and examines under what conditions the distance constraints may be alleviated or amplified. We specifically study whether and how foreign banks' performance is affected by the distance between the host market where subsidiaries are located and the home market where their headquarters are located. Note that, in the research at the domestic level, distance is conventionally defined as the closeness between a loan officer and his borrowers (e.g., Peterson & Rajan, 2002). The definition of distance and its implications in our chapter are very different one from this conventional one. Although foreign banks can substitute cross-border claims by local claims, it is far from certain that information barriers could be removed fully by a closer domestic vicinity to clients. Compared with domestic peers, foreign banks still likely face disadvantages in collecting information (especially "soft information"[1]) and identifying prime borrowers. As a result, foreign banks may still incur higher informational costs in their operation than domestic banks. The informational problem may disappear only after foreign banks have acquired the same pool of information as domestic banks, through many years of interaction with their clients in local markets.

Following Mian (2006), "distance constraints" in our chapter reflect the extent of the difficulties with which foreign banks can overcome disadvantages of asymmetric information in host markets, caused by distance from their headquarters in the home country. As a farther distance in multinational banking reflects a higher level of difficulty to know their clients and markets, one would expect that the negative effect of distance on the banking performance tends to be stronger for more distant foreign banks. How distance may constrain foreign banks' activities, if any, have important policy implications for countries that liberalize their financial sectors by allowing more foreign banks to enter the host banking markets.

Our chapter extends the extant literature in the following directions. First, using a new data set of distance between multinational bank subsidiaries and their headquarters at the individual bank level, we examine the impact of distance constraints to international banking operations. If multinational banks could overcome the informational barriers by setting up local presence, the distance between host and home markets would be insignificant in determining their banking performance. Otherwise, a negative association between distance and banking performance can be explained as consistent evidence that foreign banks are still at the disadvantages of information asymmetry. Second, we focus our analysis on foreign banks in emerging and developing economies, where economic growth is pursued by opening up their financial sectors, as a result, witnessing an increase in the foreign bank presence. As we use the samples from more than 50 emerging and developing countries, our results are more representative for developing countries in general. Third, we identify what are the specific amplifying or mitigating factors for the impact of distance in the multinational banking. These factors range from some characteristics of foreign bank subsidiaries, its hierarchical level in the conglomerate, the entry mode of foreign banks, and certain macroeconomic and financial conditions of the host countries.

The main findings of this chapter can be summarized as follows. First, we find evidence that distance constraints, indeed, adversely affect the performance of foreign banks. This finding suggests that foreign banks cannot fully overcome information asymmetry simply by establishing a local presence in the host banking market. As the distance from their headquarters increases, a foreign bank tends to lend its loans only at a lower growth rate. A longer distance also impedes foreign banks to obtain higher profit, which may reduce their capacity and incentive to supply credit over a long run. Corresponding to their lower growth rate of loans and profits, foreign banks also increase the share of nonlending assets in their portfolio, leading to inefficiency in capital allocation. Second, although in general a longer distance negatively affects foreign banks' performance, its effect is not symmetric. The following factors are found to be able to alleviate the strength of distance constraints: the entry of foreign banks through the mergers and acquisitions (M&A) mode, a longer history of presence in host markets, the existence of credit information institutions, the same language and region of host and home countries, higher financial deepening of host banking markets and highly developed stock market, a higher concentration level in the host banking market, and a higher hierarchy in its conglomerate. We also find that the effect of distance constraints becomes strong during crises than tranquil periods. Our results provide some useful policy implications for policy-makers in the host country of multinational banking.

The rest of the chapter is organized as follows. Section 2 reviews relevant literature. Section 3 introduces the regression model. Section 4 describes our dataset, and Section 5 reports the benchmark results. Section 6 examines various factors that may alleviate or aggravate the effects of distance constraints in multinational banking. Section 7 concludes.

2. LITERATURE REVIEW: DISTANCE IN MULTINATIONAL BANKING

In general, the availability and quality of information on borrowers play an important role in determining banks' credit (Stiglitz & Weiss, 1981). When banks have more accurate information about their borrowers, they tend to lend more loans. Pagano and Jappelli (1993) argue that the information exchange among banks enables them to find good borrowers and may increase their lending. Jappelli and Pagano (2002) and Djankov, McLiesh, and Shleifer (2007) show that the countries in which lenders exchange information through credit information sharing institutions (public credit registries or private credit bureaus) are associated with a higher ratio of credit to growth domestic product (GDP). Brown, Jappelli, and Pagano (2009) find that information sharing improves the availability of loans at lower costs to firms, especially for opaque firms. In addition to increasing the volume of loans, improved information availability also affects banks' performance by reducing debtors' default rates (Klein, 1992; Vercammen, 1995; Padilla & Pagano, 2000), increases the competition in banking markets and hence lowering interest rates (Pagano & Jappelli, 1993;

Padilla & Pagano, 1997), and reduces firms' incentive to over-borrow from multiple banks (Bennardo, Pagano, & Piccolo, 2008).

Banks are believed to have different abilities to collect and assess borrowers' information. For example, large banks may be able to take the advantage of economies of scale from large information technology networks and hence are better at assessing "hard information." By contrast, small banks may be better at collecting and assessing "soft information" through loan officers by personal interactions. Stein (2002) suggests that large, hierarchical banks would have comparative disadvantages in assessing soft information relative to small banks. Consistent with his argument, Cole, Goldberg, and White (1999) show that large banks tend to employ standard criteria obtained from financial statements in the loan decision process, but small banks deviate from these criteria by relying to a larger extent on the soft information such as the character of the borrower. Moreover, young banks may be less effective to distinguish good borrowers from bad ones because of their short history of presence and less often interaction with potential clients. Archaya, Hasan, and Saunders (2002) find that a bank's monitoring effectiveness is dampened when the bank expand to newly entered industries.

Distance is a practically useful proxy for the difficulties to acquire and communicate information, especially soft information (Hauswald & Marquez, 2000; Berger, Klapper, & Uddell, 2001; Peterson & Rajan, 2002; Mian, 2006; Agarwal & Hauswald, 2007). A longer distance between banks and borrowers would make information collection and monitoring more costly and then deters banks from providing more loans, especially the relationship loans that depend more on local knowledge and personnel contacts. Almanza (2002) suggests that the resources spent by banks on monitoring increases with the distance between the bank and its debtors. He also finds that banks with higher capital are more willing to lend to distant borrowers.

How distance affects the price of loans could be ambiguous. On one hand, more distant borrowers would cost banks more resources to assess and monitor; hence, banks would pass on this cost into the interest rate on loans. On the other hand, banks would extract rents from closer borrowers by charging higher rates because otherwise the borrowers would have to switch to more distant competing banks and pay higher interest rates. Degryse and Ongena (2005) find that loan interest rates tend to decrease with the distance between firms and lenders and increase with the distance between the firm and the competing banks. The reason is explained as that more distant banks have only weaker market power and hence will charge borrowers lower interest rates. Agarwal and Hauswald (2007) find results in line with Degryse and Ongena (2005) and suggest the physical distance between bank and borrowers is actually a proxy for bank's different degree of information asymmetry. Mistrulli and Casolaro (2008) find that the interest rates on loans are negatively correlated with the distance between the bank headquarters and the borrower. Hauswald and Marquez (2006) derive a negative relationship between loan rates and the distance of borrowers to relationship banks, but a positive relationship between the rates and the distance to transactional banks.

In other research (e.g., Berger & DeYoung, 2001), distance is also used as a proxy for the agency problem when a subsidiary is located far away from senior managers, hence with an increasing distance to the final decision makers, the subsidiaries may have less lending and lower profit efficiency. This strand of argument is consistent with Stein (2002). There is substantial evidence that information asymmetry would cause biases in the investment of market participants, for example, the literature on the well-known "home bias" in assets holding (e.g., French & Poterba, 1991; Gehrig, 1993; Tesar & Werner, 1995; Kang & Stulz, 1997; Lewis, 1999; Coval & Moskowitz, 1999, 2001). Portes and Rey (2005) provide an excellent survey on the literature of this issue.

It is only recent when a few empirical studies investigate the effects of distance on determining various specific types of international financial transactions. Most of these works find that distance is an important determinant of cross-border assets holding or international bank flows. Applying the gravity model methodology, Portes et al. (2001) and Portes and Rey (2005) show that geographical distance is negatively associated with the volume of international financial assets transactions, and the result is explained by a positive correlation between information friction and distance. Buch (2005) finds consistent evidence that banks hold significantly lower assets in distant foreign markets, and the importance of distance for holding assets abroad has not declined in European countries with technological progress over time. He also finds that distance constraints have not changed in its impact on cross-border asset holdings by the multinational banking sector over time during the period 1983–1999. Papaioannou (2005) also uses geographical distance to proxy the transaction and information costs and finds it is inversely associated with the cross-border bank flows. Herrero and Peria (2007) find that the informational costs significantly affect the share of local claims (to total claims) of foreign banks. Carey and Nini (2007) find that banks display home bias by providing more syndicated loans to their domestic borrowers than to foreign ones.

Siregar and Choy (2009) study the determinants of the loans from international banks from Organization for Economic Cooperation and Development (OECD) countries to East Asian countries and find a negative relationship between the source–recipient geographical proximity and the amount of loans. Similar results are also found in Wei and Wu (2001), although they do not specifically address the relationship between distance and cross-border bank lending. It is worthwhile to note that, although there is overwhelming evidence that a farther distance between source and recipient countries would negatively affect investors or banks' decision to obtain foreign assets, there is likely a positive effect as well. The correlation of business cycle may likely decline in distance; hence, a financial investment in remote countries might reward investors a higher return by portfolio diversification. If this is the case, the distance between source and recipient countries may be found positively related with international capital flows. Nevertheless, the extant empirical evidence seemingly suggests that this positive effect is practically dominated by the negative effects from information asymmetry.

However, research is still scant on the effect of distance from their headquarters on the performance of foreign bank subsidiaries that are located in host markets. If the geographical distance captures most of the information barriers between a lender and its continents-away borrowers, we expect that the distance constraints would not play any significant role if lenders could successfully know about their borrowers by setting up a local presence and narrowing the vicinity to their borrowers. So far, only a few papers have addressed the effects of the host-home market distance on foreign banks' local claims in the host country. Berger et al. (2001) find that for small business in Argentina, foreign banks headquartered in South America tend to provide more credit than foreign banks headquartered in other continents. Mian (2006) examines the credit from foreign banks in Pakistan and finds that a greater cultural and geographic distance between the headquarters and their local branches prevents foreign banks to lend to informationally opaque but fundamentally sound firms. Claessens and van Horsen (2009) find that foreign banks from a home country geographically or culturally close to the host country perform better than distant foreign banks.[2]

The interpretation of distance constraints as information asymmetry has been supported in the literature. Several studies have also presented evidence that foreign banks may only serve the sectors that are less subject to information asymmetry. Clarke, Cull, D'Amato, and Molinari (1999) observe the banking sector in Argentina and find that foreign banks concentrate their business in the industries that are less information asymmetric. Peria and Mody (2004) find that in the case of Latin American banks, de novo foreign banks charge lower spreads than M&A foreign banks and interpret that de novo foreign banks with less information on the host banking markets has to focus on the most transparent sector, which are more likely competitive sectors. Accordingly, de novo foreign banks have to charge lower spreads than M&A foreign banks. The results from these two works are consistent with the suggestion made by Dell'Ariccia and Marquez (2004) that foreign banks will enter the sectors where their information disadvantages are smaller.

3. MODEL

We set up the empirical model to examine how the distance from their headquarters affects the performance of foreign bank subsidiaries in host markets, and the banking performance is measured using four dimensions: (1) the growth rate of loans (in real terms); (2) the price charged by banks, represented by net interest margin; (3) the holding of nonlending assets, measured by the share of "other earning assets" to total bank assets; and (4) the profits of banks, proxied by the return on equity (ROE). We find that these four dimensions only modestly correlated (Table A1). We use the following benchmark model for the estimation of the role of distance constraints to the banking performance of foreign bank subsidiaries:

$$\begin{aligned} Y_{i,j,k,l,t} = {} & c + \alpha \cdot distance_{j,l} + \beta \cdot (bank\ characteristics)_{i,t} \\ & + \delta \cdot (host\ characteristics)_{j,t} + \lambda \cdot (parent\ characteristics)_{k,t} \\ & + \gamma \cdot (home\ characteristics)_{l,t} + \varepsilon_{i,j,k,l,t} \end{aligned} \tag{1}$$

where the dependent variable $Y_{i,j,k,l,t}$ represents the banking performance of foreign bank subsidiary i of conglomerate k of the home country l in host country j in year t. $distance_{j,l}$ is the geographical proximity between the host country j and the home country l. $(bank\ characteristics)_{i,t}$ is a vector of subsidiary i's bank characteristics, including its liquidity, capitalization, size, and riskiness. $(host\ characteristics)_{j,t}$ is a vector of macroeconomic variables in host market j, including the growth rate of real GDP, the change in unemployment rate, foreign exchange depreciation rate (against U.S. dollar), and a dummy of (expansionary) monetary policy with the value of 1 for an easy monetary policy and the value of 0 otherwise. $(parent\ characteristics)_{k,t}$ includes the financial strength of the parent bank k, such as the mass of the conglomerate, liquidity, and capitalization. (*home characteristics*)$_{l,t}$ represents the macroeconomic conditions in the home country l, including the growth rate of real GDP, the change in unemployment rate, and a dummy of monetary policy. $\varepsilon_{i,j,k,l,t}$ is the idiosyncratic error. α, β, δ, λ, and γ are the coefficients to be estimated.

Among the coefficients that we will estimate, α is of special interest, which is expected to reflect the sensitivity of foreign bank subsidiaries' performance to the distance constraints that they face. Distance is calculated as the geodesic distance between the geographic centers of the host and the home countries by applying Vincenty formula. We take logarithms for distance, because the marginal effect of the distance constraints may diminish as distance increases. If foreign banks are subject to higher informational costs in their operation, it is expected that a longer distance would be associated with a lower growth rate in loans. In addition, if the distance constraint hinders foreign banks to find good business opportunities, we should expect that they have to hold more nonlending assets, like deposits in other banks, securities, bonds, and government treasury bills; hence, the share of other earning assets to total assets will be increasing with the distance. Foreign subsidiaries' higher holding of nonlending assets, compared to lending assets, suggests a less efficient allocation of scarce financial resources in multinational banking.

How would the distance constraint affect the interest rate charged by foreign banks? The answer is not straightforward. On one hand, if a longer distance captures a higher cost to identify and monitor borrowers (or monitor managers), foreign banks may pass on this cost and charge a higher interest rate. On the other hand, a longer distance would cause less information about the host market and potential prime borrowers. This will drive foreign banks to concentrate their lending in more transparent industries that are more likely competitive than other opaque industries and force banks to charge only a lower interest rate. Therefore, it seems how distance would affect interest rate is left as an empirical question. If a longer distance creates the informational disadvantage for foreign banks, we may reasonably expect that profits would decrease as distance increases.

Following the standard practice, we include bank characteristics of foreign subsidiaries in the explanatory variable set to control for various types of financial constraints on the subsidiaries. It is likely that a longer distance from the headquarters actually represents a weaker financial strength of the subsidiary, especially when the conglomerate establishes a "weaker" (say, smaller, less liquid, or less capitalized) subsidiary in a distant overseas market. This possibility can be controlled by including the subsidiary-level bank characteristics in the explanatory variable set. The correlation of distance and subsidiary characteristics are reported in Table A2, which indicates that the correlations are very mild in magnitude. Another argument that may arise is that a more distant foreign bank may have a lower growth rate of loans because of a lower demand from the host market. To control for the demand effect at the bank level and the macroeconomy level, we add a riskiness measure at the individual bank level and host country macroeconomic variables. The former, measured by the ratio of loan loss provision to total loans of a subsidiary, controls for the heterogeneity across subsidiary banks' clients, whereas the latter controls for the heterogeneous demand factors across host countries. The variables of "bank characteristics" and "host characteristics" are the "pull factors" in determining the behavior of foreign banks.

The liquidity of banks is measured by the ratio of liquid assets to total assets. A more liquid bank tends to increase its credit more quickly. The capitalization of banks is proxied by the ratio of equity over total assets. A better capitalized bank is expected to have faster growth in its loans. The size of an individual bank measures the dominance of the bank in the host banking sector. The relative size of a bank is obtained by using the ratio of the total loans of the bank to the total domestic credit in the host economy. The riskiness faced by an individual bank is measured by the ratio of loan loss provision to total loans for a bank. To address the possible endogeneity problem of subsidiaries' characteristic variables in our model, we use one-year lagged values for those variables.

"Parent characteristics" and "home characteristics" are included to control for the "push factors" of foreign banks' performance in host markets. The former controls for the effects of the financial strength of the conglomerate on the subsidiaries' behavior,[3] whereas the latter controls for the force that may lead the parent banks to seek external lending (through the oversea subsidiaries).[4] The liquidity and capitalization of the conglomerates are measured in the same way for those for subsidiaries. The mass of a parent bank is proxied by the logarithm of its total assets in term of U.S. dollars. The correlation between distance and parent bank characteristics are reported in Table A3. The correlation between distance and parent bank mass is relatively large (around 0.50), probably indicating that a large multinational bank can expand their foreign subsidiary network farther than a small multinational bank. We present evidence shortly that after controlling for the effect of conglomerate mass, distance is still a significant determinant of banks' performance.

To test whether the effect of distance constraints is symmetric across banks and host markets and to identify specific amplifying or mitigating factors for the strength of the distance constraints, we extend the benchmark model by adding interaction terms:

$$\begin{aligned} Y_{i,j,k,l,t} = {} & c + \alpha \cdot distance_{j,l} + \rho \cdot factor + \sigma \cdot (factor \times distance_{j,l}) \\ & + \beta \cdot (bank\ characteristics)_{i,t} + \delta \cdot (host\ characteristics)_{j,t} \\ & + \lambda \cdot (parent\ characteristics)_{k,t} + \gamma \cdot (home\ characteristics)_{l,t} \\ & + \varepsilon_{i,j,k,l,t} \end{aligned} \tag{2}$$

where *factor* represents an examined factor that may alleviate (or multiply) the effect of distance, and $factor \times distance_{j,l}$ is its interaction term with distance. We examine various factors including (1) the entry mode of foreign banks (de novo or M&As); (2) the length of presence in host markets; (3) the existence of credit information institutions; (4) the same languages, legal systems, and religion in the host and home countries; (5) the level of financial deepening in the host banking market; (6) the level of development of stock market; (7) the degree of concentration in the host banking market; and (8) the hierarchy level of the subsidiary in its conglomerate. More detailed discussion on each of the above factors will be made when we discuss the empirical results in Section 6. A summary of all variables and their data sources is provided in Table 1.

For the estimation, we apply the feasible generalized least squares (FGLS) estimator, which allows for the AR(1) autocorrelation within banks and heteroskedasticity across banks. We introduce country dummies and time-fixed effects in the estimation to control for other unaccounted sources of the differences in the bank performance across countries and years.

4. DATA

We construct unbalanced panel dataset for the estimation by using bank-level annual observations of balance sheet and income statements retrieved from Bureau van Dijk's *BankScope* database. Our data cover 340 foreign subsidiaries of 69 multinational banks from 1994 to 2008. All selected multinational banks are universally regarded as large banks with total assets of more than \$521 billion on average.[5] We include only commercial bank subsidiaries in our dataset to reduce the possible bias due to the different nature and business scope of various noncommercial banks. We focus our

Table 1. List of Variables.

Variable	Description	Source	Mean	Standard Deviation	Median
Distance	The logarithms of geodesic distance between the geographic centers of the host and home countries (in 1,000 kilometers)	Authors' own calculation based on CIA World Factbook	1.190	1.189	1.591
Loan growth rate	The annual growth rate of real loans (in %)	BankScope	23.533	54.209	14.157
Net interest margin	The ratio of net interest income to total earning assets of banks (in %)	BankScope	5.093	4.572	4.040
Share of other earning assets	The ratio of nonloans assets to total earning assets of banks (in %)	BankScope	42.282	23.657	39.927
ROE	Return on equity (in %)	BankScope	9.416	27.531	11.450
Liquidity	The ratio of liquid assets to total assets (in %)	BankScope	38.253	19.256	35.738
Capitalization	The ratio of equity to total assets (in %)	BankScope	13.237	10.038	10.368
Size	Relative size of a bank in the banking sector, measured by the ratio of the bank's loans to the banking sector total loans (in %)	BankScope and IFS	3.827	6.848	1.244
Riskiness	The ratio of loan loss provision to total loans (in %)	BankScope	1.897	5.031	.835
Host GDP growth rate	The growth rate of real GDP in host countries (in %)	IFS	5.493	5.183	5.050
Host change in unemployment	First-order difference in unemployment rate in host countries (in %)	IFS	−.125	1.460	−.200
Dummy (host monetary policy)	A dummy = 1 if the host central bank conducts expansionary monetary policy = 0 otherwise	IFS	.588	.492	1
Host depreciation rate	Foreign exchange depreciation rate of host currency against U.S. dollar	IFS	3.810	23.415	0.000
Parent bank mass	The logarithms of the total assets of the conglomerate (in billions of U.S. dollar)	BankScope	12.583	1.177	12.714
Parent bank liquidity	The ratio of liquid assets to total assets of the conglomerate (in %)	BankScope	28.023	12.793	26.678

Table 1. *(Continued)*

Variable	Description	Source	Mean	Standard Deviation	Median
Parent bank capitalization	The ratio of equity to total assets of the conglomerate (in %)	BankScope	5.459	2.432	5.049
Home GDP growth rate	The growth rate of real GDP in home countries (in %)	IFS	2.565	2.436	2.172
Home change in unemployment	First-order difference in unemployment rate in home countries (in %)	IFS	−.290	.891	−.299
Dummy (home monetary policy)	Dummy = 1 if the home central bank conducts expansionary monetary policy = 0 otherwise	IFS	.608	.488	1
Dummy (M&A)	Dummy = 1 if the foreign subsidiary is established by merger & acquisition = 0 if established from scratch	Banks' profile, SDC platinum, annual reports	.438	.496	0
History	The logarithms of the length of presence (in years) in host countries	Banks' profile, BankScope, SDC platinum, annual reports	2.853	.975	2.639
Dummy (information institution)	Dummy = 1 if either a public credit registry or a private credit bureau exists in the host country = 0 otherwise	The World Bank "Doing Business" database	.870	.336	1
Dummy (same language)	Dummy = 1 if the host and home countries have the same official language	CIA World Factbook	.162	.368	0
Dummy (same legal system)	Dummy = 1 if the host and home countries have the same legal system	La Porta et al. (1998), CIA World Factbook	.471	.499	0

Dummy (same region)	Dummy = 1 if the host and home countries are located in a same region	CIA World Factbook	.433	.495	0
Host financial deepening	Ratio of domestic credit to private sector to GDP (in %)	Financial Structure Database by Beck and Demirguc-Kunt (2009)	39.577	29.825	29.019
Dummy (financial crisis)	Dummy = 1 if the host market experienced a systematic banking crisis in given year	Caprio and Klingebiel (2003) Laeven and Valencia (2008)	.268	.443	0
Number of listed companies in host stock market	Number of publicly listed companies per 10,000 population	Financial Structure Database by Beck and Demirguc-Kunt (2009)	.254	.456	.060
Stock market capitalization	The ratio of stock market capitalization to GDP (in %)	Financial Structure Database by Beck and Demirguc-Kunt (2009)	43.082	56.009	25.982
Stock market turnover	Stock market turnover ratio	Financial Structure Database by Beck and Demirguc-Kunt (2009)	32.494	62.529	23.397
Concentration	Assets of three largest banks as a share of assets of all commercial banks (in %)	Financial Structure Database by Beck and Demirguc-Kunt (2009)	54.962	15.613	56.141
Hierarchy	The ratio of the assets owned by the subsidiary to the total assets of the conglomerate (in %)	BankScope	1.172	2.564	.238

analysis on the foreign subsidiaries of multinational banks located in a total of 54 emerging and developing countries. The list of selected multinational banks and the distribution of their subsidiaries in the interested countries is provided in Table A4.

A bank is defined as a foreign subsidiary if at least 50% of the entity's assets are owned by a multinational bank that is headquartered in another country.[6] We take the following steps to track the affiliation of a subsidiary to its parent bank over the period of 1994–2008. First, we check the subsidiary information of selected multinational banks recorded in *Bank-Scope*, which identifies the ownership for some banks in the most recent year of recording. Second, we check the global presence of parent banks and their chronological history from their websites to pin down the establishment of their subsidiaries in foreign countries. Third, we review the profile of each individual subsidiary bank and its historical evolution from its website. In most cases, it is highlighted in the bank's profile about its incorporation and changes of its ownership. Fourth, we depend on another comprehensive database, *SDC Platinum*, which records detailed information on M&A. We collect data on when a bank in the host country was acquired by or merged into the conglomerate of the parent bank in the home country. Finally, if we are still unable to identify the ownership of the bank after going through these four steps, we resort to various other information sources such as banks' annual reports, central bank publications, and Internet news reports on changes in the bank ownership and affiliation.

We use unconsolidated data for subsidiaries in principle, and consolidated data are used only when unconsolidated data are not available for that bank. In our dataset, only 6% of observations are consolidated for subsidiaries. For parent banks, by contrast, we use consolidated data to reflect the state of the conglomerate instead of the only holding company. As all selected subsidiaries are small compositions (in terms of their assets) in the conglomerate, using consolidated data for the parent bank would not cause serious problem of endogeneity.[7]

We drop the outliers by applying the following steps: first, we remove the observations if the subsidiaries' annual growth rate of total assets exceeds 300%, which could be the result of M&A in the host country; second, we drop the data if the growth rate of loans is higher than 400%, which could occur in the early years of the subsidiaries or in the financial turmoil; third, we delete the observations when subsidiaries' riskiness is larger than 100% or lower than −100%. We lose quite a number of banks from the removal of the outliers and the usage of one-year lags for subsidiary characteristics variables, but still have around 250 bank observations for our regression.

We collect macroeconomic variables from *International Financial Statistics* (*IFS*). We resort to various sources to collect data for the factors that may affect the effects of distance constraints. These variables and their sources are represented in Table 1 and will be further explained in Section 6.

5. BENCHMARK RESULTS: DOES DISTANCE MATTER FOR THE PERFORMANCE OF FOREIGN BANK SUBSIDIARIES?

We first estimate the Eq. (1) and examine whether the distance between the host and the home markets plays an important role for the performance of foreign bank subsidiaries located in the host countries. The results are reported in Table 2.

First of all, after controlling for all other factors affecting the bank performance, we find distance is still an important determinant of banks' behavior. The coefficient on the variable *distance* is negative and statistically significant in all regressions. A more distant foreign subsidiary is shown to supply loans at only a lower growth rate. This finding is consistent with the literature of "information asymmetry" in that higher informational costs to identify and monitor borrowers would discourage banks from providing more credit. Consistent with the findings in Peterson and Rajan (2002), Degryse and Ongena (2005), and Agarwal and Hauswald (2007), distance is found negatively correlated with net interest margin, implying that a foreign bank from a more distant home country charge borrowers lower interest rates. The reason can be that a distant foreign bank is characterized with more disadvantageous informational possession and consequently only lower market power, which prevents them from charging higher interest rates to borrowers. Another explanation is that a more distant foreign subsidiary will be forced to specialize only in the most transparent industries. These industries are more likely to be competitive and hence banks have to charge only lower interest rates.

As distant foreign banks own less information to find good business opportunities, they may have to hold more nonlending assets such as deposits in other banks, securities, bonds, and treasury bills. This conjecture is supported by the positive coefficient of distance in the regression of the share of other earning assets. Finally, distance is negatively associated with ROE, which suggests that a more distant foreign bank be less profitable than other closer foreign banks. It is worthwhile to note that our results are

Table 2. Estimation Results on the Effects of Distance on Bank Performance.

Dependent Variables	Loan Growth Rate	Net Interest Margin	Share of Other Earning Assets	ROE
Distance	−4.927***	−.210*	1.224**	−1.224**
	(1.296)	(.114)	(.581)	(.574)
Liquidity	.153***	−.019***	.593***	.008
	(.044)	(.002)	(.018)	(.017)
Capitalization	.124	.024***	.085**	−.137***
	(.100)	(.006)	(.035)	(.031)
Size	−.404***	.030***	.094**	.369***
	(.122)	(.009)	(.047)	(.062)
Riskiness	−.697***	.037***	.127*	.081
	(.195)	(.011)	(.068)	(.117)
Host GDP growth rate	1.213***	−.032***	−.143**	.381***
	(.169)	(.008)	(.065)	(.074)
Host change in unemployment	−.787*	−.042	−.183	.019
	(.424)	(.026)	(.156)	(.186)
Dummy (host monetary policy)	5.642***	−.184***	.488	−.278
	(1.215)	(.062)	(.438)	(.508)
Host depreciation rate	.085***	.013***	.001	−.032**
	(.027)	(.002)	(.010)	(.016)
Parent bank mass	−1.732**	−.031	2.707***	1.347***
	(.837)	(.065)	(.315)	(.392)
Parent bank liquidity	−.190***	−.015***	.140***	−.090***
	(.066)	(.004)	(.025)	(.027)
Parent bank capitalization	−.036	.099***	−.048	.134
	(.309)	(.026)	(.114)	(.142)
Home GDP growth rate	−.323	−.003	.085	−.312**
	(.228)	(.018)	(.103)	(.122)
Home change in unemployment	−.756	.015	−.196	−.466*
	(.675)	(.040)	(.217)	(.281)
Dummy (home monetary policy)	.569	.019	.357	.351
	(1.868)	(.088)	(.690)	(.799)
Year dummies	Yes	Yes	Yes	Yes
Country dummies	Yes	Yes	Yes	Yes
Observations (no. of banks)	1307 (254)	1307 (254)	1301 (253)	1304 (254)
Goodness of fit	.183	.368	.693	.150

Note: The numbers in parentheses denote errors of the coefficients.
*** 1%, ** 5%, and * 10%.

essentially consistent with the insights of "gravity model." Multinational banks tend to allocate their loans to more proximate clients, as represented as the "home bias" proposition in that they hold financial assets issued by closer (or domestic) debtors over-proportionately.

Our finding suggests that information asymmetry cannot be completely overcome by establishing a local presence of multinational banks in the host country. As Mian (2006) pointed out using the case of the Pakistani banking, one of the policy implications is that foreign bank participation in developing countries may face a significant challenge in advancing their financial development by attracting multinational banks from abroad. As foreign banks are constrained by the asymmetric information, they may not be interested in serving some firms (e.g., the opaque small firms), which would negatively impact the economic growth in host countries. A higher holding of nonlending assets by foreign banks may also result in a less efficient allocation of scarce financial resources. Moreover, because a higher information barrier lowers foreign banks' profitability, it may undermine their incentive and capability to provide long-term credit. A pool of financially healthy domestic banks equipped with better capacity for collecting soft information for loan would compensate the disadvantage of foreign banks in assessing information and work as a necessary complement in developing host banking markets.

We also find some other interesting results. For example, it is shown that higher liquidity enables banks to increase credit at a higher growth rate and charge a lower interest spread, which is consistent with prior works like Kashyap and Stein (2000) and Gambacorta (2005, 2008). Capitalization is positively associated with net interest margin. This finding is consistent with Demirguc-Kunt and Huizinga (1998), who find that higher capitalized banks tend to get the lower cost for funding. Larger and more risky banks tend to provide more stable credit, but charge higher interest rate and possess a higher ratio of nonloan assets. Host macroeconomic conditions affect banks' loans as well. The coefficient on the growth rate of real GDP is positive and statistically significant, suggesting a higher economic growth stimulate higher demand for bank credit. The coefficient on the change in unemployment rate is negative, implying that aggregate demand and hence the demand for credit would decrease when labor market is tight.

When the host central bank conducts an expansionary monetary policy, banks significantly lend more credit at lower interest margin than when monetary policy turns tightened. Banks increase their lending when domestic currency is depreciated, probably because values for foreign banks' assets denominated in local currency increase, and at the same time increase interest spread, which reflects uncovered interest parity when foreign currencies are relatively strengthened. We also find the financial strength of parent banks affect subsidiaries' lending. Banks from a large and highly liquid conglomerate increase loans at a lower rate. The result that subsidiaries' performance is affected by the financial strength of their parent banks is in line with the literature of "internal capital market" like Gilbert (1991), Houston, James, and Marcus (1997), and De Haas and van Lelyveld (2010). We find weak evidence that home countries macroeconomic variables affect subsidiaries' behavior; hence, foreign banks are not found to import fluctuations into host countries.

6. FURTHER RESULTS: WHAT FACTORS MODIFY THE EFFECT OF DISTANCE CONSTRAINTS?

We next test if the adverse effect of distance on bank performance is symmetric across banks and countries, or put differently, if there is any factor that may buffer or amplify the impact of distance. We do that by adding the tested factor and also its interaction with distance. A significant coefficient on the interaction term can be translated as the factor would affect banks' performance through changing the effects of distance.[8]

6.1. Entry Mode

Foreign banks can set up overseas subsidiaries through either de novo establishment or M&A. Rather than gathering the information of markets and potential borrowers from scratch, a foreign bank established through the M&A entry can inherit the pool of information from its predecessor, hence largely overcome the barrier of information asymmetry. We test the effect of entry mode on the distance constraints by introducing the interaction term *distance* × *dummy* (*M&A*), where *dummy* (*M&A*) has a value of 1 if the foreign subsidiary is built through acquiring a local bank, and it has a value of 0 if the foreign subsidiary is built though de novo establishment.

The results are reported in Table 3. We find the coefficient on *distance* × *dummy* (*M&A*) is positive and statistically significant in the regressions of the loan growth rate and net interest margin, but insignificant in the share of other earning assets and ROE. These results indicate that a foreign bank entered through the M&A mode is less constrained by asymmetric information than a de novo foreign bank in providing loans and setting interest rates.

Van Tassel and Vishwasrao (2007) argue that foreign banks choose an M&A entry mode to capture the information endowment of domestic

Table 3. Estimation Results on the Effects of Entry Mode on Distance Constraints.

Dependent Variables	Loan Growth Rate	Net Interest Margin	Share of Other Earning Assets	ROE
Distance	−6.827***	−.192**	1.257**	−.962
	(1.379)	(.093)	(.617)	(.670)
Dummy (M&A)	3.618*	.166	.373	−1.601*
	(2.048)	(.118)	(.814)	(.892)
Distance × Dummy (M&A)	2.574**	.270***	.096	−.966
	(1.151)	(.079)	(.480)	(.608)
Other variables	Yes	Yes	Yes	Yes
Year dummies	Yes	Yes	Yes	Yes
Country dummies	Yes	Yes	Yes	Yes
Observations (no. of banks)	1307 (254)	1307 (254)	1301 (253)	1304 (254)
Goodness of fit	.190	.280	.695	.147

Note: The numbers in parentheses denote errors of the coefficients.
*** 1%, ** 5%, and * 10%.

banks. Lehner (2009) suggests that foreign banks with superior screening technology would prefer an M&A entry to a greenfield entry. On the contrary, Peria and Mody (2004) find that de novo foreign banks charge lower spreads than M&A foreign banks in the Latin American banking sector. They interpret the findings that de novo foreign banks possess only the least information about the host markets and thus need to focus on the most transparent sectors, which are more likely competitive sectors. Accordingly, de novo foreign banks have to charge lower spreads than M&A foreign banks. Our finding that foreign subsidiaries entered through an M&A mode are less affected by distance than those entered through a de novo mode is consistent with the arguments that foreign subsidiaries entered through M&As have better information on the host banking market than those entered through greenfields and are able to charge lower loan rates.

6.2. History of Presence

Foreign banks can accumulate information about host markets and their clients in the process of their operations; hence controlling for all else, a foreign bank that has already been operating in the market for years would possess a richer pool of information than a bank newly entered. We collect the data on banks' history from their profiles and *BankScope* and use the

Table 4. The Effects of History of Presence on Distance Constraints.

Dependent Variables	Loan Growth Rate	Net Interest Margin	Share of Other Earning Assets	ROE
Distance	−12.459***	−.341**	3.784***	−.370
	(2.190)	(.155)	(.843)	(1.142)
History	−1.253	.320***	1.597***	−.351
	(1.163)	(.082)	(.407)	(.595)
Distance × *History*	2.623***	.096**	−.949***	−.276
	(.622)	(.046)	(.218)	(.312)
Other variables	Yes	Yes	Yes	Yes
Year dummies	Yes	Yes	Yes	Yes
Country dummies	Yes	Yes	Yes	Yes
Observations (no. of banks)	1290 (251)	1290 (251)	1284 (250)	1287 (251)
Goodness of fit	.187	.264	.703	.143

Note: The numbers in parentheses denote errors of the coefficients.
*** 1%, ** 5%, and * 10%.

number of years of operation in the host markets as the history of presence variable. For foreign banks that were established by M&A, its length of history started back to the date when the acquired bank was built. The effect of length of history is detected by adding the interaction term *distance* × *history*, and the results are reported in Table 4.

As expected, the interaction *distance* × *history* is positive and statistically significant in regressions of the loan growth rate and net interest margin and negative in the share of other earning assets. A foreign bank with a longer operation history in the host market is shown to be less affected by distance and accordingly lends more loans, sets higher interest margin, and holds less nonloan assets. These results are consistent with our conjecture that "senior" banks know the market better than their "junior" counterparts.

6.3. Information Institutions

Credit information institutions can help banks to have better access to the information on potential borrowers and overcome the adverse selection caused by information asymmetry. Djankov et al. (2007) find evidence that the existence of credit information institutions boosts more private credit in their sample of 129 countries. Brown et al. (2009) find that the information sharing provided by credit information institutions improves the availability and lower cost of credit, especially to opaque firms.

In practice, credit information institutions include public credit registries and private credit bureaus. Good examples of the former institutions include databases managed by a government agency (usually the central bank) that collects information on the standing of borrowers in the financial market and make it available to actual and potential lenders. The latter institutions include private firms or nonprofit organizations that maintain databases on the standing of borrowers to facilitate information exchange among banks and other financial institutions. We construct three dummy variables – *dummy* (*information institution*), *dummy* (*public credit registry*), and *dummy* (*private credit bureau*) – to capture, respectively, the existence of either public credit registries or private credit bureaus, public credit registries only, or private credit bureaus only. The main data source for the credit information institutions, public and private, is the World Bank *Doing Business* database.

First, we only include *dummy* (*information institution*) and its interaction with *distance* in regression (Table 5, panel A). We find the existence of the information institutions dampens the adverse effects of distance on the loan growth rate and net interest margin. A same distant foreign bank located in a host country with either a public credit registry or a private credit bureau provides more loan and can charge higher interest spread than its counterparts in host countries without credit information institutions. Next, we test the separate effects of public credit registry and private bureau in affecting the role of distance constraints. We add both *dummy* (*public credit registry*) and *dummy* (*private credit bureau*) and their interactions with *distance* in regression (Table 5, panel B). We find both types of information institutions contribute to lowering the effects of distance on the loan growth rate and the interest spread. Public credit registry may also help foreign subsidiaries to hold less nonlending assets. These results are consistent with the idea that foreign banks can retrieve information from credit information institutions and use them in evaluating the loan applications. Our findings suggest that the construction of credit information institutions seems to be a valuable component for the policy of financial liberalization in developing countries.

6.4. Language, Legal System, and Region

Intuitively, if a multinational bank expands its subsidiaries into a host market that is culturally more similar to its own home market, it may incur lower informational costs. To test the proposition, we use three dimensions

Table 5. Estimation Results on the Effects of Credit Information Institutes on Distance Constraints.

Dependent Variables	Loan Growth Rate	Net Interest Margin	Share of Other Earning Assets	ROE
Panel A: Public registry or private bureau				
Distance	−10.242***	−.625***	1.206	−.539
	(2.792)	(.125)	(.816)	(1.044)
Dummy (information institution)	−5.369**	−.316**	−3.121***	1.230
	(2.611)	(.142)	(1.017)	(.950)
Distance × Dummy (information institution)	5.579**	.319***	−.336	−.946
	(2.567)	(.112)	(.794)	(.971)
Other variables	Yes	Yes	Yes	Yes
Year dummies	Yes	Yes	Yes	Yes
Country dummies	Yes	Yes	Yes	Yes
Observations (no. of banks)	1307 (254)	1307 (254)	1301 (253)	1304 (254)
Goodness of fit	.183	.322	.634	.153
Panel B: Public registry and private bureau				
Distance	−11.137***	−.656***	1.900**	−.422
	(1.994)	(.122)	(.769)	(.940)
Dummy (public registry)	−2.986	.173	.141	4.200**
	(4.235)	(.172)	(1.655)	(1.712)
Distance × Dummy (public registry)	3.965**	.349**	−2.182**	−1.510
	(1.721)	(.167)	(.863)	(.971)
Dummy (private bureau)	−2.539	−.336**	−4.259***	.381
	(2.355)	(.144)	(1.109)	(1.022)
Distance × Dummy (private bureau)	4.629***	.192*	.045	−.312
	(1.584)	(.106)	(.740)	(.807)
Other variables	Yes	Yes	Yes	Yes
Year dummies	Yes	Yes	Yes	Yes
Country dummies	Yes	Yes	Yes	Yes
Observations (no. of banks)	1307 (254)	1307 (254)	1301 (253)	1304 (254)
Goodness of fit	.164	.329	.635	.143

Note: The numbers in parentheses denote errors of the coefficients.
*** 1%, ** 5%, and * 10%.

to measure the cultural similarity between host and home countries: the (same) language and legal system in the host and home countries, and the (same) region where host and home countries are located.[9] In the extant literature, the impact, on multinational banking, of whether the borrower and the bank are located in the same region as a proxy of the cultural distance have been examined (see Mian, 2006; Claessens & van Horsen, 2009). However, the examination that whether these national features can weaken or aggravate the negative effects of distance on foreign subsidiaries behavior is still scant. We construct three dummy variables, *dummy* (*same language*), *dummy* (*same legal system*), and *dummy* (*same region*), to capture, respectively, if the host and home countries have the same official languages, the same legal origins, and are geographically in the same region.[10] The main data sources are CIA World *Factbook* and La Porta, Lopez-de-Silanes, Shleifer, and Vishny (1998).

We add these three dummies and their interaction with *distance* respectively in regressions. The results are reported in Table 6. The coefficient on *dummy* (*same language*) is statistically significant in the regressions of the loan growth rate and the share of other earning assets, supporting the idea that the same language used in both host and home countries reduces the effects of distance in credit provision and assets allocation. This result implies that foreign banks would possess and communicate more precise information about their clients by avoiding extra costs from inter-lingual translation. The coefficient on *dummy* (*same region*) is statistically significant and shows an expected sign in determining net interest margin and ROE. That is, compared to its same distant counterparts, a foreign bank can own more market power, charge higher interest margin, and earn higher profits if its headquarters is located in the same region of the host market. However, the coefficient on *dummy* (*same legal system*) is not statistically significant in any regression, providing little evidence that same legal systems may strengthen or dampen the impact of distance constraints.[11]

6.5. Financial Deepening

Banks and other financial institutions arise to ameliorate the problems created by asymmetric information; hence, the information of potential borrowers will be more transparent in a more developed financial market. We test if foreign banks face less severe or more strict distance constraints when they are operating in financially more developed host markets.

The degree of financial development is measured using the ratio of private credit by depository banks to GDP, which are collected from the financial structure database provided by Beck and Demirguc-Kunt (2009). The results are reported in Table 7. We find that the coefficient on the interaction term of *distance* with *host financial deepening* is statistically significant in determining the growth of loans, net interest margin, and ROE, suggesting that a higher financial development plays a buffering role to the adverse

Table 6. Estimation Results on the Effects of Language, Legal System, and Region on Distance Constraints.

Dependent Variables	Loan Growth Rate	Net Interest Margin	Share of Other Earning Assets	ROE
Panel A: Same language				
Distance	−7.944***	−.304**	1.378**	−1.659**
	(1.387)	(.123)	(.630)	(.729)
Dummy (same language)	−12.349	1.697**	7.940**	3.132
	(9.121)	(.760)	(3.469)	(5.024)
Distance × Dummy	9.435**	−.468	−2.969*	1.016
(same language)	(4.192)	(.324)	(1.613)	(2.087)
Other variables	Yes	Yes	Yes	Yes
Year dummies	Yes	Yes	Yes	Yes
Country dummies	Yes	Yes	Yes	Yes
Observations (no. of banks)	1307 (254)	1307 (254)	1301 (253)	1304 (254)
Goodness of fit	.179	.370	.689	.155
Panel B: Same legal system				
Distance	−5.058***	−.252*	3.101***	−1.431**
	(1.289)	(.129)	(.514)	(.670)
Dummy (same legal system)	1.233	−.444***	−.255	−.828
	(1.696)	(.141)	(.739)	(.820)
Distance × Dummy (same	−.831	.076	.236	.035
legal system)	(1.083)	(.093)	(.482)	(.569)
Other variables	Yes	Yes	Yes	Yes
Year dummies	Yes	Yes	Yes	Yes
Country dummies	Yes	Yes	Yes	Yes
Observations (no. of banks)	1307 (254)	1307 (254)	1301 (253)	1304 (254)
Goodness of fit	.176	.365	.669	.151
Panel C: Same region				
Distance	−6.364**	−1.064***	.681	−4.414**
	(2.841)	(.266)	(1.228)	(2.166)
Dummy (same region)	−4.287	−1.631***	.682	−7.185
	(6.453)	(.609)	(2.749)	(4.892)
Distance × Dummy	−3.726	1.206***	−.587	4.326*
(same region)	(3.393)	(.296)	(1.513)	(2.376)
Other variables	Yes	Yes	Yes	Yes
Year dummies	Yes	Yes	Yes	Yes
Country dummies	Yes	Yes	Yes	Yes
Observations (no. of banks)	1307 (254)	1307 (254)	1301 (253)	1304 (254)
Goodness of fit	.177	.391	.682	.152

Note: The numbers in parentheses denote errors of the coefficients.
*** 1%, ** 5%, and * 10%.

Table 7. Estimation Results on the Effects of Financial Deepening on Distance Constraints.

Dependent Variables	Loan Growth Rate	Net Interest Margin	Share of Other Earning Assets	ROE
Distance	−7.680***	−.964***	4.078***	−3.013***
	(1.903)	(.190)	(.647)	(.898)
Host financial deepening	−.067	−.041***	−.139***	−.075**
	(.088)	(.005)	(.027)	(.031)
Distance × Host financial deepening	.053**	.011***	.002	.029**
	(.023)	(.001)	(.008)	(.012)
Other variables	Yes	Yes	Yes	Yes
Year dummies	Yes	Yes	Yes	Yes
Country dummies	Yes	Yes	Yes	Yes
Observations (no. of banks)	1279 (248)	1279 (248)	1273 (247)	1276 (248)
Goodness of fit	.182	.377	.677	.156

Note: The numbers in parentheses denote errors of the coefficients.
*** 1%, ** 5%, and * 10%.

effects of distance. In a host country with higher financial depth, a foreign bank increases its credit at higher growth rate, have a larger interest spread, and hence higher profits, compared to other distant foreign banks. Our finding implies that, as the host financial sector develops, foreign banks would encounter declining information asymmetry and provide more financing in host countries.

Why foreign banks are subject to less adverse distance constraints in a more developed banking market? One explanation is that financial depth also reflects the dependence of firms on banks to finance their investment. The more firms are dependent on banks, the more actively they provide verifiable evidence for their creditworthiness, hence the less adverse the informational asymmetry is.

6.6. Crisis

Banks may encounter worse informational problem when the economy falls in crisis, which can greatly deteriorate firms' operation outcomes and obscure their business prospects. Mishkin (1990) describes the nature of financial crisis as a disruption of markets in which the asymmetric information problems of adverse selection and moral hazard become much worse. We test whether or not crises would deteriorate the effects of distance constraints.

Table 8. Estimation Results on the Effects of Financial Crisis on Distance Constraints.

Dependent Variables	Loan Growth Rate	Net Interest Margin	Share of Other Earning Assets	ROE
Distance	−4.782***	−.500***	2.152***	−1.311**
	(1.156)	(.115)	(.506)	(.570)
Dummy (financial crisis)	.978	.311**	−2.772***	.684
	(2.258)	(.151)	(.921)	(1.084)
Distance × *Dummy*	−2.339*	−.255***	−.500	.562
(financial crisis)	(1.385)	(.091)	(.504)	(.736)
Other variables	Yes	Yes	Yes	Yes
Year dummies	Yes	Yes	Yes	Yes
Country dummies	Yes	Yes	Yes	Yes
Observations (no. of banks)	1307 (254)	1307 (254)	1301 (253)	1304 (254)
Goodness of fit	.178	.360	.690	.147

Note: The numbers in parentheses denote errors of the coefficients.
*** 1%, ** 5%, and * 10%.

A dummy variable, *dummy (financial crisis)*, is constructed equal to 1 if the host country experiences a systematic banking crisis, using the data in Caprio and Klingebiel (2003) and Laeven and Valencia (2008). The results are reported in Table 8.

The coefficient on the interaction term *distance* × *dummy (financial crisis)* is found negative and statistically significant in regressions of loan growth and net interest margin, which is consistent with our expectation that information asymmetry becomes deteriorated during crisis periods. Given the same distance, foreign banks in host crises are more hesitant to expand their credit and have only narrowed the interest spread. To avoid confusion, note that our result does not contradict with the conventional observations that in crisis banks charge higher interest rate to borrowers. The individual term *dummy (financial crisis)* is shown to have a positive and statistically significant coefficient, indicating that interest rates are higher during the crisis periods. However, a negative and statistically significant coefficient on *distance* × *dummy (financial crisis)* only suggests that the adverse effect of distance on interest spread is strengthened by crises, probably because the increase in the loan interest rate is offset by an increase in the cost of funding.

6.7. Stock Markets

The development of stock market may influence the capacity of collecting information on borrowers by banks. The intuition is that a more developed stock market will have firms' financial information more transparent and easier to access by banks, especially for those publicly listed companies. In this section, we test how the stock market development influences the effects of distance on foreign banks' performance.

We use three variables to measure the development in stock market: namely, *number of listed companies* as the share of listed companies divided by total population in host countries, *stock market capitalization* as the value of listed shares divided by GDP, and *stock market turnover rate* as the ratio of the value of total shares traded to market capitalization. We collect the data from the structure database provided by Beck and Demirguc-Kunt (2009). We add these three variables and their interactions with *distance* in our regressions. The results are reported in Table 9.

We find the coefficient on *number of listed companies* is statistically significant in all regressions and show the expected sign, supporting a proposition that an increase in the number of listed companies improves the informational problem (Table 9, panel A). Given same distance as its peers, a foreign bank subsidiary in a host country where there are more publicly listed companies tends to provide more lending, be able to charge higher interest rates, hold less nonlending assets, and earn higher profits. The coefficients on *stock market capitalization* is positive in regressions of loan growth and net interest margin (Table 9, panel B), while the coefficient on *stock market turnover rate* is statistically significant in regressions of loan growth and the share of other earning assets (Table 9, panel C). Both results are in line with the proposition that foreign banks incur lower informational costs in the host country where stock markets are well developed.

Our results also shed some light on the specialization of foreign banks in serving domestic clients. As publicly listed companies are usually large companies in an economy, the finding that the effects of informational problem on foreign banks' behaviors can be improved by the development of stock market suggests that foreign banks may lend more credit to large companies and may exclude small firms whose information is limited because the financial information on those firms are not publically available in stock markets.

6.8. Concentration

The dependence of banks on the quality of information on borrowers may be affected by the competition level in the financial market. Empirical evidence on this proposition is still far from conclusive (see Archaya et al., 2002; Boot & Thakor, 2002; Hauswald & Marquez, 2006; Mistrulli & Casolaro, 2008; Zarutskie, 2008).

Table 9. Estimation Results on the Effects of Stock Market Development on Distance Constraints.

Dependent Variables	Loan Growth Rate	Net Interest Margin	Share of Other Earning Assets	ROE
Panel A: Number of publicly listed companies				
Distance	−9.276***	−.400***	4.324***	−1.643**
	(1.093)	(.135)	(.483)	(.729)
Number of listed companies	.384	−.129	−4.759**	−3.349
	(3.728)	(.278)	(2.039)	(2.097)
Distance × Number of listed companies	3.294*	.634***	−2.864***	1.964*
	(1.956)	(.171)	(1.087)	(1.190)
Other variables	Yes	Yes	Yes	Yes
Year dummies	Yes	Yes	Yes	Yes
Country dummies	Yes	Yes	Yes	Yes
Observations (no. of banks)	1285 (250)	1285 (250)	1279 (249)	1282 (250)
Goodness of fit	.158	.360	.680	.144
Panel B: Stock market capitalization				
Distance	−8.371***	−.402***	3.380***	−1.485**
	(1.109)	(.134)	(.557)	(.633)
Stock market capitalization	−.088***	−.007**	−.040**	−.003
	(.019)	(.003)	(.015)	(.012)
Distance × Stock market capitalization	.026***	.003***	.007	.007
	(.010)	(.001)	(.005)	(.004)
Other variables	Yes	Yes	Yes	Yes
Year dummies	Yes	Yes	Yes	Yes
Country dummies	Yes	Yes	Yes	Yes
Observations (no. of banks)	1267 (246)	1267 (246)	1261 (245)	1264 (246)
Goodness of fit	.164	.354	.678	.110
Panel C: Stock market turnover rate				
Distance	−8.857***	−.423***	1.450***	−1.462**
	(1.325)	(.083)	(.568)	(.645)
Stock market turnover rate	.028	−.001	−.010	.011
	(.019)	(.001)	(.006)	(.009)
Distance × Stock market turnover rate	.036**	.000	−.011**	.007
	(.016)	(.001)	(.005)	(.006)
Other variables	Yes	Yes	Yes	Yes
Year dummies	Yes	Yes	Yes	Yes
Country dummies	Yes	Yes	Yes	Yes
Observations (no. of banks)	1273 (248)	1273 (248)	1267 (247)	1270 (248)
Goodness of fit	.164	.413	.689	.130

Note: The numbers in parentheses denote errors of the coefficients.
*** 1%, ** 5%, and * 10%.

We test the effects of competition on how distance influence foreign subsidiaries' lending. We use the level of banking concentration as a proxy for the competition in host banking markets. It is widely accepted that the more concentrated the banking sector is, the less competitive it is. Concentration is defined as the share of total assets owned by the largest three banks in total assets of banking sector. The data is selected from the financial structure database provided by Beck and Demirguc-Kunt (2009).

The results are reported in Table 10. The coefficient on the interaction variable, *distance* × *concentration*, is found to be positive and statistically significant in regressions for loan growth rate and interest rate and negative in regression for the share of other earning assets. These results suggest that the adverse distance effects are less pronounced in a more concentrated (less competitive) banking sector. A same distant foreign subsidiary tends to increase its loans at a higher rate, charges higher interest rate, and holds less nonloan assets in a more concentrated market. Archaya et al. (2002) argue that a bank's monitoring effectiveness is dampened when the bank expand to more competitive sectors, results in lower quality of loans. Hauswald and Marquez (2006) suggest that banks tend to decrease their investment to acquire borrowers' information when competition is intensified. Our results are in line with this finding.

Table 10. Estimation Results on the Effects of Concentration Level on Distance Constraints.

Dependent Variables	Loan Growth Rate	Net Interest Margin	Share of Other Earning Assets	ROE
Distance	−13.518***	−1.525***	4.533***	−3.247*
	(3.199)	(.243)	(1.367)	(1.679)
Concentration	−.088	−.001	−.012	−.128***
	(.084)	(.006)	(.041)	(.044)
Distance × *Concentration*	.113**	.014***	−.047**	.024
	(.051)	(.003)	(.022)	(.027)
Other variables	Yes	Yes	Yes	Yes
Year dummies	Yes	Yes	Yes	Yes
Country dummies	Yes	Yes	Yes	Yes
Observations (no. of banks)	1289 (252)	1289 (252)	1283 (251)	1286 (252)
Goodness of fit	.175	.377	.693	.147

Note: The numbers in parentheses denote errors of the coefficients.
*** 1%, ** 5%, and * 10%.

6.9. Hierarchy

Stein (2002) shows that loan officers in hierarchically complex conglomerates will have a lower incentive to collect information about borrowers. This is because they do not generally have decision-making authority, and instead, they have to report that information to their supervisors. On the basis of this argument, we may expect that a subsidiary with higher hierarchy in the conglomerate will be less separate from the ultimate decision makers, more likely influence CEO's decisions, and hence have stronger incentive to identify potential prime borrowers. Therefore, a subsidiary with a higher hierarchy might be less affected by the distance constraint than a peer with a lower hierarchy.

We use the relative size of bank assets of the subsidiary in the conglomerate to proxy its hierarchy, that is, the ratio of the subsidiary's total assets to the total assets of the conglomerate. When a subsidiary manages more assets in the conglomerate, it implies that it is standing on a higher hierarchy.

The results are reported in Table 11. The coefficient on the interaction term, *distance* × *hierarchy*, shows an expected sign and is statistically significant in all bank performance dimensions. Compared to same distant peers, a higher hierarchical subsidiary tends to provide more loans, charge higher interest rate, hold less other earning assets, and earn higher profits.

Table 11. Estimation Results on the Effects of Subsidiary Hierarchy on Distance Constraints.

Dependent Variables	Loan Growth Rate	Net Interest Margin	Share of Other Earning Assets	ROE
Distance	−5.356***	−.489***	2.470***	−1.066*
	(1.425)	(.121)	(.516)	(.648)
Hierarchy	.566*	−.048*	.319***	.416***
	(.338)	(.024)	(.110)	(.150)
Distance × *Hierarchy*	.550**	.035*	−.199***	.249**
	(.268)	(.018)	(.075)	(.099)
Other variables	Yes	Yes	Yes	Yes
Year dummies	Yes	Yes	Yes	Yes
Country dummies	Yes	Yes	Yes	Yes
Observations (no. of banks)	1307 (254)	1307 (254)	1301 (253)	1304 (254)
Goodness of fit	.187	.362	.690	.151

Note: The numbers in parentheses denote errors of the coefficients.
*** 1%, ** 5%, and * 10%.

These results suggest that a higher standing in the conglomerate may help banks less constrained by information asymmetries. This provides consistent evidence that the managers of higher hierarchical subsidiaries have stronger incentive and capacity to collect the information on borrowers and implies that parent banks may "export" their superior expertise to higher hierarchical subsidiaries than lower ones (Berger & DeYoung, 2001; Stein, 2002).

6.10. Robustness Tests

It can be reasonably argued that the above-discussed factors may be correlated to each other and hence they actually capture something alike. In this section, we test the robustness of our finding by add all significant factors in regression. For instance, we exclude the insignificant factors and add only dummy (M&A), history, dummy (information institutions), dummy (same language), host financial deepening, dummy (financial crisis), number of listed companies, stock market capitalization, stock market turnover rate, concentration and hierarchy, and their interaction with distance into the regression of the loan growth rate.

The results are reported in Table 12. To no surprise, some factors lose their significance because multicollinearity can be hardly avoided in this regression. Even though we cannot simply rule out the importance of those variables just because they are not statistically significant in these augmented regressions, we find stronger evidence for some factors because their significance remains. It is confirmed that there are many factors that mitigate or multiply the role of distance constraints in the loan performance of foreign subsidiaries in multinational banking. They include the loan growth rate, the history of presence, the existence of credit information institutions, the same language in host and home markets, and the financial development. For net interest margin, we find robust support for the force of the history of presence, the same region where host and home countries are located, and the financial development level. For the share of other earning assets, the history of presence, the same language, the turnover rate in stock market, and the hierarchy hold on their significance. For ROE, all added factors are shown to be statistically significant, namely, the same region, the financial development, the number of listed companies, and the hierarchy of the subsidiary.

We also conduct a robustness test to check if there have been any systematic shifts over years in the role of distance constraints on the

Table 12. Robustness Tests.

Dependent Variables	Loan Growth Rate	Net Interest Margin	Share of Other Earning Assets	ROE
Distance	−31.808***	−1.470***	5.466***	−10.471***
	(6.223)	(.462)	(1.804)	(2.581)
Dummy (M&A)	7.352***	.627***		
	(2.712)	(.189)		
Distance × Dummy (M&A)	−.642	−.227		
	(1.764)	(.159)		
History	−5.121***	−.181	1.189**	
	(1.839)	(.148)	(.501)	
Distance × History	3.323***	.267***	−.691**	
	(1.013)	(.087)	(.280)	
Dummy (information institution)	−4.516	−.197		
	(3.004)	(.140)		
Distance × Dummy (information institution)	4.617*	.194*		
	(2.542)	(.116)		
Dummy (same language)	−20.521**		11.700***	
	(10.121)		(3.545)	
Distance × Dummy (same language)	11.736**		−4.218**	
	(4.768)		(1.652)	
Dummy (same region)		−.371		−14.025***
		(.558)		(5.205)
Distance × Dummy (same region)		.909***		6.252**
		(.330)		(2.626)
Host financial deepening	−.258***	−.052***		−.044
	(.090)	(.005)		(.035)
Distance × Host financial deepening	.138***	.012***		.083***
	(.049)	(.003)		(.017)
Dummy (financial crisis)	.157	.754***		
	(2.942)	(.151)		
Distance × Dummy (financial crisis)	−.529	.045		
	(1.716)	(.101)		
Number of listed companies	.107	−.153	.386	.106
	(5.412)	(.286)	(2.374)	(2.318)
Distance × Number of listed companies	4.802	−.056	2.579	2.550*
	(2.939)	(.236)	(1.614)	(1.537)
Stock market capitalization	−.040	.001		
	(.048)	(.003)		
Distance × Stock market capitalization	−.042	−.002		
	(.027)	(.002)		
Stock market turnover rate	.021		−.010	
	(.021)		(.006)	
Distance × Stock market turnover rate	.029*		−.010*	
	(.017)		(.005)	

Table 12. *(Continued)*

Dependent Variables	Loan Growth Rate	Net Interest Margin	Share of Other Earning Assets	ROE
Concentration	.157	−.005	.043	
	(.137)	(.006)	(.038)	
Distance × Concentration	.075	−.003	−.028	
	(.074)	(.004)	(.024)	
Hierarchy	1.801***	.055	.165	.632***
	(.456)	(.032)	(.146)	(.175)
Distance × Hierarchy	.351	−.033	−.174*	.279**
	(.324)	(.023)	(.102)	(.110)
Other variables	Yes	Yes	Yes	Yes
Year dummies	Yes	Yes	Yes	Yes
Country dummies	Yes	Yes	Yes	Yes
Observations (no. of banks)	1213 (235)	1217 (236)	1236 (242)	1263 (245)
Goodness of fit	.178	.382	.663	.145

Note: The numbers in parentheses denote errors of the coefficients.
*** 1%, ** 5%, and * 10%.

performance of foreign subsidiary banks. According to the estimation results, we are not able to get statistically significant evidence for the system shift over time in our sample observations. This finding is consistent with Buch (2005), which reports that the importance of distance for the foreign assets holdings of banks has not changed for commercial banks from G-5 countries doing business in 50 host countries for the period 1983–1999. However, we expect that the role of distance on the performance of foreign banks in the emerging and developing host countries diminishes over the long run due to the advancement of information technology, communication infrastructure, and globalization of the banking industry.

7. CONCLUSION

This chapter addresses the significance of the host-home distance in affecting the performance of foreign subsidiaries in host country markets. Our results suggest that, first, the distance constraint adversely affects loan growth, profitability, and performance of foreign bank subsidiaries, and second, the unfavorable information asymmetry faced by foreign banks, due to the distance constraint, in financing foreign clients cannot be smoothed out simply by establishing their presence abroad such as setting up their foreign subsidiaries. Foreign banks still need to have years of operation to learn the markets and accumulate more precise information pool for potential borrowers.

The effect of distance is not symmetric across banks and countries. We identify various factors affecting the role of distance in multinational banking. They are associated with bank characteristics (entry mode and history of presence), national features (existence of credit information institutions, cultural similarity with home countries, financial development, crises, stock market development, and the level banking market concentration), and the conglomerate structure (hierarchy). We find evidence that they play an effective role in determining the strength of distance on foreign subsidiaries' behavior and performance. Our results imply that, given the same distance from their home markets and other controlled variables, foreign banks would show heterogeneity in their performance, depending on where they are located.

Our findings in this chapter have some important policy implications. A policy that discourages M&A of foreign banks to domestic banks but encourage de novo establishment may produce less optimal outcome, because de novo foreign banks face more adverse distance constraints and information asymmetry in identifying their potential clients. Entry permission is shown not to be sufficient for good performance of foreign banks in host markets. The governments in host countries need to proactively establish and develop credit information institutions as a complement of the financial liberalization policy. Another important policy implication is that the policy-makers in developing countries should not ignore the financial health and development of domestic banks, because foreign banks are subject to the informational problem and may cause inefficient allocation of scarce financial resources in the host countries. The financial development cannot be achieved only by allowing the entry of foreign banks. A pool of strong domestic banks, with informational advantages, can compensate the disadvantage of foreign banks with distance constraints and information asymmetry and act as an indispensible participant in the financial markets.

NOTES

1. Soft information means the information that cannot be directly verified by anyone except the agent who produces it. As opposed to "hard" information, which can be credibly verified by documents or other evidence, "soft" information cannot be unambiguously documented and passed on from loan officers to their superiors.

2. Mian (2006) and Claessens and van Horsen (2009) only use dummies to measure the distance between host and home markets.

3. The effect of parent banks on the behaviors of subsidiaries is studied in the "internal capital market" literature, which argues that the financial strength in parent banks would affect the availability of resources from the parent to the subsidiaries. Related works include Gilbert (1991), Houston et al. (1997), Houston and James (1998), Campello (2002), Holod and Peek (2010), Ashcraft (2008), and De Haas and van Lelyveld (2010).

4. Related research how foreign subsidiaries may be affects by factors in their home countries can be seen in Peek and Rosengren (2000), Goldberger (2005), and some others.

5. Fifty-three out of 69 multinational banks in our sample are listed in the largest 100 banks in the world as of 2005 (in terms of the book value of equity capital). See *The Banker*, Vol. 155, No. 953.

6. Branches are not included in our dataset.

7. The ratio of a subsidiary's total assets to the conglomerate's total assets is around 1% on average and the median value is even much lower (only 0.2%). See Table 1.

8. The single item of the tested factor would be interpreted as it may affect banks' behavior through other unidentified channels.

9. Recently, the role of legal system in determining the development of financial system has received an intensive attention (see La Porta et al., 1998 and Beck, Demirguc-Kunt, & Levine, 2003).

10. The official languages in our sampled countries include English, Spanish, Italian, Portuguese, French, Chinese, and others. In total, 43 different languages. The legal origins are categorized into French, German, English, Scandinavian, and socialist legal systems, following La Porta et al. (1998) and Djankov et al. (2007). Regions are grouped into North America, South America, Central America, Europe, East Asia, South Asia, Southeast Asia, Mideast, Central Asia and Russia, Australia and New Zealand, and Africa.

11. Our results are consistent with Claessens and van Horsen (2009), who also find that the same language and region improve the performance of foreign banks, but the same legal system does not.

REFERENCES

Agarwal, S., & Hauswald, R. (2007). Distance and information asymmetries in lending decisions. *Federal Reserve Bank of Chicago Proceedings* (May), 183–204.

Almanza, A. (2002). A model of competition in banking: bank capital vs. expertise. *Journal of Financial Intermediation*, *11*, 87–121.

Archaya, V., Hasan, I., & Saunders, A. (2002). *Should banks be diversified? Evidence from individual bank loan portfolios*. BIS Working Paper no. 118. Bank for International Settlements, Basel, Switzerland.

Ashcraft, A. (2008). Are bank holding companies a source of strength to their banking subsidiaries? *Journal of Money, Credit and Banking*, *40*, 273–294.

Bank for International Settlement. (2009). *Capital flows and emerging market economies*. CGFS Papers no. 33, January. BIS, Geneva, Switzerland.

Beck, T., & Demirguc-Kunt, A. (2009). *Financial institutions and markets across countries and over time – data and analysis*. World Bank Working Paper. World Bank, Washington, DC.

Beck, T., Demirguc-Kunt, A., & Levine, R. (2003). Law and finance: Why does legal origin matter. *Journal of Comparative Economics, 31*(4), 653–675.

Bennardo, A., Pagano, M., & Piccolo, S. (2008). *Multiple-bank lending, creditor rights and information sharing*. CSEF Working Paper no. 211. Centre for Studies in Economics and Finance (CSEF), University of Naples, Italy.

Berger, A., & DeYoung, R. (2001). The effects of geographic expansion on bank efficiency. *Journal of Financial Services Research, 19*(2), 163–184.

Berger, A., Klapper, L., & Uddell, G. (2001). The ability of banks to lend informationally opaque small business. *Journal of Banking & Finance, 25*, 2127–2167.

Boot, A., & Thakor, A. (2002). Can relationship banking survive competition? *Journal of Finance, 55*(2), 679–713.

Brown, M., Jappelli, T., & Pagano, M. (2009). Information sharing and credit: firm-level evidence from transition countries. *Journal of Financial Intermediation, 18*(2), 151–172.

Buch, C. (2005). Distance and international banking. *Review of International Economics, 13*(4), 787–804.

Campello, M. (2002). Internal capital markets in financial conglomerates: Evidence from small bank responses to monetary policy. *Journal of Finance, 57*(6), 2773–2805.

Caprio, G., & Klingebiel, D. (2003). *Episodes of systematic and borderline financial crises*. World Bank Research Working Paper. World Bank, Washington, DC.

Carey, M., & Nini, G. (2007). Is the corporate loan market globally integrated? A pricing puzzle. *Journal of Finance, 62*(6), 2969–3007.

Carling, K., & Lundberg, S. (2005). Asymmetric information and distance: An empirical assessment of geographical credit rationing. *Journal of Economics and Business, 57*(1), 39–59.

Claessens, S., & van Horsen, N. (2009). *Being a foreigner among domestic banks: Asset or liability*. IMF Working paper WP/09/273. International Monetary Fund, Washington, DC.

Clarke, G., Cull, R., D'Amato, L., & Molinari, A. (1999). *The effect of foreign entry on Argentina's domestic banking sector*. World Bank Policy Research Working Paper no. 2158. The World Bank, Washington, DC.

Cole, R., Goldberg, L., & White, L. (1999). Cookie-Cutter vs. character: The micro structure of small business lending by large and small banks. *Proceedings, Federal Reserve Bank of Chicago* (May), 362–389.

Coval, J., & Moskowitz, T. (1999). Home bias at home: Local equity preference in domestic portfolios. *Journal of Finance, 54*(6), 2045–2073.

Coval, J., & Moskowitz, T. (2001). The geography of investment: Informed trading and asset prices. *Journal of Political Economy, 109*(4), 811–841.

Degryse, H., & Ongena, S. (2005). Distance, lending relationships and competition. *Journal of Finance, 60*(1), 231–266.

De Haas, R., & van Lelyveld, I. (2010). Internal capital markets and lending by multinational bank subsidiaries. *Journal of Financial Intermediation, 19*, 1–25.

Dell'Ariccia, G., & Marquez, R. (2004). Information and bank credit allocation. *Journal of Financial Economics, 72*, 185–214.

Demirguc-Kunt, A., & Huizinga, H. (1998). *Determinants of commercial bank interest margins and profitability: Some international evidence*. World Bank Policy Research Working Paper no. 1900. World Bank, Washington, DC.

Djankov, S., McLiesh, C., & Shleifer, A. (2007). Private credit in 129 countries. *Journal of Financial Economics*, *84*(2), 299–329.

French, K., & Poterba, J. (1991). Investor diversification and international equity markets. *American Economic Review*, *81*(2), 222–226.

Gambacorta, L. (2005). Inside the bank lending channel. *European Economic Review*, *49*(7), 1737–1759.

Gambacorta, L. (2008). How do banks set interest rates? *European Economic Review*, *52*(5), 792–819.

Gehrig, T. (1993). An information based explanation of the domestic bias in international equity investment. *Scandinavian Journal of Economics*, *95*(1), 97–109.

Gilbert, R. A. (1991). Do bank holding companies act as "Sources of Strength" for their bank subsidiaries. *Economic Review*, Federal Reserve Bank of St. Louis, January/February.

Goldberger, L. (2005). *The international exposure of U.S. banks*. NBER Working Paper no. 11365. NBER, Cambridge, MA.

Hauswald, R., & Marquez, R. (2000). Relationship banking, loan specialization and competition. *Proceedings, Federal Reserve Bank of Chicago* (May), 108–131.

Hauswald, R., & Marquez, R. (2006). Competition and strategic information acquisition in credit market. *Review of Financial Studies*, *19*(3), 967–1000.

Herrero, A. G., & Peria, M. S. M. (2007). The mix of international banks' foreign claims: Determinants and implications. *Journal of Banking & Finance*, *31*, 1613–1631.

Holod, D., & Peek, J. (2010). Capital constraints, asymmetric information, and internal capital markets in banking: New evidence. *Journal of Money, Credit and Banking*, *42*, 879–906.

Houston, J., James, C., & Marcus, D. (1997). Capital market frictions and the role of internal capital markets in banking. *Journal of Financial Economics*, *46*, 135–164.

Houston, J., & James, C. (1998). Do bank internal capital market promote lending? *Journal of Banking & Finance*, *22*, 899–918.

Jappelli, T., & Pagano, M. (2002). Information sharing, lending and defaults: Cross-country evidence. *Journal of Banking & Finance*, *26*(10), 2017–2045.

Kang, J-K., & Stulz, R. (1997). Why is there a home bias? An analysis of foreign portfolio equity ownership in Japan. *Journal of Financial Economics*, *46*(1), 3–28.

Kashyap, A., & Stein, J. (2000). What do a million observations on banks say about the transmission of monetary policy. *American Economic Review*, *90*(3), 407–428.

Klein, D. (1992). Promise keeping in the great society: A model of credit information sharing. *Economics and Politics*, *4*(2), 117–136.

Laeven, L., & Valencia, F. (2008). *Systematic banking crises: A new database*. IMF Working Paper WP/08/224. International Monetary Fund, Washington, DC.

La Porta, R., Lopez-de-Silanes, F., Shleifer, A., & Vishny, R. (1998). Law and finance. *Journal of Political Economy*, *106*(6), 1113–1155.

Lehner, M. (2009). Entry mode choice of multinational banks. *Journal of Banking & Finance*, *33*(10), 1781–1792.

Lewis, K. (1999). Trying to explain home bias in equities and consumption. *Journal of Economic Literature*, *37*(2), 571–608.

Mian, A. (2006). Distance constraints: The limits of foreign lending in poor economies. *Journal of Finance*, *61*(3), 1465–1505.

Mishkin, F. (1990). *Asymmetric information and financial crises: A historic perspective*. NBER Working Paper no. 3400.

Mistrulli, P. E., & Casolaro, L. (2008). *Distance, lending technologies and interest rates*. 21st Australasian Finance and Banking Conference 2008 Paper. Bank of Italy, Rome, Italy.

Padilla, A. J., & Pagano, M. (1997). Endogenous communication among lenders and entrepreneurial incentives. *Review of Financial Studies*, *10*, 205–236.

Padilla, A. J., & Pagano, M. (2000). Sharing default information as a borrower discipline device. *European Economic Review*, *44*, 1951–1980.

Pagano, M., & Jappelli, T. (1993). Information sharing in credit markets. *Journal of Finance*, *48*(5), 1693–1718.

Papaioannou, E. (2005). *What drives international bank flows? Politics, institutions and other determinants*. European Central Bank Working Paper no. 437. European Central Bank, Frankfurt, Germany.

Peek, J., & Rosengren, E. (2000). Collateral damage: Effects of the Japanese real estate collapse on credit availability and real activity in the United States. *American Economic Review*, *90*(1), 30–45.

Peria, M. S. M., & Mody, A. (2004). *How foreign participation and market concentration impact bank spreads: Evidence from Latin America*. World Bank Policy Research Paper no. 3210. The World Bank, Washington, DC.

Peterson, M., & Rajan, R. (2002). Does distance still matter? The information revolution in small business lending. *Journal of Finance*, *57*(6), 2533–2570.

Portes, R., & Rey, H. (2005). The determinants of cross-border equity flows. *Journal of International Economics*, *65*, 269–296.

Portes, R., Rey, H., & Oh, Y. (2001). Information and capital flows: The determinants of transactions in financial assets. *European Economic Review*, *45*, 783–796.

Siregar, R. Y., & Choy, K. M. (2009). *Determinants of international bank lending from developed world to East Asia*. MPRA Working Paper no. 14989.

Stein, J. (2002). Information production and capital allocation: Decentralized vs. hierarchical firms. *Journal of Finance*, *57*, 1891–1921.

Stiglitz, J., & Weiss, A. (1981). Credit rationing in markets with imperfect information. *American Economic Review*, *71*(3), 393–410.

Van Tassel, E., & Vishwasrao, S. (2007). Asymmetric information and the mode of entry in foreign credit markets. *Journal of Banking & Finance*, *31*(12), 3742–3760.

Tesar, L., & Werner, I. (1995). Home bias and high turnover. *Journal of International Money and Finance*, *14*(4), 467–492.

Vercammen, J. (1995). Credit bureau policy and sustainable reputation effects in credit markets. *Economica*, *62*(248), 461–478.

Wei, S.-Y., & Wu, Y. (2001). *Negative alchemy? Corruption, composition of capital flow and currency crisis*. NBER Working Paper no. 8187.

Zarutskie, R. (2008). *Competition and specialization in credit markets*. Working Paper. Duke University, Durham, NC.

APPENDIX

Table A1. Correlation Coefficients among Bank Performance Dimensions.

	Loan Growth Rate	Net Interest Margin	Share of Other Earning Assets	ROE
Loan growth rate	1.000			
Net interest margin	0.056***	1.000		
Share of other earning assets	−0.171***	−0.191***	1.000	
ROE	0.088***	0.109***	0.004	1.000

*** 1%, ** 5%, and * 10%.

Table A2. Correlation Coefficients among Distance and Subsidiary Characteristics.

	Distance	Liquidity	Capitalization	Size	Riskiness
Distance	1.000				
Liquidity	−0.039*	1.000			
Capitalization	0.061***	0.024	1.000		
Size	−0.282***	−0.107***	−0.173***	1.000	
Riskiness	−0.006	−0.028	0.019	−0.012	1.000

*** 1%, ** 5%, and * 10%.

Table A3. Correlation Coefficients among Distance and Parent Bank Characteristics.

	Distance	Parent Bank Mass	Parent Bank Liquidity	Parent Bank Capitalization
Distance	1.000			
Parent bank mass	0.497***	1.000		
Parent bank liquidity	−0.060***	0.024	1.000	
Parent bank capitalization	0.056***	−0.188***	−0.141***	1.000

*** 1%, ** 5%, and *10%.

Table A4. List of Multinational Banks and the Distribution of Foreign Subsidiaries in Emerging and Developing Economies.

	Multinational Bank	Home Country	Host Countries
1	ABN Amro	NL	PL, RO, HU, KZ, AR, BR, CL, CO, MX, MY, PK, PH
2	Allied Irish Banks plc	IE	PL
3	Alpha Bank AE	GR	MK, RS, RO
4	American Express	US	BR, CL, MX, UY
5	Australia and New Zealand Banking Group	AU	ID
6	Banca Intesa	IT	HR, BA, RU, RS, SK
7	Banca Nazionale del Lavoro SpA-BNL	IT	AR, BR, UY
8	Banco Bilbao Vizcaya Argentaria SA	ES	AR, CL, CO, MX, PY, PE, UY, VE
9	Banco Bradesco SA	BR	AR
10	Banco Comercial Portugues SA	PT	PL, TR
11	Banco do Brasil S.A.	BR	CL, PA
12	Banco Itau SA	BR	AR
13	Bank Austria Creditanstalt	AT	HR, SK, SI
14	Bank of America	US	BR, MX, HK, ID
15	Bank of China	CN	RU, HK, MY
16	Bank of Nova Scotia (The)-SCOTIABANK	CA	AR, CL, MX, PE, CR, JM, PA, SV, MY
17	Bank of Tokyo-Mitsubishi UFJ	JP	PL, BR, MX, IN, MY
18	Barclays Plc	GB	EG, ZA
19	Bayerische Hypo-und Vereinsbank AG	DE	BG, HR, CZ, HU, LV, PL, RO, HR, SK, SI
20	Bayerische Landesbank	DE	BG, HU
21	BNP Paribas	FR	BG, HU, PL, RU, UA, BR, MX, PE, PA, CN, ID, EG
22	Canadian Imperial Bank of Commerce CIBC	CA	JM, SG
23	Citigroup	US	CZ, HU, KZ, PL, RO, RU, SK, UA, BR, CL, CO, MX, PY, PE, VE, HK, IN, KR, MY, SG, HN, PA, TT
24	Commerzbank AG	DE	HU, PL, RU, ID
25	Commonwealth Bank of Australia	AU	ID
26	Credit Agricole	FR	AM, CZ, HU, PL, RU, RS, SK, UA, AR, BR, UY, TR, EG
27	Credit Suisse	CH	RU, BR
28	Creditanstalt	AT	CZ, HU, PL
29	Danske Bank A/S	DK	PL, RU
30	DBS Group Holdings Ltd	SG	HK, ID, PH, TH

Table A4. (*Continued*)

	Multinational Bank	Home Country	Host Countries
31	Deutsche Bank AG	DE	HU, PL, RU, AR, BR, CL, UY, MY
32	Dexia	BE	RU, SK, TR
33	DnB Nor ASA	NO	RU
34	Dresdner Bank AG	DE	HR, CZ, RU, BR, CL, MX
35	DZ Bank AG	DE	HU, PL
36	Emporiki Bank of Greece SA	GR	AL, BG, RO
37	Erste Group Bank AG	AT	HR, CZ, HU, RO, RS, SK
38	Fortis Bank	BE	PL, TR, HK
39	GE Capital	US	CZ, HU, PL, BR, MX
40	HSBC	GB	AM, PL, RU, TR, AR, BR, CL, CO, MX, PE, UY, KZ, MY, EG
41	Hypo Alpe-Adria Bank	AT	BA, HR, RS, SI
42	ING Bank NV	NL	PL, RU, UA, AR, CL, MX, PY, UY, IN, ID, SG
43	JP Morgan Chase	US	BR, MX, VE, MY
44	KBC Group	BE	CZ, HU, PL, RU, SK
45	Kookmin Bank	KR	HK
46	Lloyds TSB Bank PLC	GB	AR, BR
47	National Bank of Greece SA	GR	BG, MK, RO, RS, TR
48	Norddeutsche Landesbank Girozentrale NORD/LB	DE	LV, LT, PL
49	Nordea Bank AB	SE	PL, RU
50	Oversea-Chinese Banking Corporation Limited OCBC	SG	ID, MY
51	Piraeus Bank SA	GR	AL, BG, RO, RS
52	ProCredit Holding AG	DE	GE, MD, UA
53	Rabobank Nederland	NL	PL, BR, IN, ID, SG
54	Raiffeisen Zentralbank Oesterreich AG-RZB	AT	AL, BY, BA, BG, HR, CZ, HU, PL, RO, RU, RS, SK, SI, UA
55	Resona Bank Ltd	JP	ID
56	Sampo Bank Plc	FI	EE, LV, LT
57	Sanpaolo IMI	IT	HU, RO, SI
58	Santander Central Hispano	ES	AR, BR, CL, CO, MX, PE, UY, VE, PA, PH
59	Skandinaviska Enskilda Banken	SE	EE, LV, LT, UA
60	Societe Generale	FR	BG, HR, CZ, PL, RO, RU, RS, SI, AR, BR, MX, ID, EG
61	Standard Chartered Bank	GB	CO, PE, HK, KR, MY, TH
62	Sumitomo Mitsui Banking Corporation	JP	BR, ID
63	Svenska Handelsbanken	SE	RU
64	Swedbank AB	SE	EE, LV, LT, RU
65	UBS	CH	BR

Table A4. (*Continued*)

	Multinational Bank	Home Country	Host Countries
66	UniCredit SpA	IT	BA, BG, CZ, HR, PL, RO, RU, SK, UA, TR
67	Veneto Banca Holding scpa	IT	HR, MD
68	Volksbank	AT	HR, RO, RS, SK
69	West LB	DE	HU, PL, RU, BR

Notes: AL, Albania; AM, Armenia; AR, Argentina; AT, Austria; AU, Australia; BA, Bosnia & Herzegovina; BE, Belgium; BR, Brazil; BG, Bulgaria; BY, Belarus; CA, Canada; CH, Switzerland; CL, Chile; CN, China; CO, Colombia; CR, Costa Rica; CZ, Czech; DE, Germany; DK, Denmark; EE, Estonia; EG, Egypt; ES, Spain; FI, Finland; FR, France; GB, UK; GE, Georgia; GR, Greece; HK, Hong Kong; HN, Honduras; HR, Croatia; HU, Hungary; ID, Indonesia; IE, Ireland; IN, India; IT, Italy; JM, Jamaica; JP, Japan; KR, Korea; KZ, Kazakhstan; LT, Lithuania; LV, Latvia; MD, Moldova; MK, Macedonia; MX, Mexico; MY, Malaysia; NL, Netherland; NO, Norway; PA, Panama; PE, Peru; PH, Philippines; PK, Pakistan; PL, Poland; PT, Portugal; PY, Paraguay; RO, Romania; RS, Serbia; RU, Russia; SE, Sweden; SG, Singapore; SK, Slovakia; SI, Slovenia; SV, El Salvador; TH, Thailand; TR, Turkey; TT, Trinidad&Tobago; UA, Ukraine; US, United States; UY, Uruguay; VE, Venezuela; ZA, South Africa.